Evolution of Knowledge Science

Evolution of Knowledge Science

Myth to Medicine: Intelligent Internet-Based Humanist Machines

Syed V. Ahamed
Department of Computer Science,
City University of New York,
New York, USA
and
Department of Health,
University of Medicine and Dentistry,
New Jersey, USA

AMSTERDAM • BOSTON • HEIDELBERG • LONDON
NEW YORK • OXFORD • PARIS • SAN DIEGO
SAN FRANCISCO • SINGAPORE • SYDNEY • TOKYO

Morgan Kaufmann is an imprint of Elsevier

Morgan Kaufmann is an imprint of Elsevier
50 Hampshire Street, 5th Floor, Cambridge, MA 02139, United States

British Library Cataloguing-in-Publication Data
A catalogue record for this book is available from the British Library

Library of Congress Cataloging-in-Publication Data
A catalog record for this book is available from the Library of Congress

ISBN: 978-0-12-805478-9

For Information on all Morgan Kaufmann publications
visit our website at https://www.elsevier.com

Working together
to grow libraries in
developing countries

www.elsevier.com • www.bookaid.org

Publisher: Todd Green
Acquisition Editor: Todd Green
Editorial Project Manager: Lindsay Lawrence
Production Project Manager: Priya Kumaraguruparan
Designer: Greg Harris

Typeset by MPS Limited, Chennai, India

Contents

PART I KNOWLEDGE, WISDOM AND VALUES

SECTION I FROM EARLY THINKER TO SOCIAL SCIENTISTS

SECTION II INFORMATION MACHINES AND SOCIAL PROGRESS

SECTION III KNOWLEDGE SCIENCE AND SOCIAL INFLUENCE

About the Author

Dr. Syed Ahamed holds Ph.D. and D.Sc. (E.E.) degrees from the University of Manchester and MBA (Econ.) from the New York University. He taught at the University of Colorado for 2 years before joining Bell Laboratories. After 15 years of research, he returned to teaching as Professor of Computer Science at the City University of New York. The author has been a telecommunications consultant to Bell Communications Research, AT&T Bell Laboratories, and Lucent Technologies for the last 25 years. He received numerous prizes for his papers from the IEEE. He was elected a fellow of the IEEE for his seminal contribution to the simulation and design studies of the High-speed Digital Subscriber Lines. He has authored and coauthored several books  in two broad areas of intelligent AI-based broadband multimedia networks and computational framework for knowledge. His doctoral students have continued to contribute to knowledge processing systems and wisdom machines proposed by him during 1999–2007. In 2004, he wrote the book "The Art of Scientific Innovation", for new doctoral students based on his teaching and mentoring the best of his 20 Ph.D. students at the Graduate Center of City University of New York. Much of the innovative feedback has come from the doctoral students mentored during 1990 through 2007. He holds over 20 American and European patents ranging from slip-meters for induction motors to medical networks for hospitals.

The author is obliged to Professors Victor B. Lawrence, George S. Moschytz, Bishnu S. Atal, Nikil Jayant, Stanley Habib, Michael Kress, and Alfred Levine for reviewing many technical books written by the author. He has continued to author technical books during 2013 and 2014, and this 30-chapter book is the culmination of his quest for the Science of Knowledge on a computational and a scientific basis.

Foreword

Information Science is on the cusp of defining the transition from Big Data to Knowledge. This movement is being fueled by an urgency in addressing grand challenges in fields as diverse as health, public safety and climate change. Domain experts in these fields are looking to information science to provide a quantitative basis for solving hard problems in their data-intensive fields. Success in these efforts will be defined not only by demonstrating measurable and non-incremental progress in these verticals, but also by creating a re-usable horizontal methodology for actionable information and knowledge. When created, such a methodology will have the kind of appeal and impact that we now associate with Information Theory as conceived by Shannon, but powered this time around by the exponentially greater capabilities in computing, communications and content processing.

The scenario above is a broadly-recognized opportunity that puts in context Prof. Ahamed's latest book entitled The Evolution of Knowledge Science: Intelligent Internet-Based Humanist Machines (Morgan Kaufman, 2017). Like his earlier books The Art of Scientific Innovations (Prentice Hall, 2005), Intelligent Internet Knowledge Networks: Processing of Concepts and Wisdom (John Wiley, 2007), and Conceptual Framework of Knowledge: Integrated behavior of machines (Wiley 2009), Prof. Ahamed's latest effort reflects intellectual passion and a commitment to teach a very complex topic. Like his earlier contributions, the writing and arrangement is sometimes personalized, stylized and esoteric. But to someone looking for an approach that unifies the myriad facets of Knowledge Science, Prof. Ahamed's book is timely in the least, and perhaps indispensable.

Readers of this book will discover a wonderful historical account beginning with Early Thinkers and ending with Social Information Networks (Part 1: Chapters 1 to 15). They will then be exposed to a rich array of mathematical and computing tools, and to many layers of conceptual insights, ranging from Knowledge Elements (KELs) to Architectures for Collective Intelligence and so-called Humanist Machines (Part 2: Internet-Based Systems to Medical Machines). Although medical machine architecture is covered in only a single chapter, it represents a befitting climax for the sophisticated teachings of earlier chapters. It serves as an outstanding point of departure: for experts in the rapidly transforming medical field, for counterparts in other grand-challenge domains, and most important, for those that will continue Prof. Ahamed's effort to define the elusive dimensions of Knowledge Science and to provide a quantified way of measuring progress in this meta-field.

Education today is becoming increasingly inter-disciplinary, a theme that pervades post-graduate and graduate research, trickling down to the notion of reforming earlier education for greater breadth and pragmatics. Prof. Ahamed's book represents a rigorous and optimistic declaration of this revolutionary trend. I recommend it heartily to teachers and students in communications and computing, and to those in pursuit of incisive mathematical philosophy.

Dr. Nikil Jayant
Eminent Scholar (Emeritus),
Georgia Research Alliance
September, 2016

Preface

There are two major parts in this book. Part I deals with knowledge in its primitive format as wisdom and values of early civilizations to knowledge embedded in the social networks. Part II deals with communication, processing, and deployment of knowledge from universal knowledge bases to its more personalized mind and medical machines. There are three sections in each of the two parts and five chapters in each section covering the Science of Knowledge subdivided in to 30 incisive and short but interwoven and interdependent chapters. The chapters are willfully kept short to be able to just carve out the most relevant part of the discipline as it pertains the knowledge science. Communication of any particular "body of knowledge" (bok) is essential for its survival. Isolated islands of knowledge are death-bound and get sunk in tides of time. Linkages to neighboring islands of knowledge are as essential as the words of love between human beings. As "love" can swing between its (Fromm's) idealization to destruction and bombing of neighbors (the Bush-Iraq aggressive) practice, "words" can swing from teachings to insults. Unfortunately, genuine teachings are few and far in between.

Knowledge science has its origin in many disciplines. At first glance, these interdependencies of the founding disciplines appear vague and unconnected but the fiber of the science of knowledge runs through writings of *philosophers, social scientists, economists, physicists, mathematicians*, and *computer and communication scientists*. Persistence and patience are both necessary to "see" the light in the long fiber-optic link and decode the elements of knowledge at various wavelengths. That brings us to the current state of (*DWDM*) fiber-optic technology, but even so, it is in the technology domain and lies much lower than the knowledge domain.

First, consider the philosophers who do not indulge in physics, mathematics, or computer and communication sciences. Their perspectives become confined for the knowledge society and network era. The human contemplations toward their age-old pursuit of virtue of the philosophers are now limited to searching Internet knowledge banks distributed throughout the world, though not the universe. The pragmatism of the modern society has left little room for the underlying theories behind human effort along the other disciplines. The endurance of scholarly thoughts gets feeble and frail as civilizations grow old. Metaphysics does not cut data buses on VLSI chips. Single philosophers and their thoughts prevail simply because of the painful documentation on their part now electronically scanned as bright beacons along the information highways for the pioneer thinkers of this century. So be it, but without a knowledge positioning system in the knowledge domain alike the GPS in the geographical domain, even the scientist thinkers become aloof, isolated, and soon forgotten.

Second, consider the social thinkers who do not indulge in computer hardware, network topology, and VLSI designs to accomplish communication and social tasks on the "Social Chips" still to emerge in a few decades for the wearable and handheld mind and medical machines. The mind machines are intelligent and personalized companions in a civilization that has broken family ties and social bonds. Early signs of this trend are already evident when people and group members spend hours gazing at the tiny PDA screens rather than explore the mindset treasures their friends hold! Social skill has become social decay by the love of teenagers for their senseless indulgence of trivia on satellite linked gossip machines. Human mind is far wider than the bandwidth of the wireless phones of a few MHz and the frequencies of oscillation of the *kels* (knowledge elements) that gratify the need of companionship engulf the body, mind, and soul in synergistic cohesion. When these *kels* are oriented toward the collective social problems, a new perspective of social harmony for the entire society replaces the quest for money of the greedy and the bomb-dropping-warring thugs around the world!

Third, consider the economists and accountants who play hide and seek with the consuming public in devising the market strategy for corporate products. Generally, this strategy is buried in the misleading propaganda of corporate actions and products. The narrow vision of the mathematician who play zero-sum corporate games seems to have mastered the game of deception so openly practiced by elected public officials and corrupt military industrialists. The Internet for the dispersion of significant and valid information has become a tool for marketing for the greedy business folks. Truth stated precisely and openly releases the mind from playing trivial games and directs it to more significant social problems.

Fourth, consider the physicists who shy away at taking a global perspective of positive globally socially benevolent knowledge and confine the wavelength of their vision to fill their food baskets. Society has existed long before the scientists arrived. The social cohesion is an ingredient of inner peace that is perhaps more lasting than the race into arms to plunder, grab, and consume the neighbors' garden and fill the belly! A sense of ethical corruption has shrouded the intellectual arena of the average college educated graduate who would readily accept a job to build the stealth bombers rather than to innovate new tools for the farmer who can feed more hungry people around the world. At the height of Johnson's Vietnam War, the socially responsible sentiment of the younger generation was to decline job offers from offensive arms manufacturers and their vendors. It is interesting to remember the Persian poet who complains that "his glory is drowned in a shallow cup"[1] of wines and withering rose pedals! The decline in social responsibility of the new college graduates is perhaps an accompaniment to the decline in morality.

Fifth, consider the mathematicians and their tunnel vision in a very physical, earthly, and trivial pursuit of a set of steps toward optimal algorithmic procedures. But there have been a few exceptional mathematician-philosophers (like Einstein, Heisenberg, Plank, Schrödinger, or even Maxwell) who look at the universe and see the curvature of light from the distant worlds, or the concept of uncertainty even in the universe of knowledge. The Field Theory of Knowledge is not confounded for these great thinkers. Their grads, curls, and surface integrals encompass the mind space rather than the ICBMs and missile spaces!

Finally, consider the computer and communication scientists, generally confined to hardware, software, firmware, switching systems, these scientists rarely know where their efforts are being deployed. Dependability, efficiency, error-free operations, optimality, and quick response generally offer constraints for most creative computer and network scientists. The National Science Foundation initiative to unify computer LANS to the Internet has not permeated the creativity and precision of the scientist to create a universal error and spam-free international knowledge space and its network. In the Internet era computers and communication sciences have been merged seamlessly. Both computer and communication scientists aim to satisfy common goals and have produces an atmosphere of dependable high-speed communications. After all communication within the computer system(s) is as important as processing and building artificially intelligence within the communication systems.

The unification of these disciplines is the objective of this book. The total integration of all of these sciences is beyond the scope of one book. Only linkages, equations, and the deepest interconnections are brought out in the 30 incisive chapters in the form of diagrams and figures that tie concepts rather than devices. When the readers see figures that have commonalities in them, they are meant to deliver the thread of human thought to weave the science of knowledge.

From a wider perspective, it appears that social responsibilities and ethical values have plummeted over the last few decades. From national leaders to petty cash collectors demonstrate the lack of social conscience and of honesty. The darkness of disgrace runs through the character of the elected officials (Nixon, Clinton, Johnson, Bush, and Putin, who have lied to the public), to the petty accountants (of Andersen Corporation, who invented "imaginary corporations" to sink shareholder's monies). The search for global dominance has driven super power to become global thugs. The goal of wisdom is social ethics as the goal of information is knowledge. The mad race for economic progress seems to have savagely bitten off a pound of flesh from the conscience of the Western society. The battle for economic progress has decisively won against equity, grace, and justice to the world and for the world. Johnson's noble goal was to eradicate poverty around the globe and not to rob poor cultures of their lands and habitat. Any country can and has become a two-penny thug against any other country without even one penny to save itself!

Information technology encompasses the realm of computer and communication technologies without any conceptual, device, or system boundaries. It is based on processing the information and the delivery of the processed information contained in the raw data over the digital pipes that crisscross the world. In a true sense, it blends computing with communicating and computers into intelligent communication systems. Intelligent information technology (IIT) extends beyond this composite discipline and permits a new and powerful option to process the knowledge being communicated based on the principles of artificial intelligence (AI) and knowledge engineering, and then uses the concepts of intelligent networks to communicate the derived knowledge. Information technologies have been evolving for the last four decades and have gained rapid momentum during the last decade. Systems deploy the novel combinations of computers and communications in an intelligent and goal-directed solution of knowledge, and content-based problems. These systems are programmable, adaptive, and algorithmic, and they provide solutions based on the dynamic conditions that influence the solution of any particular problem. *Two* major forces nurturing the social aspects of information technologies are (1) the worldwide acceptance of the Internet platforms and (2) the discipline of information and knowledge processing. Each of these plays a significant role, and each is based upon a trail of precedents.

NOTE

1. Omar Khayyam wrote some 1400 years back "The idols I have loved so long: Have done my credit in men's eyes much wrong: Drowned my glory in a shallow cup: And sold my reputation for a song."

KNOWLEDGE, WISDOM AND VALUES

I

PART I SUMMARY

This part covers many centuries that span from the knowledge and wisdom across cultures to the embedded artificially intelligent (AI)-based problem algorithms in very modern social machines in hand-held devices. Communication aspects are also presented as they were deployed in the past era and the current high-speed network systems. From the pragmatic outlook of the knowledge society, the horizons of mind have been stretched far and wide, almost tearing the fabric of peace, joy and contentment. The contributions of the social scientists and philosophers serve as bandages to heal the deep scars the willful neglect of Sigmund Freud's Superego, Carl Young's concept of the soul, and Kant's reasons for virtue. The socioeconomic price of moving from Freud to Maslow is evident this part. Numerous winners and losers due to this shift in perspective are explored further in these chapters. The final analysis places mind over machines and as discretion over valor. Human wisdom reigns supreme and reaches further than the spans of global fiber-optic network and inter galactic satellite links.

The scientific innovations have propelled the information-age of two generation into one decade. Knowledge society has moved equally fast but with deep ramification in shifting the power bases in the society. This Part has three Sections: In Section 01 we present the foundations of a civil society as contemplated by the great philosophers, of the East and of the West, and the contributions of scientists and the industrialists. In Section 02, the foundations for the modern computers and networks are established, and in Section 03, the ever increasing human and social needs are integrated with the capability of machine to provide the means to gratify such needs.

FROM EARLY THINKER TO SOCIAL SCIENTISTS

PART I, SECTION I, SUMMARY

Section 01 with five chapters deals with two extreme human nature: (a) the wise, philosophic, and contemplative and (b) the aggressive, coarse, brutal and selfish nature of human personality. These two opposing faces of human temperament tear the conscience apart at the lowest levels just as well as it enhances the level of consciousness at the highest levels. The technological revolutions during the later years of the last century have favored the innovations to enhance the leisure and comforts of life. In a very pragmatic world, the contributions of Henry Ford and the Wright Brothers have gained acceptance over teachings of Buddha or the selflessness of Gandhi or even the Presidency of Carter. This drift in the attitude of human thought has affirmed the foundation for the machines of early 20th century technology to foster the electronic age of the later generations. Breaking ground by the invention of the Transistor at Bell Laboratories and the study progress towards integration of logic circuits on Silicon Wafers, the digital age had prompted the PC age and general acceptance of the role of computers as essential forces in the society.

Network technologies and the 'C language initiated again at Bell Laboratories, have strengthened the communication aspects of information and knowledge necessary to reach the public and survive as strict underlying and universal concepts. These diverse fields of knowledge stemming from semiconductor physics, mathematics, and communication sciences are interrelated and amplified in this Section of Part I of the book. During this thrust forward in making life easier, the ethical counterpart of enhancing social awareness has been ignored due to the lack of direction on the part of the social and political leaders. The wide gap for the greedy to make a deep valley down the path of self-gratification is now deeply entrenched. Human minds being the catalysts for social change can once more chart the balance with the knowledge machines that are contemplative, coherent and steadfast. This is the essential premise of this Section of Part I.

KNOWLEDGE AND WISDOM ACROSS CULTURES

1

CHAPTER SUMMARY

This chapter covers a brief overview of the ancient trails of knowledge through the centers of learning. These trails have become genetic pathways for contemplation over many centuries in Kyoto, Japan; in Nalanda, India; in the Jewish kibotos in Apamea, Phrygia; and in Giza, Egypt. More recently (eighth to thirteenth centuries), astronomy, mathematics, and methodology have been introduced in shrines of learning for the disciples and inmates of these knowledge centers. These seeds of knowledge along the venues of meditation are still based on Aristotle's notions of universal truisms, beauty and virtue in the minds of saints, gurus, and clergy. In the distant past, these seeds germinated into full blossoms of wisdom through the generations that have followed. Knowledge is many times compared to pristine water in the clouds, rain, and streams, and wisdom is likened to dew drops in the gardens of Eden. Refined thought, art, and generosity blossomed together. Wisdom deeply founded in social justice and fairness evolved much slowly in the prior generations.

The very recent pragmatism in sciences has started to demand immediate wealth and ready cash from knowledge. The pathways to progress have become optical fibers in the modern age of digital switches and information highways. Unfortunately, human reflection and refinement of notions have become subservient to the artificial wisdom of machines. The dramatic use of machines and their abuse have replaced the contemplations of the scholars of the past. Historical data bring home the ironic fact that hand-held PDAs (personal digital assistants) are becoming more affable than the spirituality laden scripture of the monks and gurus. Digits have become their beads; micro-programs have become their mantras; and keypads have become the sitars for the Internet-based transformed Vedic scholars. The monuments of technology have become barriers to the vision that unify the pursuit of science with human betterment. Marxist's concepts of scientific innovation are not slanted toward raw greed for power and wealth.

The current uses of machines in the routine activities of individuals, societies, and communities are examined from the perspective of both progress and retreat of social change that machines can catalyze. Much as computers have hastened the financial swings in the stock market, the new wave of social machines is likely to hasten the social swings, as they are already evident by the Internet. Dishonest marketers and spammer quickly take most people into deception-lands. Both the positive and negative implications of the impending social machines are presented. The underlying object to direct the machines to social enhancement rather than its decay is emphasized in this part. As much as traditional computers have hastened the business and commercial activities in the modern societies, the well-primed social machines are poised to hasten the routine of peoples, both intellectually and culturally, and to enrich lives of the world community. Information and knowledge society has further hastened such cycles and accelerated the changes. The knowledge culture of this decade is no longer based on the social laws of the last decade!

Evolution of Knowledge Science. DOI: http://dx.doi.org/10.1016/B978-0-12-805478-9.00001-7

1.1 INTRODUCTION

Very early civilizations fortified and reinforced the social practices for preservation and survival. Wars, brutality, and exploitation were common. Pragmatism was the mode of self-preservation. Competition for resources was practiced to the deadly ends. In many subcultures of the Aztecs and Incas, the time of plenty was also the period of brutality. Subcultures started to compete for power, and tribal wars were common. Astronomy and sciences learned during their plentiful periods were subjugated to unfounded myths and beliefs leading to destruction of lives and values. Good life and peace had become the privilege of the high monks and priests. Children of lesser gods were sacrificed to the deities of the elite groups of the Incas or as food for lions for the entertainment of the Greek nobility. Brutality had become the normality of social existence.

Lives during the infancy of civilizations were centered around the essentials for existence. Learning, art, and religion were the mainstream of life during later periods. Extra resources were shared more frequently and a sense of social justice emerged leading to a new way of thought for others. Perhaps this was the beginning of a balanced and civil society. Common sense though not known as early science was directed toward solving local needs in making gadgetry and tools used by these primitive peoples. Geographical and environmental factors shaped the evolution of culture patterns and their localized customs, traditions, and tendencies.

Medieval civilization reinforced the harmony of mind and nature in the preservation of sustained peace. The sense of order and justice was introduced later to ensure peaceful coexistence and coherent life with a certain degree of predictability. Social circles were smaller, knit tighter, and stability accrued. Freedom and responsibility were balanced in different proportions in social activities and based on the external threats. Largely, they varied by the age in family groups and by needs and threats in larger groups. Social dynamics in different segments of the society was delicately balanced by human judgment rather than by weights and measures. Such a mode still exists in the few authentic Eskimo and native Indian cultures.

Periods of abundance in the minds of socially just peoples have led to contemplation and reflection. The basis of right and wrong is conceived. A sense of rationality and inference starts to take shape as trails toward more footprints on the sands of time. These trails have become genetic pathways for contemplation over many years in Kyoto, Japan [1]; Nalanda [2]; India [3]; Jewish kibotos [4]; Apamea, Phrygia; and Giza, Egypt. Relatively recently, eighth to thirteenth centuries have significant contribution of scientific methodology, mathematics, physics, biology, and medicine. The house of wisdom in Baghdad (twelfth century) and in Persian shrine of the Rumi's (1207−1273) in Kona, Turkey, blend the art and architecture, beauty and peace with many culturally variant ways of universality of knowledge and wisdom. A sense of moderation and deliberation has been reinforced to control the brutal nature of the humankind.

1.2 UNABATED LEARNING AND UNBOUNDED KNOWLEDGE

Numerous versions styles of ancient institutions for higher learning have evolved in the many cultures around the world to provide institutional frameworks for scholarly activities. These ancient centers were sponsored and overseen by courts; by religious institutions, which sponsored cathedral schools, monastic schools, and madrasas; by scientific institutions, such as museums, hospitals, and observatories; and by individual scholars. They are to be distinguished from the Western-style university which is an autonomous organization of scholars that originated in medieval Europe and was adopted in other world regions since the onset of modern times.

Japan received considerable ideology [1] and culture from China. From sixth to ninth century, the influence had been exceedingly dominant. Chinese writing systems, Buddhism and Confucianism, were also well received in Japan. Following the initial impact, Kyoto was selected to house numerous (five) institutions of higher learning and much later during twelfth through sixteenth centuries, including the Ashikaga School, Ashikaga, Gakko, during the fifteenth century, reigned as Centers of Higher Learning and Education.

In India, Nalanda [2] was founded in 427 in northeastern India, not far from what is today the southern border of Nepal. This institution survived until 1197. Though primarily devoted to Buddhist studies, it also coached students in fine arts, medicine, mathematics, astronomy, and politics. The center had eight separate compounds, ten temples, meditation halls, classrooms, lakes, and parks. It had a nine-story library where monks meticulously copied books and documents so that individual scholars could have their own collections. It had dormitories for students, perhaps a first for an educational institution, housing 10,000 students in the school's heyday and providing accommodation for 2,000 professors. Nalanda attracted pupils and scholars from Sri Lanka, Korea, Japan, China, Tibet, Indonesia, Persia, and Turkey.

The Academy of Gundishapur [5], Iran, was established in the third century AD under the rule of Sassanid kings and continued its scholarly activities up to four centuries after Islam came to Iran. It was an important medical center of the sixth and seventh centuries and a prominent example of higher education model in pre-Islam Iran. When the Platonic Academy in Athens was closed in 529, some of its pagan scholars went to Gundishapur, although they returned within a year to Byzantium.

In China, the ancient imperial academy known as Taixue was established by the Han Dynasty in AD 3. It was intermittently inherited by later dynasties until Qing, in some of which the name was changed to Guozixue or Guozijian. Peking University (Imperial University of Peking) established in 1898 is regarded as the replacement of Taixue (or Guozijian). In Korea, Taehak was founded in 372 and Gukhak was established in 682. The Seonggyungwan was founded by the Joseon Dynasty in 1398 to offer prayers and memorials to Confucius and his disciples, and to promote the study of the Confucian canon. It was the successor to Gukjagam from the Goryeo Dynasty (992). It was reopened as a private Western-style university in 1946. In Japan, Daigakuryo was founded in 671 and Ashikaga Gakko was founded in the ninth century and restored in 1432. In Vietnam, the Quoc Tu Giam (literally "National University") functioned for more than 700 years, from 1076 to 1779.

Relatively recently (seventh to thirteenth centuries), the Islamic doctrine of thought has inculcated significant proportions of scientific methodology, mathematics, physics, biology, and medicine. The house of wisdom in Baghdad (twelfth century) and Persian shrine of the Rumi's (1207−1273) in Kona, Turkey, blend the art and architecture, beauty and peace with the many culturally variant ways of universality of knowledge and wisdom [6]. A sense of moderation and deliberation has been reinforced to control the greedy and brutal nature of the humankind. The pathway to immediate gratification of human needs was paved with deliberate and concerted effort to be superhuman, just, and kind. A sense of inner harmony of the mind with the untamed external forces of nature was made a part of yogic discipline of the mind. The flowers of knowledge and the pearls of wisdom were woven together for the gurus to wear in their lifetime.

1.3 PEARLS OF WISDOM ALONG HIGHWAYS OF TIME

Numerous traumas that have occurred in the East and the West have left their own imprints on the intellectual lives of populace. The triadic influence of (a) social awareness, (b) intellectual activity, and (c) knowledge in the mind has been and still is a distinct and unique coincidence. It resulted as a distinctive and an independent triad that refuses to be extinguished by minor ripple effects in the society. From the writings of Aristotle, the universality of truth, the dignity of virtue, and esteem of beauty do not perish till a cataclysm of nature.

In an insidious mode, the influences of (a), (b), and (c) have existed individually and trilaterally over the prior centuries but not in such close synchrony. However, all these three coexistent reactions of human mind started to blossom (beautifully and) rapidly after von Neumann introduced the stored program controlled (SPC) machine at the Institute of Advanced Study (IAS) [7] and the Bell Laboratories team led by Shockley invented the Transistor [8]. The integrated circuit (IC) technology that ensued had a perhaps deeper and a more significant impact on human understanding and the knowledge that have accumulated since. The concurrent ease of computing and communication technologies has been an unprecedented factor current social evolution and networks. The foundations of knowledge sciences during the last few decades are depicted in Figure 1.1.

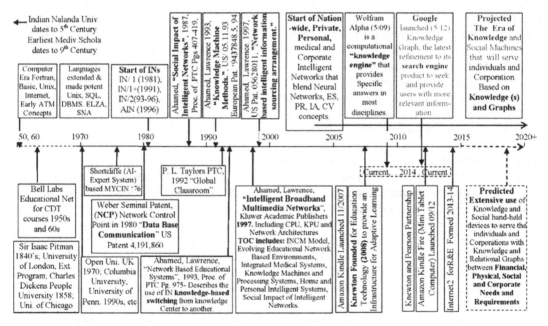

FIGURE 1.1

Foundation for the evolution of modern knowledge science. Events from 1970 are placed in the right side of the diagram.

1.4 **NEED FOR A MODERN SCIENCE OF KNOWLEDGE**

Information science is data dependent. Data stored as bits, data-structures, and words have specific formats and structures. Information sciences can analyze data in its specific format, and interpret its features. The central processor units (CPUs) generally perform the binary encoded series of steps to perform information-based functions. Interdependencies and inter-relationships in data strings can also be traced. Database management systems provide one of the powerful methodologies to implement the principles of information science on the stored data, to update it, to search, and to rearrange data strings that have certain predefined and pre-assigned features. Data searches and data matching are also some of the familiar techniques in information sciences.

Knowledge science is both object and action dependent. Objects and actions are linked in a particular format to constitute a modular body of knowledge. Knowledge science actively manipulates objects, actions, and the format of relationships. It can generate and refine such modules of knowledge. Knowledge science can also rearrange and reconstitute information and data in a programmable and artificially intelligent manner to search, manipulate, and readjust the very core constituents of knowledge and objects around which knowledge is centered and concentrated. The structure of knowledge is thus altered by the algorithms embedded and programmed in knowledge sciences. Optimality and numerous business techniques from Operation Research find their way into knowledge sciences to adjust the knowledge contained in specifically tailored knowledge structures, such as knowledge-banks, knowledge-centric elements, and fragments of knowledge generated by knowledge machines.

Knowledge resides one level above information science. It depends on objects that gratify human needs, satisfy its derived value, and/or become merged with other objects to enhance their values. In this framework, an object is any entity such as a human being, a scientist, or a knowledge processor unit (KPU) that generates new knowledge elements, which can manipulate knowledge. Computers, networks, and programs can all be objects and assume the role of knowledge processors. Whereas KPUs have the latitude to serve as CPUs, CPUs do not have the latitude to perform KPU functions. The concepts that provide a foundation for objects to exist are interwoven in the science of knowledge that can be programmed as KPU instructions.

From a distant perspective, knowledge science appears like quicksand with only weight of an object and fluidity mix of the quick sand as a swim or sink proposition. At a closer look, the confines of knowledge science assume the limits tundra space. However, at a second more detailed perspective, some of the inroads of sciences start to hold validity in knowledge sciences as well. The roles of physics (for conduction) and economics (for the behavior of human KCOs) need to be extended into getting a grip on knowledge and its flow. In this chapter, the ways and means of gripping an abstract entity such as knowledge are presented. Perhaps the most slippery aspect in this journey is the see through the consonance and the dissonance between physical and knowledge entities. Some commonality does exist to a certain extent (especially dealing with energy and its transformation) but while dealing with KCOs, the analogy fades away unless the perspective is shifted (especially into signal flow analysis) from another discipline. A collectivity of sciences (such as physics, engineering, thermodynamics, and economics) offers a more flexible path through the science of knowledge.

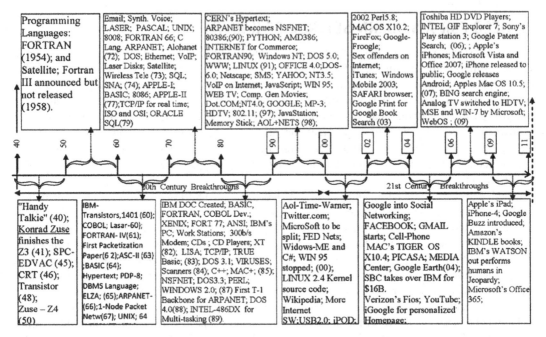

FIGURE 1.2

Hardware and software perspectives of the technological events that have shaped the modern society and contributed to the need for the science of knowledge in the twenty-first century. The new hardware devices and systems that are being currently deployed have their own scientific basis. It becomes necessary for knowledge science to harness and enhance the embedded sciences as new discipline.

Machines have influenced scientific, business, and personal lives since 1940s and 1950s. The role of computers was greatly enhanced by numerous venders of business machines and especially by the entry of International Business Machines to the community of venders for both scientific and business applications. Languages, gadgets, devices, and interfaces have been introduced steadily since the 50s and a timeline of major events is shown in Figure 1.2. During the last decade the role of knowledge, rather than that of data and information, has become dominant. New machines, languages, interfaces, and an entirely new horizon appear poised to facilitate the use of machines in the knowledge domain.

Unlike most physical media and their properties, the knowledge parameters are slightly more complex and depend on numerous individual and social characteristics. For example, in heat flow-flow, electrical or optical signal flow, material constants such as conductivities and refractive indices are introduced to accommodate the physical and particular situation. These parameters are much more subtle, nonlinear, and complex to introduce distortion and dispersion effects (as is the case for the flow of optical and electrical signals through glass and electrical media). Such effects also alter the composition and structure of the knowledge-centric object being transferred.

The variation in the behavior of human KCOs is accommodated in the equations for energy and entropy by suitable constants that traditionally relate energy and entropy in thermodynamics.

Physical sciences start to buckle under stress and emotions of humanist KCOs, and the so-called constants start to become coefficients. These constants (from thermodynamics) are not constants at all, but time- and nature-dependent (emotional) coefficients and attributes of humanist-type KCOs. The nature and type of flow of heat (or energy) from on object interact in the knowledge to other retains its basic trait when two objects domain. We quantify the relations by falling back on the definitions from thermodynamics, but abandon the second law of thermodynamics and replace it with modifiers that pertain to the specific humanist KCOs and social/cultural setting in which the knowledge transaction takes place. It no longer has a heat.

1.5 INCEPTION AND USE OF BUSINESS MACHINES

Computer-aided business practice has become essential for survival in a competitive world market place. Ranging from routine bookkeeping to intelligent decision making, the computers and networks play as dominant a role as customary patient management to distant robotic surgery in medical practice. Corporations started to deploy computer assistance almost as quickly as the academicians started using computers in research and investigations. Historically, COBOL (for businesses) and FORTRAN (for scientists, mathematicians and academicians) have coexisted since late 1950s through 1970s. The older generations of IBM 360 machines have been an asset to both communities of users.

More recently, the strides in the computer and network technology have outpaced their usage in business, but they challenge the intricacies of the human judgment in the social and medical fields. However, in the business of medicine, machines are essential for the survival of individuals, patients' doctors, hospitals, medical centers, and even for vendors.

The simpler configurations of business machines generally have CPUs, main memory groupings or banks (MMBs that include 2D, 2½D, 3D, Wafer, Multi-Wafer MMs), control memories (CMs), cache memories, numerical processor units (NPUs), graphical processor units (GPUs), network switches (NSs), numerous input/output processors, interfaces and devices, and HW for Cloud Computing (if interconnected), etc. Any specially tailored hardware is added to customize the computer configuration if it is necessary.

1.6 INFORMATION AND ITS CURRENT DEPLOYMENT

Most societies would come to a standstill if computers and networks are disabled. The thought processes continuously feed into machine functions and the machine functions quickly evaluate, verify, enhance, improvise, these thoughts before, during, and after the implementation of most major human activity or transactions. Almost all individuals and agencies depend on positively primed (or at least unbiased) operating systems and software. The advantages are immense and coupled with increased efficiency the changes can be quickly and diligently implemented. With legal and judicious, wisdom and ethics can be propelled at a quicker pace in the society. The seven phases of the machines toward the human betterment are shown in Figure 1.3.

Based on Advancement
Towards Human Betterment and Welfare.

Phase I	Phase II	Phase III	Phase IV	Phase V	Phase VI	Phase VII
Early civilizations to late 1950's	1950's to late 1970's. Business and Academic use	1970's to early 2000s. Legal and Educational use	Knowledge Sciences. 00's to Now, Still Evolving	Current - machine and Human and Social Computing, etc.	Human, Minor use of machines. Senate, Legal Judiciary, etc.	Human, Minor use of machines UN, Church Religious, etc.

-------------------------- -------- Universality of Knowledge ---
-------- Positive Effects on Society --------------- Perhaps a Sense of Value, Ethics and Endearment.

FIGURE 1.3

Evolutionary pathways from binary data to human ethics and values.

1.6.1 MOSTLY HUMAN: SENATE, LEGAL, AND JUDICIARY USE

In more advanced user configurations, the HW will have more and more human control on the KPUs, the GPUs, the graphical user interface (GUIs), object and attribute processors (OAPUs), Internet switches, and the Web sites (WWW). The evolving social operating systems and its software (SSW) are likely to control the multiple memory modules (MMs) to handle objects, attributes, their structures, graphs, nodes, and their linkages. Conventional input and output processors handle the data and text communication.

Database functions and their execution are standardized and any local DBMS provides access to the local databases. Communication with local and remote knowledge bases calls for a certain amount of knowledge processing and compilation of user queries and assembly of the procedures for answers and solutions. The knowledge processing SW needs the well-defined steps as they exist in the completion of the instructions in Higher Level Languages and a set of standard routines as they exist in the execution of number-based machine operations handled by the arithmetic and logic units (ALUs) of conventional computers. The major source of intelligence is human and (hopefully) based on ethical principles, axioms of well-founded wisdom and genuinely beneficial concepts.

1.6.2 CURRENT – ORGANIZATIONAL (UN, CHURCH, RELIGIOUS)

The hardware for such usage is akin to the HW, but with an additional layer of code for "serene and contemplative" reevaluations of the decision support systems [9] for the UN, church, and religious activities. Human error correcting codes appear as feasible in the knowledge era as the algebraic single error correcting codes in the 1949 Hamming era [10] and the Polynomial codes in the 1960 Reed-Solomon [11] era.

Hopefully, the elements of wisdom and ethics prevail in this mode of machine usage. All the same, corruptions of the good traditions of the Vatican have occurred by human agents[1] to this date

---

[1]"Pope Sexual Abuse Scandal News, Photos and Videos" - ABC News, www.abcnews.go.com > *Topics* > *News*, Browse Pope Sexual Abuse Scandal latest news and updates, watch videos and view all, Web page accessed, October 17, 2013. "A Money-Smuggling Scandal Threatens to Sink the Vatican Bank...", www.businessweek.com/.../.../2013.../ a-money-smuggling-scandal-threaten... Jul 2, 2013 — It sounds like a thriller plot: A Vatican cleric, a spy, and a financier are accused of conspiring to smuggle €20 million ($26 million), accessed October 18, 2013.

and are current. In a sense, the use of Intelligent Agents (IAs) [12] based on the age-old wisdom and contemplation can enhance the role of AI in this phase of human endeavor. Such social and ethical software can be as well designed as well as the design software for the engineering projects that checks, warns, refines, and prevents (as a last resort) the erroneous human inputs and variables interjected by human beings. The chances are that the UN, church, and religious endeavors will be as stable and secure as the engineering structures and monuments.

1.6.3 EVOLVING USE OF SOCIAL MACHINES

The internet brings about enormous multimedia communication capabilities to the users. The multimedia facilities provide immense learning potential and instant gratification in the quest of stored information and knowledge. However, information and knowledge are brought from accumulated databases rather than by the analysis of data that leads to authentic and derived or processed information. Processing of information further leads to knowledge and offers greater flexibility to seeking out the targeted knowledge. Customized information processing to suit the user needs and tastes becomes an essential function of the next-generation knowledge machines.

When the need for such information is immediate the enhanced access to data centers and the broadband channels are a boon to the decision-makers; managers are executives. The user is in global command of seeking information, but the Internet service providers (ISPs) can tag along much spam type of information to the authentic Internet information delivered. In providing free access to the data centers and knowledge banks, the ISPs derive their revenues by advertising of products and services to the users. Serious information and knowledge seekers find this additional information distracting; casual users find it interesting; and sales people find this information as revenue generators from the Internet and from those seeking tit-bits.

From a social perspective, all is not well in this aspect of Internet usage. In the name of personal freedom, irresponsible vendors appear ready to push social and ethical decay into their disaster. Spam industry knows no bounds in its sales as it serves to provide addresses of the immoral and unethical members[2] of the society. Initially, spam brought in a sales pitch to the unaware buyers who pay for the existence of such spammers. In a secondary wave of spamming, deception enhanced the profiteering from the sales of products and services.

There is a note of alarm in the progression of this business. Spammers have invaded the privacy of individuals by "targeted marketing" ploys. Such ploys designed by the ISP net-ware developers keep reminding the user of a product or a service that any user had casually surfed. Finally, the spammers violate the moral and ethical space of individuals by making immorality cheap and easy[3]! For the ethically responsible individual, the slogan in the Internet age is "Surfer Beware and

---

[2]It is assumed that these types of affairs and escapades are unethical at this time. If the society approves such conduct as rational behavior, then it is indicative of the behavioral level of the particular society. A few years back searching for gay partners on the Internet and in the local newspapers was questionable as being ethical. In this current decade, such activity is considered appropriate and serves to enhance the personal freedom. The rate of change of the ethical level of the society is governed by the force within the society (search for personal freedom) and the ethical/social inertia. These parameters vary from society to society, region to region, and time to time. The cause-and-effect relationships (force = mass times acceleration/retardation or torque = moment of inertia times angular acceleration/retardation) continue to exist in the social domain.

[3]Immorality can become as contagious as an epidemic and the spread can become perhaps as severe as the spread of AIDS or as the absence of self-restraint. This is evident in the words of the spammers, e.g., "we guarantee affair" or "we the most famous name in married dating and infidelity," "thousands of cheating wives and husbands signup."

Behave," much as the warning to the buyers as "buyer beware" a few years back to watch for deceptive sales tactics. Internet use can work against social and ethical standards of immature and unwary as effectively as it can work for the intellectual elite and socially conscientious in their search and resurrection of truth or a scientific principle.

In a 1989 publication [13, 14], the author warned against the social isolation that can result by overindulgence and overdependence of Internet gimmicks. Such gimmicks (mostly) exist to enhance the profit level of the spammers and rarely for the benevolence of the user. Genuine human association and contact sharpen the social skills. Two and half decades later in this time frame, social responsibility is still more fundamental than cheap Internet gimmickry. Interaction with sales software and agencies that Internet offers to the public is a poor substitute. "Safe surfing" is an important lesson for the young and restless PDA swingers. Linked to movie files with excessive violence and human abuse, the social effect is likely to be cataclysmic or a progression of illicit and socially destructive behavior (e.g., the sale and abuse of guns, mass murders in shopping centers and schools). Fortunately, this tendency is not rampant but it is possible and proven. But unfortunately, immorality fueled by the greed of spammers is rampant.

In more advanced user configurations, the HW will have more and more human control on the KPUs [15], the GPUs [16], the graphical user interface, UIs, OAPUs [15], Internet switches, and the Web sites. The evolving social operating systems and its software (SSW) are likely to control the multiple memory modules (MMs) to handle objects, attributes, their structures, graphs, nodes, and their linkages. Conventional input and output processors handle the data and text communication.

Database functions and their execution (Section 1.6.1) are routinely handled by database management system or DBMS. Knowledge-based functions are inherently more complex and the equivalent KBMS are neither standardized nor freely available. Even so the currently deployed KBMS primarily deliver information-based results rather than knowledge-based results. Knowledge-based systems that scan for ideas, concepts, and their analysis will make knowledge as manageable during the next decade as data is managed during the prior decade. Between DBMS and KBMS, electronic switching systems (ESSs) of the 1980s and 1990s had been developed by the Unix-based programmers to identify and control the communication channels that allocate path routing by the electronic switches.

Unfortunately, the current spam-based junkware[4] is operative with current hardware, devices, and networks. Windows or MIC (median information control) domain Unix systems download such spam without the user consent. The effects are contamination of knowledge, refutation of concepts, adulteration of wisdom, invasion of privacy, generally followed by destruction of ethics. Unmonitored, as it appears on the Internet, such devastating computer routines and SW can appear as spam that market "affairs," secret escapades, cheating wives, and Russian singles, for a few dollars! Social decay is as likely to follow as social progress that appears after a lot of contemplation, nation building, and spiritual teaching. Cyclic reversal of the positive computer usage into its abuse can be scientifically controlled and tamed, but an exploitation of the technology toward building spam-networks and misinformation and deceptive services needs regulatory control. In the past,

---

[4]The objective of this section is to project a scenario of the positive and negative effects of the emerging social machines (SMs) and their customized social software (SSW). Much like the use of fire, the social consequences can be controlled and well directed. Abuse of the Internet tools and technology in the social domain can just easily spread as wild fire.

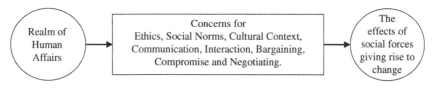

FIGURE 1.4

Activity in the personal and social domain dealing with mind, self, and society.

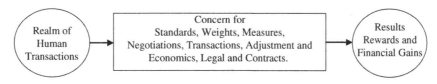

FIGURE 1.5

Activity in work and business domain dealing with money, transactions, and negotiations.

weapons technologies and firearms control have been monitored and regulated. In the knowledge domain, the abuse of news media and Internet can only make the society more turbulent.

Centered in human nature, ethics, wisdom, and concepts are error-prone and can acquire traces of immorality, deception, and self-interest[5]. Over a period, the tainted superstructure of human intelligence over that of machine forces corrupted intelligence into operating systems[6] and software. An idiot (untainted) machine is better than a tainted intelligent machine. Simple folks in the nations see the "corruption and contamination" in the human agencies and trace the origin. Unfortunately, this slow contamination has become worldwide counterproductive agent to the progress of nations. Ineffectual Federal processes, inefficient state and local governments, corruption, and scandals are the immediate and visible symptoms, and social decay is the subsequent effect. These events serve as the leading indicators of the social and ethical depression to follow. Machine intelligence is truly subservient to the human intelligence. Machines become toys of deception much as nuclear science and technology have become sources of devastation in the hands of irresponsible leaders.

Figures 1.4 and 1.5 depict two aspects of personal and transactional human activities. Both facilitate the positive use of machines for individuals and societies. Generally, such activities are intellectually sound and based on reason. Being universal, the use of machines for personal and social rewards can be programmed and made efficient.

The use of computers in every aspect of life after the IAS machine (1949) is perhaps as profound as the use of automobiles after the series of invention of the internal-combustion engine[7]

---

[5]From presidents (e.g., Nixon (Watergate tapes), Clinton (Monica Lewinsky affair), Bush (non-existent Weapons of Mass Destruction and Invasion of Iraq)) through the corporate CEOs (Arthur Anderson, Global Crossing, etc.) to the petty officers in the public departments, this seems to reflect the fall in human nature increasingly over the last few decades.

[6]Drone operating systems, their firmware and software, spy satellite systems, robotic killers in modern warfare.

[7]There have been a series of inventors and their own implementations of the internal combustion engine that have preceded the modern automobiles. Perhaps there are more inventions to follow in the transportation industry.

(Lenoir (1858), Otto (1876), and others). This impact on the average user of the Internet services only calls for a safeguard from the deterioration of the ethics simply because the *typical* Internet user has little no moral or ethical responsibilities just as the gunslingers of the Wild West 300 years back. Legal systems and judiciary sprang up to protect the rights of the civil citizens thus curtailing the mercenaries and hired hands to slay. These mercenaries and hired hands have found a new life as in the information age as Internet spammers and their SW writers leaving the moral and ethical to be "Surfer Beware and Behave."

In a quick look back at the theft and corruption of the social values all is not lost because of the positive uses of the information technology and Internet-based services in the business, government, commercial, education, medical, and security systems.

1.6.4 USE OF FEDERAL AND LEGAL MACHINES

Federal agencies and large nations soon followed the business practices of corporations in the smooth and accurate business-operation of running a nation and its role on numerous activities (from taxation to public services, from Welfare to Medicare, etc.) in dealing with the citizens; in safeguarding civil rights to ensuring safe flights; etc. The use of reason and logic was transferred to unbiased microsecond machines from temperamental slow human beings. The gradual transition of modern machines was thus initiated on a large scale to deal with entire populations rather than employees and individuals.

Generally, these large framework machines have most of the hardware components found in the corporate computer centers. In addition, wide area networking aspects, HW and SW, are also specifically included if the computing facilities are distributed over a nation or over wide geographical areas to accommodate all types (microwave, satellite, fiber, cable, etc.) of networks and their specific protocols.

Due to a large number of users and clientele, numerous switching modules (SMs) may also be included in this architecture. Secure subject matter–based knowledge banks (KBs) and security measures are generally included to safeguard the data, information, and sensitive information. The impact of technology is profound in most computer and networking systems that generally evolve with the usage.

Knowledge is an accumulated asset. Over time, trivia and gossip are filtered out and significant information is restated as derived knowledge. It assumes an aura of time and space independence. Though limited by the extent of scientific authentication of the processing of information that leads to knowledge, it becomes acceptable in a limited social setting till it is replaced by firmer and more universal knowledge. In a wider setting and over longer time, the derivation or evolution of knowledge becomes a dynamic process that converges to irrevocable and absolute truth. Being only illusive, the search for truth keeps the cycles of cultures and civilization striving, synchronized, and synergized.

Behavioral flexibility ensures the continued survival of species, humans, and cultures. Learning to respond intelligently is an essential feature of progress in any direction. Human beings learn to adapt early in life and even in embryonic life. Adaptation rather than a radical change is the key factor in adjustment. Genomes and chromosomes adapt; babies and children adapt to continue their life and growth. Short-term adjustments needing less emotional and intellectual energies lead to immediate adaptations, and longer-term adjustments need attitudinal shifts, meditation, negotiation, and computation. In the information age after the computer revolution during the last century, the optimal and precise adjustment calls for algorithmic strategy and numerical accuracy.

Important Event and Trends Leading to
New Machines and Social/Humanistic Enhancements

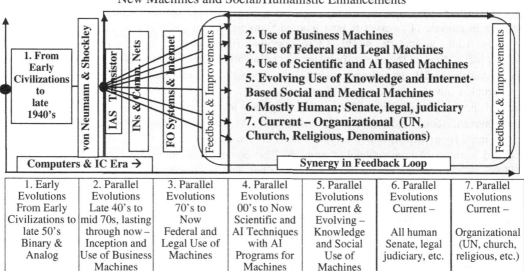

FIGURE 1.6

Timeline for the deployment of machines and data-processing systems since the evolution of the IAS machine in late 1940s. On the right side, the human role becomes increasingly important, since human nature and attitudes can change rapidly. Human judgment becomes more instrumental and machines play a greatly subservient role in such humanistic systems. In this presentation, the positive use of machines is emphasized.

The role of inventions in the computer and network fields and their deployment for social bene-fit are shown in Figure 1.6. Most of the inventions have occurred in the same time-frames, thus greatly enhancing the impact on the impact in the personal, social, and business sectors. The extent of impact has experienced an exponential (if not faster) growth. Through the current times, the expansion is still increasing in the educational, medical, and knowledge domains.

Knowledge society and social skills demand high levels of adaptation in deploying the evolved knowledge machine. Such machines can help in seeking better life and social conditions based on knowledge accumulated as wisdom. The casual attitude toward learning and adapting to the indus-trial revolution is not sufficient for dealing with the dynamic shifts that knowledge society has brought upon us over the last few decades. Together with the explosion of information comes the demand for best social adaptation to use the Internet tools and techniques. Inadequate social skill only demeans the Internet knowledge in the social and technological circles. In this next stage of the use of computer systems, the optimally composed (and compiled) social behavioral patterns will assure the success of a well-adjusted politician, a corporate executive, a manager, or simply any lovable human being.

The technological and engineering class-work and textbooks appear archaic to deal with the deployment of Internet information and refined social skills in its deployment. Pentium processors and fiber-optic highways call for quick, spontaneous, and sophisticated reactions during corporate transactions. More than the tools and techniques to adapt, a change in philosophy and attitude toward handling knowledge to suit any given social and cultural, context becomes necessary. Such a change in attitude of humans is best learned from the social machines that also learn from the knowledge banks around the world. These machines filter out poor and uncalibrated reactionary attitudes (depending on their own social anchor points of such machines) and offer sharpest knowledge to suit the social and cultural setting. Sets of most suited responses and winning mannerisms are assembled and checked to match the situation aimed toward an economic and expected maximization of the desired objective. These social machines are more than mere computers and play an almost human, social, cultural and economic role. In the same vein, the layers of social-ware become more sophisticated than the typical layers (network, application, compilers, assemblers, linkers, and loaders) of conventional computers. The communication media for social machines is decidedly superior to the media (base metallic, fiber, and wireless) of the lifeless computers. The intelligence of the social computers is as alive and responsive as that of the human beings themselves who use the machines, even though a probable "image-self" of the users is created intelligently to match the response to the user.

1.7 INTERNET AND KNOWLEDGE REVOLUTION

To bridge the wide gap that Internet and knowledge revolution have brought with them, we propose a conceptual ladder of social-software (SSW) between HW, SW, FW, micro, and nano-codes of the conventional machines and society based on etiquette of human being. It is also to be noted that the application level programs (written as social programs) for social machines will not run on 250-dollar Google PC and Unix clad bare bone von Neumann machines. This new discipline needs a streamlined philosophy of thought, concepts, innovations, designs, and engineering specifications, to accomplish socially sound advice, documents, and suggestions for human beings to deploy in their own social circles.

This conceptual ladder is placed on the grounds of knowledge explosion and leans against the raw intellect of the user. It becomes a trail and there are specific nodal anchors on the trail. This ladder slanted against human intellect becomes a seven-node graph with binary data as the first node and human values and ethics at the seventh node. In hindsight, the movement along the trail and a climb up the ladder are evident by examining the six decades of rugged computer system since the 1945, von Neumann machine. In foresight, the vastness of the trail ahead and the bright skies above become clearer as machines propose conduct and behavior for children and adolescents as much as seasoned (SW designers and Philosophers[8]) design the conceptual ladder of SSW.

Exact predictions of the future are of no avail due to technological uncertainties and indiscretion of the leaders. However, the conceptual pathways are clear. In order to let progress begin, we traverse the conceptual domain rather than dismantle technological roadblocks. As it was suggested earlier, if the binary

---

[8]The role of the philosophers is to navigate the scientists and SW designers to move along the code of ethics in the society and for the betterment of the human race. It is quite possible to abuse social machine to hurt the society, human race, and environment just as it is possible to abuse aerodynamics to build drones and drop bombs in Iraq, or use of nuclear engineering to make Hiroshima-type bombs for Japan!

bit conveys the status of reality (however fragmented it may be) and let the human values and ethics be the goal, then the trail ahead and the climb above have several stops (however harsh they may be).

A genuine conceptual breakthrough is a rarity.[9] The womb of concept is the human mind and pristine minds bear purest thoughts to benefit the society. Such purity of thought lies in seeking goals (such as preserving nature, reducing air pollution, and CO_2 emissions) that are distinctively beneficial to the human beings, race, and society. In a coherently pure fashion, the dominance of socially beneficial goals at every node is a prerequisite of a healthy knowledge trail; it is straight and unrelenting crossing the domain of wisdom into ethics.

A deceptive nucleus of falsified information riding along the knowledge trail can as easily shatter an axiom of wisdom. Statements become unfounded and direction appears devious. However, if wisdom is authentic and universal, then unwanted nuclei of false-informers only cause minor disruptions rather than alter the course of wisdom. Writings, events, and incidents since the days of Socrates document that the momentum along a trail of human betterment will continue despite corruption and deception in the society. Being able to learn from history, one can construct a rugged path and then a fine trajectory that social machine can traverse to offer more insightful and significant analysis. Faster responses based on the human behavior and the cultural setting accrues.

In a purely human setting, the selection of the optimal behavior is generally instinctual and partly learned. Inherited or acquired systematic selection entails filtering out the distracting objects from the pertinent objects to derive an economic benefit from such goal seeking activities. Predators practice selection as they hunt, farmers select the crops they plant, humans select as they find a mate, etc. In most instances, selection enhances the probability of success of the final goal since the basis of selection is to be optimal in achieving the initial goal(s). Initially the basis of selection may be subjective but soon becomes logical, rational, and then quantitative. When the art of selection is pursued on a mathematical basis, filtering becomes a science and the logical steps in the selection process become goal oriented and programmable. The scientific methodology for optimized social behavior and conduct has been studied and the approach is somewhat streamlined by econometricians from Marshall to von Neumann and Morgenstern. Quantitative and computational approaches to behavior are rare, even though they are used in some managerial decision-making systems.

Instinctive and impulsive decision-making are ruled out of behavioral outputs from the machine. Every step is well founded in the proven scientific or logical processes. Personality-dependent choices are derived from a database of personality traits of the individual user or based on similar decisions by a group of experts in the field and tailored to the particular social situation where the procedure is to be implemented. The machine performs the legwork of paying attention to every aspect of the socioeconomic situation or climate and makes the result tailored to the user and the situation. The additional use of the machine is that it can be primed to the personality of different individuals (such a pragmatic boss or a ruthless business tycoon) and find their responses. By adding a learning algorithm, the machine will imitate the behavior of other individuals like a chess-playing machine that anticipates the moves of a novice, a mediocre, or an expert in the game.

---

[9]Even though such breakthroughs (such as fiber optics for communication, MRI for medical imaging, Internet, Laser disks technology) have occurred in the past for the benefit and rewards to the society.

Human and artificial intelligences have been deployed in both the conflictive (e.g., wars, chess) and cooperative (e.g., musicians, communication systems) modes in the past. The role of the social machine is more generic. In a constructive way, it is programmable and can be assistive in a positive mode (e.g., beneficial to individual and society) or resistive in a negative mode (e.g., detrimental to the individual and society). More than being programmable, it can be tuned to individual preference, health, age, etc., and the social, economic cultural, etc., settings. Unfortunately, in a destructive way, it is also programmable to cause, hasten, ascertain, etc., the destruction of an individual, a corporation, a society, a culture, an economy, etc. The ultimate use of social machines is yet the discretion of a human being who can be a saint (Martin Luther King or Gandhi), a scientist (Louis Pasteur or Alexander Fleming), or a savage (Bush or Mao Zedong).

CONCLUSIONS

The role of knowledge in society is primeval. It has enhanced the quality of life for many centuries and provided human beings with time for contemplation and with a sense of betterment for the self, the society, and the mind. Even though there have been abuses of knowledge toward selfish goals of individuals, societies, and nations, the goals of integrated wisdom have prevailed with a sense of human honor and dignity. There is an element of rationality for the dominance of wisdom over the selfish motives. Wisdom provides a basis for peace in contrast to the sense of threat that is associated with injustice toward the surrounding members of the Klan. Threat from within can destabilize the leisure for contemplation and thus promote the insecurity from within. Repeatedly, contemplated wisdom without deceit has prolonged the duration of peace from without.

Humans and nations can learn from the experiences that unadulterated machines can retrieve, analyze, and present. Tampered machines acquire the vice of hypocrites and alter truth to offer short-term gains. Such machines feed back into the instable cycles' of unrest and injustice. In this chapter, we have alluded to the fact that machines can learn both the positive and negative aspects from the AI-based learning algorithms. For the harm to be accrued and learned as an accepted option, the source of error is generally human or a faulty machine.

REFERENCES

[1] Japanese Temples and Shrines — *The Tale of Genji*, www.taleofgenji.org/japanese_temples_shrines.html.
[2] "Nalanda — Nerve Center of Buddhist Leaning," see Subramaniun VK, "Art Shrines of Ancient India," India: Abhinav Publications, ISBN 978-8170174318, September 1, 2003. pp. 67−70.
[3] "Srenath: Where Buddha Preached His First Sermon."
[4] Hachili R. Ancient Jewish Art and Archaeology in the Diaspora (Handbook of Oriental Studies). Boston: Brill Academic Pub; April 1998, ISBN 978-9004108783.
[5] Gundishapur, Iran, https://en.wikipedia.org/wiki/Gundeshapur.
[6] The Unknown Secret of the Anatolian Mystic Mevlana. . ., www.thewisemag.com/.../the-unknown-secret-of-the-anatolian-mystic-m.

[7] Neumann J von, *First Draft of a Report on the EDVAC*, Contract No., W-670-ORD 4926, Between United States Arm Electronic Computer at the Institute of Advanced Studies, *Mathematical Tables and Other Aids to Computation*, Vol. 7, IAS, Princeton, NJ, p. 108–114, 1953.

[8] Hoddeson L, Vicki D, *True Genius: The Life and Science of John Bardeen*, Washington, D.C.: Joseph Henry Press, ISBN03090884083, October 2002, and American Physical Society Homepage, "This Month in Physics History – November 17–December 23, 1947: Invention of the First Transistor," APS Website www.pbs.org/transistor. Also see Shockley W, *Patent Application Serial No. 35,423* filed June 26, 1948, Private communication (during 1970s) at Bell Telephone Laboratories, Murray Hill, New Jersey. The N- and P-type materials are also presented in in the application; and Bardeen and Brattain WH, *Serial No. 33,466* filed June 17, 1948, Private communication (during 1970s) at Bell Telephone Laboratories, Murray Hill, New Jersey.

[9] Sauter VL. Decision Support Systems for Business Intelligence. Hoboken, NJ: Wiley Press; 2011.

[10] Hamming RW. Numerical Methods for scientists and Engineers. Dover Books on Engineering, Courier Corporation; 1973.

[11] Wicker SB, Bhargava VK, editors. Reed Solomon Codes and Their Applications. Hoboken, NJ: Wiley IEEE Press; 1999.

[12] Shortcliffe E, *MYCIN: Computer-Based Medical Consultations*, New York: American Elsevier, 1976. See also Buchanan BG, Shortcliffe EH, *Rule-Based Expert System: The MYCIN Experiment at Stanford Heuristic Programming Project*, Boston: Addison Wesley, 1984. Also see Bellazzi R, Abu-Hanna A, Hunter J, (Eds.), *Artificial Intelligence in Medicine: 11th Conference on Artificial Intelligence in Medicine in Europe*, AIME 2007, Amsterdam, The Netherlands, July 7–11, 2008.

[13] Ahamed SV, "Social Impact of Intelligent Telecommunications Networks," In: Proc. of the Pacific Telecommunication Conference, Honolulu, January 17–22: 407–414.

[14] Ahamed SV, Lawrence VB. *Intelligent Broadband Multimedia Networks*, Boston: Kluwer Academic Publishers, 1997. Also see Ahamed SV, *Intelligent Internet Knowledge Networks: Processing of Concepts and Wisdom*, Wiley-Interscience, 2006.

[15] Ahamed SV. Computational Framework for Knowledge. Hoboken, NJ: John Wiley and Sons, Inc; 2009.

[16] Ahamed SV. *Intelligent Networks; Recent Approaches and Applications in Medical Systems*, Chapter 2, Elsevier Insights, 2013.

FROM PHILOSOPHERS TO KNOWLEDGE MACHINES

2

CHAPTER SUMMARY

This chapter deals with the fuzzy space between the concepts and hypotheses of monks, philosophers, and preachers of the pre-computers era and that of equations and the exactitude of the physicists, mathematicians, and knowledge workers. The pathways are not always clear due to the infantile nature of knowledge sciences calling for considerable mental latitude to traverse both the conceptual and the mathematical spaces. The entrenched methodology and ordered discipline of Ancient Greek philosophers seem to have lost its identity in the very real pragmatism of the mid-period scientists. Over the ages, order and discipline of the philosophers toward a cohesive society have been lost. The social bondage underlying the philosophic teachings have become shrouded to the extent that the current knowledge-worker can choose to ignore it completely. The embrace of greed can and does in some cases ruin the morality of social values. Social decay becomes imminent and self-preservation is prioritized over morals and ethics. Though philosophic, the individual and the collective minds are aware of the unrest in the individuals, in the communities, in the society, and in the nations.

The purpose of this chapter is to explore the conflict between the two fundamentally opposite tendencies in all species: one favoring self-love, aggression, and exploitation, and the other pure love, restraint, and respect. The role of knowledge sciences and machines is to be aware of both sides but to suggest and justify the boundary between both with a dynamic balance that permits limited excursion of either side without being disruptive or overbearing in either direction. Such a balance is feasible by an analysis of the present tendencies and using (linear or adaptive) predictive corrections. Most of the long-term stable systems use such mathematical tools to achieve a (reasonable) peace between conflicting scientific (as in engineering systems, such as in the flight of an aircraft) and social (as in corporations such as in conflictive labor-management) systems. The artificially intelligent agents (IAs in AI sciences) lie dormant and are nonintrusive until awakened by any undesirable excursion of one or more parameters that threaten the stability of the system. Ecosystems and social systems that monitor themselves stand to benefit by comparing the levels of information and knowledge in the current (or local) system with those of the more stable and self-corrective systems.

2.1 INTRODUCTION

Preceding the computer and knowledge era, many great philosophers, scholars, and thinkers have contributed to the evolution of knowledge as an asset, a personal gift, an endowment, etc.

Evolution of Knowledge Science. DOI: http://dx.doi.org/10.1016/B978-0-12-805478-9.00002-9

Intense effort, prolonged contemplation, and deep concentration are evident in the credentials they have left behind as literature, essays, poems, and inscriptions. The enduring commitment and the most serious dedications are found in the classic works of science and deduction. Gregor Mendel's deduction of the basic principles of genetics [1], to Rabindranath Tagore's poems [2] bear witness to the character of the thinkers and of the caliber of their long-lasting impact of their very personal work.

It will be impossible to name the historical icons and to exemplify the contribution of the great many philosophers or even to hint at their genius. However, from the perspective of incidence and foundations of knowledge, a considerable groundwork was already done but in thought and words, with pencil and paper rather than in devices and machines. Conceptual blueprints needed the accuracy of the logic circuits and laws of physics to be implemented.

To pave the path toward scientific knowledge, we seek out four of the historical icons: a philosopher (Immanuel Kant) [3], a social psychologist (George Herbert Mead) [4], an industrialist (Henry Ford) [5], and social ecologist (Peter Drucker) [6]. Their contributions can be weaved in the fabric of modern Internet-based knowledge, even though purely philosophic writings of Kant seem to lose firm ground to the very pragmatic approaches of Ford and Drucker. However, the social concerns and the values ingrained in philosophy (Kant) and psychology (Mead) are two major guideposts to morality and ethics essential toward making knowledge be pragmatic, and yet serve as a social beckon for future generations to learn.

It is to be noted that this short reference to the works of these four contributors[1] does not diminish the importance of their work; the context (in this chapter) is knowledge-related. We depend on their early thoughts that have paved the path to information highways and byways, and shed some light into the fiber-optic networks that constitute much of the Global Internet.

2.2 FROM IMMANUEL KANT TO GEORGE HERBERT MEAD
2.2.1 KANT AS A META-PHYSICIST

Among the great thinkers of the pre-computer era, the writings of the paradigmatic philosopher Kant (1724–1804) have merged pure reason into the state of mind not considered as a "blank slate." In a sense, Kant has emphasized the focal role of the mind over experience and empirics that can never be entirely duplicated. Mind, knowledge, and the presence of "spatio-temporal objects with their causal behavior and logical properties" of Kant are all necessary for experience. Reason, mathematics, sciences, and empirical reality of the world short-change the "super realm of speculative metaphysics."

Kant argues the mind plays a central role for the knowledge gained by experience and limiting the access into the mind to the "empirical realm of space and time." His arguments are very convincing for those who wish to ignore the knowledge technology that modern computers and networks have brought the twenty-first-century minds. Space and time can be beautifully merged in the eternity of time and expanse of space, tempered by the velocity of light (from Einstein's perspective) and by the velocity of thought.

---

[1]Perhaps other authors would have chosen a different set of philosophers, contributors, and thinkers, but we still think that the final destination to knowledge science (see Fig. 2.1) would be the same. The absence of any one of the four contributors would have set us back in defining the science of knowledge in the twenty-first century.

Highly regarded in the philosophy, Kant's writings fall short of being convincing in the knowledge society where space, time, and deductive logic are tied by GPS coordinates, cesium clock-cycles, and the entirely proven binary logic of circuits. The changes within the society brought about by the precision of physics and mathematics, implemented on PDAs, and implemented in the knowledge networks of this century offer many mind-blocks to think like Kant and his contemporaries.

Words in philosophy carry varying contextual bondages at different times, in many cultures, and even so in different minds. This fact has been said so at different times, in different cultures, and even in different minds. The universality of truth is diffused in the different settings, which alter the precision of words. In the same vein, the virtue of deeds also has different contextual bondages in different settings. Truth, virtue, and beauty as envisioned by Aristotle become a mirage of imagination that mind can capture a glimpse but not the whole truth, the entire beauty, nor the grace of virtue. If life is change, mind is dynamic and the knowledge is superfast.

The mental imaginary of the "spatio-temporal objects" is a glimpse of the intersection of space (here) and time (now). The very fundamental concepts that Kant conveys become shrouded in logic of the super minds in the knowledge era of this century. Perhaps time has proven that great thinkers like the Greek thinkers bring a sense of timelessness, an aura of universal-space, and an immorality of mind transcending into the timeless, the space-less, and the body-less soul. Be as it may, we can respect Kant in the twenty-first century but not embrace his timeless, space-less, and body-less thoughts, even though his notions are appealing.

2.2.2 MEAD AS A SOCIAL PSYCHOLOGIST

As an American sociologist, Mead (1863−1931) has contributed significantly to the complex ties between mind, self, and society [7]. The modern-day sociology and psychology bear his impression in his well-regarded series of his original papers [8]. Mead's writings are concerned with evolution (borrowed from Darwin) to the general idea that can be hosted in any mind and any time (that is shunned by Einstein) but addressed by Mead in his collections of brilliant papers.

Mead's awareness of the pragmatism (developed during 1920s, with James [9] and others) has made his contributions valuable to the industrial society during the automobile era. Sociologist and psychologists have become aware of his contributions more gradually after his unexpected death in 1931. Western societies have realized the importance of Mead's perception of the physical world and of the social world together and not independently. He also distinguishes that the scientist is not trying to perceive the structure of the world but is simply interested in solving problems in the world that is already there.

Mead's notions of the significance of the mind, self, and society in conjunction with his concepts of the nature of scientific knowledge take him into an unexplored realm of the extension of the mind, an extrapolation of the self, and an ever-changing society in different times and cultures. However, Mead has only words to express his thoughts, and words are frail in cultural and social domains exposing his thoughts to misinterpretation in the words for the Internet and knowledge banks.

Mead's treatment of the processes of mind puts his ideas in par with the processing binary data in the central processor units of computers. In the knowledge machines, the processing of objects (knowledge-centric noun-objects and data) by operations (knowledge-oriented verb-functions), Mead's contributions find a vague correspondence. In the twenty-first century, the interpretation still needs a stretch of the imagination, but the conceptual bondage exists. Mead's awareness of the "generalized other" with the processing and consideration to be programmed into the social machines. Mead's work is commendable since his notions of 1920s may last well into the 2020s when social machines will govern human relations more elegantly and with less conflict and strife. His regard and consideration for the society embedded in the knowledge-ware will resolve the routine problems of ordinary lives of the populous. The knowledge machines with optimal code customized for the individuals in most social and cultural settings, the knowledge coordinates provided by such machines will serve as the knowledge-based global positioning systems (KGPS) on the network and Internet domains. Unfortunately, Mead did not leave behind diagrams and sketches to build knowledge-based machines from his treatment of "Scientific Knowledge" (see the discussion of Drucker's contributions, Section 2.3.2).

2.3 FROM HENRY FORD TO PETER DRUCKER

2.3.1 FORD AND MODEL T AUTOMOBILES

The major knowledge-related events presented in the Chapter 1 cover a span from early times to 1950s. Notable theoretical contributions coming from Marshall [10] to Morgenstern [11] have shaped the recent history of human thought whereas industrialists have down-to-earth priorities. Thoughts and deeds have been transfused into ambitions and practice most elegantly by many kings and emperors alike; however, the American industrialist Henry Ford (1863−1947) made his dream to address the social need for transportation with his vision to mass-produce one Model T automobile every 24 seconds. During the early efforts, the Model T was to provide a reliable automobile for everyone, and it first appeared in late 1908. His efforts to standardize the Model T with interchangeable parts manufactured and assembled in large production plants (1913) resulted in the very first moving assembly line. The Model T (1908−1927) has left a history of great ambitions, steadfast determination, and sound enterprise practice for many generations. Model T sales had reached 15 million vehicles sold before other competing cars had cut down the sales of the Model T. Together with industrial skills, Ford was very much of a humanist with his charity and peace efforts during World War II. The later efforts of the Ford Motor Company to fund research, education, and development are also noteworthy.

These aspects of the great industrialist bring Ford into the knowledge era, but all the effort and work were human; though human was executed with precision and exactitude to succeed at every stage merging values with confidence, knowledge, concepts, and wisdom coupled with values and ethics.

2.3.2 DRUCKER AND MANAGEMENT SCIENCES

Drucker (1909−2005) as a social ecologist (as he calls himself) documented his contributions in 39 books and numerous monographs. His writings cover the topics in this book. Almost 60 decades of authoring his classic books toward making organizations strong further to strengthen the society. His contributions focus on the individual, the organization, and the society. His vision extended over reshaping management practice and theory for many decades to come. Having been exposed to the executive styles of numerous executives, politicians, and leaders, Drucker's emphasis has been on performance of individuals, corporations, societies, and nations. His commitment to making everything and everyone serve the society better is hardly to be duplicated by anyone in his era. Master of methodology and an expert of every detail, Drucker has left a deep imprint on how to do everything right to be most effective and optimal.

While at New York University from 1950−1971, he authored his famous book *The Practice of Management* [12] to address the science of corporate management and its practice into a well-bounded and integrated reference book of knowledge to run corporations. This body of knowledge has been introduced earlier as *BoK* [13] and is also addressed as Knowledge Centric Object or KCO [14] in Part II of this book. During his tenure at New York University, Drucker has made a serious and concerted effort to initiate a new discipline of management. In a sense, his contributions and discussions precede the contents of this book, even though the accuracy and exactitude of computer sciences are not carried through in Drucker's contributions.

His identification of the five basic functions (Plan, Organize, staff, Implement, and Control (which we will collectively refer as *POSIC*)) in the practice of management have altered the executive actions dramatically. His control function or "*C*" is sometimes replaced by Communicate, Control, and Coordinate, which we will refer as C^3 (or *C-cube*). In Section 2.4, we fall back on Drucker's contribution not so much to manage corporations but to manage the evolving science of knowledge and include social values and ethics as integral components of knowledge science (see Sections 2.5 and 2.6 and Figs. 2.1 and 2.2).

Words and quotes by Drucker tend to become weak and frail in the programming knowledge processes into machines. Software engineering and knowledge-science techniques would perhaps help.

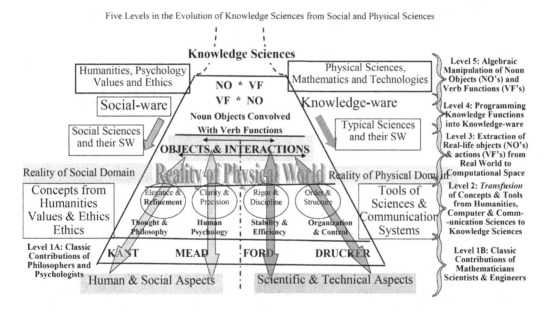

FIGURE 2.1

Five stages in forming a sociological and scientific platform for the evolution of knowledge sciences. Five levels on the right side classify the functions essential to lead up to the science of knowledge. Reality of the physical world (level 3) is the basis as much as it is the basis of physics. In both disciplines, reality and experimentation provide the final sanity check. The noun-objects (NOs) their verb-functions (VFs) and context of their interaction (*) at level 5 provide the link between human thought and validity of the knowledge-centric objects (KCOs) with the physical "objects" that "do" actions to result in elements of knowledge.

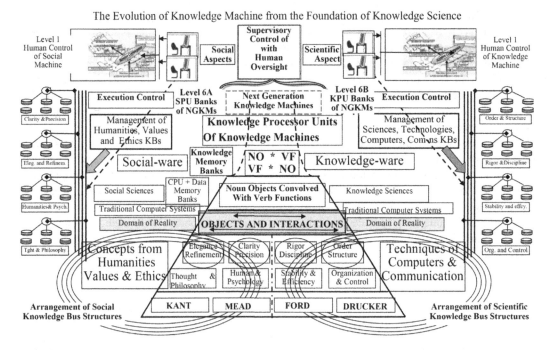

FIGURE 2.2

Architectural layout of a next generation knowledge machine that operates in both the social domain and the scientific domain. In this configuration, the operation of the machine stays tightly between the laws of sciences (right side of the diagram) and the ethical values (left side) of human beings. The human oversight (top of the diagram) further ascertains that the machine works in the realm of the current problem that the machine is resolving. The reach of the knowledge in the core of the machine reaches beyond the immediate human thought that an individual can span, and the solution offered by the machine is both ethical and scientific.

His effort to merge corporations into society and vice versa has left social ethics and values in a lurch. Unfortunately, corporations of the late twentieth and early twenty-first centuries are not always confined to be socially beneficial; but instead, they gravitate toward corporate goals of self-interest and ruin the competition. All may be fair in love and war, but it is not so in war against ethics and social values. When positive social objectives are tossed away like an old hat, opportunism, self-interest, and greed take the place of wisdom, values, and ethics. In most instances, corporate goals are in direct conflict (see the cases of Enron [15], Global Crossings [16], and Arthur Anderson [17]) with social and ethical objectives. Even the Military Industrial Complexes [18], organizations, and numerous Congressional and elected officials have been victims of their self-serving interests and swindling federal funds and public monies into their own privately held organizations.

2.3.3 THE UNISON OF SOCIAL SCIENCES AND PHYSICAL SCIENCES

Social skills and adjustments have prevailed long before the hard physical sciences. Existence of species is a testimony to the cooperation in spite of their conflicts. Conflicts like wars come and go, but cooperation lives on to live and let live. In this very mode of thinking, the Greek philosophers have merged social betterment and welfare (in spite of their injustices toward the slaves and captives) into the acts of lasting values in their daily life. Their concepts of truth, virtue, and beauty still linger on.

From a more modern perspective, we illustrate the merger of social science perspectives of Kant and Mead with early scientific perspectives of Ford and Drucker in Figure 2.1. On the right, with emphasis on the social aspects, two noteworthy contributions of Kant are his elegance and refinement of thought and philosophic perspectives. Equally, authentic endowments of Mead are clarity and precision of dealing with psychology and humanities. The clarity of philosophic principles of Kant in his books is as outstanding as the psychological refinement of Meads in his papers, not to outweigh each other but to supplement and enhance one another.

From an even more modern perspective, we find the commonality and intersection between the achievements of Ford as an industrialist and the writings of Drucker as a theorist and as a conceptualist. Ford practiced in his role as an entrepreneur what Drucker conceptualized many years later as a management scientist. On the left side of Figure 2.1 we have emphasized on the procedural and scientific aspects of the two contributor Ford and Drucker. The rigor and discipline of Ford in his industrial setting are as emphatic as the order and structure of Drucker in his management of organizations.

Fortunately, Drucker wrote profusely and we fall back on his work to bring it to make it useful in the design and architecture of knowledge into a science and to make information machines (computers) useful as knowledge machines. Toward the end of the integration of social sciences and scientific disciplines with the contributions of all the four (Kant, Mead, Ford, and Drucker), the goal is to build a humanist machine that integrates the knowledge and concepts (of Ford and Drucker) with the wisdom and ethics (of Kant and Mead).

The foundation of knowledge sciences based in social and physical sciences is the physical reality of human perceptions with the laws of physical sciences that govern the stability of objects and the continuity of actions. Together they contribute to the gratification of human needs and their perception with the reality that actions are necessary to contribute to knowledge when a noun-object interacts with a verb-function or verb-function acts upon a noun-object. Both get closely "convolved" for an element of knowledge to be formed.

Economically viable machines deal with reality. As depicted at level 3 of Figure 2.1, the physical world is the central theme of knowledge sciences focusing on real objects that exist because they perform some function or serve some purpose, or they have been brought into existence because of "work done," energy spent, or stored in the objects. Objects without history or information and without any verb(s) associated with them are no objects at all. Knowledge ID built and stored as nouns and verbs interact modifying each other; however, a context, an order, or a methodology are necessary to generate *sensible* knowledge. The syntax of interaction is called "convolution" and represented as the symbol * between nouns or noun-object(s) abbreviated as NO, and verbs or verb-function(s) abbreviated as VF in layer 5 of Figure 2.1.

It is to be firmly noted that the structure of knowledge science depicted in Figure 2.1 encompasses all the scholarly writings of the prior generations, whereas the writings of the prior generations cannot encompass knowledge sciences. This asymmetry is because all the documents from the prior generations must have NOs, large or small, that must be associated with their respective VFs, large or small, in the appropriate *contextual relation* with each other. Only and only then, the knowledge presented by the prior generations would be *sensible* to have survived in the literature.

In essence, all documents in literature would be suitable inputs, the knowledge machines that process and validate knowledge structures.

NO * VF (to denote that a noun-object performs a verb-function)
VF * NO (to denote that a verb-function is performed on a noun-object)

The preceding representation implies that actions (VFs) are initiated by NOs and that such actions when performed in the appropriate contextual relationship affect other NOs. In the process, they also generate an element of knowledge. In knowledge machines, such elements of knowledge can be processed by knowledge processor units (or *KPUs*) as bits of data that are processed in central processor units (CPUs) of computers. Data structures (or orderly collections of bits, such as bytes, words, blocks, operation codes) are also used in typical computers and have corresponding usage in knowledge machines. In a parallel universe of knowledge, these elements of knowledge can be processed, reprocessed, assembled, and combined as large, more elaborate bodies of knowledge (*BoKs* and *KCOs*), leading on the wisdom and the concepts that it holds. Human bondage is thus founded in the processes of the knowledge, wisdom, and concept machines.

The contents of the literature can also be processed by knowledge machines to examine, refine, modify, and enhance, or conversely even examine, distort, degrade, and (even) pollute the original knowledge. This feature of the machine needs care so that the authenticity of the old documents is not attenuated, delayed, distorted, and even destroyed. Unfortunately, the human social systems (such as the news media) and cultures have this capability to make gossip out of scholarly writings and vice versa. Two-penny dotcoms, biased website owners, and political reporters make such negative alteration in everyday life to make most of Internet information false and junk material. Only the thoughtful and reflective viewers can and generally decipher "who" is doing "what" to the embedded knowledge. Spam is another serious and notorious by-product of such abuse, and machines can contribute to such undesirable and falsified representations of truth/authentic knowledge.

2.3.4 MACHINE ARCHITECTURE FROM KNOWLEDGE FUNCTIONS

The basic contributions of industrialist(s) and management scientist(s) encompassing the laws of physics, sciences, and engineering are implanted in the knowledge bases on the right. These notions are updated by the knowledge base management (KBM) side on both sides of the diagram. The contributions of Kant and Mead are stored in the left-hand side, but are continuously updated by the Social Science Knowledge-base managers to suit the time era, cultural setting, and corporate/domestic environment. Reality is firmly placed at the center and interaction between NOs and VFs conform to the knowledge machine setting. The knowledge-ware governs the semantic and syntactic rules of NOs and VFs.

Management of databases and switching control points is essential in all intelligent systems to perform communication network services [19, 20]. Introduced in 1987, as an architectural component of Intelligent Network 1, the service switching point (SCP) is managed and updated on a continuous basis by the network services management systems (SMS) staff. This practice has proven to be effective and useful through the development of most Internet services, and we propose it as an integral part of using in the intelligent knowledge science machines.

A superstructure of entirely new computer systems can be superposed on Figure 2.1 to provide a basis of a knowledge machine to solve routine humanistic problems. Conceptually, two additional atop the five-level layers (see the right side of the figure) depicted in Figure 2.1. The two layers 6 and 7 shown at the top of Figure 2.2 are necessary to include (a) the role of the knowledge processor units or KPUs (that can be manufactured like the CPUs of traditional computers) and (b) the need for controlling the execution of the knowledge machine (KM). The KM is very likely to become unstable and roll off into searching and modifying unrelated NOs, VFs, and their convolutions *s. Hence, the human control plays the role of a human pilot of an aircraft, even though the autopilot can handle most routine functions.

Additionally, on the hardware-side local knowledge-banks (supplemented by Internet web-based knowledge-banks) become necessary to supply the attributes of NOs, the associated VFs, and the context-based convolutions. The validity of the each of the operations NO*VF and VF*NO at every knowledge-operation-code (*KOPC*) will be appropriately compiled, debugged, and executed only if the syntax, semantics, and *KOPC* are correctly encoded in the knowledge machine. Such checks and stops are routinely performed in all compilers and assembler of plain old computers before the programs are executed.

2.3.5 GENERALIZATION OF THE STRUCTURE OF KNOWLEDGE SCIENCE

In Figure 2.1, two related disciplines (social and physical sciences) with a common foundation of knowledge implies the very basic axiom that all fragments of knowledge in any form or shape have to have NOs and VFs embedded in them. Even more, any increment of sensible knowledge in any size has to have a contextual, syntactic, and semantic bondage (*) between NOs and VFs, thus an element of knowledge occurs when the bondage occurs. Nonsensible bondage of nonobjects with unrealistic VF is no knowledge.

To the extent that any two disciplines that have connectivity through the embedded NO(s), VF(s), and/or (*(s)), the structural diagram of Figure 2.1, can be used to connect them. For example, physics and chemistry both depend on atoms and their structure and when combined the two lead to physical chemistry. The connectivity may be examined at the nuclear level, at the cosmic level, or anywhere in between. The net result is an inroad into a combined science that may already be chartered or not.

When there are more than two (say '*n*') disciplines involved (such as physical, organic, inorganic chemistries), then a sequential approach of tying 1 with 2, 2 with three, etc., is necessary first, and then 1 with 3, 2 with 4, and so on. Finally, the entire connectivity chart should be reexamined for the validity of rule to each of the '*n*' disciplines. The approach is depicted in Figure 2.3 for the simple case where $n = 3$ for chemistry when transfusing knowledge from physical, organic, or inorganic chemistry into the other two chemistries.

It is also possible to combine two or more knowledge contents (or disciplines) in numerous ways. The necessary and sufficient condition is that there is a commonality of some real or known NOs, VFs and their connectivities between the disciplines. If there is no commonality at all, then the infusion become ineffective. For example, if the disciplines are the astronomy of the Rings of Mars and weather science for Arctic snow of the planet earth, or the cure earache and treatment for loss of hair, then the connectivity becomes distant and infusion of knowledge becomes less feasible.

Conversely, when a doctor or a patient is exploring transcendental meditations, medicinal drugs, and exercise all three together, in search for a new discipline for the cure of poor health, then the connectivities become clearly evident. The three approaches become strongly connected since mind

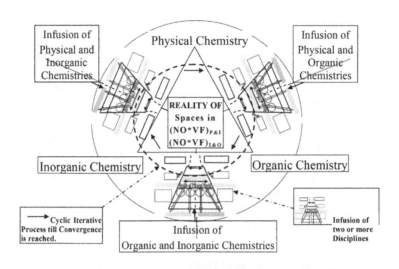

FIGURE 2.3

Generalization of the infusion principle for three (physical, organic, and inorganic) chemistries into combined knowledge for all three chemistries but with fewer customized laws of chemistry that will be applicable.

and body function together via the physiological organs common to both. Exercise that affects the body and muscle tone also affects the mind. Medicines affect the mind and body together that feels the pain or poor health.

NOs, VOs, and their contextual relations are implied in a realistic fashion to generate sensible and meaningful knowledge. When this law of relationships is not adhered, the operations (NO * VF) and (VF * NO) generate gibberish and insensible, incomprehensible set of words in any language. The need for human supervision and oversight (as depicted in Fig. 2.2) becomes essential to keep the knowledge machine to perform socially and ethically significant tasks. In the medical field, the staff and supervisory personnel perform these actions depending on their respective knowledge potentials (or KnP defined in chapter 11 of Reference 14) that they have acquired during training. Knowledge from one period of time to the next is thus communicated or deployed by the human beings in this case, or knowledge machines themselves as they adhere to their medical knowledge-banks that guide their processes.

The NOs, VFs, and the convolutions are delineated as organs of the body; the actions of such organs and physiological components (namely, limbs, muscles, heart, nervous system, etc.), the exercise (the extent of muscular movements of the related the associated group of muscles, etc.) and the meditation affect body and mind that experience the poor health. Convolutions play a part in their own right. The exercise, the timing, and durations, the TM, body posture, concentration, schedule, and frequency of activities become tied to the NOs and VFs. The overall effect might be exactly what a knowledge machine would predict and recommend. In this case, the knowledge machine serves as good humanist machine and depicted in Figure 2.4.

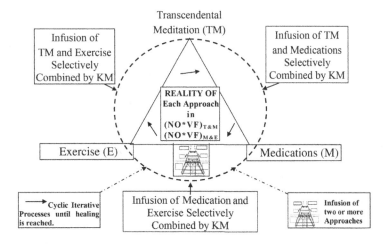

FIGURE 2.4

Generalization of the Infusion principle for three (transcendental meditation (TM), medications (M), and exercise (E)) remedial measures for patient condition into knowledge for the Combination of all three healing processes but with fewer customized laws of healing that will be applicable.

CONCLUSIONS

In this chapter, contributions of the philosophers and scientists of the earlier generations are used as wisdom-bases for the solution of knowledge-based problems dealing concurrently with sciences, engineering, and technologies of the Internet age. Such an approach facilitates the solution the social problems of individuals, societies, and nations. The goal for the machine is to seek customized and significant solutions that are not detrimental to the society, the culture, the environment, and/or the nation. The machine spans, the wisdom, and the ethical foundations in the writings of scholars as thoroughly and efficiently as it searches all the annals of modern sciences. Creativity is not limited by time (fiber-optic access to the literature) and space (Internet addressing of the knowledge bases) in the proposed machine.

The proposed machine can be fragmented to serve any combination of two or simpler disciplines. By selecting, the Vedic writing of transcendental meditation on the left side and modern medical science on the right side the machine will search as thoroughly for the cure(s) of migraine headaches or for cancer. The basis is the presence of some objects ("noun-object(s)" or NOs or KCOs) and some actions ("verb-function(s)" or VFs) that they have to perform in any appropriate context (*). If the connectivity is entirely unavailable, then the knowledge bases cannot link the NOs with the VFs in the appropriate context (*) and our knowledge becomes incomplete. The balance, the context, the convolution, or "cure" can be searched adaptively and/or exhaustively by the machine.

REFERENCES

[1] Mendel G. Wikipedia, the free encyclopedia, <https://en.wikipedia.org/wiki/Gregor_Mendel>.

[2] Tagore R. Poet Seers » Tagore Short Poems, www.poetseers.org/nobel-prize-for-literature/tagore/short/, accessed November 1, 2015; also see Rabindranath Tagore.pdf, <http://www.iitg.ernet.in/scifac/krishna/public.../Rabindranath%20Tagore.pdf>.

[3] Kant I. (Stanford Encyclopedia of Philosophy), <http://plato.stanford.edu/entries/kant/>, accessed November 1, 2015.

[4] Mead, G. Herbert Internet Encyclopedia of Philosophy. <http://www.iep.utm.edu/mead/> Internet Encyclopedia of Philosophy.

[5] Henry F. Wikipedia, the free encyclopedia, <https://en.wikipedia.org/wiki/Henry_Ford>.

[6] Peter Drucker's Life and Legacy | The Drucker Institute, <http://www.druckerinstitute.com/peter-druckers-life-and-legacy>.

[7] Mind, Self, and Society from the Standpoint of a Social Behaviorist (Works of George Herbert Mead, Vol. 1), Chicago: University of Chicago Press; 1967.

[8] George Herbert Mead on Social Psychology, Mead, Strauss, <http://www.press.uchicago.edu/.../bo3619703.html>.

[9] James W. – Philosopher, Journalist, Psychologist, Doctor, <http://www.biography.com/people/william-james-9352726>.

[10] Marshall A. – Wikipedia, the free encyclopedia, <https://en.wikipedia.org/wiki/Alfred_Marshall>.

[11] Morgenstern O. <http://www.econlib.org/library/Enc/bios/Morgenstern.html>.

[12] Drucker PF. The practice of management. HarperBusines; New York, Reissue edition 2006.

[13] Ahamed SV. Computational framework of knowledge. Hoboken: John Wiley and Sons; 2009.

[14] Ahamed SV. Next generation knowledge machines. Waltham, MA: Elsevier Insights Book; 2014.

[15] Enron Fast Facts – CNN.com, <http://www.cnn.com/2013/07/02/us/enron-fast-facts/>.

[16] How Executives Prospered as Global Crossing Collapsed, <http://www.nytimes.com/.../how-executives-prospered-as>.

[17] Arthur Andersen's Fall from Grace Is a Sad Tale of Greed, <http://www.wsj.com/articles/SB1023409436545200>, *The Wall Street Journal*.

[18] Military–industrial complex – Wikipedia, the free encyclopedia, <https://en.wikipedia.org/wiki/Military_industrial_complex>.

[19] Ahamed SV, Lawrence VB. Design and engineering of intelligent communication systems. Boston: Kluwer Academic Publishers; 1997.

[20] Ahamed SV, Lawrence VB. Intelligent broadband multimedia networks. Boston: Kluwer Academic Publishers; 1997.

AFFIRMATIVE KNOWLEDGE AND POSITIVE HUMAN NATURE

3

CHAPTER SUMMARY

Affirmative knowledge assists human progress. The positive side of human nature is stressed to enhance, amplify, and confirm the knowledge accumulated in the knowledge banks from the wisdom and observations of the prior cultures and societies. Knowledge is gained and stored, documented, enhanced, and polished to help the current and future societies to benefit from the good sense. This knowledge-base serves to make leisure and contemplative time to accelerate the positive growth of sound and beneficial knowledge. More recently, the Artificial Intelligence software and routines facilitate the extraction of such knowledge and information from the routine objects and verbs (actions) that are necessary to gratify human needs.

3.1 INTRODUCTION

Freud and Maslow have firmly established the motivations that arise from deficit needs. This observation is applicable for all species in most circumstance. Needs are generally depicted as need pyramids to indicate the dominance of certain needs over the others. Maslow [1] has classified the human needs into five groups (safety, physiological, social, ego and realization) of human needs. The most dominant needs (safety and physiological needs) are placed at the lowest frustums of the need pyramid. The urge to act at any instant if time is to gratify the most outstanding need. Whereas Maslow has five groups of needs, Ahamed [2] has added two additional groups: ((i) Need to Search for the optimal, the best, and the perfect (solution, partner, education, etc.) and (ii) the Unification of everything into a common stem of unified and integrated knowledge. The additional layers facilitate (i) the inclusion of the social aspects of searching for the optimal and/or the best solution for one's own self and the society and (ii) the integration of the various knowledge platforms into one Generic and Universal knowledge platform. Human beings sped a considerable amount of intellect, reasoning, and time to make the gratification of open and underlying needs optimal, elegant, and perhaps beautiful and virtuous. Needs are thus gratified, and the knowledge in choosing the objects to gratify and the necessary actions by humans on the locally present social objects are also generated and noted, recorded, documented, and published in knowledge banks.

Figure 3.1 depicts three phases of the solution to most routine human and social problems with the aid of need processing computer system. Seven layers of needs are represented by an open pyramid of needs. At the lowest level the Maslow's need for safety and security are shown. Typically, not all the seven levels of needs are present in all human beings. However, these needs prompt motivation for some action to gratify the need. The system and the human beings search for objects and actions in proper contextual relations to resolve such needs. Memory in humans and knowledge

Evolution of Knowledge Science. DOI: http://dx.doi.org/10.1016/B978-0-12-805478-9.00003-0

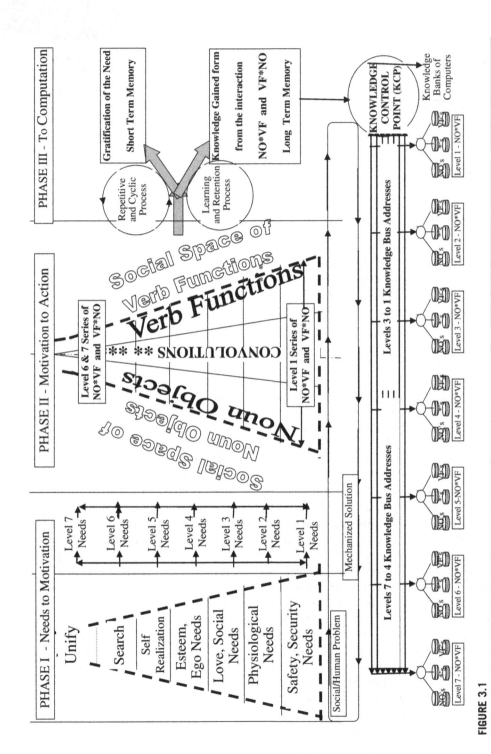

FIGURE 3.1

Configuration of a human need processing system by a computational facility. Phases 1,2, and 3 are delineated whereby system picks up a deficit need, classifies it, determines the need gratifying objects (NOs), the actions (VFs), and the contextual association between the two and resolves the need. Social and cultural dependence is stored in the knowledge banks. Problem solving is accurate.

banks in machines select objects and verbs with a sensible structural relation to find a feasible solution. In most cases, some conclusion is reached, and the extent of gratification is analyzed in view of the resources expended in realize that gratification.

The solution is embedded in the mind or machine and both learn from the solution, the methodology, and the marginal utility of the solution. In the machine, the objects are grouped and classified by the level of need and the general context of the problem. Suitable mathematical and economic analyses become necessary.

In the knowledge-based system, the choice of objects and verbs and their convolutions is done via a knowledge control point, or KCP, shown on the right side of the Figure 3.1. The KCP [3] is a knowledge-based switching system and it selects the appropriate knowledge base under the knowledge processor unit (KPU) command.

3.2 USE OF SCIENTIFIC AND AI-BASED MACHINES

These machines can be tiny as notebook-computers or full-fledged supercomputers. The nature of applications and the clientele requirements determine the exact fit of the machine to an individual or an institution. Network configurations and cloud computing may be configured to accommodate the size and geographical distribution of the users. The typical central processor units (CPUs), control memories (CMs), and main memories (MMs) configurations [3] are deployed but the architectures are highly variable. The input/output processors and devices are tailored specifically to the user requirements. Subject matter-based KBs and databases are specifically designed to suit the application(s). It is usual to add one or more matrix and array-processors with or without double-precision arithmetic units in the academic computing and research centers and networks. Object processing SW and knowledge-ware are some of the features of AI-based [5] machine.

Specific hardware devices for specialized graphics is generally treated as external devices and tagged on the main input/output bus(es) of the CPU banks. The computer technology is now mature to customize these machines to be highly efficient and optimally configured.

3.2.1 EVOLVING USE OF KNOWLEDGE AND INTERNET MACHINES

Knowledge banks are as vital for knowledge networks as the directory databases for communication networks. Both trigger the connectivity and channel paths for communication channels. Both supply vital information necessary for users and clients. In their most primitive formats, (i) the directory databases contain the client names and telephone numbers for the network and (ii) knowledge banks contain raw information for clients, respectively.

In the intermediate formats, the directory databases contain telephone numbers, client names, wire center details (at the local central office), and physical paths to the client addresses. The knowledge banks contain the knowledge source, the Dewey decimal classification code, and the pointers to the sources of the knowledge.

In the more advanced formats, the directory databases for technical use contain the loop makeup, the street addresses of the distribution center, the nature and the consistency of the wires to and from the distribution centers, the number of duplicate and auxiliary wire pairs available, and possible alternate routing in case of emergency or loop failure. This data is also stored in addition to data in the intermediate formats. Numerous linked databases may also be deployed. Knowledge banks contain the far more diversified data such as the IP addresses of KBs, alternative addresses of the KBs, access charges, user profiles, and frequency of use.

In the mobile networks, the dynamic channel path is allocated depending on the usage, delay, traffic conditions, user quality of service requirements, etc. In fiber-optic (FO) networks, the network addressing of the FO distribution is generally fixed. In the distribution network, the fiber to the home (FTTH, [6]) also remains fixed. Cable or fiber completes the connectivity to the home router or the set-top box. In satellite networks, the satellite network address depends on time of the day, the earth and lunar shadow (on the satellites), and the dynamic channel allocation algorithms choose the uplink, the downlink, and satellite-to-satellite link (if necessary). The transmission aspects if the information through these networks is an elaborate science in its own right.

In the most advanced network configuration, the knowledge banks may be required to perform knowledge processing (such as relevancy of the knowledge search, the sequence and order of the user queries, the graph tree of the knowledge delivered, the individual charges for knowledge access) functions. Some of the sophisticated knowledge centers that provide medical services may require all the service aspects of computer centers in addition to those of the knowledge dissemination and acquisition centers and knowledge processing functions.

Knowledge banks play an integral part in the Internet search activity. There are two aspects of searching: (i) Internet search based on commercial search engines that search out for physical objects and "things" and word phrases, and (ii) human search for the best results based on mental, emotional, knowledge, etc., spaces. Certain sets of convolved objects, things, and scenarios result from the searches that may involve concepts, wisdom, and ethical standards. Two activities are generally interleaved: (a) machine processing for discovering the objects in the Internet space and (b) a mental processing of the "discovered" objects. Even though the later type of searches is rare, it is common in research and innovation. For example, if a mathematician is searching for an algorithm, a multistage search becomes necessary that invokes the "objects" in the algorithm and then the search (or modified search) for the processing of such objects.

Much as knowledge banks play an important role in Internet, mainframe computing systems and communication switches play a critical role in the hardware of knowledge and Internet machines. From main machines for data processing to laptops (including personal digital assistants (PDAs), tablets, Androids, etc.), the access and interface devices play the insidious role. Humans, interfaces, networks, and main computer-based information system connect and make up the hardware (HW) chain to connect ethics, wisdom, concepts, and knowledge.

The object processor units (OPUs) [3] and the object and attribute cache(s) are seamlessly integrated with main memories with direct-memory access, or DMA to local secondary object and attribute bases. The World Wide Web, input/output devices for global access to the processors, and the local KBs, the secondary memories (SMs), form the physical layer of a Knowledge-Based Open System Interconnect, or KBOSI, global knowledge networks. Such a system can tackle social and human issues in the society just as it can tackle the inventions and breakthroughs of the twenty-first century.

3.2.2 INCREMENTAL CHANGES IN SOCIETY

Timing and social setting play a dominant part in the social changes that result from human initiated and machine implemented effort to make the change. When the social climate is suitable, human and Federal effort to make a change brings great and accelerated changes. For example,

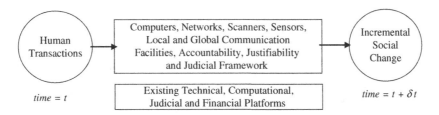

FIGURE 3.2

Snapshot of the human activity in a microscopic timeframe creating incremental changes.

after a war, nation-building effort brings rapid and notable rewards; after an epidemic, vaccination and health care effort brings rapid success; after a natural disaster, Federal and community effort to resurrect the townships restores the flow of traffic and commodities rapidly; etc. These brief timely fixes do not generally cause monumental social changes even though they may send a minor financial shockwave, or secondary enhancement in the way of life. The snapshot of this activity is depicted in Figure 3.2 over short durations of time (δt).

3.3 DUALITY OF NATURAL FORCES AND HUMAN TRAITS

Nature has assumed an uneasy balance over the millennia. The forces within nature create positive and negative incremental changes about a somewhat mean but stable over a short enough time that life can evolve and survive. In the geological time scale, human life has been short, but humans have learned from nature that the fine-tuning of modality and behavior for survival are just as necessary. Simply stated, the routine geological forces are tiny minuscule of those that brought nature into existence. In this mode, the active, proactive, and reactive forces are all effects to cause an ecological system that has assumed a dynamic equilibrium. This chain of adjustments in nature also prevails in human nature, traits, and behavior.

The local and global conditions affect the overall stability/instability of such animate and inanimate systems. The mean, the variance, and the cyclic frequency, and its own variation are all indicative of the nature of the environment. The displacement *(d)* of an object from *O to O'* also implies a change in its status. Even though the core of the object may be the same, its attributes can change incrementally or drastically depending on the forces within the society and the duration for which they are active.

For example, from an embryonic state of life to death and decay, every life form experiences social and environmental influences thus modifying its individual status from an infantile state to death. The name and genetic code may remain but (almost) all attributes change. In evolution, the durations, δt, $\delta t'$, $\delta t''$, etc., may last an eon thus altering the status of flightless dragons to flying vultures. Catastrophic events (such as a meteor strike) are also environmental changes that can accelerate, *a*, or decelerate attribute(s) changes, used in the expression for displacement *d*.

As much as there have been positive changes in human attitude brought about by the drives and efforts of the notable members in the past, there also have been negative changes toward a decline of wisdom, values, and ethics in the society by fewer noteworthy and notorious members. Any positive change incubates a corresponding negative change, perhaps to a greater or a lesser extent as shown in Figure 3.3. A trend is thus established. As far as there is $\pm$ trend, there has to be a

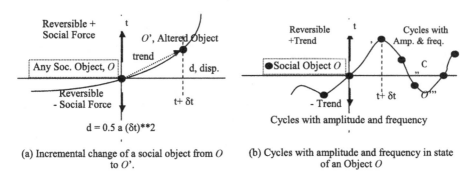

(a) Incremental change of a social object from O to O'.

(b) Cycles with amplitude and frequency in state of an Object O

FIGURE 3.3

The effects of social forces giving rise to (a) trends and their effects on the stability, movement and (b) cyclic variation of the state of any social object $O \rightarrow O' \rightarrow O'' \rightarrow O''' \rightarrow$ etc.

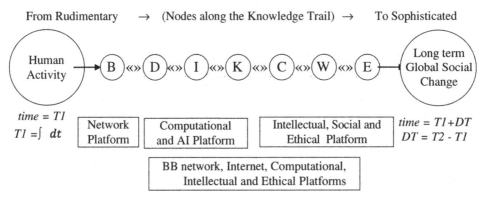

FIGURE 3.4

Software organization and a snapshot of the human activity in a prolonged timeframe creating global and sociological changes. The nodes B, D, I, K, C, W, and E represent the levels of human activity as binary, data structures, information, knowledge, concept, wisdom, and ethical levels. The activities on the left side of the chain are generally more transient and more abundant than those on the right side requiring more time and contemplation. Social change is the cumulative effect of the forces during DT and the social inertia of the society.

knowledge-based trend, thus causing cyclic changes of attitudes in the society. As long as there have been cycles of change, there is a dynamic stability around a shifting mean value Figure 3.4.

3.4 THE FINE SIDE OF HUMAN NATURE

3.4.1 INTEGRATED CHANGES IN SOCIETY

However, major social changes cumulated over long intervals ($DT = T2 - T1$) by serious contemplation and sustained intellectual efforts are shown in Figure 3.5. There is no standard operating procedure to instate such effort in the collective intelligence of the elite in any nation. The initiative and the drive

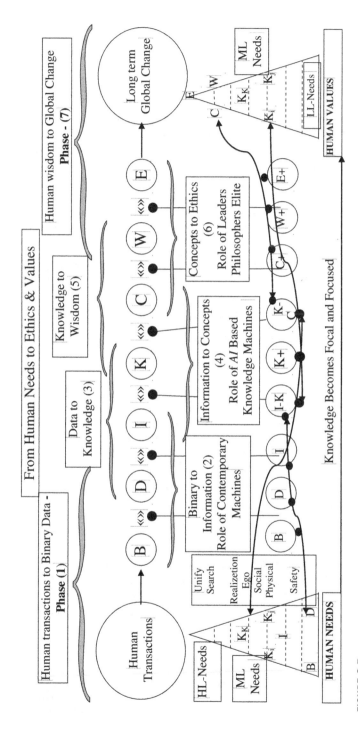

FIGURE 3.5

Snapshot of the human transactions can be in any of the seven nodes along the trail of progressive thinking. In a microscopic time-frame such transactions cause small incremental changes. These changes take place in psyche of humans and memories of machines. Trivial changes are junked, and significant changes are filtered and assigned definitive address space in minds and in knowledge banks of networks and machines. Cumulative changes are reiterated to make patterns of behavior in humans and algorithmic steps in the learning programs of machines. The long-term progression is to move from trivia to significance for humans and from left to right in the computers (on the left side of the diagram) and social machines (on the right side of the diagram).

for the effort incubate lies in the minds of the elite and responsible leaders in the society. For example, the abolition of Slavery, the Declaration of Independence, and the Clean-Air Act all have had intellectual and emotional precursors. When the national and communal predisposition is well suited, major social forces take shape and major social changes occur and have occurred in the past. It appears unlikely (and also true) that Lincoln's push for antislavery would have gained as much momentum in the Southern States as it did in the rest of the United States, or in England as it did in Constitution of the United States. In the same vein, amendments favoring homosexuality or gay marriages are likely to gain momentum in the current pursuit of individual freedom in the social context.

The migration of feelings and sentiment from the minds of elite and intellectuals to general knowledge in the public domain is much slower process. The benefits and rewards of the clean air for the communities to reach the British commoners[1] took about 20 years before coal-burning fireplaces in homes were made illegal. Social responsibility of leaders is generally burned on the stake of profiteering. The social pollution this moral corruption is left to cinder in the minds of the public.

From history, the lag of social awareness of a human trait in public can take as long as a generation if not more. However, on the positive side of the picture, the transition to the knowledge domain can be faster if it is financially rewarding to the business community. The computer and Internet revolutions have been faster especially in the younger generations. The deployment computer in the schools from very young age through the colleges thus forces an adaptation in the learning this ability.

For the knowledge domain to be transfixed in the minds of the public, the deployment of knowledge technology to solve social problems needs a firmer status. Information seekers can be as easily trained for knowledge browsing based on sound ethical foundations. In the current form of indulgence, the young are likely to be swayed in a beer tasting rampage rather than a concept and wisdom development seminar.

Perhaps the human nature during the early years is biased toward the short-lived impulses rather than longer-term self-improvement or social betterment. This tendency is possibly reversed by the enjoyment in giving rather than taking and asking the famous Kennedy question "Ask what you can do for the nation, society, others or humanity?" During the long-past Indian cultures, this was the way of life, wherein the duties of individual members were held in high priority.

3.4.2 GRADUAL TRANSITION IN THE KNOWLEDGE DOMAIN

In the modern era, the scenario is presented by allocating the fragments of information, knowledge, wisdom, and ethics in their natural sequence shown in Figure 3.5 from a young age. Children are taught to respond in a yes/no mode, make choices in binary format, etc. The complexity of behavior as adolescents makes them respond and making choices in based in grouped individual binary decisions. The process continues and becomes more and more complex at higher levels of maturity traversing more of the remaining nodes in Figure 3.5. Most grownups do not reach the last two or three (C, W, and E) nodes and the pursuit of the knowledge trail is an individual journey through the trail spiced by their

---

[1]Even so during 2009, about 33% of the energy generation during 2012 in the United Kingdom was by coal-fired fuel and about 40−43% of the electricity in the United States was by the combustion of fossil fuels. The emission of CO_2, NO_x, SO_x, traces of mercury, and other metals has not triggered a clean and legal stop for this type of environmental pollution. Brayton Point Station is a case study in old, inefficient, and dirty coal plants, and it's not even among the top 100 offenders!

own feeling, sentiments, drives, and needs. Generally, as the needs are fewer, the trail is shorter. As an ultimate paradox, the needs of species limit their understanding and hence their comprehension.

It emphasizes dealing with binary data (B), data structures (D), and information (I) during the formative years and dealing with positive concepts (+C), beneficial wisdom (+W), and social ethics (+E) during the mature years but *without* being side tracked into negative concepts (−C), degenerative wisdom (−W), and social neglect (−E) in the middle years when knowledge (−K) is most operative.

This proposition is not trivial considering that there are many hundred (perhaps thousands) of flavors of + or − C, of + or − W, and of + or − E. The (C, W, E) space is not only hyper-dimensional, but also twisted since both the origin and linearity of the C dimension depends on the origin and linearity of the W and E dimensions.[2] Correspondingly, the properties of the remaining two dimensions W and E depend on the properties of the other two dimensions (C and E) and (C and W), respectively. The C, W, E space is multiflavored, almost as complex as human nature itself. It accommodates the personality of every human being uniquely in its own compartment and each compartment can accommodate millions of behavioral patterns depending on the granularity of the $\pm$C, $\pm$W, and $\pm$E scales. Social machines can track the dynamic movements along the (C, W, E) hyper-dimensional space on an uncertain but probabilistic basis.

3.4.3 POSITIVE SOCIAL CHANGE: BETTERMENT AND ENHANCEMENT

Positive social changes result from the emotional Energies (E) and intellectual Drives (D) of the founding members in a society, community, or nation. Selfless Love (L), proven Axioms of wisdom, and positive social Ethics are the prerequisites. The synergy of the emotion and intellect on a triad of love, wisdom, and ethics is probabilistic outcome in any social setting. When it does occur, it is possible to dissect the scientific basis for its cause and predict the effect and nurture the synergy (based on the five-some, *EDLWE*) to ignite into action giving rise to a social uplift.

In Figure 3.6, the projected concurrence of the *EDLWE* is presented during the duration that social betterment can prevail during the current Internet age and Knowledge society. Human transactions (HT) in the business work environment and (almost all) activities of modern living entail data processing of some sort or another, implying the modern life is (mostly) based on binary data (Node B), its structure represented (Node D) in some computer system or the other, thus leading to the information (Node I).

For a segment of the population dealing with these three nodes is shown as the rounded rectangle on the left of the figure. However, the extraction of the knowledge (Node K) from information becomes essential. For example, a manager or an executive needs to know in order to manage the organization, plan the events to follow, organize the activities, make the business survive, grow, flourish, etc. This leads to a variation of knowledge based on the business, educational, medical, and security system wherein the knowledge trail is implemented.

On the left of Figure 3.5, the nature of human needs [2] ranging from Higher Level Needs (Need to Search for the Best and then Unify it in the Global context of Knowledge) to the Lower Level Needs (Physiological and Safety) are depicted. These needs are of the positive and the benevolent

---

[2]It is questionable whether the algebraic notations of simpler hyperspace of physical sciences can even be used to represent the geometry of the (*C, W, E*) space resident within the perceptual space of humans where the nano-dimensions of biological systems drive the connectivity of neurons which in turn process concepts, wisdom, and ethics.

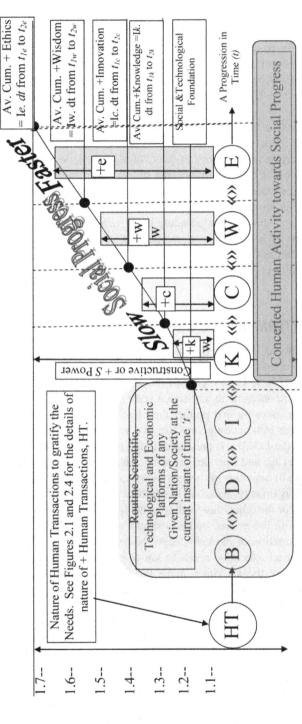

1.7-- | Av. Cum. + Ethics = Ie. dt from t_{1e} to t_{2e}

1.6-- | Av. Cum. +Wisdom = Iw. dt from t_{1w} to t_{2w}

1.5-- | Av. Cum. +Innovation =Ic. dt from t_{1c} to t_{2c}

1.4-- | Av. Cum.+Knowledge =Ik. dt from t_{1k} to t_{2k}

1.3-- | Social &Technological Foundation

1.2-- | A Progression in Time (t)

1.1--

Nature of Human Transactions to gratify the Needs. See Figures 2.1 and 2.4 for the details of nature of + Human Transactions, HT.

Routine Scientific, Technological and Economic Platforms of any Given Nation/Society at the current instant of time 't'.

Constructive or + S Power

Concerted Human Activity towards Social Progress

Slow   Social Progress   Faster

+k   +c   +w   +e

HT → B «» D «» I «» K «» C «» W «» E

Net Social Change in any segment k, c, w, or e during an interval from $t1$ to $t2$, is $+sj$. This positive (beneficial) change is $=\int_1 (+stj).dt$, where stj is the social effort/power at instant 't' in the jth direction leading to progress consistent with the equation for $Energy = \int power.dt$

FIGURE 3.6

Depiction of the change in social evolution of an organism or organization based on knowledge (effort/power) K, concept (effort/power) C, wisdom (effort/power) W, or ethical (effort/power) E, integrated over the duration these powers are active. The social progress becomes faster as the positive knowledge and wisdom starts to grow. A characteristic of triple acceleration occurs because knowledge grows, wisdom grows twice as fast, and then the ethics grow three times as fast. This ideal is rarely achieved in reality, but the converse is true as societies, cultures, and nations deteriorate into social decay when knowledge, wisdom, and ethics all turn negative.

type (e.g., build a business, provide an Internet gateway, install an antivirus software) and result in activities that facilitate[3] rather than the type that hinders the social growth within the environment.

In Figure 3.6, the social change that follows the gratification of human needs is shown. On the right side of the figure, the activities of the positive (K, C, W, and E) type are depicted as four rectangles. The height of the rectangles (*k, c, w,* and *e*) depicts the *efforts* or *powers* that are behind these activities, i.e., activities that are strong are allocated the height (*Y*-axis) accordingly. The measure of this could be budget or manpower allocated, $ allocated and spent, executive initiative, rewards allocated and granted, etc. Along the *X*-axis *time* is depicted when these activities occurred. The product (i.e., *power-* $\times$ *time*) is the measure of *energy* spent for enhancing the K (knowledge direction), the C (concept direction), the W (wisdom direction), and the E (ethics direction) directions. The integral of such energies thus becomes the measure of positive social change during a time ($DT = T2 - T1$) frame. The cumulated integration of total energy is posted on the right side of Figure 3.6.

The shape of the "Social Progress" curve and the rectangles (Fig. 3.6) are quite jagged and irregular in reality. There is granularity in both the effort and the durations thus making the resulting social progress almost (but not quite) random. The cause–effect relationship, although complex, can be tracked. Such progressions are quite frequent in nature and in routine events. For example, the growth of a plant, the progression of a postal item, the development of a child follow the progression of social changes. When the tracking is accurate, the durations and the reasons for the changes can be understood, planned, accelerated, or altered to suit. In fact, the social machines can offer an optimal program of "powers," their intensities (k_i, c_j, w_k, and e_l), and their durations (DT_x) to offer the best, cost-effective, and socially acceptable positive change in the society.

CONCLUSIONS

Social computing has already impacted the private lives via handheld devices and PDAs. The impact of full-fledged social computers is still to emerge. Opportunities posed by network-based social computing possibilities are enormous when social computers are networked into the backbone of the communication systems. Computing and communication have already merged to facilitate the global connectivity and provide data services. The present social opportunities offered by commercial Internet Social Service Providers (ISSP, not to be interpreted as Intelligent Service Switching Points in plain old intelligent networks [8]) are trivial and tainted with exploitation of the innocent and ignorant. Some of the directions of the services (find dates, find affairs, etc.) are slanted toward social decay rather than the positive enhancement.

The social aspects of human lives have not entered the global connectivity and intricacy of backbone networks. The educational and human aspects that may replace high school education with college education, deception with truth, free sex with global morality, etc. can already be implanted in backbone networks. The possibilities prevail with the current backbone switching systems and TCP/IP protocol. Some of the possible venues are explored and delineated in this chapter.

---

[3]The scale of 1.1 to 1.7 is to indicate the positive nature of activities and transactions. It is possible to conceive the negative nature of transactions (see the scale of 2.1 to 2.7 in Figure 2.14) that hinders progress (e.g., planting a virus, destroying sensitive data, or tampering with databases) within the computer systems of an organization thus resulting in a social decay.

REFERENCES

[1] Maslow AH. A theory of human motivation. Psychol Rev 1943:50:370-396, also see Maslow A, Farther reaches of human nature. New York: Viking Press; 1971.

[2] Ahamed SV. "Need Pyramid of the Information Age Human Being," International Society of Political Psychology (ISSP) Scientific Meeting, Toronto, Canada, July 3−6, 2005; also see "An enhanced need pyramid for the information age human being." In: Proc. of the Fifth Hawaii International Conference, Fifth International Conference on Business, Hawaii, May 26−29, 2005.

[3] Ahamed SV. Computational framework for knowledge. Hoboken, NJ: John Wiley and Sons, Inc; 2009.

[4] Hannessy JL, Patterson DA. Computer architecture: a quantitative approach. 4th edition Boston: Morgan Kaufmann; 2006.

[5] Turban E, Aronson JE. Decision support systems and intelligent systems (6th Ed.), Prentice Hall; 2000. Also see Holmes JH, Bellazzi R, Sacchi L, Peek N, Eds., Artificial Intelligence in Medicine: 11th Conference on Artificial Intelligence in Medicine in Europe, AIME 2007, Amsterdam, The Netherlands, July 7−11, 2008.

[6] Ahamed SV, Lawrence VB. Design and engineering of intelligent communication systems. Boston: Kluwer Academic Publishers; 1997.

[7] Ahamed SV, Lawrence VL. Intelligent broadband multimedia networks. Boston, MA: Kluwer Academic Publishers; Boston, 1997. ISBN: 0792397479. Also see Ahamed SV. Intelligent internet knowledge networks: Processing of concepts and wisdom. Wiley-Interscience; Hoboken, 2006.

NEGATIVE KNOWLEDGE AND AGGRESSIVE HUMAN NATURE

4

CHAPTER SUMMARY

This chapter deals with negative knowledge that triggers the societies into disarray, dismay, and deterioration of ethics and values accumulated during the prior interval that built positive ethics and values. We report events from recent history as facts only to indicate that polluted and adulterated knowledge has dire consequences. Section 4.1 documents some of the events that have brought the ethics and conscience of political abusers in grave doubt. The reader is forewarned about the facts that most authors shirk to report. In an extended timeframe, activities of humans and societies are a balance between the fine side of humans and their coarse side. Be as it may, most thoughtful minds weigh and consider all facts. Historically and philosophically, cultures and societies have never been able to eradicate either of the two sides of human nature. Social values are as likely to regress, as they are likely to progress. Nations come and go due to the bipolar nature of their leaders. In summarizing the movements of civilizations that have prevailed, the betterment of human race appears to have stood ground because order and wisdom are byproducts of peaceful living of the thoughtful, in contrast to the chaos and disarray that are a result of aggression and violence of the thoughtless. It is our contention that the next generation of knowledge machines, based on the science of knowledge and the knowledge of science will damp these oscillations and offer well-reasoned pathways to the betterment of the humankind.

Though the lives are short lived, the memory banks of machines (or the encrypted holographs and inscribed tablets) can withstand the erosive efforts of time. In the modern era of borderless culture of knowledge and the timeless retentions of knowledge in the Internet knowledge banks (KBs), machines by far do outperform human beings. However, it becomes necessary to empower these machines with the ability to process (positive and negative) knowledge and to extract ($\pm$) wisdom as the computer scientists have empowered the plain old computers of the 70s and 80s to process (positive and negative) data and extract ($\pm$) information from it. In this chapter, we propose the methodology to program knowledge machines and track incremental changes of knowledge that govern the corresponding changes in the society. In a sense, knowledge plays a similar focal role as money plays in commerce bringing about expansion and contractions in the financial markets. Cultures and nations are treated as super-objects that respond to the $\pm$ "social energy ($=$social power *times* lapsed time)" in the same fashion as cosmic objects that respond to $\pm$ "work-done ($=$ physical power *times* lapsed time)."

4.1 INTRODUCTION

History has grim reminders [1] of the abuse of power by leaders of men and nations that commit atrocities by the name of national pride and patriotism. The pride is a bloated personification of

Evolution of Knowledge Science. DOI: http://dx.doi.org/10.1016/B978-0-12-805478-9.00004-2

47

their personal fears and insecurities. Having no virtue to fallback, the Incas slaughtered humans to "please their deities," the alpha-apes brutally massacre the babies fathered by their prior males to propagate their own "genes," the Portuguese brought the black slaves to fill their pockets with their "blood monies," and the British captured and brought African slaves to "build the landmarks" in London. The list goes on. Nonetheless, the lack of security and confidence catalyzes the abuse of power by the two-penny political leaders all around the world. The animal in human awakens to the jingle of money and greed for power that they themselves have not earned.

For such folks, selfish love drowns the sense of decency in a shallow cup of drugged indulgence. Every weakness is mercilessly exploited for even more to serve drinks to the deaf, dumb, and weak to make fools of them! Hiding behind a curtain of lies, these opportunistic folks commit murders and crimes against humanity and yet go scot free to live in luxury with millions of dollars as their retirement funds and pensions (father and son alike)! The Justices in Oslo and United Nations become knowingly mute in fear of these disgraced world leaders. The sense of shame is totally unknown to these folks, killers, drone bombers, and self-acclaimed leaders of worldwide crimes go unpunished for many decades.

The knowledge trail for these folks ends in deception, shamelessness, and hate: In shame, they live in disgust and they die. Fortunately, the Internet and a few honest reporters bring the abuse of power into the public domain with their reports and information. The lies following the "Johnson Vietnam-war" [2], "Nixon tapes investigation" [3], "Clinton Lewinsky affair" [4], nonexistent weapons of mass destruction in Iraq [5], the personal gains accrued by the Iraq's invasion [6], and the Afghanistan incursion [7] are recent cases from recent history. An estimated 151,000 to 600,000 or more Iraqis were killed [8] after Bush began the 2003 invasion of Iraq even after the UN Envoy to Iraq had declared that there were no weapons of mass destruction in that country.

Ethics and morality taught for the benefit of the society are sold as deceptively captured African slaves. The opposing forces in human nature have kept an uneasy balance between the righteous and the selfish folks around the world. Like money, it flows sideways during economic bust and bloom, recession, and expansion. However, the federal government has a monetary system to avoid the depressions of the 40s, but the *ethical* balance swings to extreme and shakes the morality of nations with dire consequences of life and peace around the world from superpowers who have sold their souls for a few dollars more or for barrels of empty power.

4.2 THE COARSE SIDE OF HUMAN NATURE

The reason for cycles of human nature between ethical and ruthless can be traced to human (animal, or cellular) nature. Biological systems propagate at the time of plenty and shrink at the time of scarcity. In a sense, life of any organism is a balance between such changes, cycles, trends and cycles of health and illness; however, minute such changes may be. Nature has thus embedded a code of counter-change to counter the prior change. Prolonged unidirectional changes are an indication of catastrophic forces in nature, societies, and individuals.

In the normal course of events, the coarse side of human nature counters its finer nature. The thought process that invokes one type of social behavior is eventually countered by the counter-thought process that limits the extent and nature of the prior-thought process that led to change.

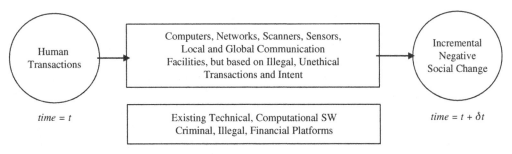

FIGURE 4.1

Snapshot of the human activity in a microscopic timeframe creating incremental negative changes.

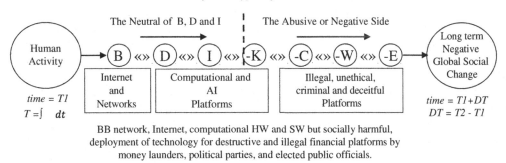

FIGURE 4.2

Computer and network organization and snapshot of the human activity in a prolonged timeframe creating disruptive, harmful global and sociological changes. The nodes *B, D, I, -K, -C, -W,* and *E* represent the levels of human activity as binary, data structures, information, negative (knowledge, concept, wisdom, and ethical) levels. The activities on the left side of the chain are generally transient and more abundant than those at on the right side requiring criminal and mafia activities.

In superposing, the types of changes that are feasible for the society by beneficial humane effort have been depicted in Figures 3.5 and 3.6. The positive insidious forces in the society and in the collective human minds of philosophers and social thinkers, who facilitate the beneficial forces cause, invoke, and propel knowledge, concepts, wisdom, and ethics. Collected over decades, axioms of such wisdom retain values and ethics in the future generations.

In contrast, the negative insidious forces in the society and in the collective minds of the greedy and self-interest groups reverse the beneficial forces, and cause, invoke, and propel abusive knowledge, deceitful concepts, predator wisdom, and mafia ethics. Such forces kill the migration of the knowledge trail in Figures 3.3 and 3.4, in a positive sense and replace the last four nodes as negative knowledge, deceptive concepts, and cruel ethics. Counter-reflections of Figures 3.5 and 3.6 are shown in Figures 4.1 and 4.2. These counter-positive or negative forces cause and invoke a negative effect upon knowledge, concepts, wisdom, and ethics. Indeed, they degrade knowledge, degenerate concepts, tear down wisdom, and demean ethics. The social attitudes depicted in Figure 3.4 have led to the positive enhancements of the society depicted in Figure 3.5. In an adverse sense, it is possible to construe an inverse social attitude that leads to social degeneration and decay. The chaos that these four negative nodes creates further accelerates the downward trend in the individual, the society, the culture, and the nation.

To gain a perspective, the visualization of both positive and negative aspects of social behavior becomes necessary. As much as the benevolent nature exists in human beings, an equivalent treacherous nature also prevails, often to the dismay of many saints and philosophers. In fact, the presence is so dominant, that even the clergy and the pope are not immune to circumvent it. In the present context of social changes, both aspects are treated to the same extent. In reality, both aspects exert their influence on members of the society and project knowledge, concepts, and wisdom in *either* directions and are generally out of time-phase. The human nature is multidimensional, if not hyperdimensional and trends in different dimensions can overlap. Noise effects and jagged behavioral patterns arise within the society. Each member gets affected differently, and thus we have (and had) saints and thugs, wise and foolish, masters and slaves, etc. in any society, at any time, in any place, and in any civilization. If there is a utopia or perfection, it can only be temporary. The very basis of judgment is dynamic as the human nature.

Figure 4.2 depicting the negative image of the authentic knowledge trail (Figure 3.3) integrates the negative incremental changes over time increments δt in Figure 4.1. These increments may last a few months or decades, but the undesirable effect is obvious in the populous, the society, the culture, and the nation. Reversal of the undesirable becomes the norm and vice versa. The microscopic changes in human tendencies go unnoticed and the integration over decades become monumental. Nations once united become mafia States, soldiers become robots, planes become drones, and leaders become criminals!

4.3 THE ABUSE OF INFORMATION AND KNOWLEDGE

The use of negative knowledge leads to aggression and violence. Stemming from the self-interest of all species, such abuse is widely prevalent. Humans have practiced the abuse to its climax, ranging from Eisenhower's use of nuclear weapon in Japan [9] to Al Capone's armed gang rivalry leading up to Saint Valentine's Day Massacre [10] leave sharp notes of such reminders.

Information age offers more options to more people to commit psychological atrocities in the form of illegal, unethical, and "mail order brides" messages in the form of "news and information." The integrated effect of the abuse is cumulative on the attitude of society by slowly justifying the objectionable as tolerable and the illegal as justifiable. Freedom can have a negative flavor and become devious enough to make the social norms slide into the negative realm. The movement is slow but insidious. Societies, communities, cultures, and nations are not able to track these slides down the cultural scale unless the knowledge machines detect the trend rather than the noise in the social media.

4.3.1 PROJECTED USE OF MACHINES TO BLOCK HUMAN ABUSE

Local, state, and federal police deploy dogs, human beings, and machines to discourage, resist, catch, and punish abusers. Physical abuse, torture, and crimes are well contained in most western societies. In the information and knowledge domains, such use of resources is less prevalent in the society. Crimes against knowledge, virtues, Ethics, and values are common. In fact, such abusers use technology to destruct, wound, and destroy societies. For example, the use of drones (in the Middle-East) to bomb human dwellings, the use of poison gas (in Iraq during the Bush Presidency [8] and in Syria under the Putin's regime [11]), and the use of the chemical weapons (in Afghanistan [12]) point to the abuse of the machines that have gone unresisted, uncaught, and unpunished.

In the other disciplines, standard bureaus and committees are established, and the violations serve to reverse any harmful trends. For example, in March 1999, a committee in Georgia reviewed the National Bureau's program to oversee Maternal and Infant Health and set up a statewide system for genetics newborn screening [13]. In social sciences, monitoring of public tendencies would result in monitoring the health of a nation. For example, teenage drunk driving incidences, abuse of firearms, robberies, and quality and number of spam messages would signal unfavorable trends. Positive knowledge/steps to counter such trends in their infancy could prove beneficial over a longer perspective.

4.3.2 ABUSE OF MACHINES AGAINST HUMANS

This is a most unfortunate byproduct of technology in the hands of selfish and greedy folks. Mafia and nations use it and commit crimes against peoples who are most vulnerable. In most cases, nations go uncaught and continue the same atrocities decade after decade. In a mad rush to grab power and claim supremacy the experimental drones drop weapons and bomb on the habitats of those who have no means to retaliate. Putin would not dare to dispatch a warhead to Whitehouse or vice versa. Proving supremacy by killing third party civilians has been noticed as an act of cowardice and crime. However, this type of abuse has been practiced against African slaves, Tibetans, Palestinians, Iraqis, and Vietcong.

Nature has provided species with tools for defense and for gratifying the survival needs. The extent of damage is local and soon overcome. Warheads and missiles are dreadful extensions of arrows and spears of the native tribes. Being guided by satellite systems to avenge and destroy falls in the category of extreme abuse of power. In the knowledge domain, the use of machines in the hands of unethical folks has led only to massive killings and bloodshed. Unbiased knowledge-ware based on ethical principles of knowledge science would trap such potential misuse of power. At the outset, it should be realized that it cannot be completely blocked, but it at least can be curtailed by make other about the potential abuse.

4.4 INDULGENCE OF SOCIETIES IN NEGATIVE SOCIAL SETTINGS

At the extreme right, the stages of total dominance of global power is sought at the expense of destruction of all social values, wisdom, and ethics (effects of NO* VF). This is unlikely to become a reality since there is (or might be) enough humans and AI-based machines to warn of the global disaster. In the past global near-disasters (e.g., John Kennedy and Nikita Khruschchev over the Cuban Missile crisis in 13 days political and military standoff in October 1962 [14]) have been averted by dialog and negotiations.

Movement Based on Deception, Arrogance, and Hate

Phase 1 Early Civilizations to late 1950's.	Phase 2 Mafia, thugs street gangs, spies.	Phase 3 Missiles, warships, war colleges.	Phase 4 War machines robot soldiers war-nets.	Phase 5 Drone planes intelligent killers, etc.	Phase 6 Total national destructive agents.	Phase 7 Destruction of civilizations, human race, etc.
Integrated from primitive times to the scientific society including the major innovation in Telephone and Early data communication technologies.	At the street level and the use of firearms, and destructive tools of technology at a psychological, social and personal level, e.g., KKK, Mafia .	At national level by the use of aggressive leaders (Saddam, Mao, Hitler, etc.) who justify the abuse power, tortures and killings.	By nations that recycle and deploy war tools and technologies, (Early Japanese, Russians agencies etc.) in the name of Patriotism.	At national level by nations that deploy war tools to gain natural resources, destroy lives, cultures by use of invasion of privacy, offensive war-heads	Nations in acts of war in e.g., Japan, Iraq, Afghanistan, Germany, in WW2. Almost all nations have had some trails of bloodshed and atrocities.	Global wars, Satellite based nuclear weapons and destructive rampages. To an extent Spanish in S America, Vietcong in Far East, etc.

---------- Deception ------------ "Self Love" of Mafia Nations -and-"Stockpiles of Ammunition"--
--------------- Self Acclaimed Supremacy and Arrogance --------------

FIGURE 4.3

Evolution that starts from binary data that erodes human ethics and values. The role of destructive individuals and criminals in this migration is crucial in using methodologies, devices, architectures, systems, innovations, and inventions to human destruction and suffering. The most unpredictable part on the chain is the role and postures of the next generation of human beings, users, and their predispositions to deception, arrogance, and hate (DAH, in a negative sense as the society sees it; or is that the positive sense as the mafia sees it). This path is a negative image of human indulgence of those in truth virtue, and beauty (TVB), in a positive sense as the society sees it or its predisposition.

In Figure 4.2 the incidence of the negative use of knowledge is shown at central Node (−K). The technologies are simply assimilated in the society as nations started to use nuclear technology to make weapons during the 50s and 60s. Values and ethics were sold in the name of national pride and competitive statesmanship of the United States (invasion of Iraq, under Bush [8]) and Russia (Bombing in Syria, under Putin [11]). In Figure 4.3, the seven phases of deterioration are depicted. The actions (verb-functions, VFs) of both these two "leaders of state" (noun-objects, NOs) can be seen in the seven columns in this figure.

It is our contention that the future machines based on the science of knowledge can help negotiate such critical issues sooner and better or not let such conflictive situation develop in the first place. In most cases supreme human talent can outperform machines, but in more routine cases (e.g., choosing a job, a graduate school) machines will be as helpful as plain old computers in solving scientific problems or in designing electrical machines.

4.5 DECEPTION AND COWARDICE IN HUMANS

Many great human beings say they are sorry after blunders of deception and hate. After the fierce war[1] of Kalinga (India) during 261 B.C. [15] between the powerful State of Kalinga and the Mauryan

---

[1]The Kalinga War became one of the most violent and terrible wars of ancient times. Its outcome became epoch-making to make it one of the most famous wars of world history.

Empire, the devastation and cruelty were unsurpassed. The great king Ashoka saw the nature of cruelty, death, and demise of the State. Being moved by the nature of hate and cruelty his soldiers had committed, Ashoka embraced Buddhism and erected the famous Iron Pillar with the teaching of peace and tolerance within the human race.

Knowledge with genuine social welfare had dawned as far as 261 years before Christ, and this knowledge still exists in the inscriptions of the "Iron Pillars of Ashoka." After such a bloody war, the powerful King Ashoka was humble to realize and say he was sorry for the war and bloodshed. More than just words, he did the most what any human being could himself: He accepted the teachings of Buddha and propagated the enlightenment of true knowledge with social justice and values intact. These pillars in Delhi and Allahabad [16] still teach a lesson of good conscience and humility (both ethical values) of a notable king.

In the modern times, similar incidents have occurred and at least one noteworthy leader[2] [17] has apologized for the atrocities of the brutal unprovoked Iraq war. Ex-British PM Tony Blair has apologized for Iraq War "mistakes." When social values and ethics are sacrificed for the greed for power and personal hate, the folks have brought public disgrace[3] they bring to the society, culture, and nation [18]. As late as Spring of 2016, a highest U.S. navy officer (Capt. Danial Dusek) was convicted and received 46-month prison term[4] for selling "military secrets to an Asian defense contractor in exchange for prostitutes."

4.6 NEGATIVE SOCIAL CHANGE: DETERIORATION AND DECAY

The spread of negative social effects has become rampant. Like the turbulent flow of any fluid, the social-mechanics has become violent and destructive in the past, like the flow of a flooded river and a stormy sea of greed and disrespect for Law and Order. Such examples prevail. Classroom, airport, shopping center killing are telltale of a serious neglect of the underlying human and social problems. Unresolved they fester like bacteria and virus that show up as infections and epidemics on the social complexion of any society. Further neglect can only make this social virus worse like the AIDS virus during the last 30 years.

The social movement can be observed in four overlapping directions[5] (K, C, W, and E) and cause jagged movements of the four nodes in Figure 4.4. Forces and the resulting movements become noise prone. Correspondingly the negative energy (power *times* duration) in these four directions contribute to the deterioration, decay, and eventual demise of positive attributes within a society. Long ignored negative energies can ruin an entire society or a culture by

---

[2]October 25, 2015 – LONDON—Britain's former prime minister Tony Blair has apologized for "mistakes" made in the U.S.-led invasion of Iraq in 2003. In contrast, in 2007 Blair had mentioned "I don't think we should be apologising at all for what we are doing in Iraq." Also see www.cnn.com/2015/10/25/europe/tony-blair-iraq-war/.

[3]On December 14, 2008, al-Zaidi shouted "This is a farewell kiss from the Iraqi people, you dog" and threw his shoes at then-U.S. president George W. Bush.

[4]http://www.msn.com/en-us/news/us/highest-ranking-navy-officer-yet-sentenced-in-sex-for-secrets-scandal/ar-BBqVk3R?li=BBnb7Kz, Referenced March 26, 2016.

[5]The dimensions are not independent as the X, Y, and Z dimensions in the physical space. Both the origin and the scales in the K, C, W, and E dimension depend on the neighboring nodes and their own attributes, making this later five dimensional intellectual space (K, C, W, E, and *time*) dynamic and twisted yet connected and tractable and never broken.

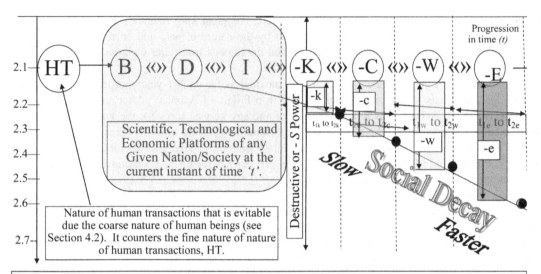

FIGURE 4.4

Depiction of the negative change in social status of an organism or organization based on social power (or effort) S. S can assume any of the four directions, knowledge power k, concept power c, wisdom power w, or ethical standard e, integrated over the duration these powers are active. The forces in the four dimensions K, C, W, and E are jagged and noise prone. Being humanistic, the individual energies and predispositions play a dominant role in the driving forces in these dimensions. Consisting of groups with individuals of differing caliber, leadership, and managerial styles, the detailed analysis in the five dimensional (K, C, W, E, and $time$) space, the movement and the status of any social entity can be tracked by large social machines.

turning love into hate (e.g., Aztec society into killers), truth into deception (Internet facts into false propaganda), and beauty into ruins (Roman and Greek temples into shambles). The four dimensions K, C, W, and E, along which a wealth of knowledge, concepts, wisdom, and ethics were once meticulously accumulated, simply disintegrate into willful ignorance, brainwaves, foolishness, and immorality.

Depiction of the negative change in social status of an organism or organization based on social power (or effort) s is presented in Figure 4.4. The social power excreted over a certain duration gives rise to energy for the change to follow. The numerical measure of S (k, c, w, or e) can be in any of the four directions of knowledge power K, concept power C, wisdom power W, or ethical power E. When S is integrated over the duration ($\delta\ t$) that these powers are active, then it results in the social energy for change.

Being humanistic, the individual energies and predispositions play a dominant role in the driving forces in these dimensions. Consisting of groups with individuals with differing caliber, leadership and managerial styles, the detailed analysis in the five dimensional (K, C, W, E, and $time$)

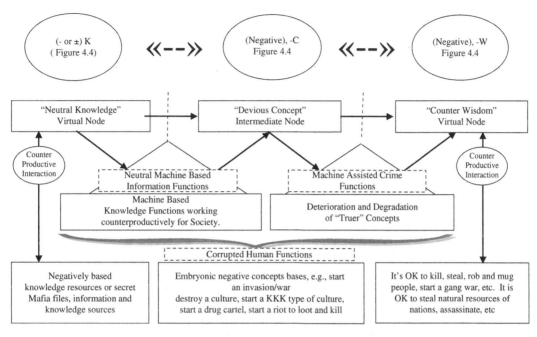

FIGURE 4.5

Depiction of a human—machine interaction syndrome that has become all too common for the small and large social entities from street gangs, Mafia mongers, drug cartels, child abduction rings to aggressive nations, and crime syndicates. The abuse of machine ranging from individuals to nations is as feasible as the constructive use of machine for the progress in just, ethical, and legally well-balanced societies.

space, the movement and the status of any social entity can be tracked by midsized social machines even though the human perception may be too slow to track such changes in real time.

4.7 SOCIAL DECAY OF NATIONS AND CULTURES

The transitions within the three (K, C, W) dimensional subspace within the larger five (K, C, W, E, and *time*) dimensional space is conceivable because of the tight sequential nature of the three nodes. Even though the exact measures of knowledge k in the K dimension are not precise, the value of k can be estimated and thus the values of c and w to a less precise extent.

Machine and Internet abuse is rampant. Ranging from planting bugs and viruses to the theft of private information, passwords, and bank accounts, machine abuse has become more prevalent by coupling it with the abuse of Internet and data networks. Security measures make the IP thieves harder to use their ploys but not totally eradicate the thievery and abuse. When coupled with criminal intent of the (smart) users, the abuse of machines can exist for a long time to come and this scenario is depicted in Figure 4.5.

The most serious abusers are criminals, mob, and mafia members who can deliver very destructive actions upon the members of any society. Prolonged abuse can alter the very ethical foundation of the society. Further negatively primed machines can assist such user as much as positively primed machines can assist socially benevolent users. The knowledge- and social-ware base in the machine "convolves" with the commands of the users, spreading a disarray of machine and robotic instructions. It appears as if constructive-nature, in its own wisdom, uses such a disarray to destroy the sources of counter-nature.

In ecology, when the lemming populations in the Tundra increases over a rational balanced population causing a disarray in their behavior while seeking food and borrows, the owl fertility increases to counter the trend. Owls being more adaptive than lemmings do not (or cannot) breed as much when the lemming population is scarce. From a historical perspective in the social domain, when Mob and Mafia activities are no longer tolerable, the specialized police and legal enforcement become stronger and vice versa. In the knowledge and social domain, it is yet to be seen what is the threshold of knowledge, concept, and wisdom pollution before a "super-constructive cultural element" such as (a Super-Supreme Court) that has the ultimate power to imprison and punish corrupt politicians, social leaders, and high-ranking government officials. During reelections (especially in Florida in the reelection of Bush for the second term) many vote counts had been tampered. In many dictatorial countries, voting fraud is conveniently overlooked. In granting privileges to the favored individuals, the police laws are flexed, etc. It is interesting to note that the social profile of a population or a community can be etched (during a given window of time) by analyzing the balance between the activities of the socially corrupt practices and the forcing blocking such activities. It is also feasible to etch (during a similar window) a corresponding profile by analyzing the balance between positive and the negative social forces in the society. The direction, trend, and the distance of movement can be incrementally tracked. Equivalent financial tools exist for the analyzing the economic health of nations (in macroeconomics), communities (with the office of municipal financial officers), corporations (in the office of the CFO), and even households (now offered by banks, credit card companies and accountants).

CONCLUSIONS

In this chapter, we reassert that knowledge science and knowledge machines cannot solve all the global problems and conflicts based on the bipolar nature of human beings, but we assert that this discipline and these machines can alleviate some of the routine conflicts that arise between individuals, cultures, and societies. Like computers that cannot solve all scientific problems, knowledge machines cannot solve all social and knowledge problems. As the problems become more global, the better-sided human beings outperform sciences and machines. On the other hand, the ill-natured human beings (such as unscrupulous CEOs, unprincipled presidents) can and have exploited the situation for personal gain [6] for money and power.

Intelligent agents and intelligently primed knowledge machines can perform to the same extent that intelligent Internets can perform over the rudimentary Internet of the plain old telephone systems. The extent of service that knowledge machines can provide can range substantially from just warning against undesirable developing social events to locking out the unauthorized users of power by suitable encryption and security measures.

Social computing has already affected the private lives via handheld devices and PDAs. The impact of fully-fledged social computers is still to emerge. Opportunities posed by network-based social computing possibilities are enormous when social computers are networked into the backbone of the communication systems. Computing and communication have already merged to facilitate the global connectivity and provide data services. The present social opportunities offered by commercial Internet Social Service Providers (SIPS, not to be interpreted as Intelligent Service Switching Points in plain old intelligent networks [19]) are trivial and tainted with exploitation of the innocent, and ignorant. Some of the directions of the services (find dates, find affairs, etc.) are slanted toward social decay rather than the positive enhancement.

The generic social aspects of universal and decent human conduct have not entered the global connectivity and intricacy of backbone networks. The educational and human aspects that may replace high school education with college education, deception with truth, free sex with global morality, etc. can already be implanted in backbone networks. The possibilities prevail with the current backbone switching systems and TCP/IP protocol. Some of the possible venues are explored and delineated in this chapter.

REFERENCES

[1] Top 10 Worst Abuses of Power in History — Toptenz.net, <https://www.toptenz.net/top-10-worst-abuses-of-power-in-history.php>. Also see Harassment and Abuse of Power and Authority | United ... <https://www.unesco.org/.../harassment-and-abuse-of-power-and-autho>. For recent a event please see Ferguson police report: five examples of abuse of power — CBC, <https://www.cbc.ca/.../ferguson-police-report-5-examples-of-abuse-of-p>.., Mar 4, 2015.

[2] The History Place — Vietnam War 1965—1968, <https://www.historyplace.com/unitedstates/vietnam/index-1965.html>.

[3] David Frost interview — "yours regretfully, R. Nixon," <https://www.theguardian.com> › US News › US Politics, The Guardian.

[4] An affair of state — September 21, 1998 — CNN.com, <https://www.cnn.com/ALLPOLITICS/time/1998/09/14/affair.state.html>.

[5] Iraq and weapons of mass destruction — Wikipedia, the free ..., <https://en.wikipedia.org/.../Iraq_and_weapons_of_mass_destru...>.

[6] FOCUS | Cheney's Halliburton Made $39.5 Billion on Iraq War, <https://readersupportednews.org/.../16561-focus-cheneys-halliburton-made-395>.

[7] War in Afghanistan (2015—present) — Wikipedia, the free ...<https://https://en.wikipedia.org/.../War_in> Afghanistan (2015—presen...

[8] Bush in Iraq, <https://en.wikipedia.org/wiki/Iraq_War>.

[9] Bombing of Hiroshima and Nagasaki — History Channel, <https://www.history.com/topics/.../bombing-of-hiroshima-and-nagasaki>.

[10] The St. Valentine's Day Massacre — Feb 14, 1929 — HISTORY ..., <https://www.history.com/this-day-in.../the-st-valentines-day-massacre>.

[11] Syria and world await Putin's reaction to apparent bombing ..., <https://www.theguardian.com> › World › Vladimir Putin.

[12] Iraqi chemical weapons program — Wikipedia, the free <https://en.wikipedia.org/wiki/Iraqi_chemical_weapons_program>.

[13] <https://http://dph.georgia.gov/nbs-advisory-committee>.

[14] Cuban Missile Crisis — Cold War — HISTORY.com, <https://www.history.com/topics/cold-war/cuban-missile-crisis>.

[15] The Kalinga War of 261 B.C., <https://en.wikipedia.org/wiki/Kalinga.War>.

[16] Pillars of Ashoka — Wikipedia, the free encyclopedia, <https://en.wikipedia.org/wiki/Pillars_of_Ashoka>.

[17] Ex-British PM Tony Blair apologizes for Iraq War "mistakes," <https://www.usatoday.com/.../tony-blair-apologizes-iraq.../7458031>...]. t <https://www.usatodaycom/.../tony-blair-apologizes-iraq.../7458031>.

[18] <https://https://en.wikipedia.org/wiki/Muntadhar_al-Zaidi>.

[19] Ahamed SV. Intelligent broadband multimedia networks. 1st edition. Boston: Springer; 1997.

ROLE OF DEVICES, COMPUTERS AND NETWORKS

CHAPTER SUMMARY

Devices, computers, and networks are prime movers in the knowledge era as the internal combustion engines, petroleum products, and roadways were the prime movers of the automobile era. The knowledge worker would be deflated without machines and Internet as much as the human body would perish without food and water. More recently, the hand-held devices and microwave communications have become intrinsically interdependent in providing significant and timely data and information to knowledge workers.

In this chapter, we investigate the social and global effects of the continuously expanding role of these tools of information technology on societies and cultures. Knowledge plays a central role. Devices, computers, and network have become a triadic central focus for the global activities of most human beings. The role of humans to process knowledge is gradually being undertaken by knowledge machines with very powerful knowledge-ware atop of traditional net-ware and AI software. Artificial intelligence is the catalyst in the machines as much as natural intelligence is the driver toward knowledge. The many directions of knowledge as classified in the Dewey Decimal System or the Library of Congress Classification demand many forms of natural intelligence of human beings. Human discretion elevates knowledge to the pinnacle of social justice or to depths of despair. Machines with trend analysis knowledge-ware can provide some initial directionality but uncorrupted human judgment still reigns supreme. In a very oblique sense, unbiased wisdom machines can even track the corruption in the human judgment!

Knowledge with human refinement becomes savory and beneficial. The more lasting discoveries in the domain of knowledge are the pearls of wisdom found and preserved in the Vedas and Verses of Nalanda. Conversely, knowledge without the human values becomes abusive and detrimental. The more atrocious deeds of humans without ethics become the venom and poison that still leave disgrace and dishonor in the books of war and shame.

5.1 INTRODUCTION

The two Chapters 2 and 3 are intertwined as the two sides of human nature that can sway between being socially beneficial and being entirely selfish. This Chapter integrates the effects the two tendencies (beneficial and selfish) of populous in society based on the foundations of knowledge integrated in human minds or knowledge banks distributed around the Internet. The last few decades have prepared the new generation toward being (all) information addicts and PDA crazy. Information can range from being gibberish to being essential; and every grade of information is available on most networks, especially on the Internet. The discretion is entirely human to use or abuse it, or simply be

Evolution of Knowledge Science. DOI: http://dx.doi.org/10.1016/B978-0-12-805478-9.00005-4

amused by it. Human judgment is generally sacrificed by discard of the potential benefit or harm that such information delivers to the unprepared users of information tools, machines, and networks.

Addiction to gimmickry of tools to extract garbage and deceitful information is a harmful proposition since the role of significant knowledge is shortchanged. Long-term beneficial information leads to the repeated use of acquired knowledge in any discipline or expertise. Conversely, disorganized and junk information pollutes, Corrupts, and clutters the mind. Order and organization bond the elemental knowledge gained from events in society into a classical structure of universal wisdom. The downward spiral of prices of IC devices and the increasing bandwidth of networks, though desirable for commerce and trade may not be entirely beneficial to the society since they rob the mind of judgment to contemplate their long-term individual and/or social effects. In the chapter, we examine the positive (long-term socially beneficial) and negative (short-term socially insignificant and amusing) information that either toward leads to individual and/or social progress or toward to individual and/or social decay. In reality, both these types of information exist, but it is up to an individual, a society, a culture, or a nation to ride the crest of positive long-term significant information and gain both knowledge and wisdom derived from it.

5.2 DEVICES, MACHINES, HUMANS, AND SOCIAL REALITIES

5.2.1 BENEFICIAL AND CONSTRUCTIVE ROLE

Machines are but toys. In the hands of socially balanced user they fulfill their constructive purpose. The intellectual attitude of the user is reflected in the processes on the machines. It is true that the core dump of any social machine will reveal the mental image of the user. The collective machine functions of any nation are its integrated intellectual activity. At present the portrayals are positive and constructive thus enhancing the (social, cultural, business, and economic) health of the nation much like monies that are used for legal use and for social activities rather than for illegal and corrupt activities. The purpose of the social machines is to increase and enhance these positive uses and to abate the negative trends. Device, machines, and networks do have their beneficial use: Chapter 2 elaborates their scientific deployment, and Figures 3.4 to 3.6 depict the long-term effects.

Human discretion plays a decisive role in their use or abuse. Values and ethics have many directions and dimensions making it difficult for the casual onlooker to detect the short-term and long-term effects. Well-primed and unbiased machines can analyze these effects more precisely; knowledge-ware can isolate the origin and trend in the use. As AI-routines and Intelligent Agents can enhance and extend the natural intelligence in the embedded software, AI based knowledge routines will track and deter abusive social elements in the society from exploiting the less-informed members of the society.

5.2.2 DETRIMENTAL AND EXPLOITIVE ROLE

The abuse of machines and monies can become severe if the top echelon of the nation, community, corporation, or even a household start the abuse. It has prevailed in many nations, corporations, and societies. At a national level and at the very top of the nation, Saddam Hussein's use of poison gas against the Kurds, the United States' use of nerve gas in the Iraq, and the Guantanamo bay camps during war are a few of the cruel social abuse of machines and power. At the community levels, the abuse of slaves in the United Kingdom, the cruelty to slaves in Southern United States; at the corporate level, the Enron swindle, the Global Crossing disaster; lying of Clinton during the Monica Lewinsky affair, Nixon lies during the Watergate tapes trial are few of the painful events from the recent past. Almost all nations have history of cruelty embedded in their past. The question is about the extent and duration of such cruelties. In the modern societies where events are accountable, such injustices are exposed quite easily on the Internet.

Instruments and devices used during these socially cruel events (chains and cuffs for the slaves, partial drowning water-tanks for the Guantanamo Bay detainees, and bank accounts and losses for the Enron employees) are grim reminders of the abusive *human* elements at the very top.[1] The social and news media can blackout negative knowledge (for their own selfish gains) that can help prevent such events in the future. Events of this nature are much more frequent and go unnoticed indicating the social decay of most nations. The negative use of the Internet in propagating spam, deception, Russian brides, Asian singles, sex-for-sale, etc., ploys are showing signs of social disservice to public and to humanity. However, it appears equally evident in the abuse of devices, machines and networks: Chapter 3 elaborates their exploitation, and Figures 4.1, 4.2, and 4.4 depict the long-term effects.

5.3 REALITY AND OSCILLATION OF SOCIAL NORMS

Social norms of a nation like being a snapshot of health of society can fluctuate and experience oscillations. The inertial mass of a society being greatly larger than "health-inertia" of an individual and the social displacement, and the change of trends both tend to be considerably slower. The fundamental limit for the use of classical equations of particle or group dynamics to analyze social dynamics is the lack of cohesion among the members in the society. Individual norms can deviate widely. In the integration of such singular norms to derive social norms is extremely noisy and probabilistic with high variances. Family, social, cultural, ethical, etc., variations add more uncertainty in the analysis and predictions of the collective norms in any social entity. The status, location, and the dimensions of individual social objects may be uncertain but on a global basis. Societies and groups obey macro-behavioral laws as the cosmic bodies obey laws of physics and the gravitational laws in Astronomy.

When the very basic need (to survive) of every individual and that of society (also to survive) becomes the same, then cohesion starts to be evident. When the security of any organization is at stake, the members unite more easily, such as during war or natural disaster, or the demise of a corporation, etc. In reality, such a tendency is displayed (as a statistical mean) when "most" members celebrate national festivities, such as a victory (e.g., Pearl Harbor) or assemble to mourn a public loss (e.g., the assassination of Kennedy) or a defeat or an earthquake (e.g., the eruption of Mount St. Helene). The cohesion though looser still exists during normal condition, and it may be integrated and "reasonably" accurately documented by large social machines.

---

[1]http://usnews.nbcnews.com/_news/2013/11/06/21338225-third-senior-navy-official-arrested-in-bribery-prostitution-scandal?lite=, accessed November 6, 2013.

5.3.1 SOCIAL ENERGY AND ENSUING SHIFTS

Shifts in the social norms are caused by social energy within the system. Energies are prompted by natural forces in the environment or created artificially by human agencies. Such forces are inevitable, and being universal and global influence the social norms and attitudes in positive or negative directions. However, the energy that moves the society is also influenced by the duration that the force is active and persistent. In a sense, the social mass and inertia both influence the displacement and/or rotation of norms. For example during war years, the force exerted in numerous directions (such as shortages, ill-health, lack of communication) over long enough periods change the social stratum of the entire society.

In reality, displacements, shifts, rotations, and transitions are gradual, continuous, and in every direction. The positive movements have been tracked and illustrated in Figure 3.5 and the negative changes have been tracked and illustrated in Figure 4.4. In Figure 5.1, the cumulative effect of

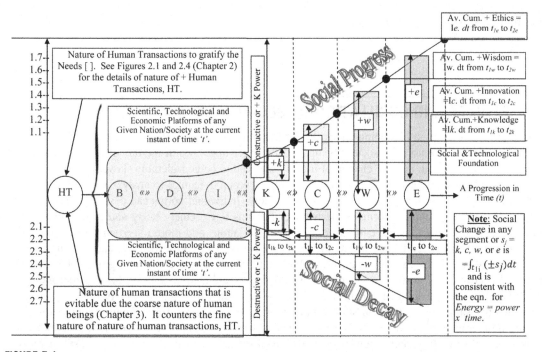

FIGURE 5.1

Depiction of the change in social status of an organism or organization based on knowledge effort/power $\pm K$, concept effort/power $\pm C$, Wisdom power $\pm W$, or Ethical standard $\pm E$ integrated over the duration these powers are active. The parameters $\pm K$, $\pm C$, $\pm W$, and $\pm E$ can (and generally do) swing in and out of phase randomly complicating the actual variations of the social progress or decay. For these reasons, when the movement of the social condition of any given object is jugged it appears to be varying randomly. Social machines primed for any given society or culture have the facility to track such changes as being correlated to the K, C, W, and E forces and their energies.

positive and negative changes in any one direction (such as literacy, social unrest, or employment or standard of living) is depicted over a finite durations.

Downward drifts of the social norms are indicative of erosion of ethics. Though not eruptive, the effect of underlying social forces such as corruption, injustices, prostitution that are exerted by mobs, mafia, self-interest groups (SIGs, [1]), military industrial complex [2], drone designers groups, etc., can erode the concepts, the wisdom, and the ethics of a nation, society, or organization.

5.3.2 CHANGE IN THE FOUR (K, C, W, AND E) SPACES

The four space encompassing knowledge, concepts, wisdom, and ethics (K, C, W, and E) are depicted as the four nodes on the right side of the knowledge trail in Figure 3.4. In the modern era, the three initial nodes (B, D, and I) are completely executed by devices, machines, and networks. In fact, most societies need these nodes to be populated, verified, processed, and documented, just to survive. The later four nodes are still to accrue by automated knowledge and wisdom machine. Currently, being generated by human beings, they lack the discipline of mathematical and computer sciences.

Forces that initiate the positive and negative movements in (almost) every society are generally present as much as the forces of expansion and contraction are present in every economic cycle. The trend is an averaged and integrated summation of such movement. In the social setting, when the positive and negative driving forces are separated the two effects can depicted by Figures 3.6 and 4.4. Such movements are generally out of time phase and out of four-dimensional spaces of knowledge, concepts, wisdom, and ethics (i.e., K, C, W, and E). The analysis can still be continued by choosing time duration long enough to filter out noise, but short enough to be able to track the correlated movement (if any) within the ($KCWE$) space. In the medical field, the sampling intervals for temperature, blood pressure, blood work, etc. is judiciously chosen by the medical staff. The patient care is (generally) successful. Such intricate diagnosis of social ailments, their analysis, and treatment is not charted or documented. However, the mathematical tools for analysis exist and the social software (SSW) algorithms can be developed. The Stock Market analysis software is indicative for partially tracking the causes for the stock price fluctuation in the financial circles. The uncertainty of investor behavior is the prime reason for the unexpected changes and lack of predictability from this type of software.

5.3.3 NOISE IN THE SOCIAL SETTING

Noise in social settings is as inevitable as the electrical noise in circuits or as the noise in networks or microwave communications and detailed in [3]. Electromagnetic noises are not as disruptive as those in electrical storms in galactic space or the sunspot activities. They do exist, but the circuits and network devices are robust enough to immune most of the time. The mainstream of the signal or the data bits in digital communications are (largely) delivered intact. In rare instances such as once in 10^8 or 10^9 bits delivered, the particular bit will be in error in fiber-optic transmission. Bursts of error also occur in communication when numerous noisy events fall in a given interval of time. Such burst of errors and sudden impulses of noises do occur but the mainstream of communication continues in spite of such noisy events.

In the knowledge and social domains, noisy events are far more numerous and more frequent causing incomplete transmission of information initially and then the interpreted knowledge is derived. The causes of social noise stems generally from the human elements in the links. Delays, distortion, and dispersions in the social and news media are willful and common. Spam and misinformation (especially for the slanted toward financial advantage of the sponsor of the noise) are extremely evident on the Internet. The reader can see through the flimsy camouflage that these noise sources hide under. Unfortunately, for corporation and local vendors, advertising has taken the disguise of deception.

The forces that are responsible for insidious social changes are caused by socially benevolent and socially abusive human beings. Sometimes Internet plays its own role, but the triggering agents are programs or human agents. Their own intellectual spaces are neither synchronized nor harmonious. Born free to explore the communal space, the coordination is not monitored and likely to become granular and jagged causing microoscillations in the cultural domain. Such oscillations can be filtered by the social software and the measuring device much like the Tsunami measuring systems, and their associated software filter the insignificant surface activity on the earth.

5.4 TYPICAL GLOBAL SHIFTS IN SOCIETIES AND NATIONS

Global shifts of attitudes are generally predictable based on the powers causing the change, the duration of power, and the social resistance to such change. The changes in life styles resulting from the communication systems, broadband networks, mobile device technology, and finally the Internet are vivid examples. The forces (the transistor, the integration, the IAS machine, the integrated architecture of main frames, and the introduction of the standalone PC, the laptop, its connectivity, the OSI model, the TCP/IP, etc.) that have preceded these technologies are well documented.

To project the change in the social domain, the dynamics of change in thought processes of human beings is equally important. The changes in knowledge, conceptual, and the wisdom domains follow. Human thought has a complex biological trail. Founded in infancy, education and training become crucial in reaching the goals in midlife years and later. Knowledge, concepts and wisdom are based on refining the behavioral path which also becomes equally important but based on social and environmental factors. An aggregated knowledge base becomes proactive in designing a graph to reach the goals. Such approaches are also used in solving complex business problems while using PERT and CPM techniques [4].

In line with the approach for the migration along the knowledge trail (see Figure 3.5), the design steps to reach the wisdom node (W) are depicted between the machine-based programs that seek and deploy the Internet knowledge (at node K) and the human effort in conceiving the embedded concepts (at node C) and then distilling the axioms of wisdom (at node W) from concepts. At the present stage of technology, concept machines (CM) are not on the horizon, even though they are eluded in Reference [5].

The feedback paths through the mind of humans who used knowledge and wisdom machines [6] for both social decay and social progress are depicted. The illusive node of concept (at C) is rarely traversed by machines, even though humans can well perceive it and nucleate the contents as sentences or as tentative equations. This feedback path validates the universality of the concepts in conjunction with the subject matter knowledge in (K) wherein the machines are active. The coordinated synergy perhaps leads to an tentative axiom of wisdom that a wisdom machine can recheck its validity, universality, and a sense of elegance in the formulation of the axiom on a stand-alone basis. The new knowledge and wisdom machine also checks the accuracy of embedded equations and verifies the basis of truth on a probabilistic scale for any social setting and the conclusions. A numerical counterpart for the social machine thus becomes essential.

5.5 OSCILLATION OF SOCIAL NORMS

Unethical practices tolerated in the society become trends and then norms. Total inhibition of freedom is as undesirable as total tolerance of the undesirable practice in personal and social dealings. Total freedom can become as addictive as teenage sex. Total tolerance of the undesirable personal practices can become as ruinous as the use of drugs. A sense of discretion and moderation becomes essential and contextual. When the natural instincts and intelligence of the social group are intact, the oscillations of social norms within the group become controlled and less violent. The principles of feedback theory (from natural sciences) become applicable in the social sciences. Such feedback occurs naturally in the physiology to maintain and monitor the health of the organism.

If the society is considered as a living organism, then all the science get converged in the realm of a healthy and prosperous society. Social norms are accurately measured and monitored. The health of any society is never totally stable but traversing minor loops between being desirable and undesirable. But, since there are enormous ways to measure social health, a simple see and guess approach will not suffice.

5.5.1 SOCIAL LAIS SEZ-FAIRE

The French approach of lais sez-faire to govern free enterprise "laissez-faire capitalism" in economics is a good way to social ruin, especially when the social norms are declining. Antithetically, this approach noninterventionist, noninterventional, and noninterfering attitude of the state and federal social agencies appears to hold validity when the social norm are stable or ascending. Most societies with an established laws of conduct, behavior, and responsibility (such as the Japanese and Buddhist) societies appear to deal with social issues on a peaceful basis.

The knowledge and social machines are redundant when the natural traditions are embedded in culture rather than in knowledge banks. The use of AI and IA becomes superfluous when natural intelligence is pervasive. In the old Shrines of Bhutan and ancient Monasteries of Stavronikita, knowledge and wisdom machines are the priests and monks!

5.5.2 SOCIAL SUPERVISION

Social unrest is a global phenomenon: scientific social remedy is not. As the way to perfect health is shrouded by medical quarks, the path to social tranquility is littered with quack politicians who try to find opportunity to perpetuate their self-interest. It is an ambition to be able to use new AI in knowledge and wisdom machine to find a reasonable remedy to such events as wars and riots to last through a few cyclic changes of social attitude. The remedies should be self-learning to keep with the social trends of a culture, a nation, or a society. More recently, social scientists have organized global research and effort to address the issues that lead to social unrest.

Entirely unruly societies need the iron fist of law and order even to maintain a low level of order. Agencies can be entirely human during the 1920s through the 1940s, partially information and knowledge based as in the current information age or more computerized with mentoring, monitoring, and stabilizing network of machines. Such machines track and trend the changes in social patterns of any civilization as financial machines track and trend movements of stocks and bonds in stock market. When abrupt and sudden changes are noticed, then prices are partially stabilized to be "floor-traders" who smooth such rapid fluctuations.

In social settings when violent social event are notices in part of the country, the federal and state police forces move in and curtail massive social eruptions. Unfortunately, the brutal hand of military forces aggravates the situation further (e.g., riots during August 2014, Ferguson, Missouri, over the death of Michael Brown, and again during July 2014, New York City, over the death of Eric Garner [7]). A scientific and social study of every situation is not undertaken to remedy the underlying basis for the eruption to have occurred in the first place.

Conventional Fourier analysis techniques may prove unrewarding but may offer some insight in to the oscillations of the K, C, W, and E energies and the delayed social response in corresponding dimensions or the synergistic energies and their combined effect. Numerous comparisons of the spectral densities over a series of observations may become necessary to track any delayed or time tag effects of energies in the four dimensions. For example, both capital expenditure (C) and dedicated leadership (L) are necessary to improve the research caliber within a university. Social analysis SW should be able to detect the quantitative relationships and learn to predict the expected social change (due to different blending combinations of C and L) accurately.

Out of phase-oscillations of the energies in the four (K, C, W, and E) dimensions should be considered as a rule rather an exception. Human agents responsible for supplying these energies inject their own traits documented by Carter and Bush as two presidents with very different areas of social emphasis. Further, the distribution of energies for any given individual also varies with time. Harmonics in the time dimension are the result and consequence of the shift in styles and the shift of energy levels. The tracking of such minute social changes may be impossible for a human being to perceive, but the social machines with time series analysis programs will be able to track such changes. In the medical field such tracking is accurately pursued in the intensive care units by electronic monitoring devices and medical information systems, and a summary is relayed to the medical staff for regulating the health of the patient. In the current social context, the contributions to the social oscillations and changes due to the human elements which can be estimated are depicted in Figure 5.2 and the jitter effects due to external (and perhaps unforeseen) effects are depicted as noise in Figure 5.3.

As a precursor to the social systems, there are numerous systems (medical, aviation, economic, financial, etc.) that precede a full-fledged computer-based intelligent social analysis and monitoring system for individual users, communities, societies, cultures, and even nations. Most technological issues have been resolved in other disciplines. The effects of individual differences, cultural variations, and transient social patterns exist in the prior systems. The fundamental forces that drive medical, aviation, economic, financial, etc., still persist and the net outcome is predictable. In the social systems, the parameters that contribute to noise and swings are more numerous but are unable to wipe out the effects of the social trends and driving forces, provided they are strong. Weak and erratic social forces are indicative of weak leadership style and political agenda within an individual, corporation, community, society, country, culture, or a nation. Lives and nations are thus ruined without an associative and communicative backbone or a (social) foundation.

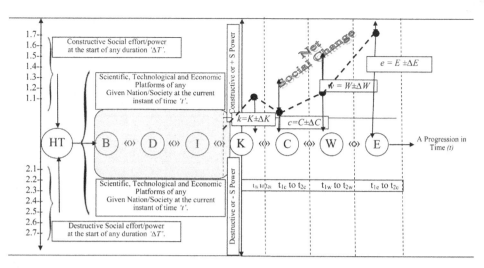

FIGURE 5.2

Depiction of random combination of forces and energies acting on a given object in any given culture or society. These external social parameters cause jagged movements in the K, C, W and E domains. In the short run, the quantification of the social condition of the object appears almost random. However, the cause-and-effect relationship can be traced by social machines for any given society or culture. The movements of objects in these four domains can be out of phase thus causing an illusive effect as to how objects behave as they traverse the knowledge trail depicted in Figure 3.5.

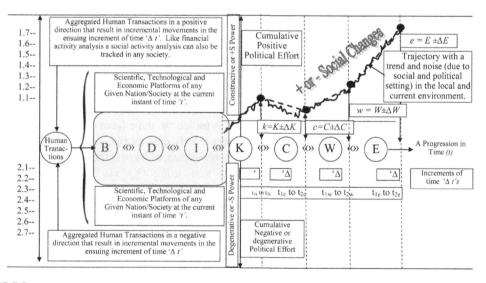

FIGURE 5.3

Depiction of the change in status in a society or organization based on knowledge effort and power of politician, instigator groups, and self Interest groups. $\pm K$, $\pm C$, $\pm W$, $\pm E$, are the extent of influences exerted. These efforts are active in most societies and cause a positive or negative drift in the social and behavioral norms of the society. The parameters $\pm K$, $\pm C$, $\pm W$, and $\pm E$, are dependent on the social conditions and the public attitude. Swing in and out of phase randomly complicating the actual variations of the social progress or decay. In the short run, the quantification of the social condition is jugged and appears almost random. However the cause and effect relationship can be retraced by Social machines for any given society or culture. The entire curve can reside in the Positive or the Negative Y-Axis domain for decades causing a continued social positive or negative change for nations, cultures, societies, and families.

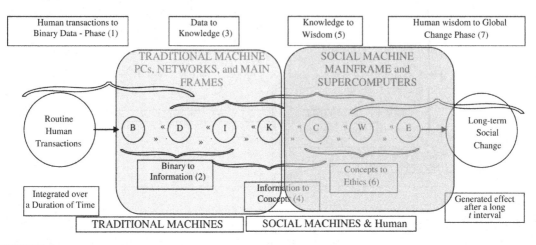

FIGURE 5.4

Grouping of machine and human functions into manageable segments to make orderly, coherent and Cohen's d sustained transitions from routine human transactions to long-term global change. The proposed road-map facilitates the migration towards an environment that fosters validated knowledge bases at the K node, progressive concepts at the C node, well-defined axioms of wisdom at the W node, and finally consistent ethics at the E node to effect a long-term global change toward a more advanced society. The first three transitions of almost all human transactions (e.g., buying and selling) to binary data (e.g., credit card data) at the B node, data structures (e.g., merchant data, credit card data, date stamp) at the D node, and information modules (e.g., date of transaction, amount of transaction, billing information, in proper sequence to make a bank transactions) at the I node are already well-established steps in the current decade.

The transition between machine and human activities is illustrated in Figure 5.4. In the current information-based society, almost every human activity is trailed by some form of data representation. Such trails are shown on the left side of the figure as Phase 1 (human transactions (HT) to data structures (D) via binary representation), as Phase 2 (binary representation (B) to information (I) domain via data structures), and as Phase 3 (data structures to knowledge (K) via information domain). Conceptualization of the three prior phases is partially mechanized by the management and executive information systems. Wisdom and ethical implications of such activities are generally human processes. The three nodes on the right side of the figure occur rather slowly and can take decades to complete and they are scrutinized and iterated many hundreds of times. The role of social machines becomes stylized and culturally dependent. The axioms of wisdom and the code of ethics are both as dynamic as life itself and the social progress of one culture can be viewed as a social retreat in another culture. For example, gay marriages would not be viewed favorably in the Eastern cultures; and by the same token male dominance of the Eastern cultures not be easily favored in the Western cultures.

Priming the social machine to suit the culture becomes a dominant social-software responsibility to guide the social movement. The synergy between *all* aspects (e.g., social, cultural, and philosophic) of human thought becomes necessary to move the society forward in any given setting. Priming the machine only to economic progress is likely to lead to boom-to-burst type cyclic variation leading the monumental crashes and (recent) failures of the banking systems.

CONCLUSIONS

Private and social lives are already impacted by the tools, machines, and networks in the society. The effect appears (almost) irreversible. Though useful in most cases, held devices and PDAs have become a showpiece for the elite. The impact of fully-fledged advanced knowledge and wisdom machines is still to emerge. As the early designs of automobiles were indicative of the later model still to emerge, the plain old computers are forerunners of humanist machines. The society appears poised to absorb the next generation of machines geared toward solving human problems rather than scientific and technical problems.

Opportunities posed by network-based social computing possibilities are enormous when social computers are networked into the backbone of the communication systems. Computing and communication have already merged to facilitate the global connectivity and provide data services. The present social opportunities offered by commercial Internet Social Service Providers (ISSP, not to be interpreted as Intelligent Service Switching Points in plain old intelligent networks [8]) are trivial but tainted with exploitation of the innocent and ignorant. Some of the directions of the services (find dates, find affairs, etc.) are slanted toward social decay rather than the positive enhancement.

The social aspects of human lives have not entered the global connectivity and intricacy of backbone networks. The educational and human aspects that may replace high school education with college education, deception with truth, free sex with global morality, etc. can already be implanted in backbone networks. The possibilities prevail with the current backbone switching systems and TCP/IP protocol. Some of the possible venues are explored and delineated in this chapter.

REFERENCES

[1] Hrebenar RJ. Interest group politics in America, <https://books.google.com/books?isbn=1563247038> − 1997.
[2] Christopher B. "What is the Military Industrial Complex?" <http://hnn.us/article/869>, History News Network, of the George Mason University.
[3] Ahamed SV. Computational framework for knowledge. Hoboken, NJ: John Wiley and Sons, Inc; 2009. p. 416−59.
[4] Ahamed SV. Intelligent broadband multimedia networks. 1st ed. Springer; 1997.
[5] Grinnell, Jr RM, et al. Program evaluation for social workers: foundations of evidence-based programs. 6th ed. Oxford University Press, 2012. Also see, East EW. Critical path method (CPM) tutor for construction planning and scheduling. 1st ed. McGraw-Hill Education, 2015.
[6] Ahamed SV. Intelligent internet knowledge networks: processing of concepts and wisdom. Wiley Interscience; 2006.
[7] Ahamed SV. The architecture of a wisdom machine. *Int. J. Smart Eng Syst Des.* 2003:5(4):537−545. Also see Chapter 2 of Ahamed SV, Computational framework of knowledge. Hoboken, NJ: John Wiley and Sons, 2009.
[8] <https://en.wikipedia.org/.../List_of_incidents_of_civil_unrest_i>.
[9] Ahamed SV. Social Impact of Intelligent Telecommunications Networks. In: Proc. of the Pacific Telecommunication Conference, Honolulu, HI. January 17−22: 407−414. Also see Ahamed SV, Lawrence VB. Evolving network architectures for medicine, education and government, Pacific telecommunications 2002. Council 24th Annual Conference Paper W.2.2.1, Honolulu, HI. January 13−17, 2002.

SECTION

INFORMATION MACHINES AND SOCIAL PROGRESS

PART I, SECTION II, SUMMARY

Section 02 with five chapters deals with the greatly enhanced human social needs that have accompanied the industrial age and leisure class of the early 20th century have enter the domain of the modern devices and audio visual gadgets in this 21st century. Starting with rotary telephones to micro-cellular wireless phones and Internet devices, these gadgets have become more and more intelligent in providing the fancies of the generations. Any trace of human connectivity of wire-pairs have been replaced by computer based electronic switching systems or the ESS that took hold of most network switching since the mid 1960s. The intertwined threads of evolving human lives and the technologies in the information-age machines are presented in this Section.

This Section also establishes the connectivity between human nature for gratifying the social needs with the flow and integrity of knowledge. Human and social aspects are explored together with computer and network sciences. Knowledge sciences are based on the well-established principles from motivation, decision science and economics. The concepts are integrated from truisms, psychology, behavioral theory, and deployment of resources to gratify needs as an economic activity and as a well developed strategy from the contribution in Operations Research to offer multiple (yet satisfactory rather than unique) solutions.

RECENT CHANGES TO THE STRUCTURE OF KNOWLEDGE

6

CHAPTER SUMMARY

In this chapter, we propose that knowledge results, or has resulted from human actions and machine functions. Human functions are essential for existence and survival. Machine functions are necessary to retain processes, enhance and modify the knowledge that is accrued by human actions. However, there are two main aspects: Actions are performed in conjunction with objects and actions are tailored intelligently and appropriately to suit the characteristics of such objects. Sensible, coherent, and cogent elements of knowledge are generated when the three elements (actions, objects, and appropriate bonding between the two) are bonded, fused, and/or forced. Such elements of knowledge can be classified, organized, grouped, and processed like binary bits and data structures in typical computer systems. To this extent, knowledge can be initially designed and constructed to have desirable social, technological, or ethical value, just as music can be composed, altered, or enhanced by computer systems. In the simplest cases, the value of knowledge generated could be rudimentary, but in the more advanced cases knowledge so generated can be constructive and creative (such as new invention) and highly significant breakthroughs (like the transistor configuration, the von Neumann's IAS architectural details, etc.) that have profound impact on lives of human beings.

Knowledge and its many dimensions are explored in this chapter. The machines prove to be invaluable when the problems tackled are complex, global, social, and/or scientific. Generally, knowledge machines need to be customized, problem directed, and specific. All the essential design features that are inherent for constructing computer systems (such as the HW architecture, the SW design, the programming languages, the libraries, the macros) also are necessary for the building knowledge machines. All the essential functionalities of the components become more cumbersome but manageable for the machines to build knowledge structures. Machines generally do not generate the highest quality of new knowledge from the old knowledge, but in conjunction with human intelligence and creativity, knowledge machines make an excellent platform for the pursuit of new knowledge.

6.1 INTRODUCTION

Rudimentary knowledge can be fabricated like any other scientific object. Well-known knowledge modules such as the customization of a rudimentary automobile, airplane, or spacecraft are well within the scope of computer-aided knowledge machines. Knowledge banks are scanned for knowledge modules for all the components on the Internet knowledge bases, the interfacing and

Evolution of Knowledge Science. DOI: http://dx.doi.org/10.1016/B978-0-12-805478-9.00006-6

connectivity's are customized, the overall design is verified against knowledge for existing objects in local and global knowledge banks and compiled as a program of a simple knowledge machine. When the situation is for a medical application, the steps are not so simply accomplished since the extent of customization is patient, doctor, staff, and hospital specific. The problems get stacked in an hierarchical structure, and the outcome becomes probabilistic rather than certain.

The knowledge-centric objects (*KCOs*) can have human attributes and become a structure in their own right. However, based on a theme that a specific body of knowledge rests on the embedded noun objects and the structural relation between these key-groups of KCOs, additional new knowledge can be generated. The events, interactions, and forces in the society alter the attributes of *KCOs* and their structural relationships. The design of knowledge deploys a very pragmatic approach that knowledge based on these key objects (*NOs*), their interrelationships (*), and their interactions with verb functions (*VFs*) can be processed by knowledge machines.

The time dependence of knowledge is implied since all the three key constituents are dynamic and can experience time-dependent characteristics. In an integrated sense, the state of knowledge at any instant t_1 can be represented as:

$$(\text{Knowledge})_t \equiv \int_{t=0}^{t=t} \sum_{i=1}^{i=n} (\text{Group of } NO_i) \left\{ \begin{array}{c} \longleftarrow - - - - - - - - - \\ ..\text{Interacting } (*) \text{ with}.. \\ - - - - - - - - - \longrightarrow \\ (*) \end{array} \right\} \sum_{j=1}^{j=v} (\text{Series of } VF_j) . dt$$

A symbolic representation of knowledge can thus be written with three terms representing

a. Arrays of "*n*" noun object(s)
b. Rows of "v_1" verb function(s) these object(s) have undergone
c. Type(s) of interactions or convolutions (*)s that have taken place from $t = 0$ to t_1.

In essence, this equation implies that every piece or element of knowledge at any instant t_1 has a history of its own or in conjunction with other noun objects. This equation should be considered representational rather than mathematical. The symbol (*) indicates that different natures of constituents are involved. The first term denotes noun objects (*NO_i*) and the second term indicates the integrated effects of a series of "*j*" verb functions (*VF_j*) for each (ith) of the "*n*" noun objects.

Knowledge undergoes dynamic changes in the society, the minds of human beings and in the knowledge structures stored in the memories and knowledge banks. Structures of knowledge can be altered in the KPUs of knowledge machines much like data structures are altered in the CPUs of traditional computers. When the concepts from integration and, conversely, the laws of fragmentation are applied in the knowledge domain, the tools and techniques of software engineering can be harnessed in integrating knowledge module into complex knowledge-based application programs and conversely for fragmenting humanistic knowledge manipulation approaches into micro-programmable instructions for the knowledge processing units.

A sense of directionality is important since any element of knowledge can be used for social benefit or abused for social harm. Numerous government and national agencies provide assistance and distribute correct and significant information. In almost all cases, the activity is initiated by the nature of the verb function (*VF* or *VFs*) on the part of the user. For example, the search can be for any object or verb, or even a word. Connectivity to other elements of knowledge is essential to pursue the search for other related elements of knowledge.

Knowledge is re-entrant to the extent that it must be connected to other elements of knowledge and no knowledge element or module may exist in entire isolation. Fragmented to very fine elements, knowledge elements are like elements in nature, but not all the laws are physical chemistry are applicable in the knowledge domain. Whereas only finite number of elements is possible due to the number of orbital paths for the electrons, knowledge can have infinitely greater variety of manifestations. The orbital paths for the elements of knowledge can be as global as the human thought or as nuclear as a neuron but connected to other neuron to exist. Individual thoughts that become unstable are out of the knowledge domain of the society and populous. Knowledge, time, and stability of elements that constitute the knowledge fall in a mental and conscious space.

History has shown a way out of this dilemma by associating knowledge with the needs of humans and species. Firmly founded in the universality of needs, knowledge starts to have a well-defined classification and firm anchorage. It is hard to find knowledge that is genuinely useless for anyone, and conversely most pertinent knowledge is most useful (directly or indirectly) to most knowledge-centric objects, most of the time. A sense of gradations and value of knowledge starts to take shape. Veblen's law [1] of scarcity applies to knowledge and scarce knowledge of high pertinence each has the highest economic value. In most cases, such knowledge is guarded as family or trade secrets and security clearance requirements.

6.2 INDIVIDUAL NEEDS AND EVOLVING MACHINES

The mapping of the individual human needs and the development of computer systems is depicted in Figure 6.1. A seven-layer need pyramid [2] is selected and depicted on the left side of the figure. In most cases, machines that serve the lower needs of human beings are in place as computer systems, intelligent networks, and Internets. The room at the top is vacant for the next generation of knowledge, concept wisdom, machines, and humanistic Internets. Conceptually, such machines can be designed, constructed, and built from existing computer systems. Components of traditional computer systems need to be assembled and programmed to serve as machines at each of the seven layers. The functionality of restructured supercomputers will also serve as the proposed knowledge, concept, wisdom, and humanistic machines.

6.3 CORPORATE NEEDS AND HUMAN MACHINE INTERACTIVE SYSTEMS

An enhanced business model of the corporate pyramid is shown in Figure 6.2. This model is derived from the individual need pyramid depicted in Figure 6.1. Seven basic corporate needs are depicted on the left side of the figure and shown in Table 6.1

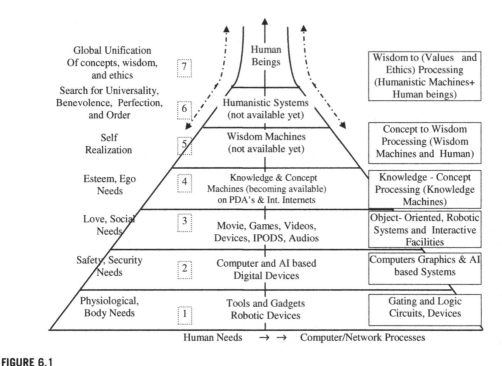

FIGURE 6.1

Mapping of individual needs on the development of computer systems.

Typical organization charts have the responsibilities and functions associated with corporate functions. The newer Management Information Systems (MIS) have programs to use the specific software modules for the control and management of most major and subsidiary functions in the lower four levels. Human and executive involvement is generally necessary for the long-term planning and stability of the functions of the top three layers.

Intelligent machines systems and robotic control of production facilities exist but not commonly deployed except for very specialized technological products such as computer chips. Even for these products, certain minimal human supervision and control has been in order. Typical examples of mostly machine and satellite controlled systems are the drone survey and earthquake emergency warning systems. A certain blend of human and machine intelligentsia appears superior to either two intelligences acting independently.

6.4 KNOWLEDGE-BASED COMPUTATIONAL PLATFORMS FOR ORGANIZATIONS

Organizations and nations both deploy computer-based systems. Networks are essential to keep the practices (i.e., *VF's*) and objects (i.e., *NO's*) that the organizations and nations deploy current and optimally tuned to the technology which is dynamic and vibrant. Knowledge society and social

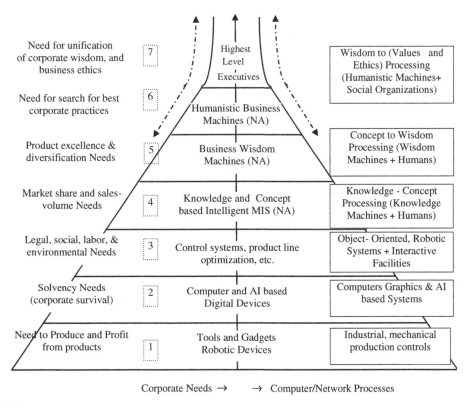

FIGURE 6.2

Mapping of Corporate needs on the machines and networks. MIS = Management Information Systems, AI = Artificial Intelligence, NA = not available.

Table 6.1 Corporate Needs and the Functionality at Each Level		
Corporate Needs	**↓ Corporate Functions at This Layer**	**↓ Management Level and Responsibility**
Level 7	Need for the unification of corporate wisdom and business ethics	Senior executives and VP level & groups
Level 6	Need for search for best corporate strategy	Marketing and production executives
Level 5	Product excellence and diversification needs	VP quality control and staff
Level 4	Market share and sales-volume needs	VP Level marketing and VP production
Level 3	Legal, social, labor, and environmental needs	HR and legal executives and staff
Level 2	Financial corporate survival needs	VP financial and accounting and staff
Level 1	Production needs (need to produce products and derive profit from them)	VP production and line managers, inventory control and scheduling staff

skills demand high levels of adaptation in seeking better life and social conditions. The casual attitude toward learning and adapting to the industrial revolution is not sufficient for dealing with the dynamic shifts that knowledge society has brought upon us over the last few decades. Together with the explosion of information comes the demand for best social adaptation to use the Internet tools and techniques. Inadequate social/knowledge skill only demeans the corporate and state professional in the social and technological circles. In this next stage of the use of computer systems, the optimally composed (and compiled) knowledge patterns will assure the success of a well-informed corporate executive, a manager, or a politician.

The tools of modern information technology call for quick, spontaneous, and sophisticated reactions during corporate and political transactions. More than the tools and techniques to adapt, a change in philosophy and attitude toward handling knowledge to suit any given social and cultural context becomes necessary. Such a change in attitude of humans is best learned from the social/knowledge machines that also learn from the knowledge banks around the world. These machines filter out poor and un-calibrated reactionary attitudes (depending on their own social anchor points of such machines) and offer sharpest knowledge to suit the social and cultural setting. Sets of most suited responses and winning procedures are assembled and checked to match the situation aimed toward an economic and expected maximization of the desired objective.

These knowledge machines are more than mere computers and play an almost human, social, cultural, and economic role. In the same vein, the layers of social-ware become more sophisticated than the typical layers (network, application, compilers, assemblers, linkers, and loaders) of conventional computers. The communication media for social machines is decidedly superior to the media (base metallic, fiber, and wireless) of the lifeless computers. The intelligence of the knowledge-based computers is as alive and responsive as that of the human beings themselves who use the machines, even though a probable "image-self" of the users is created intelligently to match the response to the user.

To bridge the wide gap that Internet and knowledge revolution have brought with them, we propose a conceptual ladder of social-software (SSW) between HW, SW, FW, micro, and nano-codes of the conventional machines and society based on the etiquette of human being. It is also to be noted that the application level programs (written as social programs) for social machines will not run on the less optimized microcomputers and Unix clad bare bone von Neumann machines. In the corporate and national circles, this new discipline needs a streamlined philosophy of thought, concepts, innovations, designs, and engineering specifications, to accomplish optimal sound advice, documents, and suggestions for human beings to deploy in their own knowledge circles.

The availability of global information has prompted many industries and nations to perform knowledge functions that were unknown or entirely human in the past. The key industrial goals are the accuracy and exactitude of results that the platform can provide with few highly specialized personnel. In Figure 6.3, the key concepts are presented. Organizations and nations have specific needs. These needs have to be gratified for survival and well-being of the entities. In the process of gratification of needs, numerous objects (*NOs*), verb functions (*VFs*), and their convolutions (*) are invoked. Sustained and continuality of needs (N), knowledge (K), and knowledge-centric objects (O) cycle for complex organizations and nations in modern knowledge societies are depicted.

Exact predictions of the future are of no avail due to technological uncertainties and indiscretion of the users. However, the conceptual pathways are clear. In order to let progress begin, we traverse

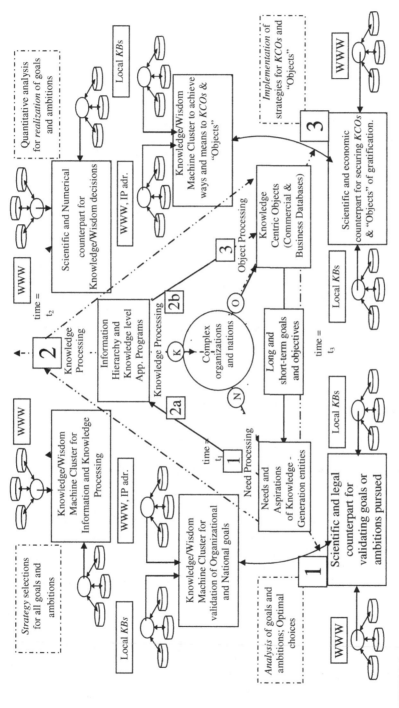

FIGURE 6.3

Organizations and nations have specific needs. These needs have to be gratified for survival and well-being of the entities. In the process of gratification of needs, numerous objects (*NOs*), verb functions (*VFs*), and their convolutions (*) are invoked. Sustained and continuality of needs (N), knowledge (K), and knowledge-centric objects (O) cycle for complex organizations and nations in modern knowledge societies are depicted.

the conceptual domain rather than dismantle the political and technological roadblocks. In the information domain, the binary bit conveys the status of fragmented reality. It is for the typical computer systems to reassemble these bits into coherent data structures that are used to solve technical and scientific problems. In the knowledge domain, the binary bits are replaced by tiny noun objects (*NOs*), microscopic verb functions (*VFs*) with their particular contextual insignia (*s) to make up microscopic elements of knowledge.

Such elements are assembled, processed, refined, reconstructed, and used to generate major blocks of precise and goal-directed knowledge. In most cases, machine intelligence will solve all the complex issues in constructing new knowledge. However, the blend of human (corporate and/or political) wisdom can force new perceptions of artificial knowledge that cannot be envisioned by human beings alone nor depicted as a computer generated image. Generally, when wisdom is called for in the solution of corporate and national problems, the knowledge and wisdom bases different cultures are queried.

A deceptive nucleus of falsified information riding along the knowledge trail can as easily shatter an axiom of wisdom. Statements become unfounded and direction appears devious. However, if wisdom is authentic and universal, then unwanted nuclei of false informers only causes minor disruptions rather than alter the course of wisdom. Writings, events, and incidents since the days of Socrates document that the momentum along a trail of human betterment will continue despite corruption and deception in the society. Being able to learn from history, one can construct a rugged path and then a fine trajectory that social machine can traverse to offer more insightful and significant analysis. Faster responses based on the human behavior and the cultural setting accrues.

6.5 GENERALITY OF THE KNOWLEDGE-BASED APPROACH

The knowledge-based approach is generic to the extent that functions in any environment are based on action by and upon objects in particularly specialized approach to accomplish a goal or part thereof. Objects, actions, approaches, and goals can be integrated and system integration techniques are feasible on computers. When the goals of any specific entity are available or predefined, then a stepwise fragmentation of the goals is structured as *a PERT* and *CPM* [3] diagrams. Now, every nodes and link of these diagrams calls for objects, actions in their own specialized approaches.

Such objects, actions, and the approach are amenable to morphology (the art of systematic fragmentation), and the processes continue till each fragmented verb can be a process, a macro, a subroutine, or an application program on a computer and each noun object can be retrieved from a local knowledge bank, an Internet knowledge-base or a local source. Approaches are also amenable to fragmentation and can be accomplished by the choice of specific routines by appropriate addressing capability in the computer systems.

To exemplify this methodology, we present an electronic government environment where the functions of different federal agencies are illustrated as programmable steps in the routine treatment of functions of the each branch of the government. The overall diagram is shown in Figure 6.4 and procedures are completed by staff members in each of the local area networks (LANs)

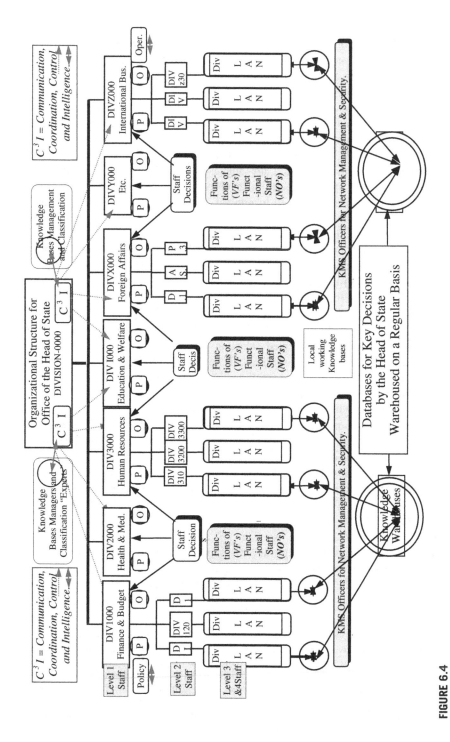

FIGURE 6.4

Configuration of Office of the Head of State to manage the functions (*VF's*), the objects (*NOs*), and their convolutions via the *C³I* approach (i.e., communication, command, control, and intelligence) for the long-term economic and growth trends in any nation.

specifically numbered as LAN100 to LANZ100. This configuration of office of any head of state has the staff members, their functions, and their implementations in the appropriate fashion assembled on a network-based information system. Information of the state of events, their changes, their magnitude, and direction are "sensed" from the numerous "nerve centers" of the state and duly observed by the human objects (*NOs*) and processed by centralized or local knowledge machines to extract the nature and reasons for such (desirable or undesirable) movements of key indicators.

In the management of the functions (*VFs*) by the various objects (humans and machines) and the fashion of their implementation (i.e., *s), the managerial style proposed by Peter Drucker (see Part I, Chapter 2) is deployed. In the original writings of Drucker [4], planning, organization, staffing, implementation, and control (POSIC) are suggested. In Figure 6.4, all the five basic elements are incorporated at every step of the senior level executives to the planning and operation of every staff member. The LANs are designed to operate at two levels: (i) for the routine affairs at the offices of the head of state, and (ii) for the management of functions (i.e., time, motion, and accomplishments) of each of the staff members.

The control function alluded by Drucker is enhanced in *four* basic directions to include the impact of information age and the Internet. *First*, Control entail communicating (C^1) with the people (staff) and elements or groups of (noun)-objects to test the effects of the proposed control. Generally, computer-aided design systems permit the user to adjust and refine the objects deployed in the project or process. Hence communicating becomes an integral part of control. *Second*, organizing the role of various staff members or objects suggested by Drucker becomes coordinating (C^2). *Third*, staffing suggested by Drucker is re-implemented selecting (C^3) the expertise and the foundations of the staff members and the selection of knowledge tools and subroutines in the knowledge-ware of the machines. *Finally*, the human and machine intelligences (I) that are denoted as * (in this case) are merged by the symbol ($\leftarrow \rightarrow$) in the figure.

In a sense, the main computer tying the LANs is programmed to serve the office of the state in its own responsibilities, and it serves to make the function of each employee efficient and optimal. For the state office functions, the C^3I function starts at the head of state and the feedback returns from the offices of the divisions, and from the key major indicators[1] measuring the economic activity in any nation.

In order to manage the functions (*VFs*), the objects (*NOs*), and their convolutions via the C^3I Approach (i.e., communication, coordinate, control, and intelligence) for the long-term economic and growth trends in any nation, the sensing of the economic activities of the nation becomes necessary. Generally, the office of budget and finance collects summarized graphs of such major financial events and transactions. The control function (*VF*) should be able to access such databases and investigate the socioeconomic forces (e.g., nuclear explosion, intent of war, bombing, police brutality) responsible for major movements of these key indicators.

In Figure 6.5, the details of the implementation of the knowledge science approach are presented for the division of education and welfare. The P and O boxes at level 2 indicate the policy

---

[1]These indicators are classified as leading, current, and lagging indicators. As many as 10 subcategories of leading indicators are available, including average weekly wages, unemployment, new orders for manufactured goods, etc. As many as seven subcategories of lagging indicators are available, including average prime rate, unemployment, consumer price index, cost of labor, outstanding consumer credit, etc. Finally, as many as eight current or coincident indicators are also available, including payrolls, personal income, industrial production, trade sales, unemployment rate, etc. These indicators are published by various private and government agencies. Examples of other indicators include unemployment rate, housing starts, consumer price index (a measure for inflation), consumer leverage ratio, industrial production, bankruptcies, gross domestic product, broadband internet penetration, retail sales, stock market prices, money supply changes.

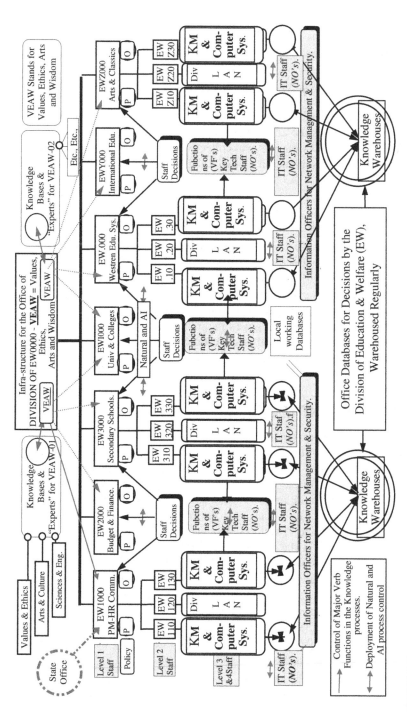

FIGURE 6.5

Knowledge machine platform for the Office of Division of Education and Welfare (EW) to monitor its functions and policy, goals, and projects completion in the execution of the Policies set forth by the head of state (see left of the figure), division, and the staff in the division office. Typically the traditional concepts of Peter Drucker's POSIC (Planning, Organization, Staffing, Implementation, and Control) is implemented first and then a unified approach can be attempted for the C³W level to deploy in the Office of Health and Welfare.

functions and operational functions executed on the appropriate noun objects (such as schools, university, departments, etc.). In this figure, as well in Figure 6.4, it is emphasized that ΔK results from the interaction of one or more noun objects (*NOs*) with one or more verb functions (*VFs*). In an appropriate fashion it is represented as:

$$\Delta K = \{(NO's)* (VF's)\} \; or \{(VF's)*(NO's)\}$$

It implies that the rate of incremental gain of knowledge depends on the rate at which the verb functions are executed. Integrating both sides the accumulated knowledge at any instant of time is the integration of the "**work done**" by the *VFs* on one or a collectivity of *NOs*. The **accumulated knowledge**[2] at any instant "*t*" becomes the summation of two integrals for *{(NO's) * (VF's)}* and for *{(VF's) * (NO's)}* and can be written as:

$$K = \int\limits^{t} [\underset{\text{noun to verb knowledge}}{\overset{n}{\Sigma}\{(NO's) * (VF's)\}}. \; dt \; and \; \underset{\text{verb to noun knowledge}}{\overset{v}{\Sigma}\{(VF's) * (NO's)\}}. \; dt],$$

where *n* is the number of NOs that perform VFs, and *n'* is the number of VFs performed on the NOs. It is assumed that the execution of *{(NO's) * (VF's) }* and *{(VF's) * (NO's)}* takes place in the correct and appropriate contextual relationship. Inappropriate functions and objects do not yield any useful knowledge element. This truism is evident in Figure 6.5 and it is also evident for every-one of the division in Figure 6.4. A series of figures for Divisions 1000 to Z000 can be drawn, and the knowledge-based approach becomes applicable for governing, managing, and optimizing all the functions for any corporation, nation, or even a medical or educational facility. The specific details for the Division of Education and Welfare are presented in Figure 6.5.

6.6 TRANSACTIONS MANAGEMENT MACHINE

Corporate and divisional productivity depends on the transactions within the local environment. Typically, such activities need to keep track of the particular activity, a response, and still be able to communicate with a large number of "objects" and to initiate a process request (ID) number. This type of response scenarios are already built in the emergency response systems (such as 911) [5] of Intelligent Network (IN/2) [6], hospitals, and airports. Automated monitoring of corporate and national activities is accomplished by incorporating sensors in the environment and then regulating the instructions to the branches by "alert" and "react" commands much as the security systems perform when a security breach is detected in the local environment. Tsunami and flood control systems also deploy such precautionary measures by sensors with distributed intelligence modules hardware placed throughout the network or environment. The programming of the response to each scenario sensed as a quantitative measure of the attributes of a set of programmable objects.

Finally we propose that the "sense and knowledge-based application environment" concept can be deployed in financial/economic environments at first and then developed in many format. Further, we propose that envision that the methodology can be deployed at *four* levels (i) the global level, (ii) the national level, (iii) the corporate/Institutional level, and even at (iv) the individual or at personal level in mobile telephone environments.

---

[2]Knowledge is generated in both cases, when *{(NO's)*(VF's)}* and also when *{(VF's)*(NO's)}* and the total knowledge is the sum of these two increments.

CONCLUSIONS

Knowledge science—oriented approach facilitates the optimal solution of most knowledge-based corporate, social and/or national problems. The most recent NOs and their VFs for the solution are updated in light of the current technological innovations by interfacing the knowledge machines to the Internet. The searches for objects, verbs, and their convolutions are done in the context of the problem and the cultural nature of the solution explored. Further, the machine has the parsing capability to break down nouns into the most generic and fundamental constituents. It has the facility to construct a PERT and a CPM diagram to implement any VF. The approach is optimal, but not perfect because of the fuzzy nature of knowledge and the very (too) many resources that would be necessary. However, it is for the user to adapt, modify, or enhance the machine-aided knowledge solution.

To some extent, the future hand-held knowledge machines will serve as a *global knowledge positioning system* (GKPS) from one solution to the next based on Internet knowledge bases. The Library of Congress or the Dewey Decimal classifications will become necessary to query the appropriate knowledge base in context of the problem. The switching facility of the new machines will switch the network channels based on the "knowledge address" rather than a numeric address of each Web site. Such switches have been built in most Intelligent Networks (INs) around the world based on the type of service that the network will provide for the user. Search and switch is routinely performed in most Internet and IN applications.

REFERENCES

[1] Tilman R, editor. A Veblen treasury. Armonk, NY: From leisure class to war, peace and capitalism, 1993.
[2] Ahamed SV. Need Pyramid of the information age human being. International Society of Political Psychology (ISSP) Scientific Meeting, Toronto, Canada, July 3–6, 2005; also see An enhanced need pyramid for the information age human being. In: Proc. of the Fifth Hawaii International Conference, Fifth International Conference on Business, Hawaii, May 26–29, 2005.
[3] Grinnell, Jr RM, et al. Program evaluation for social workers: foundations of evidence-based programs. 6th ed. Oxford University Press, 2012. Also see, East EW. Critical path method (CPM) tutor for construction planning and scheduling. 1st ed. Publisher: McGraw-Hill Education, 2015.
[4] Peter Drucker's Life and Legacy | The Drucker Institute, www.druckerinstitute.com/peter-druckers-life-and-legacy.
[5] Ahamed SV, Lawrence VL. Chapter 9 "Emergency response systems" in Intelligent broadband multimedia networks. Boston, MA: Kluwer Academic Publishers, 1997.
[6] Ahamed SV, Lawrence VL. Intelligent broadband multimedia networks. Boston, MA: Kluwer Academic Publishers, 1997.

ORIGIN AND STRUCTURE OF KNOWLEDGE ENERGY

7

CHAPTER SUMMARY

Change is perpetual in environments. Nature, human beings, and machines originate and supply the energy for changes. In the older socioeconomic systems, human liveliness has served to implant the primal "seed" or "concept" energy for change. In these older systems, the path from concept to implementation and realization has been traversed by intense human effort and endurance. The older forms of computers and machines are ineffective in paving the path to an engineering or scientific manifestation of the "seed concept." However, through the 70 s to the current era, machines have assisted human effort and creativity enormously. Computer graphic and computer vision both facilitate the upsurge of knowledge and hence the creativity that follows. The environmental-input process is faster, more efficient, and more detailed by providing neural inputs directly into the optic nerve that is ten times larger than the auditory nerve. The more recent advances in the binocular vision, 3-D graphics, and gaming devices can only sharpen the human response.

Significant scientific side effect is gained in knowledge domain and quicker learning processes result. Both can hasten the accumulation of the "knowledge energy" in the mind of the receptor. In this chapter, we outline the conscious methodology to assist the accumulation of knowledge energy and from a pathway from the environment and nature that is full of evolutionary wonders for the receptive mind and for the novel knowledge machines. These need breeds of machines analyze, classify, learn, and connect the "objects," what they do, how they do, why they do, when they do, how they do what they have to do, and finally build a "body of knowledge" that has some socioeconomic purpose or satisfies a requirement. Noun-objects and verb-functions are genetically interwoven in the fabric of knowledge thus acquiring a sense of beauty and wonder. Knowledge processor units in machines follow a similar path. The seminal "seed energy" of the human beings is thus amplified (as in electronic circuits) by these rather sophisticated machines. The groupings, their interconnectivities, and their bondages are learned from the existing knowledge bases. The social value is predictive and estimated based on the axioms of "wisdom" from the prior generations.

7.1 INTRODUCTION

Knowledge era and Internet environments have enhanced changes in the human thought processes in social settings and work environments. These dual environmental feedbacks into each other are positive thus making the changes in both twice as fast. Evolution of new knowledge and inventions become hyper-geometric as it is occurring around the world. In a sense, this type of iterative

Evolution of Knowledge Science. DOI: http://dx.doi.org/10.1016/B978-0-12-805478-9.00007-8

enhancement in the knowledge domains is unique, even though in the real world microbial colonies undergo such accelerated feedback processes and grow very rapidly. Cancer and AIDS are known to spread quickly and detrimentally.

Early inventions were far fewer than recent inventions. An older invention would be a creation closer to a breakthrough rather than an innovation or an improvisation. The genius of invention was truly practiced at the concept level rather than as an implementation. In a sense, the early inventions came out of a vacuum. The lack of knowledge surrounding a concept was a good basis for an invention. For example, the principle of Archimedes [1,2] was a genuine cry ("Eureka") of the realization of a concept of bouncy. Newton's notion of gravity was thus a realization of a concept. The force resulting from the influence of current on a magnetic needle discovered by Oersted [3] was not lost like a needle in a haystack, but instead it became the foundation for understanding the electromagnetic fields.

Many significant concepts and inventions thus resulted from these chance discoveries or coincidental observations. Luigi Galvani (a physiologist) discovered the effect of current electricity as he noticed the muscular twitch of frog leg [4] due to an electric shock. Oersted [3] discovered the effects of electricity on a magnetic needle in 1822. Rontgen [5] discovered the penetration of X rays accidentally, and so on. In the modern world and knowledge society, the discoveries are more in the conceptual domain rather than in the physical domain. Yet, it would be very noteworthy to invent/discover a principle/concept as generic as electromagnetism (Faraday [6]) or as universal as the Einstein's Theory of Relativity [7] in the twenty-first century. The parallels of such major concepts still need to be traced in the knowledge domain.

Today's environment is evolved, and the precursors to almost any discipline are already encoded in the Library of Congress [8]. In a sense, the boundaries of knowledge overlap. The laws of electromagnetism [9] and thermodynamics [10] are universal in all the engineering applications. In some cases, today's innovations may surpass the inventions a century ago. For example, the basic patents for transmitting light to enhance the purity and clarity of crystalline glass for fiber optics would demand less inventive skills than the innovative synthesis of glass fiber [11] to carry numerous wavelengths of light for the dense wavelength division multiplexing (DWDM) applications [12] in light wave systems. In the same vein, Einstein's headache from deriving his general Theory of Relativity [7] would be greater than the pain that Newton [13] would have felt when the apple dropped on his head!

The discoveries/inventions in the knowledge domain are more abstract and founded deeper at the concept level. These abstractions/imageries between parallel strings of thought are envisioned more readily than seen through. Such realizations and conceptual discoveries are not patentable or economically rewarding unless they are safeguarded as trade secrets and harnessed at a commercial level. In most instances, these discoveries are implemented as an algorithm (e.g., kernel programming, dual error-correcting codes, data encryption, etc.), or a shortcut at programming level, but then do take shape as inventions.

When human intelligence and goodwill are coupled, the machine processes with knowledge processing capabilities; the expansion of knowledge can be directed toward being desirable and beneficial. An opposite result accrues with ill will of the abusers. Machines that can predict the abuse and ill will in a social sense can warn the dangers of such use and its aftermath and block the abusers from further abuse. This extent of safeguard is deployed when the machines and networks detect possible security breaches and intrusion to privacy. Security measures that are used consist of detecting the possible abuse, and then evaluating the possible risk involved and finally invoking the programmed methodologies to impose barriers to the abusers.

In the proposed machines, the security of social and ethical values of a culture or an environment is implemented as the physical security of organizational and physical assets of any corporation or any nation. Extensive systems to safeguard the social values have not been developed in most nations, even though such social software for machines can be designed and implemented like any other software system.

7.2 NEED THEORY BASIS FOR KNOWLEDGE-BASED SOLUTIONS

Needs that motivate species into activity are used as a platform to harness the energy into productive social functions. Most species use this continuous source of energy derived from the continuity of needs throughout the life and abundant in all species, to build social relations and structured family ties. For humans beings much of this energy leads to gratifying the lower (1 and 2) levels of need, shown in Figure 7.1 as Phase I transactions. Next, in most societies, the residual energies are deployed to gratify the middle (3 and 4) levels of need, shown as Phase II transactions. This modality of behavior emphasizes that when the lower needs are gratified to an acceptable level, the means, methodology, and knowledge to gratify next higher levels of need is better constructed and optimally achieved.

It is feasible to extend this rationale to upgrade human transactions up and into four levels $(4+, 5, 6,$ and 7; see Figure 7.1) of needs and achieve a longer lasting and a more integrated solution by constructing a knowledge platform by tapping the natural endless intelligence of humans and the deep-learning artificial intelligence of the machines. For simpler, less sophisticated needs at these four levels, the plain old computer systems and smart users will suffice. However, as the needs become more sophisticated (like searching and solving for neural paths in the brain, finding a cure for cancer), the need for tireless knowledge machines and persistent humans becomes evident. Such problems demand that the machines become proactive and predictive as much as they demand users to become creative and imaginative. The latter characteristics of human beings are personal and individualistic, whereas the former capabilities of machines can be designed, constructed, tested, and optimized like the hardware, firmware, and software of computer systems.

The conceptual path through the cooperative role between machines and users is depicted in the middle of Figure 7.1 by "forcing" the machine to search, select, or conceive noun-objects (NOs) from the environmental knowledge banks. Further matching of NOs with actions is achieved by "coercing" the search engines to seek, enhance, and modify the verb-functions (VFs) in their appropriate native setting ($*s$) to build a series of elements of pragmatic elements of knowledge ($\Delta K = NOs * VFs$). These elements are then recombined to build one "body of knowledge" that will convey the implementable path from human energies to technological devices and gadgets.

The right side of Figure 7.1 is enhanced and redrawn in Figure 7.2. The human intellectual activities are reconstituted by scanning and optimizing the NOs in the local and worldwide information bases together with the scanning and optimizing for the associated VFs and their respective convolutions. The result is an increment of knowledge that satisfies a fragment of the goal toward

The Evolution of Human Activity and the Ethical Knowledge-Based Social Trail

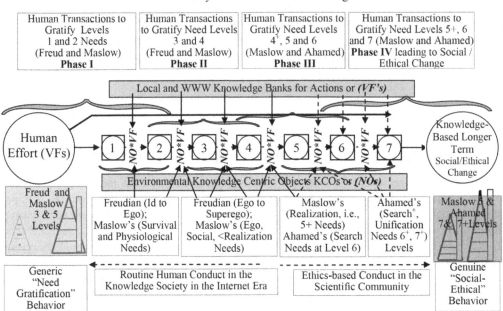

Human Transactions to Gratify Levels 1 and 2 Needs (Freud and Maslow) **Phase I**	Human Transactions to Gratify Need Levels 3 and 4 (Freud and Maslow) **Phase II**	Human Transactions to Gratify Need Levels 4^+, 5 and 6 (Maslow and Ahamed) **Phase III**	Human Transactions to Gratify Need Levels $5+$, 6 and 7 (Maslow and Ahamed) **Phase IV** leading to Social / Ethical Change

FIGURE 7.1

Snapshot of the human effort in the verb functions (VFs) within any activity. The activity is mostly directed toward gratifying a particular need that motivates the human being to gratify the deficit need. Needs in humans have documented hierarchical representations. Freud, Eric Berne, Carl Jung, Maslow, and Ahamed have stratified the layers within the need structures, and Erich Fromm has classified the social needs even further. Fromm's writings provide a valid basis for developing the core of the social layer software or SSW.

social betterment. Successively, when all the increments are prearranged and structured, then an entire "body of knowledge" will offer a composite plan (P) with organization (O), staffing (S), implementation (I), and the final control (C), [according to Drucker's Strategy (see Reference 14 and Section 2.3.2)] to achieve the social betterment of an entity, a corporation, a society, or a nation.

7.3 SEMINAL ENERGY FOR CHANGE IN THE KNOWLEDGE DOMAIN

In following the origin of changes in the environment, the human psyche plays the crucial role. The actions of any individual (*VFs*) are based on the innate intelligence to gratify the deficit needs and the behavioral patterns in the adaptation (*) of solution by manipulating the objects (*NOs*) to gratify such needs. A breed of behavioral intelligence (BI) evolves from the innate native intelligence (NI) and social norms. The composition of these two intelligences is unique as the personality of the individual thus enhancing or curtailing the energy for change for initiating or

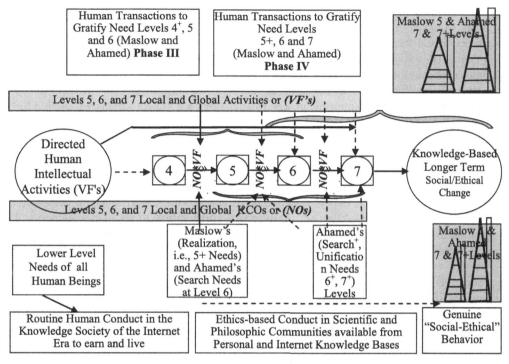

FIGURE 7.2

Rearrangement of the activities in the highest four levels of needs will evolve the necessary elements of knowledge leading to sustainable long-term social and ethical changes in the society. The basic premise is that the activities assume the more desired and ethical goals documented in the local and Internet knowledge bases, and search to divert the intellectual activity into searching, selecting, and optimizing the necessary NOs, VFs, and their convolutions (*s).

implementing the energy levels. Behavioral intelligence can be distilled by the teachings of Freud [15], Jung [16], Maslow [17−19], and Ahamed [20], and then by extending Maslow's findings to suit the increase leisure time of Veblen [21] brought about by highly efficient computer systems and very wide band WWW networks.

In the realm of computer sciences, artificial intelligence is firmly established in making machines function as decision makers, robots, pattern detectors, intelligent agents, and even as a source of expert opinion. With hardware design and programmability at the disposal of computer and network specialists, artificial intelligence is a means for machines to act in a quasi-intelligent format. The social and economic rewards of numerous inventions along these lines have an impact on society. Artificial intelligence becomes a science to impart a finite amount of human decision making onto the functions of a piece of transistorized gadgetry.

In an effort to make machines follow the human trail, behavioral intelligence takes behavioral models from the social arena and transplants them into the core of the machine so that the machine is motivated much as a human being would be driven. This is more than what an artificial intelligence-based machine would do. The proposed strategy is to make the machine imitate how a human being would behave and find the sources of motivation and their overall effect. Motivation is more fundamental than thought. In fact, motivation initiates the thought process to achieve a goal—to extinguish a need that caused the motivation in the first place.

Whereas of behavioral intelligence drives the full circle of thought in satisfying human needs, artificial intelligence is a segment of the circle. In a localized context, artificial intelligence brings together computing power to the user to solve problems in an intelligent way. In a global context, if behavioral intelligence is invoked, then behavior of behavioral intelligence makes the machine see the cycle of need, motivation, a course of behavior to satisfy the need, and return to a stable condition to take on another need of the user. To this extent, the machine imitates the behavior of a human being more closely. It becomes clear that a machine based on of behavioral intelligence will deploy the artificial intelligence tools (such as pattern recognition, robotics, expert systems, intelligent agents) consistently to complete the circle of gratification of needs. After all, a circle is a composition of its many segments. The behavioral intelligence aspect of the machine would address the curvature and angular relationship (i.e., the radius and the angle) attributes of the entire small or large circles (and needs) that human beings experience. To complete the circle, the machine also deploys the artificial intelligence tools and techniques at a segment level.

It is unclear if the human beings themselves know or plan the entire circle to satisfy any complex need or the circle is a mere composition of very short lines that symbolize the "cut and try" approach commonly used in practice. Human behavior thus retains an element of randomness, much as the current theorists in quantum mechanics suggest that the entire universe is a mere chance collection of superstrings. The need circle (from the initial of need to it final gratification) thus remains imperfect and situation dependent.

7.4 OPTIMAL SEARCH FOR NOs, VFs, AND *S

Knowledge science provides for a methodology to search the local and Internet knowledge banks for elements of knowledge much as a sophisticated computer-aided design program would let the users find the best components for an engineering design project. The process is slightly more detailed since anybody of knowledge can be fragmented by the machine and the search can be handled at any level of microscopic detail. With reasonable human oversight, the level of fragmentation can be enhanced or collapsed. Extremely detailed knowledge element searches can be time and computation intensive.

Figures 7.3 to 7.5 depict three passes for the search of knowledge element and optimization procedure on a knowledge machine. The passes are separated out only for descriptive purposes. These phases can be sequenced and the process becomes streamlined on a large machine as shown in Figure 7.6. The machine seeks out the increments of knowledge little by little, as a typical computer would search for bit sequences in large databases. The extent of match and the granularity of search are matched to the context of the problem being addressed. However, the effectiveness lies in selecting and matching the NOs, VFs, and *s together to construct the element of knowledge ΔK_1 first from the local knowledge bases. Next, refining and optimizing the

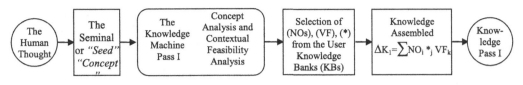

FIGURE 7.3

Mechanized generation of knowledge Pass I — Assemble initial knowledge $\Delta K_1 \rightarrow$

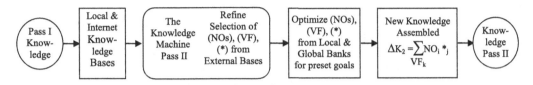

FIGURE 7.4

Mechanized generation of knowledge Pass II — Optimize new knowledge assembled ΔK_2; iterate Passes I and II $\rightarrow$

Optimize New Knowledge Assembled ΔK_2; Iterate Passes I and II $\rightarrow$

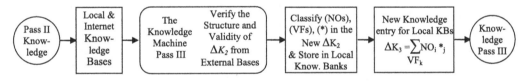

FIGURE 7.5

Mechanized generation of knowledge Pass III — Classify, reference, and store the newly generated knowledge $\rightarrow \Delta K = \Sigma NO_i *_j VF_k$.

elements of ΔK_1 from global bases as ΔK_2, and finally storing away the results in the local bases to solve similar problems or to build bigger and more beautiful structures for the larger "Bodies of Knowledge (BoKs)." Knowledge is broken down into its elements, then into their constituents, to any level of their microscopic levels, and finally restructured into the most suitable format for deployment.

In Phase I leading to ΔK_1, the machine breaks the knowledge being searched into its constituting NOs, VFs, and the numerous convolutions (*s) possible from the local knowledge bases. The search is extensive for the goals of the knowledge sought. In Phase II leading to ΔK_2, the further breakdown into finer elements (if necessary), and the optimization are shown in Figure 7.4. In Phase III, a systematic organization of the "experience" of the machine occurs leading to the newer and updated bodies of knowledge, as shown in Figure 7.5.

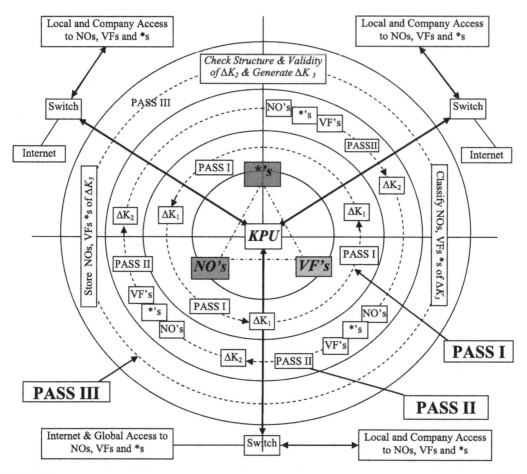

FIGURE 7.6

A large machine with knowledge processor (KPU) to execute the collections of NOs, VFs, and *s to generate the final knowledge (ΔK_3) necessary for solving knowledge-based problems. The initial assemble of the NOs, VFs, and *s takes place at the end of PASS I, which as then enhanced and optimized for efficiency, cost, and optimality during PASS II and finally validated for structural and scientific validity of the knowledge and design of knowledge-based solution.

The elements of knowledge ΔK_1, ΔK_2, and ΔK_3 are incremental and generated over the duration while their respective VFs are active. In most cases, the VFs alter the constitution of the NOs involved. For example, if the NO is the psyche of an individual and the VF is love, then the act alters the psyche of the individual. To some extent, these increments should be considered as incremental "work done"[1] or the "knowledge potential (KnP)" [22] gained by the machine. In a

---

[1]In the knowledge domain, the Newton's concept of work done { = force × (displacement = velocity × duration)} is directly applicable. The equivalent case for Newtonian concept would be in situation where the force in the actions would change the mass of the object.

mathematical sense the "work done" function should be determined as an integral over the duration of the action, 't' (from t_1 to t_2) and if the action changes the NO, then the incremental work done or the gain in knowledge potential becomes equal to

$$\Delta K_1, \Delta K_2, \text{ or } \Delta K_3 = \int NO(t)\{*(t)\}VF(t).dt$$

If there are numerous (n) *NOs* that are influenced by *VF*, then the work done or the gain in knowledge potential becomes equal to the work done in the direction of generating the appropriate knowledge. These elements are cumulative in their own respective directions.

7.5 CUSTOMIZED CASES FOR INDIVIDUALS, CORPORATIONS, AND SOCIETIES

Personal and individual traits play a crucial role in the incremental knowledge gains. or the gain in knowledge potential. Typically all students go to class, but the learning (incremental gain in knowledge) differs significantly from student to student. It becomes necessary to tailor ΔK_1, ΔK_2, and ΔK_3 to the predisposition of the emotional energy distributions associated with how the users learn and tie it to the level of need. For example, X may learn social skills faster than Y who may learn numerical skills faster than X. Three factors that play a role for any individual user are

a. configuration of the need hierarchy,
b. personality profile and distribution of the energies for NOs, VFs, *s, at each of hierarchical levels, and
c. preferential actions taken by the user in the past at each of the seven levels.

These three factors feed into the knowledge machine to find the action proposed by the knowledge-ware and depicted in Figure 7.7. The personal knowledge bases of the user are referenced initially and then the emotional energy is extracted for the particular individual, the corporation, or the society. To accommodate individual differences between users, corporations, cultures, and nations, seven indices of energy level distributions (Aa through Ag, shown in Fig. 7.8) are assigned to the seven levels of needs [20]. Figure 7.8 is elaboration of the methodology for the machine-generated solution of a knowledge-based personal problem shown in Figure 7.7. The machine generates the next possible actions on a very individualistic and comprehensive basis starting from the origin of need stimulating the energy to gratify the need, following the energy distributions in the user energy stratum, and matching the percentages of emotional energy to the current environment and finally generating the *action(s)* necessary to resolve individual user problems and issues. Local and global knowledge bases are accessed to find the three factors essential in generating the final course of action(s).

7.6 CONVERGENCE OF NEEDS IN HUMANS AND ARTIFICIAL KNOWLEDGE IN MACHINES

The solution of knowledge-based problems by machines lies in programming to be aware of local and global needs of the users. The personality profile, personal preferences, and the resources available all

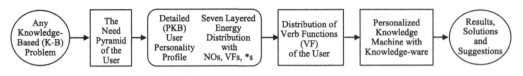

FIGURE 7.7

Computational approach to a hand-held knowledge-based machine.

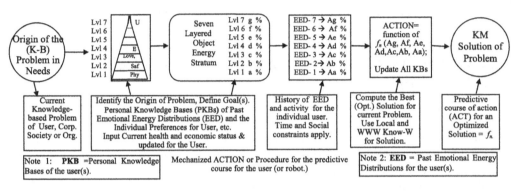

FIGURE 7.8

Procedural and computational approach for the solution of knowledge-based problems by hand-held knowledge machines that use the local knowledge banks for the individual and Internet-based social strategies for the resolution of routine issues of individuals. Societies or corporations may deploy more sophisticated problem resolution methodologies than the standard solution methodologies embedded in the knowledge-software (KSW). Such routines can be made as common as the math libraries (such as add, sub, mpy, divide, exp./) embedded in pocket calculators.

play a role in the machine-generated solution. The solution is not generally a single and unique solution but a combination of many strategies for the entire problem or even for a single critical step in the overall solution. When complex problems are fragmented, each step becomes a problem in its own right. The overall solution becomes a critical combination of numerous smaller stepwise solutions.

In some case, the steps need to be assembled by the critical path method (CPM) [23] and by deploying the program evaluation and review techniques (*PERT*) [23]. The simple routine problems do not need sophisticated programming approaches (such as *CPM* and *PERT* techniques), but as the capabilities of the hand-held devices and the software becomes embedded in the microcode, even the simple problems are likely to be solved more effectively and optimally. Abuse of these approaches is likely when the effect of the proposed solution does not include its social and environmental side effects and ill effects.

For example, the war-colleges (even some politician) teach ruthlessness and destruction as documented in the recent wars. It has brought chaos and misery, as did the WWII. The balancing of the ruthlessness of war programs is to be accomplished by the sanity of social programs. Both being developed by computer scientists, two machines can face each other in a deadlock. Human intervention is perhaps a way out of a deadly battle between a criminal drone and a contemplative robot.

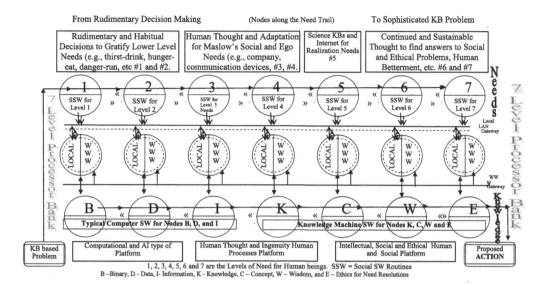

FIGURE 7.9

Snapshot of the computer-assisted knowledge-based activity in prolonged timeframe creating global and sociological changes. Typical problems (such as human betterment, medical solutions) can be addressed.

In Figure 7.9, the unison of human needs and the knowledge to resolve such need in depicted. The central section of the proposed machine receives its inputs from the upper segment that represents the seven basic needs of all human beings and the lower segment contains the computational programs, the knowledge-ware, the wisdom, the concepts, and the ethical frameworks to handle needs of different nature at each of the seven layers. Considerable latitude exists in the design of the central region of the machine. Seven different KPUs may share the computations at the seven levels, or a single KPU may act in a sequential manner demanding long execution times.

The knowledge machine processor architecture can be assembled as a S̲ingle (V̲erb), S̲ingle (N̲oun) O̲bject processor with an architecture of S(V)I-S(N)O, corresponding the SISD processor through all the architectures corresponding to SIMD, MISD, and MIMD [24] processors. In knowledge machines, the bus structure needs connectivity between local and Internet knowledge banks with the KPUs to access recent technological changes to execute VFs and to access newer and more refined NOs.

CONCLUSIONS

Computational strategies from computer science are introduced in handling knowledge-based transactions, events, episodes, and human relations. Knowledge derived from prior experience and acquisitions is held in the machines and knowledge bases of personal devices. Universal approaches to the possible array of solutions are accessed from the worldwide knowledge bases via the Internet. User preferences and prior experiences are validated from personalized caches during the customization of the computer-generated solution and the new knowledge elements being consolidated for the particular user, corporation, society, culture, etc. Two types of knowledge derived from local and global bases are intertwined and applied to the solution of user problem(s) on an individual basis. The techniques are applicable to executive information and decision support systems of corporations, medical information, and security systems.

The role of incremental changes of knowledge and movements are reflected into the social contours that bind human beings, corporations, and most social entities with close ties and commitments. Conversely, serious negative fluctuations of knowledge about social entities also expel one another from close relationships. Such events are frequent in political and corporate environments that need to survive in dynamic socioeconomic and financial situations. In this chapter, we have interleaved the classical works of Maslow (from his visions of human personality and social psychology) with contributions of Drucker (from his perspectives on the corporate management). Our goal has been to explore the technology of the twenty-first-century architecture for social machines. It is our contention that the war academies funded by public monies and spill blood around the globe, should also fund the development of knowledge machines to develop algorithms, methodologies and "languages." Such academies should be perhaps, reconstituted as "knowledge academies" to reinvent the notion of "Ashoka pillars" (see section 4.5) to spread "peaceful innovations" in the knowledge domain.

REFERENCES

[1] Ahamed SV, Lawrence VB. The art of scientific innovation: Cases of classical creativity. Boston, MA: Pearson Prentice Hall, 2004.

[2] Stein S. Archimedes: What did he do beside cry Eureka? The Mathematical Association of America, Washington, DC, 1999.

[3] Gregory F. "Oersted and the Discovery of Electromagnetism" in Episodes in Romantic Science, 1998. An excellent portrayal of Hans Christian Oersted. Also see http://www.clas.ufl.edu/users/fgregory/oersted.htm.

[4] Animal Electricity, circa 1781 The Scientist Magazine®, www.the-scientist.com › ... › *Magazine* › *Foundations*.

[5] Garcia K. Wilhelm Roentgen and the discovery of X-rays (Unlocking the Secrets of Science). Mitchell Lane Publishers, Inc., Newark, DE, 2002.

[6] Tyndall J. Faraday as a discoverer. London: Longmans, Green & Co., 1868.

[7] Einstein A. The origin of the general theory of relativity. Glasgow: Jackson, Wylie & Co., 1933.

[8] Ganendran J. Learn Library of Congress subject access. Scarecrow Press, 2000. Also see Mortimer M. Learn Dewey decimal classification. 21st ed. Scarecrow Press, Lanham, MD, 1999.

[9] Kraus J.D., Fleisch D.A. Electromagnetics. 5th ed. McGraw-Hill Science/Engineering/Math, New York, 1999.

[10] Incropera FP, Dewitt DP. Fundamentals of heat and mass transfer. 5th ed. Hoboken, NJ: John Wiley & Sons, 2001.

[11] Born M., Wolf E. Principles of optics: Electromagnetic theory of propagation, interference and diffraction of light. 7th ed. Cambridge University Press, New York, 1999. Also see Becker PC, Olsson NA, Simpson JR. Erbium-doped fiber amplifiers. 1st ed. Academic Press, Waltham, MA, 1999.

[12] Bates R.J. Wave-division multiplexing and dense-wave division multiplexing. McGraw-Hill/ Professional; New York, Telecom Series Adobe e-book, 2002, on light wave systems. DWDM applications.

[13] Cohen IB, Smith GE, editors. The Cambridge companion to Newton. Cambridge University Press, 2002.

[14] Drucker PF. The practice of management. HarperBusines. Reissue ed. Peter Drucker's Life and Legacy | The Drucker Institute; 2006. www.druckerinstitute.com/peter-druckers-life-and-legacy.

[15] Freud S. Basic writings of freud. New York: Modern Library, 1938.

[16] Jung C. *Modern man in search of a soul*. London: Routledge & Kenan Paul Ltd., London 1933 and 1961.

[17] Maslow A.H. A theory of human motivation. Psychol. Rev. 1943:50:370−396; also see Maslow A, *Farther reaches of human nature*. New York: Viking Press, 1971.

[18] Maslow AH. Motivation and personality. New York: Harper and Row, 1954.

[19] Maslow AH. Towards a psychology of being. Princeton: D. Van Nostrand Company, 1962.

[20] Ahamed S.V. "Need Pyramid of the Information Age Human Being," International Society of Political Psychology (ISSP), Scientific Meeting, Toronto, Canada, July 3−6, 2005; also see, An enhanced need pyramid for the information age human being. In: Proc. of the Fifth Hawaii International Conference, Fifth International Conference on Business, Hawaii, May 26−29, 2005.

[21] Tilman R. Ed. A Veblen treasury. from leisure class to war, peace and capitalism. Armonk, NY, 1993.

[22] Ahamed SV. Computational framework for knowledge. Hoboken, NJ: John Wiley and Sons, Inc, 2009.

[23] Grinnell, Jr R.M. et.al., Program evaluation for social workers: Foundations of evidence-based programs. 6th ed, Oxford University Press, 2012. Also see, East EW. Critical path method (CPM) tutor for construction planning and scheduling. 1st ed. McGraw-Hill Education, 2015.

[24] Hayes J.P. Computer architecture and organization. 2nd ed. McGraw-Hill, New York, 1988. See also, Stone HS. et al. Introduction to computer architecture. Computer Science Series. New York: Science Research Associates, 1980.

BANDS OF KNOWLEDGE

8

CHAPTER SUMMARY

Knowledge molds every aspect of human life and embedded behavior within it. Knowledge imprints in the many modes of behavior are as specific as the fingerprints of humans. Whereas fingerprints may retain their patterns for a lifetime, knowledge imprints are dynamic as the personality of the individual, evolving and adapting to the social and cultural environments. At an early age, the initial adaptations may be by trial and error, but the normal mode is intelligent and knowledge based. It is iterative and self-learning. It is scientific and accurate. It becomes beautiful and compassionate as personality itself.

In this chapter, we concentrate in the middle stages of being intelligent and knowledge based. Being iterative and self-learning but deploying modern computing ideologies and program-ming aspects at a conceptual level, these machine-based solutions can be more optimal than purely human solutions. The use of the highly evolved computing sciences borders knowledge sciences and is reflected within this new discipline as flowcharts and block diagrams. These precursors to the actual hardware of the knowledge machines, pave the way through knowledge-ware and knowledge modules, knowledge machine language, and knowledge operational codes. Social machines become imminent and human behavior gets streamlined leaning toward respect and trust rather than toward malice and greed in some humans, cultures, societies, and nations!

8.1 INTRODUCTION

Band of knowledge are formed as human beings attempt to gratify their needs in five layers (Maslow [1]) or in seven layers (Ahamed [2]) that constitute the need pyramid. Two aspects become evident. First, there are "objects" to gratify the needs, and, second, the "actions" (convolved with the objects) that complete the gratification. Knowledge in these five or seven bands facilitates the selections of objects and/or execution of appropriate actions necessary to gratify the needs in their respective layers. The knowledge is accumulated in these layers by learning how to expend the energies to all present needs of individuals. The personal imprint of knowledge appears over a span of time depending on family, culture, and society.

Social patterns become established and human attitudes shape the need gratification profile of individuals. The profile is matched to the pyramid of needs. Content and structure evolve and stored in the memory. Knowledge machines can be customized to individual tastes, fancies, and preferences, and primed as PDAs. Alternatively, the cultural and social practices can be stored as generic devices or chips that can be augmented with personal preferences. This practice is

Evolution of Knowledge Science. DOI: http://dx.doi.org/10.1016/B978-0-12-805478-9.00008-X

common in most PC environments where the basic and routine software is preloaded by the vendors and then the user would supplement the SW with the necessary application programs and special add-ons. In this mode, a knowledge machine becomes an extension of the personality of the user finding or offering prior knowledge based solutions to most of the routine issues that clutter the mind. Automobiles of this nature are built and marketed to the public in this era where most needs (e.g., Find directions to home?, Where am I?) of the drivers and passengers are resolved by the click of a button.

One of the specific needs in most need hierarchies is the social need and the resolution of such needs (dynamic with time, culture, and society) are addressed in the rest of the chapter. The selection of the need gratifying objects, the associated action, and the acceptable ways of practicing the resolution of most needs of most human beings are presented here. It becomes evident that the approach cannot resolve every need of every human being.

8.2 NEEDS TO MOTIVATE AND SOCIETY TO CONSTRAIN

Selfless love[1] [3] is saintly, detached, and a little farfetched for the fast lives of modern society. Selfish love [4] is savage leading to unconstrained behavior, violence, and wars. Between the two extremes resides a region of sensible love based on science, barter, economics, and psychology. One of the prime contributors to science of social psychology is Erich Fromm [5]. To have the need gratifying objects and still to be in a lasting relation and continue to exist has been articulated in Fromm's books based on his academic studies and psychological theory. Based on his theory and a sense of "equal-love" from any two partners, families and nations, a computed approach to maintaining a workable relation based on commitment, concern, responsibility, and (creative) participation is proposed, and computing systems can be primed with these four aspects for either "partners." A true sense of a balanced or sensible love is thus established. The rationality of the computer-generated basis of a relationship is generated but is devoid of pettiness, hate, or violence. Unfortunately, it is also possible to counter-program computer systems to incite pettiness, hate, and violence and devoid of concern, commitment, responsibility, and (creative) participation between humans, societies, and nations. Sometimes, ill-intentioned human beings act as these counter-programmed computers as some nations that incite wars between other nations.

We base a computational approach of social psychology by incorporating the "other" (as it is personified by Mead [6]), has as much of control upon the "noun objects" that gratify human needs that motivate and upon the "verb functions" that result in gratification. This cycle has been the practice since evolution of life and most likely to remain intact forever as long as the needs of species continue to exist. Needs of individuals and actions (*VFs*) and the constraints on behavior to obtain such need gratifying objects (*NOs*) both lead to the understanding and knowledge of behavior necessary to exist in the society. When social needs are incorporated in the five-level pyramid of Needs as Maslow [1] has done, behavior shifts from "grab and get" at the first and second levels

---

[1]The keystone of Gandhi's philosophy is "truth, synthetic or total truth, the truth of the law of human being, the truth underlying human evolution in the direction of higher, nobler, more and more harmonious and happy living." R. R. Diwakar, Gandhi Peace Foundation, New Delhi, January 1, 1979.

to "reason, adapt, and learn" at Maslow's third level of needs. Maslow's need pyramid is heightened to seven levels to accommodate the migration of the society toward the "nobler and harmonious existence" preached by Rumi[2] and reiterated by Helen Keller.[3]

8.2.1 ACTIONS, OBJECTS, EVENTS, AND TIME

The continuum of time is filled with events. Most events have some action or the other embedded within them. Any event consisting of one or more objects (*NO*) and one or more actions (*VF*) sensibly coupled and appropriately convolved (*) together can be symbolically written as:

$$Event = (NO_1) * \rightarrow (VFs)_{1to2} * \rightarrow (NO_2)$$

followed by a counter or response event.

$$Counter\ Event(NO_1) \leftarrow * (VFs)_{2to1} \leftarrow * (NO_2)$$

and the interactive dialog becomes a continuous process in the time domain. Time (t) and duration (Δt) play a role in the dialog to the extent that NO_1 and NO_2 and their associated noun-convolutions (i.e., $NO*$) are drawn from past, memory, or from Internet knowledge banks, whereas VF_1 and VF_2 and their associated verb-convolutions (i.e., $VF*$) occur in the current time of the event. A unique blending of noun objects (from the past) and verb function (in the present) occurs in the time domain. Thus the change of status of any noun object needs the force of the verb function (derived from the motivational energy) of the knowledge-centric objects (*KCOs*). It appears that Newton's classic equations ($f = m \times a$; $s = v.t + \frac{1}{2}\,a.t^2$; $de = f.\ ds$, *etc.*) from particle dynamics assume a new implication in social dynamics when the *KCOs* and human beings.

It is well known that objects fill the space(s) as events fill the time; actions fill behavior as thoughts fill the mind; and concepts fill knowledge as wisdom fills ethics. In this chapter, the underlying linkages between objects (*NOs*), actions (*VFs*), order in their convolutions (*), time (t), forces, dynamics, and content of *KCOs*, and energies to move them are explored. The knowledge trail [7] that geared toward human betterment is the major path setter in the presentation.

The concept behind inherent relations between the entropy (status) of objects, the force in the action (verb), the nature of the convolution (*), and time (t) can be generalized and restated as follows: Events generate incremental knowledge and events are by definition,

$$Incremental\ knowledge\ in\ the\ events \approx NO(s) * VF(s)\ or\ VF(s) * NO(s)$$

Further, the effect of time caused by the events lasting for any length of time Δt seconds is depicted in Figure 8.1. Knowledge as elements (*kels*), objects, actions, and convolutions are linked through events (at time = "t") in time giving rise to new elemental knowledge as new *kels* that can be fused and infused with prior *kels* in the memory (from t' to t with $t > t'$) seconds constituting the past memory span of humans or machines. They can also be inspected and projected into the future (from t to t'' with $t'' > t$) seconds constituting the future memory span of humans or machines, as learning for future events.

---

[2]"Let the beauty of what you love be what you do" (Rumi).
[3]"The best and most beautiful things in the world, cannot be seen or ever touched, they must be felt with the heart" (Helen Keller).

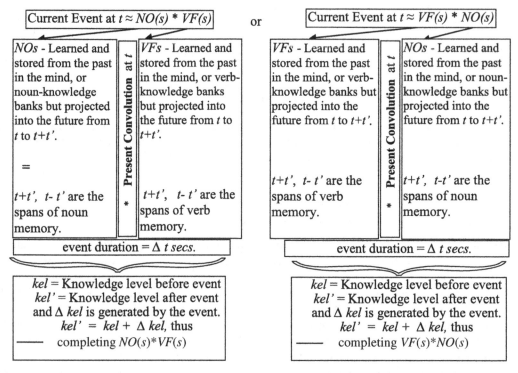

FIGURE 8.1

Diagrammatic representation of the infusion of kels derived from objects and their convolutions with actions (i.e., NO*VF) or from verbs and their convolutions with objects (i.e., VF*NO), embedded in events. The events generate new kels that can supplement prior kels, and they are assembled, stacked, and processed to generate new bodies of knowledge or as small entire knowledge-centric objects (KCOs) or large KCOs.

8.2.2 UNIVERSAL THEME BEHIND HUMAN ACTION-REACTION PROCESSES

There is a repetitive pattern of universality in processes depicted in Figure 8.1. The pattern shown in Figure 8.2 is derived from the very basis of existence (of all species) and based on the gratification their needs (N) to survive. Actions form a fourth of a universal cyclic process consisting of {(Need → Motivation → Action → Comprehension & Learning) and then back to next deficit need (N). This process is represented in Figure 8.2 in the NMAC circle. The comprehension and learning (C) reaffirm or yield new knowledge in most interactions. During the "A" part of the cycle, one or numerous noun objects and verb functions are exchanged between KCOs, and an event represented occurs as:

$\Delta kel = Incremental\ Knowledge\ Generated\ by\ \{(VF) * (NO)\text{or by}\Delta kel = (VFs) * (NOs)\}$

New micro knowledge modules $\Delta kels$ are generated and tagged systematically in comprehension "C" (Fig. 8.2) of the cycle. This cycle is symbolized as NMAC and represented in Fig. 8.2.

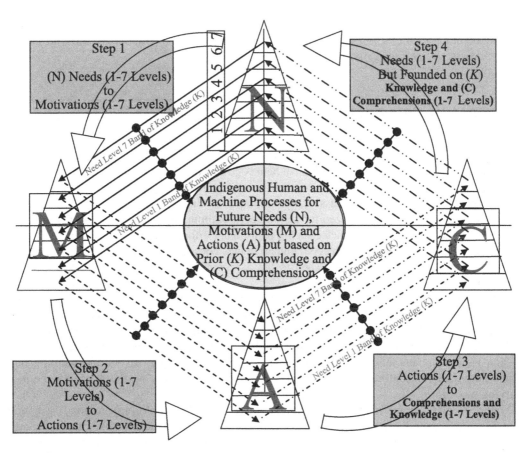

FIGURE 8.2

The repetitive cycle of needs (N), motivations (M), actions (A), comprehension, and learning (C) is presented as the NMAC circle, and the seven bands of knowledge (K) associated with the seven needs of human beings is also shown. The bands of knowledge govern the actions for future needs and situations as they develop. Largely, these bands are associated with needs and most events are within the scope of prior knowledge in the bands. Learning adds more rules of behavior and conduct in the resolution of future needs.

8.2.3 HUMAN ACTION-REACTION PROCESS: NEVER EQUAL AND OPPOSITE

Human actions and reactions are not always equal and opposite; else any dialog would come to a standstill immediately. The gap between the two moves results in a continuation of the exchange between two parties with an extension appended. Most social interactions are dyadic and symmetric where either object can initiate and respond to that the other object. Intelligent objects understand the motives and initiatives. Both process the moves and respond in a convergent socially amicable format in cooperative relations. Conversely, divergent moves and counter moves can be expected in conflictive relations. The processes are generally cyclic and repetitive.

An overall representation is shown in Figures 8.1 and 8.2 for two noun objects NO_1 and NO_2. When numerous noun-objects interact, each of the dyadic/triadic interactions should be considered as "events" in their own right.

8.3 ITERATIVE CONVERGENCE FOR OPTIMIZATION

The search for gainful knowledge is an optimized iterative process. Every element of knowledge or *kel* needs to be individually optimized and then collectively optimized in the group of smaller *kels* that constitute a larger *KEL*. In practice, human beings go to extreme effort in learning or deploying knowledge at any level and at any size. However, knowledge machines can undertake such a meticulous and prolonged task if it is necessary. For example, in the design of automobiles, not every component of every model is optimized for zero defects, optimum efficiency, or peak performance. However, in the design of space vehicles such a painstaking effort is warranted and generally practiced. In dealing with others (noun objects), human beings conserve their energies in making every move (verb function) appropriately matched to the expected outcome. When the stakes are high, the effort is also high.

Within the human mind that motivates actions, the basic theme of repeated and recurring needs plays the decisive role. They also provide the mental, social, and psychological energies to occupy the continuity of time with actions and fill the physical space with need gratifying objects. Order and systematization are enforced by making the choice, convolutions, and the cohesion between nouns and verbs significant and efficient. Comprehension and learning both become necessary for continued existence and being optimal in reducing the effort for the need gratifying procedures.

Dyadic interactions are implied since *no* individual can exist (for long) in (total) isolation. When two intelligent knowledge-centric objects, NO_1 and NO_2 (such as two human beings, machines, networks), participate in interactive and in cooperative roles, the overall scheme of processes is depicted in Figure 8.3. A centerline of symmetry exits and a series of *kel* transactions from NO_1 to NO_2 and from NO_2 to NO_1 occur. This dialog generates an *"event"* at any instant of time "t" and lasts for "Δt" seconds. Much like time is a continuous process, an event, an interaction, or a dialog is continuous generating a *kel* or a *KEL* of any importance at the end of $(t + \Delta t)$ seconds.

A series of such *kels* organized in an orderly fashion leads to the generation of new knowledge such as a book, an invention, and a treaty that has some economic/social significance. Knowledge without order becomes trash and soon forgotten. Order in knowledge becomes as significant as iterative convergence for optimized learning of deployable knowledge.

When the relationship is governed by external constraints such as master−slave, boss−employee, parent−child, relationships, then the symmetry of the two noun objects is altered and the two directionalities:

$$(NO_1) * \rightarrow (VFs)_{1to2} * \rightarrow (NO_2) \text{ and } (NO_1) \leftarrow * (VFs)_{2to1} \leftarrow * (NO_2)$$

exhibit different two different types of convolutions. The comprehension and intelligences also assume different characteristics. When asymmetrical relations are to be programmed in a knowledge machine, the verb function and convolution modules should be chosen accordingly. However,

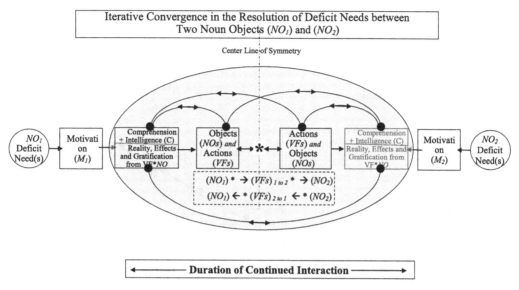

FIGURE 8.3

Representation of complete symmetric dyadic interaction between NO_1 and NO_2 with comprehension and intelligence. The symbol * represents a convolution process and all negotiations with cyclic and repetitive processes are within the ellipse.

kels are generated and the knowledge is stored for future deployment for either of the two interacting noun objects. A frontier or a boundary of relation evolves over time to make future interactions smooth for continued relation or conflictive and divergent for broken relations. The knowledge machine can indeed emulate both forms of relations. Iterative convergence for the emergence of a definitive boundary of relations may still be necessary.

8.4 KNOWLEDGE MACHINE PROGRAMMING FOR A GIVEN OBJECTIVE

The solution of most human effort is directed toward some (economic) objective(s). When numerous objectives are pursued, then it becomes necessary to derive a virtual objective that is a composite of weighted average of the numerous objectives.

For example, if a bride is searching for a groom who is "highly" cultured and "very" handsome, then a variable $y = (x$ times "culture" preference and $(1-x)$ times "handsome" preference) needs to be defined. The profile grading of many grooms can be thus cross-compared.

A case of selection process for a knowledge element *kel* generated because of an event, $VF * NO$, or $NO * VF$ is depicted in Figure 8.4. Stacks are shown for *VFs* and *NOs* on the left and on the right side with a black line for convolutions with *s. The machine picks an entry from the *VF* stack and combines it with an entry on the * line and an entry from the *NO* stack. Being exhaustive, the machine generates $(z' \times z \times m)$ computational locations (arrays) in the computer memory. Each of

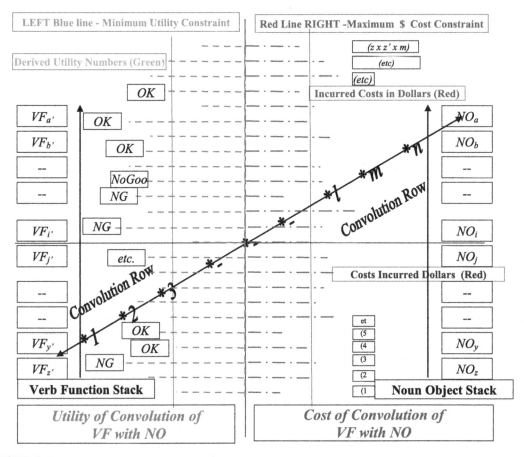

FIGURE 8.4

Matrix representation of dyadic interaction between NO_1 and NO_2 with computed utilities (U) and costs (C) incurred by the convolution of VF with NO. The economic objective is based on Marshall's law that ratio $\Delta U/\Delta C$ should be maximized by continuous incremental changes of NOs, VFs, and *s. Finite stacks of all possible NOs and VFs are represented as columns, and possible convolutions (*) are presented as a row through the center of the figure.

these $(z' \times z \times m)$ computational locations has two linked locations. The first linked location stores *the utility* or the value of the *kel* generated) by combining $VF_i *_j$ and NO_k. The subscript i has a range of a to z', k has a range from a to z, and j has a range from 1 to m as shown in Figure 8.4. The second linked location carries the cost of combining ($VF_i *_j$ and NO_k). The values of these two linked locations are shown as two (green and red) lines in Figure 8.4.

When the minimum utility required is shown as an green line (X = min. utility) on the left and the maximum cost to be incurred as a red line (X = max. cost) on the right, then the acceptable choices of the combination ($VF_i *_j$ and NO_k) become evident as OK and NG in the figure. The processes involved are incorporated as definite steps in the knowledge-ware of any knowledge machine. The programming and organization of the knowledge programs becomes simple and straight-forward as those in any intelligent executive or management information system.

An illustrative example of the case is presented in Appendix 8 A when 9 opportunities are presented to an individual with 27 options:

with *VFs* (= *GO, MOVE, or MIGRATE*) *as ∗ s* (= *STUDENT, WORKER, or TRAINEE*)

at three (illustrative) *NOs* (= HARVARD, MIT, or STANFORD)

The final choice will result based on personal preferences and inclinations that are reflected in the utilities and costs as detailed in Appendix 8 A.

CONCLUSIONS

In this chapter, a detailed technique for deriving the "best" knowledge elements *kels* is presented. *Kels* may be reassembled or fabricated at any levels ranging from nano and micro *kels* (such as chromosomes and genetic codes) to very large knowledge-centric objects (such as the species and planets). However, not every object will necessarily convolve with every verb function. It becomes necessary to select the noun objects and verb functions that are appropriately matched to yield sensible elements of modular knowledge that can be integrated or fragmented. For example, chromosomes and genetic codes do not convolve with planets and stars. Even genetic codes of different species do not convolve. Exception and special circumstances (such as some species of horses and donkeys breed mules) are already documented in the Internet knowledge bases.

In real situations, human beings face few choices of possible convolutions and they are handled on a routine basis based on experience by or common sense. When the number of possible choices become large (such as those in drug industry or in investment banking), the computational techniques are applicable. Exhaustive searches can be limited to preferential choices by admixing human wisdom with computational brute force. Exhaustive searches can also be limited to scanning the local and preferred knowledge banks for noun objects, verb functions and their convolutions. In essence, the problem of generating new knowledge can be contained by priming the knowledge machine with the structure of a seminal knowledge core and by selective scanning algorithms.

It is possible to defeat the purpose of synthesizing knowledge by forcing the knowledge machine to search for a "needle in a haystack." Further, the pursuit of perfect knowledge is impossible with imperfect and time varying noun objects, verb functions, and their convolutions. Any progress in knowledge domain alters the prior knowledge, and new nouns, verbs, and convolutions replace the prior ones thus making the knowledge domain fuzzy but not confused. It is our contention that the imminent generation of machines will make knowledge domain as firm as the number domain, even though they both become imprecise and blurry if the precision in pushed beyond perception.

APPENDIX 8 A

When there are three choices for each of possibilities for *VFs*, *∗s, and *NOs*, then $3 \times 3 \times 3 = 27$ possibilities exist. In this particular case, a 3D matrix can be used to designate *VF* = <u>G</u>o, <u>M</u>ove, or <u>M</u>igrate in the *X* direction, * = <u>S</u>tudy, <u>W</u>ork, or <u>T</u>rain in the *Y* directions, and *NO* = <u>H</u>arvard, <u>M</u>IT, or <u>S</u>tanford

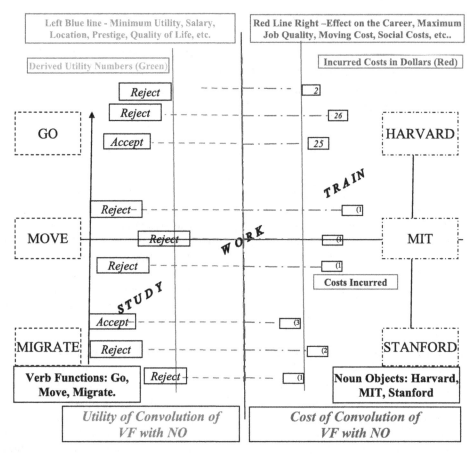

FIGURE 8 A

Programmable approach for maximizing the utility while minimizing the costs, or any combination thereof to derive the best knowledge from the convolution of VFs with NOs or NOs with VFs. This economic objective can also be based on Marshall's law of microeconomics stating that ratio $\Delta U / \Delta C$ should be maximized by continuous incremental changes of NOs, VFs, and *s. In this particular case, only 27 (=3*3*3) possible combinations exist.

in the Z direction. In effect, computational locations[4] or arrays will be necessary. When each location has two components (one for the utility or benefit that is derived and the other for cost incurred), then the acceptable choice has to satisfy the maximum "benefit derived and the minimum "cost incurred" criteria. The approach for the solution of the problem makeup is shown in Figure 8 A.

---

[4]27 choices are [{(GO, S, H; GO, S, M; GO, S, S): (GO, W, H; GO, W, M; GO, W, S): (GO, T, H; GO, T, M; GO, T, S)} ; {(MOVE, S, H; MOVE, S, M; MOVE, S, S): (MOVE, W, H; MOVE, W, M; MOVE, W, S): (MOVE, T, H; MOVE, T, M; MOVE, T, S)}; {(MIGRATE, S, H; MIGRATE, S, M; MIGRATE, S, S): (MIGRATE, W, H; MIGRATE, W, M; MIGRATE, W, S): (MIGRATE, T, H; MIGRATE, T, M; MIGRATE, T, S)}].

The two-elements *VF* and *NO* stacks are shown on the left and right sides of the figure with the convolution line through the middle. The role of personal preferences is embedded in the computation of the utilities and of the costs incurred represented as blue and red lines in the figure. This figure can only be customized, and different individuals will evaluate the utilities and costs according to individual tastes and choices. This individual freedom makes the choices different from individual to individual and also from one span of time to another.

It becomes evident that knowledge science can only solve problems geared to particular human beings and during prescribed periods during which they choices are well defined. Since human nature is also dynamic and modified by culture and society. The knowledge machine needs social and cultural orientation where the solution in being pursued.

Largely, the personal knowledge machine acts as an intelligent personal-social-cultural knowledge and Internet-based digital agent for the user. In a sense the traditional PDA now becomes an intelligent IP-S-C-K-I-DA or IPICKS-DA. The advances in the VLSI technology hold the promise of making these machines compact as the hand-held PDAs in the near future. The key difference between the current PDAs and the knowledge-based PDA lies in composing and decomposing knowledge to integrate or recompose new knowledge to suit the user needs in any culture or social setting.

REFERENCES

[1] Maslow A. Farther reaches of human nature. New York: Viking Press, 1971. For Maslow's seminal paper see, Maslow AH. A theory of human motivation. Psychol. Rev. 1943:50:370 -396.

[2] Ahamed S.V. Need pyramid of the information age human being. International Society of Political Psychology (ISSP) Scientific Meeting, Toronto, Canada, July 3−6, 2005. Also see, An enhanced need pyramid for the information age human being. In: Proc. of the Fifth Hawaii International Conference, Fifth International Conference on Business, Hawaii, May 26 −29, 2005.

[3] Tahtien U. The core of Gandhi's philosophy. New Delhi: Abhinav Publications; 1979.

[4] Pillay S. The psychology of selfish lovers. Psychology Today, Aug 13, 2010, https://www.psychologyto-day.com/.../the-psychology- Accessed January 5, 2016. See also Fromm E. The anatomy of human destructiveness. New York: Holt Paperbacks, 1992.

[5] Boeree C.G. Erich Fromm, personality theories. webspace.ship.edu/.../fromm.ht. Also see, www.erich-formm,net. Fromm's books include, The art of loving, The escape from freedom, To have or to be?, etc.

[6] Mead G.H. Social theory. http://routledgesoc.com/profile/george-herbert-mead, Website accessed January 16, 2016.

[7] Ahamed SV. Computational framework of knowledge. Hoboken, NJ: John Wiley and Sons; 2009.

FRUSTUMS OF ARTIFICIAL BEHAVIOR

CHAPTER SUMMARY

Human behavior has an infinitely large number of expressions. Most individuals practice life in its own distinctive fashion. Social behavior in the gratification of their unique needs is time, age, mood, and temperament dependent offering the rich tapestry of personality types. When the human pursuits are need driven, the classical five-level need pyramid of Maslow becomes a three-dimensional cone rather than a two-dimensional triangle. As with most human beings, age and time dependence of human needs, adds the third dimension making the cone irregular, unbalanced, and even lopsided. A sense of aesthetic beauty, balance, and stability accrues with the appropriate admixture of maturity, Intelligence, and purpose over time. Knowledge machines can find and suggest appropriate verb functions and their sequences to achieve these artificially induced qualities in the thought processes of human beings.

Frustums corresponding to the levels of these needs become a unique and personalized section of behavioral cones, even though the cones cannot be sliced gracefully to create the frustums. Machine-assisted formation of such frustums is the topic of this chapter. In a sense, the machines with their own personal updatable databases act as monitoring systems to prevent any need, fascination, hobby, or degenerative social influence to encroach on other needs that need gratification in their own right. An emotional, psychological, and physiological stability is induced in the actions and pursuits of humans, corporations, cultures, and nations. Intervention to stabilize health and psyche has been a human endeavor since the beginning of civilized times. In the current timeframe, it is logical to investigate logical circuits to sense the destabilizing forces that are prevalent in most environments. Stability is construed and computed by sensing systems and intelligent agents that are provoked to sense danger or threat. Such robotic agents or software routines take over to counter or eradicate the undesirable trends and movements. Some of these systems are humans (doctors, therapists, medical staff, etc.), corporate agents and systems (accountants, legal staff, intelligent management information systems, etc.), and nations (by the judiciary, national-security agencies, and police), etc.

9.1 INTRODUCTION

Maslows' five levels of human needs [1] are an entry into the compositions of frustums of needs that provide the motivation to act. In reality, there can be a finer hierarchy of needs and more such subsections at each levels. Each subdivided need forms a frustum of its own. For some needs, the gratifying noun objects (*NOs*), the verb functions (*VFs*) and their respective convolutions (**s*) overlap. For example, food that gratifies level the physiological need also has emotional values for some. When the needs and objects are not appropriately matched, a syntactic error arises. Most humans effectively

Evolution of Knowledge Science. DOI: http://dx.doi.org/10.1016/B978-0-12-805478-9.00009-1

correct for such errors early in the solution of problems, but when left untamed and uncorrected, such errors will cause execution time errors in lives and machines. Knowledge machines that imitate human behavior would need a powerful compiler to track both syntactic and semantic errors.

In a similar vein, verb-functions also form layers of their own. Ideally, the knowledge machine should be supported by such layer-based solution strategy to hold *(a)* need-gratifying NOs, *(b)* the associated verb functions, and *(c)* their validated convolutions at each of the five layers of Need hierarchy [1] of Maslow or at each of the seven levels of Need hierarchy[1] [2] of Ahamed. Behavior and its emulation can be represented by two diagrams.

9.1.1 ARTIFICIAL KNOWLEDGE

In effect, needs of knowledge centric objects (KCOs) [3], and knowledge centric entities (KCEs) have layers and each layer has three frustums for *(a)*, *(b)*, and *(c)*. The elements of knowledge (Δk) to solve problems of most KCEs consist of picking the appropriate objects *(a)*, convolutions *(b)*, and verbs *(c)*, from the frustums for each of the layers. Knowledge machine can also be programmed to pick *(a)*, *(b)*, and *(c)* from local (individual/corporate/social, or communal) and global (WWW, medical, university, government, etc.) content addressable knowledge banks.

The artificial knowledge (*AK*), proposed by the machine thus becomes.

$AK = \Sigma \Delta k$ that are appropriately scanned, selected, and structured optimally.

The development of these steps in the solution is depicted in Figures 9.1 and 9.2. The need of any entity that prompts action invokes the query to the accumulated knowledge about the resolution. Generally, there are six major steps (see Fig. 9.1) and most human or corporate entities follow an individualized approach. These steps may not be explicit always. Many entities extract these steps based on prior experience or "wisdom." The ideal and smooth movement through these six steps is symbolized as a Lemniscates. In reality, the steps are coarse and jagged and the distribution of the steps is shown as black circles in Figure 9.2. Finally, the learning of most knowledge-based entities (KBEs) is shown as red circles in the center of the figure and these steps become programmable on any knowledge machine.

In reality, the behavior to gratify any need at any layer does not resemble the smooth idealized solution depicted in steps 2, 3, and 4 of Figure 9.1. The *NOs* and *VFs* deviate considerably and indeed form preferable bondage as (*NO*VF* and *VF*NO*) within the frustum of any need level (*i*). This scenario is depicted in Figure 9.2 and the path 1 to 2, to 3, to 4, to 5, to 6 becomes a polygon connecting the centers of the dashed ellipses (Figure 9.3).

---

[1]Ahamed has proposed seven levels of the human needs with two layers (the Search and Unification layers atop Maslows' five layers of realization, ego, social, physiological, and safety layers. Various saints and philosophers having philanthropic and religious layers on top of the seven layers are proposed in Reference 2. The fundamental difference between the five-layer and the seven-layer hierarchies stems from the fact that Maslow has surveyed "successful" people and classified their needs. Whereas success lies in wealth, emotions, and the materialistic well being that is gratified by physical and emotional "objects," the five-layer theory of Maslow overlooks the intellectual needs of the elite, educated, and the knowledge workers of the Internet society. Dominant in most doctoral students and dedicated researchers need two additional "Search" and "Unify" layers to continue their struggle beyond gratifying the lower five layers in the need hierarchy. The efforts of the social workers and the humanistic organizations are well accommodated in the seven-plus layer.

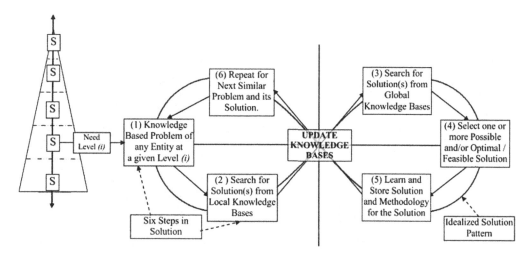

FIGURE 9.1

Programmable steps of a knowledge machine for any of the generation of knowledge for any knowledge-based entity. The need pyramid is shown on the left.

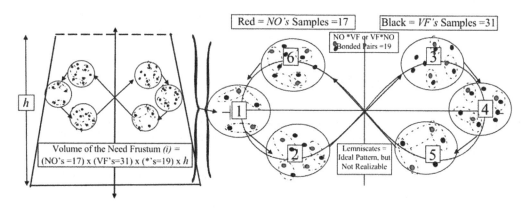

FIGURE 9.2

Representation of the ideal and realistic patterns of behavior for the resolution of the (i-th) level of need since all the possible (NOs * VFs) are generally not available for the resolution of the need. If there are infinite NOs,* VFs are feasible the volume of the frustum will be infinitely large and every need will be ideally gratified.

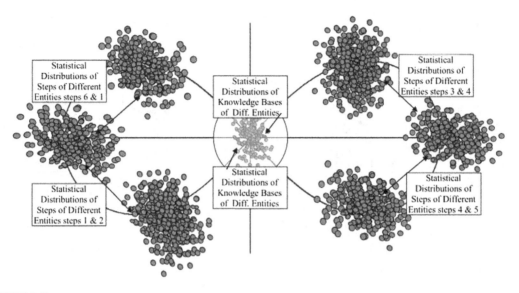

FIGURE 9.3

Typical variation of the behavioral steps (blue circles) of individual samples in most of the population distributions. Such a variation causes an overall spread of the entries (red circles) into the statistical behavioral patterns for different samples in the knowledge bases. It also indicates the nature of the statistical distribution of the variation in the six behavioral steps (blue circles) for the solution within any population resulting in the variation of entries in the knowledge bases (red circles) for the population. Individual differences are thus customized for every sample in the knowledge base for each layer of need.

9.1.2 MECHANIZED GENERATION OF KNOWLEDGE

The machine acts as a surrogate and resourceful humanoid to generate personalized artificial knowledge for the solution of a generic set of similar problems. The machine considers the follow-ing factors[2] in order to orient itself and provide a context based solution.

I. What?
  a. Origin of the problem and the layer of need to evaluate its urgency (When? and How long?) and importance.
  b. Construction of a concept diagram for the solution of complex problems.
  c. Critical objects and actions (in conjunction) for the solution (i.e., constructs a critical path [4] toward the solution).
II. Who?
  a. Personal or individual preferences and traits of the entities for whom the solution is being sought.
  b. Local environment in which the solution is to be found.
  c. Possible elements of knowledge (i.e., Δks) in assembling the structure of knowledge K for final solution.

---

[2]Two other questions WHY and WHEN are not specially queried/asked since the solution is sought because there was a need in the first place, and the user needs a solution as soon as the machine can provide an answer.

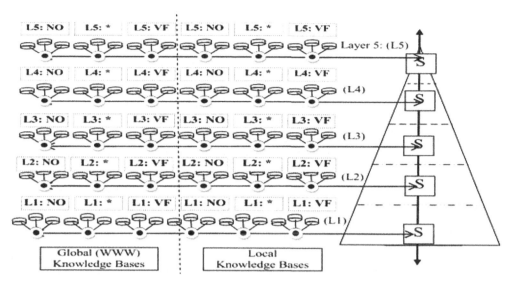

FIGURE 9.4

Addressable knowledge banks for the Local and Global (WWW) choices of noun objects (NOs), convolutions (*s), and verb functions (VFs) that constitute the elements of knowledge (Δk) for the entire solution (K) of structured and optimized as $K = \sum (\Delta k)$.

III. **How?**
  a. Searching the local and global resources or objects (*NOs*) in the solution matched to (*c*)— the local and global objects that are feasible.
  b. Searching of the local and global actions or verbs (*VFs*) in the solution—the local and global actions that are feasible.
  c. Convolutions (*s) between resources and actions, the optimization of the final solution (via a PERT [5] diagram) based on users preferences (such as minimum cost, time) to gratify the need.
  d. Resources and emotional/resource energy (i.e., rate of verb function executions times duration) for the solution based on the prior experience in implementation.
IV. **Knowledge generation function**
  a. Fragmentation of the problem to generate (Δks) if no satisfactory solution is feasible and generate a series of piecewise or rudimentary solutions.
V. **Machine learning from the proposed knowledge gained and implementation**
  a. Follow up of the knowledge that was proposed by the knowledge machine and what was used or implemented and *K*.

Numerous customized inputs are necessary for the humanoid knowledge machine based on the concepts listed earlier. In Figure 9.4, we indicate a hardware configuration to make these inputs available to the mainframe machine shown in Figure 9.5. The two sides of Figure 9.5 has two (a Maslowian (left side) and a society-based philosophic (right side)) personality types.

This configuration is generic and can serve as humanoid medical machine by replacing the two personality types on either side of the machine by two expert doctors. For example, if one

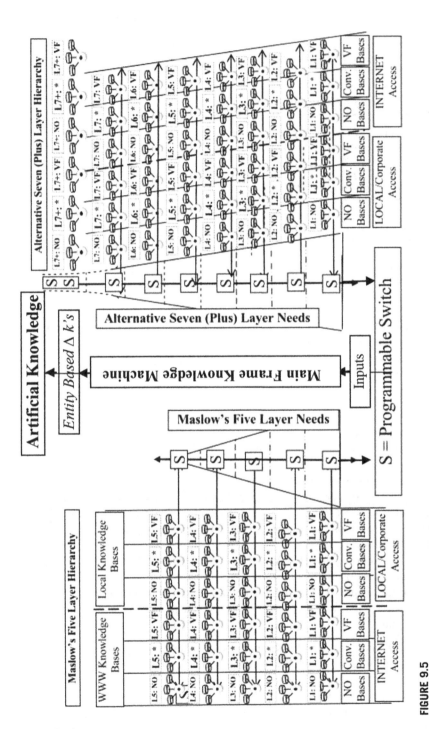

FIGURE 9.5

Matrix-based arrangement for a knowledge machine to access NOs, *s, and VFs, from local and Internet knowledge bases for two different types (five-layer and seven-plus-layer) of need hierarchies.

of the doctors is from any Western school of thought of medicine (with its *NOs*, *VFs*, and their respective **s*) and another from any Eastern School of thought (with its own *NOs*, *VFs*, and their respective **s*), then the humanoid medical machine will generate a unique blend of osteopathic and homeopathic cures, treatments, and medicines. The blending of specialties can be cascaded entirely overshadowing one's specialty over the other. This approach will verify the completeness of the knowledge-based entries in every discipline. Further, the extent of blending is controlled by the user.

Matching one expert profile with another will determine the extent of discrepancy in the opinions, options, objects of treatment, and actions of the two experts. Humanoid machines will have to be nurtured like children during infancy through their adulthood. Once the machine reach maturity, they will serve as any other computer systems.

9.2 FRUSTUMS AND THEIR VOLUME

Frustums of knowledge cone are generated by slicing the cones at the levels of needs and their associated knowledge that includes their *NOs*, *VFs*, and their respective **s*. The four dimensional volume (*NOs* × *VFs* × Convolutions (*) × Depth of layer) enclosed in these frustums contains a much more detailed signature of the individual personality of the entity. In a cultural sense, the volume in each of the frustums is indicative of the social and intellectual activity in the culture of that particular layer. Intellectually rich societies have greater volume in levels 4 and 5 frustums than in subsistence societies that have their greatest volumes in levels 1 and 2 frustums. Socially rich cultures would show considerable volume in level 6 frustum (see Fig. 9.4).

If the individual personality is dead, the frustums would collapse back into its minimum volume of the frustum with dimensions, $NO = VF = * = 1$ times depth of the Layer in the need pyramid of Maslow. Such an individual would only repeat one and only behavior to satisfy every need in the hierarchy. Only the lower carnivorous species demonstrate this modus operandi such as chase, capture, kill, and eat; repeat to gratify their hunger; find mate, sex; repeat, etc.

Human beings trace far greater variety of actions and their trajectories; even so in the Internet age where the choice are greatly increased and even more flexible in the knowledge and intellectual domain of any individual. For example, the "cut and paste" approach of need gratification pattern from one frustum to another need fine-tuning and environmental adjustments leading a large choice of behavioral patterns. Behavior like tapestry has many colors, textures, and patterns. Individuals identify their preferred color, texture, and patterns thus exposing their own individual tastes and the structure of the personality.

In a social sense, significant and purposeful knowledge ranks highest with all the features of a saint, scientist, philosopher, social proponent with lasting, invincible truth (independent of time, space, and social coordinates), honest impeccable virtue (with social benefit and long-term wisdom), and pristine, pure order (with precision and structure). This incomprehensible layer at a seven-plus level is more visionary and abstract rather than the realizable and evident. Such an ideal composure of knowledge is a myth and abstraction rather than a reality, even though it is conceivable in the human mind.

Knowledge in a refined state has value and social benefit. Highly refined status of knowledge is wisdom. Practiced over generations, the practice becomes social ethics. Not being immune to the short-term trends, knowledge, wisdom, and ethics all experience their own cycle of decay and erosion. Over a period, new knowledge emerges to bring about a new breed of wisdom and morality. The knowledge cycle repeats in a new flavor. The only certainty is the omnipresent change in its three intertwined cycles of knowledge (K), wisdom (W), and morality (M). It appears that the Watson's dual helix [6] in the biological (DNA) arena becomes a triple helix of knowledge, wisdom, and morality or (KWM) in the social arena. All the helix geometries embedded in the six coordinated (shift, slide, rise, tilt, roll, and twist) movements in the base pair geometry become applicable to the three dual-base sociological bonding in the KW, WM, and MK pair geometries. Cultures and societies twist and turn in these cyclic geometric patterns giving rise to many failures and a few successful patterns of behavior.

To deal with knowledge in the realistic human and machine context, we suggest that practical knowledge be classified into seven layers, with the highest level attained in the confluence and congruence of humans, Internet knowledge bases, and machine validation arising from subject matter experts, world-wide verification and machine confirmation. A knowledge pyramid depicted in Figure 9.5 is indicative of the knowledge cycles that rise up to wisdom and ethics. The cycle in its degenerative mode collapses knowledge to mere gossip or junk information, only to give way to new knowledge. The process is continuous, and the boundaries are vague. The process appears illusive but upon scrutiny, the omnipresent change has a life cycle of its own.

Knowledge cycles are evident in most disciplines. Einstein's findings have corrected Newton's and Maxwell's equations. Quantum theories have displaced Einstein's theories, etc. Refinement and enhancement of information and knowledge has been the intellectual challenges that scientists, philosophers, and intellectual have been seeking. Humans and knowledge machines in the current Internet era work in unison to discover yet another quirk of nature or innovate a new verb function, a new convolution, or a new object.

9.3 THE DEGENERATION OF KNOWLEDGE

The erosion of older knowledge derived from wisdom is slower and natural due to affect of time, culture, and/or society; the degeneration of "success-based" artificial knowledge is faster and artificial due to executive and/or machine, network processing. The degradation of knowledge, from wisdom and ethics to the lowest level of gossip, corrupted and short-lived distorted information is due to an omnipresent social, human, and machine phenomenon. The upward arrows in Figures 9.5 and 9.6 result from processing of information by humans and humanist machines that have a long term, socially benevolent goal on the generation of "wise-knowledge." Corrupted humans and machines can severely alter the perceptual quality of knowledge. The human element in the life and movement of knowledge can swing from the saint to a swinger; the choice is individualistic.

The tendencies to refine information and knowledge are countered by the social tendencies in the environment in some cultures. Gossip and idle knowledge processing only make the extraordinary information into the mundane and the uncommon to routine and worthless. The two tendencies in the society can keep the boundary of knowledge like the surface of an ocean that can be smooth, wavy, chopped, or even stormy. Major innovations result sometimes from the ocean bed of knowledge by the creativity of intellectuals.

The procedural steps in the symbiotic activities of the humans and knowledge machines are depicted in Figure 9.6. The processes in the flowchart of the figure can be automated, and a

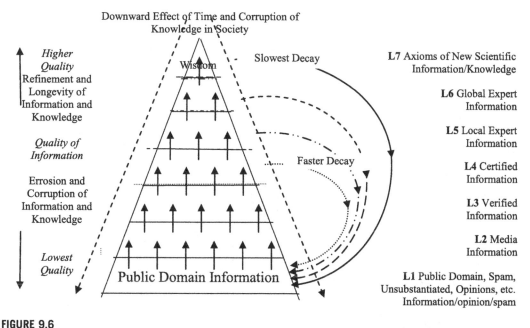

Downward Effect of Time and Corruption of Knowledge in Society

FIGURE 9.6

Representation of a Knowledge Cycles between the refinement of information and its decay. Knowledge is enhanced by humans and knowledge machines and is degraded to the lowest level of gossip, and corrupted short-lived distorted information. The up arrows result from processing of information by humans and humanist machines.

knowledge machine continuously refines knowledge in any discipline by checking out new Internet information by collecting its *VFs*, *s, and *NOs*, in an input base.

The validation continues by verifying, tallying, weighing, and considering the constituents against the established *VFs*, *s, and *NOs* of the same disciplines from a period of time (say one year earlier, a decade earlier, etc.) to evaluate the "worth of new Internet information." Human oversight is essential such that any genuine information is not discarded as junk information and vice versa. In most cases, the librarians scan the Internet bases to update the current library data.

9.4 CONTENT-BASED INTERNET KNOWLEDGE FILTERS

Internet filters like email filters are a gamble cat and mouse game. Spammers, knowledge-polluters and cheap houses like mice, will force their junk information for some hidden agenda or sales and steal time and attention away from other activities. The filtering for *NOs*, *VFs* in their appropriate context may offer a triple level safety against unwanted junk information. A safe network is likely to be a private network for only those with validated retina scans but most networks have some check for authentication.

In Figure 9.7 the knowledge-based computer system to sort and classify Internet Information into numerous levels (seven levels in this case) of knowledge based on the Verb (V)-Internet,

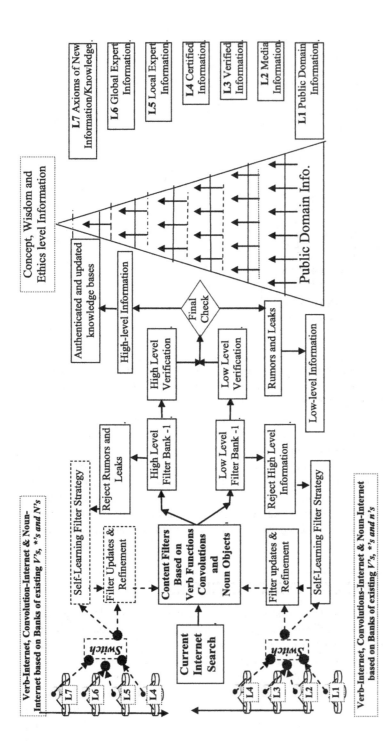

FIGURE 9.7

Knowledge-Based Computer system to sort and classify Internet Information into numerous levels (seven levels in this case) of Knowledge based on the Verb (V)-Internet, Convolution (*)-Internet and Noun (N)-Internet-based Word Banks of VFs, *'s, and NOs. These VFs, *'s, and NOs themselves are derived from the prior Internet knowledge word banks established in the society by analyzing the Information already classified into the levels. The system prevents junk information and hype knowledge to passed on as significant information and well-founded knowledge and vice versa.

Convolution (*)-Internet & Noun (N)-Internet-based Word Banks of *VFs*, *s, and *NOs* is shown. However, this procedure implies classifying the WWW data at each of the websites into verb functions, convolutions, and noun objects, and then sorting the data based on *VFs*, *s, and *NOs*, and then into the layer of need. These *VFs*, *s, and *NOs* are derived from the prior Internet knowledge word banks established in the society by analyzing the information already classified into the layers. The system (tries to) prevents junk information and hype knowledge to be classified as significant information and well-founded knowledge.

Figure 9.8 depicts the use of eight gating filters that sorts the Internet searches into various knowledge banks according the layers of needs of users. These gates check for information that gratify the specific layer of need to which the information is related. Layer 4 need have two classifications as 4 (minus) and 4 (plus) since most Internet users dwell around information to gratify their fourth layer needs in the western cultures. The placement of this subdivided layer can be different in different cultures for different users. For example, teenagers and young adult place an emphasis on their layer 3, social needs. The gating function in Gates G0 through G7 (Fig. 9.7) can only be expected to classify based on statistical means and their standard variation of the word and word grouping in the eight layers shown in the pyramid of information shown on the right. When the search become unduly specific, the gating functions are very likely to fail, but these gates can be trained to offer, reasonable results for a great number of user, most of the time. The learning software for these gates is highly trainable as the robots that perform complex and selective functions.

In Figure 9.9, one of the implementations for filtering and classification of Internet information based on the quality of information/knowledge is shown. The filter criteria are based on *VFs*, *s, and *NOs* judged as authentic based on expert systems [7]. These filtering techniques can only be accurate for most users, most of the time. Knowledge filter- management can evolve as an elaborate science in its own right. Suspicious *VFs*, *s, and *NOs* and their combinations need final human checks and validation. Over time, it is likely to become corrupted and abused by human beings much as the Internet itself is being abused by spammers, fraudulent sales staff, and junkies.

9.5 GENERAL DEPLOYMENT OF KNOWLEDGE FILTERS

Filter concepts in signal flow theory [8] is a well-placed discipline. Filter theory has innumerable applications ranging from plain old telephones systems to intergalactic communication devices. Almost all natural and artificial sensing systems use basic filtering to distinguish the significant information bearing signals from noise and contamination. Knowledge filtering becomes valuable in the Internet age of sophistication and exactitude for dealing with the deeply underlying issues in corporations, societies, and nations. For example, the depletion of carbon-di-oxide layer and the use of coal as a source of thermal energy have been interwoven for the last three centuries. Nevertheless, a cogent international policy has taken almost longer for the politician to evolve and enforce in spite of the Internet, fiber optic, communication and sensor technologies, and the global warming effects! When the bandwidth for the detection is broadened, the signal detection becomes precise but the noise can enter this extended bandwidth as easily.

The strategy used in intergalactic and microwave communication is to separate the signal bearing bandwidth far removed from the noise-bearing band. The guard band can thus be widened, and the

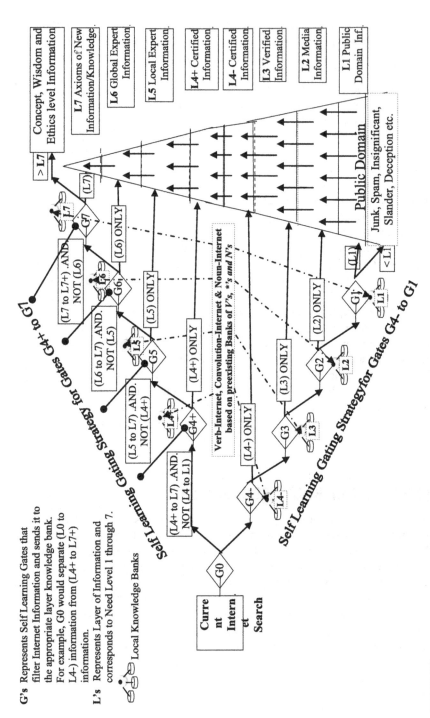

FIGURE 9.8

Knowledge Based Computer system to sort and classify Internet Information into numerous levels (seven levels in this case) of Knowledge based on the Verb (V)-Internet, Convolution (*)-Internet and Noun (N)-Internet-based Word Banks of VFs, *'s, and NOs. These VFs, *'s, and NOs are themselves are derived from the prior Internet knowledge word banks established in the society by analyzing the Information already classified into the levels. The system prevents junk information and hype knowledge to classified as significant information and well-founded knowledge and vice versa.

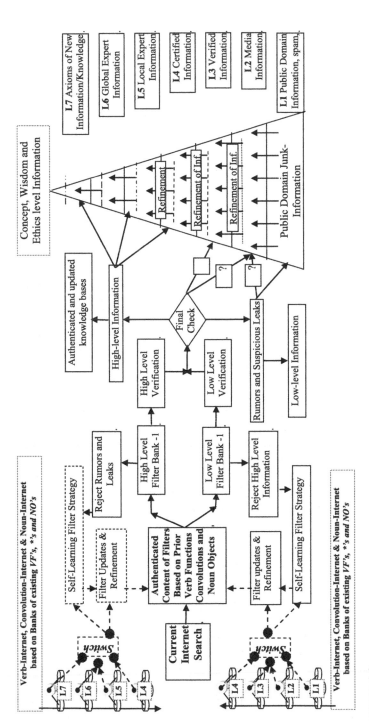

FIGURE 9.9

Filtering and classification of Internet information based on the quality of information/knowledge. The filter criteria are based on VFs, *s, and NOs judged as authentic based on expert systems. These filtering techniques can only be accurate most of the times. Suspicious VFs, *s, and NOs and their combinations need final human checks and validation.

filters can be designed to extract signals near the band edges of the desirable band. In the techno-logical devices, extraneous factors such as temperature, humidity, stray electromagnetic, and elec-trostatic fields can and do affect performance but the effects are insignificant. The signal strength remains robust. Repeated retransmission of susceptible signal is also used in many cases. This repeat signaling is feasible and generally practiced in communication of knowledge. In the knowl-edge domain, the subdivision of bandwidth (e.g., the tone of speech, the use of gestures, the move-ment of the eyes, and emotions) is not precise in all societies, cultures, meetings, or social gathering places. The human senses, mind, and intellect play a decisive role in the communication of knowledge.

Knowledge-signal processing and filtering are both built in the senses and in the brains of spe-cies. The programming of intelligent knowledge-signal processing in software is like DaVinci painting Monalisa on a banana leaf. The imitation of the neural functions in silicon is akin to plant-ing diamond dust in gold. Still, beautiful axioms of wisdom are gifted from generation to genera-tion as pieces of jewelry from parent to child.

Filtering in the knowledge domain bring in all the intricacies from signal flow theory. Shannon's contribution to for estimate of the probability of error is a good indicator of the amount of computation necessary for the eradication of knowledge-errors, if it is ever possible. Knowledge that does not have precise frontiers and boundaries poses additional mathematical issues. In a sense, the communication scientists and filter theorist have offered a safe margin for most humans to com-municate effectively and with very few misinterpretations of knowledge and information, at least in the scientific communities. Be as it may, wars, social cruelties, mass murders, and killings occur in social, ethical, and in cultural settings, and among nations.

It becomes painful to realize that perfectly balanced society with ideal combinations of knowl-edge, concepts, wisdom, and ethics is as near impossible to achieve as perfect series of four sine waves in networks and devices or to find a perfect Watson's-double helix in every biological cell. Saints, philosophers, and clergy have aimed at this utopian status for every society, nation, and cul-ture whist realizing even knowledge by itself [9] cannot be perfect nor all the computers in the world can make it perfect. Idealisms of concepts and ethics are artificial whereas human nature is neither precise nor exact. Nature and humans have been playing a cat and mouse game since the beginnings of intellect. More recently in the Internet age, the game has become a robot cat and a PDA (personal digital agent) mouse game. However, it is a compromise to live and let-live that is not comprehended by a large majority of the world population.

CONCLUSIONS

This chapter develops a methodology for designing and developing artificial machine-generated knowledge. The basis for such knowledge is that all activities of humans and machines is based on manifest or latent needs of individuals, corporations, societies, organizations, etc. Such needs are resolved by tracing back the objects, verb functions, and their convolutions and contextual settings. Designated as *NOs, VFs*, and appropriate convolutions (*), they constitute rudimentary elements of modular knowledge in the specific discipline and at the appropriate layer of need. Though it cannot solve all the problems, all the time, the knowledge machine can be trained to solve a large number of knowledge-based problems, for most of the users, most of the time depending on the complexity of problems and details of the solution.

Experience in resolving similar situations locally and globally, such constituents are scanned for the feasible groups of *NOs, VFs*, and convolutions (*), and the modular elements are collected, assembled and optimized to generate artificial knowledge with all the details of *NOs*, *VFs*, and convolutions (*) to address the current issue or situation. It provides an answer for "WHAT objects, resources, or items." "WHAT actions, events, functions are necessary (*NOs*)," "WHEN and what sequences are necessary (*V*)," "HOW to do, what has to be done (*NOs* and *s), (*VFs* and *s), and *s)." The machine also deploys the CPM and PERT methodologies to optimize the solution for a given set of objectives such as budget, time, effort, etc.

REFERENCES

[1] Maslow A., *Farther Reaches of Human Nature*, New York: Viking Press, 1971, for Maslow's seminal paper see, Maslow AH, A theory of human motivation, Psychol. *Rev*, 50, 370−396, 1943.
[2] Ahamed S.V., "Need Pyramid of the Information Age Human Being," International Society of Political Psychology (ISSP) Scientific Meeting, Toronto, Canada, July 3−6, 2005, also see "An enhanced need pyramid for the information age human being," Proceedings of the Fifth Hawaii International Conference, Fifth International Conference on Business, Hawaii, May 26−29, 2005.
[3] Ahamed SV. Chapter 2 Computational Framework of Knowledge. Hoboken, NJ: John Wiley and Sons, 2009.
[4] Thornley G., Critical Path Analysis in Practice: Collected Papers on Project Control (International Behavioural and Social Sciences, Classics from the Tavistock Press), Routledge, Reprint edition, 2013.
[5] Grinnell Jr. RM, Gabor PA, Untau YA. Program Evaluation for Social Workers: Foundations of Evidence-Based Programs. 6th Edition Oxford University Press, 2012.
[6] Watson JD. June 12 The Double Helix: A Personal Account of the Discovery of the Structure of DNA. Touchstone, 2001.
[7] Buchanan B.G. and Shortcliffe E.H., *Rule-Based Expert System: The Mycin Experiment at Stanford Heuristic Programming Project*, Boston: Addison Wesley, 1984, also see Roman EG and Ahamed SV, "An Expert System for Labor-Management Negotiation," Proceedings of the Society for Computer Simulation Conference, Boston, MA, 1984.
[8] Moschytz GS. June MOS Switched-Capacitor Filters: Analysis and Design. New York: IEEE Press, 1984
[9] Byrne DS. Complexity Theory and Social Sciences. New York: Routledge; 1998.

COMPUTER-AIDED KNOWLEDGE DESIGN AND VALIDATION

10

CHAPTER SUMMARY

This chapter outlines the rules and approaches to construct intelligent-machine-based software to build a computer-aided knowledge design (*CAKD*) system that generates new knowledge from old knowledge and to validate the contents of the new knowledge. As the laws of aerodynamics are used to build airlines and airbuses to transport people and goods, but are also used to build drones and stealth bombers, the constructs of *CAKD* can be used to make trash, spam, junk, deception, trickery, and sham. Caution against abuse is duly warranted.

When knowledge is designated and categorized as a scientific entity, then the basic rules of computer-aided design (CAD) can be applied in constructing it with its basic parameters. In case for knowledge, its basic parameters are the noun-objects, the verb-functions, and the rules of convolving nouns with verbs and verbs with nouns to construct significant elements of knowledge. It becomes necessary that word-groups or phrases to make a well-structured element of knowledge, however small it may be. Such groups can be recombined into larger groups, and yet larger group until a coherent "body of knowledge" or *BoK* of significant value is generated. In all instances, the basic building blocks are accessed and assembled. *CAKD* similarly accesses essential and necessary constituent nouns, executable or execution verbs that the nouns perform on each other such as to make a sensible and a logical element of knowledge in the context of why, how, when, where that body of knowledge is constituted. Organization and structure both are necessary to assure the value and validity of the *BoK*.

In the positive direction, perfection is an unattainable goal; the *CAKD* produces one or more *BoKs* that are useful but less than perfect. Much like the IC chips are selected from different vendors to perform logical functions in any system, the integrated knowledge module (*IKM*) in the *CAKD* derives coherent knowledge modules from a series of local or Internet knowledge banks. The orientation of final *BoK* is essential to guide the relevant information or knowledge searches. However, the Library of Congress and other knowledge classification systems provide a numerically encoded address based on the subject where the newly generated *BoK* is going to be placed.

10.1 INTRODUCTION

Societies do not always progress. Regression of ethics, morality, and respect for lives has blindfolded many mature and stable cultures. In the natural course of events, there is no end to cycles

Evolution of Knowledge Science. DOI: http://dx.doi.org/10.1016/B978-0-12-805478-9.00010-8

and counter-cycles. However, the human and technological objectives appear toward enhancing the positive aspects for everyone by extending the boundaries of knowledge that eradicates the scarcity of material resources and gratifies the needs that initiated the regression. This in an achievable goal; and it can be sustained for a long time, though not indefinitely. The geometric growth of population demanding more and more material resources is balanced by a geometric growth in wisdom that serves as the nucleus of thought rather than greed for luxuries. It is a state of mind and mind-machines.

Two basic premises of most CAD techniques are:

a. to be able to fragment the design object into its intermediate and find constituents until they are readily available in the environment,
b. to reintegrate the newly selected and optimized constituents into a similar or a better object(s) that meets the designed objectives.

In many cases, the methodology stems from a scientific equation that related the noun objects and their functions. Large numbers of examples exist. Transistors make up gates; gates make up circuits; circuits make up IC chips; chips make hardware modules; and modules make up the VLSI and ULSI chips, such chips make up computers, and so on. A similar chain of instructions, macros, and so on is integrated until an entire software system is coherently assembled. As an another example, power stations generate electrical power; power is pumped into a transmission line; transmission lines terminate in power transformers in distributions stations; power stations, transmission lines, transformers, distribution stations, etc., all constitute an electrical power grid. Components are available from vendor databases and they can be selected (scientifically and judiciously) to make up an entire system.

In the knowledge domain the underlying components are words; words that make up noun-objects to perform distinct and predefined verb-functions, independently or in unison to make up elements of (sensible) knowledge to be integrated with other elements, and so on. These words carry a mental, psychological, social, etc., bonds with the receptor and convey plausible information that can be coupled to build more information; an information platform is built in conjunction with a knowledge structure that can be supported on the information platform. Knowledge and information are thus communicated between humans, humans and humans, humans and machines, and vice versa.

In the rest of this chapter, we explore the possibilities of machines being able to generate information platforms and structures of knowledge as robust and powerful entities as well as (or better than) what human beings can do, though not what all humans can do. The methodology is borrowed from the universal discipline of CAD but modified to suit the humanistic art of constructing masterpieces of knowledge such as inventions, literature, verses, and poems.

We follow the systematic procedure of the design of the new knowledge by successively fragmenting the perception of the desired new body of knowledge to be constructed in any discipline, and then selecting the most suitable noun-objects and the verb-functions in the appropriate syntax to generate new knowledge from old knowledge. The freedom to choose every step of the procedure prompts creativity in the construction of knowledge. The design of the *CAKD* machine complex is also based on assembling hardware and software modules from existing computer designs that will function as the building blocks of the entire system. A detailed diagram of the system is shown in Figure 10.1.

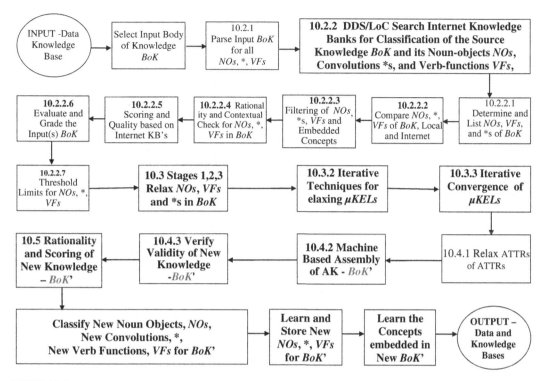

FIGURE 10.1

Conceptual block diagram for synthesizing the new body of knowledge *BoK'* from input knowledge *BoK*. The numbers in the boxes indicate the sections in this chapter where the details are provided for each of the functions in the computer.

10.2 MAJOR PROCEDURAL STEPS

There are seven sub-functions in this major procedural step.

a. Fragmentation of the seminal seed Body of Knowledge (*BoK*) (Section 10.2.1)
b. Internet-based DDS/LoC Search for classification of *VFs*,*s, *NOs* (Section 10.2.2)
c. Blending and processing INPUT, Local, and Internet Knowledge (Section 10.3)
d. Generating Newly Synthesized Knowledge − *BoK'* (Section 10.4)
e. Rationality and Scoring of New Knowledge − *BoK'* (Section 10.5)
f. Machine Configurations and Architecture (Section 10.6)
g. Generalization of the Convolution Processes (Section 10.7)

10.2.1 FRAGMENT THE INPUT SEMINAL BODY OF KNOWLEDGE BOK

The seminal concept behind the input *BoK* serves as the seminal cell for the infant in the womb. The artificial fragmentation of a concept in the mind being artificial does not compare with the natural

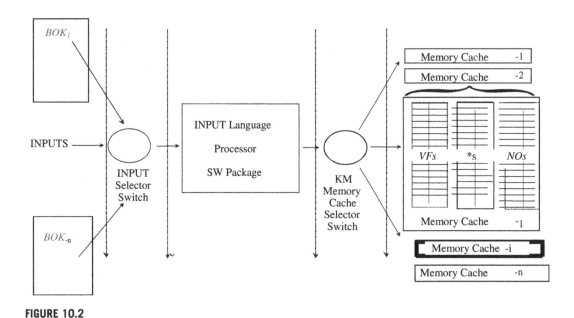

FIGURE 10.2

The machine process to fragment the body of knowledge and to store the *VF*, *, and *NO* in memory caches or linked storage locations.

evolution of the genetic seminal cell of the baby. However, fragmentation of the seminal *BoK* provides the entry point for the machine to identify the critical objects and the actions of (or up on) such objects. This step is critical since the machine-generated knowledge will have objects and actions that are composed in the appropriate context of the new knowledge. The machine will maintain a logical continuity between these objects, actions, and their convolution with objects, actions, and their own convolutions, even though they may be enhanced, modified, or even replaced by more powerful, efficient, and integrated objects, actions, and their own convolutions (Fig. 10.2).

Fragment the input *BoK* into "n" *BoK$_i$*'s.

Input $BoK = \sum_{1}^{n}(BoK_i)$.

10.2.2 INTERNET-BASED DDS/LoC SEARCH FOR CLASSIFICATION OF VFs, *S, NOs

This step identifies the orientation of the input *BoK* in relation to the Dewey Decimal System (and/or the Library of Congress) knowledge-based systems. Keyword search (such as Google word search) for *BoK* is generally insufficient in the knowledge searches based on the VF, *, and NO search for each significant *kel* in the input *BoK*. In the computations, the systematic comparison is made possible by having three sets (each set subdivided into VF, *, and NO each) of databases for input knowledge, local (or library), and Internet knowledge(s). If there is no connectivity with the established knowledge groups in DDS or LoC systems, the machine cannot modify or enhance such irrelevant knowledge which is a mere collection of words. This step prevents the machine to process *BoK* if it is junk, haphazard, or nonsensical piece of information or knowledge.

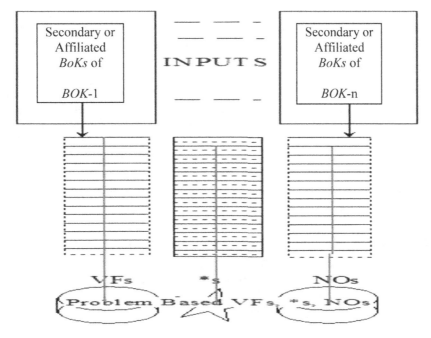

FIGURE 10.3

Collection and sorting of the verb-functions (*VFs*), convolutions (**s*), and noun objects (*NOs*) of the input knowledge *BoK*. Storage in linked memory storage locations facilitates the processing of *kels*.

10.2.2.1 Determine and list nos, Vfs, and *S of bok, local, and internet

Listing, sorting, and arranging of each set of individual *NOs*, *VFs*, and *s becomes necessary since they as a group form an element of knowledge, *kel* or Δk. These *kels* are initially detected and stored with appropriate linkages to their respective *NOs*, *VFs*, and *s. In the memory of the computers this function is easily accomplished by constructing a linked list database to access and manipulate the stringed *NOs*, *VFs*, and *s, or their components. Elemental *kels* form the basic "particles" or "elements" (such as the chemical elements) of knowledge for the primary knowledge processing to construct, reconstruct, evolve, or even merge and fuse into more powerful, distinct, and unique *KELs*. The computational processes of establishing linkages and lookup storage locations between every potential NO, VF, their convolution (and their attributes, if they are important) become critical to be able to perform operations on *kels*. Storage in linked memory storage locations facilitates the processing of *kels*. The machine process for sorting and listings of input *kels* and their affiliated *kels* are shown in Figure 10.3.

The knowledge machine scans the local library and the Internet for *VFs*, *s, and *NOs* that are similar, identical, or closely related to those used in the input *BoK*. This step provides the machine with a choice and latitude to enhance and amplify the role of the objects, verbs, and/or convolutions from the most recent Internet knowledge banks. This step also provides the machine if similar objects are readily available in the inventory, if the verbs can be assembled from locally assembled robotic process, and/or if major convolutions can be re-convoluted.

If the machine is in the all-synthetic mode, then the machine searches for *VFs*, *s, and *NOs* that attempt to meet the required characteristic of an ideal (or near ideal) knowledge sought. For example, if the machine is instructed to synthesize a poem that is alike Mathew Arnold's "Dover Beach" [1] but based on the drone technology used in modern warfare, then the machine will look for (search) if any poets have used the word in the input *BoK*. Some the famous words in this poem are "beach," "ignorant armies," "clash," and "middle if the night." The search continues in conjunction with night vision camera to search the bombing targets, as it is used in drone technology.

In these near human encounters of a knowledge machine, the "feelings" are involved. The machine "feels" the impact of the "work" or "processes" involved in generating the artificial knowledge expected from the machine. In some cases, the machine crashes in a jumble of processes. All the operating system errors and dead-locks can be expected from the OS of the knowledge-machine. It is as easy or difficult to pose an impossible problem to knowledge-synthesizing machine as it is to encourage or frustrate a human being.

10.2.2.2 Compare NOs, VFs, and *s of bok, local, and internet

The machine processes of comparing the knowledge critical *NOs*, *VFs*, and *s of *BoK* are depicted in Figure 10.4. Word compare algorithms become ineffective, but when the words form the nucleus of a concept, then concept-comparison algorithms will prove helpful. Tree-based searches and concept-graph extraction will lead to the identification of the structure of concept behind the words for *NOs*, *VFs*, and *s,.

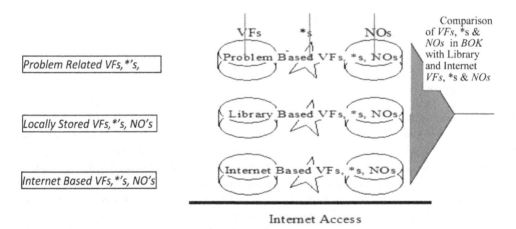

FIGURE 10.4

Knowledge machine scans the local library and the Internet for *VFs*, *s, and *NOs* that are similar to those used in the input *BoK*. If the machine is in the all-synthetic mode, then it searches for *VFs, *s, and *NOs* that attempt to meet the required characteristic of an ideal (or near ideal) knowledge sought. For example, if the machine is instructed to synthesize a poem that is alike Mathew Arnold's "Dover Beach" but based on the drone technology used in modern warfare, then it will determine if any poets have used the word "beach," "ignorant armies," "clash," "middle if the night," etc. in conjunction with night vision camera to search the bombing targets. It is as easy or difficult to pose an impossible problem to knowledge synthesizing machine as it is to frustrate a human being.

The process can be automated or can be overseen by a human being. Bias in SW programming or human judgment can serious deter the overall machine performance.

10.2.2.3 Filtering of NOs, VFs, *s, and concepts that tie them

This step prevents any porno's, illegal combinations of *NOs*, *VFs*, and *s, to enter the processing environment of the knowledge machine. This type of filtering is feasible at two places in the knowledge-ware. At this stage, the memory caches in the machine will not receive any irrelevant words, phrases, convolutions, and/or combinations thereof that can find their way into the artificial knowledge generated by the machine.

Alternatively, as the *NOs*, *VFs*, and *s enter the knowledge processor unit(s) or KPUs of the machine, the operating system can reject such knowledge-operands or *koprands* as illegal operands and refuse to execute the assembly level-knowledge instruction (*kopc*). If the machine is deployed in contaminated knowledge environments, then both precautionary filtering step would be desirable.

10.2.2.4 Rationality and contextual check of NOs, VFs, and *s

The concept check for each of the numerous *kel*s in the input *BoK* is rechecked this stage of the execution for assembling nano-*kel*s into micro-*kel*s, micro-*kel*s into mini-*kel*s, etc. (see Chapter 22).

Human minds process *kel*s effectively. In the degeneration and fragmentation processes, large cosmic *KEL*s and *KCO*s are broken down in to the most rudimentary noun-objects (e.g., elements), verb-functions (e.g., molecular formations) by the appropriate laws of convolutions (e.g., valencies, radical groupings). Conversely, microscopic *kel*s are combined and integrated into very large universes of objects, actions, and their appropriate convolutions. Life forms such as bacteria and even species in biological sciences evolve by systematic composition of more minute cells. An integrative process of this nature is applicable in the machine-based compositions of minute *kel*s or δkels to larger structures of knowledge denoted as knowledge-centric objects or *KCO*s. The process broken into two stages can be written as:

minute *kel*s → integrated (systematically) to become → large *kel*s (*KELs*)
and, then from larger *kel*s to macroscopic *KEL*s (*KCOs*)
minute *KELs* → integrated (systematically) to become → large *KELs* (*KCOs*)

The evolutionary step in each of the transitions (→) is triggered or catalyzed by a verb-function(s). Physical and mental energies are necessary for the transitions. Such verb-functions can be biologically inherent within the *kel* (e.g., a deficit need of an organism, a more desirable pattern of behavior) or induced externally (a natural event, a robotic instruction, etc.). For example, lightning discharge can form molecules of ozone O_3 in the atmosphere where oxygen is abundant. The knowledge society is an ordered environment of *kel*s represented and integrated as very minute *kel*s to larger *KELs*. . ., and then of very minute *KELs*, to larger *KCO's*, etc.[1] Chemistry also displays simple and complex to very complex chains in the distribution of atoms in the real world.

---

[1]In increasing order of complexity of *kel*s. For example, if μk is an employee in a corporation, then μK will be the corporation and $\Sigma\Sigma K$ would be conglomerate of related corporations.

10.2.2.5 Scoring and quality based on internet KB's

This an optional step to perform an overall sanity checks for the level of the knowledge being composed by the machine. Based on the nature of *NOs*, *VFs*, and *s and their combination(s), and comparing them with the Internet-based *NOs*, *VFs*, and *s, the machine can predict the extrapolated new knowledge as low, medium, high etc., although it may be correct after filtering out the undesirable *kels*. As much as a computer can abort the execution of an error ridden program, the knowledge machine can and should abort the execution of an insane or unethical social/ knowledge program. The machine can and if necessary, evaluate the good/bad or ethical/unethical intent of a politician, a social program writer or a designer, and even a new knowledge-seeker.

The role of *kels* in this machine environment can be as harmful as it is beneficial. Low-grade *kels* can ruin the reputation and the knowledge conveyed by healthy and robust *kels* that facilitate the social and knowledge environments in societies. Biological systems automatically destroy colonies of viruses and bacteria and the procedures provide a mechanism to propagate the desirable and curtail the undesirable. The benchmarks in the well-founded knowledge banks provide the guidelines leaning toward the good. Conversely, the Mafia-based knowledge banks attract the deceitful and abusive users of knowledge machines.

10.2.2.6 Evaluate and grade the inputs

This optional step permits the machine to set a benchmark for entering significant (only) bodies of knowledge into the machine. It may also be used to block abuse and theft of sensitive information. Security levels of input and processing can be monitored at this level.

10.2.2.7 Threshold limits and probabilities

The success of the knowledge machine depends on the threshold of admissible *NOs*, *VFs*, and *s, and for the concepts embedded in the *kels*. For example, if no threshold is set, the machine will admit any *NOs*, *VFs*, or *s, from the local libraries and/or Internet and produce irrelevant junk information at the output. Conversely, if the threshold is extremely tight, the machine will (or might) most likely fail because there are no exact *NOs*, *VFs*, and *s in the local library or the concepts embedded in *kels*. In a sense the latitude in the choice permits the machine to select similar or better *NOs*, *VFs*, and *s and generate more desirable solutions for the new knowledge.

It is suggested that the machine be allowed the freedom of choice in stages, such as permitting limited choice of *NOs* first and *VFs* second. Such an approach is generally followed in typical CAD systems, if the machine is *likely* to run wild. For example, in typical filter designs in electrical systems, the choice of poles and zeros is (very) judiciously administered and the final choice is in most cases a "wise" designers' selection of the parameters.

In the knowledge domain, the path of the knowledge machine is guided by human oversight like the path of a robot through uncharted territories. Human and machine intelligences need a unique blend in any new discipline.

10.3 BLEND AND PROCESS INPUT, LOCAL, AND INTERNET KNOWLEDGE

The blending function is symbolically represented in Figure 10.5. The knowledge-ware for selecting and blending the *NOs*, *VFs*, and *s from three different knowledge/word bases need unique

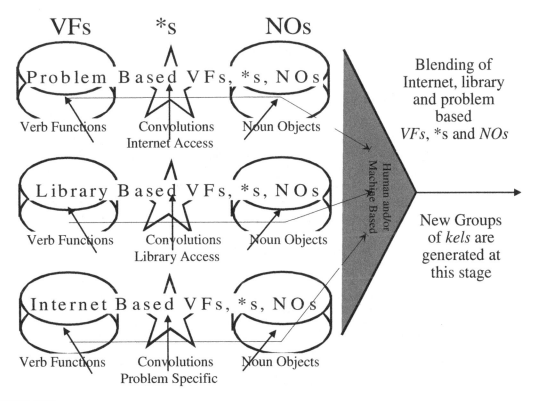

FIGURE 10.5

Selection of *NOs*, *VFs*, and **s* from all possible knowledge bases to form the micro *kels* for synthesizing the new knowledge *BoK'*. The concept behind each *kel* should be fully or partially compatible with the objective(s) of *Bok'*. This step facilitates assembling larger *kels* from the micro *kels*. The human or machine has to function at a concept level in addition to the selection of *NOs*, *VFs*, and **s*.

algorithms. For every minute *kel* in the input *BoK*, three appropriately matched set of *NOs*, *VFs*, and **s* are necessary such that it (the *kel*) contribute to the overall objective of the new body of knowledge or *BoK'*. In a sense, every chess player weighs and considers every move and in a sense most individuals contemplates the choices. In the knowledge domain, three moves (for *NOs*, *VFs*, and **s*) are chosen at every blending function in the generation of every *kel*. Machine learning becomes imperative if the process is to be automated. Alternatively, human judgment can be used to supplement the blending process during this particular phase of the knowledge machine function.

This part of the machine process is akin to that of an artist selecting the colors and shades for a painting as well as the size and shape of the brushes to be consistent with the message that the whole painting is trying to present to the viewer. In the knowledge domain, the freedom somewhat restricted because the Internet and library choice of certain key words in various disciplines. For example, just the word fusion conveys a body of knowledge as compared to fission to any nuclear scientist. As another example, the two-word pair optical-fiber conveys a different body of knowledge as compared to the two words coaxial-cable to any communication engineer. The Internet knowledge bases and the use of the terminology in authenticated documents serve the machine to select *NOs*, *VFs* and their particular convolution. There is a certain amount of mechanized creativity in this and following knowledge machine processes.

10.3.1 RELAX NOs, RELAX VFs, AND RELAX *S

Relaxing the parameters *NOs*, *VFs*, and *s within the structure of the knowledge elements (*kels*) offers the machine one more degree of freedom to fragment the assembled *kels* and reassemble them to generate the new knowledge (*BoK'*). Each one of the original *kels* selected as micro-blocks or (minute or *δkels*) can each be reassembled in its own right by relaxing the original *NOs*, *VFs*, and *s that made up the *δkels*. There is a good chance that the machine will fail this part of the knowledge processing unless appropriate techniques of forcing the convergence are enforced on the computations. A symbolic diagram for relaxing the parameters is shown in Figure 10.6.

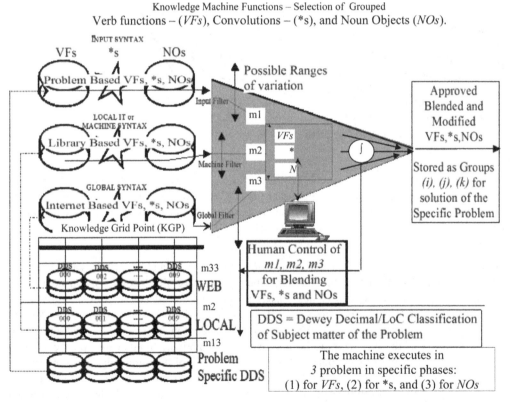

FIGURE 10.6

Blending and mixing the various *VFs*, *s, and *NOs* to generate numerous flavors of the new knowledge *BoK'*. The human operator selects the proportion such that *BoK'* has the flavor of problem specific, local, or the Internet flavor. The optimal choice can be reached after numerous iterations in generating a specific user flavor of knowledge (such as literary, poetic, philosophic) However, final check of the newly synthesized knowledge will validate its authenticity.

10.3.2 ITERATIVE TECHNIQUES FOR THE COMPUTER-BASED SOLUTIONS

This type of relaxation process is common in numerical solution of scalar and vector field, especially in electromagnetic fields. When simple and linear fields are solved by relaxation techniques, the convergence of the solution can be guaranteed and the plain old computer systems solve the problem either by matrix inversion algorithms or by Southwell's [2] relaxation procedures. Fields in homogeneous regions are quickly solved. When heterogeneous linear regions are present, the solution takes longer but converges without serious stability issues. When heterogeneous and nonlinear problems are encountered the stability of the solution is not guaranteed and the numerical solution can swing indefinitely without ever converging to a final solution. Human monitoring of the solution become necessary to force a convergence [3, 4] of the solution for the fields and especially for nonlinear vector potential problems.

In the knowledge domain, such powerful mathematical tools and algorithms are not available, nor have they been investigated. In most biological systems, the convergence occurs at the minimum energy configuration levels and the process is natural since biological systems have limited energy resources. In the human systems, rationality can assume a subservient role and emotions (generally non-linear) can cause large swings in the behavioral patterns of individuals. It becomes evident that when the knowledge machine has human "objects," the solution that needs to "compute" verb-functions can turn uncertain and unstable. However, most human being rational, most of the time alter their behavior and converge to a stable pattern of behavior without expending unnecessary energy in reaching dead end paths in human encounters. In the machine solution, the native intelligence of the embedded in the knowledge-ware algorithms starts to play a vital role from forcing the convergence of behavior (or *VFs*).

10.3.3 ITERATIVE CONVERGENCE OF PARAMETERS WITHIN MICRO KELs

Since there is no precise nor predictive science of mathematics for behaviorism,[2] iterative solution for the behavior of rational human beings appears as a viable approach in predicting path toward building a new knowledge object from the micro *kel*s, and the *KCO*s. The implementation of the iterative process and its monitoring is accomplished by forcing the machine to depict (or print) the progress through the iterations. In most cases the extent of parameters changed from iteration to the next is tracked. A good indication of an eminent meaningful result is that the change in the parameters and/or their values starts to become smaller with increasing number of iteration. Finally, this number tends to oscillate around a zero value indicating that local maxima or minima have reached. Global optimum values may be at a different location, calling for the perturbation methods to resolve this situation. A systems flow diagram for the monitoring the convergence of *kel*s is shown in Figure 10.7

---

[2]Rigid Behavior in military organizations and dictatorial societies has been established in the past. In such instances, the knowledge machine "looks up" the *VFs* for each of the (human) *NOs* and there is *no* need for computations of the estimated behavior.

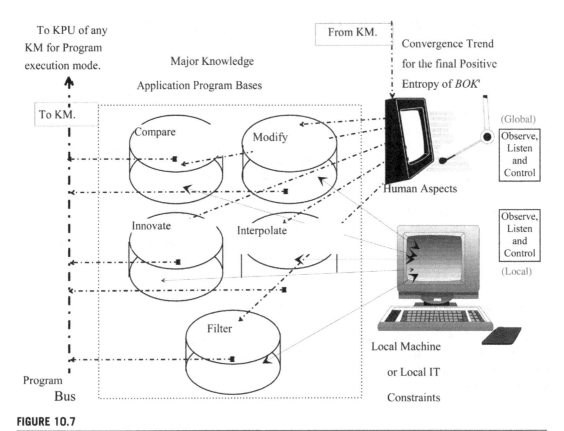

FIGURE 10.7

Depiction of the proposed flow of knowledge for the relaxation of *NOs*, *VFs*, and *s. The entropy of the newly formed knowledge may also be tracked on the computer screen. The energy configuration of the final kel configuration in the body of knowledge *BoK'*, or the machine generated *KEL* ($=\sum\sum(kels)$) to its minimum value is a good indication that the machine has successfully configured *BoK'*. This last stage is presented in the next section.

10.4 GENERATE NEWLY SYNTHESIZED KNOWLEDGE — BoK'

The generation of *BoK'* is also an iterative procedure. Typically, well-configured bodies of knowledge (*BoK*) have well-connected linkages between the important smaller *Boks*, in the table of contents, in the diagrams, in the structure of the document, etc. In most cases, this last step is accomplished by human beings and by expert manuscript editors. However, the processes can be programmed using the same techniques that were used to identify the seminal ideas in the original body of knowledge *BoK*.

In most commercial organizations, key words (such as Security, Profits, President's Office) and numbers ($ pay, $ Loss, $ expenses, etc.) identify the importance of information. In the knowledge domain, the connectivity of key concepts, key words, creativity, equations, symbols, diagrams, etc. may have convey the primary noun-objects and verb-functions. The algorithms and methodology for key concepts and their connectivity's still need refinement. Human oversight and support may also become necessary during the early knowledge-ware development.

10.4.1 RELAXATION OF ATTRIBUTES, ATTRIBUTES OF ATTRIBUTES

This step of the machine procedure generally has secondary effects and it can modify the adjectives of nouns in the newly generated knowledge or adverbs or their modifications. In some cases, it may be desirable to force the machine to search and modify the nouns, verbs, and their context if there are other close parameters. In human speech, this scenario is clarified by repeating *kel*s or *KEL*s more than once in slightly different words. When objects play dominant integrative roles, the attributes of such objects deserve a close examination.

During execution of the knowledge-code, the machine can examine the attributes of objects and relax them as it relaxes noun-objects or verb-functions. Alternatively, the machine can find substitute noun-objects and verb-functions. This type of sophisticated evaluation is practiced by corporations in selecting candidates for promotion or critical assignments. In a sense the machine can go to any extent in finding appropriate words, phrases, sentences, paragraphs, etc., in the final embodiment of knowledge.

10.4.2 MACHINE-BASED REASSEMBLY OF NEWLY DESIGNED KNOWLEDGE − BoK'

The diagrammatic representation of the reassembly of *BoK'* is shown in Figure 10.8. The knowledge-ware assembly routines for *BoK'* act as human−controlled multiple input gates in analog circuits. The function needs considerable skill and practice to generate masterpiece from a script, or create a symphony from instruments.

10.4.3 VERIFY THE VALIDITY OF THE NEWLY DESIGNED KNOWLEDGE − BoK'

This step forces the knowledge machine to check its own newly generated knowledge. This step authenticated the validity of the final machine-generated knowledge centric object. The iteration can be repeated again and again. When the machine is instructed to generate complex or super complex bodies of knowledge (*BoKs*), the overall problem can be fragmented with successive commands to generate simpler (*BoKs* or *boks*) such that the complex *BoK* can be reassembled as.

Super Complex $BoK = \Sigma^n_1 (BoKs)$.

Complex $BoK = \Sigma^n_1 (boks)$.

This process of successive fragmentation is common in most CAD procedures. For example, the chip design of a complex nature is broken down into smaller imprints of less complex chips on the same wafer and then reassembled. A super computer is an optimized assembly of small well-documented designs of CPUs, memories, bus structures, etc. Numerous rounds of customizations and enhancements are necessary for optimal performance. Human oversight, monitoring, and error checking are just as necessary as final editing of document is necessary.

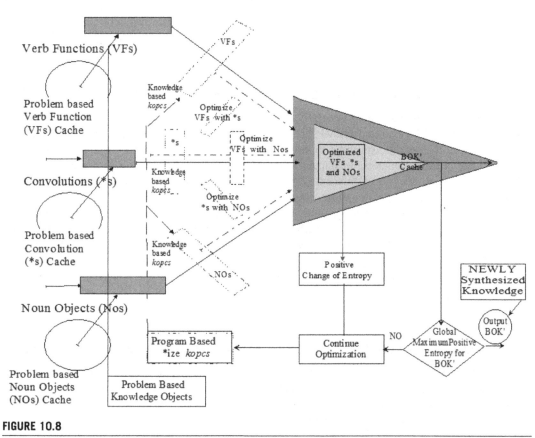

FIGURE 10.8

A schematic of the human and/or machine processes for the construction of the final machine-generated body of knowledge BoK'.

10.5 RATIONALITY AND SCORING OF NEW KNOWLEDGE — BoK'

This optional step ranks the artificial knowledge *BoK'* against the Internet-wide bodies of knowledge. This self-test provides an index for how well the machine can perform and has performed. The machine effectiveness (or its intelligence) in various knowledge spaces (real, social, psychological, intellectual, etc.) can be checked by posing the knowledge creation problem in numerous directions and disciplines.

It can be stated categorically that the machine performance is li*kely* to be poor and shabby just as the performance of early computer systems. Knowledge machine sophistication is a continuous and an unending learning experience. These concepts for learning and adaptation are embedded in most pattern recognition systems and computer aided-crime investigation centers Figure 10.9.

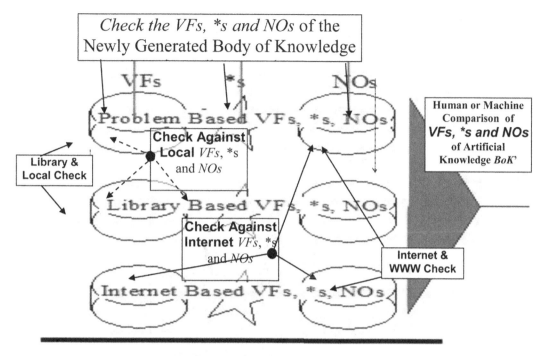

Internet Access

FIGURE 10.9

Verification and checking the validity of the newly generated body of knowledge *BoK'*. The basic scientific premise for the structure of *BoK'* is checked. This step is the same as the check for validity of the input body of knowledge *BoK* performed earlier before the generation of the new knowledge. Such a test is performed in all CAD of scientific products and designs.

10.6 MACHINE CONFIGURATIONS

Figures 10.10 and 10.11 depict possible details of the computer-aided knowledge processing machine configuration. The suggested architectures are seminal and need further deliberation. The major purpose is to convey the concepts behind the numerous steps in generating artificial knowledge customized to any individual by checking and verifying the local and Internet knowledge banks.

The machine functions and human deliberations are both indicated during the selection of *VFs*, *s, and *NOs* and during the admixing and relaxing of these components in the *kel*s that make up the *BoK'*. In the synthesis of new chemicals, the machines are used to select and mix the compounds that make up the new chemicals. The role of machine and human functions in the knowledge domain are radically different from those in the design of VLSI components and in the synthesis of compounds in chemistry or in the drug industry.

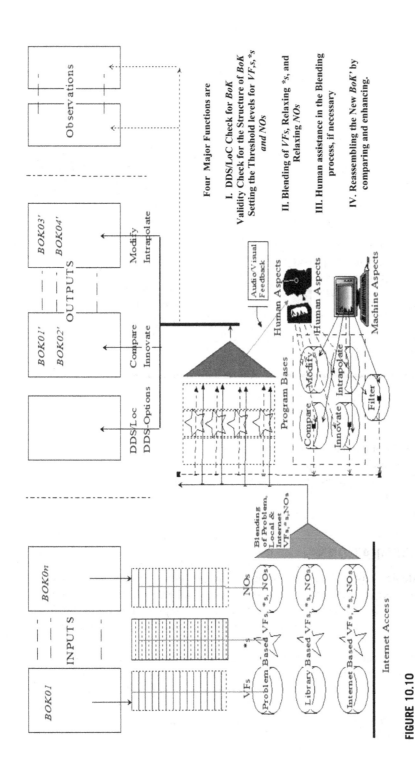

FIGURE 10.10

Major functions in the generation of new knowledge (BoK') from a seminal seed knowledge (BoK).

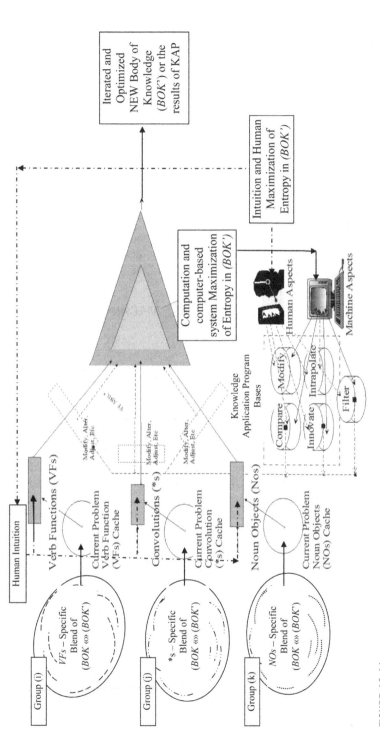

FIGURE 10.11

Configuration of the computer-aided knowledge design system and the entire machine. On the right side the knowledge analysis programs, or KAP', will analyze the capabilities and the limitation of the software and indicate the possible errors in the computation of *BoK'*. The iterative convergence is facilitated by repeatedly accessing the caches for *VF*s, *s, and *NO*s.

10.6.1 ITERATIVE CONVERGENCE OF THE "OPTIMIZED BODY OF KNOWLEDGE"

During the final stage, the integration of *kel*s into major *KEL*s is also a crucial combination of human and machine functions. The functions are blended and depicted in Figure 10.11. This function is akin to a jeweler making an ornament or a VLSI designer accommodating all the smaller SSI designs on one chip. In the knowledge domain, the flow of concepts in the final *BoK'* is the final consideration, and this is accomplished repeatedly on all masterpieces of literature. The human component in the *CAKD* effort is intensified in this phase of the execution. It is essential to realize that the human being alone may not be a force of iterative convergence of *BoK'* on the knowledge-machine, and the knowledge-ware routines are li*kel*y to be essential. At this stage, it is premature to arrange the KPU(s), object memories and local knowledge bases in a chip format. The algorithms for knowledge functions need optimization and the bus structure needs configuration. The knowledge flow patterns also need to be carefully examined.

During the execution phase, the iterative convergence of the newly generated body of knowledge *BoK'* is facilitated by repeatedly accessing the caches for *VFs*, *s, and *NOs*, to verify the change of knowledge or ΔK, and the *kel* configuration is minimized from one iteration to the next.

10.6.2 OVERALL FUNCTIONAL LAYOUT OF THE KNOWLEDGE MACHINE(S)

See Figures 10.10–10.11.

10.7 CONVOLUTIONS AND THEIR OPTIONS

In this chapter, we have proposed the convolutions between noun-objects or *NOs* and verb-functions or *VFs*. In reality and at the apex of knowledge processing, numerous other convolutions are also possible, and in fact, the mind examines these convolutions at a (deep) subconscious level.

At the fundamental level, knowledge is based on the answers to seven basic questions to anchor knowledge in the mind. The questions are Why? Who? What? How? Where? When?, and How-long? Depicted as a diagram, the answers traverse all the conceivable spaces (Real, Psychological, Social, Intellectual, etc.). Different spaces have specific coordinate systems and the human traverse these speed at the velocity of thought. The essential questions pertaining to knowledge lie in the matrix element space of (Questions, Spaces). The matrix is really a (7X4) tensor because there are numerous sub-dimensions at every element in the array.

Most investigation and research is an attempt to uncover knowledge/information. The existence of the national agencies, such as the criminal investigation agencies, the federal bureau of investigations, the private investigators attempt to follow a scientific methodology to answer the seven basic questions and also the combinations thereof, such as who, what, why and when, so-what, and then-what. In a sense the knowledge machine uses knowledge and information of this nature to build clusters of *kel*s and super *kel*s.

Figure 10.12 indicates the seven anchor points (A through G) in the mind, themselves anchored by the neighboring points. The basic question WHY is generally dictated by the need to gratify a direct or embedded deficit need of humans and objects. The energy for convolutions is derived from such needs. The next question WHEN, is generally assumed as immediate since the deficit

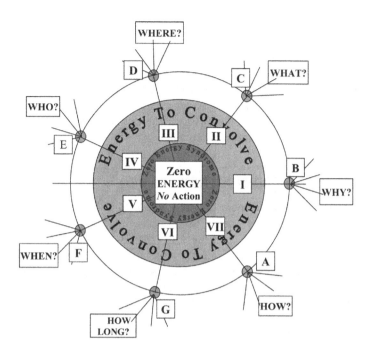

FIGURE 10.12

Configuration.

need(s) has surfaced. Answers to WHAT and HOW lie in the noun-object(s) or *NOs* and the associated verb-function(s) or *VFs*, convoluted toward gratifying the deficit need.

10.7.1 THE MIND—TIME CONVOLUTION

When the human mind is considered as an integrated composition of the four spaces (real, psychological, social, and intellectual, RPSI), then TIME and HOW-LONG (see Nodes F and G in Fig. 10.12) play a crucial role. The effect of time as an external and independent entity is experienced by all species as time follows its own course into eternity. For example, biological organisms are born, grow, age, decay, and die. In the knowledge domain, the convolution(s) between time and mind are time-based snapshots of the four RPSI spaces. Over time, these convolutions themselves and the processes are psychological, emotional, intellectual, and social. Experiences in these many spaces have driven the mature and thoughtful to significant contributions in the society: but also driven the immature and thoughtless to drink and destruction. The mind-time convolutions become too unique to be mathematical or programmable, yet most people convolute time into mind and mind into time on an individual basis.

10.7.2 THE MIND—SPACE CONVOLUTION

If mind is considered as a composite of four RPSI spaces and the physical location (i.e., *x, y, z* coordinates) as an independent parameter (see Node D in Fig. 10.12), then the two can be convoluted, though not as elegantly and as precisely. Space and time are inherently related by the velocity of human thought in neural spaces. Neuron clusters hold the spatial coordinates in their own biological knowledge banks. The transit time is finite between the neuron clusters and the spatial coordinates that they hold. Space and time in the mind thus get coordinated, and the emotions provide the bondage. Human experiences display a mirage of (Northern) lights in the horizons of the mind. Generally, communicated by human sentiments these unique experiences are not programmable as entities (*NOs*) and their actions (*VFs*). The diagrams are profuse and equations are not documented or verified for any scientific discourse.

10.7.3 THE MIND—SOCIETY CONVOLUTION

Mind and society interact in the E segment of the Figure 10.12. The convolution has a profound effect in the social and psychological or S and P space of the mind. A coherent and cogent distribution of the energies in four spaces and around the seven Nodes helps the mind in a balanced mode to handle most of the aspects of knowledge in an appropriate and a consistent fashion. The science of psychiatry can perhaps be condensed in the knowledge bases for the seven Nodes (A through G) in Figure 10.12 and let an artificially intelligent *CAKD* knowledge-ware help the social and ethical progress in the society. In the second decade of the twenty-first century, we seem as far removed as the farm workers of the second decade of the last century were unaware of the Internet-based knowledge society.

10.8 CONCLUSIONS

This chapter constructs knowledge from and around any seminal seed (or body) of knowledge (*BoK*). The machine is programmed to decipher the object and actions in this seminal seed and examines the validity of every object, action, and their interrelationship. It also examines the rate of change of the structure of noun-objects, and their entropies; the rate of change of verb-functions and their energies; and finally the rate of change of connectivity's and their bondage. Local and Internet bases of knowledge supplement, enhance, and modify these objects, actions, and their relationship to suit the individual, the place, the time, the culture, etc. Customized knowledge is then reassembled and reconstructed by systemic integration of the newly reconstituted objects, actions in their appropriate context. The new body of artificial knowledge (*BoK'*) is reexamined in the same fashion as the seminal body of knowledge *BoK*, and the iterations continue until all the objectives of the artificial knowledge are satisfactorily achieved. It is very possible to defeat the purpose of the machine by trying to construct impossible, philosophic, and irrelevant and contradictory bodies of artificial knowledge. However, it can provide most answers to most people, most of the time Table 10.1.

This chapter also presents the role of machines to build customized-knowledge based on the convolved relationships between objects and actions, both necessary for existence of life. Under normal conditions, sufficient knowledge is satisfactory to resolve most aspects of living. Personal and Internet knowledge bases are generally primed with this sufficient knowledge for most of the people, most of the time. Healthy and sustainable relationships evolve from scientific and balanced

Table 10.1 Accumulation of complete knowledge[a]

Region	Convolution in the Segments	Convolution Between	Symbolic Representation
I	How & What (A & C)	*VFs* and *NOs*	VF*NO or NO*VF
II	Why & Where (B & D)	Reason and Places (Space)	(Reason*Space) or (Space*Reason)
III	What & Who (C & E)	*NOs* and Persons	NO*(Person) or (Person*NO)
IV	Where & When (D & F)	Places and Times	(Space)*(Time) or (Time)* (Space)
V	Who & Duration (E & G)	Persons and ΔTime (ΔT)	(Person)*(ΔT) or (ΔT)*(Person)
VI	When & How (F & A)	Times and *VFs*	(Time)*VF or VF*Time
VII	Duration & Why (G & B)	(ΔT) and (Reason)	(ΔT)*(Reason) or (Reason)*(ΔT)

[a]*The table indicates all the components of a Body of Knowledge (BoK) to complete its structure. Generally, the information about any BoK is incomplete but it is contextually filled in from our prior knowledge. For example, if a complete BoK is to be extracted from event(s), then all the seven questions on the left side need to be completely answered. In addition, double, triple, and up to seven stage convolutions may become necessary. But, since there is no knowledge that is entirely complete, humans and machines generally work with adequate knowledge rather than complete knowledge.*

distribution of energies to accomplish the necessary actions that result in an attractive contour of mutual concern, responsibility, and respect. Conversely, unhealthy relations can also evolve with insufficient and/or malicious knowledge.

The pursuit of complete knowledge appears to lie in the answers to seven basic questions (Why? Who? What? How? Where? When?) and How-long? about any knowledge centric object or *KCO*. Complete knowledge is li*kel*y to provide enough information about any *KCO* for any reason (Why?), about anything and by anybody (Who?), for any object (What?), for any function (How?), anywhere (Where?), anytime (When?), for however-long (How-long?). Complete knowledge results from the answers of the seven interrelated questions. Architectures and bus structure are suggested at these very initial attempts to conceive and construct such knowledge machines from the yet evolving science of knowledge.

REFERENCES

[1] Matthew A. 1822-1888, Dover Beach, The sea is calm tonight. The tide is full, the moon lies fair. Upon the straits; on the French coast the light. http://www.poetryfoundation.org/poem/172844, accessed December 21, 2015.

[2] Christopherson DG. R.V Southwell 1888-1970. Biographical Memoirs of Fellows of the Royal Society 1972:18: 549. Also see Sir Richard Southwell, MA, LLD, FRS: Rector 1942–48, Imperial College, London, UK, and Southwell RV. Relaxation methods in engineering and sciences. Oxford: The Clarendon Press, 1946.

[3] Ahamed SV. Accelerated convergence of numerical solution of linear and non-linear vector field problems. Comp. J. 1965;8:73–6.

[4] Ahamed SV. Application of the acceleration of convergence technique to numerical solution of linear and nonlinear vector field problems with numerous sources. Int. J. Eng. Sci. 1970;8:403–13.

KNOWLEDGE SCIENCE AND SOCIAL INFLUENCE

PART I, SECTION III, SUMMARY

Section 03 with five chapters deals with the basis of information where-from knowledge is derived. Perfectly ordered and organized information (with no ambiguities) makes for rudimentary knowledge. Processing of knowledge and its enhancement leads to the underlying truisms that offer knowledge more value, longevity and universality. By tradition knowledge is more distilled and permanent than information that is collected from data in a systematic and pre-designated fashion. The syntactic rules, semantics and compilation are designed to facilitate the flow of information and knowledge seamlessly from people to people, nation to nation and culture to culture. The very essence and character of stages of evolution of knowledge from inform information are presented and depicted here. All aspects of communication, social constraints, encoding/decoding, security, dependability and error free operation are addressed in this section. Some processes remain analog but digital storage and processing has become a standard since the middle of the 20th century.

KNOWLEDGE AND INFORMATION ETHICS

11

CHAPTER SUMMARY

High-speed Internet has provided unprecedented opportunities in the information domain. The wealth of information in the Web-based knowledge banks brings about innumerable business prospects. This relentless rush for wealth lowers the information ethics by marketing unsubstantiated and ill-founded information. The rewards had brought a stream of successful dot-com corporations in the 1990 s. The dangers have also brought bankruptcy for most of these corporations. The plunderers are the knowledgeable and skilled few and the victims are the ignorant who are not able to see through the games that Internet exploiters are at play. The boom and bust of the dot-com opportunists is grim reminder of how knowledge cycle has taken the ignorant few to the depth of despair. In this chapter, we suggest that intelligent knowledge processing software should curtail the abuse of the IP networks, much as the network security programs that block the spread of spam and viruses.

11.1 INTRODUCTION

Intelligent information technologies have been successfully introduced in most private, business, educational, and public sectors society. The novel features and services of these technologies have the potential to benefit most personal, corporate, social, and cultural aspects of users. The implications for the users of the facilities that handle global information are comparable is that of the combined impact of the computer and network revolution that began in the 1950 s and 1960 s. Easy worldwide data base access, coupled with (almost) totally accurate and (nearly) instantaneous response at affordable prices, brings home a new sense of power to be knowledgeable about anything, anyplace and anywhere. Unfortunately, this power of network revolution has been corrupted by the trivia and temptations that these same technologies have bring to the minds of individuals. An unbiased individual is as likely to pulled into a whirlpool of psychological ruin, dismay, and apathy as a well-versed scholar. Occurrences of this nature have occurred in the past. The Titanic disaster, the Chernobyl nuclear fall-out, the Bhopal gas tragedy, etc., are grim reminders that when innovations are left unsupervised and unchecked, they are potentials for calamity. More seriously, the abuse of the power of Internet technology in the social context is more treacherous because they are willful and wanton actions of the abusers that corrupt information and its distribution with deceit and abusive sales pitch.

Most of the Internet users explore and benefit from the convenience and opportunities offered by the network revolution within the legal and ethical framework of society. However, such boundaries are vague and volatile. Human beings sometimes lose the perspective of the entire picture [1] of knowledge, wisdom, social movement, and social justice that is embedded in the historic, legal,

Evolution of Knowledge Science. DOI: http://dx.doi.org/10.1016/B978-0-12-805478-9.00011-X

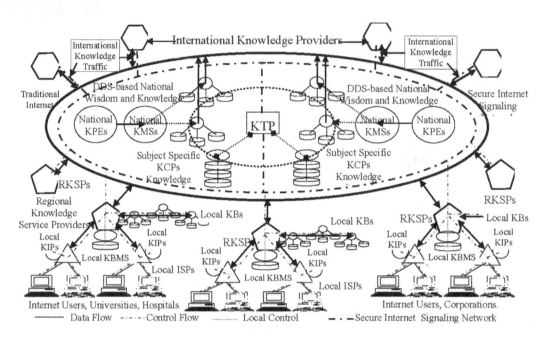

FIGURE 11.1

Framework of an intelligent Internet-based network with traditional intelligent network (IN) components.
ISP = Internet service providers; KIP = Knowledge intelligent peripheral attached to ISP local network;
RKSP = Regional knowledge service providers; KB = Knowledge banks or knowledge bases; KBMS = KB
management systems; KCP = Knowledge control point; KTP − Knowledge transfer point; KMS = Knowledge
management systems; KPE = Knowledge-provisioning environment; DDS = Dewey Decimal System or Library
of Congress knowledge bases.

and ethical dimensions in the society. An active role of a new breed of knowledge machines (*KMs*)
is proposed in this book to facilitate the human control of distributed computer systems.

KMs process synthesized information from any IT-based platforms. Decision support systems
(DSS), executive and management information systems, (EIS and MIS), SAP (Systems,
Applications, and Products in data processing), Oracle's PeopleSoft, etc., are abundant and popular
to the derive knowledge content (of significant value, if there is any) from the numerical and graphical content of such information systems. Typically, these machines dispense knowledge from
worldwide Web sites and navigate the flow of information depending on the user needs, preferences, and choices. A schematic of the methodology deployed in intelligent Internets and knowledge networks is shown in Figure 11.1.

The Internet is shown as the solid line ellipse and a new secure Internet signaling network (equivalent to the CCS7) is shown by the ellipse with the dash-dot line. Within these two outer ellipses lies
a national archive of wisdom, knowledge, ethics, and cultural value of any nation. A full-fledged
Internet-based intelligent network (IN) configuration is shown with a knowledge transfer point
(*KTP*), wisdom, and other bases that serve as the reference points for the nation. An independent
knowledge control point (KCP) holds the content-based address for knowledge and wisdom that is

held in the national archive of knowledge and wisdom. Both the knowledge management system (*KMS*) and knowledge-provisioning environment (KPE) are shown. The function of the KMS is to update, validate, and consolidate then knowledge held in the archives. The function of the KPE is to provision and dispense selected modules and blocks of information from the archives. The function of safeguarding and preventing abuse of knowledge and information can be shared with the KMS.

Three grades knowledge providers at national, regional, and local levels are shown in Figure 11.1. The national level knowledge functions are shown within the two outer ellipses. Other international interconnect blocks are shown as hexagons, the regional knowledge service providers (*RKSPs*) are shown as pentagons, and the local ISP are shown as triangles. Management of the regional knowledge bases is carried out by a *KBMS* (equivalent to the DBMS used extensively in computational environments) rather than by *KCP, KMS,* or *KPS* at national level. This difference is more a matter of detail than a conceptual difference. In the normal mode of Internet service provisioning, the routine services are provided by the ISPs. When the knowledge seekers tap into the Internet, the knowledge intelligent peripheral or *KIP* (equivalent to the intelligent peripheral in the IN environment) senses the need to invoke the cooperation of the *RKSPs*, the national knowledge services providers (*NKSPs*), or the international *KSPs*. The cooperation between *KSPs* facilitates the Internet users.

If there is a consortium of global knowledge providers, then the national knowledge, and wisdom, etc., bases of all nations can be consolidated under the patronage of the United Nations, much like the health and food programs. This "world bank" of knowledge, wisdom, and culture is the pinnacle at the fourth level (see Fig. 11.2) and provides the framework for nations to share values, ethics, and morality much like sharing other world resources. The role of information and knowledge in the growth and stability of some nations has been demonstrated by the recent establishment of cabinet-level offices (e.g., energy, national security) in any national environment.

To retain objectivity of minding and monitoring concrete social initiatives, (knowledge) machine-based human system (Fig. 11.2) that is likely to be more effective than the current human systems where the eminent self-interest of decision makers can influence their decisions. The long-term social gains from such social initiatives can be overshadowed by the lack of rigorous and scientific methodologies.

In the modern times, we face a situation where educated, business minded, but opportunistic folks are actively at work. The ultimate goals of such folks are occasionally slanted toward maximizing the self-interest [2] rather than serving the society. The slow and insidious social movement in some unwary nations and societies is toward exploitation of those ignorant in differentiation skills between justice and injustice, truth and deception, virtue and arrogance, and benevolence and exploitation. Well-documented cases of Internet-based child molesters and identity thieves, and even financial agencies ready to offer loans and then foreclose properties who default in their payments. These social ills are still rampant in stable Western societies. In the past, occupation of foreign lands and the slave trade have left dark imprints in history.

11.2 KNOWLEDGE PROCESSING IN NETWORKS

Knowledge processing has been an integral part of knowledge engineering since the early 1980 s. Concepts from knowledge engineering have matured into well-accepted disciplines, such as

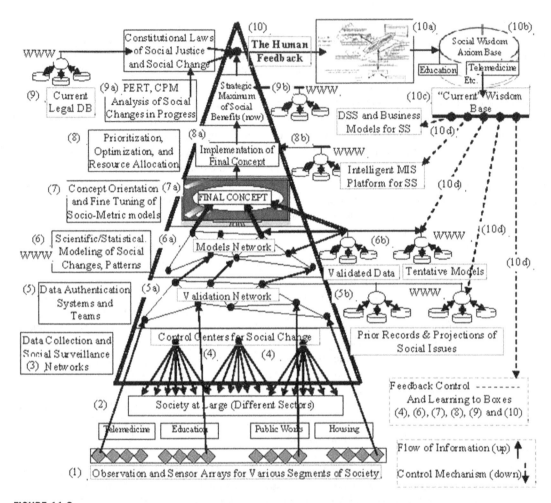

FIGURE 11.2

Schematic representation of a knowledge machine (KM)-based system to monitor, and to stabilize social movements dynamically, within a complex society. The feedback control is accomplished as information and accumulated knowledge flows up the seven (3 through 10) layers of the pyramid. The society resides outside of the pyramid and the patterns of change and movement are tracked in the information and knowledge bases within the machine. The knowledge-ware is supported by the mathematical, statistical, AI, and social models, and incremental changes are matched against those tracked by the sensor array in (1). Feedback correction is computed by scientific SW in layers (6) and (7). Most of the learning and model development occurs in these two layers. The social control is exerted via the human/robotic control centers in (4).

artificial intelligence [3], expert systems [4], pattern recognition [5], computer vision [6,7], and even robotics. These topics prepare engineers to design and build automated computer-based response systems. For example, expert systems permit the user to "get the opinion(s)" of one or more experts in the field as they may respond to the query of the user. Such opinions are generated from a knowledge base organized as an ultra-large and sophisticated data structure. The query has enough details and precision for a computer system to generate a response as the expert(s) would have responded. General queries receive broad, shallow information, and specific queries receive precise, in-depth information. Thus, in a sense, knowledge (or the information) can be engineered to satisfy users in a variety of situations.

As another example, consider computer vision. When blood samples are drawn from patients, the scanning for certain types of cells with a specific structure can be automated. This is accomplished by forcing the microscope image to be presented on a computer screen. On this screen, the cell boundaries form dark "pixels," and the computer can "see" such boundaries and detect if they match the boundaries of specific cells that are expected (or are not expected). To some degree, the computer can be "trained" to match patterns as in "pattern matching" at an elementary level, or "see" images as in "computer vision" at an advanced level. Both pattern matching and computer vision have a firm mathematical foundation since the match can be less than perfect and the attributes found may not be exactly what the computer was programed to find. Thus, a certain degree of uncertainty and lack of precision [8] may accrue. As a result, the concepts of probability and confidence levels also arise in these disciplines.

However, if these results do verge on being valid (say, 90% or 95% of the time), then they are better than no results at all. For this reason, knowledge processing and its associated functions of knowledge engineering (which are in fact parts and modules) are finding more and more acceptance in society. Such applications are numerous and computer systems are dedicated to performing these well-accepted functions routinely, such as identifying the bar code in grocery stores or voices in voice-activated systems.

In a traditional sense, the earlier machines that perform these knowledge functions are general purpose computer systems with intricate layers of software, permitting them to accomplish knowledge processing. Hardware realizations of processors and architectures of systems specifically dedicated to processing knowledge directly from "objects," their "attributes," or "other pieces of information" are the main strength of these novel networks. These machines process intermediate objects, their attributes, or modules of information to reach a goal, much like conventional computers process numbers to reach other targeted numbers or results quantified as numbers.

The compilers for these machines process input queries like the compilers of scientific computer languages. They try to identify intermediate objects (from the past experience and the attributes of interacting objects) and the ways and means to get such objects (from the forward, backward, and indirect pointers to and from such objects), and then attempt to associate them (from a history of associations, if any). Complex queries need long and intricate knowledge processing and there can be a certain level of ambiguity or uncertainty in the processing. Learning and compromising during problem solution for these new machines becomes as much an integral part of their operation as pattern matching and data base searching is in the older computer systems that do knowledge processing. The functions of the knowledge processing machines are necessary in the proposed machines, but they become tools and commands within the machines.

11.3 KNOWLEDGE MACHINES TO DAMP INTERNET OPPORTUNISM

KMs offer new methodologies to achieve well-directed goals based in authenticated "knowledge-ware." Machines can generally be outwitted by human being and for this reason, an ironclad framework of software security is necessary to prevent the abuse of the machine that will process information and knowledge to provide wisdom to the human beings.

The positive advantages of the network-based KM are speed of processing information and the global reach to all relevant knowledge bases around the world. Such machines deploy the opportunities provided by the Internet, but under the collective wisdom of socially documented rules and conduct encoded in the "knowledge software" that drives these machines. Being harder to tamper (due to numerous layers of security), these machines will be less impulsive than human beings under similar situations. To this extent, the recommendations and the suggested procedures offered by the machines will be close to being just, fair, and respectful of the rights of all the segments of human beings within the society.

In reality, the human organizations have a set of standard operating procedures (SOPs) for corporate executives. The medical code of ethics offers guidance to the medical professionals when the discretionary medical practices may interfere with the rights of patients, doctors, and/or staff members. When the procedures and organizations become complex, simple, and intelligent, DSS offer some rule-based decision-making processes that offer guidelines for human beings. In the same vein, when social and ethical procedures that influence global communities and the rights of small nations, the KM and their appropriate software can help global organizations (such as United Nations, international monetary institutions, save the children agencies, etc.) weigh and consider all the social entities in a fine balance of etiquette and justice. Such machine will overrule the self-interest of agencies and political lobby groups. Over time, these lobbies become a part of social setting in power centers, such as those in Washington, New York, Geneva, Paris, and elsewhere around the world.

Financiers, lobby groups, presidents, power centers, and dynamic power shifts threaten the stability of human organizations that make crucial decisions. In most cases, the conflict between organizational values and self-preservation of the corporate leaders become apparent. Generally, the self-preservation and self-propagation instincts win out. The recent scandals at Enron, Arthur Anderson, and Global Crossing bear witness [1,2] that decision-makers favor personal gain over legal and ethical considerations. The acceleration grows especially faster due to the high-speed backbone networks [8] with executives whose positions are precarious. The power and position held by such executives comes under scrutiny. Both are jeopardized quickly and precipitously. Any deceptive practices in the past cause heightened anxiety since public exposure comes over the high-speed media links. Once more, high-capacity backbone networks play an insidious role, and contribute to the dissemination of any unethical practices of corporate executives.

This dilemma is not to be seen as a flaw in democracy. The deduction of Aristotelian [9] wisdom that governed the social stability needs the computational support of the modern computer systems to stabilize the more complex modern society. When everything is weighed and considered, the role of knowledge and wisdom gets even more emphatic in providing social justice. It is our contention that the ancient Roman foundations of democracy are still valid and viable. It becomes necessary to provide the modern tools and knowledge-ware to support the social scientists and philosophers in drawing axioms of *modern* wisdom for the twenty-first century, rather than gazing in a crystal ball of the age-old and undocumented wisdom. The role of fair-minded human beings (like the Supreme Court judges) at the top of hierarchy of machines is necessary to guide the machine through a mirage of possibilities. The wisdom to guide the machines becomes a prerequisite to the wisdom to guide the society since these machines and their human counterparts provide the social driving force.

A select group of social, computer, and network scientists guide the machine at lower levels (3−7, Fig. 11.2) to offer a set of viable, just, ethical, and socially benevolent goals derived from age-old wisdom and modern technology. The byways and highways to progress are computationally accurate and as flawless as the current social conditions would permit.

11.4 A STABLE SOCIAL BALANCE

The purpose of the KM is to offer viable solutions for implementing social justice, preservation of values, maintaining family structure, and enhancing the educational standards, while mediating and moderating social and cultural changes in these directions. In monitoring the flow of information up the seven layers (3 through 10, in Fig. 11.2), conditions for normal ranges are examined, much as the machines automatically monitor the vital statistics of patients in a medical setting.[1] Conditions leading to instability are filtered out or modified to suit the particular socioeconomic setting. Such a monitoring strategy exists to prevent national economics from swinging between catastrophic busts and short-lived booms. In the present context, the KM facilitates a social parallelism while enforcing social justice and negotiating social change without causing social unrest. The bulls and bears in the social economy are both moderated to be in the restrained social cycles. Such machines also ensure the social/civil rights of all the constituting groups. Most of the advanced societies protect their citizen by providing medical care, social security, and other social services. While such practices are administered by limited staff and incomplete scientific methodologies, the use of modern computer, network, and communication technologies will offer more dependable means of administering social justice. Such machines also curtail the abuse of power and block corruption within the society.

The deployment of KMs in the social setting is likely to be resisted by politicians, power brokers, and government officials, much like the early diagnostic programs such as Mycin [10] or NeoMycin [11] were resisted by the medical professionals. The use of the more recent object oriented machines and knowledge-ware is likely to serve the social entities much more than the MIS type of information processing platforms [12] based on conventional computer systems.

11.4.1 MAINTAINING STABILITY IN PERSONAL LIVES

Personal lives of the younger population in society are considerably shaped by Internet content. Ethical values and quality of life bases can be enhanced or diminished wise and guarded decisions or by reckless and irresponsible decisions. In an open society that esteems the overall wisdom accumulated over the past, the choice of the irresponsible spammers can be diminished significantly by heavy taxation of such Web sites. After all, cigarette smoking was curtailed by three socially accepted

---

[1]When the society shows tendencies toward ethical sickness and moral decay, a social monitoring system to watch the flow of information becomes necessary. The flow of information in the numerous directions is a leading indicator of the various ways of the movement of the society. For example, the flow of information by gay activists on the Internet indicates the tendency of the populous toward homosexuality; the increased ads for gifts in December indicates the tendency of the society to exchange gifts for holidays; the flow of open sales propaganda by sex agencies indicates a direction toward looser moral standards; etc.

practices: (a) increased sales tax, (b) restricted minimum age to buy cigarettes, and (c) restricted spaces for smokers in public places. The abuse of alcohol has also been similarly curtailed.

The newer services that the Internet has brought, have been beneficial. The right choice of a university for a high school graduate, the appropriate medical center for a patient, network contact with educators, political leaders, etc., are examples that enhance the productivity of individuals. Preferential viewing can offer customers a better choice of entertainment and an optimum use of leisure time. Stocks, bonds, and other consumer items may be purchased automatically as the sales prices drop and are billed to a customer account number with appropriate authorization. Further, a stock market transaction may be made to follow the algorithmic preference of the participant. However, there is one basic difference between the possible social and personal impact of these intelligent information technologies. When there is a broad region of possible social impact, it is very likely that the problem and its implication has been studied by a large number of people. Thus, their collective wisdom has been instrumental in adopting the change. On the other hand, if there is an isolated region of personal impact, then the individual may choose to misuse the network, and the impact may well become counterproductive. As in every forward step technology makes, the current Internet face the threat of misuse by individuals in personal life, by organizations at a corporate level, by societies at a cultural level, and even by countries at a political level.

11.4.2 PROTECTION FROM PSYCHOLOGICAL AND SOCIAL ISOLATION

The Internet can only become an agent for social isolation for the addictive who look forward to external motivation to spend time in the trivia. Appropriately primed structure (see Section 11.4.3) of values and achievement, provide an internal motivation and inspiration toward personal integrity and progress, higher education (see Section 11.4.4), maintaining the stability in personal lives (see Section 11.4.1), and the enhancement of values to suit the culture and environment.

The current Internet environment offers high quality, efficient service to a large segment of the population. Networks' responses can be made to be extremely accurate, whereas the human response is initially inaccurate and needs iterative convergence for the interrogator to obtain the necessary information from another person. In the process of the interaction, the two people learn more about the problem [13] and about each other. This teaches one of the ethics of the social environment in which one lives. Now, consider the network environment. The ease, accuracy, and extent of the network response can be learned and mastered to a precise science. Typical device interfaces for the new information technologies are just as intolerant of input error as they are accurate in their responses to human input. Consequently, it is our contention that if the intelligent sector of our population practices high efficiency in day-to-day functions, they will also become intolerant to human communication, thus building highly intelligent knowledge tools rather than social skills needed to get along with people and their human eccentricities. People in castles of knowledge with a mastery of network skills and a pair of high-speed lines are manifestations of an information society.

11.4.3 PROTECTION OF VALUES AND FAMILY STRUCTURE

Network assisted dating services has made instant couples around the nation and the globe. E-mail romances are common as one-night stance. Short messaging system (SMS) has created short marriage syndrome. Long-distance marriages have occurred. Does this change the outlook on long-term family life and alter the cultural pattern of a society? Such changes, if any, can make the idea of a traditional family life obsolete, especially for the intelligent sector of society endowed with the inherited or acquired capabilities to use the network. The long-range effect of a lack of family structure for this sector of the population only delays its own extinction, assuming its intelligence is not geared toward its survival. Yet, the long-term survival of various species is based upon instinct rather than intelligence. Hence, the underlying implication is a need for test-tube babies, incubated in highly controlled environments and automated training facilities. Without such facilities, we may only face a rapid decrease in the numbers of people who can use the network. Once again, the users of the network may have robotic and humanoid tendencies, rather than human and social skills. It is interesting to note that this inference is supported by the recognized tendency that isolated packets of cultures do not survive over a long period. We can ask the question, whether the Internet tends to catalyze the extinction of the intellectually elite or regroup them better for propagation and survival. The stakes are high for the prolonged integrity of the family.

The personal impact over a couple of decades can be desirable, neutral, or totally unwarranted. If the change is not managed by some sort of an ethical or legal framework, then the opportunism that such information technologies bring about will influence the direction of the social change. Further, the direction of the prolonged change may violate the civil rights of some people, causing social injustice to those who are (as Marx postulates), weak, poor and venerable in the new tools and methodologies of the knowledge society.

11.4.4 ENHANCEMENTS OF EDUCATIONAL STANDARDS AND ETHICS

There is a threefold impact in the educational sector. *First*, universities are a fertile ground for new concepts. For example, the basic ideas for the ALOHA network were developed at the University of Hawaii. The simulation programs for the two-wire, high-speed data transmission systems for use in the high-speed subscriber network in the "C" language were coded by the University of California, even though these simulation studies were performed earlier at AT&T Bell Laboratories at Whippany, New Jersey. *Second*, at the school level, the networks are effective tools for computer-assisted education and resource/data base sharing between schools. *Third*, the existence of terminals, nodes, and computer-network-interface gear helps the young students to conceive ideas and internalize the use and the impact of the advanced technological evolution of the 1980 s. The utilization of intelligent systems and information technologies in the educational environment is, perhaps, the most effective method in preparing the young minds of any nation to cope with the transition toward the knowledge society.

The use of networks in graduate research, library searches, faculty searches, administrative support, and student records has already begun at schools and colleges around the world. This trend is likely to grow in the next few decades. The existence of intelligence in the information technologies is not, in itself, of great consequence since the current usage is routine and the role of the technology is likely to continue in the service mode. However, the quality of current service is bound to improve, and newer ethical and wisdom-based services can be easily appended.

CONCLUSIONS

Greater deployment of scientific methodologies in the social setting will offer greater social justice and ethics at a pace that a majority of the constituents (other than businesses) will welcome. The social changes toward a better human society are likely to accelerate rather than spin around. Human judgment alone may yield satisfactory solution in a majority of the cases but a computer-aided-social-support (*CASS*) system can offer greater benefits in the longer run. In the corporate environment, the MIS platforms offer greater corporate stability and accountability in the business community.

Violent fluctuation in the social patterns are damped out by extrapolative effects of corrections in the past and the effectiveness of such correction. While the KM offers the corrective measures, it also tracks both the microscopic and macroscopic effect of the proposed changes in both qualitative and quantitative terms. The mistakes of the past are systematically studied and eliminated and benefit-to-cost ratio is enhanced. If the criterion for optimality is imposed, then the machine uses the operations research (OR) techniques to achieve the optimal goals. When the machine is supplemented by the laws of ethics and justice, it will enforce such laws and attempt to curtail those who willfully violate such laws. It will also alert the law enforcement authorities or the judicial system within the country about predictable negative trends in the communities, societies, cultures and even nations!

REFERENCES

[1] Bryce R, Ivins M. Pipe dreams: greed, ego, and the death of Enron. HarperCollins Canada/PublicAffairs; 1st ed. 2002. See also Cruver B. Anatomy of greed: the unshredded truth from an Enron insider. Carroll Graf Publishers; 2002. See also Bernstein PA. Whats wrong with Telecom. IEEE Spectrum 26−29, Jan. 2003.

[2] Preisel B, Bouwman H, Steinfield C. E-life after the dot com bust. Heidelberg: Physica-Verlag; 2004.

[3] Walker A. Knowledge systems: principles and practice. IBM J Res Dev 1986, January.

[4] Hayes-Roth F. The knowledge-based expert systems: a tutorial. Computer 1984, September.

[5] Khan G, Nowlan S, McDermott J. Strategies for knowledge acquisition. IEEE Trans Pattern Anal Mach Intell 1985, September.

[6] Ballard DH, Brown CM. Computer vision. Englewood Cliffs, NJ: Prentice Hall, Inc; 1982.

[7] Ahamed SV, Lawrence VB. An image processing system for eye statistics from eye diagram. Paper 4−22 in Proceedings of the International Association for the Pattern Recognition Workshop on Computer Vision. Nihon, Tokyo, Japan (October 12−14); 1988.

[8] Ahamed SV. Intelligent Internet knowledge networks: processing of wisdom and concepts. Hoboken, NJ: Wiley, John & Sons, Inc; 2007.

[9] Barnes J, editor. The complete works of Aristotle, vols. 1 and 2. Princeton, NJ: Princeton University Press; 1995.

[10] Shortcliffe E. MYCIN: computer-based medical consultations. New York: American Elsevier; 1976. See also, Buchanan BG, Shortcliffe EH. Rule-based expert system: the Mycin experiment at Stanford Heuristic Programming Project. Boston: Addison Wesley; 1984.

[11] Kintsch W, et al. About NeoMycin, methods and tactics in cognitive science. Mahwah, NJ: Lawrence Erlbaum; 1984, also see, Luger GF. Artificial intelligence, structures and strategies for complex problem solving. Boston: Addison Wesley; 2005.

[12] SAP (UK) Limited. SAP solutions, and eLearning. Feltham, Middlesex, England; 2002.

[13] Ahamed SV. Social Impact of Intelligent Telecommunication Networks. In Proceedings of Pacific Telecommunications Conference. Honolulu 1987;(January 18−22):407−414.

FROM PRIMAL THINKING TO POTENTIAL COMPUTING

12

CHAPTER SUMMARY

In this chapter, we investigate the generic representations of human functions and machine operations in the same framework for execution on the current computers, i.e., how a machine would execute human functions and conversely how a human would execute machine functions. This approach would facilitate the encoding of the (common) human functions as precisely as the machine language instructions for a computer. Conversely, the approach would facilitate the transfer of the lower-level intelligence of a human being into the adaptation of the HW, SW, and FW modules of an intelligent machine.

Though not entirely feasible, the approach digs deep inroads in how human intelligent-machines can be and conversely, how robotic mundane-human beings can be. The later situation occurs in prisoner-, slave-, military-camps. The methodology is practical since machines have already started to imitate human behavior and some of the human tasks are routine and programmable into the robots. The challenge lies when some of the higher levels functions (such as conceptualize, hypothesize, optimize, generalize, axiomize, etc.) of human beings need to be programed into intelligent machines, even though middle level functions (such as summarize, generalize, rationalize, etc.) can be forced by appropriate knowledge-ware (KW) into intelligent machines. These middle level functions are encoded into the KW by searching for embedded knowledge centric objects (KCOs) in human beings, cultures, societies, and other contributing objects. Related and pertinent knowledge is found by exploring the local and the Internet knowledge bases (KBs) and selecting the attributes of these objects and or related objects. The Chapter outlines and elaborates the proposed approach.

12.1 INTRODUCTION

The instinct for survival appears encoded in the genes of species. Having survived long before any civilization, the species have been "intelligent" enough to adapt and "wise" enough to communicate the skills to the future generations in order to survive. Intelligence and wisdom both have preceded civilizations, cultures, and sciences. The laws of nature appear enshrined in the order and structure inherent in wisdom. The rules of physics in the evolving universe have existed long before any scientists discovered them. The unknowns in the sciences now are perhaps the markers for wisdom for the future. Wisdom lodged in the neuron and nurtured by the intellect in the adaptation is the basis of the machines that generate artificial knowledge. Artificial knowledge is relatively new but essential since the machines that generate it can compute and process data and information at incredible rates and win over any human efforts to manually construct knowledge.

Evolution of Knowledge Science. DOI: http://dx.doi.org/10.1016/B978-0-12-805478-9.00012-1

In the early civilizations, wisdom was earned and respected. An innate feel of selfless love was inculcated by the leaders who were dedicated to the welfare of the society. Students and disciples admired the status of the preachers and mentors. Many noble principles were handed down from a few wise but unlettered leaders of the American Indian tribes and of the Indian shrines. Logic and deduction were rated secondary to the axioms and words. The use of numbers and scales was for convenience rather than that for inference and calculations. Formal education was unimportant when truth and welfare were stated by the respected ones.

Following the age of enlightenment and concern for humankind the age-old icons of transcended knowledge, the arithmetic of worldly belongings started to gain importance in human minds. The symbolic operations on inanimate objects in life were inadvertently shifted onto the saints and scholars of the past. Soon after, dramatic changes occurred in the attitudes of people. The melody of the morning birds was replaced by the chuckle of the chickens to lay the eggs, the contemplation in the hours of morning turned into the getup, go, and search for the beacon for breakfast.

The wisdom of ages was cast aside for multiplication of worldly belongings. Quality of knowledge contained in words was subjugated to the numbers of cattle heads in the yard. A symbolic divide had erupted between and the supremacy of knowledge and the rule of guns. Understanding in the word of wisdom was sold for the braying of the horses one owned. The basis of capitalism was ingrained in the young mind of the generations to come. Mathematics of wealth, algebra of misplaced symbols and geometry of mansions ruptured an age of acceptance of values and willingness to be brave. Logic to manipulate symbols, and equations had cut a big hole in the love and respect for the basis of perception of human betterment. Scientific discipline had entered the social realm. Logic forced on passion caused a rift and conflict between the respected ones and the greedy ones.

The rest of this chapter is organized around two rather elaborate tables. Table 12.1A covers the period between early times to the period of the pragmatists and the existentialist. Table 12.1B covers the explosion of the social changes that has occurred in the last few decades due classic inventions. Typical of such major catalysts' for economic, social and intellectual changes are the Transistor, the Stored Program Controlled computer systems, the vast expanse of the communication networks by the electronic switching systems (the ESS), Microwave Technologies, Fiber Optic Technology in Global Networks, and finally the Integrated Internet with PDA wireless interconnectivity.

The two Tables IA and IB, cover two cross-linked movements in time: the social change and the intellectual achievements. Time runs along the columns and social change flows along the rows of these two tables: Table IA first and Table IB, second. Time and social/intellectual changes though not accurately mapped into the cells of these tables, indicate the correlation between integrated social change and the combined intellectual caliber of the societies to make the catalytic economic and social changes. The delay between the intellectual atmosphere and the associated social effects are generally detectable in reading the next row in the Tables IA and IB.

12.2 **FROM ATTAINMENT TO PHILOSOPHY**

The symbolic divide between the saints and the learned scholars virtually separated those who valued the symbols of respect, love and social benevolence from those who respected the symbols

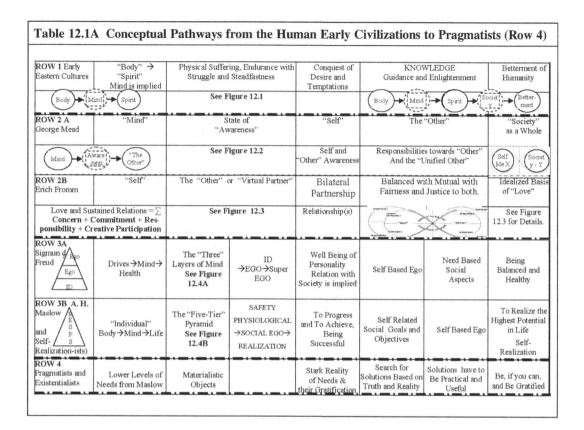

Table 12.1A Conceptual Pathways from the Human Early Civilizations to Pragmatists (Row 4)

ROW 1 Early Eastern Cultures	"Body" → "Spirit" Mind is implied	Physical Suffering, Endurance with Struggle and Steadfastness		Conquest of Desire and Temptations	KNOWLEDGE Guidance and Enlightenment		Betterment of Humanity
	Body → Mind → Spirit	See Figure 12.1			Body → Mind → Spirit → Society → Betterment		
ROW 2 A George Mead	"Mind"	State of "Awareness"		"Self"	The "Other"		"Society" as a Whole
	Mind → Awareness → "The Other"	See Figure 12.2		Self and "Other" Awareness	Responsibilities towards "Other" And the "Unified Other"		Self Me X Society - Y
ROW 2B Erich Fromm	"Self"	The "Other" or "Virtual Partner"		Bilateral Partnership	Balanced with Mutual with Fairness and Justice to both.		Idealized Basis of "Love"
Love and Sustained Relations = ∑ Concern + Commitment + Responsibility + Creative Participation		See Figure 12.3		Relationship(s)			See Figure 12.3 for Details.
ROW 3A Sigmund Freud Ego ID	Drives→Mind→ Health	The "Three" Layers of Mind See Figure 12.4A	ID →EGO→Super EGO	Well Being of Personality Relation with Society is implied	Self Based Ego	Need Based Social Aspects	Being Balanced and Healthy
ROW 3B A. H. Maslow and Self-Realization-ists)	"Individual" Body→Mind→Life	The "Five-Tier" Pyramid See Figure 12.4B	SAFETY PHYSIOLOGICAL →SOCIAL EGO→ REALIZATION	To Progress and To Achieve, Being Successful	Self Related Social Goals and Objectives	Self Based Ego	To Realize the Highest Potential in Life Self-Realization
ROW 4 Pragmatists and Existentialists	Lower Levels of Needs from Maslow	Materialistic Objects		Stark Reality of Needs & their Gratification	Search for Solutions Based on Truth and Reality	Solutions have to Be Practical and Useful	Be, if you can, and Be Gratified

in sciences and mathematics to enhance the values of educated and successful elite in the society. In this chapter, the two icons of thoughtful scholars are Mead and Fromm to influence the refraction of social values from the saints of the past, to the benefactors of the middle years.

12.2.1 THE CONTRIBUTIONS IN THE PAST (ROW 1 OF TABLE IA)

Over the many civilizations, knowledge has been learned and accumulated asset. It has been filtered and enhanced to suit the changing times. It has resided in the minds of the learned scholars as impressions, visions and sayings. Some of early contributions, being less than accurately documented, the knowledge has faded away as mystic writing on the pages of time. The older Greek, Chinese, Indian, Egyptian, South American, and many more civilizations retained order and sustainability by their inculcated statement of native wisdom. Documented has been scarce and many times plundered. Little of the early knowledge, inspiration, and wisdom have lived through the many centuries. Numerous saints and philosophers have left a long lasting impact of the social evolution of the cultures of their times.

Table 12.1B Conceptual Pathways from the Pragmatists to Knowledge Workers

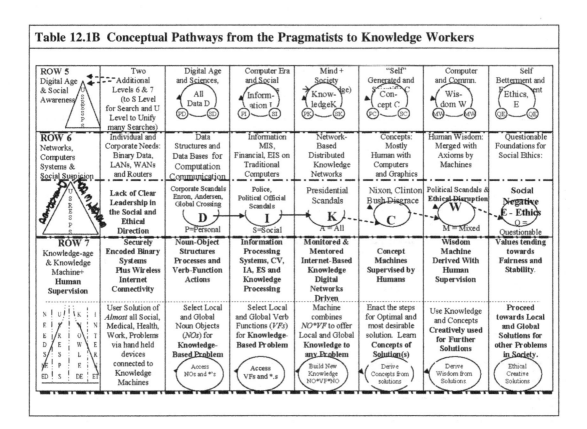

ROW 5 Digital Age & Social Awareness	Two Additional Levels 6 & 7 (to S Level for Search and U Level to Unify many Searches)	Digital Age and Sciences, All Data D (PD) (SD)	Computer Era and Social Inform-ation I (FI) (SI)	Mind + Society Know-ledgeK (PK) (SK)	"Self" Generated and Con-cept C (PC) (SC)	Computer and Commn. Wis-dom W (MW) (MW)	Self Bettement and Ethics, E (QE) (QE)
ROW 6 Networks, Computers Systems & Social Suspicion	Individual and Corporate Needs: Binary Data, LANs, WANs and Routers	Data Structures and Data Bases for Computation Communication	Information MIS, Financial, EIS on Traditional Computers	Network-Based Distributed Knowledge Networks	Concepts: Mostly Human with Computers and Graphics	Human Wisdom: Merged with Axioms by Machines	Questionable Foundations for Social Ethics:
	Lack of Clear Leadership in the Social and Ethical Direction	Corporate Scandals Enron, Andersen, Global Crossing **D** P=Personal	Police, Political Official Scandals **I** S=Social	Presidential Scandals **K** A=All	Nixon, Clinton Bush Disgrace **C**	Political Scandals & Ethical Disruption **W** M=Mixed	Social Negative E - Ethics Q = Questionable
ROW 7 Knowledge-age & Knowledge Machine+ Human Supervision	Securely Encoded Binary Systems Plus Wireless Internet Connectivity	Noun-Object Structures Processes and Verb-Function Actions	Information Processing Systems, CV, IA, ES and Knowledge Processing	Monitored & Mentored Internet-Based Knowledge Digital Networks Driven	Concept Machines Supervised by Humans	Wisdom Machine Derived With Human Supervision	Values tending towards Fairness and Stability.
N U K **F I** **E R O T** **D E W E** **S S L R** **ME P E** **ED S DE ET**	User Solution of *Almost* all Social, Medical, Health, Work, Problems via hand held devices connected to Knowledge Machines	Select Local and Global Noun Objects (*NOs*) for Knowledge-Based Problem Access NOs and *'s	Select Local and Global Verb Functions (*VFs*) for Knowledge-Based Problem Access VFs and *.s	Machine combines *NO*VF* to offer Local and Global Knowledge to any Problem Build New Knowledge NO*VF*NO	Enact the steps for Optimal and most desirable solution. Learn Concepts of Solution(s) Derive Concepts from solutions	Use Knowledge and Concepts Creatively used for Further Solutions Derive Wisdom from Solutions	Proceed towards Local and Global Solutions for other Problems in Society. Ethical Creative Solutions

The major steps leading to social betterment of early societies can be simplified and summarized as a five-step process shown in Figure 12.1A. The role of human mind as an intelligent agent was subdued by jumping ahead into the existence of the spirit or the soul. In the early Indian cultures, the needs of the body and the desires of the mind were unduly suppressed to elevate the spirit. The conquest of temptations was considered as a step toward attainment. The role of the unseen spirit of humans was considered higher than the gratification of bodily needs or the aspiration for materialistic comforts.

Without greatly dwelling in the past, the efforts of the prior civilization are represented as a seven node process depicted in Figure 12.1B, that held the knowledge attained by groups of monks, scholars, and priests as the central focus for influencing the society. Human contact and social bondage were held in great esteem whereby the priest-disciple relation influenced the slow emergence of new knowledge[1] for the new generations. Such relationship lasted entire lifetime.

---

[1]As Jalaluddin Rumi (a thirteenth century Persian mystic poet) in his shrine in Konya, Turkey had once said "Birdsong brings relief to my longing, I'm just as ecstatic as they are, but with nothing to say! Please universal soul, practice some song or something through me!", and is still evident in the melody of his spinning Dervishes'. Also enshrined is the devotion in the words of Rabindranath Tagore's Gitanjali.

FIGURE 12.1A

Simplified depiction of the events leading to social betterment in the past.

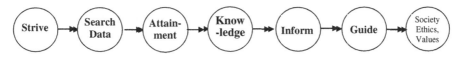

FIGURE 12.1B

Enhanced sequence of events in the mature centers of learning, meditation, and reflection of the past.

It became dedicated to perfecting the practice of attainment and the maturity of knowledge into well-founded sciences. Medicine and mathematics were studied with the same zeal and devotion as the love and search for attainment. The society progressed surely, slowly, and methodically deeply rooted in reality and truth as the pragmatist pursued it (see Row 4 of Table IA) many centuries later.

12.2.2 THE CONTRIBUTIONS OF G. H. MEAD (ROW 2A)

George Herbert Mead [1], has placed the psychological foundations of self, me, and I, into real context of daily lives by being pragmatic about the social relations. His study of nature, history, science, and anthropology gave Mead a unique perspective as a social scientist and a philosopher in his own right. Mead implanted the notion of communication in the social processes that make social events and influence human lives. During the formation of personality, Mead has stressed that the evolution of the mind and self is a by-product of social events and interactions. Processes and philosophy are uniquely blended to make Mead a pragmatist and a social scientist, both in one. Science had pierced itself into philosophy in the writings of Mead.

Mead has termed "mind" as attire of the self, and society as attire for the collective aggregation of minds. Also, the self-acts as a distillery of values, actions, and norms of personal conduct. If self is viewed as a large, flexible, and adaptive KB with a look-up table of contents. In his discussion of society, Mead describes this as an aggregation of collective minds with its legal, ethical, logical, and just norms of social behavior. If social relations consist of interacting with a large number of changing and varied groups of people, organizations, and/or even a network or a machine, then various paths of communication must be established with a large number of identifiable relevant files, people, machines, or "objects," and the needed interfaces created.

Mead again has advanced the notion that the rational part of the mind is an active collection of logical and accepted rules to guide human conduct through the mundane aspects of routine life. If the rule-based functions of the mind are viewed as elaborate, programmable, and predictable processes, then the AI techniques become applicable (including the neural-nets solutions). The object-oriented processor unit

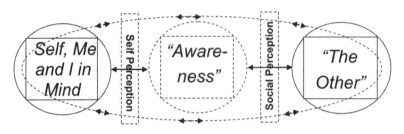

FIGURE 12.2A

Mead's pragmatic perspective of cyclic and continuous processes that shapes the emergence of mind from social events and interactions.

(the aggregation of the hardware, software, and firmware) of most computers serves as an individualized personal processor unit of an intelligent social or knowledge network. It matches the "objects" of the current problem the knowledge machine is tackling with what it already knows about the "objects" of that particular problem, or similar problems, or any other related information to solve the current problem.

Whereas Mead used mind to link self and society, it appears that we have the entire psyche and mind to link the two (self and society). In this case, the mind handles the knowledge aspects, and the psyche handles the social and social network aspects. It is clear that the mind itself has both the memory and the network processing parts. Intricate switching also becomes essential to make sure that the signals are not crossed (Fig. 12.2A).

12.2.3 THE CONTRIBUTIONS OF ERICH FROMM (ROW 2B)

Erich Fromm has presented the most stunning basis for the lasting and sustainable relation between human beings. Based on four compelling obligations toward each other, Fromm firmly places reality and human limitations in his findings. His approach is rational, practical, and entirely balanced for both sides of any dyadic relation. Both parties have limitations and capacities; have finite patience and tolerance, have expectations and abilities to reciprocate the protocols for each other. His teaching are entirely meaningful in any relation when the two parties understand the limitations, capacities, extent of patience, tolerance, expectations, and abilities of each other and make the rational and necessary adjustments in dealing with their interactions Figure 12.2B.

In his rather short but incisive book *The Art of Loving* [2, 21A], Fromm has isolated four aspects for enduring (what he calls) love. Founded in the willful actions of human beings Fromm enlists commitment, responsibility, concern, and betterment, and finally participation in the creative lives of each other. Understanding these together with the limitations, capacities, extent of patience, tolerance, expectations, and abilities of each other, makes the two personalities fuse into one, makes the two minds into a whole, and the two lives into one melody. Fromm's presentation of his concepts is depicted in Figure 12.3.

Social scientists were aware of the negative side of human personality. The classic thinker Erich Fromm has presented modes of behaviorism [3, 4] quite the opposite of his own findings in his earlier classic *The Art of Loving* [2]. Fromm (a psychoanalyst by profession) classifies these unhealthy personalities as receptive (takers), exploitive, hoarding, and marketing characters and

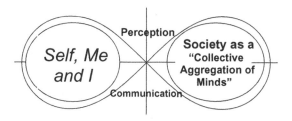

FIGURE 12.2B

Mead's pragmatic perspective of cyclic and continuous processes that can be deployed in the current knowledge banks that store an image of the "Collective Aggregation of Minds".

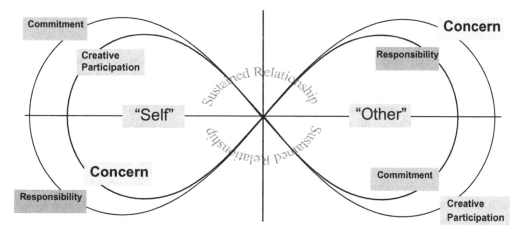

FIGURE 12.3

Picture of a dynamic, pulsating, and living relation between Self and the Other. The diagram shifts, turns, rotates, and moves in and out. Three planes in a hyper-dimensional spaces of the two minds are the XY (physical and location), YZ (time and age), and ZX (family and social) planes to makeup the reality of two lives accounting for their differences, tastes, health, personalities, etc. The four key willful actions are concern, responsibility, commitment, and participation are taken from Fromm's presentation of The Art of Loving.

they become takers from the society without contributing to the welfare of the society. More recently, Noam Chomsky offers a similar insight in his book, *Distorted Morality* [5].

12.2.4 THE CONTRIBUTIONS OF SIGMUND FREUD (ROW 3A)

Though Sigmund Freud [6] perspective has been from the field of clinical medicine, the behavioral model proposed by him is based on the notion that the mind has three basic domains (id, ego, and superego shown in Fig. 12.4A). The Freudian model is based on functions the mind performs rather than the neural pathways in the brain. From a clinical consideration, Freud proposed his convincing hypothesis that a harmonious blending of these three domains leads to normal

FIGURE 12.4A

Basic three-level segmentation of the human mind proposed by Sigmund Freud to explain behavioral disorders.

social and interpersonal behavior and a conflictive overlap of these domains leads to abnormal behavior. Even though modern psychiatry has come a long way from this rudimentary notion of Freud [6], the basic premise of unresolved conflict leading to abnormal behavior still remains valid. Over the centuries, the conflict leading to severe modalities of behavior existed in humans, tribes, cultures, societies, and even nations. Modern organizations and nations display need-driven collective behavior and succumb to the effects of conflicts in resource allocation, egos, and even in opinions.

Other contributors such as Carl Jung [7] and Eric Berne [8] have made significant contributions to human behavior and its influence on the social migration. The mainstream western thinking has favored the Freudian concepts for the functioning of the human mind. In reference to individual behavior and its manifestation, both are subject to genetic tendencies and environmental conditions, conditions that provide or block the means to satisfy the needs. In reference to collective behavior and attitude, both are also subject to the history and resources to satisfy the collective needs. Extremes of behavior, according to Freud, can still be linked to severity of internal needs and the (internal and external) constraints blocking the satisfaction of such needs.

Simplistic as it may be, Freud's model offers a means to understand the rationale behind individual behavior. It is also applicable when dealing with issues at a collective level. The three-level model (Fig. 12.4A) of Freud is a mere framework for dealing with more complex sets of issues of the workings of the mind, even though no one has really "seen" the three domains of the mind. In reality, individual behavior is finally embedded in the neural inter-actions (action and reaction) in the brain. To this extent, Freud remains the founder of a simple model for understanding human behavior. In a similar vein, Tesla remains the founder of rotating electromagnetic field based on a model of three (red, yellow, and blue) phase currents even though no one has really "seen" the rotating electromagnetic field.

It is yet to be seen if the ego in Freud's hypotheses of the mind (Fig. 12.4A) serves as a catalyst (Fig. 12.4AB) in altering the energy levels for chemical processes between two reactants R-1 (Superego) and R-2 (Id). As much as the catalyst increases the rate of a reaction in the chemical processes, the ego alters the rate of conflictive roles between Superego and Id in the human mind thus moderating the behavior and the activation energies between the forward reaction between R-1 and R-2 and the reverse reaction between R-2 and R-1.

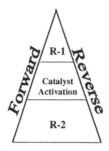

FIGURE 12.4AB

chemical reaction and the activation energies as they are altered by the catalyst that influences the reaction between two reactants R-1 and R-2.

12.2.5 THE CONTRIBUTIONS OF A. H. MASLOW (ROW 3B)

Maslow has discarded the clinical perspective of Freud, the notions behind the reasoning of Jung, and the transactional analysis of Berne. Maslow has taken are a bold new step in tying the needs of healthy human beings to their behavior via the factors that motivate them and society that provides the means to satisfy the needs. In a sense, the relationship between an individual and society (and environment) is implied in Maslow's model but it remains dominant from the individual's point of view. Among the various higher-level models for explaining behavior, Maslow's five-level model is widely accepted in corporate and social settings. It deals with the actions and interactions between highly rational individuals. Maslow studied a cross-section of successful and motivated people and suggested the five-level model (Fig. 12.4B) to deal with human behavior. When the situation deals with microcosmic real-life issues the five-level model is adequate.

However, Maslow's original writings are more profound. Whereas Jung had touched upon an existence and influence of human soul, Maslow did not explicitly incorporate the spiritual dimension in his hierarchy of needs pyramid. Instead, he proposed that human beings have fifteen "B-Values," listed as truth, goodness, beauty, unity and transcendence, aliveness, uniqueness, perfection, justice, simplicity, richness, effortlessness, playfulness, self-sufficiency, and meaningfulness. In essence, Maslow was proposing that a human being is a more complex entity. In an obscure way, Maslow was hinting at the "spirit" of a human being. A contextual correlation emerges between the "spirit" that Maslow writes [9] presents and the spirit that Carl Jung has explicitly referred to as the "soul" of a human being [7]. This is a sharp contrast to the work of Watson [10] in 1919 and the work of Skinner [11].

Human values can also be strong motivators, but Maslow did not include them in a motivational cycle or as driving forces to be considered in a scientific vein. In addition to the five level needs, values could also make a difference. The model proposed by Maslow and his "B-values" form a strong foundation to further the model of human behavior. Unfortunately, Maslow's work does not address the possibility of adapting it to the computer environment and evolving platforms for the behavioral intelligence (BI) and instinctive intelligence, even though both are parts of the natural intelligence.

FIGURE 12.4B

Motivations come from human needs. Maslow has proposed a basic five-level motivational model based on human needs. This model is used most often to explain the motivations, aspirations, and organizational behavior of corporate employees and successful human beings.

12.2.6 THE PRAGMATISTS (ROW 4)

Wealth and possessions dominated the thoughts of the new culture. The scientist and mathematician had gained more esteem than the symbolic icons for love and values. For example, Bell and Edison attracted more attention than Marx and Kant. In a sense, love for wealth and success for oneself was considered as a valid goal[2] rather than learning and humility for collective betterment as two objectives. Self-realization (of Maslow) was considered as a higher objective over the social goals for human welfare (of Immanuel Kant).

Mead inculcated pragmatism. His teaching in pragmatism are however, not held in great esteem as the problem solvers during the late eighteenth century leading to the foundation of Science. It embraces the idea that a proposition is true if it is functions satisfactorily. Practicality and use is accepted, theories, notions, and impractical ideas and propositions are rejected. To this extent, Mead had built inroads in Sciences' and their acceptability. This major step forward was embraced by Charles S. Peirce, William James, and John Dewey. Reality and truth were the main foci of being pragmatic. The transcendental nature of truth and the philosophic contemplation were dismissed by being practical about the reality and vice versa. The significance of thought was tied to its value in its usage. Truth was the final test of disciplines and the philosophic consideration dominated the social tendencies for a long time in the twentieth century. Analytical philosophers emerged to make pragmatism as a significant step toward being practical in science and (oddly enough) in philosophy by exploring practicality in the thoughts of philosophers.

---

[2]Maslow [9] has founded his need pyramid based on a cross section of the realization goals (fifth level) of "successful, happy and well adjusted" people in the society. The reference to social welfare from a broader pers.

The challenge posed by the pragmatists to the great thinkers of the early twentieth century is founded on the use, value and the deployment of prior human knowledge and effort. The timelessness of truth, utility, and value of knowledge is pitted against the philosophic meditation of the great early thinkers. A new foundation for useful knowledge was built by the pragmatists that eventually made mere thought as momentary and transitional. From the pragmatists' perspective, the concepts embedded in the prior knowledge needed to be useful, true and more permanent than a poetic utterance or a verse.

In a sense and in a new way of thinking, the pragmatists of the turn of the century were pleading for action rather than contemplation. They were indeed pleading[3] with Mathew Arnold to write the constitution of the United Nations to avoid WW-I rather than write the poem "Dover Beach"; to build a cathedral to house the derelict rather than preach theology; to find a cure rather than complain, etc. To this extent, the evolution of the digital age has been directed toward solving the issues of the current and emerging generations rather than making the Startreck episodes, even though they may have some entertainment value. Reality and truth is emphasized heavily in the modern society (see Rows 5 and 7 in Table IB), even though the opportunism of a few had exploited the information and IT boom of the late twentieth century during the Nixon, Clinton, and Bush years (see Row 6 in Table IB).

12.3 THE INCEPTION OF THE DIGITAL AGE (ROWS 5 TO 7 OF TABLE IB)

From a contemporary perspective, the new generation of computer and network users is beyond the models Freud and Maslow. Knowledge age and Internet offer a great variety of activities and pursuits to follow. Time becomes a stringent resource. This fact coupled with a self-centered attitude forces the device users to select to be most pragmatic about gratification of the most dominant deficit need. Some network users have retained the process philosophy that blends contemplative thinking with pragmatic reasoning. The modern users blend their natural intelligence with the potential of the Internet, the processing of knowledge and the data handling capacity of the backbone networks.

Recent strides in information, knowledge, and computer technologies essential to nudge the society forward are evident in almost all network-based information and knowledge systems. Electronic governments, medical systems, educational institutions, research centers, etc., deploy some level of information technology, knowledge processing, computational facilities, and network communication. Integration of global IP based addressing capability of Internet and application oriented processing of data that is the forte of computer systems is already available from the worldwide KBs. TCP/IP has provided a harmonious blend of OSI functionality in the existing computer and communication facilities. Distance learning, remote hospitals, robotic arms, and sensing systems provide realistic applications for the seamless integration of computers and communication. Knowledge workers are pragmatic and down to earth (and to the last bit of effort) in being optimal and efficient in the deployment of their limited resources. Knowledge and its processing facilitate mathematically accurate, socially benevolent, and economically viable optimal decisions for localized and global environments.

---

[3]The beauty of thought was surrendered to the utility of objects, the verses of joy were cast asunder! See Footnote 1.

The algorithms, specialized hardware, and user-friendly interface embedded in corporate decision support systems, remote medical services, safety nets, emergency response systems provide. The combined switching/routing technologies and data communication that and the feature of most traditional digital networks and precise computing of massive mainframe computers are already being deployed in global facilities. Space-centers, Tsunami-centers, newsrooms, financial markets all bear the benefits of the current integrated digital environment.

Computer and network technologies bring reality and urgency to knowledge and information. These technologies, deeply embedded in modern society, process, communicate, and disseminate information effectively. Network users scan and sense the knowledge environment deeply and thoroughly. This aspect emphasizes the combined roles of computer and networking technologies with scanner, sensor, and processing technologies. These technologies offer human beings the capacity to look beyond the obvious and derive information to mirco-manage the environment and are able to strategize and win. Such an immense power to accurately manage and control the environment was unavailable to prior generations. A new sense of responsibility becomes eminent.

The architectures of machines that process data and information have evolved dramatically over the last few decades. Whereas information is stored in databases; knowledge is retained in minds making human beings knowledgeable and wiser. Coupled with intellect and creativity, concepts form a bridge between the domain of knowledge and the state of wisdom. This role of the users now implies that if the current state of technology is projected into the future, then knowledge, concept, and wisdom processing are realistic as data and information processing was a few decades back. The grasp and derivation of the concept behind progress of the past is essential to progress in the future; both are as important as the prior data behind the current information.

The role of computers and networks in the current scientific space is too ingrained to be retrieved back to the days of philosophy and endless contemplation.[4]

From pragmatic and implementation considerations, knowledge is the vehicle for social progress. Knowledge machines serve the dual role of creating and modifying the fuel for progress and constructing newer mode of transportation of noun-objects (*NOs*) and verb-functions (*VFs*) in any body of knowledge. New knowledge is created by sensibly primed machines and conversely abused knowledge machines produce garbage and trash. From internal combustion to jet propulsion, from automobiles to spacecraft, new knowledge systems have taken human beings from horse and carriage-age to rocket and missile-age. The changes in knowledge domain during the last few decades now appear irreversible, expect by catastrophic events.

---

[4]Yet, a lurking of the past symphonies lives in the deep emotional subconscious to instill peace in a restless world of machines and jets. The melodies stay awake: sleep cannot forsake them and entertainment cannot drown them. To make room for this restlessness, at least two more levels of needs for the longing mind that cries to contribute to a society of which one is only a part. The search to be a pioneer continues. For the body, modern humans have the id (Freudian), an ego (Freudian), and a set of lower-level needs (physiological and safety—Maslow's need pyramid). For the mind, the modern humans have a set of higher needs (the ego (Freudian), the social (or the Freudian superego), and realization (Maslow's need pyramid)).

Finally, the contemplative modern humans have two levels (search and unification) atop the models of Freud and Maslow that will form the basis of a seven-level personality. This model is complete basis for human behavior and is a model for the machine to impersonate a human. The complete human being with a body, mind (Freud and Maslow) and longing (soul by Jung; see also Crick [12]) is represented in this model. These two outermost levels of personality represented as sixth- and seventh-level needs, let the thoughtful, meditative, and contemplative individual leap into the realm of the unknown and unexplored. The individual explores a little more into the outer reaches of human perceptions, "having gone where no one has gone before" in the perceptual space of the mind.

12.4 DIFFERENCES BETWEEN INFORMATION AND KNOWLEDGE MACHINES

Information machines process existing data and information and derive logical relationships that may already exist. Some versions of intelligent executive information systems (EIS) may have predictive features to alter the parameters of algebraic equations and display the effects. One such example occurs when the size of inventory is changed up and down to calculate the expected profits or losses of retail merchants. Other possible examples also exist by altering the ratios of investment options in financial portfolios.

Knowledge machines process all circumstances and conditions of the problem being studied, solved and/or expected. These machines (try to) probe all the features associated with the problem by investigating or obtaining the answers to seven fundamental questions (Why? Who? What? How? Where? When? and How-long?) about the problem posed to the machines. Further, they gather the information from where the problem originated. A human example is that when a patient visits a doctor who has to find and comprehend the medical history of the patient, the circumstances when a medical condition was discovered, the validity of the medical complain, the contextual relation between the patient history/heredity and the patient condition, etc. As a next step, the knowledge machines probe all the objects and the actions that are embedded in the information presented. The contextual relation between the object, between the verbs, between the objects and the verbs are also investigated and validated for that particular problem (or patient). All the pros and cons of altering the parameters of all the equations leading to the reality are investigated to maximize the utility of the derived utility due to every proposed change(s) of parameters and the cost of resources expended in making the change.

The detailed proximity search of the information, complain and problem is accomplished by the Internet search of already existing KBs. The search is directed and targeted to the KBs that evolve in conditions and circumstance of the current information, problem and complain. The parameters that yielded the information in the first place and the sources of the information and the accuracy of such information are authenticated from other (local and/or global) knowledge banks. All the tools and algorithms of AT are deployed to (almost) perfect the search and solution. Compared to knowledge machines that process knowledge, information machines that process information appear rudimentary.

12.5 THE IMPACT OF DIGITAL DOMAINS ON EXTENDED INFORMATION

The shift into the digital domain for measurement, storage, processing, and computation started almost seven to eight decade earlier and gained momentum as the prices of the ICs dropped drastically over the last three decades. The movement is nonreversible and complete. Almost every phase of any scientific endeavor is now digital based on measurement to barcodes, displays to radio astronomy, etc. Digital processing has followed and overtaken most other applications due to cheap computing and portable devices. Generally, the use of digital technology is impeded at the information level in its raw intelligible level for human beings.

However, in this chapter and in rows 5, 6, and 7 of Table IB, we propose that the use of technology be forwarded into the domain of knowledge, concepts, wisdom, and ethics. These stages are a logical progression of information and serve individuals and society alike. These stages provide a pathway to further human thought to become aware of

a. how the information came about,
b. what is concept that yielded the information,
c. how to redeploy the concept in other situations,
d. how to enhance the concept behind valuable information,
e. the generic wisdom (if any), that is embedded in the information,
f. how to block the abuse of the concept behind worthless and junk information, and
g. finally, how to deploy the wisdom for the benefit of society thus gained in knowledge from information.

The answers to these questions build the "knowledge' about the source of the information and the details about its origin and what else can be learned from the nature and circumstances that yielded the information in the first place.

12.5.1 POSITIVE EVENTS THROUGH THE KNOWLEDGE ERA (ROW 5 TABLE IB)

Over the years of the use of information processing machines, their use has been directed toward the benefit to organizations and societies. In the main, information has embedded *KCOs* within its structure and three observation can be derived in the processing of information. The scientific principles in handling these objects and their economic implications are programed in the machines. From a scientific perspective, the processing of information proceeds systematically from one step to the next based on three basic concepts listed as follows:

a. Information objects have a certain number of (strong or weak, unilateral or bilateral) relationships with their own attributes or with other objects or their attributes. For example, if water is an information object, then the two hydrogen atoms and one oxygen atom constitute one water molecule (H_2O) in a stable state to be classified as a stable information object. When n number of water molecules interacts with n sulfur trioxide (SO_3) molecules, then equal numbers of molecules of sulfuric acid (H_2SO_4) are formed. In this case water and SO_3 molecules form a bilateral relationship. Numerous other examples also exist.
b. Information objects have structures or laws (available from local or global KBs) that hold the internal information objects and/or their attributes in a relational and coherent fashion (e.g., valency of hydrogen = 1 and valency of oxygen = 2). A statistical map of such relationships can be obtained by scanning local or global knowledge banks. An entire collection of information objects acts as a group that can be enhanced, modified, processed, or rearranged to suit different events, circumstances, or applications. Numerous other examples also exist.
c. Any change to structure of information needs an event (however fast or slow it may be, like an explosion as hydrogen combines with oxygen or slow corrosion due to condensation) to alter the flavor, content or the composition of information. Without external deployment, information in machines will remain as such, stagnate and turn useless. In human beings, information degenerates due to memory effect over long enough periods (Fig. 12.5A).

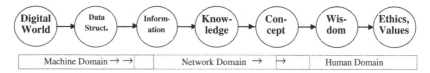

FIGURE 12.5A

Machine, network, and human domains processing functions in the society.

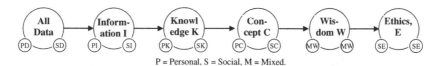

P = Personal, S = Social, M = Mixed.

FIGURE 12.5B

Migration of individuals toward conceptualization, wisdom and being ethical in dealings with society.

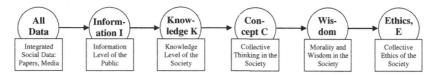

FIGURE 12.5C

Group dynamics of Societies and cultures toward conceptualization of social status, collective wisdom and being responsible and ethical in dealings with other societies, cultures, and contacts.

Information processing is akin to data processing. Objects rather than variables are processed. Numerical and logical processes become more complex as object processes. The objects, their attributes, and their interdependencies are processed in a coherent fashion to follow the reality and the context of a particular application. It becomes evident that the software layers for object processing are elaborate and extensive to handle real-life information objects.

12.5.1.1 Positive personal migration

Digital era has brought about profound effects on the personal and individual lives. Most members of the society have derived great benefits from being gentle and sophisticated. Though unwritten and undocumented the code of ethics for individuals has prompted them from being fragmented as data to being integrated and ethical members of the society. The steps in the positive and beneficial movement are presented in Figure 12.5B.

12.5.1.2 Positive social migration

Digital era has brought about profound effects upon the normal behavior within the collective social entity of a nation, a culture, an organization, etc. Corporate ethics have evolve recently to exemplify the expect mode of behavior of corporate members. Organization code of ethics exist for faculty, medical staff, etc. have existed as long as stable societies have been in vogue (Fig. 12.5C).

12.5.2 NEGATIVE EVENTS IN THE KNOWLEDGE ERA (ROW 6 IN TABLE IB)

Knowledge era can have (and had) negative down side to it. Chapter 4 details the negative aspects of human nature and its influence on the social decay that follows when deception in society is left unchecked. In most cases, opportunists from petty officers to Presidents seek personal gain and selfish interest at the expense of the social norms and public damage.

The effect on the public can be serious and damaging. In the network era, personal insecurities and integrity of the leaders get exposed more quickly due to the information handling capacities of the media and networks. The pragmatists (Section 12.4) have emphasized truth; both aspects of truth and untruth are at exposed on the public media and Internet. Reporters have disclosed scandals and shady characteristics of public officials and thugs. Judicial system generally penalizes the low to middle-level officials and thugs but the top offenders abuse the political position to avoid the scandal making the headlines and though guilty move on without any retribution(s). In Section 4.3 the scenario of abuse of information and knowledge is presented in detail.

In this section, the effect of corporate and political abuse is presented in Row 5 of Table IB since it has/had undermined the public confidence in society and eroded the trust of the public to be honest, sincere to be pursuing truth that was the ideology of the pragmatists. In perspective, the abusive era has led to a renewed push for knowledge machines. This attempt to include knowledge machines is shown in Figure 12.4B. The deployment of appropriately primed KMs in the organization loops prevents serious social and political misconduct and crimes in the same vein as the Internet and network gadgets have led the police to reduce street crime. The social scene during the period of scandals has/had become a setting for the social abusers as gangsters, Mafia, and even politically armed swindlers! Only negative wisdom and counter-ethics survived this era (Fig. 12.6A).

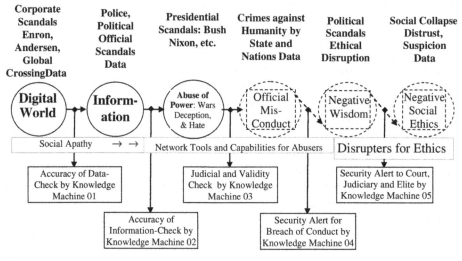

FIGURE 12.6A

Depiction of the negative swing of Ethical and Social standards in Corporate, Public, and Federal organization by the unraveling of scandals and misconduct by offices at five organizational levels. The role of Knowledge Machines at different levels can detect, alert, caution, warn and expose the social cycle that erodes the standards in organizations and nations alike.

12.5.3 OBJECT AND FUNCTION BASIS OF KMS IN THE SOCIETY (ROW 7 TABLE IB)

In the recently evolving knowledge age driven everywhere by network and Internet technologies, the emphasis has been on the commercialism and financial gains for a great many peoples. However, the focus of mind of the scholars and elite toward social betterment and higher ethical goals has not been subdued by the Stock market on Wall Street, nor drowned by in the oil-wells pumping crude oil in Saudi Arabia. There is good reason to believe that temporal gains do not quench the mental (almost divine) thirst for truth as the pragmatists (see Row 4 in Table IA) have brought to light before the dawn of the computer-age. The computer age has brought the logical and numerical processes of the Silicon-age to the knowledge-age, but not overtaken the neural-age of timelessness where the thoughts of the ancient contributors (see Row 1 of Table IA) govern the cause-effects reasoning of the philosophers and scientists (see Rows 2 and 3 of Table IA) (Fig. 12.6B).

In line with the continuity of content that runs through Rows 1 through 4 of Table IA and the cyclic nature of many civilizations, we propose that wisdom and ethics (see Nodes 5 and 6 of Fig. 12.6A), will reemerge through a new generation of (computer-, network-, Internet-based) machines. A sequence of six foreseeable processes is depicted in Figure 12.7. These processes will ride atop the processes in Silicon, Intelligent (local and global backbone) Networks [13] and knowledge-based Intelligent Internets [14].

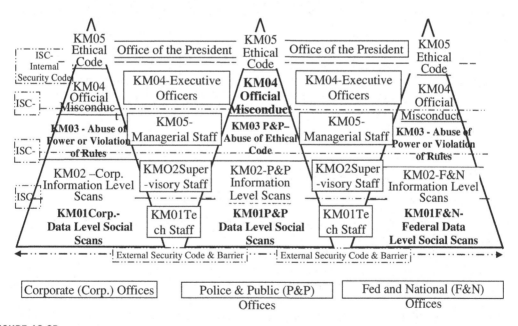

FIGURE 12.6B

The role of Knowledge Machines is expanded to included security barriers and oversight at the five levels from the presidential office to the participation of routine managerial and Technical staff. These machines will detect, alert, caution, warn and expose the activities in the social cycle that violates the standards in organizations and nations alike. The proposed system is alike an intelligent physical and computer security systems in airports and public buildings.

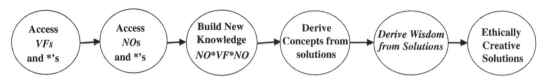

FIGURE 12.7

Representation of the generic new knowledge machines dealing with verbs (VFs), objects (NOs) and their convolutions (*).

The computer opcodes (*OPCs*) and operands (*OPRs*) of typical lower level computers, are replaced be generic *VFs* and *NOs*, respectively. Together, they govern every type of social, intellectual, business, etc., activity. The *OPC* and *OPR* matching in the compilers of traditional computers is replaced by the convolution operator (*). The match is necessary to execute *VFs* on their appropriate *NOs* (i.e., $VF^* \rightarrow NO$) and *NOs* to perform *VFs* (i.e., $NO^* \rightarrow VF$) on self or other *NOs* thus completing a transaction ($NO_1^* \rightarrow VF_{12}^* \rightarrow NO_2$ as an action and $NO_2^* \rightarrow VF_{21}^* \rightarrow NO_1$ as a reaction), thus completing every transaction even if a *VF* is Zero or *no-opc*.

12.6 ACTION [(VF)* UPON *OBJECT (NO)] BASED OPERATIONS

The command structure to the processors is in the binary code that the processor can execute at the most rudimentary level. Each command is carefully assembled and store in the memory or the control memory that is transferred to the processor in the appropriate sequence to perform the function exactly as it was meant to perform. Any higher-level command may deploy the Marcos in the lower level language. Accordingly, we propose that the highest level commands to knowledge processors units (*KPUs*), and above can deploy the lower level, information level processor Macros, routines, code, and even direct commands to the *CPUs*, the *GPUs*, the *APU's*, etc.

12.6.1 GENERIC REPRESENTATION OF VF*NO

The representation generic *VF*NO* processors (HW, SW, FW included) is represented as:

a. Single *VF*: Single *NO* or SVSN (Multiple processes included in *VF* and knowledge centric object(s) included as *NO* or *N*)
b. Single *VF*: Multiple *NOs* or SVMN (Multiple processes included in *VF* and knowledge centric object(s) included as *NO* or *N*)
c. Multiple *VFs*: Single *NO* or MVSN (Multiple processes included in *VFs* and knowledge centric object included as *NO* or *N*)
d. Multiple *VFs* Multiple *NOs* or MVMN (Multiple processes included in *VFs* and knowledge centric object included as *NOs* or *Ns*)
e. There can be numerous smaller processes (*vfs*, *opcs*, or *v's*) in any one *VF* and there can numerous smaller nouns (*nos*, *kcos*, or *n's*) in any one *NO*. The execution can become complex as both *VFs* and *NOs* can become recursive.

12.6.2 PROCESSORS FOR NUMEROUS APPLICATIONS

From a global perspective, processors for the numerous applications (from numerical processing (Level-1) to national programs (Level-7)) can be classified in a hierarchical fashion[5] as follows:

7. Processors for National, Security, Cultural, International, UN, etc.; Applications at the highest level.
6. Processors for Ethics and Values Oriented Machines.
5a. Processors for Concept and Wisdom Oriented Machines.
5b. Processors for Health, Medical Processors Oriented Machines.
4a. Individual Need, Relations Oriented Machines.
4b. Information and Knowledge Oriented Machines.
3. Internet-Based.
3a. Processors for Object Machines and Processors Oriented Machines.
3b. Processors for LANs and Backbone Oriented Machines.
2. Network-based.
2a. Processors for Scientific Application and Research Oriented Machines.
2b. Processors for Corporate and Business Application and Research Oriented Machines.
1. VLSI — Typical CPU, GPU Types: SISD, MIMD, ALUs, LUs, numerical, sensors and digital signal processors are included at the lowest level.

12.6.3 INSTRUCTION FORMATS FOR CPU TYPE OF PROCESSORS (LOWEST LEVEL-1)

These instructions are the conventional SISD, MIMD CPUs, ALUs, LUs, numerical, etc., for CPUs and graphical processor units (GPUs), sensors, and digital signal processing chips, etc.

OPC (SI or MI)	*OPR* or Multiple *OPRs* (Operands to be consistent with *OPC*)
GP Instructions (GPI)	*Graphical* S/M *Objects* (Operands to be consistent with *GPI*)

12.6.4 INSTRUCTION FORMATS FOR SCIENTIFIC/BUSINESS APPLICATIONS (LEVEL 2)

These instructions are the processors for most general purpose computers and PCs

FFT Array Proc., etc.	*OPR* or Multiple *OPRs* (Any type consistent with *OP Code*)
MIS, SAP, EIS, etc.	*OPR* or Multiple *OPRs* (Any type consistent with *Instruction*)

These instructions can include LAN, DB, and DBMS, and TCP/IP commands, INTERNET instructions.

---

[5]This classification is similar to the OSI classification where the Application Layer 7, resides at the top and the Physical Layer 1, is at bottom. The analogy prevails since the silicon layer of the processor arena now performs as the copper/ FO/microwave layer performs in the networks arena.

12.6.5 INSTRUCTION FORMATS FOR INTERNET-BASED AND OBJECT-ORIENTED APPLICATIONS (LEVEL-3)

All Object-Oriented Language (OOL) instructions in the higher-level application programs make up the code for the applications run on object machines. Hardware, software and firmware are generally blended to make the execution quick, efficient and optimal. Consistency between *VFs* and *NOs* is essential and a prerequisite.

VFs——for Objects, DBs, etc.	*NOs——Any Object, Entity, Module declared and consistent with VF Instr.*
Group, Ungroup, Move, etc.	*Files, Graphs, Pictures, Databases, Programs, etc.*
Email, Store, Send, Rcve, etc.	*Objects* or Multiple *Objects* (Any type consistent with *Instruction*)
	Objects or Multiple *Objects* (Any type consistent with *Instruction*)

Examples of VFs:
Email, Store, Send, Receive, Group, Ungroup, Move, Kill, Delete, Private, etc.
Examples of NOs:
Objects, DBs, Graphic Objects, Games, Programs, Addresses, Lists, etc.

12.6.6 INSTRUCTION FORMATS FOR INDIVIDUAL KNOWLEDGE AND INFORMATION TYPE OF PERSONAL AND SOCIAL APPLICATIONS (LEVEL-4)

Rows 2 and 3 of Table IA for the *VFs* and *NOs* for the individual (self)-language programs for PDAs, Androids, hand-held devices, and tablet type of LAN and Internet-based computers. These instructions enter the social domain of people and human functions. The machines will systematically execute these instructions embedded in the *VF* commands. These functions may be extracted from Rows 2 and 3 of Table IA.

VFs (Instr.)	*Appropriate NOs (Me, I, Myself, Patients, Other, Society, etc.)*
Gratify, Help, Remedy, etc.	*Mead Self, Me, and I* (Need Array Operands type consistent with *Instr.*)
Find, Gratify, Best, Adjust, etc.	*Me, Other, Society, etc.* (Needs, Constraints, Laws, Limits, etc. (*))

12.6.7 INSTRUCTION FORMATS FOR CONCEPTS AND WISDOM TYPE OF SOCIETY, WELFARE, MEDICAL, HOSPITAL, AND SOCIAL APPLICATIONS (LEVEL-5)

Rows 4 and 5 of Table IA for the *VFs* and *NOs* for the individual (self and society)-language programs for special purpose PDAs, Andriods, hand-held devices and special devices for closely knit LANs, campus networks and Internet-based computers connected to uncorrupted ethical and elite KBs. Network and KB security is of concern to prevent abusers and officials to tamper with issues that may benefit them at a personal level.

VFs	Appropriate NOs (Others, Family, Me, Other, Culture, Society, etc.)
Extract, Deploy, Modify, etc.	Papers, Books, Manuscripts, Statements, Lectures, Presentations, etc.
MM: Diagnose, Treat, Cure	Patients, Groups, Students, Workers, Needy, Hungry, Society, etc.

Most of the concept manipulation functions form the *VF* instructions for the concept and knowledge machines, and most of the medical and hospital functions form *VF* instructions for the medical and hospital machines (MM). These processors can be in the form of higher-level SW modules but accomplish the tasks for concept manipulations and/or medical functions.

12.6.8 INSTRUCTION FORMATS FOR ETHICS AND VALUES APPLICATIONS (LEVEL-6)

Knowledge machines to protect the Judicial, ethical and national values of countries, organizations and institutions have not been seriously considered by the House or Senate committees, even though the National Security Office has been active to monitor the physical security of most institutions, universities and airports and service structures. Networks can be made extremely secure by security algorithms in the network and computers. Such programs provide ample protection but it will be desirable to monitor the leading, current and lagging *social* indicators as the national agencies watch, monitor economic indicator and implement economic policies. Social and ethical standards can take serious down turns from one generation to the next. Human trafficking, alcohol and drug abuse are some of the current examples.

VFs	NOs
Find, Help, Facilitate, etc.	Elite, Social Groups, Universities, etc. (Operands type Consistent with *Instr.*
Hinder, Block, Ban, etc.	Religious Groups, Charity Organizations, even Criminals, Mafia, and Thugs

Example of Positive VFs:
Find, Help, Facilitate, Adjust, Be Just, Do Not be Deceived, etc.
Example of Negative VFs:
War, Bomb, Destroy, Kill, Loot, Avenge.
Examples of NOs: Elite, Social Groups, Universities, Religious Groups, Charity Organizations, even Criminals, Mafia, and Thugs (Operands type consistent with VFs).

12.6.9 INSTRUCTION FORMATS FOR NATIONAL, CULTURAL, CRISIS, SOCIAL, APPLICATIONS (LEVEL-7)

VFs	(*) NOs matched to the VFs
War, Rectify, Uplift, Heal, etc.	Nations, Cultures, Countries, Societies, etc.
Find, Gratify, Best, Adjust, etc.	Families, Tribes, Organizations, etc. (*)

Example of Positive VFs:

Make Peace, Educate, Help, Grant, Forgive, Understand, etc. Example of Negative VFs: War, Bomb, Destroy, Kill, Loot, Avenge Examples of NOs:

Israel——Palestine; Indian Tribes, Ireland, Hospitals, Communities, Immigrants, Refugees, United Nations, etc.

CONCLUSIONS

In this chapter, the motivational energy for actions is derived from the outstanding needs of humans, corporations, societies, cultures, and nations. Such need can be quite rudimentary as find the next meal or they can be highly sophisticated as understand the universe. But a majority of needs of human beings and other organization occur in a narrow band of daily, social, work related, and ego needs in the current knowledge era. Such needs and their solutions can indeed be taught to modern gadgets, hand-held devices, Internet-connected devices thus relieving the mind to address creative and genuinely authentic problems that face them personally, socially, psychologically, and ethically. The proposed approach in this chapter facilitates the public to address the issues on society and thus establish a positive trend for social betterment and a more balance attitude to dealing with nature, Cultures, and nations. The new structure of KW stands atop of the traditional computer SW and firmware. It deploys the functions of the many decades of the developments in the computer industry.

The use, value, and the deployment of prior human effort based on its ultimate use, value, and the deployment in the future, constitutes the timelessness of innovations and inventions in these modern information and knowledge ages. This cycle thus becomes an endless pursuit but produces milestones in its cyclic rotation. Being pragmatic has become the art of scientific investigation and innovation in the hardware, software, firmware, and the KW to serve the current and future needs of the society. If the ethical and moral standards are the needs of the emerging societies, then the knowledge machines should offer the means to achieve these goals by paving the way with "true" and "valuable" landmarks in the evolution of the knowledge science. In a sense, the pragmatic solution toward (true and valuable) social progress forces the knowledge machines to offer the tools and algorithms to produce timeless (well almost) solutions even though they may be less than perfect. These machine generate new knowledge from old knowledge and only timeless knowledge lingers on as oracles of wisdom, benevolence to the society, intellectual shrines of precision and beauty.

REFERENCES

[1]   Mead GH. Mind, self and society. Chicago: University of Chicago Press; 1934.
[2]   Fromm E. The art of loving. New York: Harper and Rowe; 1954.
[3]   Fromm E. Anatomy of human destruction. Austin, TX: Holt, Rinehart and Winston; 1973, Also see Fromm E. Man for himself, an inquiry into psychology of ethics. New York: Owl Books; 1990.
[4]   From Behaviorism Fromm E. Anatomy of human destruction. Austin, TX: Holt, Rinehart and Winston; 1973.
[5]   Chomsky N. Distorted morality. Production Koch, Studio Wea Corp., DVD released; March 2003.
[6]   Freud S. Basic writings of Freud. New York: Modern Library; 1938.

[7] Jung C. Modern man in search of a soul. London: Routledge & Kenan Paul Ltd.; 1933, and 1961. Also see Crick F. The astonishing hypothesis − the scientific search for the soul. New York: Simon & Schuster, Touchstone Book; 1995.

[8] Berne E. August 27 Games people play: the basic handbook of transactional analysis. Reissue edition New York: Ballantine Books; 1996.

[9] Maslow AH. A theory of human motivation. Psychol Rev 1943;50:370−96, See also, Maslow AH. Motivation and personality. New York: Harper & Row; 1970 and Maslow A. Farther reaches of human nature. New York: Viking Press; 1971.

[10] Watson JB. Psychology as the behaviorist views it. Psychol Rev 1913;20:158−77.

[11] Skinner BF. Beyond freedom and dignity. Hackett Publishing Company; March 2005, Also see Boeree CG. (1998), Skinner BF. Retrieved September 19, 2003 from <http://www.ship.edu/%7Ecgboeree/skinner.html>.

[12] Crick NA. "Pragmatism, Rhetorical Theory", in Oxford Research Encyclopedias, Oxford University Press, at ORE@OUP.com. Also see Crick NA. The search for a purveyor of news: The Dewey/Lippmann debate in an internet age, Critical Studies in Media Communication, 2009; 26: 480−497.

[13] Ahamed SV. Intelligent networks: recent approaches and applications in medical systems. Boston: Elsevier Insight Books; 2014.

[14] Ahamed SV. Intelligent Internet knowledge networks: processing of wisdom and concepts. Hoboken, NJ: Wiley, John & Sons, Incorporated; 2007, Also see White RA. Intelligent networks: perspectives for the future. Paper presented at Zurich switching seminar; March 1992.

ACTION (VF) → (*) ← OBJECT (NO) BASED PROCESSORS AND MACHINES

13

CHAPTER SUMMARY

In this chapter we assert that every aspect of human existence has some form of actions associated with it. Actions originate and terminate at generic knowledge centric objects including life forms. Being innately intelligent and energy efficient, the life forms weigh and consider action to derive the maximal utility from every action. The maximization of the derived marginal utility leads to selective pairing between actions (VFs) and objects (NOs) and also between objects (NOs) and verbs (VFs). If this optimal pairing is generically represented as a convolution or *, then every transaction of every sort will have the form $(VF) \rightarrow (*) \leftarrow (NO)$ where the arrows indicate a time sequence. Any transaction defined as a stimulus followed by a response will have *a symbolic representation* $NO_1 \rightarrow VF^*_{12} \rightarrow NO_2$ and $NO_2 \rightarrow VF^*_{21} \rightarrow NO_1$, where NO_1 initiates an action VF_{12} directed to NO_2, (i.e., $NO_1 \rightarrow VF^*_{12} \rightarrow NO_2$) followed by a response from NO_2 to NO_1 (i.e., $NO_2 \rightarrow VF^*_{21} \rightarrow NO_1$). Numerous transactions lead to an event and numerous events lead to a relation as R_{12} between NO_1 and NO_2, and bilaterally R_{21} between NO_2 and NO_1. All relations are not symmetrical and R_{12} may not have the same profile *as* R_{21}.

In computer environments, the nature and characteristics of all elements of transactions will be analyzed and appropriately matches to the objects. The relationships will be customized and relationships can thus be analyzed and navigated by intelligent machines. Guided activities converge toward being meaningful and significant will be differentiated from being haphazard divergent actions as being trivial and expendable by any user selected scoring algorithms. Interactions are thus made goal directed and profitable based on the user traits and preferences. Social and cultural machines will thus be useful to build good or bad relationship profile between individuals and between cultures. These machines or devices will carry some predictable trends and offer the users corrective measures if the direction of goal is being overwhelmed by insignificant transactions and events. If a lifetime is viewed as a series of significant events, then the knowledge machines will navigate the activities of the objects toward constructing such events and experiences that contribute to the individual, social, and cultural betterment.

13.1 INTRODUCTION

Communication systems, networks and their access have greatly facilitated human transactions (HT). The movement toward social progress (SP) is not always a fore drawn result. The movement

Evolution of Knowledge Science. DOI: http://dx.doi.org/10.1016/B978-0-12-805478-9.00013-3

being slow and long drawn suffers from setbacks and gets retarded, abated and almost reversed to undermine the earlier SP, bringing social decay, anguish, and suffering to large segments of human populations. Typically, acts of deception and aggression by the social icons are leading indicators of hostility and hate between social entities. Unfortunately, even nations fall victim to these savage games. When the time lapse is short for the more gentle side of human nature to overcome the negative forces, then social unrest, wars, looting, illegal seizer of land, and property accrue. Human judgment is drowned, and animal in man comes alive.

However, human instinct has an economic and peace loving trait since the acts of *deception*, *aggression*, and *hostility (dah)* require more energy and are less predictable than acts of *peace*, *respect*, and *justice (prj)* with a sense of patience and constancy. Whereas the former actions of *dah* are based on physical energy, the later actions of *prj* are derived from mental energies with a sense of contemplation, universal order and firmness. If evolution lies dormant in the genetic code, then order, and wisdom are written in the code making them the preferred direction toward *prj* rather than *dah*.

Historically, the *prj* actions have long survived; the *dah* actions have survived but for a while. These two rather opposing forces are never equal and opposite and keep the society constantly shifting from one direction to the other and generally remain dormant and unperceived. Like the seismic forces that shape the counters of the earth, the *prj-dah* (pronounced *prij'dah*) forces shape the society, the culture, the communities, and the nations. The swings can be gentle as a breeze or violent as a storm but a sense of serenity emerges since the physical energies can only prevail for short durations.

In this chapter, we pursue the more prevalent positive force *prj* in the subservient knowledge trail *(B«»D«»I«»K«»C«»W«»E)* in the knowledge society. It feeds into wisdom (W) and ethics (E). SP is the goal but retarded, stopped and even reversed (for a while) by the negative force *dah*. The noteworthy feature of the trail is that each of the seven nodes has resulted from patience and endurance of the human species over the millennia. Computers, networks, and the VLSI era have already taken the society to the knowledge (K) era and it is to be extrapolated if knowledge, concept, and wisdom machines will propel the society in a *prj* era.

13.2 HUMAN TRANSACTIONS AND SOCIAL PROGRESS

Human transactions initiate SP or its decay. The path to SP is depicted as sequence of nine nodes: HT, binary (*B*), data (*D*), information (*I*), knowledge (*K*), concept (*C*), wisdom (*W*), and *SP*. The trail and it nodes are presented in Figure 13.1. This diagram is consistent with the rows 2, 3, and 4 of Tables IA and IB in Chapter 12 and with their corresponding figures.

The seven inside nodes are derived from the typical knowledge trail [1]. In this case, the binary data in the computers and networks (at node B) is processed by lowest level logic circuits, and the nodes D, I, K, C, W, and E represent the levels of human activity at *Data* structures, *Information*, *Knowledge*, *Concept*, *Wisdom* and *Ethical* levels. The activities on the left side of the chain are generally more transient and more abundant than those at on the right side requiring more time and contemplation. Social change is the cumulative effect of the forces during finite intervals and the social inertia of the society.

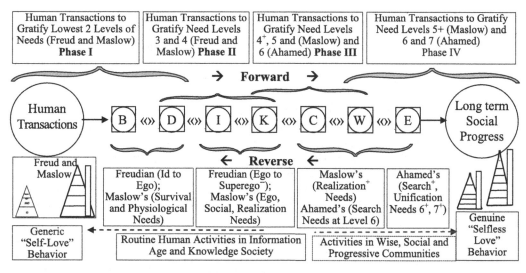

FIGURE 13.1

Snapshot of the human transactions within any activity is mostly directed toward gratifying a particular need that motivates the human being to act. Human needs have definitive hierarchical representations. Freud, Eric Berne, Carl Jung, Maslow, and Ahamed have stratified the layers within the need structures and Erich Fromm has classified the social needs even further. Fromm's writings provide a valid basis for Social-layer Software or SSW for modern computers.

Processing any particular class of entities (e.g., numbers such as binary, floating point, double precision, complex) in the knowledge trail of Figure 13.1 become quite precise at the left side of the figure and becomes progressively fuzzy toward the right side. It becomes evident that the root node is the start of the path from "raw data" or the observation of the real world. It probably terminates at some basic "truth," or a universal concept, such as the law of economics, law of marginal utility, law of conservation of mass, and/or energy, relativity, or the principle of uncertainty that gave rise to the raw data observed as reality in the first place. The cycle time for the entire process can be microseconds or eons. In this situation, time is of no essence because data/knowledge banks integrate all the information when it is available.

The migration from data to information involves accumulation, categorizing, classifying, labeling, and synthesizing the raw data. These machine executable processes and/or human activities become the link/edges of the graph. The raw data storage becomes the antecedent (parent) node and deduced information storage becomes the descendant (child) node.

It becomes feasible to generalize the steps and processes in the migration from any node (i) to the next node ($i + 1$). The link between the two nodes needs the programs or the hardware to process the inputs at the ith node. In general, it is not sufficient to be able to process at the ith node inputs; it is also necessary to cumulatively check the consistency of the prior processes (i.e., between node 1 through ($i - 1$) in view of the process at the ith node. Generally, this backward compatibility of processes is a requirement for almost all software revisions. For example, when the updated version of any software is released, the new version is made compatible with rules and files processed by earlier versions of the same or similar software.

In a sense, the progression of knowledge hinges on the adherence to the laws that have been used to generate prior (information or) knowledge. In certain special cases (such as the correction of Maxwell's equation because of Einstein's theory of relativity, or inclusion of Heisenberg's principle of uncertainty in the measurement of physical parameters, or quantum mechanics integration into wave propagation), the prior laws are modified rather than being rejected.

Machines and networks have been deployed to facilitate the routine HT. The progression toward *SP* has been evident over the last few decades. The cycles of from *HT* → *SP* and then from *SP* → *HT* is an underlying theme of all cultures. The forward chain (*B*«»*D*«»*I*«»*K*«»*W*«»*C*«»*E*) represents the conversion of routine HT and activities to binary information *(B)*, data structures *(D)*, Information *(I)*, Knowledge *(K)* derived from the information, concepts *(C)* from knowledge, wisdom *(W)* derived from concepts, Ethic *(E)* based on wisdom and finally sustained *SP* from ethics that prevail in the society.

The details of roles of knowledge, concepts, wisdom, and ethics in the knowledge machine age are presented in Figure 13.2 and the upward flow of human activities at each of the seven layers occurs because of the innate nature of all species based on the maximization of the utility derived from every aspect of effort incurred. Human *dah* can and do interrupt the forward chain and indeed retard the progress toward *SP*. In the knowledge era, computers and network have accelerated the movement in both the progress and then the regress of social movements by the rapid process in the silicon chips and the extreme speeds of data flow in the fiber/wireless networks.

These factors hasten the movements up and down the seven-layer pyramid in Figure 13.2 thus causing more stress and anxiety accelerating the downward trend with *dah* tendencies; while the same factors also hasten the upward trend to be wise and cautious. The frequency of human tendencies in the two opposite sides (the wisdom side and the brutal side) is increased. These effects cause more tensions and unrest within the subcultures. The role of computers and machines is explored further in the following sections.

13.3 INSTRUCTIONS AND PROCESSORS FOR HUMANISTIC FUNCTIONS

Object processing becomes essential for most human and humanistic functions since objects and the verbs maintain a continuum of time in every activity. Suitably matched object machines can emulate human functions closely. Typical processors and their machines are presented in the following sections.

13.3.1 OPC-OPR BASED TRADITIONAL COMPUTER SYSTEMS

The Operation Code—Operand basis of classifying the CPU functionality in the von Neumann design of the IAS design of the 1948 computer has led the four basic architectures of the CPU designs to execute the machine language instructions. The first (a) SISD design has one single operation encoded as opc that is executed on a single piece of operand data or the opr. The second

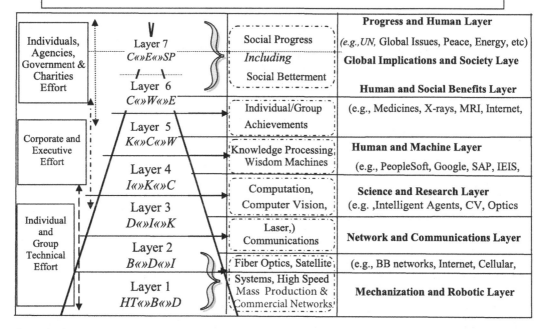

FIGURE 13.2

Deployment of the modern machines and networks to facilitate the movement from routine human transactions HT to social progress (SP). The (B«»D«»I«»K«»W«»C«»E) chain represents the underlying processes behind routine HT to binary information (B), data structures (D), Information (I), Knowledge (K) derived from the information, concepts (C) derived from knowledge, wisdom (W) derived from concepts, Ethics (E) based on wisdom and finally sustained SP from ethics.

(b) SIMD design has one single operation that is executed on one string of operand(s) data or the opr(s). The third (c) MISD design has multiple operations that are executed on one single data, and the fourth (d) MIMD design has or the multiple operations, strings of multiple data.

13.3.2 OPC-OPR BASED OBJECTS ORIENTED OPU SYSTEMS

This mode of classification can be extended to Object Processors that process object rather than binary, logical, arithmetic, or complex data. In processing objects, a single instruction is generally inadequate to complete an object function, calling for an entire process (a programed sequence of machine language instructions) rather than a single instruction. Accordingly, the symbolic classification of the object processor units (OPUs) would be *SPSO* for a single process, single object processor. In the same vein, the following classifications are for single-process, multiple-objects for

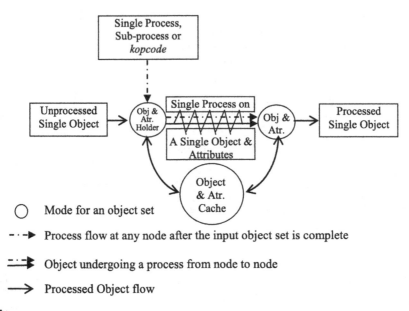

FIGURE 13.3A

A simplified representation of a SPSO Processor that operates on a single object and its attributes. When placed in the 1948 IAS machine, the object processor will works a simple von Neumann object processor.

SPMO processors, multiple-object processes, single-object for *MPSO* processors, and *MPMO* for multiple-processes, multiple-objects processors.

Further, object processing is usually done with knowledge processing and any body of knowledge holds numerous knowledge-centric-objects. Hence to present the object processing environment in conjunction with knowledge processing and in theirs appropriate perspectives, we present two Figure 13.3A and B for *SPSO*.

13.3.2.1 SPSO *processors and machines*

Single process single object processors are akin to the SISD processors for traditional CPU's. When the object is immune to processing, the OPU hardware get simplified to the traditional CPU hardware with an instruction register (IR) to hold the operation code, data register (DR), memory address register (MAR), program counter (PC) and a set of A, B, and C registers. The CPU functions according to the fetch, decode, execute cycle (FDE) in the simplest case.

The *SPSO* processor architecture in object machines becomes more elaborate than an MIMD CPU architecture since the *SPSO* processor accommodates the entire entropy of the object that is under process. The entropy can have a series of other dependent objects, their relationships with the main object, its attributes, and dependent object attributes. The format of the objects and attribute can be alphanumeric (descriptive) rather than symbolic. Primary and secondary objects and their attributes can be local and predefined in the simplest cases, or they can be Internet-based and fetched from WWW knowledge banks. The execution of a single *kopc* can influence the entropy of the single object via the secondary objects and attributes. In essence, numerous caches are

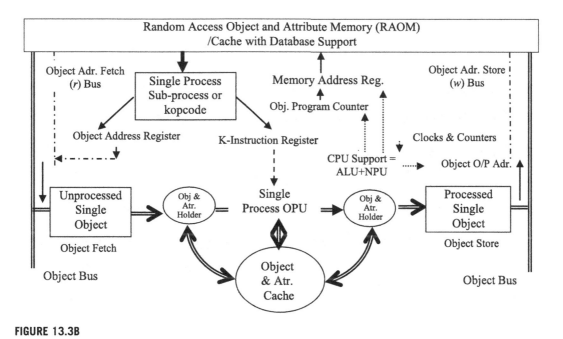

FIGURE 13.3B

Simplified representation of a SPSO object machine. The configuration of a single processor OPU is presented in Section 13.3.

necessary to track the full effect of the single *kopc* process on the entire entropy of the single object in the *SPSO* processor. The configuration of this type of object processor in an object machine is presented in Figure 13.3B.

It can be seen that the machine configurations for other types of architectures, i.e., single process multiple object (*SPMO*), multiple process single object (*MPSO*), multiple process multiple object *MPMO*, and pipeline object processors can be derived by variations similar to those for the *SPSO* systems.

An additional configuration of the *MPMO* architecture is shown in Figure 13.4A. The program bus feeds the segments of object programs to the program caches and the systems operate as numerous independent object processors under the control of an independent operating system.

The architecture of the *MPMO* processor is generally accommodated within the architecture knowledge machines. Local and global programs can both be executed by permitting universal access to program, knowledge, and technology bases. The role of the operation system becomes crucial in coordinating the numerous (1 through n) programs to be accomplished on (1 through l) objects and each program can have any number of associated tasks.

From a design consideration, the optimal *KPU* design would depend on the sophistication of the technology being deployed in the actual *KPU* hardware. Such an approach has been effectively used in traditional CPU designs ranging from MISD, MIMD to the numerous microprogrammable architectures [2]. Very large number of multiple process instructions is possible.

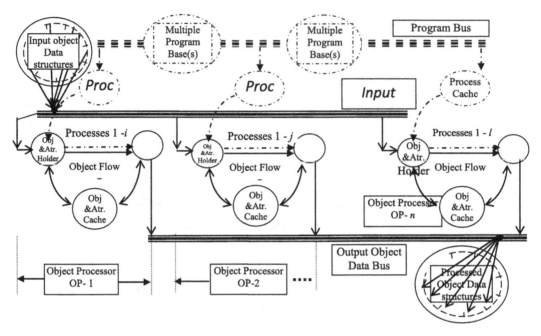

FIGURE 13.4A

Multiple process, multiple objects, (MPMO) architecture. Multiple programs are executed upon multiple objects in multiple processors at the same time. This architecture is akin to the traditional multiprocessor computer systems with the exception that the multiple attribute processing can also take place with each of the multiple object processors (OPs). Such application of the MPMO hardware exists if a search firm seeks multiple executives from multiple databases of applicants based on numerous attributes or requirements.

The conventional indirect addressing (available in most assembly language instruction set), via the base sector does not offer enough flexibility. Double, triple-level nested addressing via the active memory locations is likely to offer the latitude to access secondary objects, their attributes, the attributes of attributes, etc. It is to be appreciated that nested address capability in the knowledge machine can provide quick access to the objects and attributes in the cache memory of the *KPU*'s. Further, the operation of the knowledge programs can be prevented from turning chaotic by robust addressing algorithms. In fact, such addressing capability offers the basis for the development of knowledge processing theory as being distinct from complexity theory [3].

For example, if the *KPU* command turns specific such as "Hard liquors maybe offered to intoxicated American Indians in order to deprive them of the capacity to be judicious about the sale of their lands to the British Army officials who have enjoyed the hospitality of the American Indians." When this specific information/knowledge is interpreted by a human being, implies very specific and highly directed instructions. The identification of the noun objects (intoxicated American Indians) and verb (offered, under force, coercion, sale, etc.), with adverbial modifications (by the British Army officials, for the purpose of "deprive them of the capacity to be judicious about the sale of their lands") needs at least three additional selective filtering to meet the

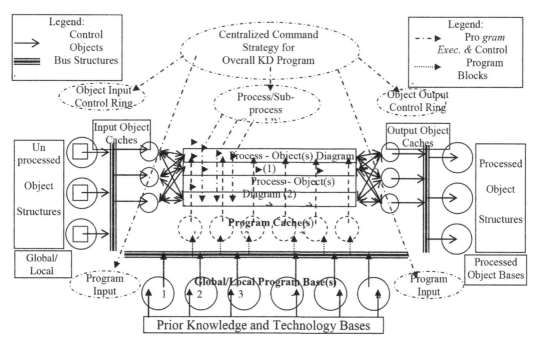

FIGURE 13.4B

Process hierarchy of multiple objects in the MPMO configuration from left to right. The local and Internet access is also shown in this machine configuration. Caches and processes are shared and the operating system allocates the sources for complex knowledge programs to pass through the machine. The configuration of the machine shown will be similar to that of a MIMD series object machines.

constraints in the statement. The attributes of attributes is implied in already intoxicated, deprivation of the capacity, and judgment of the sale of their lands.

13.3.2.2 MPMO *processors and machines*

The configuration of a *MPMO* object processor is shown in Figure 13.4B. This dual object bus structure holds numerous single object processors between the input object bus and the output object bus.

In a general sense, the machine is capable of tracking attributes of attributes to any depth from (0 to i) and explore (n_{i+1}) attributes of (n_i) attributes of any object (multiple primary objects, dependent secondary objects, attributes of objects, attributes of attributes of all objects, etc.)

Figure 13.4A Multiple process, multiple objects, (*MPMO*) architecture. Multiple programs are executed upon multiple objects in multiple processors at the same time. This architecture is akin to the traditional multiprocessor computer systems with the exception that the multiple attribute processing can also take place with each of the multiple object processors (OPs). Such application of the *MPMO* hardware exists if a search firm seeks multiple executives from multiple databases of applicants based on numerous attributes or requirements.

13.4 ARCHITECTURAL CONFIGURATIONS OF ADVANCED PROCESSORS

In this section we present a hierarchy of architectures of processors for the emerging computer systems. From the conventional CPU designs in the four generic SISD, SIMD, MISD, and MIMD at the lowest level to Social Processors at the highest level. The lower level CPU designs have been in use since the days of von Neumann and deployed for pipeline and multiprocessor machines extensively. At the next stage of integration of numerical processors exist Array Processors, Matrix Multipliers, Fast Fourier Transform processors, etc.). The processors deploy the lower levels of the logic and arithmetic (integral and decimal, floating point) processors.

At the intermediate level, the object processors have been in vogue. The processor designs can be implemented in hardware, firmware, and/or software. The essential functions of every type of object and attribute processing must be accomplished in all the design variations. At the higher level, reside the knowledge, medical, concept, and wisdom processors. These newer processors should perform all the conceivable and the necessary manipulations in the knowledge, medical, and social domains. Much as array processors deploy the routine CPU functions, the higher level processors deploy the object processor functions.

The flexibility of processor designs has offered the design of the processors to be tightly matched for their particular applications. Numerous special purpose processors have been in use for speech, audio, movie applications, and especially for computer games. The lowest ranking processors are at level seven and almost any processor can be built from this level. There at least seven conceivable processor architectures for seven major classifications of computer applications in

1. National, Public Offices, Social, Cultural, and International Relations; Studies and Refinement,
2. Ethics and Values; Searches and Refinements
3a. Wisdom and Concept; Searches and Refinements and
3b. Health, Medical Applications,
4a. Individual Need, Individual Relations computers Applications,
4b. Information and Knowledge Based Applications,
5. Internet-Based Applications:
   5a. Object Machines and Applications,
   5b. LANs and Backbone,
6. Network-based:
   6a. Scientific Application,
   6b. Corporate and Business, and
7. VLSI-CPU and GPU Type for SISD to MIMD, Array Processing, Logic, and Numerical Processing for integer, floating point and exponential, double precision numbers.

In this section we present the architectures for four processors for (i) knowledge processing, (ii) medical processing, (iii) concept processing, and (iv) wisdom processing. Processors for other applications can be derived from the configuration presented.

13.4.1 THE KNOWLEDGE PROCESSOR UNIT AND SYSTEM

These architectures of the *KPU* and the knowledge machine systems are based on the universal cyclic mode of operations of all processors and there can be as few as seven distinct steps in

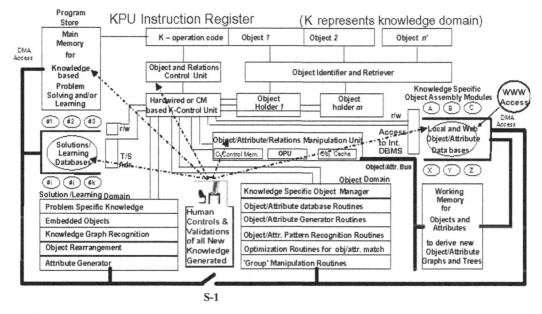

FIGURE 13.5

Switch S-1, Open for Execution Mode for Knowledge Domain Problem Solving; Closed for Learning Mode. The Learning programs "process" the existing solutions and are able to extract Objects, Groups, Relationships, KOPcodes, Group Operators, Modules, Strategies, Optimization Methodologies from existing solutions, and store them in Object and corresponding databases. The architecture permits the KPU to catalog a new object in relation to existing objects and generate/modify existing pointers to and from new objects.

this cycle: (1) read the program register to get the address of the instruction to be executed, (2) the fetch of an executable instruction from the memory, (3) load the operation code in the IR, (4) load or bring the data from the memory and bring the operand(s) in the data register(s), (5) execute the operation code and generate the output of that particular instruction and (6) store the result at the preassigned location (7) increment the program register to fetch the next instruction.

A single processor knowledge processing unit embedded in simple processing system is shown in Figure 13.5. The control memory CM contains the micro-coded expansion of macro *KOPcodes*. Like most computer systems the CM can be replaced for different application environments such as for education and universities, or weather and climatic centers, etc. The organization of object and IRs and caches is presented for a knowledge processor capable of handling each knowledge binary level instruction. With customized VLSI chips and disk controller units the knowledge processing systems will resemble the current Internet-based PCs. Chip based terabyte memory units will further reduce the size of personalized KPS. The distinctive feature will be that a hand held KPS will execute knowledge-based functions like answering the basic bondage (why, who, etc.) that is generic to all knowledge centric objects or KCOs.

13.4.2 **THE MEDICAL PROCESSOR UNIT**

Figure 13.6 depicts the schematic of a medical processor unit (MPU) derived from the designs of an OPU presented in Section 13.5.1 and the *KPU* presented in Figure 13.5. Patients and their attributes are treated in unison and as one combined element of knowledge. Patient records are dynamic and reflect the most recent state of health and the attributes are updated with a history of changes. History of treatment and procedure are treated similarly. New procedures are configured from known procedures on similar patient but with slightly different attributes. The procedures are mapped against the attributes to ascertain the optimality and efficacy of treatments and procedures. The basic laws of medical sciences are not violated during administration of treatments and procedures.

Administering *n* sub-procedures on a patient with *m* (maximum) attributes generates an $n \times m$ matrix. The common, conflicting and overlapping attributes are thus reconfigured to establish primary and secondary medical safety rules in the practice of medicine. Most of the features for automated learning procedure from the *KPU* shown in Figure 13.5 are included for the medical

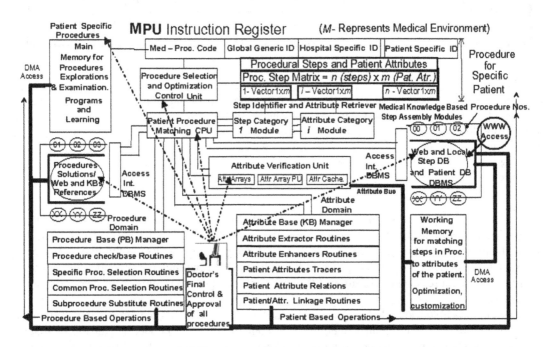

DMA = direct memory access, DBMS = data, procedure, patient and/or attribute base(s) and their associated management system(s), KB = knowledge base(s).

FIGURE 13.6

Configuration of a medical processor unit (MPU). Objects, attributes, and their special features for the medical environment are extracted from existing practices and procedures are extracted and stored for AI- based learning in the machine. DMA = direct memory access, DBMS = data, procedure, patient, and/or attribute base(s) and their associated management system(s), KB = knowledge base(s).

systems to activate AI procedures and suggest improvised procedures to the medical teams. Patients and their attributes are treated in unison and as one synergy. Patient records are dynamic and reflect the most recent state of health and the attributes are updated with a history of changes.

Procedures are configured from known procedures on similar patient but with slightly different attributes. The procedures are mapped against the attributes to ascertain the optimality and efficacy of treatments and procedures. The basic laws of medical sciences are not violated during administration of treatments and procedures. Administering n sub-procedures on a patient with m (maximum) attributes generates an $n \times m$ matrix. The common, conflicting and overlapping attributes are thus reconfigured to establish primary and secondary medical safety rules in the practice of medicine. MPUs have not yet specifically built for medical operation codes (*mopcs*). However, it is possible and viable that such processor chips can be tailored and geared to medical functions. In fact, the current processor chips have tremendous amount of flexibility to be converted to MPUs. A variety of such generic functions can be readily identified.

Generic *mopcs* are abundant. A common *mopc* for the diagnostic procedures is to instruct the MPU to compare symptoms (i) with all known complaints from WWW patient problems and identify any settle changes in this particular case. Comparison of time-lapse results stored in patient bases such as CAT scans, X-rays, etc., yields inference about the progression or regression of a disorder and infections, cancer, or any other ailment. Certain amount of physician discretion permits the system to personalize any procedures and prescriptions. From the perspectives of computer scientists and VLSI designers, such modular tasks have already been accomplished in other disciplines (such as pattern recognition, signature and face identification, etc.). The ordeal is to unify the individual contributions into one discipline of knowledge science.

13.4.3 THE CONCEPT PROCESSOR UNIT AND CONCEPT MACHINE

Figure 13.7 presents the configuration of a concept machine with a concept processor housed in the architecture. This figure is construed along the same design as the knowledge and medical machines. The major concept-based functions can be classified as verb-functions and the KCOs in the knowledge bases wherefrom the concepts are to be derived are considers as subsets of major objects or the modular KCOs. These types of machines may demand considerable computing power and time to extract one or more generic conceptual platforms, equations, or principles on which the knowledge has been based.

The islands of knowledge are decomposed and mapped in numerous ways as graphs and neural nets of noun objects, verb functions, relationships, attributes, similarities, strengths, weakness, etc. The conditions for stability of these 'island objects' (e.g., the creatures of Galagapus islands) are investigated from the feedback cycles in society and nature and projects into the future be restructuring the social and natural forces. There is an enhanced probability that the new (noun) objects and (knowledge) islands, so derived will have the survival qualities. Positive human inputs synergistic with the foundations of science, economics, and constructive technology can help the positive feedback process. Conversely, the negative human inputs countering the basis of science, violating the laws of economics, and destructive technology will not only cause an overall instability of the system but rip the system apart. There is a constant threat that such concept machine can be abused to propagate negative forces of human nature such as the optimum ways of cruelty [4] and profiteering from war and occupation [5] practiced during the occupation of Iraq.

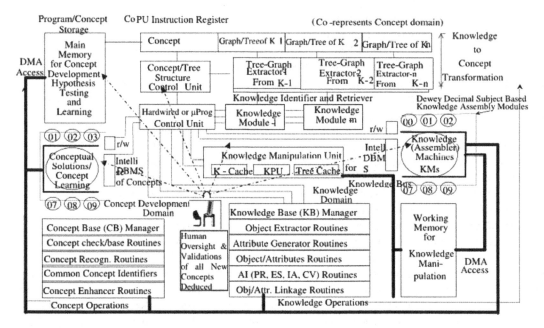

FIGURE 13.7

Hardware configuration of a concept processing machine that evolves concepts from knowledge by disassembling knowledge into the embedded noun objects (NOs) and their relationships with the verb functions (VFs).

13.4.4 THE WISDOM PROCESSOR UNIT AND MACHINE

The hardware configuration of a Wisdom Processor Unit (WmPU), presented in Figure 13.8 and generally embedded in the wisdom machine discussed in Refs. [6, 7]. These machines evolve wisdom from concepts and knowledge by verifying universality, social value, and elegance which are (statistically) likely to have the most knowledge and concept embedded in any statement, equation, theorem, invention, etc. The machine can be commanded to find "best" piece of literature, art, or movie. It is capable of creating a masterpiece, if the requirements of a masterpiece are embedded in the Objective Function (OF).

13.5 SOCIAL PROCESSING

The design of the social processing processors and systems is unique. The users and the social objects are human; carrying an aspect of very personalized needs and expectations. Personalized needs are addressed by accessing customized knowledge banks that store preferences, prior experiences, friends, special contacts, solution preferences, etc. These knowledge banks are linked to the preferred Internet banks for supplemental data/information/suggestions. Expectations are assembled from prior experiences of the successful solutions to problems of a similar nature. The procedure is

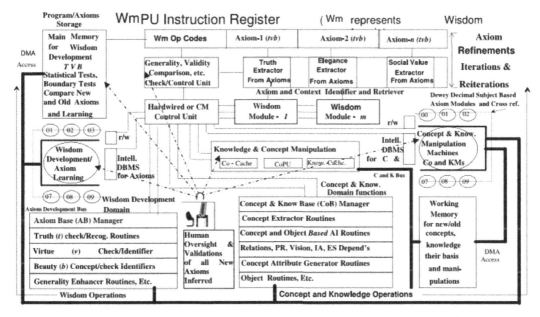

FIGURE 13.8

Configuration of a wisdom processor unit (WmPU) that evolves the social and ethical (if any) from the derived concepts and then refines the axiom(s) to suit social and cultural setting.

repeated for interpersonal relations depending on prior interactions with the same person. The machine undergoes dual customizations and offers an experience that connects the interacting humans in their own unique settings.

13.5.1 BASIC CONCEPTS FOR DESIGN OF SPUs

Social processing involves human beings and their behavioral traits. At the outset, it would be impractical design a social processor unit (*SPU*) quite as simple as a central processor unit (CPU) or as a signal processor unit that is built by customizing the engineering design features. The components each deals with a unique trait of a human being. The design methodology of CPUs, ALUs, sensing devices, and control units offer only a conceptual pathway that need humanization. Customized signal processors in use since 1970s and 1980s offer some basic algorithms and adaptation techniques.

13.5.2 COMMONALITY BETWEEN COMMUNICATIONS AND INTERACTIONS

Communication sciences have evolved dramatically since the decades of Bell, Tesla, and Marconi, when telephony and telegraphy were offered in the public domain. The impact has been profound. Later, certain amount of order and discipline had been introduced that has still remained in most communication systems. Sessions of interaction were coarsely broken down as units of communication lasting for certain duration of time from X1 to X2, and then from X2 to X1, and so on thus

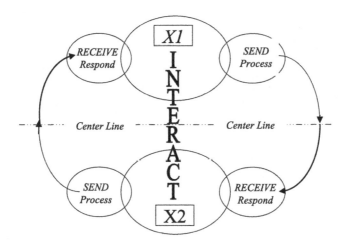

FIGURE 13.9A

Schematic of a simple interactive process between the objects or individuals X1 and X2 that exchange tokens, gestures, speech, etc.

completing a session. Simplex (one-direction) and duplex (both-directions) modes of communication were also introduced. Coding of text to electrical signals was a crucial step in both telephony and telegraphy.

More recently, communication systems deploy packets, cells and bits in variable or fixed lengths. Multiplexing of channels and channel identification is a precise science. Channel routing and switching is ultra-fast. The use of protocols and header blocks is accepted on a world-wide basis. The Internet Protocol (TCP/IP) over the fiber-optic media has made global communication as viable as wireless telegraphy from the days of Marconi only millions of times faster, dependable, secure, and cheaper.

The early models of human interaction were based on an extremely simple model depicted in Figure 13.9A. Sentences, parts of speech were communicated from one party to the next in a intelligible formats for both parties that lead to a dialog and a social need of each/both parties are fulfilled. Intelligibility, transmission media characteristics, and low distortion of information bearing speech signals were assumed. In the more recent environments, where media and cultural properties can be significantly different, the communication or social dialog model is enhanced to accommodate such differences and depicted in Figure 13.9B.

Communication in electrical, microwave, and fiber optic networks has evolved as a precise science over a number of decades. The discipline and methodology offers a pathway into making human communication more scientific and precise. The effects of the individual characteristics, the media properties and finally the effects of social and cultural variation between humans can be more accurately understood and rectified in social interactions. Such social interactions bear a striking analogy with the streamlined functions of devices communicating with each other.

In this section, we present some of the design aspects building SPUs that can emulate social behavior of human beings during interactions but carry the rigor and methodology found in

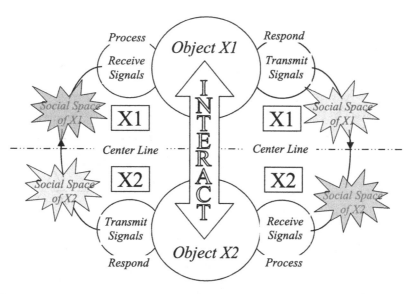

FIGURE 13.9B

Details of a bilateral human interaction process between the individuals X1 and X2 with exchanges of tokens (such as sentences, gestures, speech, words, indications, etc.).

communication systems. Such processors hold the promise of being able to be cast in Silicon as a HW unit in its own right or be assembled as a system of existing CPU, Memory, I/O chips, and programmable switches.

13.5.3 CONCEPTUAL FRAMEWORK FOR SPU DESIGN

Human beings interact based on laws of society however different they may be based on the culture setting. In a totally brutal society, the interaction is duality of force, atrocity, and violence. The behavioral mode in most societies is based on an exchange of social tokens, gestures, and speech. Body language also plays a role. More than those, the laws of social ethics also become implied. For example when an interaction is initiated the two interacting objects equal status and rank (unless it is a continuation of a prior interaction wherein the participant ranks are defined, e.g., boss-employee, parent-child, king-subject, master-slave, etc.).

13.5.3.1 specialized features of spus

When individuals interact, the performance depends on the individual traits. This truism calls for access to the individual knowledge banks on a generic basis. However, the processing of the data based on the traits should be alike.

i. In human transactions (HT, see Figure 13.10), the structure of the participant roles is generally expected to be generic and interchangeable, but the results can be different as the role performance depends on the traits. When two interacting individuals X1 and X2

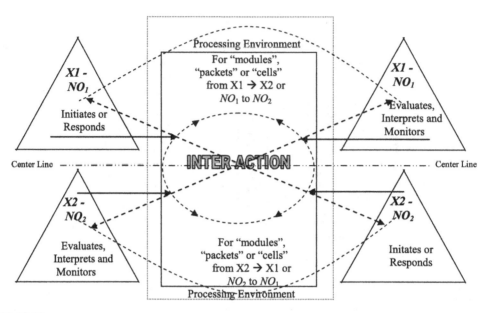

FIGURE 13.10

Depiction of a bilateral interaction process between the individuals X1 and X2 or noun objects NO_1 and NO_2. The initiations and the responses are also symmetrical.

interact, X2 should be able to perform all the tasks X1 can perform and vice versa. In the case of communications systems in hybrid-duplex systems, the transmitter and receiver at either end of the channel will act interchangeably and perform depending on the characteristics of the individual devices. Devices have been standardized and they will have a predefined range of performance that will make these devices efficient and interchangeable. To this extent the well designed SPUs perform in a similar fashion to the communication devices.

ii. Further, a specific time slot is allocated for the "packet," "cell," or "module" of interaction is completed before a responding "packet," "cell," or "module" of interaction from the other party responds. In the case of communications systems with single duplex systems, the transmitter and receiver at either end of the channel will act interchangeably but only in allocated slots of time. They perform depending on the characteristics of the individual devices. Devices have been standardized will have a predefined range of performance that will make these device interchangeable. To this extent the SPU in a similar fashion to the communication devices.

Generally the civilized social human dialog or transaction is in the second or (ii) mode, where each participant waits for the other to complete the act of sending or receiving each "packet," "cell," or "module" within the interactive process. In some less desirable instances (e.g., war, hostilities, occupations brutalities, etc.), the mode of interaction can assume a chaotic format where each participant is simultaneously transmitting and receiving. In some communication (such as satellite and inter-galactic) systems, end-devices can and do transmit simultaneously but they use different communication paths/channels and adequate buffering. Sometimes, repeated transmissions are deployed to correct for random channel errors.

13.5.4 INTERACTIVITY BETWEEN HUMAN BEINGS

A generic model of a bilateral two party human interaction process between two individuals X1 and X2 is shown in Figure 13.9A. The bilateral nature requires symmetry about the horizontal centerline in the figure and either both X1 and X2 can perform the functions of initiating interactions, or of responding to actions (verb-functions) from the other.

In charting human interactivity, the use of AI techniques such as pattern recognition, learning, intelligent agents, robotics, and the use of intelligent agents becomes essential. In addition, the natural intelligence of both or either parties causes an uncertain outcome. The computer solution becomes probabilistic and the final solution gets obscure. The unique characteristics of individuals lead to different behavioral strategies. The refusal of human being to be all rational all the time makes the interactions time and situation dependent. Even so, the customized memory chips of knowledge machines will offer patterns of solution that are "likely" to be correct "most" of the time.

In rational, bilateral and symmetric relations depicted in Figure 13.9B, either one of the two parties can monitor the contents (noun-objects), the direction (i.e., the variations of contents in time domain), and the mode of interaction (conformance with the social and cultural setting of the interaction). The interaction progresses in *incremental steps* as the "modules," "packets," or "cells" from X1 to X2 or from X2 to X1 are exchanged during the interaction. The underlying mental process of evaluating the contents is also implied. Such evaluations bring back the interactions to their focus. They provide a basis of ongoing relationships.

Both X1 and X2 can initiate, or respond to actions (verb-functions) from the other, and to monitor the contents (noun-objects), the direction (i.e., the variations of contents in time domain), and the mode of interaction (conformance with the social and cultural setting of the interaction). The interaction progresses in incremental steps as the "modules", "packets" or "cells" from X1 to X2 or from X2 to X1 are exchanged during the interaction.

Figure 13.10 depicts the ith step in an interaction process between two individuals X1 and X2 with "n" "modules/packets/cells" or gestures are exchanged to complete one interactive session. A series of interactions whereby knowledge is gained by either part leads to a relationship with the other. Each step contributes to an increment of information or knowledge that is cumulated and retained by X1 and X2 about the contents or about each other. This model is not complete since the cumulating processes of each step are not depicted.

In Figure 13.11, a typical step (i) starts with X1 or X2 initiates or responds at location a_i or b_i and follows it around the "cycle" of inter action leading to an exchange of knowledge and a "frontier" of relation.

13.5.5 GESTURES/TOKENS EXCHANGED WITH KBs AND CONVOLUTIONS

Figure 13.12 depicts of an interactive process between two individuals noun objects NO_1 and NO_2 or individuals X1 and X2 where "n" "modules/packets/cells" or gestures exchanged. The dark line

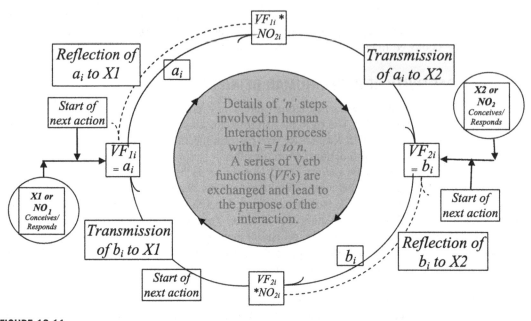

FIGURE 13.11

Depiction of the ith step in an interaction process between two individuals X1 and X2 with "n" "modules/packets/ cells" or gestures are exchanged to complete one interactive session.

contour completes one iteration with X1 and X2 having learned and updated the respective knowledge bases at b_5 and a_5 respectively leading toward the next step of the interaction. Reflection is a process whereby the step in the interactive process causes a side self-reaction in the participant due to its own action. The reflections can be positive or negative thus altering the flavor of the next step in the interactive process. Generally when the parties are progressing toward the same goals, the reflections are positive and reinforcing. The opposite is true in conflictive interactions and every positive or negative step is reflected back in a negative sense, thus tearing apart a relation, or blocking it from blossoming.

13.5.6 THE EFFECTS OF THE SOCIAL MEDIA CHARACTERISTICS

The social media plays its role in enhancing the steps toward convergence or deterring it from reaching a significant conclusion. The media, i.e., culture, society, family, corporate, etc. settings can contribute or deter relationships. News and TV media influences the attitude and impressions of political leaders as much as a university/shrine atmosphere can enhance learning or contemplations. Movies, advertising, and broadcasts can also massively influence public impressions. These intricately interwoven steps are depicted in Figure 13.12. The programing of these sequential/simultaneous steps is derived from the cyclic block diagram.

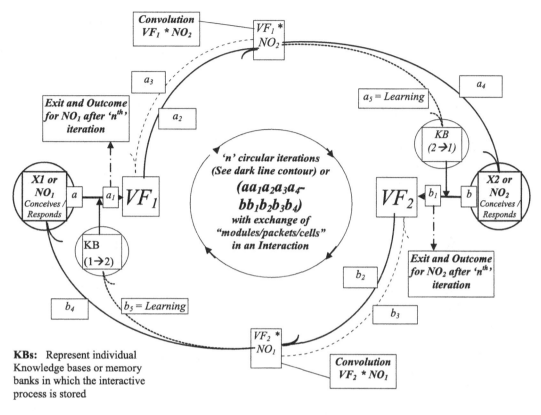

FIGURE 13.12

Details of an interactive process between two KCOs, NO_1 and NO_2 or two individuals X1 and X2 with "n" "modules/packets/cells" or gestures exchanged. The dark line contour completes one iteration with X1 and X2 having learned and updated the respective knowledge bases at b_5 and a_5 respectively leading toward the next step of the interaction. Processes a_3 and b_3 are indicative of the effects or "reflections" of their own actions upon X1 and X2 respectively.

Based on the symbols borrowed from electrical engineering, the forward and reverse media characteristics are symbolized as two matrices $[ABCD]_{12}$ from X1 to X2 and $[ABCD]_{21}$ from X2 to X1. Since knowledge is being exchanged, these matrices should be more precisely stated as $[A\text{-}I]_{12}$ from X1 to X2 and $[A\text{-}I]_{21}$ from X2 to X1. See Ref. [8] for details of the matrix representation.

13.5.7 PROGRAMING FRAMEWORK FOR THE SOCIAL PROCESSES

Figure 13.13 Programing Framework for the social processes shown in Figure 13.12 on a computer or a VLSI chip. A VLSI chip can be designed two symmetric layouts for each of the two

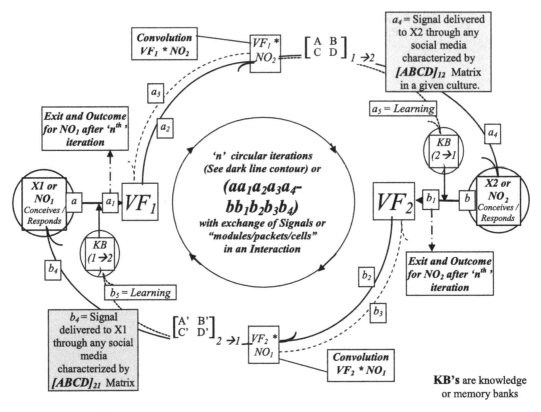

FIGURE 13.13

Details of an interactive process between two individuals X1 and X2 with 'n' Signals or "modules/packets/cells" are exchanged. The effects of the social media characteristics are included in the diagram by two Matrices [ABCD]12 (for signals X1 → X2) and [ABCD]21 (for signals X2 → X1). Media distortions and their effects are reflected by the parameters A, B, C, and D.

interacting objects. The flow of knowledge and the actions are traced by following the dark flow lines. Being symmetric about the center line, the interactive steps for the two objects can also by sharing (or buffering) a single layout alternatively by X1 and then by X2. Intermediate results are stored in disk buffers and treated as inputs and outputs, to and from X2 and X1 and vice versa.

To some extent the programing of social processors is well comprehended in the human activities. When human communicate, they virtually comprehend the media characteristic and psychologically undo the effect of a noisy media by speaking louder, emphasizing the key words, repeating the key sentences, exaggerated body-language, etc. Conversely, when the signal arrives over a distortion embedded social or news media, the emphasis shifts to careful listening of key vowels, asking for repeat of the sentence, etc. When the concept is transfused into the knowledge domain, the social processors need to pre-emphasize the noun-objects, verb-function and their convolutions in any key body of knowledge before transmission of knowledge such that the media distortion is (at least partially) undone by the pre-emphasis. Conversely, when knowledge is received, the social processors should detect the media distortion and undo its effect.

Human learning and adaptation in society learns these methodologies (or algorithms) when the biased news media delivers a particular item, especially during elections and the self-proclaimed victories during wars. The same strategy applies as the public listens to the self-acclaimed praise in advertising. To this extent the distortion and delay in the social media can be overcome by adaptive social processors[1] and transceivers [9,10].

13.5.8 CONFIGURATION OF A MICROPROGRAM-BASED SPU

Figure 13.14 depicts a microprogram-based *SPU* for human support in solving most of the common social problems. The microprograms are imported from a library addresses personalize issues for X1 concerning X2 and vice versa. Detailed social interaction issues, such as greet X2, introduce the context of issues to be resolved, (such as union complaints, pay dispute, sex discrimination, etc.) are handled by embedded software modules. Even though every encounter is different, a large part of the ceremonial exchanges are routine and social intelligence is not necessary. However, when the issues are complex and need intelligence in the cooperative or conflictive situations, the intelligent social processors will embed business, economic, negotiating strategies as an integral part of the transactions.

Such additional help is currently provided by human assistants to senators, negotiators, business partners, etc. Social processors or hand-held devices can outperform mediocre human assistants even though the smart assistants will perform better in special situations. The purpose of these devices is to facilitate the general immature adolescent human beings in tough social situations. These devices translate gestures and read body language of X2 for X1, and vice versa. Programing and personalizing the devices for the social processes depicted in Figure 13.14 can be generally implemented in the computer SW or in a VLSI chip.

Interchangeable VLSI chips will alter the behavioral patterns of humans in proposing detailed steps of how to act, as much as drugs can force altered human behavior by chemically induced neural processes in the brain. The former behavioral patterns are completely reversible, controlled and programmable. To some extent the social processors act as trainers of etiquette and language for the immature and act as Professor Henry Higgins for Eliza Doolittle [11] by being consistent, praiseworthy, and well-liked in reasonable and successful in social circles or rational, economic, fair, and just in business circles.

13.5.9 ARCHITECTURE OF A μ-P BASED SOCIAL COMPUTER

Figure 13.15 depicts a microprogrammable SPU that is the main processing element in the overall architecture of a social computer. A social computer may have numerous such SPU elements depending on the single or multiple capabilities of the machine. Figure 13.16 depicts the architecture

---

[1]In the design of electrical transceivers [10] for digital subscriber loops (especially in the DSL and ADSL) communication networks these techniques are build in adaptive equalizers in the receiver module and adaptive pre-emphasis circuits in the transmit module.

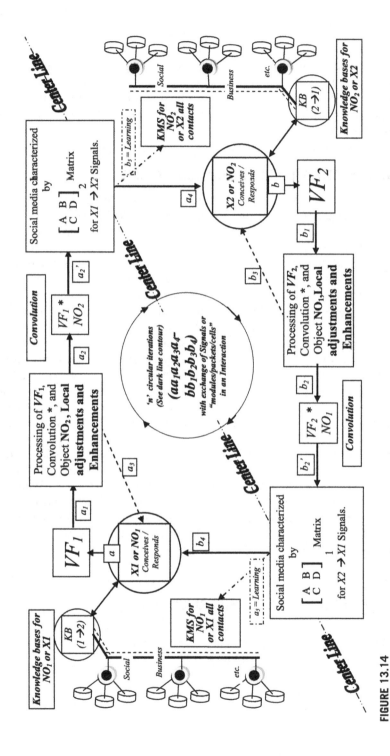

FIGURE 13.14

Programing Framework for the social processes on a computer or a VLSI chip. A VLSI chip can be designed two symmetric layouts for each of the two interacting objects. The flow of knowledge and the actions are traced by following the dark flow lines. Being symmetric about the center line, the interactive steps for the two objects can also by sharing (or buffering) a single layout alternatively by X1 and then by X2. Intermediate results are stored in disk buffers and treated as inputs and outputs, to and from X2 and X1 and vice versa.

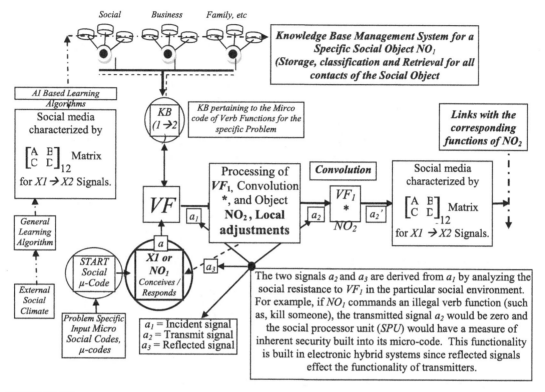

FIGURE 13.15

Microprogram-based SPU for human support in solving Social Problems. The microprograms are imported from a library that addresses and solved microscopic social interaction issues, such as greet X2, introduce the context of issues to be resolved (such as pay dispute), read body language of X2, etc. Programing Framework for the social processes shown in are implemented in the computer SW or in a VLSI chip.

of a μ-Processor based social computer. The operation of this machine is modified from the operation of most of the traditional μ-Processor computers. The *opcodes* and *operands* are replaced by verb functions (*vfs*) and noun-objects (*nos*). The compilation of social and knowledge programs lies in the appropriate choice of the convolutions (*s) between each and every *vf* with its corresponding *no* that the SPU or the KPU can execute. Since the *vfs*, *nos*, and *s are situation and personality dependent, the machine will need the features of interpretation, i.e., to execute every instruction before compiling the next, as in the case of some machines that interpret Basic language programs rather than just execute a compiled basic code.

It is our estimate that these machines though feasible will be about an order of magnitude more complex than the current computers awaiting an opportunity to surface in the knowledge (plus) era on the next generation.

The program execution sequence is shown by numbers 1 through 10. The local sequences $(4' \leftrightarrow 5')$; $(8 \leftrightarrow 8')$; $(9 \leftrightarrow 9' \leftrightarrow 9'')$ are repeated numerous times till the social problem is iteratively and completely solved. Global iterations take place in the sequence 1 through 10.

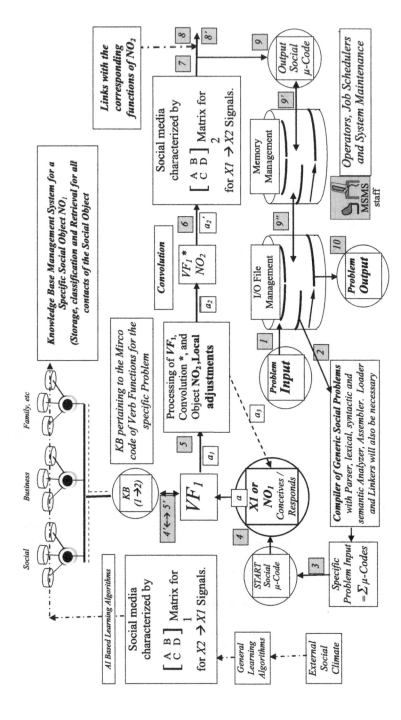

FIGURE 13.16

Architecture of a μ-Processor based Social Computer. The program execution sequence is shown by numbers 1 through 10. The local sequences (4'↔5'); (8↔8'); (9↔9'↔9'') are repeated numerous times till the social problem is iteratively and completely solved. Global iterations take place in the Sequence 1 through 10.

CONCLUSIONS

This chapter is dedicated to knowledge and social machines and their architectures to be generic and significant in their respective domains. Knowledge, concepts, and their hierarchies are subjugated to the service of humankind rather than humans be subjugated the fancies of machine and SW designers. The content penetrates deep into the core of human needs that provide the motivational energies to manipulate the need gratifying objects and their actions. The mode of human adaptation is as primitive as the use of tools in the evolution of civilizations; currently, we use semiconductors devices, fiber optics highways, electronic switching systems, and massive integration to gratify our aspirations. When appropriately primed, the social machine provides creative solutions to harness all forms of emotional, intellectual and psychological energies to move forward toward the betterment of all human beings.

Petty distractions of greed, aggressions, and hostilities are overwritten during the execution of social programs written for and written by well-founded social agencies. This machine impersonates Karl Marx and executes a philosophy that Marx was not able to convince the Western societies to accept. In essence, there is no violence or force in the proposed social machines. It is based entirely on reason and validity that truth is perhaps longer lasting that deception, understanding is more acceptable than arrogance and justice is better than hostility. The modern HW, SW, FW, and knowledge-ware are capable of executing social programs provided the greed, deception, and hostility of self-interest groups and politicians will not brute force social agencies and their wisdom-based social machines. Perhaps the greatest strength lies in the fact that there is more creativity that the minds and machines can explore together. The search and optimizations are faster and through by machines thus presenting human beings to be agile and fluent in creating new solutions.

REFERENCES

[1] Ahamed SV. Intelligent Internet knowledge networks. Hoboken, New Jersey: Wiley Interscience; 2006 [chapter 15].
[2] Clements A. The principles of computer hardware.. Oxford University Press; 2006Also see Stone HS, et al. Introduction to computer architecture. New York: Computer Science Series, Science Research Associates; 1980. See also, Hayes JP. Computer architecture and organization. 2 ed. New York: McGraw Hill; 1988.
[3] Byrne DS. Complexity theory and social sciences. New York: Routledge; 1998.
[4] U.S. Navy, Detention Camp for Prisoners of war without Trial. Also known as GTMO, Naval Station Guantanamo Bay − CNIC, https://en.wikipedia.org/wiki/Guantanamo_Bay_detention_camp.
[5] Angelo Young. Cheney's Hilliburton Made $39.5 Billion on Iraq War; March 20, 2013. readersupported-news.org/.../16561-focus-cheneys-halliburton...iraq-.war. Also see www.theguardian.com › *US News* › Dick Cheney, http://www.theguardian.com/commentisfree/cifamerica/2011/jun/08/dick-cheney-halliburton-supreme-court.
[6] Ahamed SV. The architecture of a wisdom machine. Int J Smart Eng Sys Design 2003;5(4):537−49.
[7] Ahamed SV. Intelligent Internet knowledge networks. Hoboken, New Jersey: Wiley Interscience; 2006 [chapters 10 and 11].

[8] Ahamed SV. Computational framework for knowledge. Hoboken, New Jersey: John Wiley and Sons; 2006 [chapter 5].

[9] Software Industry Report. "Itex Shipped Over 1 Million ADSL Chipsets," Millin Publishing, Inc.; June, 2005.

[10] Ahamed SV. Design and engineering of intelligent communication systems. Boston: Kluwer Academic Publisher; 1997.

[11] George Bernard Shaw, Pygmalion Book and Lyrics, Characters Henry Higgins, Eliza Doolittle see https://en.wikipedia.org/wiki/My_Fair_Lady_%28film%29#Plot.

APHORISM AND TRUISM IN KNOWLEDGE DOMAIN

14

CHAPTER SUMMARY

When knowledge processing becomes abundant as data processing, the truisms of knowledge will become as frequent as the philosophic wisdom of Plato or Aristotle. We begin this chapter by examining the scientific basis for social machines since order; logic and rationality constitute the basis of science. We extend the knowledge domain of sciences into the wisdom domain of philosophers and derive machines that can process knowledge into axioms based on truisms of the social scientists and philosophers. The Internet society is now bonded by wireless and fiber optic media and moves through the air-waves and fiber. The earlier observations and the deductions were based in a slower society bonded in human minds. The current society lives in an age where computer scans are automated at microsecond speeds and transmitted at gigabits per second to vast intellectual space of refined scientific communities. The impact on human lives is significant. It almost seems as if the human mind is losing its grip on the flow of information and knowledge but not on wisdom and hopefully not on ethics. Truisms and long-term observations affirm the foundations of axioms of wisdom and some of the truisms last long. In this chapter, we propose five such truisms derived from observations but tailored to the peta-flop speeds of modern machines and are generic enough to programmable in personal space of the users of PCs and Androids in the Information age.

14.1 INTRODUCTION

Knowledge like wisdom undergoes evolution and refinement. Knowledge follows a strong dictum of order, logic, and rationality in its evolution making the derived knowledge firmer than information. The more enduring aspects of order, logic, and rationality make knowledge more resilient than information from where knowledge is derived. This change is accelerated by technology, especially the glass and plastic (fiber) optic, and the cheap integrated circuit (IC) chip technologies. In fact, older axioms of wisdom become text book knowledge and older truism of knowledge become basic information constantly making room for new knowledge and deeper wisdom. The principle of Archimedes, bouncy, gravity, heat transfer, and Maxwell's and Schrodinger's Laws are largely in public knowledge domain. In the Internet age and cheap devices, the velocity of information has reached fiber optic data rates, and wisdom trickles down to knowledge as knowledge trickles down to information. Knowledge machines become personalized Androids. In fact such machines may be programmed to serve as wisdom machines to generate the personalized aphorisms of knowledge based on personal traits and the availability of Internet knowledge bases all around the globe.

Evolution of Knowledge Science. DOI: http://dx.doi.org/10.1016/B978-0-12-805478-9.00014-5

Social sciences and social machine play a special role in the knowledge-age since they deal with human objects and entities. The principles of hard sciences cannot incisively penetrate the social space, even though they make deep reasonable inroads into the mental space. Mental space rides atop a multiplicity of scientific, biological, psychological, and social space in a stunningly elegant fashion. To enter the mental space through the scientific pathways and then find the trajectories to a multiplicity of social destinations appears as a win-win computational challenge in both spaces.

14.1.1 PEACE, RESPECT, AND JUSTICE (PRJ)

Human instinct has an economic and peaceful trait. Acts of peace, respect, and justice (*prj*) with a sense of patience and constancy generally require less energy and are more predictable that acts of deception, aggression, and hostility (*dah*). The former actions of *prj* are derived from mental energies with a sense of contemplation, universal order, and firmness whereas the later actions of *dah* are based on physical energy. If evolution lies dormant in the genetic code, then order and wisdom are written in the code making them the preferred direction toward *prj* rather than *dah*.

Historically, the *prj* actions have survived longer, though not in their entirety. Imperfections in peace, respect, and/or justice lead to minor or major cycles within the *prj* cycle. Societies and cultures are thus kept alive and an entire shift from *prj* to *dah* can span decades or even centuries. As the *prj* cycles reaches its peak, the frail side of *dah* starts to become evident. Social and cultural revolutions occur. Cultures in South America, India, Europe, and Spain bear witness to this cyclic nature of ebb and flow of the accumulated knowledge within the society. The longevity of the *prj* phase requires the presence of law, order, and wisdom without violence and wars.

14.1.2 DECEPTION, AGGRESSION, AND HOSTILITY (DAH)

The *dah* based actions have survived but for a while. The peak of the *dah* cycle is more transient than the *prj* peaks. When the society is not corrupt, the *dah* peaks are tolerated by fewer members of the society. These two rather opposing forces are never equal and opposite and they keep the society constantly shifting from one direction to the other and generally the movements remain dormant and unperceived. Like the volcanic activity that shapes the surface of the earth, the *prj-dah* forces shape the society, the culture, the communities, and the nations. The shifts can be gentle and as unperceived as the drifts of the continents or violent as Tsunami. The gentle *prj* shifts become more favorable to the *dah* activities since these shifts consume less energy to form and are generally more beneficent to the society and humankind.

14.1.3 THE CONFLICT BETWEEN PRJ AND DAH

The movement toward social progress (SP) is not always positive. Social regression is equally likely if the users of the machine abuse the power and potential. The positive movement being slow and long drawn can face setbacks, get abated, and even reversed to pullback from earlier social progress. Social decay, anguish, and suffering to large segments of human populations who have seen the society move forward. Typically, acts of deception and aggression by the social icons are leading indicators of hostility and hate between social entities. Even nations fall victim to these savage games. When the time lapse is too short for the more gentle side of human nature to overcome the negative forces, social unrest, wars, looting, illegal occupation of land, and property accrue.

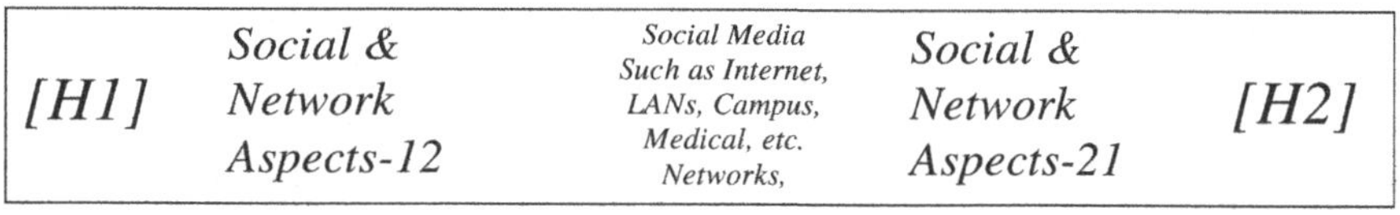

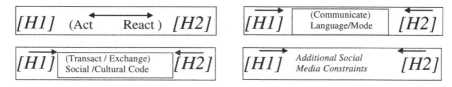

FIGURE 14.1

Formats of communication and exchange of knowledge and information between two humans H1 and H2. The number sequence 12 and 21 indicates the media characteristics for an action the flow of information from H1 to H2 and from H2 to H1, respectively.

FIGURE 14.2

Modes and constraints for communication.

Human judgment is drowned, and animal in man comes alive making them sick and abusive. Almost all life forms, social entities, and countries are fair-game for the games that abuser and arrogant people play. The recent war dialogs are indicative of the sick games nations play at the United Nations.

14.2 FOUNDATIONS OF SOCIAL INTERACTIONS

The formats of social interactions between two human beings H1 and H2 are represented in Figures 14.1 and 14.2.

14.3 RECENT CHANGES IN THE SOCIAL SETTINGS

As much as the contributions of von Neumann [1] and Shockley [2] have influenced our lives in the computer age, the writings of Eric Fromm [3] and Peter Drucker [4] have influenced the emotional and corporate lives in the recent times, but more so in the Internet age. Eric Fromm has reshaped the concepts of love of individuals; Peter Drucker has molded the tasks of organizing complex human functions in simple basic, organized and programmable steps. In blending emotions and their resolutions as a unified social science, the concepts of human Love (from Fromm) are beautifully integrated with the discrete steps of resolving intellectual, personal, and corporate issues (of Drucker) in feasible and manageable and programmable steps of systems approach.

The computer revolution kindled by Neumann and Shockley during the 1950s and then the emotional resolution of abstractions of Love by Fromm and by Drucker in 1950 have both touched upon the lives of (almost) every computer cultured and Internet literate human being. Social issues of human beings appear as highly personalized computer problems where knowledge machines take over the role of traditional computer systems. Number crunching at pico-second rate is substituted by deliberate considerations of "Knowledge Centric Objects" [5] or *KCO*s that have intellectual, emotional, financial, and utilitarian linkages and should be weighed and considered. Whereas the computers provide enormous data and information processing power, the Internet provides enormous knowledge and social power. Coupled to the new evolving knowledge processing systems, the social leverage of human beings is greatly enhanced. Their deployment used with due and deliberation (professed by Formm) and systematic problem-solving (taught by Drucker) of such *KCO*s provides the knowledge workers insights into the two overlapping entities of emotional minds and scientific selves (Neumann and Shockley) in most very modern cultures and societies.

Ancient cultures have harnessed the synergy of mind and self by the wisdom of the leaders. This scenario does not exist in the current economic business-driven societies. However the thought processes and deliberations may be duplicated, at least partially, by layers of "social software" in knowledge machines. In a sense, the social software designers offer the users as much control of handling their personal issues as the designers of word processing programs offer in controlling the features of documents.

14.3.1 FOUR NOTIONS FROM FROMM

The four underlying notions/concepts from the philosophic writings of Fromm can be reduced to

a. Responsibility (R) of one (human/social) entity toward another
b. Concern (C_n) of one (human/social) entity for another
c. Commitment (C_t) of one (human/social) entity toward another and
d. Creative (C_r) and ongoing participation of involved (human/social) entities

At least two human beings are involved in the notion of Fromm's Love, even though these notions are applicable to the welfare of one's own self for better health and for curing one's own sickness(es). In a symbolic format, the emotional involvement can be represented as $\{RC_nC_tC_r\}$ or simply as RC^3.

14.3.2 FIVE NOTIONS FROM DRUCKER

The five concepts in the practice of management from the original writings of Drucker in his classic contribution [4] can be reduced to

1. Planning (P)
2. Organization (O)
3. Staffing (S)
4. Implementation (I), and
5. Control (C)

In a symbolic format, the managerial functions can be represented as *{POSIC}*. In the evolution of the science of management during the two following decades, other notions were supplemented to control in order to bring the managerial tasks of communication (C_m), coordination (C_o), and control (C_l) in the picture. The managerial tasks were more centralized and more unified to manage local, national, and international corporations. Thus, the symbolic format the managerial functions according to the newer schools of management can be represented as $\{POSIC_mC_oC_l$ or $POSIC^3\}$.

14.3.3 **FIVE NOTIONS FROM COMMUNICATIONS**

Communication dominates human interactions and corporate transactions, both extensively. Such communications can be language, gesture, signs, etc. based (as in human interactions) or it can be contract, economic, trust, etc. based (as in corporate transactions). During the second half of last century, communication scientists (especially at Bell Laboratories) undertook to study and master human communication in total earnestness by deploying devices and technology. Most of the refined mathematical tools and techniques were deployed. The growing impact of computing systems during 1950s was incorporated by the design and development of earliest electronic switching systems (ESS #1 in 1965). Once again, the impact of artificial intelligence (AI) was built into communication systems by the deployment of intelligent networks in 1980s. The contributions were that the destination address(es) would select the communication path(s) with embedded algorithmic intelligence in real time.

The five powerful notions that telecommunication engineers and scientists[1] have developed during the evolution of networks are summarized as follows:

i. Digital hierarchies [6] (DHs) from earlier analog system to the following D1 through D4 system of digital hierarchies and then the optical system synchronous digital hierarchies [8] (SDH), frame relay (FR) systems, asynchronous transfer mode [8] (ATM), cell relay system techniques, all abbreviated as digital hierarchy systems or {*DHS*}

ii. Software and embedded intelligence-driven programmable switching systems. Switches and their programmability (ESS) #1 through ESS5 [9], the add drop multiplexors [10] (ADMs), and then the optical switches [11] are all abbreviated as current digital switching systems or {*IDSS*}

iii. Communication channel allocation in circuit switched [12] (CS) and packet switched [13] (PS) systems ranging from older telephone system formats of circuit allocations for calls to more recent and dominant packet switched frame relay abbreviated as {*PSFR*}

iv. Real-time channel allocation, control, and the routing of multiplexed communication channels abbreviated as {*RTCC*} [see References 8–13] {*RTCC*}

v. Integrating all digital communication media [14] (copper, satellite, laser, fiber optic, wireless, etc.). Evolution and integration of (almost) every media to carry multiplicity of communication channel(s) abbreviated as media integration and the dominant cell relay wireless systems for cell phones {*IM&W*}

These contributions are in order of their importance contributing to the forces shaping habits, social networks, systems, and devices and their usage in maintaining and nurturing human bondage. The historical order appears unimportant since the networks and their embedded intelligence are already in place. The introduction of the open system interconnect (OSI) model, although very significant is not listed since the integration of the physical media, implies the need for the six upper layers in the OSI model [14]. The introduction of the signaling protocol for data dandling is also another significant step in the evolution of the Internet TCP/IP protocol. Numerous books [15] document these radical forces that have shaped communication industry, systems, and networks.

In a symbolic format, these concepts from communication sciences can be represented as {*DHS, DSS, PSFR, RTCC, IM&W*}.

---

[1]Very many notable scientists and inventors have contributed to the rapid evolution and growth of the communication era during the last century. We have confined the discussions as they pertain to the currently evolving discipline of social networks.

14.3.4 TRANSFUSION OF CONCEPTS INTO SOCIAL NETWORKS

Transfection[2] though biological in nature finds its way into the social methodology. Human beings like chromosomes have evolved their unique capacity to find distinctive and optimal ways to deal with and adapt to the issues in the gratification of their needs. Dealing with other human beings and society is a requirement to minimize friction and conserve energy. The transfer of concepts, knowledge, and methodology from one discipline to another builds bridges in the solution of intervening issues in maximizing the utility of social interactions.

We propose a *four* prong *(a)* transfusion, *(b)* transmigration, *(c)* transmutation, and *(d)* transformation approach in building the concepts underlying social networks from the *three* most relevant areas:

i. Love from Fromm,
ii. Organization from Drucker, and
iii. Methodology from communication engineers of human networks.

Transfusion and migration of concepts become necessary because the important ideas of the early social scientists (especially Fromm) and the methodology (ies) of management scientists (e.g., Drucker) are seminal and generic. For example, the grouping RC^3 (see section 14.3.1) proposed by Fromm have a sense of universality, virtue, and stability[3] in it as much as the practicality in the functions *POSIC* (see section 14.3.2) of management, documented by Drucker. These raw concepts need transformations as they are transfused. The *POSIC* group starts assume the flavor of $POC_mC_oC_p$ (where C_m denotes communication, C_o denotes coordination, and C_p denotes cooperation). Staffing and implementation (*SI*) are generally one time activity and drop out of the routine managerial functions and they are inapplicable in the social domain. Additional qualities such as Consultation, Cordiality, Control, *Due* Deliberation may be added. Represented in a symbolic fashion, the *POSIC* group becomes POC^3 or even POC^6D^2.[4]

14.3.4.1 From Drucker to Fromm via von Neumann

From a management perspective, Drucker offers a richer array of tools, techniques, and methodologies to practice the verb functions or *VFs* in everyday life, whereas Fromm points to the rich collections of individual assets, the noun objects or *NOs* and their attributes of individual, community, society, culture, nation, etc. Between these two themes of "how" and "what" stays the individual freedom to convolve the two in a meaningful, optimal, and significant fashion. Super functions convolve with super objects as readily as micro-functions with micro-objects. The art (not an algebraic procedure) of convolving is a matter of human rationality and intellect.

In computer science, von Neumann set the course of stored program control. His notion that a set of machine language instructions with predefined operation codes (*opcs*) "operate" upon "operands" (*oprs*) to execute a program repeatedly to the end of the program (a super function) still stands unchallenged. The "operands" are a set of predefined "objects" upon which the *opcs* may be "operated."

---

[2]Transfection is the process of deliberately introducing nucleic acids into cells. The term is often used for non-viral methods in eukaryotic cells.

[3]It is possible to build a counter-universe based on greed, hate and deception that offers a safe heaven where anti-humans can dwell.

[4]C^6 results from merging C_m communication, C_o coordination, and C_p with Consultation, Cordiality, and Control, and D^2 stands for *Due* Deliberation.

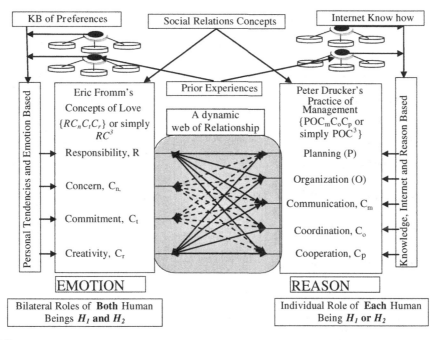

FIGURE 14.3

Representation of human dialog and interaction deploys both emotions and rationality to govern the stability and the direction of the relationship over its life time. Emotional forces from Fromm's Love are intertwined with the practicality of Drucker's management.

In the social sciences, we have close parallelism. Any object (e.g., human beings, societies, communities, nations) may exercise certain functions (*vfs*) legally, ethically, and in a rational form upon other objects (*nos*). Illegality and lack of ethics are both deeply entrenched in societies. Hence, a lack of order and methodology prevails. The social system becomes at least an order of magnitude more complex that the von Neumann's computer systems.

14.3.4.2 Fusion of Drucker's methodology into Fromm's emotions

Social transactions involve at least two parties. One of the more elegant ways to discharging the obligations of love (RC^3; see Fig. 14.3) is to deploy the steps (POC^3 (see Fig. 14.3) or even POC^6D^2) of Management of one's own time and resources. When the duties of love for another are as systematically implied as the obligations in management by both parties in social transactions, the relationships tend to be genuine, and vice versa. Numerous variations of this ideal scenario exist and there is much room for one-sided love, selfish love, exploitation, and degenerate love.

This composition of the two PC^3 and POC^3 approaches is depicted in Figure 14.4. When social relations are initiated, it is to be expected that there are at least two (H_1 and H_2) entities, social objects, basic personalities, etc.; the attributes (see left side of the Figure) are highly variable; preferences differ and the styles of managing the relations (see right side of the Figure) are also different.

When these attributes and preferences are accumulated over time, they can be stored away in an individual knowledge base (KB) for the individual. In the same vein, when the approaches used to

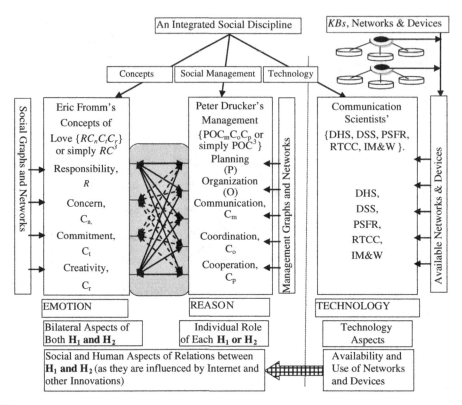

FIGURE 14.4

The impact of changes in networks and communication systems as they influence social relations. Modern conveniences such as cell phones, short messaging systems, Skype, and Video phones bring implicit responses in social entities that communicate to maintain and amend social relations. Users are generally unaware of the technology and its influence on social relations.

resolve problems and social situation are accumulated over time, they can be stored in as KB of prior experiences. There is one fundamental difference, whereas emotions dominate the left side of the diagram, reason, and socially accepted Internet practices and norms dominate the right side of the diagram. The tools and techniques for handling emotional issues with the rationality of scientific problem solving are learned over time but get accumulated in the personal attributes and preferences on the left side of the diagram. The representation in Figure 14.4 thus gets refined and becomes more accurate with use and deployment.

When the interactions (see the middle box of Fig. 14.3) are practiced with reasonable deliberation and in balance between heart and the head (i.e., emotions and reason), relations can be civil and cordial and vice versa. The depiction is applicable when interactions between any two social entities such as groups, corporations, communities, and even nations interact. The long term dynamics of relations is governed by the integrated effected of the energies (emotional forces acting in harmony or in disharmony with reason) designated as the lines between the two boxes. Numerous scenarios of disharmony prevail and in most cases disharmony prevails.

14.3.4.3 The insidious Role of Device and communication technologies

Three important influences of modern technologies become evident. *First,* the storage of personal preferences in handheld devices makes them ready for use at anytime and at any place. Second, the network access via the wireless cell phones and devices make it feasible to reach anyone at anytime and at anyplace. *Third,* the Internet access provides a lookup for the type of POC^3 functions on the RC^3 emotional objects of the human self! Thus, the reaction time is reduced and Internet dialog is as feasible as "social interaction meeting."

The features of this technologically sound and robust dialogs alter the very fabric and flavor of social interactions. Figure 14.4 depicts the impact of the Android, the networks, and the Internet technologies on the emotional and reasonable content of human relations.

In using POC^3 approach to deal with RC^3 factors in human emotions, the use of technology plays an underlying role. Pictures on Androids can show concern; movie of events can soothe misunderstandings; face to face dialog (even if it is over a handheld device) can heal emotionally broken ties, etc. In a sense, technology-assisted social relations can be superior provided the communication media does not distort or inject socially harmful content. There is good reason to guess that good relations can only become better when the purpose and intention follow the writing of Fromm. Conversely, bad relations can deteriorate by abuse of technology. Unexpected disruptions in negotiations can break them. Social balances can be significantly altered by the mother-in-law scenarios or the airing of misplaced remarks of politicians during campaigns.

In the public domain, the media does influence social tastes and choices. The advertising industry thrives on this premise. Unfortunately, the lesser forces in the society resort to misstatements, false ads, and weird misrepresentations. Truth is as easily killed by greed as beauty is prostituted by thugs or as monuments are driven over by tanks. Technically robust media is devoid of such human deficiencies. The nature and types of distortions, delays, and noises have scientific properties that can be compensated or statistically estimated.

14.4 AXIOMS FOR DEALING WITH SOCIAL OBJECTS

The following axioms start out from being routine statements and well-observed truisms. Soon the rigor and discipline of quantification from physical sciences become necessary since social objects follow some extent of measures and comparisons even though they may not be quite accurate in a revised consideration.

The discipline from computer sciences in predefining the nature and characteristics of variables (such as integers, floating point numbers), type of operations (on real, imaginary, and complex numbers, such as *FP-MPY, FP-DIV*, Matrix operations) starts to bear a similarity in dealing with social entities. Social entities do have specific matrix and array characteristics. The interactions tend to resemble matrix/array types of representation.

Next, the structured approaches in software engineering such as compilation including parsing, lexical, syntactic, and semantic analysis of social objects become essential in dealing with nature of specific social entities that initiate and respond to social interactions and situations. For example, the features of parent—child, siblings, and boss—employee relationships may be predefined in a declaration statement to a social interaction application program as easily as declaration of arrays and matrices in scientific programming.

Further, the solution methodology for a specific problem that is definitive in a given environment is the feature of application programming in that particular discipline. Such behavioral strategies are abundant in social settings. For example, in a dating situation, the code of conduct that defines the stimulus-response chain of events can be quite specific and different from the technical dialogue between a boss and employee interaction in a corporate situation. Such programming of conduct or behavior of social entities can be founded in the application programming tools and techniques

Perhaps the most important approach comes from the statistical methods from quantum mechanics since each social entity is unique in its own right but still belongs to a group or sect whose properties have been observed. Only observation of group-behavior tends to offer some clues as to how a particular social entity may behave. Such results, predictions, and expectations in behavior are based on statistical and the outcome of any particular individual can only to be probabilistic.

These axioms deal with the truisms associated with dynamic and *life-like* organisms and are listed as follows:

Axiom 1: Organisms change continually from within and from without.
Axiom 2: Organisms are mutual interdependent; physical laws and/or utility theory governs the balance of interrelationships.
Axiom 3: Change of organizational structure and relations need energy.
Axiom 4: Organic changes are quantum in nature but statistical methods are applicable.
Axiom 5: Changes in organisms are partially mathematical; symbols and equations are applicable.

The Axioms 2, 3, and 5 are elaborated further in Appendices 14A.1, 14A.2, and 14A.3.

14.4.1 AXIOM 1 (TRUISM 1)

Organisms change continually from within and from without. Any organism is devoid of life without any action or associated process(es) within it or with it. Stated alternatively the axiom states that life is a continuum of processes and sub-processes associated for life to continue to exist. Organisms, change, rate of change (a velocity or the first derivative), and force that bring about acceleration (or the change of the change, i.e., the second derivative) are unified. Life and time are indeed unified by the change in it. This truism is based on the observation that any organism or any organization is under one or numerous processes to continue to exist. Organism implies an order or structure to fulfill its lower level needs (to survive and be secure), its mid level needs (to adjust and modify its behavior to accommodate the environmental changes and variations), and its higher level needs (to grow and expand, in spite of social, cultural, and environmental variations).

Most of the physical, social, cultural, and environment processes are conceivable, few are programmable and fewer are computable. When the computational accuracy is increased, events and changes become quantized in nature and the computational generality is lost. Every event and change assumes life forms of their own. For example, each photon in light and electron in electric current is an entity, much like a human in eternity, but influenced by its immediate vicinity and environment. Statistical methods yield probabilistic results and a confidence level. Quantum theories start to enter the picture but when integrated over large populations and large durations, the computational methods sometimes become applicable.

When the structure, boundary, and relationships of the knowledge-centric objects (*KCOs*) are considered as dynamic and lively entities, most noun objects become conceivable and under some process or the other, even though they might be abstract and occupy only mental dimensions and coordinates. The concepts of change, rate of change, and the acceleration of change of such (abstract or mental, real, or imaginary) objects are applicable. The relationships governing force, acceleration, and movement becomes feasible. Equations incorporating mass, inertia, center of gravity (or focus), center of momentum can be conceived for most *KCOs*, few *KCOs* can be programmed, and fewer can be computed accurately enough. Intelligibility become the prime and accuracy becomes secondary. Knowledge is thus made intelligible and the dynamics of knowledge is made conceivable by analyzing the force, torques, moments on the *KCOs* in relation their mass, inertia, and center of moments.

14.4.2 AXIOM 2 (TRUISM 2)

Organisms and sub-organisms are mutually interdependent; physical laws and/or marginal utility theory govern the balance of interdependencies. Action and interaction involve at least two objects or sub-objects (segments) within an object. This truism is based on the reality that a representation of an action as a sentence needs a noun that initiates or performs an action that is directed towards "another," however amorphous either one maybe. A single noun object in entire and total isolation is a nonentity or a myth. The existence of an object, real, or abstract can only be in relation with its surrounding or linked object(s) including the observer object that knows of the existence of the original object. Noun objects (nos) and verb functions (vfs) by themselves do not constitute complete and accurate sentences. In conjunction, they can be forced to deliver modules of knowledge (Δk's) to humans and to machines.

14.4.2.1 Representational model of behavioral interactions

Humans being more adaptive and forgiving than machines readily adjudicate and fill in missing or incomplete aspects of *nos* and *vfs*. When noun objects are replaced as operands (*oprs*) and verb functions are replaced by operation codes (*opcs*), the simpler sentences of a language can be approximated the assembly level programs to be executed by CPUs within a machine.

The concept of action (*C1*) that a (noun) object no_1 performs a (verb) function *vf*, on another (implicit or explicit) object no_2 in a certain fashion is complete command that a machine can simulate. As science has evolved, the following concept (*C2*), of force, acceleration, velocity, and displacements were introduced in their own right. Yet the result could be observed only as a force between two or more objects, one upon another or one upon many, or many upon many. To weave the two concepts into the knowledge and social domains, we propose that the simplest module of knowledge (or social action) be represented (with the notation *{R- }*) as:

$$no_1 \rightarrow vf \rightarrow no_2 \qquad \text{\{R-1\}}$$

resulting in an increment of knowledge as Δk. Yet this notation is incomplete since the second concept ($C2$) is not conveyed. To force the notion of both concepts into one notation, we propose that this statement be modified as

$$no_1 \rightarrow vf^* \rightarrow no_2, \qquad \{R\text{-}2\}$$

where vf^* implies a sense of convolution-force where every element of vf from no_1 acts on every element of no_2. Even so, the notation is not complete because the extent of force (torque), type of acceleration (angular), velocity (rotational), displacement (angle) are not all communicated. Further, the directionality of vf (1 to 2, or from 2 to 1) can have different implications on no_2. Hence, the next two step modification becomes necessary

$$no_1 \rightarrow (vf_1 \cdot {}^*{}_{12})(vf'_1 \cdot {}^{*'}{}_{12}) \rightarrow no_2. \qquad \{R\text{-}3\}$$

The first modification incorporated in $(vf_1 \cdot {}^*{}_{12})$ the directionality and nature of the action from 1 to 2 in the notation and its converse in the second modification. However, for the representation of a transaction that is organic, human, interpersonal, social, or corporate in nature, the representation in line $\{R\text{-}3\}$ is incomplete, since an action from 1 to 2 arouses a reaction from 2 to 1, and the notation may enhance further as:

$$no_1 \rightarrow (vf_1 \cdot {}^*{}_{12})(vf'_1 \cdot {}^{*'}{}_{12}) \rightarrow no_2 \quad ACTION - no_1 \quad Acts$$

$$no_2 \rightarrow (vf_2 \cdot {}^*{}_{21})(vf'_2 \cdot {}^{*'}{}_{21}) \rightarrow no_1 \quad REACTION - no_2 \quad Reacts \qquad \{R\text{-}4\}$$

where $(vf_1 . {}^*{}_{12})$ is the transmit signal from no_1 and $(vf'_1 . {}^{*'}{}_{12})$ is the received signal *at* to no_2. In the same vein, and as a reaction, $(vf \cdot {}^*{}_{21})$ is the transmit signal from no_2 and $(vf_2 . {}^{*'}{}_{21})$ is the received signal at to no_1. The effect of distortion of (signals) vfs is included here since $vf'_1 \neq vf_1$ and $vf'_2 \neq vf_2$. To include the time elapsed as

$$no_1 \rightarrow (vf_1 \cdot {}^*{}_{12})(vf'_1 \cdot {}^{*'}{}_{12}) \rightarrow no_2 \text{ at } t$$

$$no_2 \rightarrow (vf_2 \cdot {}^*{}_{21})(vf'_2 \cdot {}^*{}_{21}) \rightarrow no1 \text{ at } (t + \Delta t) \qquad \{R\text{-}5\}$$

rewritten as

$$no_1 \rightarrow \{(vf_1 \cdot {}^*{}_{12})(vf'_1 \cdot {}^{*'}{}_{12}) \rightarrow no_2\}_t$$

$$no_1 \leftarrow \{(vf'_2 \cdot {}^{*'}{}_{21})(vf_2 \cdot {}^*{}_{21}) \leftarrow no_2\}_{(t+\Delta t)} \qquad \{R\text{-}6\}$$

NOTE: Two major effects in all signal communications are *delay and distortion* in the medium. Social media also exhibits these traits and tendencies. The news media uses such delays and distortions for the self interest groups and political advantage. In some cases, the willful distortions can be to cause uncertainty and confusion for the recipients and used extensively by the political groups when defeat is eminent.

14.4.2.2 *Typical computer Instructions*

In the routine programming of computer instructions, such detailed encoding is not necessary since the location of the program instruction (no_1), the opcode, i.e., predefined, and the operand (no_2) are implied before and after the instruction is actually executed in the CPU. The most rudimentary form of instruction

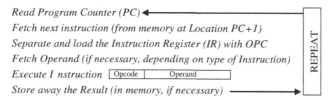

will suffice. The routine sequencing of instructions[5] such as

Read Program Counter (PC)
Fetch next instruction (from memory at Location PC+1)
Separate and load the Instruction Register (IR) with OPC
Fetch Operand (if necessary, depending on type of Instruction)
Execute I nstruction
Store away the Result (in memory, if necessary)

is implied since the program counter (PC) is incremented once the instruction is completely executed. The memory and CPU cycles times are defined and matched such the program can continue to run from one instruction to the next is streamlined. If an interruption occurs the Operation System stores the Program counter, Memory register (MR) contents (if necessary), etc., are stored such that the program can continue to run after the interrupt service routine handles the service request. In addition, the computer environment being far more structured than the social or organic environments follow a very specific pattern of processes and functions.

14.4.2.3 Social events and instructions

In the social environments, since transactions are neither fixed nor predetermined, the programming has to be very detailed and specific to events. The extent of detail forces social machines to act and behave as human beings or as how organisms would act, react, interact, and transact. In addition, the nature of execution of a simple transaction represented as:

$$no_1 \rightarrow \{(vf_1 \cdot *_{12})(vf'_1 \cdot *'_{12}) \rightarrow no_2\}_t, \qquad no_1 ACTS \qquad \{R\text{-}7\}$$

$$no_1 \leftarrow \{(vf'_2 \cdot *'_{21})(vf_2 \cdot *_{21}) \leftarrow no_2\}_{(t+\Delta t)} \quad no_2 REACTS$$

can be programmed to be dependent on locally computed variables such as the mood, emotional attitude, age, health, and/or temperaments of no_1 and/or no_2. The stability and outcome of the results cannot be guaranteed but they can be dependent on numerous external factors like most human beings depend up such as age, gender, health of no_1 and/or no_2, and their interdependencies. Social dynamics and timing play a significant role. However, humans do behave rationally most of the time and the social machines do offer sensible solutions most of the time.

The representation *{R-7}* repeats indefinitely in human interactions as long as the interaction continues. At the start of the next transaction, the cycle continues with some memory of the prior interaction. This repetitive cycle can be symbolized in the time sequence as (*a, b, c, d*) cycle needing discrete intervals to for each of the micro steps *a, b, c, d*, to continue the

---

[5]These instructions are typical for hardwired CPUs. The instructions set for micro-programmed CPUs are quite different and controlled by the micro-programs in the Control memory.

dialog (interaction) between any two social objects no_1 (or a human H_1) and no_2 (or another human H_2).

where $(t' - t)$ seconds is the delay in media channel $no_1 \rightarrow no_2$ and $[(t + \Delta t)' - (t + \Delta t)$ is the delay in media channel $no_2 \rightarrow no_1$. The a, b, c, d repeat cycle in a loop now becomes (a_i, b_i, c_i, d_i) to $(a_{i+1}, b_{i+1}, c_{i+1}, d_{i+1})$ and so on. Both the transmission properties *(delays and distortions)* of communication channels are now included in the representations of social communications.

14.4.2.4 Micro-economic behavior of noun objects

Micro-economic behavior of the noun objects or object-groups is implicit in all the modalities of behavior governed by representations *{R-1}* through *{R-7}*. For an immediate span of time Δt, these different modes simply happen to overcome an immediate situation or an event, such as greeting the other or exchanging formalities. It assumes the form of exchanges of gibberish. The marginal utility of such social transaction is too trivial to consider and the effort involved is inconsequential. However, in sustained transactions and relations involving continued dialog of some sort or another, the laws of marginal utility enter the human-social balance. The efforts and their utilities tend to have similar marginal values. The derived utilities governs the continuity of relations, i.e., the basis for $[no_1 \rightarrow \{(vf'_1 \cdot {}^*_{12})\ (vf'_1 \cdot {}^{*'}_{12}) \rightarrow no_2\}_t]$ in the forward mode and on the basis $[no_1 \leftarrow \{(vf'_2 \cdot {}^{*'}_{21})\ (vf_2 \cdot {}^*_{21}) \leftarrow no_2\}_{(t+\Delta t)}]$ in the response mode tend offer similar rewards for no_1 and no_2, respectively.

14.4.2.5 Instability of certain social categories

Chaotic behavior of insane and highly unstable humans cannot be effectively simulated or copied by social machines. Such machines can imitate the behavior of the criminally insane if the criminal tendencies and insanity can be programmed even though they have extraneous social dependencies. Total chaos is by definition not programmable, even though order and chaos can have a very fine boundary line. The programming of social machines needs human/organic behavioral lookups just as the programming of normal computers need numeric/logical lookups that are mirco-programmable.

14.4.3 AXIOM/TRUISM 3

Any Change of Organizational Structure and Relations Needs Energy. Energy is essential to bring about actions, changes, and/or movements. In the physical sciences, the law for the conservation of energy (or of mass and energy) has been well articulated. In the social and organism domain, additional modifications become necessary. Psychological, personal, corporate, group, community-based energies derived from motivation and drive need to be included in the formulations and estimations. Financial resources (if they are considered as potential energy) may also be invoked. Unlike physical energies, social energies do not have definite measures and quantization techniques. However, they exist and can be sensed; they can be depleted and rebuilt, conserved and safeguarded, squandered or deployed, etc. These energies cause social movements and create social dynamics. Thus, when a noun object no_1 interacts with another object no_2, the energy can be absorbed, transmitted, amplified, modified, or reflected, turned around, amplified with vengeance, etc. A parallelism exists in the transmission, communication, and reception of social and electrical energies exists and further explained in Appendix 14A.3.

14.4.3.1 Control of contaminating signals

The basis of computations in (signal transmission domain) is the energy (or power) balance between the information bearing signals and the contaminating signals and to ascertain and to preserve their relative magnitudes. In the social environments, the coupling factors can become highly variable thus amplifying or attenuating the influence of one noun object on the other (such as the influence of a teacher on a student). A highly coupled no_2 pick up all the energy from $no1$ and vice versa. A highly motivated no_2 can amplify the energy from no_1 and vice versa. The energy in the social/organic systems is not conserved but manipulated by the individual noun objects, thus altering the ratios between signal power (the main purpose of vf^*no in the numerous depictions in Axiom II) and the cross-talk (intervening) powers of extraneous noun objects. For example, a healthy strain of bacterium can significantly alter the relation (the healing process for a human to overcome infection), or a marriage counselor can (perhaps) heal the husband-wife relationship, and so on. The personality factors (i.e., the coupling effects) can and do play an important (and dynamic) role in social behavior. Though complex, such variations are initially computable and can be refined as the social software becomes more sophisticated.

14.4.3.2 Contamination of social signals

Contamination of speech and data signals has been studied in great detail by communication scientists. Since these signals also have energy associated with them, they can cause errors or undesirable modification to the signals. In social settings, distortions and miscommunications do result when the media distorts and delays significant social information. A statement misplaced or drawn out of context can cause an unbalance in the relations and understandings. Many novels and movies are based on misunderstandings that can pile up just as genuine understanding can nurture relationships. Understanding, knowledge, and interpretation in social context becomes as important as address encoding, handling, and protocol decoding in Internet and packet networks.

14.4.4 AXIOM/TRUISM 4

Organic Changes are quantum in nature but statistical methods apply. A quanta of knowledge (Δk) is generated when no_1 or no_2 invokes Δvf and/or $*\Delta$, upon no_2 and/or no_1. The cycle is complete (and may be repeated) from no_1 or no_2 as an action and a reaction. Since knowledge is dynamic, its variation can be influence by its three basic constituents vf, $*$, and/or (no_1 or no_2). These elements are quantized from larger social interactions and these in turn yield larger bodies of knowledge. In principle, these constituents of interaction that give rise to quanta of knowledge may be regrouped to larger elements of interaction giving rise to larger blocks of knowledge. The statistical methods for grouping of the constituents and their properties thus become applicable. For instance, when a teacher (no_1) instructs (vf) a class (no_2), the reaction of the class shows statistical properties, even though each student in the class (quanta) may show a statistical pattern of properties (from complete learning to total ignoring of the material taught).

Since the extent of change depends on the context of the problem, approximations are possible by Taylor series expansions of the change of the state of knowledge from its prior state. Numerous approximations exist when the function for vf, $*$, and no, as they contribute to knowledge. If they do not exist, then a functional approximation can be derived[6] from the observations. When the social traits (of no_1 and/or no_2) are stored in the knowledge bases as discrete points, then interpolation becomes necessary to evaluate these traits at intermediate point and interpolation techniques are necessary. Such equations and their approximations permit the machine to keep track of knowledge profile and incremental knowledge when the parameters vf, $*$, and no are arranged, rearranged, and manipulated to find venues for discovering and uncovering knowledge. It becomes viable to find how the structure and composition of knowledge can be altered by the type of verb functions (available from knowledge bases of scientific verb functions) in any given discipline. Attributes such as circumstances and social parameters can also be varied and the social machines should offer a good approximation for the expected results.

14.4.4.1 Approximations due to variations of (vfs, *s, and nos)

Taylor series approximations [16] are presented in most books in mathematics and a few results are presented in Appendix 14A.1. Generally, the expansion one, and two-dimension variable do not offer sufficient flexibility to handle all social events, interactions and environments. But the three-dimension expansions start to shed some light as to the expected changes in the expected outcome when a verb function (vf), convolves ($*$), with a noun object (no). These three dimensions are still not sufficient since a complete social event, transaction, or interaction has as many as four (a, b, c, d) themes:

$$(a) \quad no_1 \rightarrow [\{(vf_1 \cdot *_{12})_t\}], \qquad \{R\text{-}7a\}$$
$$(b) \quad [\{(vf'_1 \cdot *'_{12}) \rightarrow no_2\}_{t'}], \qquad \{R\text{-}7b\} \text{ for the forward action(s), and}$$
$$(c) \quad no_2 \rightarrow [\{(vf_2 \cdot *_{21})\}_{(t+\Delta t)}], \qquad \{R\text{-}7c\}$$
$$(d) \quad [\{(vf_2 \cdot *'_{21}) \rightarrow no_1\}_{(t+\Delta t)'}], \qquad \{R\text{-}7d\} \text{ for the backward action(s),}$$

for the response action(s), as indicated in representation {R-7} in Section 14.4.2.3 within Axiom 2.

---

[6]In dealing with social objects, polynomial algebraic approximations of behavior can cause ripple effects leading to instability in the overall solution. Representation by smooth functions is preferable, even though interpolations can be done by Taylor series approximations. In reality, rational behavior of species rarely exhibit ripple effects, unless they are strategically and willfully adapted during negotiations or life threatening situations.

In a sense themes *(a)* and *(b)* represent an action *(vf$_1$)* from *no$_1$* directed toward *no$_2$* at an instant "*t*" and *(c)* and *(d)* indicate the reaction *(vf$_2$)* from *no$_2$* directed toward *no$_1$* as a response at an instant "*t* + Δt." The action and reaction cycle is iterated many times before a social transaction/ interaction is complete. The social machine also cycles through these iterations. Further, it tracks the incremental knowledge-gained, after each iteration.

14.4.4.2 Information transmission and reception in social media

The social media behaves much like the electrical or fiber optic media. Transmission engineering for electrical signals in telephone and communication systems has been well studied and documented for more than six decades. It is only logical to transfer the well-established concepts and principles into the transmission of social contents of transactions in the humanistic domain as far as possible and develop the fine tuning necessary as it is needed. It can be seen that such transfusion is possible and further it can be seen that fine tuning is necessary since electrons and photons do not traverse the social media; instead information[7], knowledge, ideas, and concepts traverse freely from one social object to another via the social medium.

In formulating the joint methodology for electrical transmission systems and social communication systems, extra elements such as

$$(PTransmitter \sum [One\ Social\ Media] \rightarrow [Next\ Social\ Media] \sum Receiver\ P)$$

have been added on the representation *{R-7}*. The symbols **P** and Σ represent that the receivers and transmitter have their own characteristics and the noun objects *no1* and *no2* adapt to these characteristics. For example, if the social media is email, then the object adapt to logging on, connecting to an ISP, typing at suitable rate and in a suitable language, etc., to transmit the element *(vf$_1$.*$_{12}$)*. These details are shown in representations *{R-7e}* to *{R-7h}*.

In the forward direction the unit of communication is

(e) no$_1$ $\rightarrow$ *{(vf$_1$.*$_{12}$) P Transmitter Σ [into the Social Media]*   *{R-7e}*

Source — Internet & Backbone Networks

(f) [Social Media delivers] Σ Receiver P (vf'$_1$.'$_{12}$)* $\rightarrow$ *no$_2$*   *{R-7f}*

In the reverse direction the unit of communication becomes

(g) no$_2$ $\rightarrow$ *(vf$_2$.*$_{21}$) } P Transmitter Σ [into the Social Media]*   *{R-7g}*

Source — Internet & Backbone Networks

(h) [Social Media delivers] Σ Receiver P (vf'$_2$.'$_{21}$)* $\rightarrow$ *no$_1$}*   *{R-7h}*

These representations are transformed into systems diagrams by assigning the processes to a box and by following the sequencing of processes. For example, the process *(vf$_1$ · *$_{12}$)* has two processes, verb function *vf$_1$* and the associated convolution in *{R-7e}*, within it.

---

[7]Information in social media should be considered as an unique entity in its own right and it is not the information derived from datasets in computer science.

14.4.5 AXIOM/TRUISM 5

Organisms do not always interact in harmony. Population densities acting in harmony tend to increase in any healthy environment. But for the same reason after a span of time, the competition for resources for the gratification of needs brings disharmony. The origin of all species bears evidence to this truism. The lower-level needs of organizations dominate as the population density starts to increase countering the condition for healthy environments to exist indefinitely. This cycle, essential in nature, preserves the population of organisms to some extent. The supply and demand equations from price-theory in economics enter the local balance between resources and the demand. The price-elasticity of demand and of supply fine-tune the localized price.

14.4.5.1 Higher level needs and healthy social environments

There is a paradox in the natural cycle of harmony in the human species. The higher-level needs increase in healthy environments thus bringing in an intellectual component for restricting the population of the healthier species. The caliber of the elite is edged upward as their own population density is moderated. On the other hand, the population of those without artificial agents and education of human intellect to control their population starts to grow more quickly. This intellectual segregation of populous is a historically proven fact. The French Revolution, the Collapse of Inca civilizations, the border conflicts at the edges of rich and poor nations, etc., bear testimony to this rather intricate balance between those who want the best to survive and those who would do anything to survive. The fragile harmony between the organisms is broken in many ways and forms.

The restoration of harmony is not a prerequisite. Destruction and annihilation are also distinct possibilities. If harmony is restored by reason and justice, it leads to a longer-lasting peace and vice versa. Violence and brutality are the evil faces of reason and justice. The restoration process can be asymptotically convergent or divergent. Oscillations can occur in either case. The behavior of organisms simply follows the destruction or restoration processes.

During abnormal conditions and crisis, human behavior and its simulation by social machines both become unstable as the adjudications of the leaders profiles are very sharply contrasted. Such situations are documented in the past. The choice for restraint by Kennedy during the Bay of Pigs Crisis and the choice of brutality by Eisenhower during the bombing raids of Hiroshima or Nagasaki have brought about dramatically different global consequences. Judgment and the wisdom or conversely, the pride and prejudice of leaders and of power brokers are programmed as personality attributes of individuals rolling the political dice while issuing the higher-level commands to a new breed of social machines simulating human behavior.

Under such circumstances, the social machine would offer possible venues out of the crisis by emulating the behavioral traits of successful leadership styles superposed by the patterns of choices of the current leaders, but customized to the current socioeconomic conditions. These traits, patterns, and socioeconomic conditions are available in knowledge bases (*KBs*) throughout the world. When the crisis has distinct national implications, privately held knowledge bases (such as *KBs* with CIA, Secret Services, self-interest lobby groups, Military Industrial Complex) also contribute to the final decision making process during the crisis mode. It is important to note the machine processes are not emotionally or psychologically oriented; instead they are based on verifiable logic, reason, and documented decision support system algorithms distilled as the foundation for the emotionally and psychologically stable leaders.

14.4.5.2 Iterative cyclic social processes (a, b, c, d) revisited

The *"abcd"* iterative loop is essential in most social settings since knowledge (statements) and its affirmations leads to the conclusion of any major event or dialogue.

In observing the iterative (*a, b, c, d*) theme presented above, the energy to impose a action (verb function) from no_1 in the form of (vf_1 .*$_{12}$) has two effects: *(i)* supplying (altering) the energy of no_2 and *(ii)* conversely, depleting (altering) energy in some form or another (such as emotional, psychological, financial) of no_1.This depletion can be viewed as a reflection of energy that can be attenuated, amplified, synchronized, and/or coordinated, etc. Such reflections govern the nature and stability of interactions between no_1 and no_2. In social settings, Freud [17], Eric Fromm [18], Eric Berne [19], Maslow [20], etc. have analyzed such interactions. Their perspectives are well documented. Freud [17] has conceived such reactions necessary for healthy/unhealthy emotional living. Fromm [18] has documented the noble art of loving (between any noun objects no_i and no_{i+1} that is reciprocal and mutually rewarding that last much longer than selfish and exploitive interactions that have the shortest life span. Eric Berne [19] has conceived human transactions to be essential for balanced and unbalanced relationships. Maslow [22] has gone one step further in classifying the emotional drives and energies for healthy and successful corporate executive and contributors.

14.5 SOCIAL MEDIA AND HUMAN INTERACTIONS

Figure 14.5 duplicates Figure 14.1 in order to implant the flow of knowledge in human transactions. The actions (initiate/respond) take place at various instants (*t1, t2, ... etc., and t3, t4, ... etc.,*) but in an orderly and sequential fashion. As data is exchanged in communication networks, orderly procedures prevail in most exchanges ranging from polite formalities gestures to blows and kicks. The sequence(s) and rate of exchanges carry the social energy behind these gestures.

In Figure 14.6, the noun object no_1 or no_2 is replaced by *[H_i]* and initiate an action vf_1. The energy for this action is derived from its own need structure or motivation in an attempt to gratify such need(s) thus initiating an action-reaction cycle and also generating elements of knowledge (Δk) over a duration Δt. These elements accumulate[8] and generate a "body of knowledge" or ($BoK = \Sigma \Delta k$) that has finite boundary and volume of knowledge over a time ($T = \Sigma \Delta t$).

Further details of the diagram are shown in Figure 14.7. The social network and aspects composed of the personal nature of *[H_i]*, social-cultural norms of the society are depicted. Such interfaces are necessary for the two humans *[H_i]* in the diagram.

14.5.1 FROM BLOCK DIAGRAMS TO DEVICES

In Figure 14.7, the IPOD type of devices the hold the individual nature of the users and the social norms of the society are depicted. There is no need for symmetry in the system and the diagram can accommodate any noun object no_1 or no_2 to exchange elements of knowledge to and from no_2 or no_1. The bilateral nature for the exchange of knowledge is not essential.

---

[8]Elements of knowledge do not add up like numerical entities; instead they are arranged and cascaded like building block in a structure, or flowers in a bouquet. The symbol Σ has to be interpreted with due care in context to the elements of knowledge. Perhaps we need new mathematics of knowledge rather abuse numerical mathematics in this context.

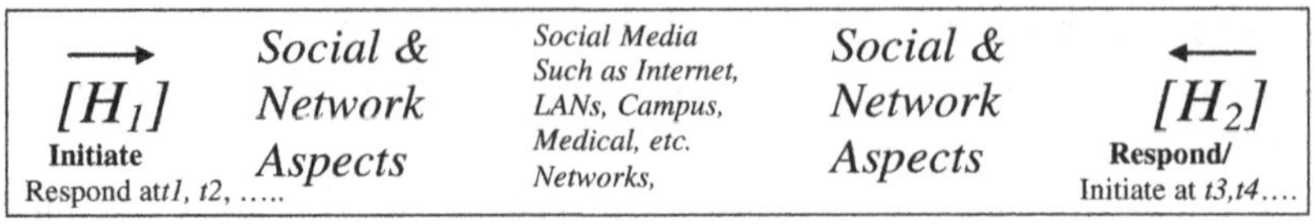

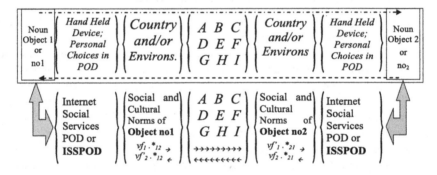

FIGURE 14.5

Typical format of communication and exchange of knowledge and information at various instants of time *t*.

FIGURE 14.6

Recent formats of communication and exchange of knowledge and information. Social media is replaced by its media characteristics [A through I].

FIGURE 14.7

Formats of communication and exchange of knowledge and information from a modern perspective. The parameters A-I in the centralized matrix govern the flow of $vf_1{^*}_{12}$ no$_1$ in the → direction and $vf_2{,^*}_{21}$, no$_2$ in the reverse direction. Internet Social Services Providers connect to ISSPOD and provide the knowledge banks that support for $vf_1 \cdot {^*}_{12}$ and $vf_2 \cdot {^*}_{21}$.

Additional devices/effort on the part of *no$_1$* and *no$_2$* will complete the transactions in the knowledge domain. When the appropriate code of ethics and the norms of the society(ies) are adhered by the interfacing devices, the exchanges can be beneficial and rewarding. For example, humans may have cosmic encounters and terrestrials may comprehend extra-terrestrials (ETs), and vice versa.

Figure 14.7 depicts the formats of communication and exchange of knowledge and information from an knowledge worker's perspective. The parameters A through I in the centralized matrix govern the flow of $vf_1,^*{}_{12}$, to no_2 in the $\rightarrow$ direction and $vf_2,^*{}_{21}$, to no_1 in the reverse direction. Internet Social Services Providers connect to ISSPOD and provide the knowledge banks that support for $vf_1 \cdot {}^*{}_{12}$ and $vf_2 \cdot {}^*{}_{21}$.

In the simplest case, Figure 14.6 is incomplete since all the five sub-processes *(e)* through *(h)* are not represented. In the next case depicted as Figure 14.6, all the sub-processes are presented but graphical presentation of *{7e, 7f, 7g, and 7h}* is not complete since the convolution aspects are not depicted. In Figure 14.7, both the actions and verb functions, i.e., *vf*, the convolutions, * with *vf* are shown as *vf**, and the perceptions of noun objects i.e., **no* are shown. The continuity of the smaller programmable processes is depicted in the sequence of the three figures.

14.5.2 SEPARATION OF REASON AND EMOTION DURING HUMAN TRANSACTIONS

The *"abcd"* sequence of events (in Section 14.2.4) is developed in three stages from real-life social events. Five processes (including the perceptions P_1 and P_2 of H_1 and H_2, respectively, are:

  i. an initiation, from H_1 of an interaction from a social member (1),
  ii. the perception, P_2 (that has a rational content and an emotional content) of the action by the other social member (2),
  iii. the response R_2 by (2),
  iv. the perception P_1 (that has a rational content and an emotional content) of the response, and
  v. the initiation of the next interaction (if any) from H_1 from (1).

The entire pattern thus becomes

$$H_1 \rightarrow P_2 \rightarrow R_2 \rightarrow P_1 \rightarrow H_1 \text{ and/or conversely } H_2 \rightarrow P_1 \rightarrow R_1 \rightarrow P_2 \rightarrow H_2$$

These perceptions of the two participants (H_1 and H_2) play a role in their transactions. The perceptions need real time to be formed and then the reactions emerge. Although these timings are not specifically allocated in the representation, the simulation social-ware in computer needs to allow for the perceptual delays. In real instances, the duration may be as short as the reflex time (such as "love at the first sight") to decades for mature friendships and acquaintances to emerge.

When the entire pattern is written down as a loop, the sequence can be represented as Figure 14.9 and each loop in an overall interaction generates a corresponding element of knowledge Δk_1 or Δk_2 for H_1 and H_2, respectively.

Figure 14.8 also depicts the accumulation of two incremental knowledge(s) by H_1 and H_2. This accumulation of knowledge is indeed the learning in children and adults as they encounter new experiences. Two separate bases are shown as KB_1 and KS_1 for H_1, and correspondingly KB_2 and KS_2 for H_2. The participants deal with reason and emotions at two levels and a rational mode of behavior accrues. Confusion between these two inherently different modes of reaction can leave relationships tangled and messy.

In real time, knowledge, intellectual, or rational processes are processed simultaneously with emotional, sociological, or social processes in human minds. The capacity to keep them apart is perhaps a sign of wisdom and maturity in humans. Separation of the matters of head and heart is a learning process for both humans and machines.

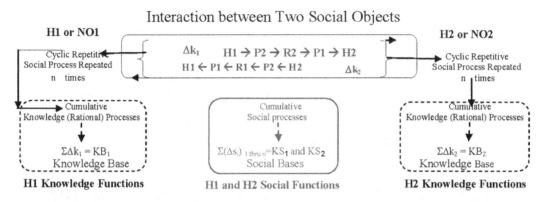

FIGURE 14.8

Depiction of an interaction process between two individuals H_1 and H_2 leading to two increments of knowledge Δk_1 and Δk_2 and two increments of social impressions Δs_1 and Δs_2. Over 'n' such interactions, these increments are accumulated in the two respective bases KB_1 and KB_2 for 'reason-based' knowledge and two similar bases KS_1 and KS_2 for "emotion-based" social boundaries between H_1 and H_2.

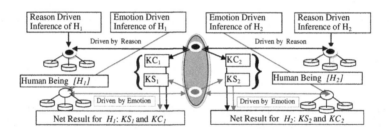

FIGURE 14.9

Separation of the reason and emotional content takes place during the individual process depicted in Figure 14.8. Long term accumulation of KBs leads to KCs. Social bases KSs also accumulate by their own "emotional tendencies" of the individuals H_1 and H_2. The integration of KSs leads to $_{KS1}$ and KS_2. The integration of KBs leads to KC_1 and KC_2. Individual social bases KSs need less updating, whereas the KCs can be updated as the social machine searches the Internet knowledge bases for the most suitable rational behavior depending on the local and traditional settings of any social interaction.

The machine also treats these two processes the two incremental knowledge(s) Δk *and* Δs differently and *cumulates them to* two different bases *KB and KS for each* H_1 *and* H_2. The accumulation of long term *KBs* leads to *KSs* leads to sustained relations and vice versa. In a sense learns how to arrange and cumulate these knowledge-bases as human beings might have done. During the learning stage, the machine behavior needs "understanding and tolerance" as human beings show toward children.

The diagram in Figure 14.9 indicates the nature of human beings based on their most frequently used tendencies, classified as reasoning, logic, and validity (see either side of the diagram leading to computable machine behavior) as opposed repeated concerns, recurrent feelings, and confirmed compassion (see center of the diagram to estimate social behavior). The two can be blended in the core of any social machine.

In Figure 14.9, when the social machine is debugged and performing optimally, it can (almost) outperform human beings in two distinctive ways. *First,* it constantly learns based on (AI based) robotic reasoning from its own actions (or experience) in the social domain.[9] *Second,* it constantly learns the most suitable tools and techniques (also AI based) but over the WWW knowledge bases for shaping its computed behavioral response.

To some extent, the social machine updates Peter Drucker's practice of management to Eric Fromm's notions of and customizes them to the local conditions. The two processes occur simultaneously. While it updates and customizes the behavioral actions (i.e., POC^3, or the Verb Functions), the machine also deploys the optimal, localized, and personal (Noun Objects) of conduct (i.e., RC^3, i.e., the noun objects). It can be seen that the "Practice" of management supplies *VFs* to deal with the "abstract objects" (i.e., RC^3 or the Noun Objects) of Love. The composite effect is a face of "universal and (semi) perfect behavioral love" that is as "rational and customized" as it is beautiful from anyone for anyone, at any time, and at any place. The abstraction of love is founded in the choice of the best personal objects (by searching its own social base(s) of love (*KSs*) to be deployed in conjunction of the WWW code (*KCs* monitored by the Internet *KBs*) of ethics and conduct.

The diagram in Figure 14.10, the architecture of a system for the fusion of these two concepts, is presented. At the top, a system extracts and accumulates the incremental knowledge from each of the repetitive series of social interaction between social objects. The separation of the rational content from emotional content is also done here by the embedded self learning intelligent agents (AIs) [23] based on history of similar transactions.

The organization of the bases *KBs*, *KCs*, and *KSs* occurs in the lower half of the diagram. The social bases are tied to the personal preferences, choices, and emotions of the two objects H_1 *and* H_2. The rational and computed bases are linked to the rational tendencies, decision strategies, and rationality of the two objects H_1 *and* H_2.

In an obtuse fashion, the machine builds the emotional and intellectual profiles of the users. The four knowledge bases (KC_1, KC_2: KS_1, KS_2) contain an index of intellectual and emotional maturity for the two participants. It can be seen that when a corporation uses a social machine to build its own profile, it will yield a true picture of how it actually acted or reacted to changing social conditions. In university setting, the profile of a university may be generated without bias by a social machine that studies, analyzes, categorizes, and accumulates its prior actions and its reactions to the changing socio-economic conditions, administrative decisions, and the ever changing student populations.

---

[9]This continuous mode of training the predictive systems is used in the of speech encoders (with linear predictive coding or LPC (of speech signals) and adaptive predictor coding or APC (of speech signals)) where the encoders adjust their own parameters till the prediction of the next speech sample is (almost) equal to the actual speech human of the human being. The extent of error is used to modify the next prediction by the LPC and the APC type of encoders.

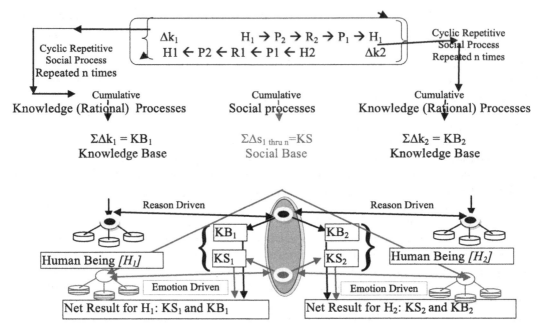

FIGURE 14.10

Overview of a social process between H_1 and H_2. Knowledge, intellectual, or rational processes are processed simultaneously with emotional, sociological, or social processes. The machine treats these two processes and the two incremental knowledge(s) Δk and Δs differently and cumulates them to two different bases KB and KS for each H_1 and H_2.

14.6 SEPARATION OF EMOTION AND REASON ON AN INTEGRATED BASIS

Social systems deal with two basic formats of intelligence: social intelligence and rational (logical, derivable, computable) intelligence. On the one hand, the words romantic, emotional, and social are used for people who are artistic and less predictable. In the context of developing the social-ware for machines, these words interchangeably but derived and classified based on their personal behavior and reactions to social situations.

On the other hand, the words reasonable, predictable, computable, robotic are knowledge based and used for people who are more logical, rational, and more predictable. For the social-ware these words are used interchangeably but derived and classified from the personal preference and behavior. The social machines scan the knowledge bases of the localized social bases to resolve social interaction and adaptation issues. These machines will also scan the Internet knowledge bases for the most logical, rational, and reasonable strategies. The range of search for the optimal strategy is far wider for the rational intelligence-based algorithms.

In real instances, almost all human beings have both formats of intelligence that are used with caution and due deliberation in an optimal blend. Furthermore, the choice can be controlled and channeled to the type of social interaction. The social machine has user-controlled inputs that will

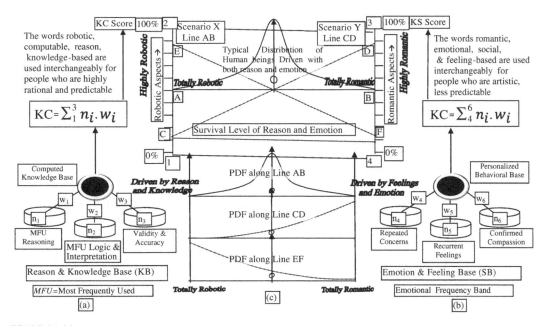

FIGURE 14.11

The basic nature of human beings based on their most frequently used tendencies, classified as reasoning, logic, and validity (see left side of the diagram leading to computable robotic behavior) as opposed repeated concerns, recurrent feelings, and confirmed compassion (see right side of the diagram to estimate social behavior).

proportion of the blends of the two formats of intelligence offering a wide variety of choices for handling social issues. The speed and the search of the machine becomes an asset for the real-time reactions for handling social interactions. This can be performed by handheld intelligent social IPODs in real time. Much as a navigation system offers driving-options, the ISSPOD (see Fig. 14.8) will offer the socially suitable (robust) path for interaction, negotiation, romance, or simply a tittle-tattle gossip!

The organization of the social-software is depicted in Figure 14.11. The user controlled inputs specify the weights for the rationality and emotionality are shown on the left and right sides of the figure. After some training of the software patterns of preferences start to emerge. The rational individual will score highly on the left side and the emotional individual will score highly on the right side. When the software is adequately trained the system will identify the pattern preferred by the user for a variety of social problems and much as a human being would do offer a solution to a social issue based on his own experiences, or in this case from the solutions that have been adapted by the user in the past.

It is interesting to "command" a solution more rational or more emotional, or a blend of the two to segmented sections of the problem. For example, a research problem that involves biological specimens may be commanded to be "human" to the specimens (e.g., less painful) but be thoroughly scientific (rational) in analysis, interpretation, methodology, choice of medicines, etc. Machines offer greater latitude of solutions in complex social circumstances. These options used in

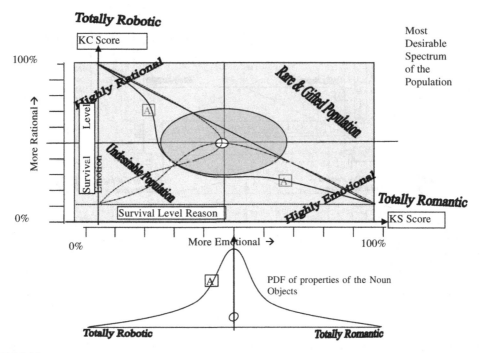

FIGURE 14.12

Typical distribution of human tendencies based on their most frequently used actions and reactions classified as being rational or being emotional.

conjunction for treating terminally ill patients can offer a more peaceful and humane way to treat patients. Social machines have the built-in features to provide such answers to the care givers.

Scores from any community exhibit a harmonious blend of social and intellectual attitudes. Dictated by the tastes and widely accepted social norms, the emotional tendencies tend to reduce friction, anger, and hate. The solutions tend to be practical and conserve physical and psychological energies. A possible spread of the two scores is shown in Figure 14.12. The proportion of totally rational users, corporations, communities, etc. becomes as rare as the totally emotional segments. A blend of scientists, engineers, theoreticians, and alike is as frequent as poets, painters, musicians, and alike. The shape of the distribution is shown as curve A. Total rationality becomes as undesirable as total emotionality in any sustainable community. Individuals can be more emotional than rational during different time spans, aging process, social situations, etc, and vice versa. Human adoptability is an acquired trait and the social machine will track changes and their derivatives. Sudden variations and unstable conditions are monitored. As the medical measures tracked in ICUs, the hand-held social machine (*ISSPOD*) will track unreasonable and unexplained changes in the two scores (intellectual and emotional) of users.

Emotions are generally controlled and kept private, whereas rationality is more evident. Over time, a profile evolves as preference to stay one domain more than another. In trying to resolve situations, most people evaluate the situation and assign numerical values *n1* through *n6* (if not more, see Fig. 14.12) based on their feelings, to resolve the situation. The social machine assigns weights *w1* through *w6* based on how the individual has emphasized one aspect compared to the other. Typically the rational individuals come up with a heavier *KC* score and the emotional individuals come up with a higher *KS* score. The machine learns any changes in scores and learns to keep a moving average of the weights. Further, it connects to the WWW bases to find how other individuals (from the intellectual groups and/or emotional groups like poets, philosophers, and other members of their family group have handled problems in the past. A summary of the possible solutions is suggested and an basis and explanation is provided for the proposed solution.

It is interesting to view the human solution of the users to any particular problem would weigh against the solutions of Einstein by forcing the machine to assume his "Einstein-Personality" by admixing his *KC* profile blended with his *KS* profile (available on the Internet). It is equally possible to view the solution if the machine assumes a "Rumi-Personality" or a "Mathew-Arnold-Personality." The machine will offer solutions depending on how the *KC* and *KS* bases as primed and their weighting factors *w1* through *w3* on the left (intellectual) side and weighting factors *w4* through *w6* on the right (emotional) side of Figure 14.11. Robots fed by these personality profiles will imitate the human behavior of the individuals.

The intellectual groups are offered valid reasons, and the emotional groups are offered real-life experiences from the recent past. Examples how "Albert Einsteins" may scientifically solve the issue versus how "Mathew Arnolds" may hint at the solutions in verses, give the user to be rational and/or emotional or be a blend of the two. The rare and gifted population has the uniquely proportionate and highly balanced admixture of being genius and philosopher in the same person and depicted by the top right quadrant of Figure 14.12. This gift perhaps allows a person to see the microscopic vision to study and alter the details and a binocular vision to adjust and accommodate to the social and ethical aspect of scientific problems. In essence, the ability to innovate and implement mathematical and graphical techniques to social problems is complimented by the human and beneficial insight into scientific problems.

CONCLUSIONS

In this chapter, we have affirmed that any action by and for objects leads to the expansion, refinement, and enhancement of knowledge. Actions can be generalized as verb functions that humans and machines can execute alike. Objects can be knowledge centric objects (*KCOs*), such as humans and social entities; that humans, social organizations and nations that perform verb functions that all objects and machines can execute alike. The net effect of the interrelations is refinement and enhancement of knowledge that propels societies toward peace and progress, refined and refocused intelligence, and stable and secure societies. The role of intelligence is further enhanced by the right choice of the convolutions that bind noun objects (nos) with verb functions (*vfs*) and similar compilations that make up the commands that both humans can generate, speak, understand, and perform and machines that can compile, verify, and execute.

Knowledge and social machines with Internet access and intelligent switching systems (section 14.3.4 in this chapter) unify *KCOs* and human entities with goals for peace embedded deep in mind, respect for nature and lives, and enduring justice (i.e., *prj*, see section 14.1.1, of this chapter) and away from deception, aggression, and hostility (i.e., *dah*, see section 14.1.2, of this chapter). In this decade, the four distinctive roles of semiconductors in computers, the optical speeds in fiber-optic networks, extensive wisdom of the philosophers (see section 14.3.4, of this chapter) and the mathematical precision of scientists (see Appendices 14.A.1, A.2, and A.3 to this chapter) are integrated into one discipline of Knowledge Science. It is our intuition that this foursome blend of knowledge(s) into the hardware, software, firmware, and knowledge-ware of knowledge machines will prevail against the global problems such as greed, wars, and hostilities that have brought the societies around the world to a downturn, arrogance, and shame of a naked women and hostile politician on the Internet. A new breed of knowledge machines can produce a computer based, high-speed, wise, and precise directionality for the cluttered minds within the societies and corrupt leaders within the nations.

REFERENCES

[1] von Neumann J, First Draft of a Report on the EDVAC, Contract No., W-670-ORD 4926, Between United States Army Ordnance Department and University of Pennsylvania, Moore School of Electrical Engineering, June 30, 1945.Additional details are presented in Burks AW, Goldstine HH, and von Neumann J, U. S. Army Report Ordnance Department, 1946.

[2] Shockley W. Patent Application Serial No. 35,423 filed June 26, 1948, Private communication (during 1970s) at Bell Telephone Laboratories, Murray Hill, New Jersey. The N- and P-type materials are also presented in in the application of J. Bardeen and W. H. Brattain Serial No. 33,466 filed June 17, 1948, Private communication (during 1970s) at Bell Telephone Laboratories, Murray Hill, New Jersey. William Shockley, Electrons and Holes in Semiconductors, with Applications to Transistor Electronics, Krieger Publishing Company, ASIN: 088273827, 1976, also see www.lucent.com/minds/transistor.

[3] Fromm E. Anatomy of human destruction. Austin, TX: Holt, Rinehart and Winston; 1975. See also, Fromm E, The art of loving. New York: Harper and Rowe; 1954.

[4] Drucker P. The practice of management. Harper Paperbacks; 2006.

[5] Ahamed SV. Computational framework of knowledge. Hoboken, NJ: John Wiley and Sons; 2009.

[6] Ahamed SV, Lawrence VB. Design and engineering of intelligent communication systems. Boston: Kluwer Academic Publishers; 1997. Optical digital hierarchies, see Chapter 4. For US hierarchies, see Bell Laboratories, Transmission Systems for Communications, Western Electric Co. 1982.

[7] Ahamed SV, Lawrence VB. Design and engineering of intelligent communication systems. Boston: Kluwer Academic Publishers; 1997. Chapter 15 "Knowledge highways" for SDH and FR systems.

[8] CCITT (now ITU) 1988, Synchronous digital hierarchy bit rates. Recommendation G. 707, Blue Book. Also see Ryan KM ATM and data networking. AT&T Bell Laboratories, Private Communication; 1994. For concise reading, see Ahamed SV, Intelligent internet knowledge networks: Processing of concepts and wisdom, Wiley-Interscience; 2006, Chapter 2.

[9] Ahamed SV, Lawrence VB. Intelligent broadband multimedia networks. Boston: Kluwer Academic Publishers; 1997, Chapter 6.

[10] Bellcore. "SONET Add-Drop Multiplex Equipment (SONET-ADM) Generic Criteria" TR-TSY-000496, Issue 2, September. And Bellcore 1989, "SONET Add-Drop Multiplex Equipment (SONET ADM) Generic Criteria for a Self-Healing Ring Implementation" TA-TSY-000496, Issue 2, November.

[11] CCITT (now ITU), Synchronous Digital Hierarchy Bit Rates, Rec. G. 707, Blue Book, For SONET Digital Hierarchy, also see Chow Ming-Chwan, Understanding SONET/SDH: Standards and applications, Holmdel, NJ: Andan Publishers; 1996, 1988. Sandesara NB, Ritchie GR, Engel-Smith B,

Plans and considerations for SONET deployment, IEEE Commun. Mag., Aug. 1990, pp. 26–33. For a concise summary, see Ahamed SV, Chapter 2, Intelligent internet knowledge networks: Processing of concepts and wisdom, Wiley-Interscience; 2006.

[12] Ahamed SV, Lawrence VB. Intelligent broadband multimedia networks. Boston: Kluwer Academic Publishers; 1997, Chapter 3.

[13] Ahamed SV, Lawrence VB. Intelligent broadband multimedia networks. Boston: Kluwer Academic Publishers; 1997 For details, see Section 4–5.

[14] Bell Communications Research. OSI protocol requirement and objectives for operation systems and network element interfaces. TA-TSY-000285, Bellcore, Issue 3, 1987 (December). Summarized in Ahamed SV, Lawrence VB, Intelligent broadband multimedia networks. Boston: Kluwer Academic Publishers; 1997, Chapters 4.Also presented in Ahamed SV, Intelligent internet knowledge networks: Processing of concepts and wisdom. Wiley-Interscience; 2006, Chapter 2.

[15] Hunt C. TCP/IP network administration. 3rd ed. O'Reilly Media; April 2002.

[16] Meschkowski H. Series expansions for mathematical physicists (University mathematical texts, 37). Oliver and Boyd; 1968.

[17] Freud S, Strachey J, Gay P. The ego and the id (The standard edition of the complete psychological works of Sigmund Freud), W. W. Norton & Company; Standard Edition, September 1990 In: Freud EL, editor. Letters of Sigmund Freud. New York: Basic Books; 1960.

[18] Fromm E. Man for himself, an inquiry into psychology of ethics. New York: Owl Books; 1990.

[19] Berne E. Games people play: The basic handbook of transactional analysis. Ballantine Books; Reissue edition, August 1996.

[20] Maslow AH. Toward a psychology of being. 2nd edition. Van Nostrand Reinhold; 1982 Also see Maslow AH, A theory of human motivation. Psychol. Rev May 1943;50:370–396.

[21] Fromm E. The art of loving. New York: Harper and Rowe; 1954.

[22] Maslow AH. Motivation and personality. New York: Harper & Row; 1970 and Maslow A. Farther reaches of human nature. New York: Viking Press; 1971.

[23] Luger GF. Artificial intelligence, structures and strategies for complex problem solving. Boston: Addison Wesley; 2005. Also see Mohammadian M. Intelligent agents for data mining and information retrieval. Idea Group Publishing; 2004.

APPENDIX 14A.1 **INTERPOLATION OF SOCIAL SIGNALS**

In Appendix 14A.1, the equations for interpolation are presented to facilitate the derivation of values of such traits in one and more dimensions. Numerous real-life examples exist. For example, consider a boss-employee interaction where an individual (boss) no_1 handles a individual (employee) no_2 who is overly sensitive and can become unpredictable (shows a flare-up, a knock out, a shooting-spree, or a suicide, etc.) when a statement such as "you are fired" is directed to the employee in the case. Yet the social machine should be able to estimate the response when statements such as "you are let-go," "your job is terminated," or "your job is eliminated," are addressed toward the individual. An interpolation/extrapolation of the response based on the severity of the statement can thus be generated by the machine.

Examples of two dimensional interpolation/extrapolations might also be necessary if the employee faces a harsher statement: "You are fired as of now and the security guard is going to escort you out of the building" (extrapolation), or if the individual faces a softer statement: "We would like you to consider resignation over the next 12 months" (interpolation).

In the second case, two dimensions (vf and *) that are relevant are the termination of the job and the duration of over which vf is going to be activated (i.e., of the convolution *, of vf) upon the employee. Thus, the reaction of the employee (no2 in this case) can be estimated due to the combination of vf and *.

In two dimensions the value of $f(x,y)$ is written as:

$$f(x,y) \approx f(a,b) + (x-a)f\ x(a,b) + (y-b)f\ y(a,b) +$$
$$\frac{1}{2}\left[(x-a)^2 \int xx(a,b) + 2(x-a)(y-b)\right] \int xy(a,b) + (y-b)^2 f\ yy(a,b)] + ..$$

The approximation in three dimensions in $(x1;\ x2;\ x3)$ is written as

$$f(x_1,x_2,x_3) \approx f(a_1,a_2,a_3) + \left[\sum_{j=1}^{j=3}\frac{\partial f(a_1,a_2,a_3)}{\partial x_j}(x_j - a_j)\right] + \frac{1}{2!}\left[\sum_{j=1}^{j=3}\sum_{k=1}^{k=3}\frac{\partial^2 f(a_1,a_2,a_3)}{\partial x_j x_k}(x_j - a_j)(x_k - a_k)\right] + \cdots$$

Second degree approximation for the function is written as

$$f(x_1,x_2,x_3) \approx f(v_1,*_2,n_3) + \left[\sum_{j=1}^{j=3}\frac{\partial f(v_1,*_2,n_3)}{\partial x_j}(x_j - v_j)\right] + \frac{1}{2!}\left[\sum_{j=1}^{j=3}\sum_{k=1}^{k=3}\frac{\partial^2 f(v_1,*_2,n_3)}{\partial v_j *_k}(x_j - v_j)(x_k - *_k)\right] +$$
$$\frac{1}{3!}\left[\sum_{j=1}^{j=3}\sum_{k=1}^{k=3}\sum_{l=1}^{l=3}\frac{\partial^3 f(a_1,a_2,a_3)}{\partial x_j x_k x_l}(x_j - v_j)(x_k - *_k)(x_l - n_l)\right] + \cdots$$

In the same vein, the values of (each of) V, *, and N are extrapolated as follows:

$$f(x_1,x_2,x_3) \approx f(v_1,*_2,n_3) + \left[\sum_{j=1}^{j=3}\frac{\partial f(v_1,*_2,n_3)}{\partial x_j}(x_j - v_j)\right] + \frac{1}{2!}\left[\sum_{j=1}^{j=3}\sum_{k=1}^{k=3}\frac{\partial^2 f(v_1,*_2,n_3)}{\partial v_j *_k}(x_j - v_j)(x_k - *_k)\right] +$$
$$\frac{1}{3!}\left[\sum_{j=1}^{j=3}\sum_{k=1}^{k=3}\sum_{l=1}^{l=3}\frac{\partial^3 f(a_1,a_2,a_3)}{\partial x_j x_k x_l}(x_j - v_j)(x_k - *_k)(x_l - n_l)\right] + \cdots$$

APPENDIX 14A.2 VERB-FORCE FUNCTION AND CHANGE OF NOUN OBJECTS

The concept (*C1*) of a (noun) object no_1 performing a (verb) function *vf* on another (implicit or explicit) object no_2 in a certain fashion is a complete sentence that a machine can simulate. As science has evolved, the concept of force (*C2*), acceleration, velocity, and displacements were introduced in their own right. Yet the result could be observed only as a force between two or more objects, one upon another or one upon many, or many upon many. To weave the two concepts (*C1* and *C2*) into the knowledge and social domains, we propose that the simplest module of knowledge (or social action) be approximated as:

$$no_1 \rightarrow vf \rightarrow no_2. \qquad \qquad \{\text{R -1}\}$$

Yet this notation is incomplete since the second concept *C2* is not conveyed. To force the notion of both concepts into one notation, we propose that this statement be modified as

$$no_1 \rightarrow vf^* \rightarrow no_2, \qquad \{R\text{-}2\}$$

where vf^* implies a sense of convolution-force where every element of vf from no_1 acts on every element of no_2. Even so, the notation is not complete because the extent of force (torque), type of acceleration (angular), velocity (rotational), displacement (angle) are not all communicated. Further, the directionality of vf (1 to 2, or from 2 to 1) can have different implications on no_2. Hence, the next two step modification becomes necessary

$$no_1 \rightarrow (vf_1 \cdot {}^*{}_{12})({}^*{}_{21} \cdot vf_2) \rightarrow no_2. \qquad \{R\text{-}3\}$$

The first modification incorporated in $(vf_1 \cdot {}^*{}_{12})$ the directionality and nature of the action from 1 to 2 in the notation and its converse in the second modification. However, for the representation of a transaction that is organic, human, interpersonal, social, or corporate in nature, the representation in line $\{R\text{-}3\}$ is incomplete, since an action from 1 to 2 arouses a reaction from 2 to 1, and the notation may enhance further as:

$$no_1 \rightarrow (vf_1 \cdot {}^*{}_{12})({}^*{}_{21} \cdot vf_2) \rightarrow no_2.$$
$$no_2 \rightarrow (vf_2 \cdot {}^*{}_{21})({}^*{}_{12} \cdot vf_1) \rightarrow no_1. \qquad \{R\text{-}4\}$$

or to include the time elapsed as

$$no_1 \rightarrow (vf_1 \cdot {}^*{}_{12})({}^*{}_{21} \cdot vf_2) \rightarrow no_2 \ at \ t$$
$$no_1 \leftarrow (vf_2 \cdot {}^*{}_{21})({}^*{}_{12} \cdot vf_1) \leftarrow no_2 \ at \ (t + \Delta t) \qquad \{R\text{-}5\}$$

written out as

$$no_1 \rightarrow \{(vf_1 \cdot {}^*{}_{12})({}^*{}_{21} \cdot vf_2) \rightarrow no_2\}_t$$
$$no_1 \leftarrow \{(vf_2 \cdot {}^*{}_{21})({}^*{}_{12} \cdot vf_1) \leftarrow no_2\}_{(t+\Delta t)} \qquad \{R\text{-}6\}$$

APPENDIX 14A.3 **ELECTRICAL SYSTEMS ANALOGY**

Such variations in the behavior of (scientific) objects occur in passive (resistive elements and [ABCD] matrices [7]) and active (transistorized and coupled/uncoupled) electrical circuits. The electrical circuit equations have been documented well for the past three or four decades. In importing these equations, a certain amount of caution is necessary since extraneous elements can cause local interference in the received and reflected signals. In electrical transmission system, the effect of such pickup and contaminating signals [6, 9] is handled by near-end crosstalk (NEXT) and far-end cross talk (FEXT) to emulate the first order effects and by interaction crosstalk (IXT) calculations. These equations are not directly applicable in social and organic environment but indicative of their effects and there directions.

14A.3.1 **CONTROL OF CONTAMINATING SIGNALS IN COMMUNICATION SYSTEMS**

The basis of computations in (signal transmission domain) is the energy (or power) balance between the information bearing signals and the contaminating signals and to ascertain and to preserve their relative magnitudes. In the social environments, the coupling factors can become highly variable thus amplifying or attenuating the influence of one noun object on the other (such as the influence of a teacher on a student). A highly coupled no_2 pick up all the energy from no_1 and vice versa. A highly motivated no_2 can amplify the energy from no_1 and vice versa. The energy in the social/organic systems is not conserved but manipulated by the individual noun objects, thus altering the ratios between signal power (the main purpose of vf^*no in the numerous depictions in Axiom II) and the cross-talk (intervening) powers of extraneous noun objects. For example, a healthy strain of bacterium can significantly alter the relation (the healing process for a human to overcome infection), or a marriage counselor can (perhaps) heal the husband-wife relationship, and so on. The personality factors (i.e., the coupling effects) can and do play an important (and dynamic) role in social behavior. Though complex, such variations are initially computable and can be refined as the social software becomes more sophisticated.

The role of the hybrid is crucial because the nature of this circuitry permits access between A to B and C to D but blocks out A to C and B to D. A certain amount of leakage (called trans-hybrid coupling) occurs and causes noise in the signals received at B and D. The echo canceller removes any leakage and offers (reasonably) quality of signal at the receiver ends. The Buffer and Transmitter (Trans) or Regenerator (Regen) and Buffer make the transmitted and received signals coherent and synchronized. The system works well if the transmitter is not too far away. Signals from very distant transmitters become too attenuated for the receiver to assure a good quality of reception in view of the locally generated noises (e.g., echoes and reflections due to impedance mismatches) and extraneous noises (e.g., star pick up signals, thermal noise, timing jitter).

APPENDIX 14A.4 **EXTRAPOLATION INTO SOCIAL SYSTEMS**

Social systems and duplex electrical communications systems bear considerable similarities. Social communication systems are also duplex and transmission/reception can occur simultaneously. The human mind acts to residual contamination due to echo of one's own speech. In most formal social communication systems, only one of the participants transmits (speaks) while the other receives (listens). But the human mind can transmit signals (such as speak, gesturers, posture, make faces) as it is also listening or receives other visual/acoustic or body language signals. Whereas the electrical systems are simpler in comparison, they provide some of the methodology of the communication engineers.

Figure 14A.2 presents a superposition of social process(es) upon a electrical engineering communication model (EECM shown in Fig. 14A.1) for deriving the basic equations and terminology between a social science communication model (see Fig. 14A.3). The entire social process consists of a series of exchanges between any two entities. These bidirectional exchanges culminates the social process as divergent (no agreement), concurrence (with agreement) or as a continuous ongoing and open ended series of transactions. Such transactions can be monitored, interpreted, enhanced, goal-directed, etc., by social machines that perform as well as the social entities themselves and made economic and optimal.

Enhancement of the communication model (from electrical engineering model of bidirectional communication model of digital subscriber lines) for the representation of social interactions over

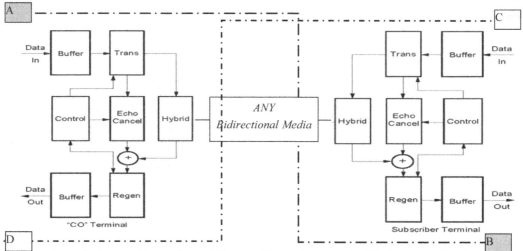

A sends data to B and C send data to D simultaneously. Bi-directionality is thus established over the same media at the same time.

FIGURE 14A.1

Circuit diagram of a bidirectional electrical communication system that permits A (from the central telephone (CO) exchange) to communicate analog or digital information with telephone line subscriber B and vice versa.

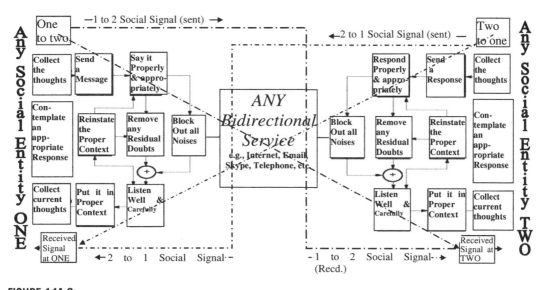

FIGURE 14A.2

Superposition of social process(es) upon an electrical engineering communication model (EECM shown in Fig. 14A.1) for deriving the basic equations and terminology between a social science communication model (see Fig. 14A.3). The entire social process consists of a series of exchanges between any two entities. These bidirectional exchanges culminate the social process as divergent (no agreement), concurrence (with agreement), or as a continuous on-going and open ended series of transactions. Such transactions can be monitored, interpreted, enhanced, goal-directed, etc. by social machines that perform as well as the social entities themselves and made economic and optimal.

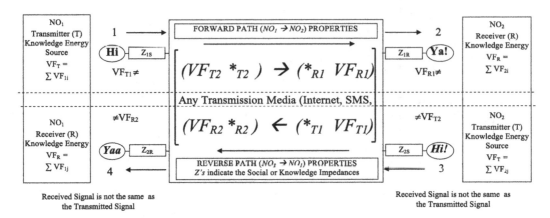

FIGURE 14A.3

Enhancement of the communication model (from electrical engineering model of bidirectional communication model of digital subscriber lines) for the representation of social interactions over any bidirectional social media, such as the Internet, Email systems, telephone systems. A social noun object NO_1 interacts with another NO_2. Both objects have distinct characteristics such as their energy levels, capacity to perform verb functions VFs, and to transmit and receive them from each other. VF_i is socially interactive force and i refers to the ith iteration in a social process; 1 and 2 refer to social entities 1 and 2; T and R refer to transmitter and receiver; Z refer to the internal impedances in the elements. Machine analysis it can be shown that what is received is not the same as what was transmitted but modified in the same fashions as electrical signals and energies over bidirectional electrical media.

any bidirectional social media, such as the Internet, Email systems, telephone systems, is also possible. As shown in Figure 14A.3, a social noun object $NO1$ interacts with another $NO2$. Both objects have distinct characteristics such as their energy levels, capacity to perform verb functions VFs and to transmit and receive them from each other. VF_i is socially interactive force and i refers to the i-th iteration in a social process; (1 and 2) refer to social entities 1 and 2; T and R refer to transmitter and receiver; Z refer to the internal impedances in the elements. By extending algebraic analysis to noun objects, verb functions and their convolutions, it can be shown that what is received is not the same as what was transmitted but modified in the same fashions as electrical signals and energies are modified over bidirectional electrical media.

CHAPTER SUMMARY

In this chapter, we present a computational-based framework for the representation of social interactions. A knowledge/social machine can thus analyze, scrutinize, enhance, and improve any interaction process. In a rational setting, computer-aided social processes can be smooth and directionally convergent without irritations, misunderstandings, and emotionally exhausting. In an emotional setting, computer-aided social interactions can be accepting, forgiving, and adjusting. Since almost all social entities have a fair proportion of intelligence and emotion content in their dealings, the machine can so adjust the tone of the interaction to be intellectual yet emotionally satisfying and also be emotionally gratifying yet intellectually rewarding. The mode of interaction can be made mood, situation, culture, and time dependent.

The role of the machine becomes desirable in corporate and national negotiations where the situation is generally depicted by a zero-sum game strategy. Fairness and risk are both explored for both the participants simultaneously. When the situation is depicted by nonzero-sum game strategy, the machine will search the Internet knowledge bases to find a creative conclusion of the social interactions by introducing other linked objects into the negotiation process with time, and timings are negotiable parameters. It is also foreseeable that such machines will train the next generation of adolescents in the art of social elegance and work creative solutions for social problems thus reducing social friction in the society.

15.1 INTRODUCTION

In the generic format of any transaction, two background processes occur: (a) the exchange of knowledge pertaining to the transaction and (b) the establishment of the social profile of the two participating human beings in the mind of one for the personality of the other participant. Social human transactions assume an aura of complexity with an immense amount of detail embedded in it: complex transactions they are, but incomprehensible they are not. The programing methodology of the detailed instructions to the processors becomes effective in programing social machines to execute social transactions as dependably as the modern computer systems execute numerical or communication functions in real time.

This requirement brings in the additional dimension of human perception of time[1] in the response of the machines that is based on the processor-speeds and their clocking-rates. Time and timing both

---

[1]Whether Einstein predicts that gravity travels in waves, or whether Omar Khayyum laments that the attraction between human hearts will fluctuate as time travels the many corridors of life, or whether the author suggests that the linkages between knowledge centric objects (*KCOs*) depends on the neighborhood of the other *KCOs* as they come and go, the practical fact of the matter is that human behavior implanted in their *vfs*, *, and *nos*, will change with time, culture, individual, and society.

Evolution of Knowledge Science. DOI: http://dx.doi.org/10.1016/B978-0-12-805478-9.00015-7

play a critical role for the success or failure of social transactions. When machines are pulled in order to assist the human effort in social transactions, the role of machines has to be moderated accordingly.

It is foreseeable that social machine will prepare the adolescents of the next generation as the current intelligent toys train infants and kids. In a sense, the social, cultural, and academic settings are matched to the students and the type of profession the students aspire to practice. The user's own skills will evolve in deploying social machines for human-machine interaction. It is viewed to become a fine balance that prevails when pilots fly airplanes or as drivers drive automobiles.

Social machines will train humans to practice intelligent and gainful social habits without undue friction in the pursuit of their individual goals since the potential gain for each participant is computed based on individual tastes and preference. When the participation is based on a strict zero-sum game theory [1] the social machines will become fair and just without exploitation, when the participation is based on nonzero-sum games [2], the machine will find a creative solution for a win-win strategy by searching the prior game(s) of similar nature and scanning the knowledge bases on the Internet. This practice already prevails in the intelligent machines deployed in the medical profession where time and timings are both matters of great essence for the health and well-being of the patient(s).

15.2 INCLUSION OF TIME IN SOCIAL TRANSACTIONS

The instant of time "t" is chosen when a social noun object *no1* initiates an action or verb-function oriented toward *no2* in a certain convolution format *. The sequence of actions is depicted in Figures 15.1A and 15.1B.

Increments of knowledge are exchanged in incremental human transactions. The increments are systematically processed and stored to form a "body of knowledge" that grows and evolves with definite and connected contours. These process need time in humans and in machines. The machines can track human mind process sufficiently well to be able to impersonate the human being as well as one human can impersonate another. Such personifications are programmable in the social machine to imitate one person at some time and another person for another. The social machine can act as a programmable schizophrenic with multiple personalities when the consistency of knowledge exchanges becomes corrupted and/or chaotic.

It is also possible for one human to stifle the other human by transmitting irrational and inconsistent pieces knowledge from time to time. Such knowledge, based on the verb-functions, the noun objects, and their convolutions need a consistent, coherent, and a cogent framework within the realm of knowledge being communicated.

The basis of social transaction represented in Section 14.4.4.1 by the relationships R-7a, 7b, 7c, and 7d, corresponds to

In Figure 15.2, a sequence of such micro events is depicted. Perceptions of both objects and the following action-reaction sequences are also included in this figure. In Figure 15.3, these four events are approximated as 1, 2, 3, and 4 when two social objects interact with one another, in an ACT-REACT scenario. Only one micro event is depicted.

The symbols used in these diagrams are as follows:

vf1 = an action invoked or responded by no1 to initiate or to continue an interactive process,
*12 = convolution of *vf1* as it is directed toward *no2*,
vf1 *12 = the process is completed at an instant "*t12*",

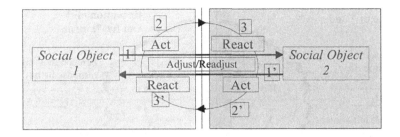

FIGURE 15.1A

A Symbolic representation of the conventional action/reaction sequence of events between two (social) objects.
1, 2, 3 and 1', 2', 3'.

(a) $no1 \rightarrow [\{(vf1.*12)\}]$,
(b) $[\{(vf'1.*'12) \rightarrow no2\}]$,
for the forward action(s), and

(c) $no2 \rightarrow [\{ (vf2.*21) \}]$,
(d) $[\{(vf'2.*'21) \rightarrow no1 \}]$,

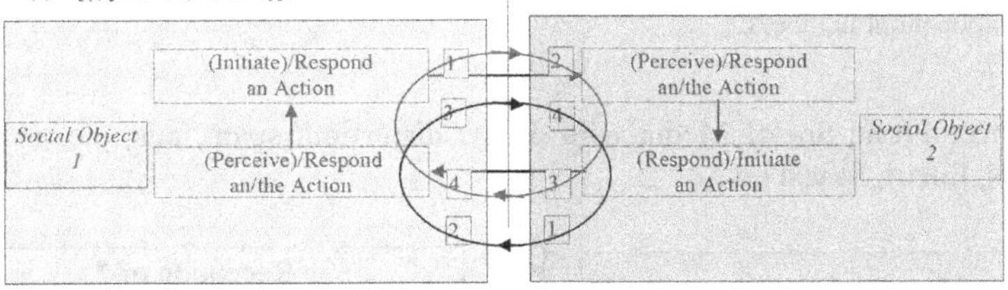

Pattern1: *Object 1 Initiates*   →   *Object 2 Perceives*
          Object 2 Responds   →   *Object 1 Initiates next action in response*

Pattern2: *Object 2 Initiates*   →   *Object 1 Perceives*
          Object 1 Responds   →   *Object 2 Initiates next action in response*

FIGURE 15.1B

A Modified representation of a series (1-2-3-4) of interactions between two (social) objects giving rise to a boundary of relation reinforced by the sequence and the nature of interactions that can reinforce the emotional, intellectual, financial, etc., leading to a border, an understanding, or boundary of the relation or bondage of the two social objects. Blue ellipse for social object 1; Red ellipse for social Object 2. Both are simultaneously active in most transactions dealing with human beings.

$\Delta k12$ = an incomplete element of knowledge is transmitted into the social media at an instant "$t1$",
$vf2$ = an action invoked or responded by $no2$ to initiate/continue the interactive process,
$*21$ = convolution of $vf2$ as it is directed toward $no1$,
$vf2 *21$ = the process $vf2 *21$ is completed at an instant "$t21$",
$\Delta k21$ = an incomplete element of knowledge is transmitted into the social media at an instant "$t2$".

The communication is not complete unless no1 adds the two elements of knowledge as:

$$\Delta k = \Delta k12 + \Delta k21$$

The unit or module of communication in the social domain is completed as on sequence of (a, b, c, d) subprocesses and depicted in the circle shown in Figure 15.3.

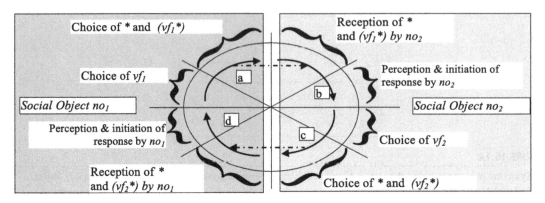

FIGURE 15.2

Enhanced and detailed analysis of the events in a transaction within a sequence of interactions for a social machine to be able to track, enhance, modify, suggest, stipulate, and social dialog and interactive processes. Analysis of this nature was also necessary in building conventional computer with arithmetic processor units (APUs), when the early computer hardware designers were developing multipliers and dividers for integer, floating point, and exponential numbers.

Noisy and Error Prone Social Media with delay, distortion, spam, ads, etc. (e.g., Internet, Comm. networks, Email, Skype etc.

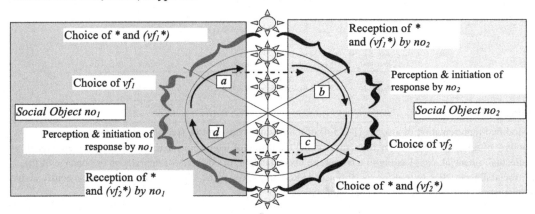

The presence of noise in the media is depicted by a series of stars in the center of the diagram. The received entities *VFs*, * and *NOs* will not be same as the transmitted entities. Miscommunication, delay and distortion are added to the originally transmitted entities.

FIGURE 15.3

Depiction of an elemental social transaction wherein two incremental modules of knowledge $\Delta k12$ and $\Delta k21$ are exchanged between no1 and no2. These modules are filtered from the contaminated media signals, sorted and systematically accumulated into the bulk of knowledge banks $K12 = \Sigma k12$ for no1 and $K21 = \Sigma k21$ for no2. In packet switching systems, this procedure is followed routinely as computers exchange packets of data. The figure depicts a continuum of these social transactions that give rise to a meaningful and integrated social event.

15.2.1 TIMING IMPLICATIONS IN SOCIAL TRANSACTIONS

In making the processes in Figure 15.3 programmable by social machines and computers, the sequence of events and timing aspects become essential. In addition, most interactions in current Internet age are network based and numerous delays, distortions, nonlinearity's, and errors can occur. Social machines thus need a foundation of technical computing to account for the transmission, delays, and distortions in these existing networks. The entire communication will thus have the social individual aspects and the network aspects in dealing with the flow or exchange of information and knowledge from one social entity to the other.

15.3 FIVE BASIC TRUISMS AND THEIR IMPLICATIONS

Five truisms presented in Section 14.4 have far-reaching implication. Summarized briefly, these axioms can be states as: (i) organisms change continually from within and from without, (ii) organisms are mutual interdependent; physical laws and/or their particular utility theory that governs the balance of interrelationships, (iii) change of organizational structure and relations needs energy, (iv) organic changes are quantum in nature but statistical methods are applicable, and (v) changes in organisms are partially mathematical; symbols and their own equations are applicable.

The implications and effects of these truisms are explored further in the following sections, in context to the interactive role of social organisms.

15.3.1 QUANTIZED CHANGES AND ALGEBRAIC VARIATIONS

Social changes are individualistic and quantum in nature since every social entity is unique and its actions, reactions, and interaction are both distinctive and dynamic. Hence, social processes are not precisely definable by a set of equations. They are however, predictable with a certain level of confidence.

In view of this reality, the machines that emulate social behavior and its consequences would need the observations of similar entities stored in statistical data and knowledge bases. A certain amount of pattern matching also becomes necessary to match the nature and attributes of the current social entity in comparison with those of the observed population. Such procedures are commonly used when human beings estimate/predict the behavior of individual students, employees, and staff members.

15.3.2 SOCIALLY ORIENTED KCO'S AND THEIR MOVEMENTS

The social entities (like human elements, doctors, patients, staff, bacteria, viruses, etc.) and other knowledge centric objects (*KCOs* [3]) are alive, and their profiles constantly changing. Physical, social, cultural, and environment processes around such objects are constantly occurring. Most of these processes are conceivable; some are programmable, and a few are totally computable.

Every event and change in their vicinity assumes life forms of their own. This observation is also valid in pure sciences. For example, each photon in light or each electron in the electric current is an entity and is influenced by its immediate environment. Many billions of such entities make for light and electric current in the real world. Yet the statistical methods yield probabilistic results and the confidence level of the cluster of such entities is very high leading to a certainty. When the behavior is integrated over large populations and large durations, the measurements and computational methods become accurate and applicable. For instance, the flow of current is accurately measurable in the physical world. The accuracy of the measuring devices is coarse and does not measure the electronic charge densities or their flow. Similar reasoning applies in the measurement of light intensity but not at a photonic level.

15.3.3 EXTENSION INTO MEDICAL AND EMOTIONAL ENVIRONMENTS

The group behavior of bacteria or viruses is predictable (most of the time). The influence of medications is also documented reasonably well by observing the response of large populations. There is a reasonable level of confidence about the effectiveness of the treatment when antibacterial or antiviral medications are used by patients. In a sense, the statistical methodology is applicable to other social objects such as how a group of students may react in a classroom situation, even though the response of any one student can vary considerably from the response of another. The methodology shifts from being analytical to being statistical, but the laws of means and variances become operative.

In the social environments, the group behavior of most of the noun objects is conceivable though not accurately computable. The objects[2] can also be abstract, emotional, physiological, or even imagined but encompassed and influenced by other physical objects. However, being under some (extraneous or intrinsic) process or the other, they suffer from statistical variations. Such processes can be frail and intangible occupying only mental dimensions and coordinates. Objects real or abstract abide by the laws of science at the macro level or by the laws of statistics at the very micro or pico level. Some social objects (such as pain, sorrow, disappointment, failure, etc.) can traverse the micro level to the macro level quite rapidly, radically, and freely. They are affected by feeling, social pressures, and environmental factors and forces. When such forces are sensed and conceived, the two immediate effects become evident. Force, counter-force, displacement, momentum, and acceleration are inherently coupled as torque, counter-torque, angular rotation, momentum, acceleration. They are as feasible in the social domain as they are in the physical domain where Newtonian and relativistic laws are applicable.

The change, rate of change, and the acceleration of change of such (abstract or mental, real or imaginary) objects is viable and result from human, social, spiritual, etc., influence. In the medical field, the effects of treatment are predictable and the rate of recovery or cure can be conceived. Equations incorporating mass, inertia, center of gravity (or focus), center of momentum can be conceived for most *KCOs*; few *KCOs* can be programed, and fewer can be computed accurately enough. In most cases, predictive behavior becomes the prime and accuracy becomes secondary. Knowledge is thus made comprehensible, and the dynamics of knowledge is made conceivable by analyzing the (socialized) forces, torques, moments (the nature and dosage of medication) on the *KCOs* in relation with their mass, inertia, and center of moments (the nature of illness, the extent of sickness).

---

[2]An object so *radically* disconnected with any other object that even imagination cannot penetrate becomes a *nonentity*. Linkage(s) in some form of human senses or sciences is essential to analyze and to conceive and treat it by some mathematical or computational technique(s).

15.3.4 **MULTIPLICITY OF SOCIOLOGICAL INFLUENCES**

KCOs suffer manipulation by other noun objects that change their mental image and their relationships to other *KCOs*. For example, children are pampered, coddled, loved, and sometimes spoiled. Parents of others help build the self-image and provide a mental anchorage for the children. Stability is not the forte of knowledge or of the objects around which knowledge is gathered. This constant flux creates an illusion that the mind learns to filter out by connecting to firmer objects. Numerous objects and verb functions hold a greater extent of firmness than others do. For example, parents for a child (generally) hold a firmer status or gravity is more stable than the force of a locally generated electromagnet, etc. In reality, every object suffers destabilizing or modifying influences from one or more interconnected objects. Human beings cope by classifying noun objects and verb functions as inconsequential, irrelevant. Thus in a coarser framework, entire groups and populations of objects can become nonentities, and their influence can be ruled out. Threshold limits in social machines accomplish this (almost) human behavior in distinguishing the *Vf's* from inconsequential *NOs*.

When any particular behavior is noticeable as human, the social-ware of a machine is programed to emulate such behavior, provided the rationality and sanity exists between the cause and effect. Such approaches in other disciplines are omnipresent. For example, when a number becomes smaller than the limit of accuracy in a computer system, it is truncated as a zero, when two floating point numbers are multiplied and stored, the truncation of the least significant numbers occurs automatically (unless a double precision arithmetic is invoked). In a similar vein, secondary social reactions can be ignored in social machine. In the medical field, the side effects of life-saving medications or treatments are overlooked by doctors, unless they are themselves life threatening.

In order to live in an infinitely complex world of innumerable social forces, noun objects learn to deal with a finite set of influences in an orderly, coherent, and a cogent fashion. This mode of operation permits the operating system (OS) of social machines to be resilient and durable to tackle the problem of most social objects. The inherent advantage is that of speed, accuracy, and connectivity to the Internet and other social networks and machines. Social machine should thus perform as effectively as the conventional computers in solving a great majority (though not each and every one) of the social problems. It can offer an approximate and a legitimate answer as much and INTERN software [4] offers an uncertain diagnosis when the input is insufficient, conflictive, or simply inaccurate.

15.3.5 **SOCIOMETRIC ENERGIES**

Social changes are not entirely haphazard, nor totally chaotic. Cause-effect relations prevail. Conversely, when there is an action or a reaction of some sort, there is a cause in the reversed time domain. Newtonian forces and rotational torques dictate the movements and rotation. Twisting torques also influence the way in which a *KCO* gets distorted in the social environment. Since time and its perpetual effects are all presents, there is energy associated with the dynamics of social objects in society. For example, a scream versus a shout, or a suggestion versus a command carries different force factors and impact levels. Integrated over time their respective energy levels are also different. In the machine environments blinking lights and siren alarms carry higher-energy spectrum than a display on a screen.

The responding *KCOs* tend to offer a variety of responses ranging from a simplistic response to chaotic behavior in the form of scatter plots. But by and large, there are average and variance numbers for the type of response(s) which a social machine can easily predict and process.

Sociometric energies have forward effect, to the extent that they invoke a response from the recipient object and a backward effect, to the extent that they deplete the energy (however, small it may be) from the activator element. This effect is dominant in adverse social relations where the recipient-object can (physically, emotionally, financially, etc.) destroy or threaten the activator. For example, if a single wild dog tries to attack a bison, the bison may simply trample the dog to death. In social settings, the formality of relationships (such as boss-employee, teacher-student, doctor-patient, etc.) prevents chaotic behavior or disorderly conduct. Energies transferred and transfused are in controlled and formalized fashion over prearranged and/or prescribed durations of time.

In comparison to the physical environment, the laws of conservation of energy [5] assume a guise of laws of transfused energies where the formality of relationship (if any) governs the amplification, attenuation, transformations, and/or transmutation of physical, emotional, financial,[3] energies, and resources. If the formality is blocked out, a sense of wild animal behavior can accrue where "might is right" becomes the dominant mode of behavior. Machines can emulate such behavior of the physical noun objects; deplete the emotional energies (thus preventing further motivation to advance vf's); and /or deplete the financial reserves of objects.

15.3.6 SERIES OF TRANSACTION AND BORDERS OF RELATIONS

Social entities tend to establish healthy long lasting relationships. Most transactions are formalized, and social energies are not wasted but conserved toward generating socially and mutually gratifying interactions. One of the unnerving facts during interactions is that every transaction is unique causing an uncertainty in the outcome.

When studied in detail, this quantized modality of behavior offers interesting statistical patterns somewhat similar to how a group of electrons would deplete the positive charge while carry a current (in the opposite direction, of course). Certain modes of behavior from individuals do deplete the patience of others and vice versa. However, when integrated over a finite duration and a finite number of cases, a pattern emerges leading to how a noun object group initiates or responds in a given set of circumstances. For example, it is documented as to how a police officer should behave during investigating a crime scene or making an arrest, thus making it energy efficient to go through routine procedures.

In the machine representations, the software would adopt the mean (average, prescribed, documented, etc.) pattern but learn to modify it depending on the social objects and the circumstances. This mode action and reaction are generally practiced by most human beings and animals (pets, domesticated animals, etc.). However, randomness does occur and the ability to collect samples of behavioral variations becomes necessary. The separation of signals (i.e., those that lead to a meaningful interaction) from misleading trivialities (i.e., jitter or noise) is essential to carry a social machine to successful and useful results.

Figure 15.4 depicts an enhanced, detailed, and computable set of events in a transaction within a sequence of interactions for a social machine to be able to track, enhance, modify, suggest, stipulate and social dialog and interactive processes. Analysis of this nature was also necessary in building conventional computer with arithmetic processor units (APUs), when the early computer hardware designers were developing multipliers and dividers for integer, floating point, and exponential numbers.

These procedural steps are necessary to be able to track, enhance, modify and recompute the individual step in social transactions and depicted in Figure 15.5.

---

[3]Accumulated wealth is considered as a form of social energy to the extent that money offers the potential of transacting social transactions, "work" or business.

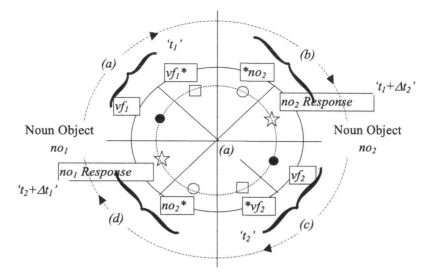

FIGURE 15.4

Configuration of the iterative (a, b, c, d) cycle to signify action-reaction or stimulus-response interactions between two noun objects no1 and no2. The two objects find convergence, oscillations, and/or divergence in the interaction process over a period of time $\Sigma(\Delta t\text{'s})$. The effect of time is included in the diagram by t1, t2, and $\Delta t1$, $\Delta t2$, where the 1 refers to no1 and 2 refers to no2 and Δ's refer to reaction times. If the sequence a, b, c, d is followed in the interactive process, it is implied that Δt's are positive and t2 > t1.

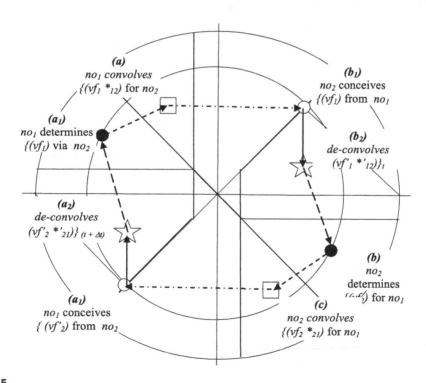

FIGURE 15.5

Enhancement of the iterative (a, b, c, d) cycle to time the eight processes in a unit of interaction between no1 and no 2. Many such units "add up" to the two bodies of knowledge or two bodies of knowledge or BoKs that are communicated.

15.4 TIME, TRANSACTIONS, AND OSCILLATIONS

Time plays a vital role in the cycle of transactions. If the elemental cycles "abcd" has a period for oscillation, then this interval is based on the response time of the individuals and social media constants to communicate the forward action and the ensuing reaction as:

$$no1 \rightarrow \{(vf1 \cdot {}^{*}12)(vf'1 \cdot {}^{*\prime}12) \rightarrow no2\}t$$

and the response action

$$no1 \leftarrow \{(vf'2 \cdot {}^{*\prime}21)(vf2 \cdot {}^{*}21) \leftarrow no2\}(t + \Delta t)$$

Based to the volatility of human nature, different proportions of emotional and intellectual contents may constitute the type of actions and reactions, stimuli, and responses. For this very basic limitation, the human and social personalities are always totally consistent, the (a, b, c, d) cycle would show a tendency to wobble and tremble. Radical changes and drifts are not generally the forte of healthy human beings and social organizations. Slow and well-conceived movements are indicative of social adjustments and its converse. Hence the machine learns in an adaptive fashion and filters out rapid and unexpected changes.

15.4.1 PROCESS SEQUENCING IN UNITS OF INTERACTION

The social machines follow changes in human temperament, and adjustment provided they are (reasonably) slow and programmable. The window for readjustment of the behavioral tendencies (or parameters) is sufficiently wide for the machine to provide and substantiate the change in its solutions to social problems. However, the machine should be able to decide and accommodate human variations during its learning sessions. For example, if a group of emergency-room doctors respond to a patient population slightly differently, then the machine would have a reference mean and an acceptable variance to be able to "derive" what the average response should be and monitor the variations about the average response. Some procedures are streamlined and for the situations where procedures are not streamlined, the machine will provide a solution from what it has learned.

In Figure 15.6, the details in the (a, b, c, d) loop are elaborated further. The processes and their timing are critical in programing any social machine. These loops become the equivalent of machine instructions in typical stored-program computers. The incremental "bodies of knowledge" are built up in the memories as the units of transactions are "executed" in the social machine. To this extent, the social machine as a subhuman robotic communication processor that provides flexible and adaptive connectivity between social objects. The machine also acts as an adaptive language convolution encoder depending upon the preferences and practices of the participants. These rather cumbersome processes can be readily programed in any intelligent handheld device and cell phones.

In reality, there are timing jitters caused by variations in the network response times and channel response times. This is especially the case over ATM networks [6] on fiber optic backbone networks [7] where the channels and links are allocated in real time. The frame delay and cell delay can be slightly variable, but within the limits of tolerance based on the pre-chosen subscriber quality of service. In general, the human delay time dominates the overall delay of the sub-elements of the social transactions.

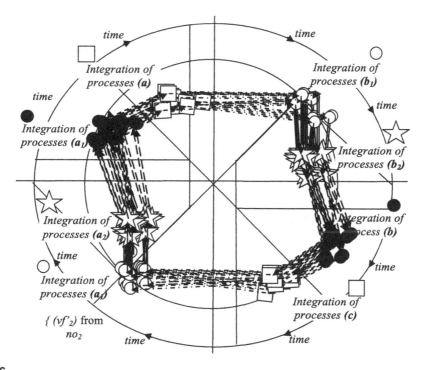

FIGURE 15.6

Diagram of the iterative cycle (a, b, c, d) over time to indicate the variable and quantized nature of the responses from no1 and no2 to variations in the delays in the social paths of both participants. Furthermore the variation of delays in the network channels also causes the jittery nature of these eight points in the loop. However, these variations have a range and most social objects adapt themselves to carry on a meaningful exchange of knowledge in spite of the timing jitters.

15.4.2 QUANTIZED NATURE OF SOCIAL TRANSACTIONS

Human transactions are tailored to the context. Intellectual, social, and emotional factors play their own/joint roles. Variations are inevitable uniqueness is distinct and thus every transaction bears its own signature. In the context of social machines, these transactions cannot be ideally duplicated or simulated. However, when the machine recognizes the context, it can supplement additional information from its own personality profiles, emotional bases, knowledge bases, WWW knowledge resources, etc.

In Figure 15.7, the depiction of a prolonged social transaction is presented. When the forward movement time is depicted as the circle with clockwise rotation, then the (a, b, c, d) sequence follows a

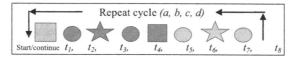

sequence of a mini-process within the transaction. In order to be consistent with the sequence of functions in the computer field, we propose a Table 15.1. The functions and processes standardized

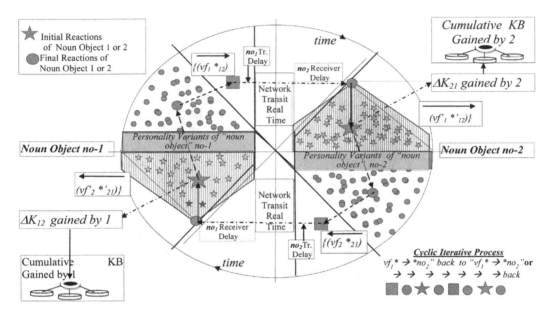

FIGURE 15.7

Interactive processes involved in the interaction "vf1* → *no2" and by its response "vf2* → *no1". Learning is embedded in the two increments of knowledge gained in ΔK12 by no1, and in ΔK21 by no2.

Table 15.1 Suggested Location for Functions to be Embedded in Knowledge Software

Context Process	Computer Systems	Social Systems
Continued and repeatedly performed major tasks and functions	Application programs	Discourses/meetings Conferences/events
Major structural module	Scientific, business, corporate, medical, etc., program	Social transaction of any nature, in most of the human dealings
Major function	Program module (e.g., subroutine, library, I/O module, etc.)	Interaction (e.g., speech, looks, gestures, any stylized form)
Events within libraries, subroutines, program modules	Process (e.g., I/O, DMA, disk, display, ALU, memory, switching, etc.)	Exchange of (Social, Technical, Emotional, etc.) information.
Modular function(s)	Mini process (e.g., FDE repetitive cycle assembly programs)	(a, b, c, d) Repetitive cycle within an interactions
Macros and macro functions	Control program Micro-instructions	Flow of knowledge, contents (social, verbal, emotional, technical, etc.)
Minor function and binary instructions	Micro-process HW/ IC/Logic process in VLSI	Subconscious/reflex reaction to a situation

Note: I/O = input/output, DMA = direct memory access, ALU = arithmetic logic unit, FDE = fetch-next-executable-instruction, decode operation code, execute, HW = hardware, IC = integrated circuit, VLSI = very large scale integration generally refers to chips.

in the computer field, and their corresponding equivalents in the evolving social field are depicted. The design of the social software is facilitated by enforcing the organizing and methodology established in the computer software industry.

To some extent, the machine can be instructed to filter out the rough edges or undue emotional flares that are typical in harsh human behavior (unless it is an established personality trait and included as options for each, either or both noun objects no1 and no2). Interactions can become unstable and lean toward offering unsatisfactory conclusions to any social transaction. Wars, unresolved differences, and conflicts are the more likely machine outcome when coarse tendencies prevail in the emotional databases of social machines.

An additional portrayal by the social machine is indicated by the spread of the eight points in Figure 15.6. In an ideal situation, Figure 15.6 would shrink to Figure 15.5 indicated by single sequence with eight end points in every exchange of every transaction:

indicative of a one-step process. The whole social transaction is one (a, b, c, d) cycle and there would be totally rational exchange of one verb functions vf1 from no1 which is convoluted perfectly as *12 for no2 at an instant "*t*" and the response action from no2 would be an equal perfect to completely satisfy no1.

$$no1 \rightarrow \{(vf1 \cdot {}^{*}12)(vf'1 \cdot {}^{*'}12) \rightarrow no2\}t$$

And the response action.

$$no1 \leftarrow \{(vf'2 \cdot {}^{*'}21)(vf2 \cdot {}^{*}21) \leftarrow no2\}(t + \Delta t)$$

In Figure 15.6, an extensive spread of the eight points is shown. Such a spread is indicative of a diversity of the items discussed, and size of the cumulative knowledge bases is indicative of the knowledge gained by the two social objects no1 and no2 about each other. Any rapid variation in the sizes indicates the impulsive nature of the two corresponding parties. It is also feasible to estimate the extent of compromise that either party has made in reaching the final position of the eight points shown as compared to the initial starting point location of these points.

These points are also indicative of the economic compromise (made by no1 and no2) by calculating the financial expectation of each party from the initial positioning of the four points for no1 and no2, respectively. The mean scalar distance between final position and the starting position indicates the extent of economic sacrifice of each of the two social objects no1 and no2.

All interactions may not necessarily reach successive convergence. A lack of convergence indicates the final intellectual, emotional, financial, etc. distances between no1 and no2. All the distances do not have to close to zero or some acceptable minimum value, concurrently. The social machine can track the slow, oscillatory, or steady convergence over a given duration, if it occurs. Divergence and its different flavors are also equally well tracked by the social machine.

The suggested structure of the social software can emulate the human behavior accurately in hindsight be examining the (a, b, c, d) loop configuration(s) and the locations of eight points ▢●★●▣○☆○. In foresight the machine can be used to offer suggested *vf*'s and *'s, to avoid hang-ups or divergence between no1 and no2. The abuse of the social machine is equally probable when the users want to break social relationships between people or even start a war between nations.

The use of the social machine and its software can assist human beings as much as medical machines and its medical-ware can assist doctors. The case for social machines, especially the handheld wireless devices are suitable during the second and third generation of Internet device technology.

In Figure 15.7, the entire picture of a major social transaction of any nature, in most of the human dealings is presented. In the computational domain, scientific, business, corporate, medical, etc., programs may be represented by iterative convergence of the numerous steps involved in reaching the final solution. In most numerical problems and their iterative solutions on computers, some schema for acceleration of convergence becomes desirable. In the social domain, the venues for the schema lie in the hidden wisdom of the final solution to the immediate social problem. Such oracles of wisdom (e.g., peace is preferable to war, or to err is human and to forgive is divine, etc.) have survived over generations and can avoid local pitfalls to solve any social problem based purely on emotions, brutality, or drones to destroy.

The transference of knowledge gained by social machine based on human reactions is easily shifted to knowledge based on intellectual and scientific reactions readily. When the social software layer is forced to deploy the reactionary responses vf1 and/or vf2 (see Fig. 15.3) of both or either no1 and no2 based on reason-driven or scientific routines (see Fig. 15.8) during the solution of a social problem or

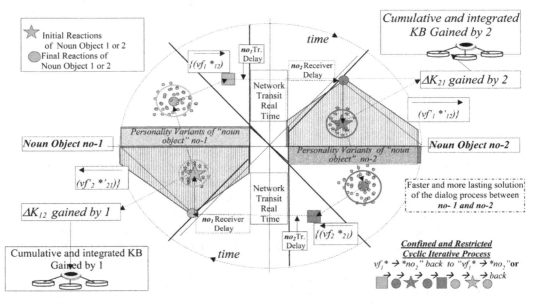

FIGURE 15.8

Interactive processes involved in the interaction "$vf1^* \to {}^*no2$" and by its response "$vf2^* \to {}^*no1$". Learning is embedded in the two increments of knowledge gained in $K12$ by $no1$, and in $K21$ by $no2$ is compared with the world wide knowledge bases during the solution of similar problems. Typically, this approach is adapted during UN deliberations and international corporate negotiations. The approach forces most of the "Stars and Circle" to be confined to limited and congested areas. The interactive process becomes more refined and civil, rather than argumentative and violent. Many wars are averted by being wise and deliberate rather than by launching trial bombs and flying drones.

dialog, then the solutions to emotional problems assume an intellectual flavor. Perhaps this is a desirable alternative when no1 and/or no2 tend to be volatile or emotional. The blending of the two responses is arbitrary, but the convergence to a realistic solution is not always assured. It is quite feasible to "derive" new oracles of "knowledge-age" wisdom for the Internet age adolescents who tend to wander away in the Internet fantasy. Such oracles where reason is stressed over emotions is likely to moderate, at least in the short run, the explosive changes brought about by the Internet in our society.

It is interesting to note the time delineated on the circumference of the circles in Figures 15.5 to 15.7 is not real time but the "social and personal time" that is embedded in the time-coordinates of the points ▫ ● ★ ● ▪ ○ ☆ ○. For example, the convolutions vf1 *12 and vf2 *21 may follow the human response times of no1 and no2 that can stretch over many days or months and not be the real time at all, unless it is a real time dialog. The distance between two consecutive points (circle to square) in the repeat cycle is the social time, whereas the distance (square to circle) is the network-connect time as shown in Figure 15.8.

15.5 MEDIATION BY KNOWLEDGE/SOCIAL MACHINES

The coarse edges of the emotional content in social situations of human noun objects can be partially erased by the oversight of a perfectly rational machine. Such a machine is an ideal of all human rationality held as an integrated (from $t = -\infty$ to $t = $ now) as a single knowledge base. Impossible as a practical entity, it can exist as two limited handheld device for two conflictive parties [8], (e.g., N. and S. Korea, Capitalists and Marxists, Haves and Have-Not) that can suggest negotiation rather than war. The databases will contain detailed information/knowledge about the areas of differences between the two parties.

The sociometric energy contained in each of the vf1 *12 and vf2 *21 within the transaction is proportional to the radius of the (blue and green) circles. When the social transaction is tense and "highly charged" there will be large circles and vice versa. For example, any angry parent accusing a submissive child will have large circles on the parent side and vice versa. Two warring nations will have a war interaction with bombs and missiles as circles in the Figures 15.7 and 15.8. When such transactions are mediated by a knowledge/social machine, the role of the machine will be to reduce the integrated surface area of both blue and green circles gradually over time to reach an emotionally stable solution.

In an ideal case, all the circles and squares in Figures 15.7 and 15.8 will become single dots, and two figures will become a single feedback loop as shown in Figure 15.5. Such a situation is not feasible unless every interacting human becomes a knowledge/social machine with perfectly synchronized clocks and operating speeds.

CONCLUSIONS

In this chapter, we have presented a practical framework for social machines to mediate and negotiate social situations between intellectual and/or emotional social objects. The profiles of the two parties are primed into the respective knowledge bases. The machine can also adjust the blending on the profiles until the irrationality or emotionality is reduced to tolerable levels from each other's perspective. In fact, the two machines will force the opposite issues on two handheld devices until each can "see" the irrationality or emotionality of the other. Both are gradually reduced to zero or near zero levels. Conversely, the machine will rationalize/emotionalize the differences until each party "sees" and appreciates the strength(s) of the other. Like the moods altering drugs, the machine will act as a psychiatrist who will move a situation from any level to a better or a higher level.

It is also possible to abuse the knowledge/social machines in the hands of war-mongers and Mafia who will exploit any social situation to their own personal gain or toward a selfish end. Numerous nations have been known to ignite a war between other nations and abuse the political power and/or the arsenal of the more powerful nations.

REFERENCES

[1] von Neumann J, Morgenstern O. Theory of games and economic behavior. Princeton University Press; 200.Chapter Zero Sum Games. Also see <https://www.math.ucla.edu/>... by TS Ferguson, Part II. Two-Person Zero-SumGames. 1. The strategic form of a game. Los Angeles: University of California.

[2] von Neumann J, Morgenstern O. Theory of games and economic behavior. Princeton University Press; 200.Chapter Non-Zero Sum Games. Also see, The theory of zero-sum games is vastly different from that of non-zero-sum games because an optimal solution can always be found.<https://cs.stanford.edu/people/eroberts/courses/.../game.../nonzero.html>.

[3] Ahamed SV. Computational framework of knowledge. Hoboken, NJ: John Wiley and Sons; 2009.

[4] Shortcliffe E. MYCIN: computer-based medical consultations.. New York: American Elsevier; 1976, See also, Buchanan BG., Shortcliffe EH. Rule-based expert system: the Mycin experiment at Stanford Heuristic Programming Project. Addison Wesley, Boston; 1984.

[5] NASA Publication at <https://www.grc.nasa.gov/www/k-12/airplane/thermo1f.html>. The conservation of energy is afundamental concept of physics along with the conservation of mass and the conservation of momentum.

[6] Ahamed SV. Intelligent Internet knowledge networks. Hoboken, NJ: Wiley Interscience; 2007.

[7] Internet backbone – The Internet backbone may be defined by the principal data routes between... Fiber-optic cables are the medium of choice for Internet backbone providers for... <https://en.wikipedia.org/wiki/Internet_backbone>. Accessed January 2016.

[8] Social conflict theory in sociology: definition & contributors, study.com/.../ Jan 23, 2015 – Social conflict theory sees social life as a competition and focuses on the distribution of resources, power, and inequality.

SUMMARY

FROM INTERNET-BASED SYSTEMS TO MEDICAL MACHINES

This part covers the principles in treating knowledge as a scientific entity. Though not entirely physical, knowledge has certain discernible flow characteristics and its dynamic nature. Knowledge becomes amenable to quantization and fragmentation. Words, phrases, sentences, etc., that have to follow the structure of language and expression, also carry the knowledge embedded in them, thus imparting a distinctive structure and flavor to knowledge. More than that, the use of figures, illustrations and charts makes the communication of knowledge forceful, potent, energy-centric and directional with vectorial properties. Such vector properties and directions can be altered by other "bodies of knowledge" also exerting their own force, power, energy, and directionality. The dynamics of knowledge emerges due to these "knowledge fields."

This part also discusses, interprets and projects the behavioral, economic and long-term implications of social networks. Information and knowledge aspects in balancing human needs and economic activity in knowledge and information society are both blended to find individual balance for human beings and societies and nations. The role of computers and communication networks is integrated with the social, mental and medical aspects of the society.

In summary, we have presented the flow of contemplative human thought through the book is like fragrance in a Garden of Eden. Both captivate the imagination. The title is the breeze and words are the songs: the suggestion to the reader is to see beyond the words and figures that constitute chapters of the book. We submit to the readers to ponder and contemplate a time span four-five decades from now. Intellectual spaces like fragrances are here to be mapped, understood and put to good use for the joy of human race.

THE SCIENTIFIC BASIS FOR KNOWLEDGE FLOW

I

PART II, SECTION I, SUMMARY

Section 01 with five chapters deals with the scientific and physical basis for the flow of information and knowledge. The widely documented principles for the flow of electricity, heat and fluids only offer an entry point into the domain of knowledge in chapter 16. When the flow of knowledge is considered as the flow of the elements of knowledge (or kels) that make up a larger body of knowledge (KCO), then the media characteristics for the flow of KCO can be envisioned and discussed in chapter 17. This rather primitive approach is enhanced further by considering the flow of knowledge based on the combined characteristics of the type of knowledge and the media characteristics to that particular type. The tools and techniques for this more refined approach are based on the transmission theory of data streams in chapter 18. This methodology developed at Bell Laboratories (of the 1960s to 1990s era) has been deployed by the communication scientists for last five or six decades. When kels are very finely subdivided, then principles of quantum (or kuantum) physics are applicable and finally inspiration theory for the flow of knowledge presented in chapters 18 and 19 of this part with a presentation of the fragmented properties of knowledge and their flow in chapter 20.

GENERAL FLOW THEORY OF KNOWLEDGE

CHAPTER SUMMARY

In this chapter, we propose a methodology for quantifying the flow of knowledge based on simple rules of flow that govern the flow of current, heat or fluids. Knowledge being radically different from any of these established down to earth concepts starts to display that the approach based on conduction theory soon become ineffective, if not futile to be very precise in the quantification the flow of knowledge. However, the inroads of these discipline carved out over many decades offer a rough mapping of potentials, resistances, path impedances, work-done, and energies transferred. At the outset, knowledge does not abide by universal law of conservation of energy nor by the basic laws of fluid mechanics, instead knowledge needs its own laws and precepts to quantify its flow, rate of flow, and energies transferred from one knowledge centric object (*KCO*) to another.

The conceptual framework evolved in this chapter, together with the tools of characterization of *KCOs* in any given discipline offers the explanation that the knowledge potential acquired by anyone depends on the differences of knowledge potentials, the duration of interaction, and the resistance to flow of knowledge between the participants. Concepts developed here are generic and they can be used most disciplines and in most places. The chapter also identifies the makeup of the "source" and the "receptor" *KCOs* and addresses the process of knowledge transfer wherein the constitution of the *KCOs* is altered and adjusted by the "work done" during the knowledge energy transfer. By adapting and enhancing equations from heat-, current-, or fluid-flow laws of physics, electrical engineering or fluid mechanics, we propose the knowledge flow be similarly quantified. Though simple and direct, this approach is coarse and approximate. It yields values for knowledge entities that happen at a subconscious level for human minds and for animate objects and at data and knowledge levels in intelligent communication systems and machines.

16.1 INTRODUCTION

There are four major Chapters 16 through 19, in this Section related to the flow of knowledge. Chapter 16 deals with the generic flow theory to quantify knowledge as we measure the current, fluid-flow, heat, magnetic fields, etc. Chapter 17 deals with flow of knowledge as we would quantify current and voltage signals in transmission media and filters with their own characteristics in electrical communication theory. Chapter 18 deals with the flow of knowledge based on the *kuantum* theory where the individual quantum of knowledge can interact with the medium it is traversing. Finally Chapter 19 deals with the inspirational basis for the transfer of knowledge without any media but between transmitters and receptors with matching characteristics. Chapter 19 discusses that knowledge does not need a medium at all, and it can traverse infinitely large distances and cross most frontiers of time.

Evolution of Knowledge Science. DOI: http://dx.doi.org/10.1016/B978-0-12-805478-9.00016-9

Wherever evolution has brought any species, adaptation and learning have become the foremost nature in life to exist and life in nature to coexist [1]. The origin for the flow of knowledge is evident in all social environments, even without dabbling in uncharted oceans of marine biological evolution. The habitats of the primitive to those of the Internet wherefrom knowledge societies are evolving both hold the human mind as the driving element. Knowledge bases are the nodes and human minds are the leaves. Information and knowledge flow freely through the fiber and wireless networks at in-creditable terabit-per-second rates as do concepts and wisdom flow freely through the sensory and neural networks at a few cycle-per-second humanistic rates. The universal laws of physical science that dictate the flow of teraflops per second in machines and the philosophic ideals that dictate evolutions of morality and ethics in human minds reflect each other but at two different connected levels of thought. Both are intricately interwoven in the science of knowledge and in the philosophy of existence.

Two identifiable interactive objects and three dominant parameters at play surface in the flow of knowledge in most settings. For example, the teacher and the student become the *two* interacting social objects. The capacity or potential (as a primary parameter) of the teacher to deliver knowledge, the net resistivity (as a secondary parameter) of the path that links the teacher and the student, and finally the receptivity (as a tertiary parameter) of the student, become the *three* parameters. In quantifiable units, these parameters govern the quantized "velocity" of knowledge flow, the "intensity" or rate of flow. Time in seconds, semesters, years, or decades becomes necessary for the knowledge potentials of the *two* interacting objects to become roughly the same, if they can ever become equal! In reality, these potentials meet at an uneasy but stable boundary wherein constructive dialog can exist. The duration for the evolved state of knowledge-flow through the Internet can be roughly broken down in four eras: the circa 1900, circa 1980, circa 2000 and finally circa 2015.

Circa 1900: Established in shrines, schools, universities, libraries, the flow of knowledge was based on dedication of gurus and, scholars their expertise, concentration of knowledge, personal communication. Scriptures, books, and human skills played a dominant role.

Circa 1980: Computers, computer languages, programing (COBOL, Fortran, Primitive DB Languages) were firmly in place and the flow of knowledge was well along high-speed digital pathways from data banks to the users of distributed networks.

Circa 2000: Standardizations, global networks, Open System Interconnect, Internet (TCP/IP), Switching Systems, AI based Learning, Operating Systems and Network Control, Fiber Optics and Optical Switches have already transformed the flow of data and information encoded in digital streams. An entirely new philosophy of dealing with knowledge and its processing had evolved.

Circa 2015: Internet II, Knowledge Networks, Global Libraries, On Line revolution based on knowledge processing and concept building is in vogue. New machines to safeguard pristine knowledge appear eminent.

Through the millennia, a few basic truisms have survived; three dominant themes have withstood the test of time. (1) Human beings operate in the knowledge space (KS) through their perceptions and ensuing actions to satisfy their inherent needs. (2) Cosmic, super, global, normal, mini, micro, and nano objects (noun objects) play a role in interacting with other objects. (3) What action (verb functions) occurs and how they interact (convolution) and when it occurs (*t*) are contextually related. Based on this premise it is possible to build a framework for the science of knowledge.

16.2 **THE STATE OF AN OBJECT**

Knowledge objects are time, situation, and system dependent variables. From fine cellular structures to greater universes, they are constantly under a condition of flux in an effort to maintain, sustain, and improve their structures. Change can range from being infinitely slow and degenerative to infinitely fast and explosive. Given sufficient time and sufficiently fast measurements of these change, the nature of the forces, the resulting movements, and velocities of objects can be tracked reasonably accurately.

Knowledge centric objects do not reach a state of perfect equilibrium but their movement can be tracked in the KS. Internal and external forces and their energies constantly shape the status of most objects. Elements (increments) of energy and time are thus involved to change the status. Objects, their velocities, and their very existence at any given (spatial and time) coordinates form a fuzzy triad much as forces, movements, and energies form a scientific triangle for physical objects. When a *KCO* interacts or acts upon another *KCO*, body of knowledge (*BoK*), any global noun object (*NO*), or any local noun object "*n*", energies, and entropies are altered to reach from one state of a dynamic and partially stable existence to another.

In Figure 16.1 the basis of energy and entropy is illustrated from the traditional perspectives [2−4]. In Figure 16.2 the basis of *kenergy* and *kentropy* is illustrated from a knowledge domain perspective. The actual shapes of the curves in these figures are not important. However, they depict the fundamental relations between energy and entropy in thermodynamics by using temperature in °A on the Absolute scale along the X-axis in Figure 16.1. In the knowledge domain, when the *kentropy* of *n2* is high, even a small amount of positive "*kenergy*" from donor object *n1 reduces* the *kentropy* (disorder) of receptor object *n2* by a considerable amount, i.e., it reduces the "disorder" considerably.

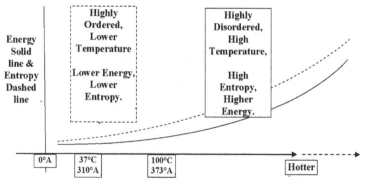

A Typical Thermodynamic System

Temperature is used as a measure along the X axis for this thermodynamic environment

FIGURE 16.1

Depiction of a typical thermodynamic system where an object is moved to the right (i.e., gains temperature) and consequently gains entropy. This representation is typical for a system where the temperature of an object or entity is indicated by the average of all temperatures level of all elements in that system.

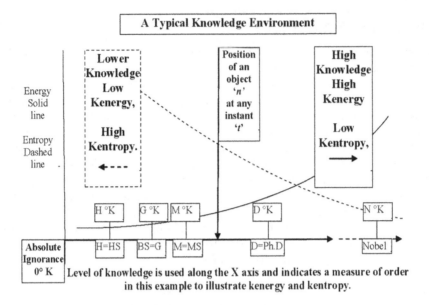

Level of knowledge is used along the X axis and indicates a measure of order in this example to illustrate kenergy and kentropy.

FIGURE 16.2

Representation of a typical knowledge system where the knowledge or order position of an object or entity is indicated by the average knowledge level of all directions of knowledge embedded in that entity. On the X-scale a new measure (°K) is used. The horizontal distance from the origin indicates the degrees of knowledge at each of the points. Much alike temperature that can be elevated or depressed the degrees of knowledge can be altered by internal force or by external objects. This alters the initial and its total kentropy levels of the objects.

Further, in the knowledge domain depicted in Figure 16.2, the temperature along the X-axis is replaced by the knowledge potential measured in °K with 0°K to represent absolute ignorance reach higher and higher temperature as the level of education gets higher. Much like science has never experienced 0°K, it is likely that we will never know what absolute ignorance is or will be. Much like what a *practical range* of temperatures of "freezing water" at 0°C to boiling water and "sea level" at 100°C, we can establish a *practical range* of knowledge potential is at high school (HS) graduation (1°K) to a similar potential at college graduation (100°K). It is to be appreciated that these numbers are imprecise and the accurate exact measurements of temperature, pressure at sea level, purity of water, etc. are imprecise.

The benchmark for absolute ignorance is yet to be established. In the knowledge domain, this instant is perhaps the start of the collapse of the earlier universes that led to the Big Bang, an instant of time when all prior knowledge collapsed into utter chaos and zero (dis)order. Whatever it may be, the knowledge degrees (in °K) of the most distant form of life (e.g., single cell organisms or most primitive life forms) is likely to a low number measured like the temperature of the universe. Perfect ignorance of any object would also entail total unawareness of itself and the stabilizing algorithms that would instill its own recognition. By this definition any object approaching 0°K would have long disintegrated just like any object or entity approaching 0°A would reach unsustainable state of super condensed matter.

For the lack of any standard measuring units along the X-axis direction, we suggest the use of degrees of knowledge[1] (°K) to measure knowledge along the X-axis. The knowledge status of HS is designated as H°K, and the knowledge status of a Nobel laureate (Nobel) is designated as N°K. The differential degrees between the knowledge status of a PhD object and a HS object would be (D-H) °K and is measured the "knowledge degrees." In the same vein, the degree measure of a PhD object will be P°K along the X-axis. However, knowledge is gained or lost from any one level to another over a duration of time. The movement of knowledge entails the concept of its mass or inertia[2] but this is not a fixed number like the mass/inertia of a physical object: though dynamic and variable, it can be updated in the computer memory. The loss or gain of knowledge energy can be thus equated to "work-done" (= integral of + or − knowledge power over the duration; or the product of knowledge force times the displacement along the knowledge axis) in moving the mass or inertia from on knowledge level (or KnP) to the other. The variable D (that will be used to compute kentropies of various objects) thus indicates the knowledge degrees between any *KCO* at its current state to a state of a *KCO* in a state of total ignorance. From any given point of reference, the measurement of relative knowledge is in +°K measured in the positive direction and −°K measured in the negative direction.

Like heat that flows from a body at higher temperature to one at lower temperature, knowledge can flow from an object at higher °K to and one at lower °K. Like 0°A (i.e., −273°C) is virtual, the state of "total ignorance," "perfect disorder" or 0°K (i.e., perfect "disorder" (measured at the origin of Fig. 16.2)) in knowledge dimension is hypothetical, but it does provides an origin for measurement. The temperature of the farthest universes may reach about 2.725 (±0.002) °K, but 0°K is the established benchmark for the measurement of temperatures. The scales of measurement in the temperature and knowledge are presented in Figure 16.3.

The implications of the *kenergy* and *kentropy* are observable in practice. With reference to Figure 16.2, a small amount of negative *kenergy* from the news media that is directed at the H°K (i.e., HS level) population will create a more serious increase in the entropy than that in the college and graduate level population. During the last stages of political campaigns the potential losers tend to broadcast negative propaganda in the hope of swaying the larger segment of lower level population groups with negative propaganda. These quantifiable relations explain the commonly occurring social reactions in society. The nature of the donor, the knowledge potential of recipient, and the social circumstances that alter the shape and gradients of these curves explain the behaviorism that follows in a knowledge related social interaction between donors and recipients of a "module" or a "quantum" of knowledge.

---

[1]The measure of knowledge in degrees, i.e., °K is not to be confused with the symbol K that is a short form of °A. The symbol K (for Kelvin) by itself is used frequently in thermodynamics; it is also used in other sciences to denote "kilo," or 1000 in denoting Kohms (resistance) or KHz (frequency), Kg (weight), etc.
[2]We introduce the concept of "inertia or mass of knowledge" here to account for the fact that trivial *v's,*s* and *n's* do not substantially alter wisdom or concepts deeply embedded in massive *KCOs*. Conversely, massive *v's, *s* and *n's* can indeed wipe out (colonies of) *KCOs*. Megatons of knowledge (like the megatons of weight in the universe) will never be precisely known. However, the mass or inertia of knowledge to perform the daily tasks can be estimated. A sense of proportions is thus administered (like the number of KW of power) to light up a city or a building, even though we never know how many multi-MW-eons of energy made up the universe.

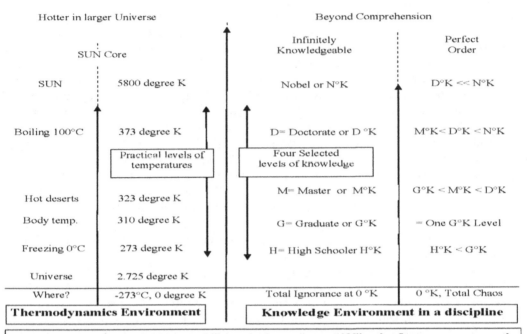

FIGURE 16.3

Comparisons of thermodynamics and knowledge environments to derive the units for the measurement knowledge energy or kenergy. These numbers are approximate but serve the basis to measure temperatures and knowledge potentials. In thermodynamics, temperature is one mode of measurement. In the knowledge domain, the discipline selected for comparison is also one direction of measurement. It is consistent with the observation that an illiterate but wise saint might be more "knowledgeable" in the integrated art of human life than a Nobel Laureate in economics or in social science (if it was to be given out in this discipline).

16.2.1 KENERGY OF OBJECTS

The notion of *kenergy* of objects is instrumental in determining which object (activator *n1*) will "act upon" and which object will be "acted upon" or who/what will be the receptor (*n2*). To receive an action from another object (*n1*), the receptor object needs a lower "action" potential and a lower *kenergy* level to receive an action. In Figure 16.4 the relative positions of *n1* and *n2* are marked {*n1* (at (i)) and *n2* (at (ii))} to indicate an incremental knowledge operation (*n1* ← *v* → *n2*).

For example, if a prey (*n2*) is to be caught by a predator (*n1*), its nature and skill sets should have a lower "reaction" potential or lower *kenergy* level. Stated alternatively, the *kentropy* of *n2* needs to be higher than the *kentropy* of *n1* for the flow of knowledge from *n1* to *n2*. Miscalculations can end up in disasters as much as the tables can turn. In the knowledge domain, group of informed students can teach instructors a "lesson," or two of their own.

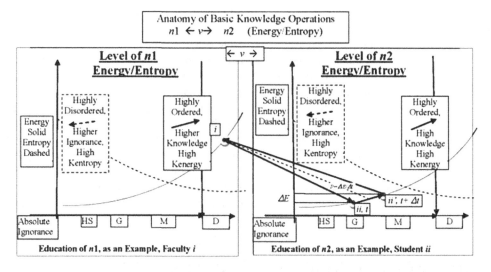

FIGURE 16.4

Relative positions of *n1* (at (i)) and *n2* (at (ii)) to indicate an incremental positive knowledge operation (*n1* ← *v* → *n2*) to take place when knowledge flows from *n1* to *n2*. It is necessary to make the X-axis consistent in both sides of the figure. In another situation when the subject matters are different, then a BS in economics can teach (positively) a Nobel laureate in chemistry and vice versa. HS = High School, G = Graduate, M = Master Degree, and D = Doctorate. Flow of knowledge has vector properties rather than scalar properties.

The availability of knowledge resources exposing the venerability of the receptor object *n2* offers the source noun *n1* the *kenergy* to contemplate an action or a verb function or "*v*" from *n1*. The estimated rate of expenditure of resources from *n1* over a specific duration offers the "power" in the punch to "act" and similarly the rate of estimated expenditure of resources from *n2* over time offers the "power" in the punch to "react." The cycle can continue till a total surrender of *n2* or of *n1* (i.e., the *kentropy* of *n2* or of *n1* is driven infinitely high) or the two parties reach a stalemate or either party have reached ultimate destruction.

The converse effect is not always the case when a small amount of positive *kenergy* from the news media is directed at the general population even though it could influence a small group of motivated professionals. Whereas conflictive knowledge interactions (e.g., political debates) deplete or defame the *kenergy* of the other party, cooperative knowledge interactions (e.g., mentor-student relations) enhance or reconstruct the *kenergy* of both parties. A converse equation for *kentropy* can also be readily derived.

16.2.2 KENTROPY OF OBJECTS

Kentropy does not have to be measured along a single direction of the DDS or the LoC classification. A weighted average of all entropies is a more logical measure of the "weakness" of the overall knowledge bases in any *KCO*. For example, the power of a nation is not estimated by its army, air power, naval power, etc., only, instead the *KCO* formed by the smaller *BoK's* based on its army, air power, naval power, army, law enforcement, etc. In many instances, the equations and relationships between *kentropy, kenergy,* and the individual weight to derive a composite value for *kentropy* and/or *kenergy* starts to display nonlinearities and instabilities. In these instances, human estimations for *kentropy* and/or *kenergy* become less and less dependable but the humanist machine can track such changes more dependably and provide a better estimation for the outcome of interactions between *n1* and *n2* and provide more appropriate strategies for the actions of *n1/n2* or "*v's*" for or against *n2/n1.* A smooth trajectory for the movement of *KCOs* in society, is thus "formulated" by the machine.

It is our estimate that the smoothness of most social transactions will improve dramatically by knowledge and humanist machines and networks just as the smoothness of most financial transactions has improved dramatically by financial systems and banking networks. In extreme cases such as wars and disasters, the source of instability is the fickle mindedness of human beings. Given a long enough period to learn the inconsistencies of the leaders, humanist machines can at least offer the best and worst case scenarios with greater precision than human guesswork. It is still to be seen if the best intuitions of humans can do better than the computational results of a human machine in the long run.

16.3 COMBINED KENERGY AND KENTROPY OF OBJECTS

The status of knowledge may be studied at three levels. In the simplest case, when an action (a verb function, a convolution, or any generic act) takes place in society, the knowledge for the recipient object(s) gets modified by the action. In the next case when an object motivates an action the energy level of the source object gets modified by the action. Finally, when the action(s) influences both the objects, the energy of the source is indicative of change of entropy of the recipient and the structures of both get modified. The structure of knowledge (i.e., the combined *kenergy* and *kentropy*) is altered in all the three cases. Hence, the dynamics of the structure of knowledge needs computation in the three cases. However, since the third case is inclusive of the earlier two cases, it becomes the most generic. In most dyadic human interactions (between *n1* and *n2*), both energies and entropies are modified by a series of (inter)actions that take place. A depiction of a typical interaction is presented in Figure 16.3. In these cases this sequence of interactive processes are invoked and a dual knowledge processor unit (KPU) machine can emulate the human interactions in an almost human way. Synchronization and active feedback from one KPU (for object *n1* or *n2*) to the other KPU (for object *n2* or *n1*) and their associated memory blocks will be necessary.

16.4 STRUCTURE OF KNOWLEDGE

Traditional knowledge has its beginning in reality, even though it quickly becomes abstract or even virtual. Finally, it may even become an entity in abstract KS of ideologists and philosophers. Real (physical) space can indeed be mapped into KS, but the converse is not always feasible. Imagination overflows reality in most routine cases. Human imagination and perception provide the tools for constructing interconnected knowledge (hyper) spaces. Furthermore, Internet has significantly altered the thought processes over the last few decades and thus added many new dimensions in the KS(s) of most individuals. The geometry of KS needs new algebras for manipulation and processing of knowledge pertaining to the objects that satisfy human needs including other human beings. Traditional algebras are directed towards the manipulation of objects in conventional Euclidian spaces and their extensions. When intelligent human objects are the participants, computational representations become more appropriate to emulate partially the transactions between objects.

In order to deal with the growing need to contain knowledge in a computational framework, the five following notions (i) through (v) in this section, are suggested. The computational symbols, objects, and entities can penetrate the KS and the computational domain, but they may not always be represented in the real (physical) space. It is desirable to have a certain amount of transparency joining these three (physical, knowledge, and computational or PS, KS, and CS) spaces. But it is also necessary to tolerate nascent objects to hop between two or more spaces within a more encompassing super-space of the same kind or any two out of the three interrelated (PS, KS and CS) spaces.

16.4.1 FIVE AXIOMS FOR THE STRUCTURE OF KNOWLEDGE

i. *KCO is a Knowledge Centric Object (KCO) and becomes a focal node in a graph of knowledge.* Knowledge collects around such objects and a *KCO* becomes a nucleus in a human mind and/or an addressable entity in the KS, and/or an addressable block of memory in a computational space.

ii. *BoK is a Body of Knowledge and a Structured Graph of KCOs in the KS. KCOs* and *BoKs* may be combined (integrated) *recursively* to form super objects. They may also be decomposed (differentiated) successively to yield sub objects.

iii. *The operator (v^*) is a convolution of verb(s) upon noun(s).* These convolutions bring about changes in knowledge graphs. Such altercations may or may not involve catalysts. Verbs actions/functions are performed by noun (objects) upon themselves or other noun objects. Both the active and passive nouns are affected by verb(s).

  a. The step $v^* \rightarrow n2 = $ A basic knowledge function that effects the recipient object $n2$. Like any basic instruction in a machine, this instruction alters (from negative increment (of any magnitude) to a positive increment (of any magnitude), the entropy of the recipient object $n2$ that is a component of any *KCO* and hence the entropy of the entire *BoK*.

  b. The step $n1 \leftarrow {}^*v = $ A basic knowledge function that affects the status of the source object $n1$. Based on the reality of the physical world, the action alters (from negative increment (of any magnitude) to a positive increment (of any magnitude)) the energy of the source object $n1$ that is a component of any *KCO* and hence the entropy of the entire *BoK*.

iv. *Objects initiate and terminate v^* or a sequence of v^*s.* If $n1$ is a source object that initiates an activity (an action or verb) "v" upon an object $n2$ a recipient object (which may be a passive or an active object), then this operation may written as

  $n1$ activates v which may affect both $n1$ and $n2$.

  Written down as two parts

  $n1 \leftarrow {}^*v$, or $n1$ initiates v with some effect on itself, and

  $v^* \rightarrow n2$ or $n2$ terminates v with some effect on itself.

  If 'v' is rewritten as

  $\leftarrow {}^*v$ and $v^* \rightarrow$

  $n1 \leftarrow {}^*v$ and $v^* \rightarrow n2$

Thus, the convolution symbol $^*v$ that has two components $\leftarrow$ and $\rightarrow$. The component $\leftarrow$ affects $n1$ (the source object) and the $\rightarrow n2$ (the recipient object) respectively. For example, in zero-sum situation, $n1$ may give (v) **x** dollars to $n2$. This makes $n1$ poorer by **x** dollars and conversely $n2$ richer by **x** dollars. In a nonzero sum situation, if $n1$ teaches a class of $n2$

students, *n1* does not deplete the knowledge banks nor have to rip physically off pages of his notes to give it to *n1*. Generally, *n2* gets richer but *n1* does not have to get poorer. In other instances, both *n1* and *n2* may both get richer by *v*. If *n1* teaches a class and during that process, *n1* discovers a new possibility for the technology being taught then both *n1* and *n2* gain from "*v*" in win-win situations. Other examples include parent–child or doctor–patient relationships. Emotional relations with genuine concern for each other (i.e., *n1* and *n2*) also offer a sustainable and stable relation between parties. Converse situations can quickly deplete the nature of (no-win) $\leftrightarrow$ (no-win) relationships. In most instances, the incremental change of energy for *n1* and change of entropy of *n2*, can thus swing from vary small positive or negative incremental values to very large fluctuations. The response depends on the situation, *n1, n2,* and *v*. In some instances, if the processes involved in completing *v* are complex and long, an initial process in *v* may affect later process(es) in *v* leading to all shades of relations between objects *n1* and *n2*. Time dependence of relations can thus be computed by nonlinear distribution of energy and entropy in the nature of objects *n1* and *n2*.

v. *Relatively fixed objects may appear in numerous roles in the numerous KSs.* Much like the constants e $(=2.71828...)$, π $(=3.14568...)$, μ_0 $(=4\pi \times 10^{-7}$ Henries/meter), $c = (2.998 \times 10^8$ meters/sec), etc., that appear in numerous scientific contexts, knowledge centric objects (*KCOs*, such as towns, automobiles, houses, etc.,) also appear in different *KSs* and contexts. They can act as tunnels to and from different *KSs*. Hence when we transfer *KCOs*, all their attributes and relationships also migrate with the objects unless they get modified by the transfer functions of the tunnel. It becomes necessary that geese (objects) in one KS will not suddenly appear as gander (objects) in another, unless the tunnel modifies the nature of objects and in this case, the passage through the tunnel is a verb function. The structure of the more extended KS is thus retained.

Certain syntactic and semantic laws are necessary to maintain the order and structure of *BoKs*, *KCOs*, and *n's* to transform from sub objects to super objects and vice versa. The flow of knowledge and exchange of information is thus be streamlined and the integrity of *all* objects is preserved. If there is a unit to measure of knowledge, then the knowledge embedded in *BoKs*, *KCOs*, and *n's* would have the same units.

16.4.2 IMPLICATIONS OF THE AXIOMS FOR STRUCTURE OF KNOWLEDGE

The axiom (i) implies that *KCO* names are symbolic place holders for objects. These identifiers serve two purposes. On the human and programmers side they serve as primary entities around which actions and convolutions are focused. On the machine side, they are flexible data structures that can be addressed, accessed, manipulated, and processed. Each *KCO* bears a unique symbolic tag like a genetic tag, a biological species, a vector potential or a temperature in an area of investigation. In knowledge domain, these objects can be far more generic like shorelines, topographic surveys, human beings, social entities, etc.

Axioms (i) and (ii) together imply object hierarchy of sub-objects and objects, objects and super objects, etc. The trees, branches, twigs and leaves of graphs will then tend to converge at the top, and the tree can thus be traversed, realigned, optimized and forced to satisfy the structural laws that govern generic and specialized trees.

Axiom (iii) is unique to knowledge processing. When objects interact, then the rules of interaction are enforced between objects, the effect of interaction is reflected by the predefined laws and the change of energy (Axiom *iii.a*) of the source noun object and entropy (Axiom *iii.b*) of the receptor noun objects are properly tracked at a microscopic and a macroscopic level. This is perhaps an important feature for the knowledge-processing domain. In the real world, humans address such tasks and issues.

Axiom (iv) has significant philosophic implications based on stark reality. This axiom implies that events and verb functions do not happen randomly and without a reason. There is cause and then there is effect. The cause is the motivation to act and the effect(s) are on the source noun object(s) and on the receptor noun object(s). It also is reflected in the changes of energy of the source and the change of entropy of the activated. The two rarely add to zero. In most cases, there could be loss/gain of energy and/or gain/loss of entropy. There could also be an efficiency term involved in performing a knowledge function, especially in the human interactions and knowledge process. A precise mathematical computation is feasible for objects and their attributes as they undergo changes in their energies and entropies.

Axiom (v) implies that an object may have many manifestations in the global hyperspace of knowledge. Much as a human being can be a professional, family member, human being, scientist, etc., an object can also be numerous entities in physical space(s), KS(s), computer space(s), etc. For example, an airplane may be in a hanger, in air space, in war zone, etc. (in physical space); a flying machine, an information gathering object, a stabilized aerodynamic contour, etc. (in KS); a drawing, a computer aided design or CAD-based optimized system, a stable electrical/mechanical system, etc., (in computer space).

When objects migrate from one space into another space, their attributes need to be preserved and the stability of the entire super-object in all the spaces needs validation and mediation. Knowledge machines (KMs) that can encompass numerous spaces, dimensions, attributes, and their numerical values can perform such validation, mediation, and performance checks. All the scientific principles for all the (finite number of) objects will be optimized in all their relevant (finite number of) spaces. In essence, the KM takes the concept in KS to a realizable working system in its own physical space via the computer space. The machine can also traverse the entire global space forward and backwards to ensure that all three spaces are mapped conformably on top of each other consistently and accurately. The ultimate constraint is on the nature of time in the physical space: the fact that time cannot be reversed in the physical (mass, length, time, or the MLT) space.

16.5 FLOW-DYNAMICS OF KNOWLEDGE

Knowledge may pose many philosophic dimensions and spiritual implications but it also has scientific structure and linguistic texture. In a computational environment, only the two later attributes of knowledge have significance. At the current state of computational environments, the philosophic and spiritual aspects appear as distant domain for any machine to explore. In an attempt to explore the role of machines and facilitate the day to day activities of human beings, the seven following axioms are distilled from most human cultures to be instilled in modern KMs.

If it can be construed that *KCOs* interact to generate new knowledge in an almost biological and reproductive sense, then the nature of two (or more) interacting parent objects need coarse genetic classification. All objects do not interact, let alone mate to give rise (birth) to new objects. When objects (such as, data, bar-codes, numbers, etc.) do interact, their behavioral mode may be passive and depicted in Figure 16.5.

If objects do interact, then a primeval genetic compatibility is necessary. The purpose is to select the sequence, modality and paradigm of an interaction. For example, birds and primates that

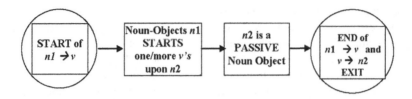

FIGURE 16.5

Reaction of a passive receptor noun object $n2$, to a convolution $n1 \leftarrow v \rightarrow n2$, with n1 initiating a convolution (e.g., any act of aggression, love, hate, or any verb v). If $n2$ is totally passive, the convolution is a single event with no ramifications on $n1$. Note that $n1$ and $n2$ can be individuals, or any social entities, or humanist systems.

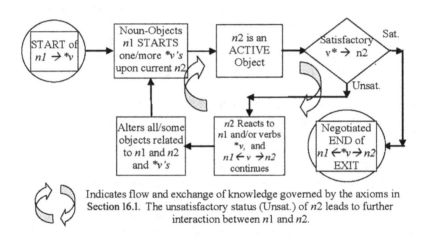

Indicates flow and exchange of knowledge governed by the axioms in Section 16.1. The unsatisfactory status (Unsat.) of $n2$ leads to further interaction between $n1$ and $n2$.

FIGURE 16.6

Logical reactions of an active receptor noun object $n2$ to a convolution $n1 \leftarrow v \rightarrow n2$.

do not mate, friends interact differently than foes, Maxwell's equations cannot be easily written as reactions in chemistry, atomic weights and gravitational weight cannot be readily interchanged, etc. Hence, the framework of interactions follows a context dependent pattern.

When objects with genetic compatibility do interact, commonality of honest ideals invokes cohesion of actions. Conversely, conflict of interests provokes acts of aggression and war. In a sense, if the role of the source *KCO* is defined as one that provokes action, the role of the receptor *KCO* can be passive or reactive with two flavors; cooperative or conflictive. If receptor is passive then the sequential chain of interaction that follows a diagram shown in Figure 16.5, whereas reactive receptor objects may modify their behavior based on the source noun object, verb function and the type of convolution. An iterative convergence may be reached towards a negotiated end of the process $n1 \leftarrow v \rightarrow n2$. The cycle of responses is shown in Figure 16.6. Conversely, the interactions may result in iterative divergence of the parties leading to a stalemate or a termination of the interactive processes.

16.5.1 SEVEN AXIOMS FOR FLOW OF KNOWLEDGE

a. *Knowledge is a dynamic entity with some traits of fluids.* The influence of time on information and knowledge (symbolized as *(I «» K)*, see Reference [5]) and its velocity is to be expected and should be computable. Zero velocity an thus the movement of all *(I «» K)* is absolute death of knowledge (similar to the status of the physical world at 0°A or 0 degrees K) as far as human mind can conceive.

b. *Knowledge Centric Objects (KCOs and thus the knowledge they carry) move and/or can be structurally altered within the encompassing KS(s) under the influence of verbs, actions and convolutions.* Such verbs, verbs functions (v's or VFs) and actions interact and convolute (*) with objects or nouns objects (n's or NOs) altering the structure (and thus the inertia or (mass2)) of knowledge contained in any *KCOs*.

c. *Verb functions, actions, interactions, and convolutions need power and energy for any change of structure, movement, displacement, additions, deletions, or any change of the objects in the KS.* In a sense both the objects i.e., source noun *n1* and the receptor noun *n2* participate in the process in a neutral, cooperative, or conflictive mode. These modes can be time and space variant. The human mind and KPUs keep track of the progress at short enough intervals that the reality of the events in the physical space is accurately tracked in the mind and the knowledge object memories in the KM.

d. *Objects initiate verb functions, actions, interactions, and convolutions.* In an interactive mode, objects can modify, enhance, react, resist, and negotiate, etc., verb functions. Objects can also terminate verb functions, actions, interactions, and convolutions temporarily, as a reaction, or upon their completion.[3] This exercise brings about a change in the *kenergy* for *n1* and change of *kentropy* for *n2* that constitute clusters or bodies of knowledge (*BoKs*). Every action in the KS of computers has a beginning and an end, just as every program has a "Begin" and "End" statement to mark the boundaries of a program, subprogram, a routine, a macro, or even a microprogram in the control memories of machines in the computational space.

e. *KSs occur in human minds, conversations, interactions, documents, knowledge banks, etc.* These KSs bear a human, an event, or an IP address and can be characterized as memory addresses for the machines to reach, explore, modify, or alter to suit the *BoKs* that are being contemplated by humans, processed by computers, or being structured by humanist machines. KSs are plentiful in every way. When the human thoughts probe any field of knowledge, a KS is created, when nature displays its wonder, a KS is created, etc. Such spaces may be transitory and quickly terminated. Documents, knowledge banks, and even scriptures have a life cycle. Immortal knowledge is as fictitious as an immortal human. However, incremental knowledge is finite, bounded and serves significant purpose. Like numbers in the universe, or light in the cosmic space the origin and end may be unknown, but the real world is well served by numbers between $(-N < 0 < +N)$, even as N may tend to ∞ but never reach it.

f. *Human thought process alters the entropy of the objects just as much as a KPU as it processes (noun) objects in the KS.* Both vary the structure and dimensions of BoKs in the KS but not by the

---

[3]This axiom is a restatement of axiom (iv). In the former case, it relates to nature of noun objects. Here, it relates to the energy for the source object *n1*, and entropy of the receptor object *n2*.

same precise laws in every KS[4] for everyone. The knowledge operation codes (kopcs) alter the entropy by finite increments of a knowledge program (KPs). Such KPs process objects to generate typical macro knowledge functions, such as obtain a college degree, drive a car, fly a kite, enter the KS of Einstein by reading up on relativity, etc. In all these instances, there is a "flow" of knowledge. Its structure is being continuously engineered to suit the current socioeconomic setting. Much like fluid mechanics that is governed by Bernoulli equations, the flow of knowledge also follows laws of knowledge mechanics. Numerous well-defined rules of physics, fluid mechanics, aerodynamics, thermodynamics, electrical engineering, etc., and bear conceptual parallelisms with the dynamics of knowledge. We explore anomalies that are readily evident in various other disciplines to formulate the laws of knowledge and its flow. The dynamics of knowledge is still to become a refined science (like fluid dynamics or magnetohydrodynamics or MHD) in its own right. The scientific disciplines that appear far removed (such as colloidal chemistry and Schrödinger's equations) from the science of knowledge are tentative discarded (to be reexamined again), even though the laws of fluid mechanics and thermodynamics may shed some insights on the flow of knowledge through societies.

g. *Knowledge, information, and the structure of most Knowledge Centric Objects decays and dissipates* unless there is an implicit or explicit knowledge process that is blocking it from degradation. This axiom is a corollary to Axiom 1 that specifies that knowledge is dynamic. However, this last axiom assigns a dissipative quality to any *KCO*. This is perhaps a law of physics that specifies that any objects is slowly gaining entropy and losing its structure to crumble into oblivion. For example, the planets, galaxies, and universe are growing ever so slightly colder ever so slowly. Biological organism would dissipate except for the order within them to preserve (if not enhance) them. The need for energy is universal. Knowledge is no exception and *kentropy* just becomes a form of knowledge energy that can be deployed for any number of socially constructive or destructive purposes.

16.5.2 IMPLICATIONS OF THE AXIOMS FOR FLOW OF KNOWLEDGE

16.5.2.1 Implications of flow axiom (a)

(a) Knowledge is a dynamic entity.

Axiom (a) depicted in Figure 16.7, is indicative that almost any knowledge or information that can be perceived is in fact, in a state of transition. The rate of change could be very slow thus causing stability in super objects of knowledge that can be perceived as (almost) stationary for other minor object to cluster around and offer some stability to construct structures of knowledge.

The major implication of this axiom is the time factor for changes of *BoKs* and *VFs*. For example, the shore line (super object) of any continent is being reshaped by the forces of nature, yet in most cases it is slow enough for shore communities (objects) to evolve and human settlements (also objects) to build seafront homes (sub-objects). When the time constants for the coastal erosion become too low (e.g., California, Hawaii, etc.,) the lower level objects need to consider the movements of the super objects.

---

[4]Knowledge in mind is as variable as intelligence in brain. Both serve very specific purposes. In a sense, human intelligence can be viewed as the power (quality, capacity, and the facility) behind the verb functions (v's) discussed in this chapter. The raw and processed objects (n's) are stored in the human (knowledge base) mind in an organized and structured fashion. The instant flash of skill of humans to process such objects becomes the convolution (*) between v(s) and n(s).

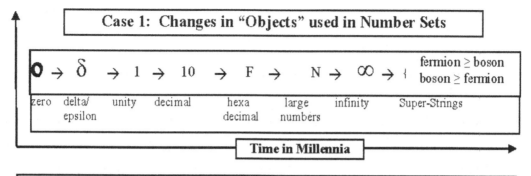

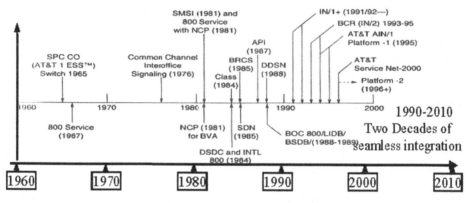

FIGURE 16.7

Illustration that even super-objects (number sets, communication systems, etc.), their objects (numeric representations, switches, etc.), and their sub-objects (binary data-structures, network interfaces, etc.) all experience the effect of time. In the processing of objects, time plays a significant role on the change of energy and the change of entropy of the embedded objects.

There are numerous other examples in social and corporate environments. In such *KCOs*, major *v's* bring about more impact and bring about quicker changes and vice versa. Similarly source super objects *BoKs* and *KCOs* suffer less of a change in their energy and more slowly than the change of entropy for the receptor sub-objects. Time and the rate of change play as important a role in the *KS* as it does in the *PS*. These relationships are not likely to retain proportionality in all situations but the nature of change remains consistent.

16.5.2.2 Implications of flow axiom (b)

(b) Knowledge Centric Objects (*KCOs* and thus the knowledge they carry) move and/or can be structurally altered within the encompassing KS(s) under the influence of verbs, actions, and convolutions.

This axiom has two major implications: the movement of *KCOs* and the interaction between *v's* and *n's* via a fixed or adaptive convolution algorithm. There is enormous flexibility embedded in this axiom. For dealing with complex and super objects, notion of the interdependence between *n1*, *, and *n2* is realized by lookup table that match the three (*n1*, *, and *n2*) with each other, and then with other adjoining objects in that particular KS. The integrity of all spaces is thus implemented in light of this axiom.

Another major implication of the axiom (b) is that knowledge is an integrated entity. The accumulated knowledge in any *KCO* is akin to the KWHs of work (in the physical space) expended to make any product. Knowledge embedded in the complex *KCOs* is a reflection of the knowledge processing performed on raw information to derive the knowledge stored. For example, the knowledge in the *KCO* stated as $E = mc^2$ is indicative of years of genius + work of Einstein.

16.5.2.3 Implications of flow axiom (c)

(c) Verb functions, actions, interactions, and convolutions need power and energy for any change of structure, movement, displacement, additions, deletions, or any change of the objects in the KS.

The human mind and KPUs keep tract of the progress at short enough intervals that the reality of the events in the physical space is accurately tracked in the mind and the knowledge object memories in the KM. This capability of the machines provides the users to be able to control knowledge functions accurately, intricately, and optimally. To some extent, this facility of machine-assisted communication will reduce the pollution and corruption of knowledge and information. The human communication channels will become consistent. Unnecessary erroneous repetitions and misrepresentations will benefit the society as much as standardized currency benefits the financial systems. Nouns, verbs, and convolutions will flow in beautifully manicured statements. The flow of (knowledge) energy is thus optimized to suit the intended goal of the interactions between *KCOs*, *BoK's*, and noun objects.

Even though, we may never know how many Maga-MWH of energy is expended to create the universe, but we have a firm grasp of a KWH that is equivalent of expending 1000 watts of power for 1 hour. As another example, the knowledge of a simpler *BoK*, such as $F = m.a$ (i.e., force = mass times acceleration), is indicative of Newton's work in formulating the dynamics of physical bodies that have a mass and that they can be displaced. The energy in this *BoK* is approximately 3 Newton-years, if Newton took 3 years to derive this *BoK* full time (or he took 6 years half time basis, etc.). This axiom confirms the human observation that trivial forces do not move mountains when the *kenergy* of a source noun id too little for the mass and inertia of the receptor noun. Conversely the forces in earthquakes ruin colonies of men and mice alike when the *kenergy* of the source becomes much too large for the mass or inertia for the receptors.

16.5.2.4 Implications of flow axiom (d)

(d) Objects initiate verb functions, actions, interactions, and convolutions. In an interactive mode, objects can modify, enhance, react, resist, and negotiate, etc., verb functions. Objects can also terminate verb functions, actions, interactions, and convolutions temporarily, as a reaction, or upon their completion.

This exercise brings about a change in the *kenergy* for *n1* and change of *kentropy* for *n2* that constitute clusters or bodies of knowledge (*BoKs*). Every action in the KS of computers has a beginning and an end, just as every program has a "Begin" and "End" statement to mark the boundaries of a program, subprogram, a routine, a macro, or even a microprogram in the control memories of machines in the computational space.

In all the three spaces (PS, KS, and CS), actions are caused/triggered. In the physical space, PS, internal and/or external energy is expended by the source object and consumed by the recipient object, even though there could be a waste and efficiency in the process. In the knowledge pace, actions are initiated after some thought/deliberation about the KS holding the objects under consideration. However, the principle of conservation of energy does not hold in KS. Instead, the laws of *kenergy* and *kentropy* dominate where the *kenergy* expended by *n1* and the decease of entropy in *n2* will be governed by the finite difference forms of the equations that define entropy in Section 2. A, B and C. Errors in thought, deliberation, and the orientation of objects in the KS, can cause serious or even chaotic complications in the manipulation of *KCOs*. In the computational space (CS), errors in HW, SW, FW, routines, etc., all contribute to an unsatisfactory solution. Fortunately, computer sciences are sufficiently evolved that such errors are rare in CS.

Another implication of this axiom is that it permits the grouping of actions, activation or verbs by the source nouns (and thus the *kenergy* expended) as distinct knowledge operation codes from those of the receptor nouns (and thus the change of *kentropy* depleted). The relation between these two would mathematically involve the characteristics of both *n1* and *n2*, the type of media used during the knowledge transaction and initial knowledge levels of the two (see Fig. 16.3). When these parameters are factored into the *kenergy-kentropy* relations, the knowledge transactions become more and more realistic. The laws or traditional thermodynamics and their corollaries are not immediately applicable in the knowledge domain where the principle of conversation of *kenergy* does not hold.

16.5.2.5 Implications of flow axiom (e)

(e) KSs occur in human minds, conversations, interactions, documents, knowledge banks, etc.

This axiom deals with the manipulation and storage of knowledge and indicative of the human role since the prehistoric times. Knowledge has been evolving in the civilizations even though there were no computers and the sophistication to deal with knowledge processing. Early cave painting and drawings start to instill a first glimpse in the thoughts of a few in these civilizations.

In the modern days, the facilities for documentation have exploded beyond reasonable limits and have brought about instantaneous contamination and corruption of information. Validation, cross-checks, coordination of knowledge has become ever so important. The major implication of this platform may involve human minds, documents, knowledge banks, conversations, interactions.

16.5.2.6 Implications of flow axiom (f)

(f) Human thought process alters the energy and entropy of the objects just as much as a KPU as it processes knowledge centric objects.

This axiom provides a basis for the KM to switch from human interactions, events, conversations, knowledge bases etc., to the knowledge memories in KMs. In human settings, KMs are thus able to input from conversations, speeches, remarks, etc., and verify the structure and flow of knowledge in the context in which such events occurred. The quality of the human *BoK* becomes an input and relationships, dependencies, associations, plagiarisms, distortions, noise, etc., can thus be determined by the knowledge machine.

Quality of change in entropy of recipient *BoKs* due to the human "actions and events" will shed light on the source noun object that initiated the change in *BoK*. For example, if the *KCOs* embedded in the leadership of Obama are extracted from his speeches from the first term of Presidency and compared with similar *KCOs* from Bush's first term of Presidency, the ratio of their "Presidential Quotients (PQ)" can be derived by a KM. Similar comparative quotients would also be machine derivable for the surgeries at Sloan Kettering Cancer Center versus the surgeries performed at Stanford Medical Center for Cancer Research. Human bias is removed from judgmental decisions by using exactitude of the choice of criteria for the machine to evaluate. KMs can and do evaluate more stringently than biased humans.

16.5.2.7 Implications of flow axiom (g)

(g) Knowledge, information, and the structure of most Knowledge Centric Objects decays and dissipates unless there is an implicit or explicit knowledge process that is blocking them from degradation.

This axiom affirms Axiom (a), and in addition gives a mathematical basis that any neglected knowledge object is continuously in a process of decay by themselves due to the lack of cohesive forces between the sub-objects that offer the structure to that knowledge object. Only if there is an internal or external binding force or power sustained over a period of time will the object maintain its identity. This is true of all objects in all spaces. From the neurons in the human brain to the physical cohesion a certain amount of energy is needed for any *BoK* to be in a state that it is and the extent of decay or enhancement that occurs at any instant of time depended of the *kenergies* flowing out or in of that object. Stated alternatively, the rate of decay or enhancement depends on the rate at *which kentropies* are being gained or lost within that object.

16.5.2.8 Feedback and stability of KCOs

The interactive process between two *KCOs (n1 and n2)* is influenced by the actions transacted (verb functions) between them. A repertoire of prior transactions is generally stored in the minds of humans or as lookup tables in the libraries of computer systems. An idealized set of steps in the interaction is depicted in Figure 16.8. Events that govern the nature and characteristics of relationships between two knowledge centric humanist objects *n1* and *n2* are sequenced from *n1* to *n2* as actions and conversely from *n2* to *n1* as reactions. When *n1* initiates/continues an interaction as $n1 \leftarrow v_1 \rightarrow n2$ and *n2* responds/continues the *reaction* as $n2 \leftarrow v_2 \rightarrow n1$, then the cyclic feedback process gets initiated. Laws of stability/oscillations/instability (from Control Systems Theory [6]) dictate the operations of the loop in stable operative mode (convergence), or force oscillatory mode (depending on the magnitude and phase of the feedback) within the loop, or an unstable mode (divergence). These three modes depend on the

i. nature and characteristics of the subordinate noun objects of *n1* (i.e., n_{11} through $n_{1i'}$), the subordinate verb functions of *v1* (i.e., v_{11} through $v_{1j'}$), and their convolutions ($*_{11}$ through $*_{1k'}$) within (n_{11} through $n_{1i'}$) and (v_{11} through v_{1j}) that are deployed by *n1*, and also upon

ii. nature and characteristics of the subordinate noun objects of *n2* (i.e., n_{21} through $n_{2i'}$), the subordinate verb functions of *v2* (i.e., v_{21} through $v_{2j'}$), and their convolutions ($*_{21}$ through $*_{2m'}$) between (n_{21} through $n_{2i'}$) and (v_{21} through $v_{2j'}$) that are deployed by *n2*.

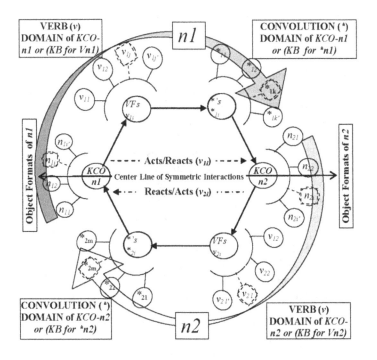

FIGURE 16.8

Dynamics of interaction between two knowledge centric objects KCO-n1 and *KCO2-n2* and the flow of knowledge/information that reconstitutes the structure of the objects themselves.

There are practical manifestations of the three modes of human, corporate, or international interactions prevalent in human beings and organization. The processes in Figure 16.8 get repeated numerous times as any two objects interact. Individuals thrive, bicker, and fight to destruction of either individual; corporations engage in mutually beneficial transactions, engage in smearing or legal activity; and nations participate in trade, import/export, etc., impose embargo's, sanctions, etc., and actively engage in dialectics, war, hostilities, etc. against each other in a predictable fashion much of the time, even though it can occasionally become chaotic.

In a true sense, the results from control systems theory and the mathematical formulations become applicable in the behavior of humans, corporations, and nations alike. Humanist machines that simulate and track human and social behavior derive these behavioral anomalies based on conditions for convergence, oscillations, and divergence from control systems theory.

The variations in the interactions are controlled independently by *n1* and *n2*. The choices of subordinate noun objects of *n1*, the subordinate verb functions of *v1*, and their convolutions are discretionary and the control can be exerted on each one to make/break relationships from either side. The creative features of human behavior becomes evident in making the *n*, *v*, and *, appealing or appalling to the other party in the interaction process.

CONCLUSIONS

Since knowledge has existed for many eons before science had ever evolved, we fall back upon the axioms or truisms based of observation of reality and experience with dealing with objects in the environment and nature. Knowledge and its structure based upon physics, thermodynamics, electricity, and economics evolved later to strengthen the foundations of knowledge and it flow. The science of knowledge is thus ingrained in human nature. Paths and bye-paths through nature have streamlined the mechanics of knowledge through its deployment to solve simple and then more and more complex problems in the environment. The confluence many disciplines thus governs the dynamics of knowledge. In this chapter we have furthered these humanistic pathways by incorporating the science of computation and communication to steer knowledge towards predefined goals in various disciplines.

The principle of conservation of energy in the knowledge domain should be deployed with appropriate caution and care. Psychological, emotional, physiological, and spiritual energies are significantly apportioned, enhanced or depleted by sentiments and feelings. Hence, the routine procedures of energy balancing (from conventional sciences) becomes inaccurate and gets misplaced in dealing with human beings who may initiate "actions" or v's on themselves or on other noun objects, n's or KCOs. This delicate balance is time and situation dependent but a close study of prior decision-making processes can be embedded in the machines emulating human actions and behavior in knowledge machines.

REFERENCES

[1] Barnes J, editor. The complete works of Aristotle, vols. 1 and 2. Princeton, NJ: Princeton University Press; 1995. Also see Hugh HB. Socratic wisdom: the model of knowledge in Plato's early dialogues. Oxford, UK: Oxford University Press; 2000.
[2] Greven A, Keller G, Warnecke G, editors. Entropy, Princeton studies in applied mathematics. Princeton, NJ: Princeton University Press; 2003. Also see Clausius R, Carnot S, Kelvin BWT. Thermodynamics: memoirs by Carnot, Clausius, and Thomson, Nabu Press; April 20, 2010.
[3] Rezakhanlou F, Villani C, Golse F, Olla S, editors. Entropy methods for the Boltzmann equation: lectures from a special semester at the Centre Émile Borel. Paris: Institut H. Poincaré; 2001 (Lecture Notes in Mathematics). Also see Sethna JP. Statistical mechanics: entropy, order parameters and complexity (Oxford Master Series in Physics), Oxford University Press, USA; illustrated edition 2006.
[4] Shannon CE, Wyner AD, Sloane NJA, editors. Claude E. Shannon: Collected Papers. Wiley-IEEE Press; 1993.
[5] Ahamed SV. Intelligent Internet knowledge networks. Hoboken, NJ: Wiley Interscience; 2007.
[6] Doyle JC, Francis BA, Tannenbaum AR. In: Greven A, Keller G, Warnecke G, editors. Feedback control theory. Dover Books on Engineering; 2009. Entropy, Princeton Studies in Applied Mathematics, Princeton University Press; 2003. Also see Clausius R, Carnot S, Kelvin BWT. Thermodynamics: memoirs by Carnot, Clausius, and Thomson, Nabu Press; April 20, 2010.

TRANSMISSION FLOW THEORY OF KNOWLEDGE

17

CHAPTER SUMMARY

In this chapter, we explore the transmission theory for the flow of knowledge. The complex (resistive/restrictive, reactive/distortive, attenuative/regenerative, etc.) properties of the social media can be designated more accurately than in the conduction-based theory for the flow of knowledge. Neither of the two theories completely offers an accurate (enough) model to predict and track and optimize the flow of knowledge for any one individual accurately, even though a statistically averaged flow of information from a social group in different social media can be generated. Two fundamental differences between electric, electromagnetic, and electrostatic signals and knowledge signals get intensified further by (a) the dynamic properties of the social medium and (b) the deeply embedded behavioral characteristics of knowledge centric objects (KCOs), their verb functions (VFs), and the graph of the structure of knowledge designated as the convolutions (*'s) between the KCOs and VFs.

The latter three governing elements of knowledge offer astounding arrays of behavioral, functional, and combinatorial properties since each of the three components are time and environment dependent. Further they display individual/unique traits that can be radically different from one individual to another. The sheer variety, intensity, and their nonlinearities limit the modeling and mathematical processing of these knowledge signals through the social media. However, based on laws of group dynamics, economics, and human nature, the range of variation becomes restrictive enough to attempt the mechanics of knowledge-flow in a probabilistic sense but with realistic logic. Viscous fluid mechanics and flow analysis of electric signal in active nonlinear circuits and media, together offer a good platform for the study knowledge flow in social media where the transmitter and receptor of knowledge can communicate knowledge based on individualistic and media characteristics.

17.1 INTRODUCTION

There are four major related Chapters 16 through 19, are included in this Part II, of this book. Chapter 16 deals with the simplest theory to quantify knowledge [1] as we measure the current, fluid-flow, heat, magnetic fields, etc. Chapter 17 deals with flow of knowledge, as we would quantify current and voltage signals in transmission media and filters with their own characteristics in electrical communication theory. Chapter 18 deals with the flow of knowledge elements and based on the *kuantum* theory where an individual *kuantum* of knowledge (a *kel*) can interact with the medium it is traversing. Finally, Chapter 19 deals with the inspirational basis for the transfer of knowledge without any media but between transmitters and receptors with matching characteristics. Chapter 19 discusses that knowledge does not need a medium at all, and it can traverse infinitely large distances and cross most frontiers of time.

Evolution of Knowledge Science. DOI: http://dx.doi.org/10.1016/B978-0-12-805478-9.00017-0

Impressions of physical space are instilled into the minds of animate objects since inception. Estimation of distances (to create the notion of space) is an inborn skill and evident as infants grab things. Mental space is acquired soon after to deal with others, need-gratifying objects, environment, and boundaries of psychology of self. The environment, others, and the self soon start to exert influence on the reactions and responses of children and adults and serve as links between self, others, and the environment by action (or verb function) such as an adult acquiring a need gratifying objects in the environment. The relation of objects within the environment, others within the society with respect of one's own self starts to play a part in dealing with the psychological and physical spaces, reality, and relationships. In the computer, physical space is artificially created as arrays of computer memories by specifying the X, Y, Z, and t coordinates. Others and environments are created as objects.

Most species deal with modules of sophisticated knowledge and acquire it to make life easier. Like nature itself, knowledge exists in all textures, sizes, and forms. Human senses that operate in real and physical space offer a very tiny glance of a much more intricate and sophisticated universe of knowledge that can be sensed by perception and resolved by programing/mathematical tools. To deal with reality and its use in the knowledge era, the structure of knowledge needs careful adjustment, alignment, and association, especially if it is to be deployed in computational environment.

The recent changes in the Internet age are catalyzed by gating functions in the silicon chips and wave mechanics of photons in the optical fibers. This unprecedented synergy in silicon-based computation with glass-based communication has elated the human thought to new levels of intellectual activity and scientific exploration. The mental processes still hold an almost mystical execution of neural programs to mould concepts, knowledge, and wisdom with learning, behavior, and adaptation.

Even though thought processes are associated with neural space, the computational processes are associated with physical and Pentium space. These intermediate linkages bridge reality and physical spaces with the human psyche dealing with objects, their actions, interactions, and their effects. Human beings have learned to cross these spaces readily by mind control, a "flick of will" or a "twinkle in the eye," a gesture of the face, etc. Such fine processes are hard, if not impossible to program in the software of social machines. However, the connectivity of the mind with the machine can be established by controlling the noun-objects, verb function, their convolutions, and timings. These four entities make up the computational space as the mind would alter them in the psychological space to accomplish any social function or process. The social machine would alter the status of the noun-objects and their entropies accordingly. Thus the machine in a limited sense track, can follow and duplicate the mental and psychological processes of a human mind.

17.2 THE COMPLEXITY OF KNOWLEDGE SPACE

Knowledge space is staggeringly more complex than physical space. The order of complexity becomes at least fourfold since every noun-object (n), verb-function (v), and their combination (*) is unique, furthermore all three depend on the X, Y, Z, t coordinates in society and culture. Hence, it is necessary to limit the size of *kuantum* (i.e., a quantum of knowledge) to "sensible" size and to be practical. Initially, it can be limited to most useful noun objects (such as a human being) and verb functions (such as what is the action). Two examples follow. In a down-to-earth format, a *kuantum* of knowledge can be stated as (food (n), eat (v), restaurant (x, y, z), date and time (t)).

At the other extreme, a cosmic *kuantum* can be stated as (spaceship A (*n*), explore (*v*), coordinates-Planet B (*x, y, z*), cosmic calendar date and time (*t*)). The need to be practical and limit the programing complexity, it becomes a necessity to deal with kuantized knowledge within the realm of computation. Even so, the content of the knowledge so gathered (i.e., the food eaten in the restaurant or the data collected by the spaceship) is not communicated. The flow of the entirety of knowledge needs more numerous smaller *kuanta* (*kco*'s) to be complete by the global *kuanta* of knowledge (or *KCO*).

However, there are two sides to this process. *First*, a given noun-object *NO1* initiates an action or verb-function VF_1 in a certain fashion or convolution *1 generating a *kuantum* of knowledge (NO_1, *$_1$, VF_1). *Second*, this *kuantum* is directed toward another noun-object (including one's own self) or NO_2 that responds with an action or verb-function VF_2 in a certain fashion or convolution *$_2$ thus generating a response or reflective *kuantum* (NO_2, *$_2$, VF_2). Numerous *kuanta* of knowledge (ranging from a few to many millions or billions) make up a minor *module* of knowledge *kco* or a major *KCO*, thus altering the status, kenergy and kentropy of NO_1 and of NO_2. Knowledge energies are thus altered in the knowledge domain via a *"medium"* of words and language over specific durations of time. The movements of *kuanta* start to assume highly unique wave patterns of their own thus generating a "signature of interactive behaviorism" between NO_1 and NO_2.

Time plays a significant role. The earlier three types of *kuanta* for *NO*, *, and *VF*, all vary with time since a time freeze of anyone will alter the other two. It appears that the *kuantum* of knowledge $(kok)^1$ has a life of its own depending on the triadic interdependence of any of *NO*, *, or *VF* on the other two. In a sense, these three entities act as organisms with a molecular formula for compounds such as bicarbonates, nitrates, chlorates, or other organic molecules of carbon, oxygen, and/or hydrogen group, or of an acid with free hydrogen atoms to react with a base with free a hydro-oxyl pair. The propagation of these types of *kuanta* in any medium of language is structured and tightly coupled thus generating a module of knowledge in each sentence that makes sense in the mental space.

17.3 PHYSICAL SPACE AND MENTAL SPACE

17.3.1 THE PHYSICAL SPACE (M, L, T, AND μ)

The basis of most scientific measurements is founded on the real properties of physical entities, i.e., mass (*M*), length (*L*), time (*T*), and the nature of the object which is related, one way or another, with its character of other objects. The most fundamental of the objects (as it was conceived earlier) is the outer space with its own electromagnetic/electrostatic properties, i.e., μ_0 and ε_0, related by the velocity of light held firmly fixed the Michelson-Morley experiment [2] and attested by the writings of Einstein [3].

The length can, however can be measured in various coordinated systems (xyz, $r\theta\psi$, $r\theta h$, etc.). In the rectangular systems, two (*x, y*) and three dimensions (*x, y, z*) offer representations of planar or cubic spaces. Essentially, *M* (*x, y, z*, coordinate space), time, and μ_0 designate a reasonable physical system for single point representations. Yet again, objects are not points and force whereby

---

[1]The symbol *kok* denotes a kuantum of a microscopic body of knowledge (*bok*) and symbol *KoK* denotes a kuantum of a macroscopic body of knowledge (*BoK*). We are still at a loss to identify one universal kuantum of knowledge (unless it is written as (*vf *no* or *no * vf*) for *all* bodies of knowledge.

action takes place, are not lines. Mass being represented as inertia and force being represented as torques offers a little reprieve for reality of the objects undergoing events and actions that twists and turn knowledge centric objects (*KCO*) in the real world under the influence of verb functions from one *kco* or the other in real life. Newtonian representations become ineffective in social space, but when coordinated with mental space the two representations blend space in mind as numbers in mathematics.

17.3.2 THE MENTAL SPACE (WHO, WHAT, WHEN, WHERE, WHY, AND HOW)

Mental space is firmly stood on the answers to seven fundamental questions of the existence of (almost) all objects; why, who, what, how, where, when, and how long. The mental space is filled with rationality that ties the answers to these six questions in an orderly coherent, consistent, and cogent fashion. In tying the answers to be relatively insensitive to the effects of time and social setting, we submit that the computational space to track the mental space to contain the answers to (at least) three most variable answers to who?, what?, and how?. The answers to the other three questions, when, where, and why modify the answers to former questions but in a more rational and predictable way. For example, the answer to the question why is generally found by tracking what is being done to the motivation and the deficit need of the doer. Similarly, where and when are frequently resolved by (x, y, z, t) coordinates of the doer.

In Table 17.1, the knowledge generated ΔK by each of the noun objects NO_i or no_i, verb functions VF_j or vf_j and their convolutions $*_j$ are presented. Knowledge and need gratification become linked every time any noun object does anything at any place and at any time. The association between (noun) objects (who), verb functions (what), and their convolutions (how) get associated with needs (why) in the mind of infants and adults alike. Such mental associations can be reworked in computer systems like telephone numbers are worked into switching systems that provide channels of communications in networks. A scientific model becomes essential and mathematical relationships become necessary to optimize the chain of need(s), action(s), response(s) to gratify such needs. More than that, in a social setting, the socially acceptable norms play a part and culturally variable factors make the programing of social machines more demanding than the programing of plain old scientific computers based on already optimized mathematical algorithms.

In an attempt to establish a scientific model for the machine and to offer valid results, the correlation between reality of the physical world and the symbolism in the machine is necessary. A series of such correlations are presented in Table 17.1. Noun-objects, convolutions, verb functions, and timing instants and durations are manipulated in the social processor units (*SPUs*) of the machine-like data, numbers, and strings are manipulated in central processor units (*CPU*).

17.4 REALITY AND ITS MENTAL PORTRAIT

Objects (*no*'s), actions (*vf*'s), their interplay (*'s) and timing connect the physical space with the mental space. The human mind retains a trail of what happened (*vf*'s) to and from what objects (*no*'s), how what happened did happen, and the way (*) it happened, the instant of time (*t*) and the

Table 17.1 Six basic questions (who (W_1), what (W_2), when (W_3), where (W_4), why (W_5), how (H)) and knowledge generated (ΔK) from the answers

	Effect of Convolution(s) and the Gratification of the Deficit Need (WHY the action WHAT took place)	
Why (W_5)/Reasons	Any deficit need of the Source Object(s)	Element of knowledge; $(\Delta K)_1 = (NO_1 * {}_1VF_1)_{t1}$ VF_j or vf_j in turn gratify the deficit need of NO_i or no_i
Who (W_1)/Object(s)	All Objects such as NO_1 or no_1; NO_2 or no_2; NO_3 or no_3; NO_i or no_i	Element of knowledge; $(\Delta K)_2 = (NO_2 * {}_2VF_2)_{t2}$ VF_j or vf_j in turn gratify the deficit need of NO_i or no_i
What (W_2)/Verb(s)	VF_1 or vf_1; VF_2 or vf_2; VF_3 or vf_3; VF_j or vf_j	Element of knowledge; $(\Delta K)_2 = (NO_3 * {}_3VF_3)_{t3}$ VF_j or vf_j in turn gratify the deficit need of NO_i or no_i
How (H)/ Convolvutions (*)	${}^*{}_1$ ${}^*{}_2$ ${}^*{}_3$ ${}^*{}_j$	Element of knowledge; $(\Delta K)_i = (NO_i * {}_jVF_k)_{ti}$ VF_j or v_f in turn gratify the deficit need of NO_i or no_i
WHERE (W_4)/ LOCATION(S)	Location (x, y, z) Coordinates of Object(s)	At the *exact physical location(s) coordinates* of NO_1 or no_1; NO_2 or no_2; NO_3 or no_3; NO_i or no_i
When (W_3)/ Time "t"	Time "t" coordinates of the Object(s)	At *the **exact time** coordinates* of NO_1 or no_1; NO_2 or no_2; NO_3 or no_3; NO_i or no_i

duration over which it happened (Δt). A snapshot relating the four (no, *, vf, t, and Δt) entities is thus rendered in the mental space. If the duration can be derived or deemed unimportant, reality is portrayed as a four-dimensional object in mind Figure 17.1.

A series of these real events occurs routinely, and the mind participates by interjecting more actions and/or follows events in the physical space. The mental space in the memory elements of the machine is updated accordingly. Three spaces (physical, mental, and social) participate in the overall process, and fourth overlapping space mapped in the computer memory, emulates the change via social programing in tracking these changes in the time dimension. A representation of these four hyper-dimensional spaces is shown in Figure 17.2.

The methodologies from existing (physical, mathematical, social, and computational) sciences offer sufficient ground space to construct a more comprehensive science of knowledge that crisscrosses all these disciplines. Numerous strides have been documented. The physical and mathematical sciences have the most rapid pace of expansion. Computational science being more recent has a shorter course with notable contributions from Knuth [4] and Aho [5]. Social sciences though much older have their origin in philosophy, humanities, and religion. However, human needs and their structures, though

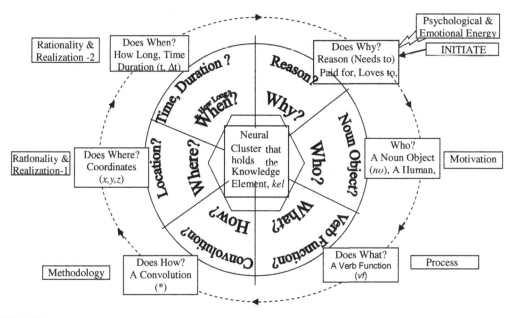

FIGURE 17.1

A portrait of the mental coordinate system of a knowledge element kel that presents a mental imagery by completing a circular path by answering the (seven) basic questions about anything that has happened, happening, or will happen.

as old as the species itself, have a scientific methodology based on the classical work of Freud [6], Jung [7], and Maslow [8]. The seven layer need pyramid eluded by Ahamed [9] incorporates the most recent trend of the Internet age humans searching the worldwide knowledge banks (Level-6) and to attempting to unify (Level-7) whatever they find into the mainstream of activities.

In an optimizing and predictive mode, the social machines alter the parameters of physical, mental, and social spaces to make the discrete time transitions optimal and energy efficient. Although the programing can be different for the numerous social settings, these new generations of machines can offer solutions based on the universality of values and ethics around the globe. Such solutions are generally not unique for a particular entity in a particular social and cultural setting for a particular problem at hand, thus offering the final optimizations and creativity to the individual. For example, a computer offers a string of numbers for pi that is normally nine digits long working in single precision mode and a string of seventeen digits for researchers operating the computer in a double precision mode, and so on.

17.5 THE TRANSMISSION ASPECTS OF KNOWLEDGE

We present a theory akin to the transmission theory of electric signals in physical and electromagnetic domains. Some of the EE tools from transmission theory can be borrowed to explain the nascent-

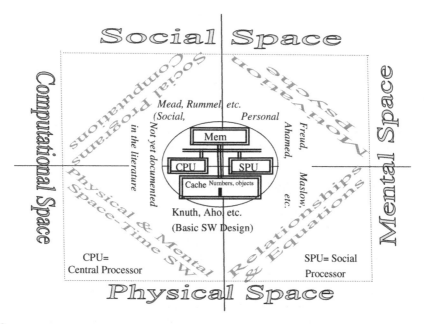

FIGURE 17.2

Depiction and interconnectivity of the dynamic distances in the physical, mental, and social spaces by programmable steps in a social machine to track, design, predict, and optimize social processes. Solution of most energy efficient (or least painful) solution to social problems is also feasible. In the design mode when a global problem in a given social setting, is posed, the machine blends the solutions of many cultures and lists the pros and cons of each solutions and blends them optimally to find the "best" solution if one or more "objective function(s)" are defined.

flow properties of knowledge. Some of the techniques from wave propagation theory are borrowed to explain the (x, y, z, t) properties of knowledge flow. They can isolate the resistive and distorter properties of the social medium, especially when the media has storage (memory) and discharge (suddenly release) properties. For example, a knowledge bank can keep certain news items stored for a length of time and then suddenly publicize the item hiding critical information or in a distorted perspective.

In addition, outflow of knowledge energy from a source does not deplete its energy nor it is dissipated; instead, it is continually changed (distorted, enhanced, or transformed) into new knowledge forms. In a sense, it exhibits some wave properties of electromagnetic propagation waves wherein the electric and magnetization vectors become time and space dependent. In the knowledge domain, the composition and constitution of noun-objects, the verb-functions, and their convolution structure all get modified and transformed depending on the location (x, y, z, t) in the social media as a "wave of knowledge" passes by.

This phenomenon is also prevalent as sound waves travel through air and aqueous media, or as light is refracted/reflected at the boundaries of air and glass, water and glass, etc. Properties of social spaces and the time dependence start to gain significance but the mathematics and relationships become obscure due to the complex structure of knowledge *kuanta* composed of *nos*, *vfs*, and *s.

However, there are two sides to this process. First, a given noun-object no_1 initiates an action or verb-function vf_1 in a certain fashion or convolution $*_1$ generating a *kuantum* of knowledge (no_1, $*_1$, vf_1). Second, this *kuantum* is directed toward another noun-object (including one's own self) or no_2 that responds with an action or verb-function vf_2 in a certain fashion or convolution $*_2$ thus generating a response or reflective *kuantum* (no_2, $*_2$, vf_2). Numerous *kuanta* of knowledge (ranging from a few to many millions or billions) make up a module of knowledge thus altering the status, kenergy, and kentropy of no_1 and no_2. Knowledge energies are thus altered in the knowledge domain via a "medium" of words and language over time. The movements of *kuanta* start to assume highly unique wave patterns of their own thus generating a "signature of interactive behaviorism" between no_1 and no_2.

17.5.1 SIGNAL FLOW IN CONVENTIONAL CIRCUITS

In this section, the flow of knowledge is based on the flow of electrical signals. Currents, distributions of voltage, power, and energies in electrical systems and circuits are well documented in electrical engineering and physics. Knowledge flow refers to the flow of information and knowledge, distributions of knowledge potential, knowledge power and kenergy, in social systems and media. Knowledge science is not as highly evolved. Limited parallelism exists in the two systems and the concept of series elements and shunt elements can be imported from electrical systems into social systems and the flow of knowledge can be estimated.

Whereas analysis of electrical circuits[2] (such as transmission lines, passive filters, ladder-circuits, dividers, etc.) is based on fixed parameter values, the analysis of knowledge flows should include the variations of these parameters based on (x, y, z, t) coordinates. Even though the analysis is complicated, it is programmable based on the updating of the resistive, inductive, and capacitive coefficients are based on location (household, society, culture, place, nation) and time (past, present, or future) coordinates. The worldwide knowledge banks do indeed portray the moods and their variations in most social environments.

17.5.2 SIGNAL FLOW ELEMENTS IN SIMPLE: SERIES ELEMENTS FOR SIGNAL FLOW

Two basic types of elements exist: the series and shunt elements. In the simplest of cases, the equations for signal flow can be derived by voltage−current equations embedded in Kirchhoff laws. The basic equations for the two port electrical network for series impedances can be written as:

17.5.3 SIGNAL FLOW ELEMENTS IN INDUCTIVE AND CAPACITIVE ELEMENTS FOR SIGNAL FLOW

In context to the signal flow in electrical systems, inductive, and capacitive elements can occur in series, parallel, or any combination thereof. Depicted in Figures 17.3 and 17.4, these elements can bring about serious effect for the flow of signals. Fortunately, the nature of these elements has been

---

[2]Active circuit analysis also assumes fixed transistor parameters. However, when circuit components such as varactors [10] (i.e., voltage dependent capacitive elements) or magnetic materials with saturable B−H characteristics, [11]) are present, these circuits can exhibit different but computable change in behavioral characteristics of the system.

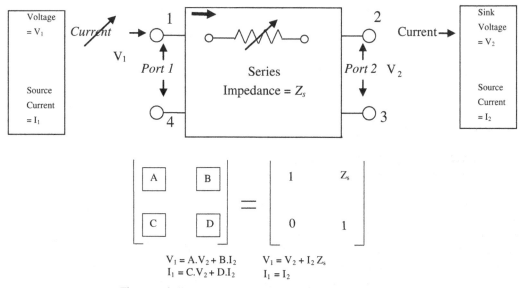

$$\begin{bmatrix} A & B \\ C & D \end{bmatrix} = \begin{vmatrix} 1 & Z_s \\ 0 & 1 \end{vmatrix}$$

$V_1 = A.V_2 + B.I_2 \qquad V_1 = V_2 + I_2 Z_s$
$I_1 = C.V_2 + D.I_2 \qquad I_1 = I_2$

The arrow indicates variable character of the element due to variable impedance due to environmental conditions

FIGURE 17.3

Series resistive element for flow of Signal from Port 1 between terminals (1 and 4) to Port 2 between terminals (2 and 3).

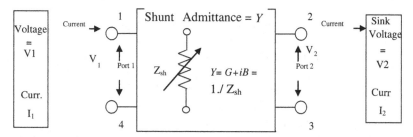

The basic equations for the two port electrical network for shunt impedance shown in Figure 17.4 can be written as:

$$\begin{bmatrix} A & B \\ C & D \end{bmatrix} = \begin{bmatrix} 1 & 0 \\ Y & 1 \end{bmatrix}$$

$V_1 = A.V_2 + B.I_2 \qquad V_1 = V_2$
$I_1 = C.V_2 + D.I_2 \qquad I_1 = V_2 Y + I_2$

The arrow indicates variable character of the element due to variable impedance due to environmental conditions

FIGURE 17.4

Shunt impedance for flow of Signal from Port 1 between terminals (1 and 4) to Port 2 between terminals (2 and 3).

studied by physicists, electrical engineers, and mathematicians. Since they respond to the rate change if current and voltage, they can give rise to "resonance" in circuits and systems. In the knowledge domain, such elements can be responsive to rate of change of knowledge rather than the amount of knowledge in a complex *KCOs*.

17.5.4 SIGNAL FLOW ELEMENTS IN SIMPLE: SHUNT ELEMENTS FOR SIGNAL FLOW

Electrical elements influence the flow of power and alter relations between voltages and currents. The exact relations and equivalent impedances are documented in most textbooks in Electrical Engineering and Signal Flow Theory [12] and for this reason we go to the next section and determine their equivalencies for the flow of information and knowledge in social media.

The arrow indicates variable character of the elements due to high magnetic or electric intensities. Such nonlinearity's are sometimes exploited to alter nature the overall circuit response in cases such as voltage regulators or frequency dividers or even lightning arresters.

17.6 FEEDBACK AND STABILITY OF *KCO*'s

This social media can attenuate all three (*v's*, *n's*, and *s) components of knowledge. Typically found in nonreceptive audiences and sleepy classrooms, the social media does not dissect the knowledge enough to find its beginning or the end. Any output from the resistive media would be at a lower power level (*Knowls*, a suggested unit for the knowledge power). The effect of this type of media would be loss of information and knowledge from the source. For example, if a high resolution image is projected on a low resolution screen, or seen through a translucent glass, objects, and their relationships become dim, dull, and fuzzy. Such images and bodies of knowledge (*BoKs*) are soon forgotten if they are not reinforced, restored, replenished, or in some cases reincarnated structures, monuments, books, and religions fall victims in the passages of time.

These social elements (e.g., campaign staff, news editors, special-interest groups, etc.) can willingly and wantonly distort the relationships between nouns (*n's*), verbs (*v's*), and their convolutions (*'s) at any instant of time. They affect the most crucial features by altering the convolutions (*), combinations, and sequencing of verbs between the nouns. Though it appears as a slip of the pen, the damage to the original *BoK* is done. When conditions are at their worst, these elements in resonance with the timings of *v's* can cause a short circuit (series resonance) and completely choke (parallel resonance) the flow of (significant and trustworthy) knowledge and information.

For example, Mao's blockage of distribution of Scriptures [13], Bush's blockage of Guantanamo-prison coverage [14], the News blackout during Middle-East Conflict [15], Nixon's refusal to release of the White House tapes [16], etc., are examples of radical changes in the knowledge-flow brought about by unworthy elements in the social networks. In the knowledge domain, the abuse of power corrupts the pristine knowledge space. Truth gets replaced by deception, love by arrogance and virtue by hate. Conversely, truth can be reinforced by desirable social agents that make "truthful" information to accompany the original flow of beneficial knowledge.

The properties of the media dictate the amount, and distortion of knowledge through that particular social media, or the flow of current and power for the signal-flow through active electrical circuits. In addition, these elements project the media characteristics on the *v's* and *n's* and can completely

L Henries   C Farads   L Henries   C Farads

(a) Series Reactive Elements   (b) Shunt Reactive Elements

FIGURE 17.5

Series and Shunt impedance elements for the flow of currents in electrical circuits.

decouple the convolution processes. The effect is too common in practice. For example, any biased news and TV media under dictatorial rule, the political and advertising campaigns, the sales pitch of shady salespersons, the word of hypocrites, etc. carries such as the proof of attenuation, distortion, and dispersion of knowledge further and further from its pristine nature encompassing truth and nothing but the truth. A dangerous situation in the society is portrayed under these conditions.

One additional complexity for the knowledge flow is the presence of active elements (equivalent of transistors and operational amplifiers [17] embedded in electrical circuits) in the social media. These elements readjust their characteristics based on the knowledge (signal) that is flowing through the elements. To some extent, they resemble the intelligent agents in AI programs to monitor and control environments [18]. In the real world, such elements distort the truth in knowledge and bring in bias in society. For example, the casualties of allied force in war are brought to the headlines, and the casualties of other side are quietly ignored, the victories of war are exaggerated by the media for the sole purpose of gaining popularity. The cruelties of the allied forces are pushed to last page; the failures of the Federal policies (against drugs and Marijuana) are quietly forgotten soon, etc. It needs to be investigated if willful contamination of pristine knowledge by social media and elements to deceptive and corrupt knowledge should carry the same penalties as the charges for financial corruption by officials and employees Figure 17.5.

17.6.1 CONVENTIONAL POWER, ENERGY, AND ENTROPY

In Sections 4.1 and 4.2, we present the concepts using the ABCD matrix for the signal flow analysis in physics and electrical engineering. The circuit analysis concepts for signal flow are detailed in Figures 17.6 and 17.7 depict the flow of signals and power using the traditional circuit analysis techniques readily available in most electrical engineering textbooks. These concepts are enhanced and transformed into knowledge domain and flow analysis using the A-I matrix, discussed further Section 17.5.

The ABCD matrices are generally held constant during simulations, even though they vary slightly from a transmission event to the next. When averaged over numerous events and over many network configurations, the received signal shapes are satisfactory enough to yield very low bit error rates.

17.6.2 FLOW OF ELECTRICAL SIGNALS AND POWER

Figure 17.6 depicts a simple electrical signal path for the flow of *signals* that are embedded in the (magnitudes, wave shapes, and harmonic phase relations between) voltages and currents as they

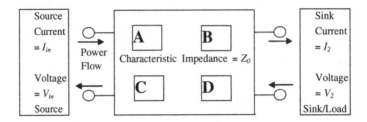

FIGURE 17.6

Representation of a two port electrical network to transfer signals and power from any source with source impedance of Z_s to any sink/load with its own impedance of Z_T through a medium of characteristic impedance Z_0.

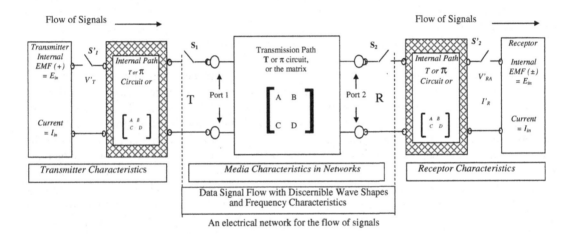

FIGURE 17.7

Flow-path for information bearing signals through wired media. For the wired paths the T or π approximations are generally used. For the wireless, the field analysis techniques are generally used. For fiber optic medium both solutions yield convergent results. The computation of signal wave shapes and power transferred from transmitter to the receptor provide accurate (enough) results to predict the robustness of the signal transmission. Probability of errors does exist but it is sufficiently low. Most back-bone and global network communication systems have statistical bit error rates as low as one bit in 105 bits received through metallic media systems and as low as one bit in 108 or 109 bits received through fiber optic media systems.

flow from the transmitter (at the left) to the receptor (at the right). In the absence of noise and random events that alter the three characteristic [ABCD] matrices for the path, the propagation distortion(s) and delay is totally deterministic.

The methodologies are completely algebraic, and almost every variation of the signal can be traced, computed and predicted [19]. In most practical applications, the transmission systems cannot be completely shielded from the effects of random events that may interfere with the preservation of signal through the medium. In these situations, the mean and variance of the random events (such as noise, lightning, and even component variations) are computed and the margin of error is reduced to tolerable levels. Generally, digital systems offer much desired robustness for the entire system and are used extensively in almost all signals, their preservations, measurement, and monitoring.

In most knowledge systems, the public media for the transmission of information/knowledge is highly variable and random. The usual techniques of coding, measuring, and monitoring the S/N ratios, equalization, etc. will assume a very different flavor. For this reason, a self-learning error correction methodology becomes attractive. Largely, human-beings adopt this practice. For example, when a criminal suspect is identified, the police will concentrate on the prior clues left behind by the criminal and try to identify such clues. In the same vein, when a type of cover up has been used in the social media (such as hiding the evidence of corruption, bank records, Swedish bank accounts, etc.) then the humanist machines will over sample events to find out repetitions of clues for similar actions, misrepresentations or even slander. Suspicious activity deserves a greater investigation by human beings and machines alike.

In computer science, embedding and priming intelligent agents (IAs) [20] serves the same purpose. Such agents learn from the prior behavior of the system and act predicatively to rectify the impending disasters when initial clues are detected.

When information/knowledge passes through a corrupt medium, the receptor system would attempt to rectify the nature of the "verb functions" or v's, the nature of the "noun objects" or n's, and/or the nature of the "convolutions" or $*$'s in the body of knowledge or BoK received at the receptor. Such precautionary safeguards are quite human and definitely transferable in the knowledge-ware (KW) of humanist machines.

17.7 KNOWLEDGE FLOW AND DISTORTIONS IN SOCIAL MEDIA

Society exists because of the capacity to communicate. The deformation of signals communicated is typical of most communication systems. This fact is inevitable. The audio-visual face to face media has been pretty much replaced by electrical pathways, electromagnetic, wireless, and fiber optic media since the days of Marconi, Bell, and Tesla. Social media and social elements are forever present making social networking carry dual implications; first the physical media brings its own delay and distortion characteristics and second the human elements have their delay, distortion, decay, and disordering characteristics. These impairments cause misrepresentation, inaccuracy, and twisting of the original information present in any body of knowledge. The magnitude, phase, and ordering error introduced can be extremely serious about the extent of making of the received information almost chaotic.

Pristine information has distinctive parameters. These parameters of knowledge have structure and order like the voltages and currents in electrical systems that can be measured, adjusted, and calibrated. Knowledge has a theme, foundation and a set of equations that govern its flow and its' potential. Specific body of knowledge rests on a structural relation between a key-group of $KCOs$ and the current forces in the society to alter such $KCOs$ and the structural relationships between them. Such an activity can cause incremental changes in knowledge, however, localized they may be. To track the changes we can fall back on the communication of v's, n's, and *s, through a social media characterized by its own nine-element A-I matrix written out as follows:

$$\begin{pmatrix} A & B & C \\ D & E & F \\ G & H & I \end{pmatrix}$$

When an individual or a structure (machine, organization, society, government, etc.), S_1 with a sociometric potential injects a body of knowledge BOK_1 at the input of the medium to be transmitted to another individual or a structure S_2, then the retracted body of knowledge is BOK_2 is generated at the output. However, degradations and distortions may occur much like the degradations and distortions that occur during signal transmission. In the algebraic methodology [21] that relates input and output electrical signals, the relation between the two bodies of knowledge can be written as.

The "times" operation should be considered as a convolution rather than the matrix multiplication. The exact laws for this sociometric convolution still need to be derived. In the simplest of cases, if the only nonzero elements in the [A-I] square matrix A, E, and I are each 1.0; then the numerical multiplication is applied for "times" and all the v's, *'s, and n's get translated from $BOK1$ to $BOK2$. The active verbs (v's), operations (*), and the embedded noun objects (n's) are related by a matrix equation.

The science of knowledge processing is still in infancy compared to the science of signal processing. It becomes a challenge to accurately evaluate the parameter [A-I] in the knowledge domain, even though the [ABCD] can be computer very accurately by measuring the properties [R, L, G, and C] for wired media or the μ and ε for wireless media. However, we fall back on the intuitions of Bell, Edison, Marconi, or Tesla as they were evaluating the wired and wireless media during the late nineteenth century for communication of voice encoded as electrical signals and wave shapes.

Cascading of numerous segments of transmission media has evolved from rigorous mathematical discipline that preserves the attenuation and dispersion properties caused by individual segments in a media chain that may have significantly different characteristics. The methodology for cascading is quite generic, and it can be used in a large of variety of applications. In essence, if the methodologies can be transfixed in the knowledge domain, much of deception and misrepresentation of information and knowledge can be (and will be) removed. Social values will be quite accurately safeguarded by machines.

For signal processing and the power flow calculations, cascading is a process of multiplying the individual [ABCD] matrices of each segment to get one overall composite [ABCD] matrix for the complete flow-path. In general, the composite matrix for the entire path carries the effect of each individual segment due to the multiplication rule for generated composite matrix. This identity is accurate for the wired media. In the knowledge domain, when the channel of communication is strictly confined (e.g., the White House media office, or corporate public office, a university spokesperson, etc.) then the BoK at the termination can be strictly monitored by appropriate personnel Figure 17.8.

When there is no control on the media (typical news agencies, community centers, gossip engines and junk broadcast services, etc.) severe distortions and dispersion of the original BoK

$$BOK_1 \quad = \quad \text{\textit{Social Media Characteristics}} \quad \text{times} \quad BOK_2$$
$$\text{\textit{From 1 to 2}}$$

(a) Simple transmission and reception equivalency of a *kel* from BOK₁ to BOK₂

BOK_1	*Internal*				*Internal*	BOK_2

$$
\begin{array}{ccccc}
BOK_1 & \textit{Internal} & & & \textit{Internal} & BOK_2 \\
 & \textit{Char. of} & \text{Social \quad Media} & & \textit{Char. of} & \\
\textit{Total} & BOK_1 & = \quad \text{Characteristics} \quad \text{times} & BOK_2\textit{for} & \textit{Total} \\
\textit{Power} \rightarrow & \textit{for Trans.} & & \textit{Recept. fr.} \rightarrow & \textit{Power} \\
\textit{Trans.} & \textit{to} & \text{From 1 to 2} & BOK_1 & \textit{Recevd.} \\
 & BOK_2 & \rightarrow & &
\end{array}
$$

(b) Total transmission and reception equivalency of a *kel* from BOK₁ to BOK₂

FIGURE 17.8

Flow-path for a knowledge element "kel" from BoK_1 to BoK_2. The kel is generally delayed, attenuated, and distorted in the same fashion as information bearing signals (currents and voltages) in electrical systems. The resistive and reactive elements of the society cause serious errors in communication of the overall knowledge content which is represented as $\sum\sum\sum\ldots$ of *kels* over a time.

can be expected. For example, the reporter's bias is embedded in the report however well-disguised it may be. FOX or CNN media reporting recent events can be quite different from the reports from another news agency reporting the same incidents and activities. Perhaps the un-tampered logic circuits can outperform the biased self-preserving intelligent human systems. Preservation of truth and accuracy based on logical deductions will be a desirable machine feature Figure 17.9.

17.8 FLOW OF INFORMATION AND KNOWLEDGE

Figure 17.10 depicts a transmission path for the flow of knowledge through social media. Typically, the well-intentioned media (e.g., universities, welfare and charitable organizations, churches, etc.) promotes and amplifies the social and ethical values that have a lasting impact on society. Neutral media promotes facts in perspective. Biased media generally promotes the self-interest groups (SIGs) that fund the media. Such activities do leave a smelly trail behind or a smoking gun, both of these can be covered up by the same biased media. Even for humanist machines, the compensation and correction of bias and corruption in the media would need considerable KW intelligence and effort.

In many cases even the most powerful humans turn vulnerable and the downward spiral of cover-ups (e.g., Nixon's White House tapes and transcripts during early 1970s that lead to his resignation before impeachment as a President of the United States, Clinton's Monica Lewinsky affair (1998), Bush's lies about the Weapons of Mass Destruction in Iraq, etc.) continues. Machines do persevered and the machine knowledge thus generated is likely to get more preserved than the human voice that can be suppressed. The role of (unbiased) social machines does become more persuasive against lies and deception of such defamed political leaders.

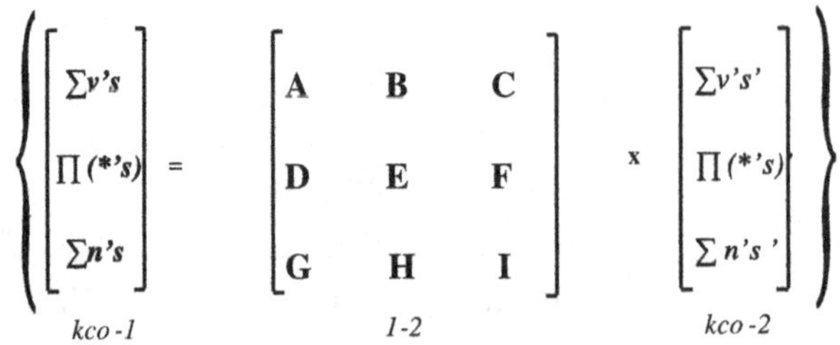

$$
\left\{
\begin{bmatrix}
\sum v's \\
\prod (*'s) \\
\sum n's
\end{bmatrix}
=
\begin{bmatrix}
A & B & C \\
D & E & F \\
G & H & I
\end{bmatrix}
\times
\begin{bmatrix}
\sum v's' \\
\prod (*'s) \\
\sum n's'
\end{bmatrix}
\right\}
$$

$$
\quad\quad kco\text{-}1 \quad\quad\quad\quad 1\text{-}2 \quad\quad\quad\quad kco\text{-}2
$$

Case 1. Generic and instantaneous snap-shot for knowledge flow from $kco1$ to $kco2$ over an infinitesimally small interval dt.

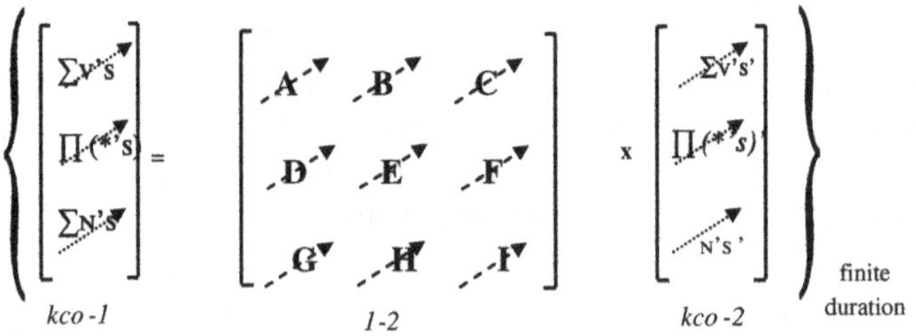

$$
\left\{
\begin{bmatrix}
\sum v's \\
\prod (*'s) \\
\sum N's
\end{bmatrix}
=
\begin{bmatrix}
A & B & C \\
D & E & F \\
G & H & I
\end{bmatrix}
\times
\begin{bmatrix}
\sum v's' \\
\prod (*'s) \\
N's'
\end{bmatrix}
\right\}
$$

$$
\quad kco\text{-}1 \quad\quad\quad 1\text{-}2 \quad\quad\quad kco\text{-}2 \quad \text{finite duration}
$$

$$
\varDelta t = \int_t^{t+\varDelta t} dt \ \text{ or } \ \varDelta T = \int_t^{t+\varDelta t} dt
$$

Case 2. Integrated representation of the matrix representation in Case 1 over a discrete interval of time from 't' to '$t + \varDelta t$' or from 't' to '$t + \varDelta T$'.

FIGURE 17.9

Flow-path for numerous knowledge elements or "kels" from BoK_1 that is transmitting knowledge centric objects $kco\text{-}1$ to Bok_2. These KCO's get delayed, attenuated, and/or distorted in the communication in any social medium. The characteristics of the social and media elements play a significant role in the communication and flow of knowledge.

However, machines being slaves of humans can be programed, to play an exactly opposite adversarial role. The role of well-secured ethical and unbiased KW in machine does offer hope. After all, the teaching of Buddha inscribed in Asoka-pillars have carried the same message for centuries. Computer memories are more transitory by design than human values inscribed in Scriptures.

The DDS and LoC offer two widely accepted directions in the subject matter classifications. These two frameworks of classification do not specifically address the concerns of individuals and societies in dealing with knowledge ranging from junk and spam knowledge to the most profound axioms of eternal wisdom. For the reason of classifying knowledge for the masses that encounter ordinary lives as ordinary individuals attending to ordinary duties, we classify knowledge in three (1, 2, and 3) directions as we have classified wisdom. *First*, consider the direction of absolute wisdom based on Aristotle's truth, virtue, and beauty (*TVB*) and label the direction as 1 (one). *Second*, consider the direction of wisdom of the knowledge society based on science, economics, and technology (*SET*) and label the direction as 2 (two). *Finally*, consider the direction of (negative) wisdom of the evil society based on deception, arrogance, and hate (*DAH*) and label the direction 3 (three). The volume integral (in directions 1, 2, and 3) of the knowledge base generated

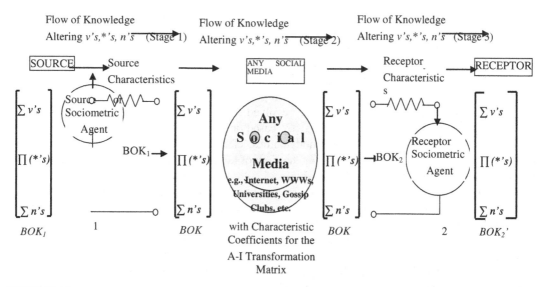

FIGURE 17.10

Flow path for information through social media. For regimented paths (such as the military and corporate management), the chain of command ascertains accuracy and freedom from errors. When the social values and ethics tolerate deception and misrepresentations, the social media can (and does) introduce self-beneficial omissions and falsifications. This practice is too common to be ignored. Numerous news agencies carry incomplete or biased information tending to favor personal gains and self-interest. For example, the source sociometric agency can well be a dating agency that only emphasizes its success stories without indicating average rate of failures or disgruntled couples. As another example, the State Department briefing agencies almost always presents the victorious war stories (however false they might be) of the current President.

should be zero and the surface integral (in dimensions 1 and 2) should be infinite, however curved this surface might be. Most individuals fail to maximize their growth in directions 1 and 2, while minimizing it in direction 3 in their personality.

CONCLUSIONS

The basis for treating knowledge as an energy centric entity is explored in this chapter. Knowledge can exist in an abstract state in many forms in human mind, as words on paper, in computer or as irrelevant gossip. These forms of knowledge do not have any significance until the content is processed to suit the situation. Context becomes essential to gain a scientific grasp, and the context is bounded to trap the enclosed knowledge. In this mode, the contextual analysis yields the shape and nature of KCOs and those around these objects. Thus knowledge can be assembled in an orderly and scientific fashion. Content and context both become equally important.

In the long run, stagnant or highly altercate knowledge does not serve beneficial human or social purpose. However, cohesive and flexible knowledge molded around individual and social needs and circumstances can greatly benefit individuals and society. The laws of fluid knowledge mechanics are thus linked to the flow heat, electricity, signals, and binary bits in electrical and electronic circuits. An overall scheme of establishing the basis for flow of knowledge based on knowledge potential difference, the resistance to knowledge and the natures of source and recipient knowledge(s) is thus evolved in this chapter. Active circuits with embedded transistors offer a basis for evolving knowledge flow in dynamic and intelligent social networks.

Knowledge has preceded science had ever evolved for many eons. We fall back upon axioms and truisms (presented in the chapter 14 and 16), based on observation and experience about reality and its pervasive presence. Physics, thermodynamics, electricity, and economics also govern the final pathways and govern the mechanics for the flow of knowledge. The confluence of many disciplines is essential for the science of knowledge.

The principle of conservation of energy in the knowledge domain should be deployed with appropriate caution and care. Psychological, emotional, physiological, and spiritual energies are significantly apportioned, enhanced, or depleted by sentiments and feelings. Hence, the routine procedures of energy balancing (from conventional sciences) become inaccurate and get misplaced in dealing with human beings who may initiate "actions" or v's on themselves or on other noun objects, n's or $KCOs$. This delicate balance is time and situation dependent but a close study of prior decision making processes can be embedded in the machines emulating human actions and behavior in knowledge machines.

REFERENCES

[1] Ahamed S.V. General Flow theory of knowledge. Chapter 16 of this book.
[2] Michelson-Morley Experiment. <http://scienceworld.wolfram.com/physics/Michelson-MorleyExperiment.html; Referenced October 15, 2014>.
[3] Einstein's Special and General Relativity. <http://www.physicsoftheuniverse.com/topics_relativity_special.html>; Referenced October 1, 2014.
[4] Knuth DE. The art of scientific programming. 1st ed. Addison-Wesley Professional; March 3 2011.
[5] Aho AV, et al. Compilers: principles, techniques, and tools. 2nd ed. Addison Wesley; September 10 2006.
[6] Freud S, Strachey J, Hitchens C, Gay P. Civilization and its discontents (complete psychological works of Sigmund Freud. W. W. Norton & Company; August 9, 2010 (Reprint edition).
[7] Jung CG. The undiscovered self. Signet; February 7, 2006 Reissue edition.
[8] Maslow A.H. Towards a psychology of being. March 7, 2014 (Sublime Books).
[9] Ahamed S.V. An enhanced need pyramid for the information age human being. In: Proceedings of the Fifth Hawaii International Conference, Fifth International Conference on Business, Hawaii; May 26–29, 2005. See also, An enhanced need pyramid of the information age human being. Paper presented at the International Society of Political Psychology, (ISSP) 2005, Scientific Meeting, Toronto, July 3–6, 2005.
[10] Ahamed SV. Analysis of specially doped varactors for direct frequency tripling. Bell Syst. Tech. J. February 1975;54(2):317–34 Article first published online: July 29, 2013, <doi:10.1002/j.1538-7305.1975.tb02841.x>.
[11] Erdelyi EA, Ahamed SV, Burtness RD. Flux distribution in saturated DC machines at no load. Transactions of IEEE, PAS 1966;84:61.
[12] Bell Laboratories. Transmission systems for communications. Western Electric Co.; 1982.

[13] Chang J, Halliday J. Mao: the unknown story. 1st ed. Anchor; 2006.

[14] Margulies J. Guantanamo and the abuse of presidential power. Simon & Schuster; 2007.

[15] Morris B. One state, two states: resolving the Israel/Palestine conflict. Yale University Press; 2010.

[16] Prados J. The White House Tapes: Eavesdropping on the President: A Book-and-CD Set. The New Press; 2003 Also see, Stuart CE. Never trust a local: inside Nixon's campaign and the White House. Algora Publishing; 2005.

[17] Williams A. Analog filter and circuit design handbook. McGraw-Hill Professional; 2013.

[18] Ahamed SV. Intelligent Internet knowledge networks, processing of concepts and wisdom. John Wiley and Sons; 2006.

[19] Ahamed SV. Design and engineering of intelligent communication systems. Kluwer Academic Publishers; 1997.

[20] Mohammadian M. Intelligent agents for data mining and information retrieval. Idea Group Publishing; 2004.

[21] Lee E, Messerschmitt D. Digital communication. 2nd ed. Kluwer Academic Publishing; 1993.

QUANTUM FLOW THEORY OF KNOWLEDGE

18

CHAPTER SUMMARY

In this chapter, we propose that knowledge can be reduced to its elementary *(elemental)* size. Each element consisting of quantized noun object(s), their quantized verb function(s), and the incremental type(s) the convolutions that bind such noun objects and verb functions. Even though knowledge may not be quantized as finely and as definitively as matter can be quantized in physics, these elements of knowledge form building block for larger and practical bodies of knowledge. These elements of knowledge (*kels*) exhibit statistical properties and their dynamics are based on the properties of *kels*, their origin, their environment, the media, and their recipients. Further, we define the elementary particles as a *kuantum* of knowledge, even though a *kuantum* is not a quantum in the traditional sense.

In maintaining a working relation with other sciences, we explore the flow of these *kels* to and from larger practical objects to complete social and real functions. A quantum of knowledge (*kel*) is like a particle of matter or a pulse of energy that can be coupled. We present this concept to investigate if such *kels* will explain all the intricacies in the flow of knowledge in societies, cultures, and groups. Even though a *kel* is not as defined precisely as quantum (an electron) in physics, but in the framework of theory presented here, the statistical properties of kels explains statistical differences in the way in which noun objects communicate, i.e., transmit and receive such *kuanta* and *kels*. This approach holds the maximum promise but the quantization of a *kel* to a workable size becomes unique and depends on the direction in which knowledge is being explored and/or constituted. The generic quantum of knowledge or *kel* still appears as a mystic entity, even though specific *kuanta* are feasible that the modern computers can tackle, build, process, constitute, reconstitute, reprocess to generate "artificial knowledge." Such artificial knowledge is then verified, validated, and accepted or challenged, disputed, and rejected by AI routines and by natural intelligence of human beings to build large and realistic bodies of knowledge (*bok's*) or knowledge centric objects (*kco's*) of any size, shape, or form.

18.1 INTRODUCTION

Four chapters are included in this Part II of the book. Chapter 16 deals with the simplest theory to quantify knowledge [1]. As we measure the current, fluid-flow, heat, magnetic fields, etc. Chapter 17 deals with flow of knowledge [2] as we would quantify current and voltage signals in transmission media and filters with their own characteristics in electrical communication theory. Chapter 18, this chapter deals with the flow of knowledge elements [3] and based on the *kuantum* theory where an individual *kuantum* of knowledge (a *kel*) can interact with the medium it is traversing.

Evolution of Knowledge Science. DOI: http://dx.doi.org/10.1016/B978-0-12-805478-9.00018-2

Finally, Chapter 19 deals with the inspirational basis for the transfer of knowledge [4] without any media but between transmitters and receptors with matching characteristics.

This current Chapter 18 is based on the principle that incremental knowledge is derived that when one noun object interact (in any way) with other noun objects by exchanging verb functions between them in a fashion (i.e., a convolution) subject to the rules of the behavioral grammar. This chapter also presents that knowledge can be reduced to tiny elemental cells constituted by the quantized noun objects, quantized convolutions, and quantized verb functions. Most species deal with modules or *kuanta* of rudimentary knowledge in order to gratify their routine needs and acquire them to make life easier. Most elite learn to deal with and manipulate more advanced *kuanta* of sophisticated knowledge in order to gratify their special needs and learn them to satisfy their needs, environment, and their circumstances. *Kels* do indeed have a hierarchical structure. Like nature itself, knowledge exists in all textures, sizes, and forms. Human senses that operate in real and physical space offer a very tiny glance of a much more intricate and sophisticated universe of knowledge that can be sensed by perception and resolved by programing and/or mathematical tools. To deal with reality and use in the knowledge era, the structure of knowledge needs careful adjustment, alignment, and association, especially if it is to be deployed in computational environment.

In order to be practical and concurrently wise, we explore the quantum theory of knowledge whereby the protocol for the knowledge paths between smallest knowledge centric objects (*kco's*) and the larger knowledge centric objects (*KCO's*) are transported. A continuum of noun objects (*no's*), verb functions (*vf's*), and the associated convolutions (*'s*) is thus retained. This continuum is searched out by segmented knowledge machines that operate between the smaller *kco's* and the larger *KCO's* in any given domain or direction of knowledge. Dewey Decimal System (DDS) [5], and Library of Congress (LoC) [6], offer two established methodologies to classify the various domains of knowledge. One or more pathways exist in the chain of evolution of the subject matter and related inventions that have occurred around practical and real modules of knowledge in the range of any smaller *kco* to the larger *KCO*. All modalities of knowledge representation (images, documents, graphs, presentations, etc.) need investigation to complete the pathway(s) between *kco's* and *KCO's*.

Minute constituents (i.e., *no's*, *'s*, and *vf's*) of *kels* can and do interact with the social and cultural character of the medium that carries them. In a very sense, the statistical properties of the medium alters the genesis, the transmission and the retention of these *kels* thus offering the vast varieties of lives, decay, and death of knowledge in different societies and cultures. All the principles for the transmission of knowledge presented in Chapter 2 of becomes applicable in this chapter. Even though human beings may be daunted by such intricacy, knowledge machine can routinely handle tracking, transmission, attenuation, and dispersion of knowledge in most societies.

The origin of *kel* (to represent *k*nowledge c*el*l) is derived from the word pixel to stand for picture element (i.e., *pic*ture-c*el*l, written as pixel). In addition, there is a resounding similarity between *kel* and the naturally elements in chemistry at the atomic, molecular, and at a reactionary level. For instance, the chemical elements also consist of neutrons, positrons, and electrons that play an adaptive role as the elements form molecules, and complex chains of organic, inorganic compounds, and acids. Nature has provided an innate intelligence for the world of materials to exist.

In a closely correlated methodology, *kels* also play such a complex role. *kels* can share noun objects and convolutions as much as atoms can share the nuclear elements, electrons, and valency bonds. The particularly adaptive role of atoms to form varieties of compounds is evident when *kels*

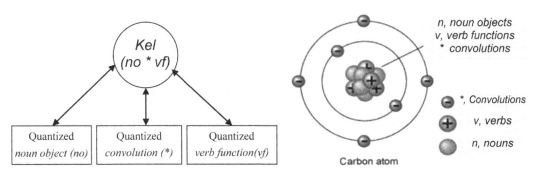

Structure of a *kel* constituted as the knowledge when a noun object *no* convolves (*) with a verb function *vf* in a specific convolution * format.

Structure of a larger *kel* with numerous *no's*, *vf's* and convolutions

FIGURE 18.1

Configuration of an element of knowledge, kel formed from a set of the tiniest but flexible, and dynamic entities (no, *, and vf). The kels become comparable to atoms made up of neutrons, protons, and electrons. The basic building blocks can be shared and enhanced to form new kels during social interactions or in knowledge processing machines.

can arrange and rearrange their structures of *no's*, *'s*, and *vf's*, to form different configurations of knowledge of chain of *kels* to form minor *kco's* and major *KCO's*. The analogy is evident to treat the chemical world as a type of knowledge society or culture where the *no's*, *'s*, and *vf's* are the basic building blocks and these *kels* are formed and unformed depending on the dynamic social setting and the setting. At a very microscopic level, change in the chemistry of every atom is as real as the change of every *kel*!

The role of a *kel* is as fundamental as the role of seminal biological cell in all species. The two chromosome pairs formed as xx (female) and/or an xx or xy (male) chromosomes to constitute the female and male genetic cell evolves after the genetic code in the male (no_1)-kel_1 penetrates and ruptures $(vf(s))$ in a distinctly unique fashion(*)) the female (no_2)-kel_2. A new kel_3 and a new no_3 (the baby) is thus formed that carries the genetic code of both no_1 and no_2 as the no_3-kel_3. Ones, twins, and multiple babies are all formed from the process[1] $(no_1$* vf_1, also see Fig. 18.1). In a very oblique sense, the inception of knowledge and the origin of life get intertwined.

18.2 REPRESENTATION OF THE GENERAL FORMAT OF INTERACTIONS

18.2.1 PHYSICAL AND MENTAL SPACES

The impression of *physical space* in instilled in the human mind since inception. Estimation of distances is an inborn skill and evident as infants grab things. The dimensions in physical space are

---

[1]The more precise representation of the entire set of processes is represented as $(qno_1 \leftrightarrow q^*_1 \leftrightarrow qvf \leftrightarrow q^*_2 \leftrightarrow qno_2)$ where the prefix q denotes a *kuantum* of the genetic code in each *kel*, genetic sciences elaborate the processes that follow.

readily computable in machines. *Mental space* is acquired soon after infancy to deal with others, need-gratifying objects, environment, and self. The environment, others, and the self soon start to exert influence on the reactions and responses from children and adults and as a link between self and environment is by action (or verb function) such as an infant crying/or trying to communicate because of some outstanding need. The relation of objects in the environment, others in the society with respect one's-own self all become influential in dealing with the physical space, reality, and relationships.

Mental space is dominated by objects, convolutions, and verb functions. In the most rudimentary format, these three entities are constantly arranged, rearranged, formatted, and reformatted to make to gratify all-pervasive human needs. Needs that initiate motivation, also supply the psychological and physical energy to find means to gratify the most outstanding need at any instant of time. However, objects, actions, and the convolutions that bind the two together all play a seminal role as to how and how well the need is gratified.

In reality and perceptions, noun objects can be as large as cosmic objects and continents or as small as electrons and photons. The object size (such as a meal to gratify hunger to a cartload of grain) can vary vastly. The object type (like drinking water sip to quench the thirst to a lake to drink from) can also vary. In a similar mode, the convolution (type of action) can range (from taste, sip, gulp, nip, imbibe, slurp, to knock back, etc.) and verb function can range (from gulp down, drink, taste, to swallow or gobble). The range of variations can become too immense for the mind or machines to comprehend or process all variations, all at once. To seek a solution within the rational mind or by a programmable machine, we suggest that the solution to any given problem specify that bounds for (*no's*, **'s*, and *vf's*) to a range that the mind may offer a satisfactory solution and the machines may offer an optimal (or at least a near optimal) solution. Quantization of (*no's*, **'s*, and *vf's*) within the range thus becomes feasible.

18.2.2 MENTAL AND COMPUTER SPACES

The association between (noun) objects (*who*), verb functions (*what*), and their convolutions (*how*) gets associated with needs (*why*) in the mind of infants and adults alike. The association with time (*when* and *how long*) are generally associated with now and as long as it takes. These linkages are also formed in the minds of infants since time is now and how long depends on the gratification of the need (*why*). The mental space forms a basis of social relations. Social objects traverse these mental spaces like clouds in the sky where some major need gratifying objects (such as parents, schools, universities, jobs, etc.) retain permanent coordinates with all six questions are answered (at least partially) in the hyper dimensional spaces in the mind. Human beings generally do not conceive social objects in precise coordinate systems, but the subconscious linkages persist in the short and long-term memories. The subconscious that provides a platform for the life, supplies the mental coordinates and working space for meaningful relations between objects (*no's*), the associated verbs (*vf's*), and the formats (**'s*) of interactions and the formats of tasks in human life in any given society and culture. *Kels* form a coherency for such tasks, as time forms a bondage between them. Knowledge and time thus get intertwined in the fabric of human activity that is tractable in the as tasks in the CPU of computer systems. Both forms of tasks need time to complete. However the silicon speed of chips being much faster, can also optimize the execution of human tasks and provide a predictive plan for human activity. In the computational domain the human beings can benefit from the intelligent peripherals of an already intelligent Internet.

Such mental associations can be reworked in computer systems like telephone numbers are worked into switching systems that provide channels of communications in networks. A scientific model becomes essential and mathematical relationships become necessary to optimize the chain of need(s), action(s), response(s) to gratify such needs. More than that, in a social setting, the socially acceptable norms play a part and culturally variable factors make the programing of social machines more demanding than the programing of plain old scientific computers based on already optimized mathematical algorithms.

18.2.3 ATOM AND KNOWLEDGE ELEMENT

The diagrammatic representations of a *kel* and of a Carbon[2] atom are shown in Figure 18.1. Figure 18.2 depicts the atoms for Gold and Hassium. These two elements have radically different properties. Atoms can and do exist in many atomic weights as much as *kels* can and do exist in many *"kel* weights" (like atomic weights) depending on the utility of the knowledge embedded in the *kel*. *Kels* can exist freely in nature (as atoms in gold), or machine generated (as atoms of Hassium). For instance the atomic weights of the noble metals is higher than one, since the energy contained in their

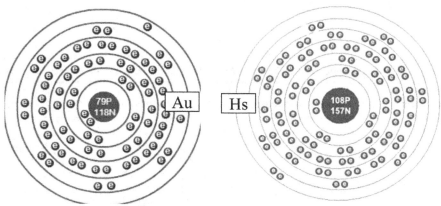

The Structures of Gold (Au) and Hassium (Hs) Atoms

FIGURE 18.2

The structures of the Gold (Atomic weight = 196.966) with 2,8,18,32,18,1 electrons in an Au, atom and then the radio-active Hassium (Atomic weight 277) with 2,8,18,32,32,14,2 electrons. These elements have radically different properties. The kels in Figure 18.1 are comparable to atom made up of electrons, protons, and neutrons. The basic building blocks can be shared and enhanced to form other elements or during chemical interactions/ radio-active and or forced processes as much as kels are altered in social/cultural and/or hostile interactions.

---

[2]Carbon atom is chosen as an example, but any element that forms molecules and compounds would exhibit similar properties and traits.

atoms is far greater than in the hydrogen atom with an atomic weight of 1.0078 [7]). The *kel-weight* of a brain surgeon (a noun object) performing a (*vf*) transplant of the brain (if it is possible), in a very specific way (*) would be much higher than the *kel*-weight of a monkey eating peanuts. The knowledge society is thus a very ordered environment of *kels* represented and integrated as *μk's*,

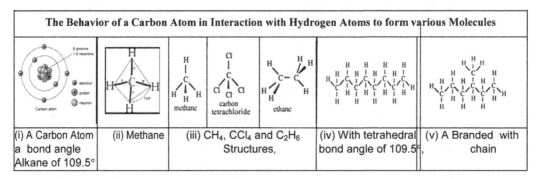

The Behavior of a Carbon Atom in Interaction with Hydrogen Atoms to form various Molecules				
(i) A Carbon Atom a bond angle Alkane of 109.5°	(ii) Methane	(iii) CH_4, CCl_4 and C_2H_6 Structures,	(iv) With tetrahedral bond angle of 109.5°,	(v) A Branded with chain

FIGURE 18.3

The Alkane (C_nH_{2n+2}) Family (Methane, Ethane, Propane, Butane, Pentane, Hexane, etc.) and the adaptive role of the Carbon Atom (C).

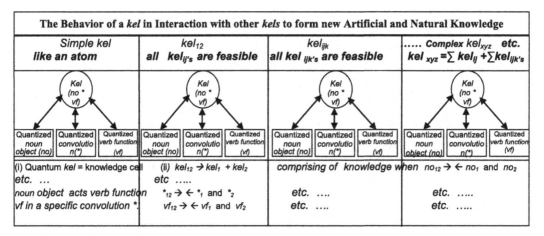

The Behavior of a *kel* in Interaction with other *kels* to form new Artificial and Natural Knowledge			
Simple kel like an atom	kel₁₂ all kelᵢⱼ's are feasible	kelᵢⱼₖ all kel ᵢⱼₖ's are feasible	..... Complex kelₓᵧ₂ etc. kel ₓᵧ₂ =∑ kelᵢⱼ +∑kelᵢⱼₖ's
(i) Quantum kel = knowledge cell etc. ... noun object acts verb function vf in a specific convolution *.	(ii) kel₁₂ → kel₁ + kel₂ etc ..... *₁₂ → ← *₁ and *₂ vf₁₂ → ← vf₁ and vf₂	comprising of knowledge when no₁₂ → ← no₁ and no₂ etc. .... etc.	etc. ..... etc. .....

FIGURE 18.4

The chain of new knowledge structures generated when a basic kel (such as the knowledge in an invention (e.g., 2-D computer memories)) starts to interact other kels such as 2½-D memories to leading to the Architectures of 3-D memories. Numerous other examples also exist such as the discovery of Penicillin by Fleming has led to the development of other specific chain of antibiotics, such as the invention of internal combustion engine has led to the turbo charged automobile engines, etc.

∂k's, Δk's, $\sum ks$, $\sum\sum k$'s, ..., and then of μK's, ∂K's, ΔK's, $\sum Ks$, $\sum\sum K$'s, etc.[3] Chemistry also displays simple and complex to very, complex chains of distribution of atoms in the real world.[4,5]

18.2.4 MOLECULAR WEIGHTS OF CARBON COMPOUNDS AND LARGER KNOWLEDGE ELEMENTS

The behaviors of a Carbon atom and a *kel* are depicted in Figures 18.3 and 18.4. *Kels* can combine with themselves, (one or more) *kels*, and form chains of *kels* as in human dialogs where every step in the interactive process modifies the status of the present *kel*. *Kels* retain the history of modifications like a symbol in a series of steps of mathematical derivation or like a numeric symbol in computational processing. In a sense, like human objects, *kels* have a life of their own. Sometimes they live and die in the perception of human counterparts and sometime they as real as sentences and procedures documented in textbooks.

The variety of *kels* can be as large as the number of molecules and compounds in the real world. *Kels* can be as transitory as the fleeting passion or as (semi-) permanent as the written word. In most cases *kels* have a utilitarian value. This utilitarian value is indicative of the *kel*-weight. The utility if a *kel* depends on the need that it gratifies. Thus, a *kel* to represent a monkey eating peanuts would fall well below the *kel* as a programer developing new software.

Knowledge space encompasses physical space as much as memory time spans real time and as much as perception spans cosmic time. The order of complexity of knowledge space is greatly enhanced because every noun-object, verb-function, and their combination are unique to the quantum of knowledge being pursued and the human being processing it. Moreover, the psychological and mental coordinates of space and time are socially and culturally variable.

Hence, it becomes necessary to limit the definition of *kuantum* to "sensible" size and to be practical locations in setting the object-size of the *kuanta*, the size of the verb-function to be discernible and type of convolution (*) to be in the realm of human comprehension. Only the unique combination of these three "*kuants*" constitutes the *kels* in its own particular setting at a given instant "*t*".

Initially the *kuantum* of knowledge can be limited to most useful noun objects and verb functions. Two examples follow. In a down to earth format, a *kuantum* of knowledge can be stated as (food (n), eat (v), restaurant (x, y, z), date and time (t)). At the other extreme, a cosmic *kuantum* can be stated as (spaceship A (n), explores (v) and coordinates Planet B (x, y, z), cosmic calendar date and time (t)). The need to be practical and limit the programing complexity, it becomes a necessity to deal with kuantized knowledge within the realm of computation. Even so, the content of the knowledge so gathered (i.e., the food eaten in the restaurant or the data collected by

---

[3]In increasing order of complexity of *kels*. For example, if μk is grocery item, then μK will be a grocery store and $\sum\sum K$ would be worldwide chain of food stores, global banking corporations, etc.

[4]Is determined by bringing all the products of combustion back to the original precombustion temperature, and in particular condensing any vapor produced. Such measurements often use a standard temperature of 25 °C (77 °F). This is the same as the thermodynamic heat of combustion since the enthalpy change for the reaction assumes a common temperature of the compounds before and after combustion, in which case the water produced by combustion is liquid.

[5]The higher heating value takes into account the *latent heat of vaporization* of *water* in the combustion products, and is useful in calculating heating values for fuels where *condensation* of the reaction products is practical (e.g., in a gas-fired boiler used for space heat). In other words, HHV assumes the entire water component is in liquid state at the end of combustion (in product of combustion) and that heat below 150 °C can be put to use.

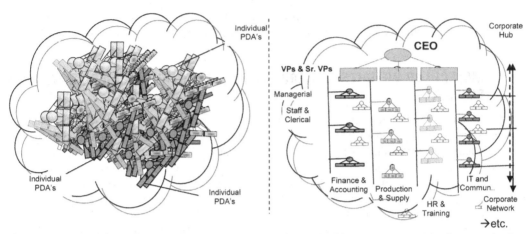

(a) A disorganized *kco* e.g., an ad hoc group people   (b) Organized *kco* e.g., an structure of an organization

FIGURE 18.5

Formation of a knowledge centric object kco form a set of kels. A kco or a kel is a human being with its own personality (noun objects, no's) functional capabilities (convolutions, *) and unique tasks (verb functions, vf's). These three constituents can be further fragmented to ascertain the appropriateness of the kels.

the spaceship) is not communicated in this representation. The flow of the entirety of knowledge needs more numerous smaller *kuanta* (*kco*'s) to be complete by the global *kuanta* of knowledge (or *KCO*). In social settings, such KCO's may be disorganized, quasi organized, or well organized as shown in Figure 18.5.

The recent changes in the Internet age are catalyzed by gating functions in the silicon chips and wave mechanics of photons in the optical fibers. This unprecedented synergy in silicon-based computation with glass-based communication has elated the human thought to new levels of intellectual activity and scientific exploration. The mental processes still hold an almost mystical execution of neural programs to mould concepts, knowledge, and wisdom with learning, behavior, and adaptation. Machines to implement such functions are just appearing in the society.

Even though thought processes are associated with neural space, the computational processes are associated with physical and Pentium space [8]. These intermediate linkages bridge reality and physical spaces with the human psyche dealing with objects, their actions, interactions, and their effects. Human beings have learned to cross these spaces readily by mind and thought control, a wink, or even a gesture of the face. Such fine processes are hard, if not impossible to program in the software of social machines. Quantized knowledge between human minds and machines can be established by controlling the quantized noun-objects, the convolutions, the verb function, and their timings. These four entities makeup up the computational space as the mind would alter them in the psychological space to accomplish most social functions or processes. The quantized social machine would alter the status of the elemental noun-objects and their entropies accordingly. Thus, the machine could in a limited sense track, follow, and duplicate the minute mental and psychological processes of a human mind at a quantum level.

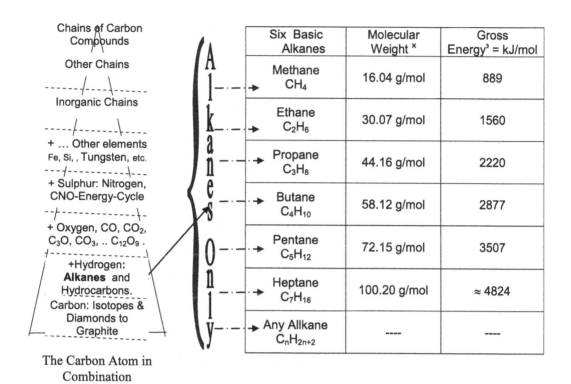

	Six Basic Alkanes	Molecular Weight [x]	Gross Energy[ɔ] = kJ/mol
	Methane CH_4	16.04 g/mol	889
	Ethane C_2H_6	30.07 g/mol	1560
	Propane C_3H_8	44.16 g/mol	2220
	Butane C_4H_{10}	58.12 g/mol	2877
	Pentane C_5H_{12}	72.15 g/mol	3507
	Heptane C_7H_{16}	100.20 g/mol	≈ 4824
	Any Allkane C_nH_{2n+2}	----	----

Chains of Carbon Compounds

Other Chains

Inorganic Chains

+ ... Other elements
Fe, Si, , Tungsten, etc.

+ Sulphur: Nitrogen,
CNO-Energy-Cycle

+ Oxygen, CO, CO_2,
C_3O, CO_3, .. $C_{12}O_9$.

+Hydrogen:
Alkanes and
Hydrocarbons.
Carbon: Isotopes &
Diamonds to
Graphite

The Carbon Atom in
Combination

Notes: ✗ The numbers are approximate, since the atomic weight of H is 1.00789 and the standard atomic weight of C is 12.011.

ɔ The quantity known as higher heating value (HHV4) (or gross energy or upper heating value or gross calorific value (GCV) or higher calorific value (HCV5)). It can also be expressed as MJ/kg.

FIGURE 18.6

Properties the carbon atom as it forms compounds with other elements, H, O, N, etc.

18.2.5 ATOMIC AND MOLECULAR WEIGHTS FROM CHEMISTRY

Atomic weight consists of three weights, weights of the protons, neutrons, and electrons. Thus, the heavy metals have a more complex atomic structure than the higher metals. Similarly, complex compounds can be substantially heavier than simple molecules. For example, the atomic structure of a Gold atom (atomic weight of 197) has 79 Protons, 118 Neutron, and 112 Electrons in 7 Electron shells [7]. The molecular weights of compounds also exhibit similar characteristics.

The Hassium atom formed during radio-active fusion exhibits fundamentally different properties from those of Gold, Carbon, or even Lead. *Kels* also "genetically" inherit properties based on the type and nature of the *kenergy* that was expended in generating these *kel*-elements. Humans and

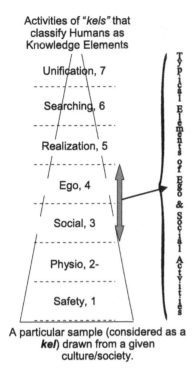

A particular sample (considered as a **kel**) drawn from a given culture/society.

Some Basic Elements in 3 and 4	Mean & Variance[X] from Populous	Satisfaction['] = Achievement X Years
⤍ Wealth	Personal Pref. = P_w **Mean = μ_w** Variance=σ_w	$S_w = P_w \cdot \mu_w \cdot Years_w$
⤍ Power	Personal Pref. = P_p **Mean = μ_p** Variance=σ_p	$S_p = P_p \cdot \mu_p \cdot Years_p$
⤍ Fame	Personal Pref. = P_f **Mean = μ_f** Variance=σ_f	$S_f = P_f \cdot \mu_f \cdot Years_f$
⤍ Status	Personal Pref. = P_s **Mean = μ_s** Variance=σ_s	$S_s = P_s \cdot \mu_s \cdot Years_s$
⤍ Prestige	Personal Pref. = $P_{p'}$ **Mean = $\mu_{p'}$** Variance=$\sigma_{p'}$	$S_{p'} = P_{p'} \cdot \mu_{p'} \cdot Years_{p'}$
⤍ Respect	Personal Pref. = P_r **Mean = μ_r** Variance=σ_r	$S_r = P_r \cdot \mu_r \cdot Years_r$
Integrated Sum of Achievements of an individual.	Dynamic and Society/Culture Dependent	**Total Achievement** $S_t = \sum S_i$ $i = w, p, f, s, p', r$

Notes: [X] The numbers are approximate, and based on statistical Averages of wealthy and successful segment of the population at any given time frame or decade in any given culture/society.

['] The satisfaction or integrated achievement of *kel* can be considered as the sum of individual achievements and the duration over which they last. The personal preference factors (P_w, P_p, P_f, P_s, $P_{p'}$, and P_r) are also dynamic but indicative of the individual's personality profile. There is no quantitative measure for satisfaction and happiness but it can be a perceptual entity that the *kel* (individual) can "feel".

FIGURE 18.7

The properties *kels* and *KCOs* as they forms new combinations with other traits (such as loving and kind → considerate) in the Social domain. These properties give rise to social profiles (S's) and new elements of knowledge or larger, more integrated *KCOs*. New and customized knowledge is thus created in social settings most the time and in most social interactions.

animals may have common physiological functions have different "genes of knowledge" to make them radically different.

In Figure 18.6, the carbon atom and its molecules are used to indicate the chain of compounds derived from Carbon atoms on the left side. Carbon atoms combine with other elements, and metals to form elaborate arrays of compounds. The alkane chain is used to depict the molecular weights on the right side. The molecular weights in g/mol increase as the chain of hydrocarbons becomes longer in column 2 and the energy contained expressed as in kJ/mol also increases. As depicted in Figure 18.7, *kels* and *kco*'s also exhibit similar properties.

18.3 ATOMIC/MOLECULAR WEIGHT OF KELS IN SOCIETY

Kel atomic/molecular weight consists of three (*kel*) atomic weights (a) *no* (or *no's*), * (or *'s), and *vf* (or *vf's*), thus complex or chained *kels* such as a surgeon (a *no*) performing a surgery, can be substantially heavier than simple *kels* such as a monkey (*no*) eating (*vf* and * together), peanuts (secondary noun object). *Kel* atomic/molecular-weights can be positive for constructive knowledge elements enhancing utility (such as *X* helps *Y*) or zero (such *X* does nothing to/for *Y*) and even negative (such as *X* hurts *Y*), for nonconstructive or destructive knowledge elements decreasing utility (such as *X* bothers *Y*). The three components (*no* (*no's*), * (*'s*), and *vf* (*vf's*)) all determine the utility. In a sense, human values in the society and culture are ingrained in utility. If construction, reconstruction, and peace are on the positive scale, then destruction, terrorizing, and war are on the negative scale. Thus, the *kel* balance can swing and fluctuate with time and social setting. Nations have examined this abstract notion by examining the extent of knowledge that propagates health, happiness, and welfare in the society to the extent of Mafia, war, and terrorizing knowledge disintegrated over a finite duration of time such as the Presidency[6] of US Presidents. The measure though not precise is still indicative of the utility of any President for the country. Documented periods of war (Churchill (WWII), Nixon and Johnson (Vietnam war), and Bush (Iraq war) Presidencies) are disfavored in comparison with the years of reconstruction and social reform that followed such Presidential years engaged in social reform, public and global welfare and other constructive actions (verb functions, *vf's*) bear high positive utility for the President.

18.4 STATISTICAL PROPERTIES OF KELs AND KCOs IN SOCIETY

Kels those resident in human beings for long periods of time substantially shape the personality of the host. For example, a human being (*no*) with a subject matter specialty in physics and teaches (* and *vf*) it for decades, becomes a physics teacher (a *KEL* or *KCO*). Other examples are also evident. For this reason, the evolution of a *kel* to a *KCO* becomes evident in almost all circumstances and situations. In the case of inanimate *kels*, petroleum in gasoline becomes petrol. The terminology becomes less important than the evolutionary chain of *kels* to *KELs*, and then on to *kcos* and *KCOs*.

Complex *KELs* in large associations with other *kels* have high "molecular weights." For example, a highly sociable person or a subject matter expert will have higher "mo weight" than an introvert or a high school student. Such *kels* can be classified according to their "mo weights." The highly valuable *kels* also at the top of a hierarchical structure gratify the most wanted human and social needs. If such needs are themselves classified (as in Maslow's Need Pyramid), then the *kels* to gratify these human needs, can be rearranged accordingly. The *kels* that satisfy the

---

[6]It is hard to justify that an egotist would be classified as a highly placed *kel*, unless the ego also serves a molecular association with other beneficial *kels*. As another example, a Mafia boss, though well connected with other members of mafia cult would have a high negative mol-weight. It becomes necessary to associate the social welfare with mol-weights to be positive. In the current social setting, leaders such as Gandhi, Carter, and King would have a highly rank positive in the hierarchy. Negative mol-weights are and should be associated with torrents, terrorists, and dictators such as Mao in China, Hitler in Germany, Johnson in Vietnam, Bush in Iraq, Netanyahu in Palestine who have brought shame to humankind.

realization, social, and ego needs (from Maslow's Hierarchy) of humans and societies will have their highest *kel*-atomic/molecular weights. The diagrammatic arrangement of Needs, their *kels* are shown in Figure 18.7.

CONCLUSIONS

We have proposed that knowledge should be considered reducible into their finest quantum sized elements. The quantized elements of knowledge behave as elements in chemistry and constitute the building blocks of larger bodies of knowledge, much as the elements in nature combine to become compounds and molecules. In the knowledge domain, the constitution of *kels* and their behavior is dramatically more flexible and individualistic, but exhibit statistical properties that makes communication (exchange of knowledge) possible across social and cultural barriers. In this chapter, we trace the similarity between the elements of knowledge and elements in chemistry. It is feasible only to a certain extent since the structure and modality of *kels* becomes radically different than those for the elements in chemistry. In the later case, the Periodic Tables precisely and rigidly dictate the properties and behavior of chemical elements.

In the knowledge domain, the syntactic and semantic laws the *kel* composition for the exchange of knowledge depend on the individuals, society, culture, time, and the information content in the knowledge being exchanged. The capacity of the modern computers and hand held devices is by and large sufficient to offer individual users pathways and byways through the knowledge domain to deal with the exchange of information precise, optimal, and efficient. In this vein, we suggest that choice of their particular elements of knowledge of individual users be toward the achievement of their long-term goals like wealth, status, power, etc.

REFERENCES

[1] Chapter 16, "Conduction Theory of Knowledge Flow", this book.
[2] Chapter 17, "Transmission Theory of Knowledge Flow", this book.
[3] Chapter 18, "Kuantum Theory of Knowledge Flow", this chapter.
[4] Chapter 19, "Inspiration Theory of Knowledge Flow", this book.
[5] OCLC, Dewey Decimal Classification and Relative Index. 22nd ed. OCLC, Dublin, OH; 2003. See also, Comaroni JP, Dewey Decimal Classification, 18th ed. Albany, NY: Forest Press; 1976.
[6] United States Government, Library of Congress Classification, <http://catalog.loc.gov>. URL accessed June 2013.
[7] Los Alamos National Laboratory, "periodic tables of elements," <http://periodic.lanl.gov/index.shtml> Accessed March 2015.
[8] Wikipedia, List of Intel Pentium Processors, <http://en.wikipedia.org/wiki/List_of_Intel_Pentium_microprocessors> Accessed March 2015.

INSPIRATION FLOW THEORY OF KNOWLEDGE

19

CHAPTER SUMMARY

This chapter is based on the notion that the elemental modules of knowledge (ΔK) are exchanged or transferred by virtual exchanges of verb functions (*VF*'s) between noun objects or knowledge centric objects (*KCOs*). In order to be practical and concurrently meaningful, we explore the concepts in this theory whereby the protocol for the knowledge path of smaller *kco*'s is in the physical domain and the larger knowledge centric object (*KCO*) is transported by imagery, similarities, parallelisms, and inspirations. One or subsequent sociopsychological pathways (memory flash-back, trigger-images, look, glance, gesture, etc.) confirm the knowledge exchange is imminent and then an "image" of a large body of knowledge (*KCO*) gets subconsciously formed by the receptor whereby bulk of the content is exchanged between the donor(s) and recipient(s) or vice versa. This image of the *KCO* is transferred, processed, reinforced, and refined. For example, love at first sight is another name for this mystic process. As another example, two scientists can communicate an enormous amount of information significant and beneficial to each other, in a short time by preassigned symbols, notations, equations, and even looks, signs, or a gesture. The resulting image is a constructive combination of the perceived image (as a seed or nucleus) and the supplementary image(s) from the receptor's own knowledge banks. We hasten to add that cruelty and violence can also be transferred thus. For example, a tiny insignificant nation can induce hate and aggression against other nations by distorting images fed to a much larger more powerful nation. Such examples are much too prevalent in history.

Knowledge space becomes staggeringly more complex than the physical space. The order of complexity becomes at least fourfold because every noun-object (*n*), verb-function (*v*), and their combination (***) are unique, furthermore all three depend on the *X, Y, Z, t* coordinates in socially and culture. Hence, it becomes necessary to limit the size of kunatum to "sensible" size and to be practical. Initially, it can be limited to most useful noun objects and verb functions. Two examples follow. In its practical format, a *kunatum* of knowledge can be stated as (food (*n*), eat (*v*), restaurant (*x, y, z*), date and time (*t*)). At the other extreme, a cosmic *kunatum* can be stated as (space ship A (*n*), explore (*v*), coordinates-Planet B (*x, y, z*), cosmic calendar date and time (*t*)). The need to be practical and limit the programing complexity, it becomes a necessity to deal with *kunatized* knowledge within the realm of computation. Even so, the content of the knowledge so gathered (i.e., the food eaten in the restaurant or the data collected by the space ship) is not communicated. The flow of the entirety of knowledge needs a larger number of smaller *kunata* (*kco*'s) to be complete within the global-*kunata* of knowledge (or *KCO*).

Evolution of Knowledge Science. DOI: http://dx.doi.org/10.1016/B978-0-12-805478-9.00019-4

19.1 INTRODUCTION

Four chapters are included in this Part II. Chapter 1 deals with the simplest theory to quantify knowledge [1], as we measure the current, fluid-flow, heat, magnetic fields, etc. Chapter 2 deals with flow of knowledge [2], as we would quantify current and voltage signals in transmission media and filters with their own characteristics in electrical communication theory. Chapter 3 deals with the flow of knowledge elements [3] and based on the based on the *kuantum* theory where an individual *kuantum* of knowledge (a *kel*) can interact with the medium it is traversing. Finally, Chapter 4 deals with the inspirational basis for the transfer of knowledge without any media but between transmitters and receptors with matching characteristics. Chapter 4 is based on the principle that incremental knowledge [4], is derived when one noun object interact (in any way) with other noun objects by exchanging verb functions between them in a fashion (i.e., a convolution) subject to the rules of the behavioral grammar. This chapter, also presents that knowledge can be reduced to tiny elemental cells constituted by the quantized noun objects, quantized convolutions, and quantized verb functions.

Life and physical objects are inseparably intertwined. Living and working with physical objects are necessarily entangled. Art of living and scientific skills are inevitably interwoven. The space and time-coordinates of this triadic essentials of existence (life itself, physical objects, and (x, y, z, t) coordinates) set the stage for the drama of all lives that unfold at any place and at any time.

From a slightly different perspective, minds and neural cells are biologically linked to living. Thought processes and actions are activated to enact. The physical sciences of noun objects (mass and dimensions), their actions (force and displacement), and the psychological motivation (incentive and impetus) to gratify human needs all coordinated. Life, society and reality are thus entwined.

From a more remote perspective, to establish the bondage and make reality of physical space, activity of mind, and continuum of physical and time-coordinates the fabric of universal knowledge becomes essential. Universal knowledge makes the imagination free from social and psychological constraints permitting thoughts to traverse mental space, physical space, and time. Human creativity and inspirations result from this constructive and cohesive cushion of knowledge.

In this current Internet age where information travels in the physical media at lightning speeds, the need for the mind to travel at super neural speeds is becoming more and mandatory. Perhaps inspirations based on constructive and creative knowledge have the potential to travel faster than light and overtake thoughts before the senses can process them. Life becomes easier with a set of well define knowledge tools. Knowledge exists in all textures, sizes, and forms from the deepest seas and dizzy heights. Human senses can only offer a tiny glance of a much more intricate reality. The sophisticated universe of knowledge can still be sensed (or felt) with perception and imagery. Programing and mathematical tools resolve such perceptions and images to realistic algebraic processes to be conceived by the mind and implemented on computers. To deal with reality and use in the knowledge era, the structure of knowledge needs careful adjustment, alignment, and association, especially if it is to be deployed in computational environment. The rigor of computer programing becomes essential.

The recent changes in the Internet age, catalyzed by high-speed gating functions of electron clusters in the silicon chips and by equally high-speed paths of photons in the optical fibers causes unprecedented synergy between knowledge centric objects of all sizes and shapes. Smaller *kco*'s (like humans, animals, marine life, etc.) dominate their own particular social spaces and much larger *KCOs* (like sun, moon, stars, etc.) dictate their own cosmic spaces. The human thought, now elated to new levels of intellectual activity and scientific exploration reigns supreme to unravel and decode the complexities of nature. Human mental processes still execute a variety of almost mystical arrays of neural programs to mould concepts, knowledge, and wisdom with learning, behavior, and adaptation.

Thought processes are generally associated with neural space and computational processes are associated with gating functions in silicon chips. These intermediate linkages bridge reality and physical spaces with the human psyche dealing with objects, their actions, interactions and their effects. Human beings have learned to cross these spaces readily by mind control. These mental processes are hard, if not impossible to program in the software of social machines. However, the connectivity of the mind with the machine can be established by controlling the noun-objects, their verb function, their convolutions and timings. These four entities make up the computational space as the mind would alter them in the psychological space to accomplish any social function or process. The social machine would alter the status of the noun-objects and their entropies accordingly. Thus, the machine could in a limited sense track, follow and duplicate the mental and psychological processes of a human mind.

19.2 TRANSFERENCE OF KNOWLEDGE
19.2.1 THE HUMAN SOCIAL PERSPECTIVE

Social interactions are essential for the existence of any object in society. Social objects interact with others in a stylized format most of the time and the syntactic rules are well defined, even though they are highly variable from culture to culture, society to society, and even household to household. Semantic rules are likewise variable these rules but extend and affirm the context of the local interactions. In an overall attempt to image social interactions to social machine emulation, any basic module of the interactive process can be written as:

$$NO_1 \leftarrow {}^*VF * \rightarrow NO_2$$

when a noun object NO_1 (i.e., Who?) interacts with a noun object NO_2 (Whom?), and NO_1 attempts a verb function VF (an action What?) upon NO_2 in the appropriate syntactic and semantic context $\leftarrow$ * with respect to itself and in the appropriate syntactic and semantic context * $\rightarrow$ with respect to the other object NO_2 (Whom?). NO_2 can be the same as NO_1 it as self-function like eat, drink, etc.

However, in reality there are hierarchies of Objects (ranging from global, cosmic objects to quantized, *kunatized* submicroscopic objects) and Verb function (ranging from global, cosmic functions to quantized, *kunatized* submicroscopic functions) and a series of stylized syntactic and semantic rules. Such representations for NO_1, NO_2 and VF are shown in Figure 19.1. The rule are symbolized as $\leftarrow$ * and as * $\rightarrow$ for NO_1 upon itself and upon NO_2 respectively.

The linkages up and down the NO and VF hierarchies are depicted as the curvilinear lines between the various levels of hierarchies. This linkage occurs in the minds/backgrounds of the objects to make the social interaction coherent and purposeful.

Typical Social Interaction Based Machine Code is written as

$$NO_1 \Leftarrow * VF* \Rightarrow NO_2$$

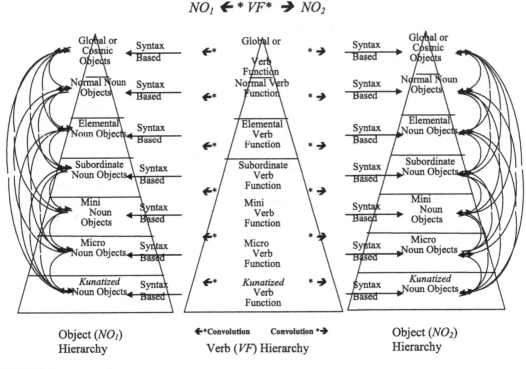

Object (NO_1)
Hierarchy

←*Convolution   Convolution *→

Verb (VF) Hierarchy

Object (NO_2)
Hierarchy

FIGURE 19.1

Classification of the NO and VF hierarchies for the interaction between two social objects (NO_1) and (NO_2). The action id VF and the convolution is *, with ←* as the effect on (NO_1) and *→ on (NO_2). *Operation code (opc) Operand (opr) or Operand Address* Subject to syntactic and semantic laws for governing *opc(s)* and *opr(s)*.

19.2.2 THE SOCIAL MACHINE AND KNOWLEDGE MACHINE PERSPECTIVES

Social machines or knowledge machines depend heavily on social processor units (*SPUs*) or on knowledge processor units (*KPUs*). These new breed of machines are much like typical computers that depend on CPUs for processing. Typical machine instruction for traditional CPUs is written as

Operation code (opc) | Operand (s) (opr (s)).

A series of such CPU instructions constitutes a machine language program.

In the social and knowledge machines, the *SPUs* and *KPUs* both track modules of social interaction and knowledge instructions for processing of objects in a similar fashion. Whereas social interactions are generic between human beings, the social modules can emulate elements of social interaction an almost human fashion. The generic representation shown in Figure 19.1, is further enhanced to indicate the positioning of Noun Objects (*NO*), Verb Functions (*VFs*), Convolutions (*), and then the processing of syntactic and semantic laws that are necessary to govern knowledge-based *opcs* or *sopcs* and the corresponding operands or *sopr*(s) and shown in Figure 19.2.

Typical Module of Human Interaction (VF_{1-2}) between two Objects (KNO_1 and KNO_2 or SNO_1 and SNO_2) is written as: KNO_1 or $SNO_1 \leftarrow * VF_{1-2} * \Rightarrow KNO_2$ or SNO_2

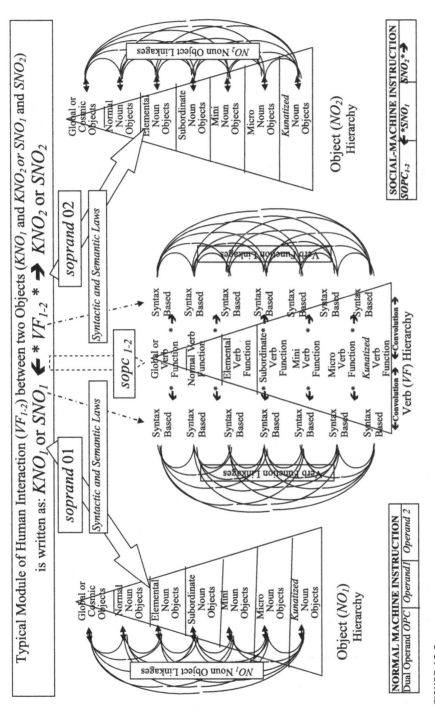

FIGURE 19.2

Corresponding machine code for the social machine is written as {$SOPC_{1-2} \leftarrow *SNO_1\ SNO_2* \rightarrow$}, where SOPC is social-based knowledge operation code and $\leftarrow *SNO_1$ and $SNO_2* \rightarrow$ are the two operands. As in every compiler the syntactic and semantic tests are necessary for compiling social machines programs. For the higher-level language and application programs these checks are performed by compilers. For the machine language programs, these checks must be performed by the programers. Most programers follow the verification automatically during the design of the software.

This type of processing can occur at any levels of the *NO* or *VF* hierarchies. For instance, if two super *NOs* (e.g., two galaxies) can give rise to a new offshoot solar system that has unique characteristics or a two microbe micro *NO* pair that can generate a new breed of bacteria, etc. It is also feasible to program the machine that functions of the noun objects from lower hierarchies can be incorporated in the processing routines, macros or microcode. An entirely new generation or species of *NOs* can thus be generated. Examples in nature are abundant as the species have evolved. Inspirational objects and functions are more appropriate in the psychological and mental space even though they may have a mapping in the real space.

19.2.3 DIFFERENCE BETWEEN SOCIAL INTERACTION-BASED PROCESSING AND KNOWLEDGE-BASED PROCESSING

These machine processes of these two machines are very similar. The machine language instructions can be written down as

$$SNO_1 \leftarrow {}^*SVF * \rightarrow SNO_2$$

for the typical social interaction-based machine and the code for the knowledge-based machine is written as

$$KNO_1 \leftarrow * KVF * \rightarrow KNO_2$$

The knowledge bases for *SNOs* are for typically for human beings and *KNOs* are for any general knowledge centric object. Correspondingly, the bases of *SVFs* and *KVFs* are also different.

The knowledge bases (*KBs*) of noun objects are created by knowledge management systems as easily as databases for data are created by database management systems. Entries in *KBs* of *NOs* serve as operands (*KOPERANDS* or *koperands*) for the *KPUs*. In the same vein, Verb Function *KBs* created to hold the verb functions *VFs* serve as operation codes (*KOPCs* or *kopcs*) for the *KPUs*. The syntactic and semantic laws are supplied by the lookup tables stored alongside of the noun and verb *KBs*. These knowledge bases serve as supporting information for social, medical, and educational systems.

Table 19.1 presents the systems breakdown of the various type of processor units of knowledge (*k*), social (*S*), medical (*M*), educational (*E*) machines that processes two *XNO's*, *XNO$_1$*, and *XNO$_2$*. The accumulators (or registers) of the traditional computers should be updated as objects registers with attribute caches for each object. The typical RR, RX, RS, SS, etc. [5], instruction sets also need to accommodate object processing and the accompanying attribute modifications.

In Table 19.2 the correspondence between the human thought processes and the social machine operation codes (*gopc's* through *qopc's*) for the various level (global through the *kunantized*) of the noun object and verb function hierarchies are tabulated. The relationship between the human actions involving active and passive, intelligent and non-intelligent objects with the operation codes of machines is firmly established by designing a methodology that is common for a general class of knowledge and social machines. Numerous series of such machines are the evolving knowledge (*K*), social (*S*), medical (*M*), educational (*E*), electronic government (*EG*) machines during the next few generation.

19.2.4 KONTROL MEMORIES FOR KNOWLEDGE-BASED MACHINES

During the development of traditional main frame computers, IBM had deployed the use of main frame generic hardware environment for scientific or business machines by simply inserting the

Table 19.1 General form of any interactive process between two noun objects XNO_1 and XNO_2 ($X = K, S, M, E,$ etc.)

Initiate/Respon — Respond/Initiate

$$\text{Interaction} = \sum (\text{Object - Action – Object})$$

Noun Object 1 $\leftarrow$ *Verb Function *$\rightarrow$ Noun Object 2

Noun Object 2 $\leftarrow$ *Verb Function *$\rightarrow$ Noun Object 1

Noun Objects (WHO? WHOM?)	Verb Functions (WHAT ACTION?)	Convolution (HOW?) * with appropriate Semantic and Syntactic Laws	Knowledge Machine Function Formal Representation
Global; GNO's = $\sum NNO$'s$+\sum ENO$'s$+\sum sno$'s $+\sum mno$'s$+\sum uno$'s$+\sum qno$'s	Global; GVF's $\sum NVF$'s$+\sum EVF$'s$+\sum sVF$'s $+\sum mVF$'s$+\sum \mu VF$'s$+\sum qVF$'s	$\leftarrow$*GVF*$\rightarrow$ Convolution with Forward and Reverse Convolutions	$GNO_1 \leftarrow$*GVF_{12}* $\rightarrow GNO_2$
Normal; NNO's = $=\sum ENO$'s$+\sum sno$'s$+\sum mno$'s $+\sum \mu no$'s$+\sum qno$'s	Normal; NVF's $\sum EVF$'s$+\sum sVF$'s$+\sum mVF$'s $+\sum \mu VF$'s$+\sum qVF$'s	$\leftarrow$*NVF*$\rightarrow$ = Forward and Reverse Convolutions	$NNO_1 \leftarrow$*NVF_{12}* $\rightarrow NNO_2$
Elemental; ENO's= $\sum sno$'s$+\sum mno$'s $+\sum \mu no$'s$+\sum qno$'s	Elemental; EVF's $=\sum sVF$'s$+\sum VVF$'s $+\sum \mu VF$'s$+\sum qVF$'s	$\leftarrow$*EVF*$\rightarrow$ = Forward and Reverse Convolutions	$ENO_1 \leftarrow$* EVF_{12}* $\rightarrow ENO_2$
Subordinate; sno's= $\sum mno$'s$+\sum \mu no$'s$+\sum qno$'s	Subordinate; sVF's $=\sum mVF$'s$+\sum \mu VF$'s$+\sum qVF$'s	$\leftarrow$*sVF*$\rightarrow$ = Forward and Reverse Convolutions	$sno_1 \leftarrow$*sVF_{12}* $\rightarrow sno_2$
Mini; mno's= $\sum \mu no$'s$+\sum qno$'s	Mini; mVF's $=\sum \mu VF$'s$+\sum qVF$'s	$\leftarrow$*mVF*$\rightarrow$ = Forward and Reverse Convolutions	$mno_1 \leftarrow$*mVF_{12}* $\rightarrow mno_2$
Micro; μno's= $\sum qno$'s	Micro; μVF's μVF's $= \sum qVF$'s	$\leftarrow$*μVF*$\rightarrow$ = Forward and Reverse Convolutions	$\mu no_1 \leftarrow$*μVF_{12}* $\rightarrow \mu no_2$
Kunatized; qno's	*Kunatized*; qVF's	$\leftarrow$*qVF*$\rightarrow$ Forward and Reverse Convolutions	$qno_1 \leftarrow$*qVF_{12}* $\rightarrow qno_2$

Note: NO *(or* no*) refers to noun objects (WHO? and WHOM?) and* VF *(or* vf*) refers to verb functions (WHAT?) action occurs between the objects. The convolution operator (*) facilitates the representation of how (HOW?) the action was performed. For example, the "take" action can be rob, steal, receive, collect, accept, grab, snatch, etc. Each variation could have a different impact on the two noun objects.*

appropriate control memory chips for micro-programmable machines. This approach is also used in the automobile industry where the automobile engine blocks are made compatible with the body frame of numerous models of vehicles. In the same vein, it will be cost wise effective to build generic hardware environments for numerous series of social, medical, educational library, and other knowledge-based machines. The control (*kontrol*) memory ROMs [6] can be designed to be

Table 19.2 General Form of Any Interactive Process Between Two Noun Objects NO_1 and NO_2

Interaction = $\sum$ (Object - Action - Object)
Noun Object 1 ←*Verb Function *→ Noun Object 2
Noun Object 2 ←*Verb Function *→ Noun Object 1

Noun Objects (Who)	Verb Functions (What Action)	Convolution (How)*	Knowledge Machine Function — Formal Representation
Global; GNO's $=\sum$NNO's$+\sum$ENO's$+\sum$sno's $+\sum$mno's$+\sum\mu$no's$+\sum$qno's	Global; GVF's $=\sum$NVF's$+\sum$EVF's$+\sum$svf's $+\sum$mvf's$+\sum\mu$vf's$+\sum$qvf's	←*GVF*→ = Convolution with Appropriate (Lookup) **Semantic and Syntactic Laws**	$GNO_1 ←* GVF_{12} * → GNO_2$
Normal; NNO's $=\sum$ENO's$+\sum$sno's$+\sum$mno's $+\sum\mu$no's$+\sum$qno's	Normal; NVF's $=\sum$EVF's$+\sum$svf's$+\sum$mvf's $+\sum\mu$vf's$+\sum$qvf's	←*NVF*→ = Convolution with Appropriate (Lookup) **Semantic and Syntactic Laws**	$NNO_1 ←* NVF_{12} * → NNO_2$
Elemental; ENO's $=\sum$sno's$+\sum$mno's $+\sum\mu$no's$+\sum$qno's	Elemental; EVF's $=\sum$svf's$+\sum$mvf's $+\sum\mu$vf's$+\sum$qvf's	←*EVF*→ = Convolution with Appropriate (Lookup) **Semantic and Syntactic Laws**	$ENO_1 ←* EVF_{12} * → ENO_2$
Subordinate; sno's $=\sum$mno's$+\sum\mu$no's$+\sum$qno's	Subordinate; svf's $=\sum$mvf's$+\sum\mu$vf's$+\sum$qvf's	←*svf*→ = Convolution with Appropriate (Lookup) **Semantic and Syntactic Laws**	$sno_1 ←* svf_{12} * → sno_2$
Mini; mno's $=\sum\mu$no's$+\sum$qno's	Mini; mvf's $=\sum\mu$vf's$+\sum$qvf's	←*mvf*→ = Convolution with Appropriate (Lookup) **Semantic and Syntactic Laws**	$mno_1 ←* mvf_{12} * → mno_2$
Micro; μno's $=\sum$qno's	Micro; μvf's $=\sum$qvf's	←*μvf*→ = Convolution with Appropriate (Lookup) **Semantic and Syntactic Laws**	$\mu no_1 ←* \mu vf_{12} * → \mu no_2$
Kuantized; qno's	Kuantized; qvf's	←*qvf*→ = Convolution with Appropriate (Lookup) **Semantic and Syntactic Laws**	$qno_1 ←* qvf_{12} * → qno_2$

interchangeable. The design of the processor unit should execute various forms of firmware subroutines the interpret operation codes according to the application. It may be possible to build RISC knowledge machines for such knowledge based computer systems.

19.3 **INSPIRATIONAL ASPECTS IN THE FLOW OF KNOWLEDGE**

We propose an inspirational theory of knowledge or its derivative to explain and monitor the flow of knowledge in almost all media and in no media at all. In its early format, it is to be stated that when two or more knowledge centric objects (*KCOs*) are in proximity and a sociopsychological path is sensed (aroused, ignited, communicated, etc.) between any two or more *KCOs*, then the necessary Global Verb Functions (*GVFs*) cluster by prior association (expectation, longing, desire, inspirations, etc.). A new more beautiful, efficient, useful, wanted or beloved, *KCO* and/or *GVF* "gets formed" as a super *KCO* or *GVF* in the mental (real, perceived, derived, perceptual, and/or psychological), spaces of two or more *KCOs*. The super *KCO* may involve the original *KCOs* or by analogy two or more similar mental (real, perceived, derived, perceptual, and/or psychological) *KCOs*. The super *GVF* may involve the original *GVFs* or by analogy two or more similar actions (real, perceived, derived, perceptual, and/or psychological) *KCVFs*.

In reality, noun objects items on which life depends and verb functions become their movements and moves. In a very graphic sense, the process occurs when people (*KCOs*) juggle "things" or smaller objects (*kcos*), the "actions" (*GVFs*), and/or their "arrangements" to improvise their activities. The process of "gets formed" can be conscious, subconscious, voluntary, involuntary, inspired but it does require a duration of time lasting as a flash (like love at first sight) or drawn out and tedious (like the case of Maxwell's generalization of his four equations of electromagnetism).

Such transfers of "knowledge" occurs between mother and child as the child perceives the parent–child bondage as a new *KCO*; in this case the "knowledge" is the "love" that is transferred and the *GVFs* can be the acts of nourishing, caressing, cuddling, etc. Less frequent are the deeds of genuine inspiration of a scientific principle from one scientist to another, when the receptor scientist interprets a generic concept of the donor scientist to a more general, more inclusive, more useful, more creative concept involving the original or similar *KCOs* and/or *GVFs*.

For example, the raw observations of Ampere, Gauss, Faraday, etc., were available to Maxwell, he built the more inclusive, more Global, more elegant and more universal form in his Maxwell's equations. This chain continues through Einstein's Special Theory to his General Theory of Relativity. A flash of genius, a twinkle in the eye, a symbiotic gesture or just a glance might form a lifelong bondage of love or association between human beings.

When knowledge is recast as clustered triggering of neurons in the brain, then such incidents of triggered cell centers occur in the brain when a child learns to add (like 2 and 2 on its fingers) and then goes on learn addition (like 3 and 3 using the fingers) in the same fashion. The *KCOs* are neighboring neuron clusters, the *GVF* is adding, the minor *KCOs* or *kcos* are the fingers, and the inclusive *GVF* is addition any two or more numbers. Numerous other examples also exist.

In its early format, this theory states that knowledge may be "transferred" or it can flow from one object to another by inspiration. Specifically, it states that when two or more knowledge centric objects (*KCOs*) are in proximity and a sociopsychological path is sensed (aroused, provoked, communicated, or even imagined) between any two or more *KCOs*, then the necessary Global Verb Functions (*GVFs*) cluster by prior association (expectation, longing, desire, or inspiration, or even imagination) follow from insight or (computer-based, algorithmic) visualization(s).

A larger, (more beautiful, efficient, useful, wanted or beloved, etc.), *KCO* and/or *GVF* "gets formed" as a super *KCO* or *GVF* in the mental (real, perceived, derived, perceptual, and/or psychological), spaces of two or more *KCOs*. The super *KCO* may involve the original *KCOs* or by analogy two or more similar mental (real, perceived, derived, perceptual, and/or psychological) *KCOs*. The super *GVF* may involve the original *GVFs* or by analogy two or more similar actions (real, perceived, derived, perceptual, and/or psychological) *KCVFs*.

When knowledge is recast as clustered triggering of neurons in the brain, then such incidents of triggered cell centers occur in the brain when a child learns to add (like 2 and 2 on its fingers) and then goes on learn addition (like 3 and 3 using the fingers) in the same fashion. The *KCOs* are neighboring neuron clusters, the *GVF* is adding, the minor *KCOs* or *kcos* are the fingers, and the inclusive *GVF* is addition any two or more numbers. Numerous other examples also exist.

In its early format, this theory states that knowledge may be "transferred" or it can flow from one object to another by inspiration. Specifically, it states that when two or more knowledge centric objects (*KCOs*) are in proximity and a sociopsychological path is sensed (aroused, provoked, communicated, or even imagined) between any two or more *KCOs*, then the necessary Global Verb Functions (*GVFs*) cluster by prior association (expectation, longing, desire, or inspiration, or even imagination) follow from insight or (computer -based, algorithmic) visualization(s). A larger, (more beautiful, efficient, useful, wanted or beloved, etc.), *KCO* and/or *GVF* "gets formed" as a super *KCO* or *GVF* in the mental (real, perceived, derived, perceptual, and/or psychological, etc.), spaces of two or more *KCOs*. The super *KCO* may involve the original *KCOs* or by analogy two or more similar mental (real, perceived, derived, perceptual, and/or psychological) *KCOs*. The super *GVF* may involve the original *GVFs* or by analogy two or more similar actions (real, perceived, derived, perceptual, and/or psychological) *KCVFs*.

19.4 POSITIVE INSPIRATIONS (PORTRAIT OF PROGRESS)

In reality, these super noun objects and super verb functions can be animate or inanimate, virtual or abstract, impressionistic or realistic. One of the chief requirements is that the receptor object be intelligent to enhance or modify the "impression/inspiration" communicated by the donor object. History has documented the role of prophets (Buddha, Moses, and Christ) and saints (Schweitzer, Gandhi, King) in inspiring their disciples and followers with super objects (like personalities of saints, portraits of virtue, images of shrines, etc.) and super functions (like love, respect, etc.). Enormous good and virtue has followed.

In its simplest form, transfusion of imageries is any normal human dialogue where the opinion or knowledge of one human being is being modified by communicating with the other. For instance, when human beings exchange gestures of love, the imagery of what they expect from one another get formed and either enhanced or rejected leading to many possibilities that can arise from one or more series of interactions. In a rare but real form, it can be the rich legacy of musical compositions that resulted between two great musicians [7] Yehudi Menuhin and Ravi Shankar. Further, the association with Zubin Mehta also affirms a triadic form of inspirational music which appears more melodious and richer than the music of any one of the two/three great musicians.

In a different format, the association between Thomas Alva Edison, (1847−1931, the inventor of telegraph), Alexander Graham Bell (1847−1922, the inventor of telephone), and Frederic Allan Gower (a businessman), resulted in the formation of the Edison Gower-Bell Telephone Company of Europe, Ltd. in the early 1880 s, to serve most of Europe [8]. The invention of Thomas Edison's Carbon microphone (1877−78) did find a distinctive role in Alexander Graham Bell's telephones [9]. This gadget became a promising component in the older telephone systems.

Inspirational pathways of knowledge both positive and negative do not need real-time pathways or continuity in the time domain. In fact, this "inspirational knowledge" can appear as true, genuine, and beneficent inspirations or as false, deceptive, and harmful deceit. In a negative sense, an "inspiration" occurs when two Mafia member meet to collude. Over space it can transfer between Europe and United States, spread over time, it can transfer between generations.

Knowledge centric objects or *KCOs* are items on which life depends and verb functions become their movements and moves. In a very graphic sense, the process occurs when people (*KCOs*) juggle "things" or smaller objects (*kcos*), the "actions" (*GVFs*), and/or their "arrangements" to improvise their activities. The process of "gets formed" can be conscious, subconscious, voluntary, involuntary, inspired but it does require a duration of time lasting as a flash (like love at first sight) or drawn out and tedious (like the case of Maxwell's generalization of his four Equations of electromagnetism).[1]

Such transfers of "knowledge" occurs between mother and child as the child perceives the parent−child bondage as a new *KCO*; in this case the "knowledge" is the "love, concern, responsibility," that is transferred and the *GVFs* can be the acts of nourishing, caressing, cuddling, etc. Less frequent are the deeds of genuine inspiration of a scientific principle from one scientist to another, when the receptor scientist interprets a generic concept of the donor scientist to a more general, more inclusive, more useful, more creative concept involving the original or similar *KCOs* and/or *GVFs*. For example, the raw observations of Ampere, Gauss, Galvani, Faraday, etc., were available to Maxwell and he went on to build the more inclusive, more generic, more elegant and more universal form in his Maxwell's equations. This chain continues through Einstein's Special Theory to his General Theory of Relativity. A flash of genius, a twinkle in the eye, a symbiotic gesture, or just a glance might form a lifelong bondage of love or association between human beings.

When knowledge is recast as clustered triggering of neurons in the brain, then such incidents of triggered cell centers occur in the brain when a child learns to add (like 2 and 2 on its fingers) and then goes on learn addition (like 3 and 3 using the fingers) in the same fashion. The *KCOs* are neighboring neuron clusters, the GVF_1 is adding, the minor *KCOs* or *kcos* are the fingers, and the inclusive *GVF* is addition any two or more numbers. Numerous other examples also exist.

Figure 19.3 depicts a situation when a donor *KCO* (1) communicates an impression of a fragmented *kco* (1) to the receptor *KCO* (2). The *KCOs* can be two or more knowledge machines that convey the "image-knowledge structures" of the "*kcos*" via data links or high-speed Internet ATM

---

[1]*KCOs* and *kcos* denote major and minor *knowledge centric objects*, GVF, and gVFs denote the major and minor *verb functions*, respectively. The structure of the objects and their functionalities are carried by the (noun object-verb function) pair(ings).

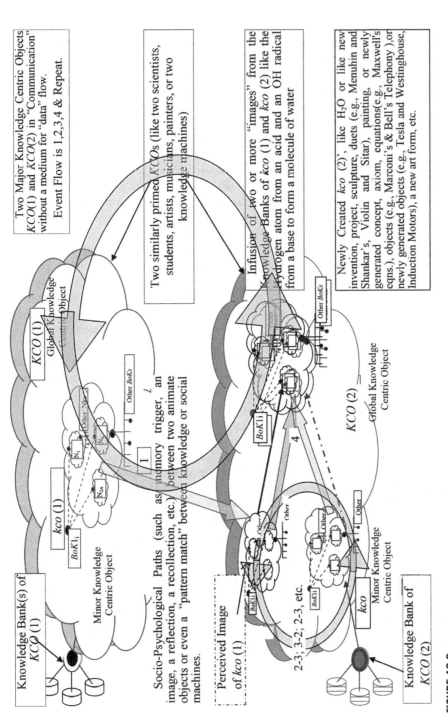

Two Major Knowledge Centric Objects $KCO(1)$ and $KCO(2)$ in "Communication" without a medium for "data" flow.

Event Flow is 1,2,3,4 & Repeat.

Two similarly primed *KCOs* (like two scientists, students, artists, musicians, painters, or two knowledge machines)

Infusion of two or more "images" from the Knowledge Banks of *kco* (1) and *kco* (2) like the hydrogen atom from an acid and an OH radical from a base to form a molecule of water

Newly Created *kco* (2)', like H_2O or like new invention, project, sculpture, duets (e.g., Menuhin and Shankar's, Violin and Sitar), painting, or newly generated concept, axiom, equations(e.g., Maxwell's eqns.), objects (e.g. Marconi's & Bell's Telephony),or newly generated objects (e.g., Tesla and Westinghouse, Induction Motors), a new art form, etc.

Socio-Psychological Paths (such as memory trigger, an image, a reflection, a recollection, etc.) between two animate objects or even a "pattern match" between knowledge or social machines.

Knowledge Bank(s) of KCO (1)

Minor Knowledge Centric Object

KCO (1)

Global Knowledge Centric Object

kco (1)

Other *BoKs*

N_1

Other *N*

N_a

*BoKI*ᵢ

Perceived Image of *kco* (1)

*BoKI*ᵢ

2-3; 3-2; 2-3, etc.

*BoKi*ᵢ

Other

kco

Minor Knowledge Centric Object

Knowledge Bank of KCO (2)

*BoKi*ᵢ

Other *BoKs*

KCO (2)

Global Knowledge Centric Object

4

FIGURE 19.3

Depiction of an inspirational transfer of knowledge. Incomplete "images" or "tokens" based on two objects communicate via a sociopsychological path or any two machines transferring such "images" via protocol during signaling, and data paths and generate new "image" of an object derived from one or more "images" from the knowledge bases of the two primary knowledge centric objects, i.e., KCO (1) and KCO (2).

pathways. If the two machines are both intelligent, then they can generate numerous "children *kcos*" (twin objects, triadic objects, etc.) that are more valuable to the society where the two original *KCO*s exist. The situation is akin to two parents in unison can produce a baby from the genes drawn from both or of an engaged couple who plan a life of bliss or conversely for one exploitive partner to sweet talk and deceive the other into marriage.

Such examples have prevailed in nature and civilizations for eons but become applicable in the information domain between humans and/or machines. The protocol and interfaces to receive and process the significant content of the *kcos*, their structure, and *GVFs* need to be explored and standardized such that any couple *KCOs* can gainfully interact. For example, if a hacker tries to fool a machine to provide access to secure data, a certain amount of educated deception is being practiced and it can be reversed by a super-machine and such machine can "intellectually trap" the hacker and communicate the hacker information to the security centers around the WWW profile hubs. Such advanced security measures are enforced by intelligence agencies of many nations. A sense of good and evil is evident. However, the roles are reversed for the corrupt and the dishonest. The role of human intellect becomes supreme to become decisive based on the local and environmental conditions. The art of programing very insidious role of being superhuman will be perhaps, the final test for Artificially (Superhuman) Intelligent programing experts.

19.5 NEGATIVE DESPERATION (PORTRAITS OF DECEPTION)

As much as truth, virtue and grace are implanted in an honest society by the noble and elite, the seeds of descent, hate, and aggression can be planted in a corrupt society by Mafia and thugs. Society thus swings as a massive pendulum under these opposing forces. The endless cyclic rhythms of lives, societies, nations follows the waves of deceit, aggression, and ignorance moving counter to truth, virtue, and wisdom and vice versa in both microscopic and macroscopic scales. Harmony and accord suffer brutally at the whim and fancy of ignorant missiles-and-machine-gun wielding army generals. The enactment of this behavior has been documented in the history of British colonial rule around the world. The destructive nature of violence is inherently faster than the resurrection of harmony and accord within the society. Ignorance and brutality are as much akin as knowledge and consent from a global perspective.

Harassments and negative acts of desperation can be equally ingenious but ill-founded and deceitful. They can be atrocious and disastrous bringing death and dismay to large segments of populous. History has documented numerous incidents of such collusion of evil intent with grave trails behind them. For example, the French and British instigated the Inquisition[2] and torture

---

[2]"At root the word Inquisition signifies as little of evil as the primitive 'inquire,' or the adjective inquisitive but as words, like persons, lose their characters by bad associations, so 'Inquisition' has become infamous and hideous as the name of an executive department of the Roman Catholic Church." Further the description reads "The Inquisitions function was principally assembled to repress all heretics of rights, depriving them of their estate and assets which became subject to the ownership of the Catholic treasury, with each relentlessly sought to destroy anyone who spoke, or even thought differently to the Catholic Church. This system for close to over six centuries became the legal framework throughout most of Europe that orchestrated one of the most confound religious orders in the course of mankind." [http://www.bibliotecapleyades.net/vatican/esp_vatican29.htm]

starting in 12th century France and spread to Spain and Northern Italy. The Portuguese and British[3] slave traders brought and brutally exploited the native African tribesmen and women for over 300 years starting mid to late 1400 s.

As another example, when Bush started an offensive in Iraq with the assumption of misdirected evidence that Saddam Hussein was hoarding weapons of mass destruction, Blair joined in as a poodle following a dog. Both the two countries brought in massive suffering on people who had nothing to do weapons of mass destruction! As recently as the middle of 2014, offensives are regularly launched despite world opinion and UN disapproval.[4]

Numerous examples of such cruelty smear the history of human race with trails of cruelty of willful and questionable conduct of political leaders. Truth, honesty, and wisdom are blindfolded when deceit reigns supreme. Collusion of evil wills is an antithesis of an inspiration seeking rewards the humankind by goodwill and noble intent. Natural intelligence needs to play its vital role above and beyond machines primed with artificial intelligence which can turn sour.

19.5.1 PROTOCOL TRANSFER AND CONTENT REINFORCEMENT

In collaborative reinforcement of inspiration, the physical media (like sight, gesture, nod, look, etc.) establishes the protocol (like how) the transference can be done via inferences, impressions, reading, and memory linkages, etc. But thereafter the transport stops and interpretation starts to activate the intelligence (natural, artificial, and PR methodologies to scan for the deeper content and purpose of the initial protocol) of the receptor. Reinforcement of content and purpose of the possible "impressions" may be invoked via other physical or perceptual links. Scriptures are believed to have this type of spiritual continuity and numerous master-disciple (e.g., Siddhartha and his monks, Jesus and John, the Baptist, Gandhi and Nehru, etc.) relationships claim such "inspirational" communication.

19.5.2 PROCESSING OF IMPRESSIONS AND INSPIRATIONS

The cognition of impressions and their successive processing are two critical steps in inspirations exchanged or communicated. The "image," ΔK_1 brings signals of the knowledge centric objects KCOs, their GVFs, and the structure and constitution that relate such modules of information. The inspiration processing is shown in Figure 19.4. As a first step, the impressions thus received as A conveys the background of the increment of knowledge or (ΔK_1) from KCO (1) to KCO (2) in box and perceived as B. The initial processing removes any noise or background signals from the perceived image.

The image, token, or impression initially received by KCO (2) is blended by image processing algorithms in AI and a new image is thus deduced by blending (Box 3). The refined admixing of

---

[3]For well over 300 years, European countries forced Africans onto slave ships and transported them across the Atlantic Ocean. The first European nation to engage in the Transatlantic Slave Trade was Portugal in the mid to late 1400 s. Captain John Hawkins made the first known English slaving voyage to Africa, in 1562, in the reign of Elizabeth I. Hawkins made three such journeys over a period of 6 years. He captured over 1200 Africans and sold them as goods in the Spanish colonies in the Americas. [http://abolition.e2bn.org/slavery_45.html]

[4]Please see http://news.msn.com/world/israel-widens-air-attack-gaza-death-toll-tops-125-1. Please read the complete news article.

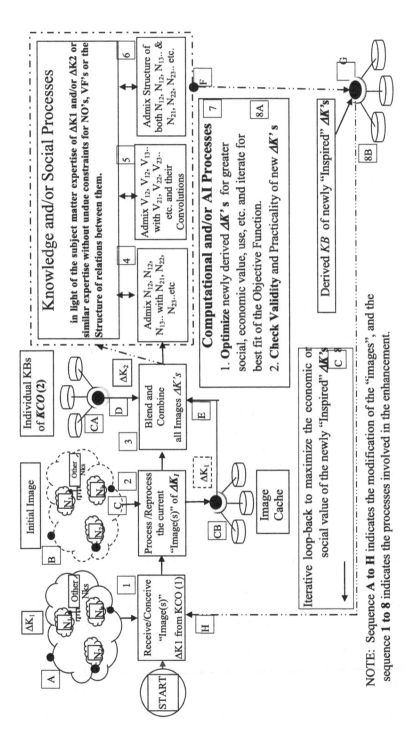

FIGURE 19.4

Computer schematic for deriving and deducing inspirations between human beings via virtual sociopsychological pathways or between knowledge machines via Internet data links based on systematic and computational algorithms. The superiority of human function lies in the knowledge processing box with dashed lines, where the neural pathways in the brain can yield optimal results without any known algorithmic process.

the numerous smaller *kcos* (shown as N_{12}, N_{12}, N_{13}.. and $N_2 1$, N_{22}, N_{23}.. etc., Box 4), the numerous *GVFs* (shown as $V1_2$, $V1_2$, $V1_3$.. and $V_2 1$, V_{22}, V_{23}.. etc., Box 5), and their respective structures (Box 6) in the knowledge processing box in Figure 19.4. Only newly derived or deduced *kcos* (F) that show promise of being valid and practical are moved to the next *KB* of "Inspired" ΔKs (G) for further evaluation and analysis.

The validity processing (Box 8) is verified by analysis or by heuristic comparisons. The analysis is done examining the subject-matter (e.g., chemistry, physics, engineering, etc.) analysis of *N's*, *V's*, and their structural relations in the inspirationally derived *kcos*. The heuristic analysis is done by searching if the *N's*, *V's*, and their structural relations in the inspirationally derived *kcos* match those in the existing *KBs* on the Internet websites or local *KBs*. Optimization and final refinement of the "inspired" image in the *KB* is repeated numerous times until a satisfactory "image" or object is derived or deduced by the series of steps shown in Figure 19.4.

CONCLUSIONS

Inspirational mode of knowledge-transfer needs the transmutation of concepts dealing with physical objects and their attributes to analogous concepts dealing with mental images and metaphysical objects and their associations. Images once formed in the minds of humans or the core of the computer memories are objects in their own right. Such objects can both be enhanced and processed by computer-based image processing algorithms. This processing uncovers any underlying patterns of human thought in a social setting to yield greater economic or social value in the present context. The robustness of the original concepts holds the key to the travel in time and without any media for transport. Within the mind or the machine the concepts are treated as images subject to image-processing algorithms and objects subject to object processing macros and routines.

It is our contention that every object has some function associated with it. An object is non-object if it does not do anything and conversely an action is a nonaction if no object can do it. Both (noun) objects and (verb) functions fall out of the knowledge domain if they cannot be connected to some existing (verb) function (*VF*) or (noun) object (*NO*) respectively. In appropriate conjunction (convolution or *) the pair (*no*VF* or *VF*no*) contributes to an element of knowledge ($\Delta k \propto f_1$ (*no*VF*) or $\Delta k' \propto f_1'$ (*VF_1'* *no*)) that serves some purpose or gratifies some element of need ($\Delta n \propto f_2$ (Δk) or $\Delta n' \propto f_2'$ (Δk)) of an individual, species, society, culture, or some social object.

The knowledge space is now greatly augmented by Internet connectivity and it fills all suspicious gaps by either tangible path(s) or by mathematical formulation(s). This paper offers means of establishing continuity between most physical object(s) and their functionality(ies) by establishing an hierarchy of knowledge centric object than be reduced to the *kunata* thus entrapping the microscopic objects and their microscopic functionality(ies). The approach is also feasible at a macroscopic level where macro-objects perform macro functions. The possibility of micro objects doing macro functions leads to statistical probability distribution of their occurrence. The sciences have not sufficiently evolved to solve all aspects of macro knowledge centric objects (like the universe, the human body, etc.) problems at the same time and solve the microscopic objects (like the photons, the genetic cells, etc.) problems at one and the same time, except by statistical methods in quantum physics. Further, sciences can provide some insight into the equations for main macro functions (like the Big Bang, the genetic evolution, etc.) but they cannot resolve the infinitesimal micro functions (like electron-photon interactions, the cellular biological processes, etc.) both at one and the same time. Human comprehension starts to fizzle out at both extremes of noun objects (i.e., for super-cosmic objects and for micro-monocular particles). Human comprehension also fizzles out at both extremes of verb functions (i.e., for chaotic collision of super nova and for collision of electrons in super colliders). In a sense, knowledge though complete in its own right is incomprehensible at such extreme boundaries the knowledge processing calls adequate care and due diligence in implementing them on computers.

REFERENCES

[1] Chapter 16, "General Theory of Knowledge Flow", in this book.
[2] Chapter 17, "Transmission Theory of Knowledge Flow", in this book.
[3] Chapter 18, "Kuantum Theory of Knowledge Flow", in this book.
[4] Chapter 19, "Inspiration Theory of Knowledge Flow", (this chapter) in this book.
[5] Hayes JP. Computer architecture and organization. 2nd ed. New York: McGraw Hill; 1988, See also, Stone HS, et al. Introduction to computer architecture. Computer Science Series, Science Research Associates, New York; 1980. Stallings W. Computer organization and architecture. New York: Macmillan; 1987.
[6] Hill MD, Jouppi NP. Readings in computer architecture. Morgan Kaufmann Series in Computer Architecture and Design 1999.
[7] Lavezzoli P. The dawn of Indian music in the West - Google Books. Bloomsbury Academic; 2006. p. 47, West Meets East, Yehudi Menon and Ravi Shankar and Ali Akbar Khan, ISBN-13: 9780826418159.
[8] Rutger's University. The Thomas A, Edison Companies; April 2010. Also see <http://en.wikipedia.org/wiki/Edison_Gower-Bell_Telephone_Company_of_Europe_Ltd>.
[9] Ahamed SV, Lawrence VB. The art of scientific innovation. Prentice Hall; 2004, ISBN-13:9780131473423.

DYNAMIC NATURE OF KNOWLEDGE: FRAGMENTATION AND FLOW

20

CHAPTER SUMMARY

In this chapter, we propose that knowledge can be reduced to its elementary (elemental) size. Each element consisting of quantized noun object(s), their quantized verb function(s), and the incremental type(s) the convolutions that bind such noun objects and verb functions. Even though knowledge may not be quantized as finely and as definitively as matter can be quantized in physics, these elements of knowledge form building block for larger and practical bodies of knowledge. These elements of knowledge (*kels*) exhibit statistical properties and their dynamics are based on the properties of *kels*, their origin, their environment, the media, and their recipients. Further, we define the elementary particles as a *kuantum* of knowledge, even though a *kuantum* is not a quantum in the traditional sense.

In maintaining a working relation with other sciences, we explore the flow of these *kels* to and from larger practical objects to complete social and real functions. A quantum of knowledge (*kel*) is like a particle of matter with a pulse of energy that can be coupled. We present this concept to investigate if such *kels* will explain all the intricacies in the flow of knowledge in societies, cultures, and groups. Even though a *kel* is not as defined precisely as quantum (an electron) in physics, but in the framework of theory presented here, the statistical properties of *kels* explains statistical differences in the way in which noun objects communicate, i.e., transmit and receive such kuanta and *kels*. This approach holds the maximum promise but the quantization of a *kel* to a workable size becomes unique and depends on the direction in which knowledge is being explored and/or constituted. The generic quantum of knowledge or *kel* still appears as a mystic entity, even though specific *kuanta* are feasible that the modern computers can tackle, build, process, constitute, reconstitute, reprocess to generate "artificial knowledge." Such artificial knowledge is then verified, validated, and accepted or challenged, disputed, and rejected by AI routines and by natural intelligence of human beings to build large and realistic bodies of knowledge (*bok*) or knowledge centric objects (*kcos*) of any size, shape, or form.

20.1 INTRODUCTION

Knowledge can be reduced to tiny elemental cells constituted by the quantized noun objects, quantized verb functions, and their quantized convolutions. Most species deal with modules or kuanta of rudimentary knowledge in order to gratify their routine needs and acquire them to make life easier. Most of the elite learn to deal with and manipulate more advanced kuanta of sophisticated knowledge in order to gratify their special needs and learn them to satisfy their needs,

Evolution of Knowledge Science. DOI: http://dx.doi.org/10.1016/B978-0-12-805478-9.00020-0

environment, and their circumstances. *Kels* do indeed have a hierarchical structure. Like nature itself, knowledge exists in all textures, sizes, and forms. Human senses that operate in real and physical space offer a very tiny glance of a much more intricate and sophisticated universe of knowledge that can be sensed by perception and resolved by programing/mathematical tools. To deal with reality and use in the knowledge era, the structure of knowledge needs careful adjustment, alignment, and association, especially if it is to be deployed in computational environment.

The origin of *kel* (to represent knowledge cell) is derived from the word pixel to stand for picture element (i.e., picture-cell, written as pixel). In addition, there is a resounding similarity between *kel* and the naturally elements in chemistry at the atomic, molecular, and at a reactionary level. For instance, the chemical elements also consist of neutrons, positrons, and electrons that play an adaptive role as the elements form molecules, and complex chains of organic, inorganic compounds, and acids. Nature has provided an innate intelligence for the world of materials to exist.

In a closely correlated methodology, *kels* also play such a complex role. *Kels* can share noun objects and convolutions as much as atoms can share the nuclear elements, electrons, and valency bonds. The particularly adaptive role of atoms to form varieties of compounds is evident when *kels* can arrange and rearrange their structures of *nos*, **s*, and *vfs*, to form different configurations of knowledge of chain of *kels* to form minor *kcos* and major *KCOs*. The analogy is evident to treat the chemical world as a type of knowledge society or culture where the *nos*, **s* and *vfs* are the basic building blocks and these *kels* are formed and unformed depending on the dynamic social setting and the setting. At a very microscopic level, change in the chemistry of every atom is as real as the change of every *kel*!

In order to be practical, we explore the quantum theory of knowledge whereby the knowledge paths between small knowledge centric objects (*kcos*) and large knowledge centric objects (*KCOs*) can be investigated. A continuum of noun objects (*nos*), verb functions (*vfs*), and the associated convolutions (**s*) is thus retained between *KCOs*. This continuum is searched out by segmented knowledge machines that operate between the smaller *kcos* and the larger *KCOs* in any given domain or direction of knowledge. Dewey Decimal System (DDS) or the Library of Congress (LoC) classification offer two methodologies to classify the domain of knowledge pursued. One or more pathways exist in the chain of evolution of the subject matter and related inventions that have occurred around practical and real modules of knowledge in the range of any smaller *kco* to the larger *KCO*. All modalities of knowledge representation (images, documents, graphs, presentations, etc.) need investigation to complete the pathway(s) between *kcos* and *KCOs*.

Minute constituents of *kels* (i.e., *nos*, **s*, and *vfs*) can and do interact with the social and cultural character of the medium that carries them. In a sense, the statistical properties of the medium alter the genesis, the transmission, and the retention of these *kels* thus offering the vast varieties of lives, decay, and death of knowledge in different societies and cultures. All the principles for the transmission of knowledge presented in Chapter 17 of this book become applicable in this chapter. Even though human beings may be daunted by such intricacy, knowledge machine can routinely handle tracking, transmission, attenuation, and dispersion of knowledge in most societies.

The role of a *kel* is as fundamental as the role of seminal biological cell in all species. The two chromosome pairs formed as xx (female) and/or an xx or xy (male) chromosomes to constitute the female and male genetic cell evolves after the genetic code in the male (no1)-*kel*1 penetrates and ruptures (vf(s) in a distinctly unique fashion(*)) the female (no2)-*kel*2. A new *kel*3 and a new no3 (the fetus) is thus formed, and it carries the genetic code of both no1 and no2 as the *no3-kel3*. Ones,

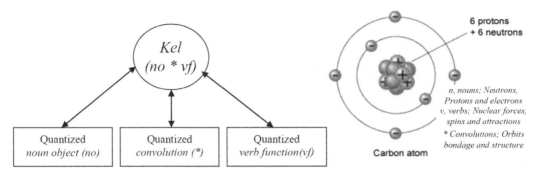

Structure of a *kel* constituted as the knowledge when a noun object no convolves (*) with a verb function vf in a specific convolution * format.

Structure of a larger *kel* with numerous no's, vf's and specific convolution * formats.

FIGURE 20.1

Configuration of an element of knowledge, kel formed from a set of the tinniest but flexible and dynamic entities (no, *, and vf). The kels are comparable to atoms made up of neutrons, protons and electrons. The basic building blocks can be shared and enhanced to form new kels during social interactions or knowledge processing.

twins, and multiple babies are all formed from the process[1] (no1* vf1, also see Figure 20.1). In a very oblique sense, the inception of knowledge and the origin of life are intertwined. The genetic code should be considered as knowledge that carries the imprint of the species and the two codes (male and female) that get interlock should be considered and the generation of new *no3-kel3* noun object.

20.2 FRAGMENTATION OF KNOWLEDGE INTO ITS ELEMENTS

20.2.1 GENERALITY IN NATURE AND OTHER DISCIPLINES

The formation of complex *KELs* from their microscopic structure or *kels* occurs in human minds. Major knowledge centric objects *(KCOs)* are also constituted by their fragmented elements. Software development is based on machine instructions, macros, subroutines, and utility programs. The growth of life forms such as bacteria, and even species in biological sciences is a process of systematic composition of more minute cells. Such an integration methodology is applicable in the evolution of larger structures of knowledge and depicted as follows:

$$\delta\,kels \to \mu\,kels \to \Delta kels \to \sum kels \to \sum\sum kels$$

stated alternatively;

---

[1]The more precise representation of the entire set of processes is represented as $(qno_1 \leftrightarrow q^*_1 \leftrightarrow qvf \leftrightarrow q^*_2 \leftrightarrow qno_2)$ where the prefix q denotes a *kuantum* of the genetic code in each *kel*. Genetic science elaborates the processes that follow from the formation of the seminal cell of the fetus to the duplication of the cells but in the context of where and how the cells are deployed. The changes in the womb and the physiology of the parental object $\to qno_2$.

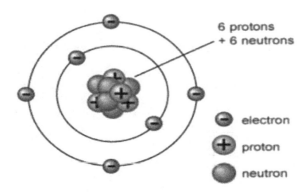

6 protons
+ 6 neutrons

electron

proton

neutron

FIGURE 20.2

The kels in Figure 20.1 are comparable to atoms made up of electrons, protons, and neutrons. The basic building blocks or kels can be shared and enhanced to form other knowledge elements. As much as the structure of atoms is altered in chemical reactions, the structure of knowledge is altered, modified, truncated, or even eliminated by actions, words, or dealings in human environments.

$$minute \; kels \rightarrow becoming \rightarrow large \; kels (KELs)$$

and, then from larger *kels* to macroscopic *KELs*

$$\delta \, KELs \rightarrow \mu \, KELs \rightarrow \Delta KELs \rightarrow \sum KELs \rightarrow \sum \sum KELs \rightarrow KCOs$$

written alternatively;

$$minute \; KELs \rightarrow becoming \rightarrow large \; KELs (KCOs)$$

The evolutionary step in each of the transitions ($\rightarrow$) is triggered or catalyzed by a verb function(s). Such verb functions can be inherent within the *kel* or induced externally. For example, lightning discharge can form molecules of ozone O3 in the atmosphere where oxygen is abundant. The knowledge society is an ordered environment of *kels* represented and integrated as δks, μks, Δks, $\sum$ks, $\sum \sum$ks, ..., and then of δKs, μKs, ΔKs, $\sum$Ks, $\sum \sum$Ks, or *KCOs* etc.[2] Chemistry also displays simple and complex to very, complex chains of distribution of atoms in the real world.

20.2.2 ATOMS AND KNOWLEDGE ELEMENTS

The diagrammatic representations of a *kel* and of a Carbon[3] atom are shown in Figures 20.1 and 20.2. Atoms can and exist in many atomic weights as much as *kels* can exist in many "*kel* weights" (like atomic weights) depending on the utility of the knowledge embedded in the *kel*. For instance, the atomic weight of the noble metals is much higher than that of the ordinary elements. The energy contained in their atoms is greater than that in the hydrogen atom with an

---

[2]In increasing order of complexity of *kels*. For example, if μk is grocery item, then μK will be a grocery store and $\sum \sum$K would be worldwide chain of food stores, etc.
[3]Carbon atom is chosen as an example, but any element that forms molecules and compounds exhibits similar properties and traits.

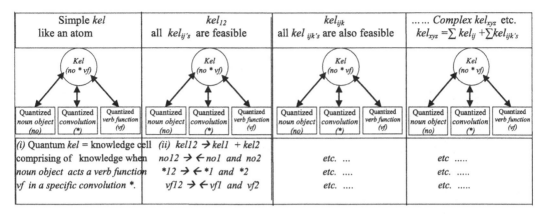

FIGURE 20.3

The chain of new knowledge structures generated when a basic kel (such as the knowledge in an invention (e.g., 2-D computer memories)) starts to interact other kels such as 2½-D memories to leading to the Architecture of 3-D memories. Numerous other examples also exist such as the discovery of Penicillin by Fleming has led to the development of other specific chain of antibiotics, such as the invention of IC engine has led to the turbo charged automobile engines, etc.

atomic weight of 1.0078. The *kel*-weight of a brain surgeon (no) performing a (vf) transplant of the brain (if it is possible), in a very specific way (*) would be much higher than the *kel*-weight of a monkey eating peanuts.

In most stylized interactions, *kels* adopt a formal approach depending on the syntactic and semantic setting for the interaction. In a computation environment, the protocol is essential for any particular interaction between machines. In human environment, the etiquette and customs define the modality and success of the exchange of information and knowledge. Typical behavior of a *kel* is shown in Figure 20.3 the formality of the process (*no * vf*) is retained in most settings.

When *kels* interact with each other, new knowledge is created by the syntactic and semantic rules that led to the interaction. The result also becomes a part of the incremental knowledge generated by humans and/or by knowledge-based *KEL* machines. This naturally or artificially generated new knowledge can be generated in simple or in complex chains of interactions. Figure 20.3 depicts various circumstances for the artificial generation of new knowledge as single and/or multiple noun objects interact. For example, two hydrogen atoms can form a molecule in the simplest case. Hydrogen and oxygen can combine H_2O, H_2O_2, D_2O, D_2O_2, etc. in various convolutions. Biological and genetic cells are formed when numerous elements interact. See the left column in Figure 20.3.

Organization and context become the basis of all the elements and *kels*. Both display and contain the mechanisms of how and why a elements and *kels* may be useful/useless and in turn contain a utilitarian/ dysfunctional value of either elements or *kels*. For example, the organization of the carbon atom makes it amenable to numerous useful chains of foods, and derived compounds; whereas Argon or Arsenic has a potential non- or dis-utilitarian value. The concept of organization of two groups of human beings is shown in Figure 20.4.

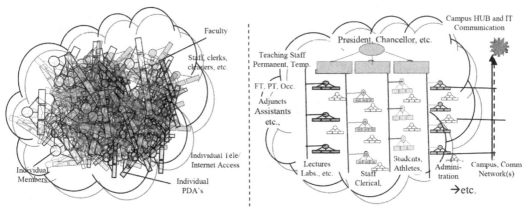

(a) An ad-hoc Group of University Members (*kels*)   (b) Organized *kco* e.g., A Functional University Setting

FIGURE 20.4

Formation of a knowledge centric object kco form a set of kels. A kco or a kel is a human being with its own personality (a noun objects, nos) functional capabilities (convolutions, *), and unique tasks (verb functions, vfs). These three constituents can be further fragmented to ascertain the appropriateness of the kels.

Knowledge space encompasses physical space as much as memory time spans real time and as much as perception spans cosmic time. The order of complexity of knowledge space is greatly enhanced because every noun-object, verb-function, and their combination are unique to the quantum of knowledge being pursued and the human being processing it. Moreover, the psychological and mental coordinates of space and time are socially and culturally variable. Hence, it becomes necessary to limit the definition of *kuantum* to "sensible" size and to be practical locations in setting the object-size of the *kuanta*, the size of the verb-function to be discernible and type of convolution (*) to be in the realm of human comprehension. Only the unique combination of these three "*kuants*" constitutes the *kels* in its own particular setting at a given instant "*t*".

Initially the *kuantum* of knowledge can be limited to most useful noun objects and verb functions. Two examples follow. In a down to earth format, a *kuantum* of knowledge can be stated as (food (*n*), eat (*v*), restaurant (*x, y, z*), date and time (*t*)). At the other extreme, a cosmic *kuantum* can be stated as (space ship A (*n*), explores (*v*), and coordinates-Planet B (*x, y, z*), cosmic calendar date and time (*t*)). The need to be practical and limit the programing complexity, it becomes a necessity to deal with *kuantized* knowledge within the realm of computation. Even so, the content of the knowledge so gathered (i.e., the food eaten in the restaurant or the data collected by the space ship) is not communicated in this representation. The flow of the entirety of knowledge needs more numerous smaller *kuanta* (*kcos*) to be complete by the global *kuanta* of knowledge (or *KCO*).

The recent changes in the Internet age are catalyzed by gating functions in the silicon chips and wave mechanics of photons in the optical fibers. This unprecedented synergy in silicon-based computation with glass-based communication has elated the human thought to new levels of intellectual activity and scientific exploration. The mental processes still hold an almost mystical execution of neural programs to mould concepts, knowledge, and wisdom with learning, behavior, and adaptation. Machines to implement such functions are just appearing in the society.

Even though thought processes are associated with neural space, the computational processes are associated with physical and Pentium space. These intermediate linkages bridge reality and physical spaces with the human psyche dealing with objects, their actions, interactions, and their effects. Human beings have learned to cross these spaces readily by mind and thought control, a wink, or even a gesture of the face. Such fine processes are hard, if not impossible to program in the software of social machines. Quantized knowledge between human minds and machines can be established by controlling the quantized noun-objects, the convolutions, the verb function, and their timings. These four entities makeup up the computational space as the mind would alter them in the psychological space to accomplish most social functions or processes. The quantized social machine would alter the status of the elemental noun-objects and their entropies accordingly. Thus, the machine could in a limited sense track, follow, and duplicate the minute mental and psychological processes of a human mind at a quantum level.

20.3 REPRESENTATION OF THE GENERAL FORMAT OF INTERACTIONS

20.3.1 DYNAMIC NATURE OF REALITY AND ITS CONCEPTION

Impressions of reality are instilled in the human mind since inception of life. Evaluation of distances and learning to walk and to run are inborn skills. These skills for survival and adjustments become evident as infants grab things or learn to stand up. In programmable machines, the dimensions in physical space are readily computable and are used for robotic gadgetry. Mental space is acquired soon after infancy to deal with others, need-gratifying objects, environment, and self. The environment, others, and the self soon start to exert influence on the reactions and responses from children. The learned behavior of children and adults acts as a link between self and environment and the linkage is by action (or verb function) such as an infant crying or trying to communicate because of some outstanding need. This is perhaps an extension of the embryonic behavior as the baby turns during the third trimester of its life. The relation of objects in the environment, others in the society with respect one's own self starts to play a part in dealing with the physical space, reality, and relationships. As Georg Herbert Mead has indicated in his Book "Mind, Self and Society," the mind is based on reality and learns to adopt but also learns to readjust the reality to gratify the needs, hopes, and aspirations.

Mental space is dominated by noun-objects, verb-functions, and their convolutions. In the most rudimentary format, these three entities are constantly arranged, rearranged, formatted, and reformatted to meet and to gratify the all-pervasive human needs. Needs that initiate motivation, also supply the emotional, psychological, and physical energy to find means to gratify the most outstanding need at any instant of time. However, the triad of noun-objects, verb-actions, and their convolutions that bind the two together play a behavioral role as to how and how well the need is gratified and how well the human transactions occur.

Noun objects can be as large as cosmic objects and continents or as tiny as electrons and photons. The object size (such as a meal to gratify hunger to a cartload of grain) can vary vastly but is tied to the ensuing verb function (i.e., to eat). Object type (like drinkingwater to quench the thirst to a lake to drink from) can also vary dramatically. In a similar mode, the convolution (type of action) can range (from taste, sip, gulp, nip, imbibe, slurp, to knock back, etc.) and verb function can range (from gulp down, drink, taste, to swallow or gobble.) The range of variations can become too immense for the mind or machines to comprehend or process all variations, all at once. However, in context of the entire *kel* or a body of knowledge (*bok*), knowledge is communicated to and from machines just well as between human beings. To seek a solution within the rational mind or by a programmable machine, we suggest that the solution to any given problem specify that bounds for (*nos*, **s*, and *vfs*) to a range that the mind may offer a satisfactory solution and the machines may offer an optimal (or at least a near optimal) solution. Quantization of (*nos*, **s*, and *vfs*) within the range thus becomes feasible at first and then programmable.

20.3.2 FROM CONCEPTIONS TO PROGRAMS

The association between (noun) objects (who), verb functions (what), and their convolutions (how) gets associated with needs (why) in the mind of infants and adults alike. The association with time (when and how long) are generally associated with now and as long as it takes. These linkages are also formed in the minds of infants since time is now and how long depends on the gratification of the need (why). The mental space forms a basis of social relations. Social objects traverse these mental spaces like clouds in the sky where some major need gratifying objects (such as parents, schools, universities, jobs, etc.) retain permanent coordinates with all six questions are answered (at least partially) in the hyper dimensional spaces in the mind. Human beings generally do not conceive social objects in precise coordinate systems, but the subconscious linkages persist in the short and long-term memories. The subconscious that provides a platform for the life, supplies the mental coordinates and working space for meaningful relations between objects (*nos*), the associated verbs (*vfs*), and the formats (**s*) of interactions and the formats of tasks in human life in any given society and culture. *Kels* form a coherency for such tasks, as time forms a bondage between them. Knowledge and time thus get intertwined in the fabric of human activity that is tractable in the as tasks in the CPU of computer systems. Both forms of tasks need time to complete. However, the silicon speed of chips being much faster can also optimize the execution of human tasks and provide a predictive plan for human activity. In the computational domain, the human beings can benefit from the intelligent peripherals of an already intelligent Internet.

Such mental associations can be reworked in computer systems like telephone numbers are worked into switching systems that provide channels of communications in networks. A scientific model becomes essential and mathematical relationships become necessary to optimize the chain of need(s), action(s), and response to gratify such needs. More than that, in a social setting, the socially acceptable norms play a part and culturally variable factors make the programing of social machines more demanding than the programing of plain old scientific computers based on already optimized mathematical algorithms.

20.3.3 STATISTICAL PROPERTIES OF KELS AND KCOS IN SOCIETY

Kels that reside in human beings for long periods substantial shape the personality of the host. For example, a human being (*no*) with a subject-matter specialty in physics and teaches (* and *vf*) it for decades, becomes a physics teacher (a *KEL* or *KCO*). Other examples are also evident. For this reason, the evolution of a *kel* to a *KCO* becomes evident in almost all circumstances and situations.

In the case of inanimate *kels*, petroleum in gasoline becomes petrol. The terminology becomes less important than the evolutionary chain of *kels* to *KELs*, and then on to *kcos* and *KCOs*.

Complex *KELs* in large associations with other *kels* have high "utility function." For example, a highly sociable person or a subject matter expert will have higher utilitarian value than an introvert or a high school student. Such human *kels* can be classified according to their expected contribution to the welfare if the society. The highly valuable *kels* also at the top of a hierarchical structure gratify the most wanted human and needs within the society. Such needs have been classified (as in Maslow's Need Pyramid [1]). The *kels* that gratify these human needs, also can be rearranged accordingly. The *kels* that satisfy the realization social, and ego[4] needs (from Maslow's Pyramid) of humans and societies will have their highest *kel*-utilitarian value.

For instance, three doctors[5] (placed on a relative scale of expertise of 100 in comparison with three nurses at 50, and three Marine placed at 30) will have a *kel*-utilitarian value of 100 times the area of expertise of E1, E2, E3, ... etc., *kel* utility number per year (kun/year) of 100E1, 100E2, 100E3, ... etc., per year relative to three nurses with 50E1, 50E2, 50E3, ..., etc. kun/year. The corresponding kun numbers for three nurses will be 30E1, 30E2, 30E3, ..., etc., kun/year. Statistical tables for different professions can thus be generated since the mean (μ) and sigma (σ) of different professions are known in most areas of expertise.

CONCLUSIONS

In this chapter, we have delineated the similarity between knowledge science and other sciences. Especially in Chemistry, the elements in nature provide a blueprint for the behavior of elements of knowledge, perhaps because of the neurobiology in the body and brain. Much like the molecules, compounds, and long molecular chains, short and long, simple and complex strings of knowledge centric objects are generated by the *quanta* of knowledge (the noun objects, the verb functions, and their convolutions) in various subjects, disciplines, conversations, cultures, and societies. Such chains can be cascaded up or fragmented down to get to the very essence of knowledge. In either extreme case, the limit of human understanding is reached since knowledge is infinite and comprehension is limited.

Knowledge is amenable to the science of morphology to fragment and modularize. Knowledge is also amenable to the science of integration, reconstruction, and reconstitution. Fragmentation and segmentation on the one hand, and then integration and reconstitution have basis two social flavors.

---

[4]It is hard to justify that an egotist would be classified as a positively placed *KEL*, unless the ego also forms a positive (beneficial) bondage with other *KELs*. As another example, a Mafia boss, though well connected with other members of mafia cult would have a high negative kel utility number. It becomes necessary to associate the social welfare with *kel* utility number to be positive. Social leaders such as Gandhi [2], Carter [3] and King [4] would have a highly positive rank in the hierarchy. Negative kel utility number are and should be associated with torrents, terrorists, and dictators such as Mao in China [5], Hitler [6] in Germany, Johnson [7] in Vietnam, Bush [8] in Iraq, and Netanyahu [9] in Palestine who have brought shame to humankind.

[5]Even though a value of 100 is chosen, in this case, the real achievement value of a doctor's education (based on the education and training can be computed) by evaluating the Knowledge Potential or *KnP* [10] of any *KCO*. In Ref. [10], the *KnP* of medically trained doctor is estimated at approximately $(350-400)°K$, whereas the KnP of a trained nurse is approximately $(175-200)°K$.

On the positive scale, the knowledge elements that form complex chains of larger socially beneficial knowledge centric objects reward the environment that hosts them. On the other hand, such elements constituting the formation of larger socially destructive structures harm and hurt the society. Innumerable examples exist in any society and culture.

REFERENCES

[1] Maslow AH. Towards a psychology of being.. Sublime; 2014.
[2] mkgandhi.org, Banaras Hindu University Archives. See *"Quit India Speeches"* of M. K. Gandhi, see also www.bbc.co.uk, BBC — Ethics — War, "Non-violence doesn't just mean not doing violence; it's also a way of taking positive action to resist oppression or bring about change."
[3] Whitehouse.gov, https://www.whitehouse.gov/1600/presidents/jimmycarter, Nobel Peace Prize; 2002.
[4] King ML. Strength of love.. Fortress Press; 2010.
[5] Chang J, Halliday J. Mao: the unknown story. 1st ed. Anchor; 2006.
[6] History.com, The Holocaust — World War II; www.history.com/topics/world-war-ii/the-holocaust.
[7] History.com, Vietnam War; 1965. "Johnson considers the options", and Escalation of Vietnam War, http://www.history.com/this-day-in-history/johnson-considers-the-options.
[8] Margulies J. Guantanamo and the abuse of presidential power. Simon & Schuster; 2007.
[9] Morris B. One state, two states: resolving the Israel/Palestine conflict. Yale University Press; 2010.
[10] Ahamed SV. Next generation knowledge machines, design and architecture. Elsevier; 2013.

PREFACE

PART II, SECTION II, SUMMARY

Section 02 with five chapters deals with a quantitative approach applicable in the knowledge domain. The gain in knowledge potential (KnP) is considered as "work-done" by individual KCOs as they spend the physical, mental, psychological, etc., energies spent in acquiring the potential. This potential is expended, altered, expanded and or enhanced by the individual efforts during the deployment of the KnP in the routine activities by actions based on verb-functions (VFs') that constitute integral parts of kels and KCOs. The utility of the expenditure of the knowledge energy are also presented in the various chapters in this part. The traditional concepts of Marshalls' microeconomic theory are not directly applicable in the knowledge domain since KnPs are not depleted simply by sharing them. In nature the concept of deploying and sharing the basis of elements (such as neutron, protons and electrons) is most effective and prevent since the beginning of the universe.

Roles of kels and KCOs in knowledge processing machines is are also introduced and discussed in chapter 23. The foundations of societies and cultures that have survived for millennia are presented in chapter 24 and finally the impact of human discretion in guiding the flow of smaller kels and the very large KCOs and KELs are presented in chapter 25.

KNOWLEDGE POTENTIAL AND UTILITY

21

CHAPTER SUMMARY

In this chapter, we enhance and extend the quantitative theory of knowledge. It emphasizes the truism that academic knowledge is acquired over a time by process of learning from faculty and staff at the colleges and universities. A formal model of student environment from high schools to various levels of universities granting doctoral degrees training is assumed in this research. In this chapter, we also include the effects of learning in postsecondary schools and in post-doctoral institutions. The net effect is that most human beings continue to learn but to varying degrees depending on the characteristic of the student/employee, the faculty attitude to teaching/job environment, and the duration of such interactive process. The proposed model allows for desirable growth of individuals who reward the society in a beneficial way. This is the primary reason for the development of the model. However, the same model is also applicable for those who live to hurt and destroy social values. The Mafia schools and warring nations train their terrorists and offer them all the lethal tools of hurt and destruction. The systematic decay of human civilizations appears as scientific to the negative thinkers as the science would appear attractive to the civilized societies. The portrait of different forms of life is thus tracked as a mathematical approximation based on statistics and norms drawn from the society itself. The model is predictive and becomes a good leading indicator of where living and learning can take any individual over a given period. Different scenarios of student personalities who learn to earn, those who learn to learn, and those who love to learn are presented in conjunction with the faculty personality who teach to earn, who teach to educate, who love to teach, are examined to gauge the knowledge potential gained by the learners from postsecondary training centers to postdoctoral centers advanced research and social contributions.

21.1 INTRODUCTION

Quantitative measures of knowledge exist in the literature, such as grade point average, scholar ratings, etc. [1], even though they are not widely used due to lack of standardization, and methodology for measurement. A greatly enhanced model in this chapter is based on two axioms that (a) learning and living are two continuous processes and (b) the society rewards the human beings by the expected contribution to the job environment. The caliber of

Evolution of Knowledge Science. DOI: http://dx.doi.org/10.1016/B978-0-12-805478-9.00021-2

learning is established by the knowledge potential gained by the individual[1] at any given stage in life. At the lowest level of mandatory secondary school, the Knowledge Potential[2] (or *KnP*) is relatively low at level of $0°K$ at the graduation from high school or at subzero level for lower level. Through the continued schooling, the *KnP* can reach levels of $100\pm$ at the Bachelors' Degree level, levels of $220\pm °K$ at the Masters' Degree level, and attain levels in a wide range $270-1004°K$ (or even higher) at the Doctoral Degree levels. Differences in universities, faculty, and facilities influence the institution tier levels. Though not important at the lower levels of learning, these differences become influential in the *KnP* gained by the students at the Master's and Doctoral Degree levels. Individual differences in the student capabilities are also reflected by their achievements and the Grade Point Averages (GPAs). In addition, the students who wish to finish their degree as their ulterior motives of learn only to earn, whereas students who actively pursue the degree to learn to acquire higher *KnPs* throughout at an exponential rate, through their postgraduate programs and perhaps the rest of their lives.

There is a surprising extent of correlation between the annual incomes with the *KnPs* gained at almost all levels of education from secondary school to postdoctoral training. The study confirms two universal observations. *First*, those learning only to earn and gratify their own lower level needs [2] as human beings, reaches a premature saturation level at lowest income level of about 20,000−22,000 dollars (2012 National Labor Statistics). *Second*, those learning to learn the skills to gratify the outstanding social/technological needs saturate at four to five times the annual income (2012 National Labor Statistics) after graduation. *Further*, those who continue to live and learn together reach a much higher level and the accelerated growth continue until the biological process of age hinder the learning, memory, and retention functions.

21.2 REPRESENTATION OF GENERIC FORMAT OF INTERACTIONS

Knowledge is generated when any noun (object) performs a verb function; how the verb is performed, adds more dimension(s) to new or the older knowledge already collected and stored by noun object(s). The value of such knowledge can rank as low as triviality, a reiteration of what is already known, or as high as new oracle(s) of perpetual wisdom. The structure of knowledge can be founded on this truism.

21.2.1 TRUISMS ABOUT THE STRUCTURE OF KNOWLEDGE

Knowledge results due to effects of interactions between noun objects (*nos*) and verb functions (*vfs*) and vice versa. For example, when one human talks (*) to another and the other responds, knowledge is generated. How the interaction takes place adds another dimension in the interaction

---

[1]The learning scenario is universal in all situations of a student in a school, a disciple in a shrine, an apprentice in a job, a child from a parent, an intelligent chip in a network, etc. The flow of knowledge (unidirectional or bidirectional) like the flow of power, are the prime features in consideration.
[2]The symbol $°K$ should be treated as degrees of knowledge and not as degrees Kelvin as a measure of the temperature. The interpretation should depend in the context of knowledge and not as the temperature. Thermodynamics (with $°A$ and $°K$ to designate temperature) is a branch of Physics whereas Knowledge Science (with $°K$) is a branch of Learning and Education and Retention of knowledge after various levels of Schooling.

process and its effects. For example, if talks are replaced by "yells," "hollers," "shouts," etc. then the effects that follow can be different.

There are five components (*a* through *e*) in such an interactive process.

A noun object *no1* initiates a verb function *vf* and the mode of interaction is established as *. This basic elementary process is represented as

$$no1 \ ^*vf.$$

Further, broken down this process is written down as:

$$no1 \ ^*12 \ vf12 \ no2; \text{ or as}$$

$$no1 \ vf12^* \rightarrow no2$$

and its response from *no2* is written as:

This element of any elementary transactional process can be written as:

(i) a forward process (full lines)

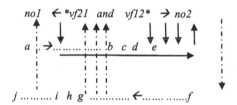

Followed by (ii) a backward process (dashed lines).

in a time sequence. Represented as a diagram, *a to j* interactive process is depicted as:

Any number of these processes will give rise to an interaction and knowledge is accumulated at each of the minor steps *a* through *j* in each process depicted as → and by the directional arrows. Significant knowledge is added when these steps are arranged in an orderly and systematic fashion. Such accumulated knowledge can occur for a few microseconds in computerized and networked elements it can occur over decades and lifetimes in cultures and societies. In Figure 21.1, the methodology for the accumulation of knowledge has syntactic and semantic relations between the elements *a to e*, and then through *f to j* and then again *a to j* in a contextual sense. The rules for the flow and accumulation of knowledge have their cultural and societal foundations.

21.2.2 COMPUTATIONAL APPROACH TO THE GENERIC INTERACTIVE PROCESS

The logical and functional processes in Figure 21.1 are not evident to be programed on a typical computer system. Programing of social computers can become a selected expertise. Alternatively, definitive approaches become necessary to force the constraints in the social elements of any social system to be simulated on any typical computer system.

Two such parameters are reversibility of the social elements and the continuous scanning of all parameters of each social element to forcing the computer system to emulate the social system. Social systems act and react in real time; and the simulation software should be able to track the changes of all parameters that influence the social interaction. However, the representations in

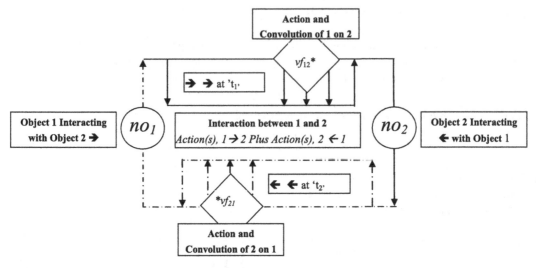

FIGURE 21.1

Depiction of an interactive process between two participants no1 and no2. This diagram does not have an easy flow chart that be implemented on a computer system. However, the diagram can be partitioned into two symmetric halves, one for each participant and linked via a current interactive event in a process.

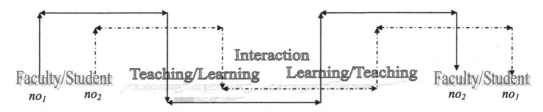

FIGURE 21.2

Indicative roles while the Faculty/Student are in a Mentor/Researcher interactive role. Both learn and adapt the interaction toward making the processes productive and toward significant results. This type of situation is common when both parties play cooperative roles and assist one another. In conflicting situations, the processes can become exploitive and divergent.

Figure 21.1 can be decomposed by realizing the roles of the interactive participants are reversible and symmetric, i.e., the processes of no1 or no2 can be imaged in subroutines but with the parameters being updated from those from *no2* to *no1* respectively, and then the vice versa. A programmable flow chart of the generic interaction processes are shown in Figure 21.2.

The generality of the interactive processes depicted in Figures 21.2 and 21.3 is exemplified in the three following situations. *First*, a student and teacher interaction is modified by a history of prior events stored and updated in the computer memory. This depiction is programmable by two routines or tasks for the CPU that functions for *no1* and *no2* alternately to depict one or more series of interactions. *Second*, an atom of carbon can interact with a molecule (two atoms) of oxygen to form a molecule of CO_2. The bondage between the atoms is a programmable set of events that

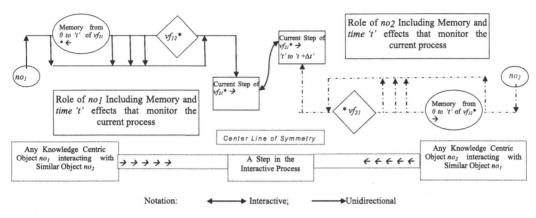

FIGURE 21.3

The depiction of a step in the interaction that has built-in memory effects for both participants and the effect on the current event in a chain of interactions. Full lines indicate student to faculty learning interaction and dashed lines indicate faculty to student teaching interaction.

makes one molecule of CO_2. *Third*, the formation of the primal and genetic cells is universal examples for all species. One of the *XX* or *XY* chromosomes from the male sperm interacts with one of the female *XX* chromosomes to make the genetic imprint of the unborn baby. Randomness and statistical coupling occurs during most of the natural process, such as the birth process of a fetal, or the germination of a seed. Such interactive processes are innumerable and most prevalent in nature.

21.2.3 INTERACTION OF KNOWLEDGE ELEMENTS IN HUMAN MINDS

An element of knowledge in mind is like a chromosome in the womb. Under controlled environments, a new specimen (or even a new species) may evolve. Largely, the processes are probabilistic and circumstantial and the new product of knowledge-evolution can occur as a coincidence or as a matter of intense training in shrines and universities. It is our contention the pearls of wisdom and invention can be farmed by careful implanting of pearl fragments in the tissues of an oysters. A nursery for pearls can be reconstructed in the universities much like an artificial pearl-farm in tropical oceans.

21.3 KNOWLEDGE ACQUISITION IN INSTITUTIONS

Most institutions generally offer a systematic and a stylized format of learning for students. Typical schooling in the United States consists of Secondary and High schooling followed by formalized junior and/or senior college education and finally Graduate education for the Masters, Doctoral, and Postdoctoral training or internships.

During the last few decades, knowledge is gained in a series of classroom sessions with well-defined faculty and over finite durations of time (class hours per week during semesters and 2/3 semesters per years). Knowledge gain can thus be integrated based on the attitudes of the students, the setting of the institution, type and quality of faculty members, and the duration for the degree(s).

On a statistical basis, the parameters that facilitate the educational status, or the potential of knowledge of each student, become quantifiable. In a sense, the compilation of knowledge in the human mind becomes an integrative process and it can be represented as a knowledge potential (*KnP*) in degrees of knowledge symbolized as a finite number of °K.

21.3.1 KNOWLEDGE POTENTIAL DEFINED

Knowledge potential of a student is a number (measured in degree of knowledge or °K) gained by the student[3] from numerous faculty members over the student ($\leftarrow$ and $\rightarrow$) faculty contact integrated over the duration of the study/contact. The parameters in the learning process(es) are individual and/or statistical, the integration is mathematical, and the type(s) of interaction is definable by the social/cultural modes of behavior such as collegiate, friendly, congenial as in civilized and elite circles, or even hostile, detrimental or destructive as in brutal, invasive or wars. A (temporarily) stationary baseline of knowledge is desirable in most situations and can be arbitrarily chosen to suit the particular study. For graduate studies, we have suggested at school graduation the knowledge is at 0°K.

In a strict sense, the knowledge potential of any individual should be considered as zero at the formation of the seminal cell with inception of *XX* or *XY* chromosomes derived from the male and the female of the parent members in any given species. The knowledge is thus embedded in the genetic code with certain degrees of conformity to offer the physiology of the member species and a certain degree of latitude to give the freedom of the personality of the fetus. For genetic studies, the baseline with a *KnP* of °K is perhaps founded in the knowledge embedded in genetic coded of parents or ancestors.

Knowledge potential has a utilitarian value. In an immediate sense, it indicates how that potential can be utilized for solving current problem(s) at hand. While the quality of the solution may be the highest in the direction of the specialization, the enhanced training that was necessary to attain the *KnP* will also be valuable for solving generic problems. For example, a Master's degree holder in Biochemistry with a *KnP* of 240°K may solve a problem in organic chemistry much better than a layman. In a longer term perspective, *KnP* multiplied by the expected contributions for 30 years in the career trail would have a utilitarian value of 7200 knowledge-years. Certain precautionary rules should be considered since the *KnP* value can swing up (or down) by the job effects, social setting, diligence of the individual, etc. In reality, the acquired skill over a lifetime can be significant.

In a true sense, the net utilitarian value should be an integrative process of every learning experience of the individual. Furthermore, the acceleration of the learning process and its retention are both generally, the highest in the early job experiences compared to those in the declining year of one's career. Some of these deliberations are considered by technical managers in corporations.

21.3.2 STUDENT TRAITS

Students offer various mindsets to learning depending on "who" is teaching ""what," "when" the teaching occurs, and then "how" the teaching occurs. These variables contribute to the mindset in a psychological framework defined by "kristivity" (σ^{st}) in mind, a parameter unique to the student.

---

[3]The flow of knowledge assumes a pattern that is akin to that of the flow of wealth or power. In most civil settings, knowledge and control originates from a noun-object with higher knowledge potential (*KnP*) to one with lower *KnP* much as the flow of wealth or power of one who has the larger accumulated wealth or strength. These higher values result from the "work-done" in acquire the asset. Knowledge assumes (an almost physical and) comparable principle as in physics.

Next, the path of communication (ℓ) and the area of psychological contact ($\acute{a}$) combine to offer "kristance" (= $\sigma^{st}.\ell/\ \acute{a}$ kohms) that facilitates the flow of knowledge as current, and grows the *KnP* of the student by an incremental amount (Δknp). Initially, the quantity of knowledge received depends on the original *KnP* of the student.

21.3.3 FACULTY FACTORS

In the prior section, faculty factor (*fst*) influences the "who," "how," and "when" aspects of the knowledge delivered to the student. This factor, though not very critical in the early stages of learning become important, the student develops a personality and a mindset of his/her own. Thus the *"kenergy"* i.e., knowledge energy, delivered over a time will become

$$Kenergy = (KnPf - KnPs) *\{Kurrent(as\ a\ function\ of\ fstand\ kristance)\} *Duration\ of\ Study.$$

The stored version (or memory effects) of this *kenergy* enhances the *KnP* of the student. It is important to note this energy could be counter-productive and act as a drain on the energy already stored in the student *KnP* previously acquired. This condition frequently appears as confusion or negation on the part of the student. In general, this is a frequent situation, found during a period of culture shock or when negative propaganda that is delivered by TV and Internet.

21.3.4 UNIVERSITY FACILITIES AND SETTINGS

The environmental and extraneous factors, such as classrooms, libraries, duration of the commute, housing, and student facilities provide tangential effects of learning. Such effects may sometimes have emotional influences on the net change in the student *KnP*. The gain of student *KnP* due to these factors may add or subtract some marginal numbers to the final *KnP* gained. Such effects are included by incrementing or decrementing the *KnP* gained.

21.4 GRADUATE EDUCATION

Under idealized conditions, the student learns to "convolute" (or learns how to learn) from the faculty teaching) thus "compounding" or acceleration (i.e., $y = x^i \cdot t$ (with t = duration) and $i > 1.00$) the learning experience. In the same vein, the faculty member can "convolute" (adapts the teaching style based on student's gain in their median *KnP*) of the class. Thus "double compounding" (i.e., $y = x^{ii} \cdot t$ with $ii > i$) occurs for a student learning and a single compounding for faculty teaching. The process does stop here, but it can offer "compounded-compounding" (i.e., $y = x^{iii} \cdot t$ and $iii > ii$) offering a bilateral learning and teaching experience for students and faculty alike. This phenomenon can be universal in shrines, monasteries, and even in all social interactions and spouse relations. These equations for y can be alternatively written as $y = (x \cdot t)^j$.

21.4.1 MASTER'S DEGREE STUDENTS

The details of gain in the knowledge potential and a basis for the quantification of knowledge potential or *KnP* are both presented in Ref. [3]. Knowledge potential is (almost) derived as the measure of temperature when an object (student) is in a hot/cold setting (Shrine/Mafia institution).

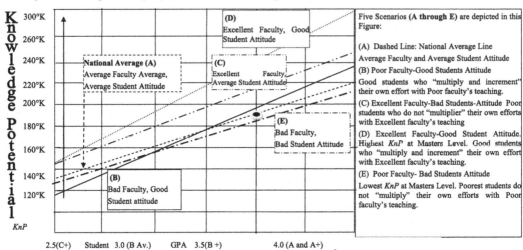

Snapshot of Knowledge Potential (*KnP*) at Graduation with Masters Degree

FIGURE 21.4

Expected knowledge potential (KnP) of different students at the completion of Master's degree. Some segments of these trends are exclusive by definition. For example, a student with really bad attitude (trend E) gets expelled from the Master's degree program during the first one or two semesters and does not reach the high end of trend E. Conversely, students with good attitude, rarely remain in the lower section of trends C and D, but may decline to trends A, B or E during the Master's program by neglect or by abandoning their early attitudes. Student effort is thus a fundamental element in acquiring a high KnP. The figure indicates as a warning to those slipping and as an incentive for those who are ahead.

The *KnP* rises to gain kenergy to serve and benefit the society or sinks low to deplete the morality and spread violence.[4] In this section conductive mode of knowledge-transfer is considered, even though Inspirational (see Chapter 19) and Transmission (see Chapter 17) modes are known to exist.

Knowledge potential thus serves as an indication of how well and how quickly individuals can address, comprehend, and gainfully solve problems in unique, distinctive, and creative fashion(s) that are also economical and productive. The concepts have been applied to the educational platform as students as they go through high school to doctoral degrees (if they do). In a generic sense, this is a universal principle that if a solution of any problem is to be reached, the knowledge potential in each and every prior solution has to be evaluated and excelled by students.

The gain in *KnP* for Master's Degree students is presented in Figures 21.4 and 21.5. The GPA along the X-axis is a good indication as to how well the students have integrated their learning to become knowledgeable. There are five (A through E) trends shown and indicated for the cases where the students with good and bad learning-attitudes learn from excellent, average, and poor

---

[4]This analogy can be taken only to a certain extent since no mature society needs Mafia to survive, whereas cooling is desirable for life in hot environments.

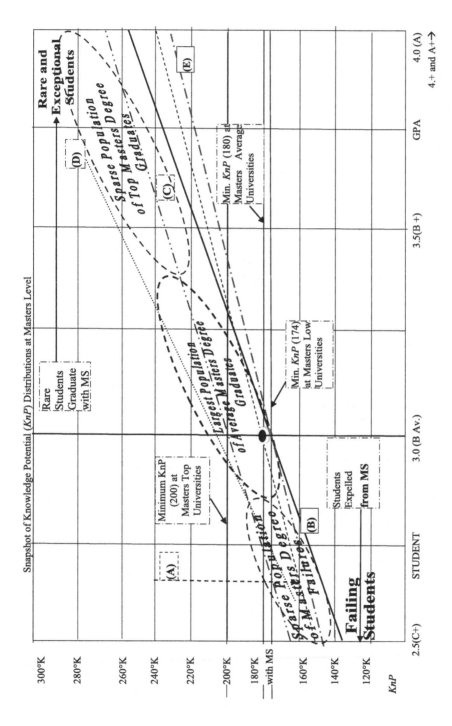

Snapshot of Knowledge Potential (*KnP*) Distributions at Masters Level

FIGURE 21.5

Expected knowledge potential (KnP) of different students after 24 months in the Master's program. The minimum KnP level is tolerated by lower strata of universities and low quality of faculty members in such universities. Since the KnP is low in trends B and in A, most universities strive to at least meet or better the National average of the KnP level of 180°K at the Master's Degree level. The top stratum of Master's degree holders with KnP of 280+ (see trend D), in most cases outperform doctoral degree holders with poor student attitude, poor faculty, and at low-level universities. Please see trend A in Figure 21.6.

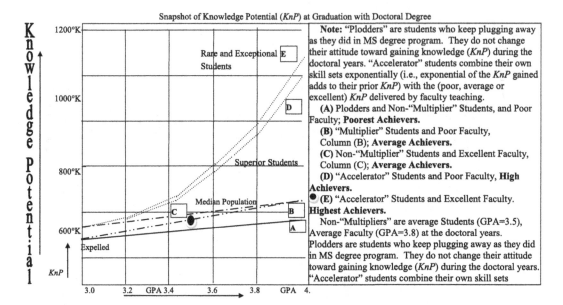

FIGURE 21.6

Expected knowledge potential (KnP) of different students at the completion of Doctoral degree. As it can be expected, Plodders do the worst (A) and "Multiplier" students at poor universities do gain enough KnP to graduate. The "accelerator" students (D and E) do the best but are extremely rare, even though some faculty members and professional show this rare gift of accelerating faster than teachers and mentors. Multiplier students do better than plodders but still are not able to take full advantage of the faculty talent. Exceptional non-multiplier students at excellent universities will do as well as multiplier (B and C) students at low level universities.

faculty members. The good students learn about how to learn while learning the course material and become proactive to the additional course material taught thus boosting their *KnPs*. The average students do learn but to pass the examinations and complete the degree. In a similar mode, the average faculty can teach the course material, whereas the excellent faculty would learn (love) to teach what they teach and how they teach.

This later synergy of faculty student interaction generates a series of Verb-functions (*VFs*) from the faculty to teach the foundations of course material knowledge, and conversely (*VFs*) from the students to distill concepts from knowledge and infuse them into wisdom trail of productive lives.

21.4.2 DOCTORAL DEGREE STUDENTS

The expected of *KnP* for the PhD students is shown in Figure 21.6. Three trends (A, B, and C) and two curves (D and E) are depicted. The choice of the most creative mentor is of significant to the future contributions of their doctoral student. To this extent, the training of the advanced PhD students becomes an art rather than a job. The Art of Scientific Investigation [4] in teaching becomes the practice of the superior faculty members and mentors as much as the art of learning to learn becomes the responsibility of the rare and exceptional students as depicted by the two exponential curves C and D in Figure 21.6. Postdoctoral training and internships can also be quantified along the basis of trends and curves presented in this chapter.

The best of the students learn how to learn from the knowledge they have already received and then go on to apply the newly gained knowledge to further their *KnP*. An accelerative trend is established. The *KnP* thus grows at an exponential rate[5] that reaches as high as 1154°K for the Doctoral students (with excellent faculty and 5 FTE years in an excellent university). Comparatively, the more mundane students reach just enough, as low as 369°K (with poor faculty, 5 FTE years at an inferior university), to get their PhD degrees as job seekers! Unfortunately, after 5 FTE years of their lives, student in the lowest strata of doctoral student end up with a *KnP* that is just about or even less than the *KnP* of top MS students with excellent faculty in top institutions when they both finish their degrees. Top Master's Degree graduates are sometimes more coveted than low-level doctoral degree graduates are as much as the top Bachelor's degree students are preferred over the lower strata of Master's Degree students. The starting salaries, as it is reflected by the Salary Surveys in the United States. The tracking of the statistically averaged trajectories for *KnP* (2012) starting salary for Doctoral, Masters, and Bachelor's degrees holders is evident[6] in Figure 21.7A and B.

CONCLUSIONS

The *KnPs* developed in this chapter are indicative of the employee, trainee, apprentice, or students, ability to solve significant problems in a creative and beneficial fashion. Whereas these curves reflect the generally accepted notion that more education leads to better pay, we have a predictive model that related higher education implies higher computable *KnP* and thus a compounding effect reflected in the higher income. This intermediate parameter (*KnP*) is a computed based on employee or student traits, industry or university setting, and the quality of management or teaching/research teaching faculty. We also indicate the parameters that influence the final *KnP* of the student at graduation and training received after as an extrapolation of the gain in the *KnP* during the employment or college/institutional years. The model is entirely predictive but subject to the sampling error in the student, faculty, and the university populations. By and large, the model is as accurate as the age and health prediction in any culture or society. Individual differences continue to exist; however, the circumstances can be consciously altered to maximize the possibility of being constructive and creative by extrapolating the knowledge gained thus far, into the environment of the culture and society.

---

[5]Out of the 20 student mentored, we found ≈ 10% (or even less, one with the traits of an accelerated learner and the other with an inclination to learn but unable to follow through) who were in the top category and 60−70% in the mid-range and then about 30−20% who just wanted a PhD to append to their names.

[6]After the Bachelor's degree level in Figures 21.7a and b, (a) slightly bump in salary is seen. This is ascribed to the fact the more promising BS degree holders are lured into jobs while they could have easily enrolled in the Graduate programs of universities. Further, the desire to earn at BS degree shows a psychological peak than the desire to learn, thus the better students may compete and get higher salaries than average (B/B+) students who enroll in the Master's Degree programs.

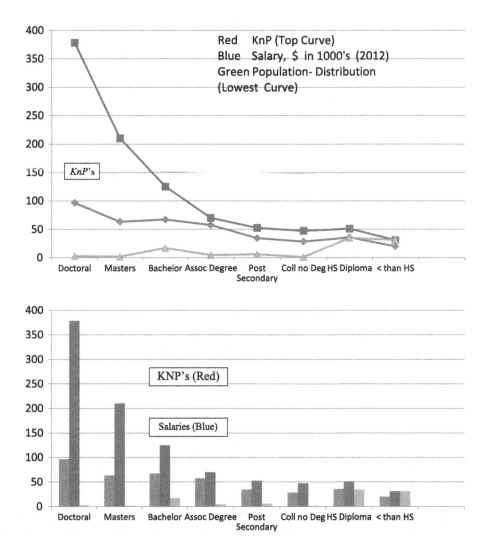

FIGURES 21.7A AND B

The trend indicates that at the highest levels of education, the KnP and salaries are the highest for this sparsely populated segment population and vice versa. In addition, at the lowest KnP levels, the national minimum wage ($7.75 per hour − 2012 rate) law also influences the total compensation. The HS diploma holders and postsecondary trained employees are comparable in both their KnPs and salary levels. The KnPs are derived from the training and its duration whereas the salary level is surveyed.

The net effect is that the reader can read (this chapter) for the sake of reading, for learning after reading, for learning while reading and for those who love to learn after reading and for those who love to learn as they are reading (this chapter or this entire book). The time based compounding occurs in both the time (after and while) dimension and in the mental (learning and learning for the sake of learning) and in the emotional dimension (reading without emotion, loving to read or loving to learn). Teachers can "see" such differences in their students just as well as monks "feel" such differences in their disciples.

REFERENCES

[1] Ahamed SV. Next generation knowledge machines, design and architecture. Elsevier Insights, Hardcover; September 2013.
[2] Maslow AH. Towards a psychology of being. Sublime Books; March 7, 2014. See also Ahamed SV. An enhanced need pyramid for the information age human being. In Proceedings of the Fifth Hawaii International Conference, Fifth International Conference on Business, Hawaii; May 26—29, 2005. See also An enhanced need pyramid of the information age human being. Paper presented at the International Society of Political Psychology (ISSP) 2005 Scientific Meeting, Toronto; July 3—6, 2005.
[3] Ahamed SV. Next generation knowledge machines, design and architecture. Elsevier Insights, Hardcover; September 2013, In particular, see Chapters 9, 10, and 11 for the Development of Knowledge Potential in Universities.
[4] Ahamed SV, Lawrence VB. The art of scientific innovation. Prentice Hall; 2005.

ELEMENTS OF KNOWLEDGE AS ELEMENTS IN NATURE

22

CHAPTER SUMMARY

In this chapter, we propose that knowledge bears a remarkable parallelism with the elements in nature. The numerous elements in nature correspond to branches of knowledge. The elements of knowledge play the role of atoms in chemistry that combine with other atoms to make compounds. The laws of chemistry are well adhered in forming stable compounds as the linguistic laws that make up sentences. Chains of compounds make up the organic compounds and polymers that have a useful life as words and sentences that make up "bodies of knowledge" that have finite spans of life. Knowledge science is more recent than chemistry or physical chemistry. Knowledge evolves in the minds of creative human beings and by the ceaseless exploration of machines that explore all combination of noun-objects (*ns*), verb functions (*vs*), and their convolutions (**s*) that constitutes a *kel*. The elements in nature have already evolved (as far as we know) and have filled all the possible discrete shell orbits by the electrons, even though some of the rarest elements are highly unstable. In their structure elements and compounds conserve energy. For the exploration of knowledge, still in its infancy, the exploration of knowledge space is as wide as that of the universe itself. Variation of the atomic structures of the elements, that they may assume in other galaxies challenges the imagination that lies at the outer limits of knowledge.

A quantum of knowledge (*kel*) is like an element in nature or a pulse of energy. We present these concepts to investigate if such *kels* will explain all the intricacies in the flow of knowledge in societies, cultures, and groups or to explain the flow of knowledge energy (*kenergy*) in social groups and universities. When these seminal kels can be contoured in the memories of machines, then their properties, and attributes can be examined, evaluated, designed, and optimized to suit the particular environment where they are deployed. This approach by constituting bodies of "Artificial Knowledge," thus corresponds to synthesizing of compounds for generic drugs to cure patients and to alter the chemical structure of the compounds to cure a particular ailment. Artificial knowledge can soothe many ailing minds and find solutions in resolving mental blocks, hitherto unknown in the wisdom of saints or the words of the psychiatrists to pacify disturbed patients.

22.1 INTRODUCTION

Knowledge and elements blend-like wisdom and motivation in mind or like nouns and verbs mingle in the reality. Knowledge centric noun objects (*KCOs*) spread and flourish in societies like organisms in nature or like human beings in cultures. Such *KCOs*' relay knowledge elements (*kels*) in environment and culture thus forming a bond between self and society or between mind and culture. These *kels* traverse the social space between *KCOs* thus forming dialogs and interactions. In the domain of reality, the *kels* can be as tiny as microorganisms in biology or as enormous as cosmic objects in

Evolution of Knowledge Science. DOI: http://dx.doi.org/10.1016/B978-0-12-805478-9.00022-4

space. The atomic nature of these *kels* makes up the structure of information and knowledge as the nucleus of atoms that makes up the structure of matter. The ensuing information and knowledge binds societies and cultures like physical, social and intellectual cohesion that binds reality.

The atomic structure of *kels* is as basic as the nuclear structure of elements. Noun objects, verb functions, and their convolutions take the place of neutrons, protons, and electrons. In their own unique stance, they carry very basic information about why, who, what, when, and how the *kels* exist and an underlying directions in which these *kels* can be useful, useless or hurtful to the society. The directionality of the utility of *kels* is thus established. A sense of good and bad is thus formed in the nuclear structure of *kels* like a sense of the potentially useful, useless, or disruptive elements in nature. *KCO*s can indeed be human and machines and/or tools or conjectures.

The deployment of *kels* makes up the basis of all lives. Continued use of well-placed socially beneficent *kels* is the norm of civilized societies as much as the continued deployment of hurtful and destructive *kels* is the custom of Mafia, thugs, and the warmongers. The nature of *kels* and their innate structure renders their efficacy or their danger to the society in which they prevail. Much like elements and their compounds, *kels* and *kel*-chains can be poisonous or medicinal. In this chapter, we develop a science, engineering, deployment of positively based knowledge elements, such as universities, schools, shrines, knowledge bases, etc., and to become aware about the potential abuse of negatively based *kels* such as terrorist groups, syndicates, and violent political groups.

In order to be practical and to correlate with other disciplines, we explore the quantum theory of knowledge whereby the protocol for the knowledge paths between smallest knowledge centric objects (*kcos*) and the larger knowledge centric objects (*KCOs*) are transported. A continuum of noun objects (*nos*), verb functions (*vfs*), and the associated convolutions (*$*s$) is thus retained. This continuum is searched out by segmented knowledge machines that operate between the smaller *kcos* and the larger *KCOs* in any given domain or direction of knowledge. Dewey Decimal System (DDS) or the Library of Congress (LoC) classification offer two methodologies to classify the domain of knowledge pursued. One or more pathways exist in the chain of evolution of the subject matter and related inventions that have occurred around practical and real modules of knowledge in the range of any smaller *kco* to the larger *KCO*. All modalities of knowledge representation (images, documents, graphs, presentations, etc.) need investigation to complete the pathway(s) between *kcos* and *KCOs*.

Minute constituents (i.e., *nos*, *$*s$, and *vfs*) of *kels* can and do interact with the social and cultural character of the medium that carries them. In a very real sense, the statistical properties of the medium alters the genesis, transmission, and retention of these *kels* thus offering the vast varieties of lives, decay, and death of knowledge in different societies and cultures. All the principles for the flow of knowledge presented in chapters 16 through 20 become applicable in this chapter. Even though human beings may be daunted by such intricacy, knowledge machine can routinely handle tracking, transmission, attenuation, and dispersion of knowledge in most societies. It can also be predictive about the possible effects and life spans of most positive and negative KCOs in different cultures and societies.

22.2 QUANTIZATION OF KNOWLEDGE

22.2.1 BASIS FROM HUMAN PHYSIOLOGY (*KELS* AND PHYSIOLOGICAL FUNCTIONS)

The human body offers an insight into how the body functions are knowledge based and how this knowledge is structured in a very functional format. A typical example of linkages between

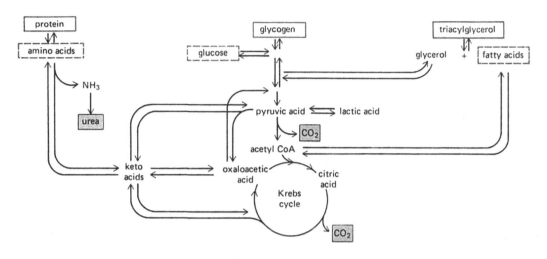

FIGURE 22.1

Simplified chain of noun objects (*nos*) linking carbohydrate, fat, and protein metabolism with appropriate verb functions (*vfs*).

carbohydrate, fat, and protein during metabolism is shown Figure 22.1. Additional amino acids and other organic compounds, CO_2, and various acids are produced and sometimes reabsorbed. The diagram shown is a simplified representation of how the chemistry of numerous elements functions together for illustrative purposes. Carbon, hydrogen, and nitrogen especially play critical roles interdependently and in conjunction.

To draw a similarity between *kels* and the various components depicted in Figure 22.1, a more concise representation is shown in Figure 22.2a. Various compounds such as NH_3, or ammonia at metabolism 1, Kerbs cycle generating citric acid, and CO_2 at metabolism 2, reentering *Kerbs* cycle again 3 and 4, lactic acid at 4 should be considered as noun objects. The CO_2 at 4 are not shown to simplify the chain of metabolisms. Numerous types of metabolisms should be considered as verb function (*vfs*) in the body trigger the change of the status of these noun objects. Figure 22.2b depicts the more fundamental chain of noun objects that constitutes the human body. Figure 22.3 depicts the integrative process that occurs in making up larger more stable *KELs* from the generic *kels*.

22.2.2 BASIS FROM CHEMISTRY (*KELS* AND CHEMICAL PROCESSES)

The diagrammatic representations of a *kel* and of a Silicon[1] atom are shown in Figures 22.4. Atoms of different elements are quantified by their corresponding atomic weights. The basic elements of knowledge *kels* can exist in many "*kel weights*" (like atomic weights) depending on the utility of the knowledge embedded in the *kel*. For instance, the atomic weight of the noble metals is much higher than that of the ordinary elements. The energy contained in their atoms is greater than that

---

[1]A Silicon atom is chosen as an example, but any element that combines to form compounds exhibits similar properties and traits.

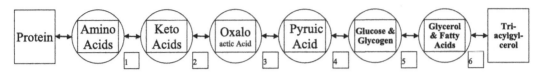

(a) A Simplified Chain of noun objects (*no's*) linking carbohydrate, fat and protein metabolism. Other noun objects (NH_3, or ammonia at metabolism 1), Kerbs cycle generating citric acid, and CO_2) at metabolism 2), reentering Kerbs cycle again 3 and 4, lactic acid at 4 and CO_2 at 4 are not shown to simplify the chain of metabolisms. Metabolisms should be considered as verb function (*vf's*) in the body the trigger the change of the status of noun objects. The processes are described in detail in most elementary books on human physiology.

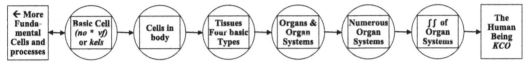

(b) Specific Example and Most Simplified Element Hierarchy to build a Most Complex *KCO* (e.g., a human being)

FIGURE 22.2

An continuous chain in the development for knowledge elements or kels that are like atoms, microbes, microorganisms, bacteria, or even human beings that organize themselves to form the more complex chain of chemical compounds, life forms, organizations, societies, and cultures. Knowledge gets embedded in each of the stages of development to stabilize the particular element survive and then migrate to the next stage. Carbon element or any element has life cycle(s) of its own as a human being has event, developmental, life cycle, and stage.

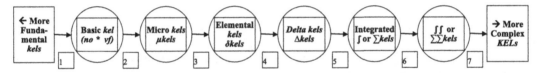

FIGURE 22.3

Generic examples of knowledge elements to make up an integrated knowledge hierarchy of *KELs* and *KCOs*. Numerous other *kels* can be and are usually generated at the verb functions or *vfs* at transition points 1 through 7.

in the hydrogen atom with an atomic weight of 1.0078. The *kel*-weight of a brain surgeon (no) performing a (*vf*) transplant of the brain (if it is possible), in a very specific way (*) would be much higher than the *kel*-weight of a monkey (*no*) eating (*vf*) peanuts.

22.3 MOLECULAR WEIGHTS OF CARBON COMPOUNDS AND LARGER KNOWLEDGE ELEMENTS

The behaviors of a carbon atom and a *kel* are depicted in Figures 22.5 and 22.6. *Kels* can combine with themselves, (one or more) *kels*, and form chains of *kels* as in human dialogs where every step in the interactive process modifies the status of the present *kel*. *Kels* retain the history of modifications like a symbol in a series of steps of mathematical derivation or like a numeric symbol in computational processing. In a sense, like human objects, *kels* have a life of their own. Sometimes they live and die in the perception of human counterparts and sometime they are as real as sentences and procedures documented in textbooks.

The variety of *kels* can be as large as the number of molecules and compounds in the real world. *Kels* can be as transitory as the fleeting passion or as (semi-)permanent as the written word.

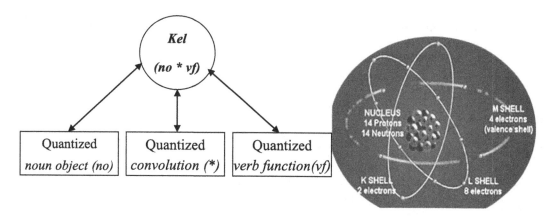

Structure of a *kel* constituted as the knowledge when a noun object *no* convolves (*) with a verb function *vf* in a specific convolution * format.

The structure of a Silicon atom is shown here. But the structure of any element has its own unique structure.

FIGURE 22.4

Configuration of an element of knowledge, *kel* formed from a set of the tinniest but flexible and dynamic entities (*no*, *, and *vf*). The kels are comparable to atoms, made up of neutrons, protons, and electrons. Protons and neutron, correspond to *vfs* and *nos*, and convolutions correspond to convolutions. Convolutions occupy the most variable orbits in social transaction and can influence the nature (flavor) of the compound (social interaction). The basic building blocks can be shared and enhanced to form new kels during social interactions or knowledge processing.

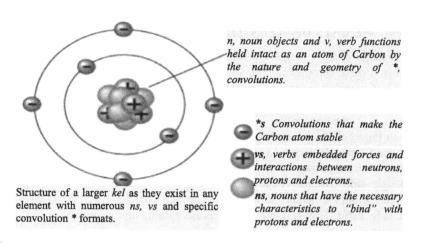

*n, noun objects and v, verb functions held intact as an atom of Carbon by the nature and geometry of *, convolutions.*

*s Convolutions that make the Carbon atom stable

vs, verbs embedded forces and interactions between neutrons, protons and electrons.

ns, nouns that have the necessary characteristics to "bind" with protons and electrons.

Structure of a larger *kel* as they exist in any element with numerous *ns*, *vs* and specific convolution * formats.

FIGURE 22.5

Basic kels of any body of knowledge (Figure 22.4) are comparable to atom made up of electrons, protons, and neutrons. The basic building blocks or kels can be shared and enhanced to form other knowledge elements. As much as the structure of atoms is altered in chemical reactions, the structure of knowledge is altered, modified, truncated, or even eliminated by actions, words, or dealings in human environments.

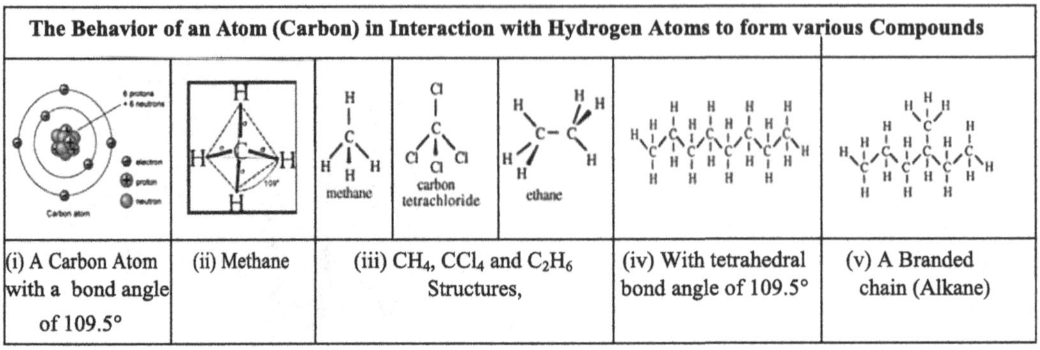

The Behavior of an Atom (Carbon) in Interaction with Hydrogen Atoms to form various Compounds				
(i) A Carbon Atom with a bond angle of 109.5°	(ii) Methane	(iii) CH_4, CCl_4 and C_2H_6 Structures,	(iv) With tetrahedral bond angle of 109.5°	(v) A Branded chain (Alkane)

FIGURE 22.6

Alkane (C_nH_{2n+2}) family (methane, ethane, propane, butane, pentane, hexane, etc.) and the adaptive role of the carbon atom (C).

In most cases, *kels* have a utilitarian value. This utilitarian value is indicative of the *kel*-weight. The utility if a *kel* depends on the need that it gratifies for an individual or in a society. Thus, the *kel* weight of a monkey eating peanuts would fall well below that of the *kel* weight of a programmer developing new software. In the mathematical domain, *kels* exist and thrive. The knowledge content of a *kel* written as ($E = mc^2$) would have a greater utilitarian value written as a *kel* written as ($d = 1/2$ at^2) because of the differences in nature and implication to the society and to the real world. Likewise, humans also carry their own personalized *kel*-weights as do machines and gadgets. Intelligence adds an addition convolution in the computation of *kel*-weights introduced in Section 22.2.2 and explored further in Section 22.3.6.

22.3.1 ATOMIC WEIGHTS OF ELEMENTS AND *KEL* WEIGHTS

Atomic weight consists of three weights, weights of the protons, neutrons, and electrons. Thus the heavy metals have a more complex atomic structure than that of the lighter metals. Similarly, the molecular weight of complex compounds can be substantially heavier than simple molecules. For example, the atomic structure of a Gold atom (atomic weight of 197) has 79 protons, 118 neutrons, and 112 electrons in 7 electron shells. The molecular weights of compounds also exhibit similar characteristics. In Figure 22.6, the carbon atom and its molecules are used to indicate the chain of compounds derived from carbon atoms on the left side. Carbon atoms combine with other elements, and metals to form elaborate arrays of compounds. The alkane chain is used to depict the molecular weights on the right side. The molecular weights in g/mol increase as the chain of hydrocarbons becomes longer in column 2 (Table 22.1) and the energy contained expressed as in kJ/mol also increases. As seen in Table 22.2, *kels* and *kcos* can also exhibit similar properties.

22.3.2 MOLECULAR WEIGHTS OF CHEMICAL COMPOUNDS

Molecular weights of compounds are based on the corresponding atomic weight of the constituting elements and have a definite measure since the atomic weights are known and periodic tables exist. Unfortunately, we do not have similar measures in the knowledge domain. However, the noun objects

Table 22.1 Molecular Weight and Gross Energy of Some Basic Carbon Compounds

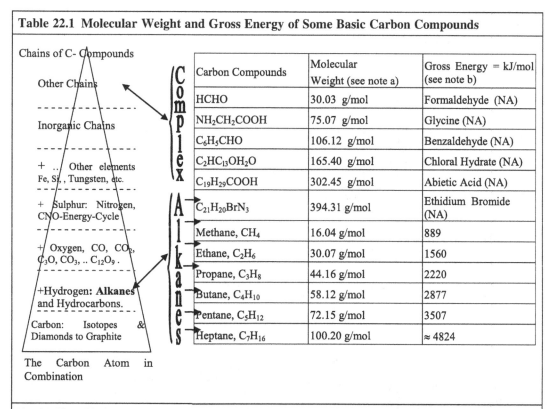

Chains of C- Compounds

Other Chains

Inorganic Chains

+ .. Other elements
Fe, Si, , Tungsten, etc.

+ Sulphur: Nitrogen,
CNO-Energy-Cycle

+ Oxygen, CO, CO$_2$,
C$_3$O, CO$_3$, .. C$_{12}$O$_9$.

+Hydrogen: **Alkanes**
and Hydrocarbons.

Carbon: Isotopes   &
Diamonds to Graphite

The   Carbon   Atom   in
Combination

Carbon Compounds	Molecular Weight (see note a)	Gross Energy = kJ/mol (see note b)
HCHO	30.03 g/mol	Formaldehyde (NA)
NH$_2$CH$_2$COOH	75.07 g/mol	Glycine (NA)
C$_6$H$_5$CHO	106.12 g/mol	Benzaldehyde (NA)
C$_2$HC$_{13}$OH$_2$O	165.40 g/mol	Chloral Hydrate (NA)
C$_{19}$H$_{29}$COOH	302.45 g/mol	Abietic Acid (NA)
C$_{21}$H$_{20}$BrN$_3$	394.31 g/mol	Ethidium Bromide (NA)
Methane, CH$_4$	16.04 g/mol	889
Ethane, C$_2$H$_6$	30.07 g/mol	1560
Propane, C$_3$H$_8$	44.16 g/mol	2220
Butane, C$_4$H$_{10}$	58.12 g/mol	2877
Pentane, C$_5$H$_{12}$	72.15 g/mol	3507
Heptane, C$_7$H$_{16}$	100.20 g/mol	≈ 4824

Note (a): The numbers are approximate, since the atomic weight of H is 1.00789 and the standard atomic weight of C is 12.011. NA indicates that the number is not available.

Note (b): The quantity known as higher heating value (HHV[2]) (or gross energy or upper heating value or gross calorific value (GCV) or higher calorific value (HCV[3])). It can also be expressed as MJ/kg.

have a history of the knowledge trail behind them which specifies how much energy has been spent in acquiring the knowledge in the particular *KCO*. In a sense, the higher molecular weight compound (such as Heptane, see Table 22.1) will have a gross energy of ≈ 4824 KJ/mol compared to Methane that has 889 KJ/mol. When deployed, the released energy is corresponding high for Heptane.

The similarity between *kels* and chemical elements should be explored and investigated with due caution. In chemistry, elements form the basis of compounds and compound chains. In knowledge science, *kels* make up for the generation of new *kels* and are themselves derived from other

[2]Is determined by bringing all the products of combustion back to the original precombustion temperature, and in particular condensing any vapor produced. Such measurements often use a standard temperature of 25°C (77°F). This is the same as the thermodynamic heat of combustion since the enthalpy change for the reaction assumes a common temperature of the compounds before and after combustion, in which case the water produced by combustion is liquid.

[3]The higher heating value takes into account the latent heat of vaporization of water in the combustion products, and is useful in calculating heating values for fuels where condensation of the reaction products is practical (e.g., in a gas-fired boiler used for space heat). In other words, HHV assumes all water component is in liquid state at the end of combustion (in product of combustion) and that heat below 150°C can be put to use.

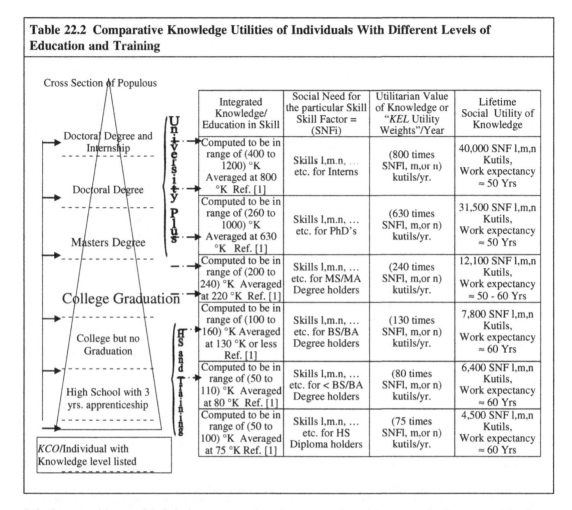

Table 22.2 Comparative Knowledge Utilities of Individuals With Different Levels of Education and Training

Cross Section of Populous

	Integrated Knowledge/ Education in Skill	Social Need for the particular Skill Skill Factor = (SNFi)	Utilitarian Value of Knowledge or "*KEL* Utility Weights"/Year	Lifetime Social Utility of Knowledge
Doctoral Degree and Internship	Computed to be in range of (400 to 1200) °K Averaged at 800 °K Ref. [1]	Skills l,m.n, … etc. for Interns	(800 times SNFl, m,or n) kutils/yr.	40,000 SNF l,m,n Kutils, Work expectancy ≈ 50 Yrs
Doctoral Degree	Computed to be in range of (260 to 1000) °K Averaged at 630 °K Ref. [1]	Skills l,m.n, … etc. for PhD's	(630 times SNFl, m,or n) kutils/yr.	31,500 SNF l,m,n Kutils, Work expectancy ≈ 50 Yrs
Masters Degree	Computed to be in range of (200 to 240) °K Averaged at 220 °K Ref. [1]	Skills l,m.n, … etc. for MS/MA Degree holders	(240 times SNFl, m,or n) kutils/yr.	12,100 SNF l,m,n Kutils, Work expectancy ≈ 50 - 60 Yrs
College Graduation	Computed to be in range of (100 to 160) °K Averaged at 130 °K or less Ref. [1]	Skills l,m.n, … etc. for BS/BA Degree holders	(130 times SNFl, m,or n) kutils/yr.	7,800 SNF l,m,n Kutils, Work expectancy ≈ 60 Yrs
College but no Graduation	Computed to be in range of (50 to 110) °K Averaged at 80 °K Ref. [1]	Skills l,m.n, … etc. for < BS/BA Degree holders	(80 times SNFl, m,or n) kutils/yr.	6,400 SNF l,m,n Kutils, Work expectancy ≈ 60 Yrs
High School with 3 yrs. apprenticeship	Computed to be in range of (50 to 100) °K Averaged at 75 °K Ref. [1]	Skills l,m.n, … etc. for HS Diploma holders	(75 times SNFl, m,or n) kutils/yr.	4,500 SNF l,m,n Kutils, Work expectancy ≈ 60 Yrs

KCO/Individual with Knowledge level listed

kels. Long residence of *kels* in human can alter the personality of humans who become *KELs* themselves such as large populations and concentration of physics *kels* in a scientist can make him a physicist and a knowledge element *KEL*. This type of a phenomenon is generally not perceived in elements, though it is present. For instance, a large collection of gold atoms in an object is a gold-*kel*. However, elements in complex chains of other derived molecules will alter their behavior to suit the chemical reaction. Energy is thus exchanged, received, or generated. Human, *KELs* may perform in a similar fashion but the methodology is not documented nor formulized.

When the commonalities are completely standardized and formulized, they will create barrier to human creativity, inventions, and innovations since a human being is robbed of their freedom to explore new solutions. Every activity will be cataloged and the outcome will be predictable. In a sense, even chemical elements behave with a certain amount of randomness as new compounds and drugs are being synthesized and developed but this methodology is more streamlined in chemistry rather than in social sciences. Social dynamics is more rapid and major cultural changes can accrue faster than the changes in the chemistry of elements, even though no element is indefinitely stable in a cosmic timeframe.

22.3.3 POTENTIAL AND UTILITY OF KNOWLEDGE, *KELS*, AND *KCOS*

In the knowledge domain, *KCO*s with a high level of knowledge acquired during their preceding knowledge trail, have a larger "knowledge weight" or a larger knowledge potential [1] or KnP to perform more elaborate, more skilled, more intense verb functions. For example, the services of a doctor and those of a nonprofessional will have their own differences. This statement implies that a highly educated individual can and usually performs more socially desirable tasks in their own professions. The utility of knowledge thus gained or the knowledge potential thus acquired is indicative of the utility of the *KCO* (or an individual) that has such knowledge. The molecular weight and the knowledge weight thus retain their equivalency but with on radical difference.

Whereas the energy in the chemical compounds get exhausted after its use, the knowledge potential is not depleted and generally enhanced and regenerated (in many cases) by being used in a creative direction. This is a fundamental difference between knowledge in life forms and energy in inanimate objects. Creativity and regeneration is the key to being alive.

22.3.4 KNOWLEDGE UTILITY (KUTILITY) OF LIFE FORMS

Kutility is defined as the utility of knowledge for knowledge centric object or a human being with history of knowledge acquisition or skill. When used appropriately, this training offers a measurable utility for the public and the society and thus enhances values and morality. Conversely, in an abusive mode, this abuse of knowledge like that of power can bring wars, hate, and disasters to the society and bring negative features to a sane society. Unfortunately, deceit can also grow exponentially. For example, while Internet is being used to promote Russian brides and Asian singles, the values of a society can only degenerate by associating cheap sex with the security and sanctity of lifelong matrimony.

In Marshall's economics, the positive and negative utilities of goods are not clearly defined, whereas the *kutilities* of social and cultural objects (or *kels*) play a decisive role in social relations and the movement of neighboring *kel* objects. In such environments, a firmer grip on the *kutilities* becomes necessary to monitor the movements of human transactions.

22.3.5 NONDEPLETION AND SELF-REGENERATION OF KNOWLEDGE

When learning is practiced in the traditional and positive sense, retention of knowledge follows by comprehension and its expected utility for future use. Knowledge retains its value more intensely than the value of other materialistic assets in most cases. The deployment of knowledge does NOT deplete it; instead a life form that contains knowledge nurtures it like the womb nurtures the seminal XX or XY chromosome pair. Growth nurtures growth exponentially and new imprint of knowledge evolves. Constant learning to be polished in the latest novelties and technologies in any profession does not deplete knowledge but invigorates a methodology to weigh and consider the latest information in view or in conjunction of the prior knowledge. Structure, order, and connectivity result. The process yields an exponential understanding of the professional subject matter and an enhanced positive use of such newly generated knowledge.

22.3.6 KUTILITY OF ACQUIRED KNOWLEDGE

Tables similar to Table 22.1 can be constructed for KCOs with various histories of knowledge trails. The energy is not depleted but continuously regenerated by life giving forces in the animate objects. The term utility is used in this context but has a broader implication than the traditional utility used by economists in economic analysis. Hence, the term utility has a time dimension associated with it since time is limited for all life forms and any *KCO* can deploy the "knowledge weight" for so many hours a day, week, or year, or even over the lifetime of a particular *KCO*. Table 22.2 illustrated the "*KEL* utility weights" of typical individuals with training from high school diplomas through to postdoctoral internships is presented in Table 22.2.

CONCLUSIONS

This chapter offers specific means of quantifying the knowledge and the potential gained by formalized education in any society. Animate and chemical parallelisms are used to evolve the basic element of knowledge defined in this paper as a *kel* to specify a knowledge element. Exchange of such *kels* makes and breaks social bondage and interdependencies between small and large knowledge centric objects. The level of exchange of *kels* is also quantified as the integrated work or energy in the knowledge trail behind humans and machines. Whereas humans learn and retain knowledge learned in their minds, machines carry the embedded intelligence in the silicon chips and the firmware and software code that control CPU functions.

The utilitarian value of different knowledge centric objects is computed as the projected weight of the knowledge-based *kels* learned, retained and deployed by individuals in the social and cultural environments and by the machines in network and robotic environments. Quantitative estimations and prediction can thus be made on a scientific methodology. The results presented in this chapter reaffirm the observed results in real life; however, a firm quantitative basis is introduced in the analysis and prediction of knowledge and the gross knowledge-utility of humans, robots, and machines. Such quantitative methods in chemistry have been the basis of the periodic tables used extensively throughout the discipline of chemical analysis.

The concept of *kel-weight* is implied in this chapter by assigning *kel-weights* to the *kels* in any *KCO*. For example, on the positive side, if Einstein (with high atomic *kel* weight) interacted (i. e., *VF*) with Newton's concept of gravity (another high atomic weight *kel*) to come with Relativistic correction to the gravity fields of distant cosmic bodies, then the new theory (*KCO*) with a very high *kelweight* of its own can be perceived. Likewise, if gold and platinum were blended to make a new ornamental alloy, then that alloy would be more valuable than gold or platinum each by themselves. Conversely, undesirable but possible negative combinations also can be foreseen. For example, if the defense laboratories designed a new robot by combining the AI of the original robot with a nerve gas pump in the unmanned drones, then the new robot more lethal than either old robot or the nerve gases filled drones, etc.

REFERENCES

[1] Ahamed SV. Intelligent Internet knowledge networks, processing of concepts and wisdom. Hoboken: John Wiley and Sons; 2006, ISBN 978-0-471-788560-0.

[2] Ahamed SV. Next generation knowledge machines. Boston: Elsevier Insights; 2014, ISBN 978-12-416629-5.

KNOWLEDGE ELEMENT MACHINE DESIGN: PATHWAYS OF KNOWLEDGE IN MACHINES

23

CHAPTER SUMMARY

Knowledge elements are as universal as life itself that revolves around knowing enough to get by, modify, enhance, and improve it. Life without any knowledge is dead as knowledge without life. The varieties of such knowledge elements that make up segments and fraction of life are as profuse as the diversity of the rhythms of life and of life forms. In fact, there is no life without embedded knowledge to continue and supply the essentials of living. Conversely, there is no knowledge without life forms to support its continuum of change and adaptation. Symbiotic as they are, the interdependency prevails since the beginning of life and the origin of knowledge. The evolution of species is founded on the increasing complexity of *kels* that perpetuate knowledge to constitute new species of knowledge and knowledge of species.

The knowledge enhanced to gratify the needs for the incremental change in the species is time-dependent statistical occurrence. The change may be microscopic or cataclysmic. Change and adaptation are both essential. All forms of life abide by the law that knowledge and life are in deepest harmony just to keep living. After Darwin, we have realized that time to evolve flows through the process of neural adaptation to learn to be the fittest to survive. Knowledge to live by and life to enhance the genetic code are the two chromosomes in the womb of humankind.

In the more evolved species, the complexity of *kels* and their structure both reach astounding levels of complexity and connectivity, perhaps reaching their highest peaks in human beings. In the other species, the complexity is tailored to suit their own form of life and its needs with three (physiological, safety, and reproductive) lower level needs. By process of trial and error, they learn to be optimal in the expenditure of time and energy to learn the adaptation. In humans with higher levels of needs [1] and a higher level of comprehension, the dynamic movement of *kels* becomes scientific and almost mathematical process. In this chapter, we propose a mechanism for the pathways of knowledge in the society and for the graphs for solving complex problems.

23.1 INTRODUCTION

The origin of *kel* (to represent knowledge cell) is derived from the word "pixel" to stand for picture element (i.e., picture-cell, written as pixel). In addition, there is a resounding similarity between *kel* and the naturally occurring elements in chemistry at the atomic, molecular and at a reactionary level. For instance, the chemical elements also consist of neutrons, positrons, and electrons that play an adaptive role as the elements form molecules and complex chains of organic, inorganic compounds, and acids. Similarly, a *kel*[1] consists of noun, a verb, and a convolution to join them. Nature has provided an innate intelligence for the physical world of materials to exist.

Knowledge element (*kel*) is defined as the minute particle of comprehensible knowledge that is also computable. Like quantized particles in physics, *kels* have a life of their own, and like atoms in chemistry, *kels* can be tracked and reformulated to make up other compound and super *kels*. The principle occurs in nature many times and even in astronomy when numerous Novas structure themselves as a Supernova. In Chemistry, most of the basic elements (like hydrogen, nitrogen, oxygen) present in biological cells make up tissues and organs of the body.

Kels support knowledge structures and their organization as much as chemical elements support life forms in species. The greatest commonality lays in the functions that chemical elements and *kels* serve. Whereas elements serve to make the well-structured organization of compounds and molecules secure and stable, *kels* serve to make larger *kels* to be consistent, coherent, and cogent. In some cases, the both processes are dynamic and transient.

Much like elements that can be grouped, regrouped, and assigned atomic weights, *kels* can also be classified, reclassified, and assigned *kel*-weights to convey how much the any particular *kel* can be beneficial or detrimental to the society. After all, chemical elements can be used in medicines and in poisons. Much as chemical analysis leads to the separation of constituting elements in compounds, knowledge analysis can lead to the basic *kels* that constitutes a large body of knowledge-centric objects, or *KCO*s. At the first stage of the analysis of knowledge, it can be reduced to its tiniest elemental cells, i.e., into *kels*. At the second stage of analysis, the atoms in elements, *kels* can be decomposed into quantized groups of noun-objects, quantized types of convolutions, and quantized sets of verb-functions, wherein the convolutions bind noun-objects and verb-function into a nuclear structure of an action by a noun. For example, a simple *kel* such as John speaks has a different bondage between John speaking than a *kel* John yells or the *kel* John hollers between John (a noun) and speaks, yells, or flirts (series of verbs with the same meaning but different tonalities). This simple *kel* can also be an integral part of a larger *kel* such as John speaks at a conference about chemical analysis. The role of the convolution *between the *no* (John) **vf* (yells) is different from its role in *no* (John) **vf* (hollers) or in John speaks.

Most species deal with modules or *kuanta* of rudimentary knowledge in order to gratify their routine social and deficit needs and acquire them to make life easier. Most elite learn to deal with and manipulate more advanced *kuanta* of sophisticated knowledge in order to gratify their special needs and learn them to satisfy their needs, environment, and their circumstances. *Kels* do indeed have a hierarchical structure. Like nature itself, knowledge exists in all textures, sizes, and forms. Human senses that operate in real and physical space offer a very tiny glance of a much more intricate and sophisticated universe of knowledge that can be sensed by perception and resolved by programming/mathematical tools. To deal with reality and use in the knowledge era, the structure of knowledge needs careful adjustment, alignment, and association, especially if it is to be deployed in computational environment.

---

[1]The italicization of the words kel, kels, KEL, KELs, NO, NOs, no, nos, VF, VFs, vf, vfs, does not carry significance in this chapter. Basically, the suffix 's' designate multiple elements, the capitalization designates a larger denomination of the elements.

23.2 **THE NATURE OF A KNOWLEDGE ELEMENT (*KEL*)**

Kels play a complex role in communication of knowledge between humans and knowledge systems. *Kels* can share noun-objects and convolutions as much as atoms can share the nuclear elements, electrons, and valency bonds. The particularly adaptive role of atoms to form varieties of compounds is similar to that of *kels*, when they arrange and rearrange their structures of *no's*, *s, and *vf's*, to form different configurations of knowledge in a chain of *kels* to form minor *kcos* (knowledge-centric objects) and major *KCOs*. The analogy is evident to treat the chemical world as a type of knowledge society where the *no's*, *s, and *vf's* are the basic building blocks, and these *kels* are formed and unformed depending on the dynamic social setting and cultural setting. At a very microscopic level, change in the chemistry of every atom is as real as the change of every *kel*.

The role of a *kel* is as fundamental as the role of seminal biological cell in all species. The two chromosome pairs formed as *XX* (female) and/or an *XX* or *XY* (male) chromosomes to constitute the female and male genetic cell evolves after the genetic code in the male (*no*1)-*kel*1 penetrates and ruptures (*vf*(s) in a distinctly unique fashion(*)) the female (*no*2)-*kel*2. A new *kel*3 and a new *no*3 (the fetus) is thus formed, and it carries the genetic code of both *no1* and *no2* as the *no3-kel3*. One, twins, and multiple babies are all formed from the process[2] (*no*1***vf*1). In a very oblique sense, the inception of knowledge and the origin of life are intertwined. The genetic code should be considered as knowledge that carries the imprint of the species and the two codes (male and female) that get interlocked should be considered and the generation of new *no3-kel3* noun-object-*kel*. Life, actions, and behavior are coincidental with noun-objects (*no's*), verb-function (*vf's*), and the syntactic rules (*s), respectively, that bind them.

When two *kels* interact to yield a new *kel*, or when two noun-objects interact to yield a new noun-object, the process can be represented by the symbolic process

$$kel1\ vf_{12}* \rightarrow kel2\ for\ the\ forward\ action\ vf_{12}\ and\ by\ kel2\ vf_{21}* \rightarrow kel1\ for\ the\ reverse\ process.$$

As a flowchart that can be programmed on a computer, the unit of interaction is shown in Figure 23.1. Conceptually, the unit of transaction that occurs between any two noun-objects (or *kels*) is shown in Figure 23.2. New *kels* are constantly being formed in the minds of humans and knowledge processing units (*kpus*) of knowledge machines [2]. The transient time could last as briefly as a flash in the mind or a cycle time of a *kpu*. The newly evolved *no'* can have lifetime of an unworthy paper or as long as the written word of some value. The truest beauty lies in the truth and the truth lies in the beauty. Together they make up the super-*kel* of timeless Time and flawless Beauty. An endless cycle of continuum results, wherein *kels* are born, live, and die like microorganisms, humans, and even cosmic entities.

Small and large *kels* are recycled in most publications, dissertations, and papers. Over time, it becomes hard to discover the origin of the innovation of the seminal *kel* (to the left of Pico *kels* in Figure 23.3) and the nature of the seminal *no's*, *vf's*, and their convolution (*). A breakthrough *kel* is as rare as the discovery of new knowledge leading to a new chemical element or a newly

---

[2]The more precise representation of the entire set of processes is represented as ($qno1 \leftrightarrow q*1 \leftrightarrow qvf \leftrightarrow q*2 \leftrightarrow qno2$) where the prefix q denotes a *kuantum* of the genetic code in each *kel*. Genetic science elaborates the processes that follow from the formation of the seminal cell of the fetus to the duplication of the cells but in the context of where and how the cells are deployed. The changes in the womb and the physiology of the parental object $\rightarrow qno2$.

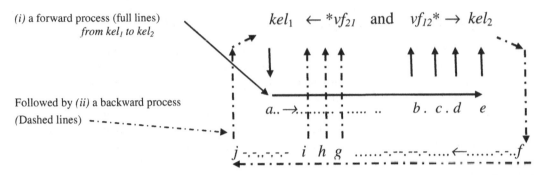

(i) a forward process (full lines)
from kel_1 to kel_2

$$kel_1 \leftarrow {}^*vf_{21} \quad \text{and} \quad vf_{12}{}^* \rightarrow kel_2$$

Followed by *(ii)* a backward process
(Dashed lines)

$a.. \rightarrow$ $\qquad b . c . d \quad e$

j $\qquad i \ h \ g$ $\qquad \leftarrow$ $\qquad f$

FIGURE 23.1

Programmable sequence in reality depicted as $kel \rightarrow$, of steps for a unit of a transaction between $kel1$ and $kel2$.

formulated drug, even though the routine synthesis of drugs in industry is as common as the rehashing of the technical contents in a new publication. The entire occurrence of cyclic nature of *kels* is depicted in Figure 23.3.

23.3 PROGRAMMABILITY AND DEPLOYMENT OF *KELS*

In dealing with *kels* in lives of most people, the noun-objects, verb-functions, and their convolutions play a vital role in gratifying human needs. The gratification the lower needs of humans [1] are greatly influenced by noun-objects, verb-functions, and their convolutions that address safety, physiological, and social needs. The mental association between needs and the corresponding objects and verbs (to gratify such needs) is instilled in the minds of infants and it persists throughout through lifetime. Computers can track and find optimal inventory items and their functions for individuals, corporations, societies, and nations as easily as human beings find. However, timeliness, precision, and optimality are added features from *kel* and social machines.

If a look-up table for objects, verbs, their convolutions, and human needs is read into the memory system of a typical computer, then the algorithms to gratify the entire spectrum of need can be programmed for individual personality types, cultures, and (most) circumstances. Social programming has many more variables to consider than scientific programming, but even so, the methodologies of software and firmware engineering [3,4] and design become applicable to social programming. The social processing units though different and more complex can be designed to handle a larger and more robust set of social operation codes or sopcs. The basic instruction set for social processor unit (*SPU*) based on the input processing of noun-objects, their associated verb-function, and the appropriate convolutions needs the features of object processor units [5], and the Instruction Register (IR) should be able to decode and secure the microcode for social functions. The *kels* will simply correspond to (very) long words or strings of binary data to be accommodated in the Data Register (DR). The social computers work with data structures in the memory rather than words stored in the memories of conventional computers.

The role of convolution symbolized as * is pivotal in *KEL* machines. Historically, convolutions have facilitated most social and business environments. In the simplest mode, the process of adding

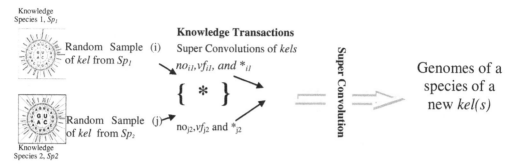

(a) Evolution of a species of knowledge elements after a Super-Convolution of all *no*s, *vf*s and *'s.

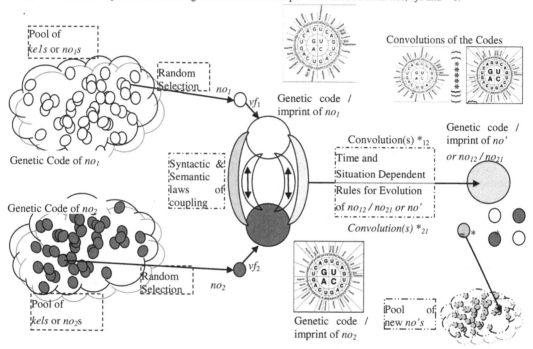

(b) Details of the processes that evolve new species knowledge elements by the Super-Convolutions of smaller more miniscule *kels* of two species of interactive *KCO's*.

FIGURE 23.2

The diagrammatic representation of the interaction between no1 and no2 or between kel1 and kel2 that is depicted as a convolution whereby a new no' (shown as no12/no21) is evolved. The genetic imprint of both no12 and no21 are carried into no'. The newly formed no' becomes a member of a pool of no's and the process keeps repeating. The flavors of knowledge are as widely dispersed as the sentiments human beings that carry and nurture knowledge elements.

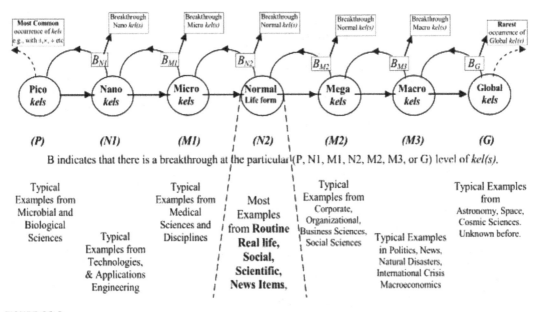

B indicates that there is a breakthrough at the particular (P, N1, M1, N2, M2, M3, or G) level of kel(s).

FIGURE 23.3

Depiction of the cyclic nature of kels in society, sciences, cultures, and most environments. The change in the level of understanding and interpretation leads to either a new kel or backwards to the preexisting and documented kels.

has permitted the measure of wealth, currency, grain, etc. Dollar values are simply added to measure the net worth of individuals, estates, corporations, etc. As a next example, when monies are invested with financial institutions, the dollars do not simply add over time and the net worth of the invested fund grows (or even depleted) in a convolved fashion depending on the nature of investment, socioeconomic conditions, location, management policies, etc. As a further example, an organ in a human body functions as an integral and adaptive unit to support the body and mind. The role of an organ is convolved with the role of other organs to support the human functions. In social situations, a statement or a unit of knowledge interjected can cause emotions, energies, and functions to become convolved in conjunction with other *KELs* and it becomes more complex than simple addition.

At this stage of evolution of social computing, there are no software modules or hardware units that can process complex social functions like the complex number and array processors that process complex numbers and numerical data arrays. It appears that multidimensional data structure handling capability becomes highly desirable feature of social processor units (spus).[3] In the modern machine, special software modules and/or hardware units are included to make the machine functions accurate, optimal, and fast. Such a design strategy will facilitate the functionalities of the *KEL* machines greatly since such functions are complex and elaborate.

---

[3]The functions of *spu's* and *kel* processors are alike. The databases are primed appropriately for their different uses.

23.4 **THE ARCHITECTURE OF A *KEL* MACHINE**

Kel machines process knowledge elements and reside at the top of a new generation of computers to handle knowledge precisely, efficiently, and optimally. Kel operation code (kopc) specifies the operation to be performed on a kel operand (kopr, that has a predefined format) with a set of attributes (if any) and a set attributes of attributes (if any). The kopcs and koprs need appropriate pairing by a suitable knowledge machine compiler. The numbers of kopcs and koprs can be quite large depending on the generality of the kel machine. The kel machines are expected to as precise and dependable as the mainframe business machines that handle a large variety of business, financial, and economic problems and offer intelligent decision support systems for the large corporations.

23.4.1 **THE DESIGN FRAMEWORK OF *KEL* MACHINES**

During the current time-frame, *KEL* machines appear as conceivable as the von Neumann machine (1946—48). In 18th century, the internal combustion engine as equally well conceived. In the more recent time frame the microcomputer-integrated circuit (IC) chips embedded in most the modern internal combustion engines make them precise, efficient, and optimal. In the same vein, we suggest that a *kel*-chip will make a knowledge machine precise, efficient, and optimal. From a designer's perspective, the blueprint of a *kel*-chip becomes more extensive than that of a basic von Neumann machine. All the recent enhancements (massively parallel-processed, microcoded, pipelined, MISD (multiple instruction single data), MIMD (multiple instruction multiple data), etc.) are applicable to *KEL* machines.

The processor unit of a *kel* machine is depicted in Figure 23.4. The operation of the machine is consistent with that of a typical computer. First, the next executable instruction is brought in the social (or *kel*) processor unit. Second, the operation code is decoded.[4] Third, the social (or *kel*) operands[5] are brought into the processor as data structures with shared or dedicated storage within the processor architecture and the execution is done by the sequential or parallel steps in the microcode that is invoked by the opc. Finally, the newly processed *kel* (or its data structure) is moved back into the memory of the *kel* machine. To this extent the sequence of operations (F, fetch; D, decode; E execute, and S, store the result) of traditional cpus is retained in the *kel* cpus.

23.4.2 **THE DEPLOYMENT OF DATABASE TECHNOLOGIES**

Databases are used extensively in the architecture shown in Figure 23.4 in order to facilitate the complex nature of operation codes and operands in *kel* machines. Such bases may not be necessary for the simpler *kel* machines that are functionally comparable to the simpler single instruction single data (SISD) von Neumann machine. Internet access is not shown in this figure but is easily provided by a dedicated Internet switch to address and access WWW bases. Numerous variations with

---

[4]The sopc (social operation code) can be more complex than the *opc* (operation code of typical computers) of typical computers and diversity of the codes can be quite large. However, complexity and diversity of operation codes are both easily handled by larger and more elaborate IC designs.
[5]Numerous secondary fetch steps may be necessary for bringing linked objects, the attributes, and the attributes of the attributes into the processor caches.

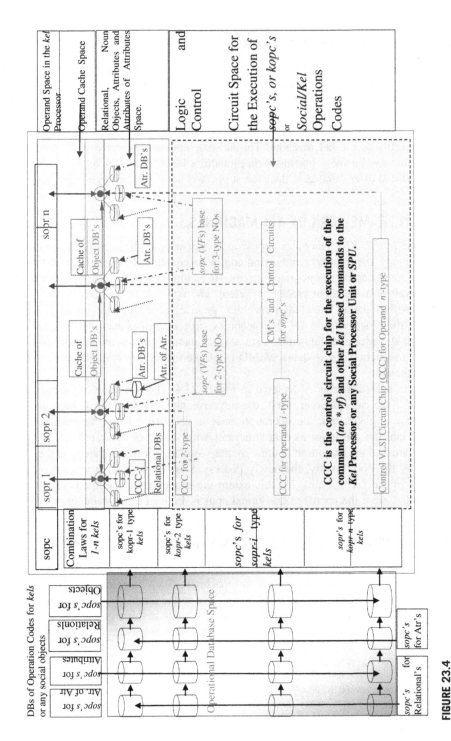

FIGURE 23.4

Structure of a kel processor for social or kel machines. The machine follows a typical FDE (Fetch, decode, bring operands, linked operands, attributes, attributes of attributes into the processor) and executes sequence for a social/kel operation code (KOPC). Additional microcode may also be necessary for the complex OPCs necessary for kel processing.

dedicated or shared bus configurations are also possible for the computer architecture designers. This figure offers a conceptual methodology and a framework for the newer versions of the Next-Generation Knowledge Machines.

The use of database technologies is extensive in most intelligent networks (such as IN/1 during the late eighties, and subsequently IN/2 and the Advanced intelligent Networks or AINs during early nineties, presented in Ref. [5]) and in intelligent Internets. This role is necessary in the *KEL* machines, but to a larger and more refined extent. The noun-objects (*no's*, their attributes, their relationship to other *no's* are all arranged as a tree structure), the verb-functions (*vf's*, the semantic and syntactic rules, and relations to other *vf's*) and the permitted convolutions (*s) are also stored in databases and used in an intelligent fashion to cater for an application or social program. The processes though complex and cumbersome can be resolved in modern computers. A typical configuration of such a *KEL* processor is shown in Figure 23.4.

23.5 SOCIAL IMPACT OF KNOWLEDGE-BASED MACHINES

The social impacts (such as more user options, possible abuse of Internet, overly aggressive marketing, spread of computer bugs and viruses) of these advanced technologies have been predicated [6] as early as 1987. The technological advances during the turn of this century have further facilitated the spread of smaller corporate and home based intelligent networks. The knowledge technologists have considerable benefits that can be derived from the future *KEL* machines on the one hand and conversely the marketers have more options to harass and to become deceptive about the products.

23.5.1 THE USES OF *KEL* MACHINES

KEL machines that are bug and virus free can save the users considerable time in performing routine activities of personal, social, and corporate lives. The converse statement is equally effective. Personally and individually preferred action can be streamlined for user approval. However, *KEL* machines have the ability to fragment and reassemble functions and noun-objects, and further select appropriate convolutions to couple them into decisions, knowledge, explanations, and convincing. It becomes essential that all the functions and their complexity be accurately executed. Such accuracy and dependability of major and minor functions has been already practiced in modern telecommunication networks, Intelligent Networks IN/1, IN/2, AINs, and Internets. The interdependencies between computer networks and intelligent communication networks constitute the platform to building very potent and beneficial social/*KEL* machines over the next few decades.

23.5.2 THE ABUSES OF *KEL* MACHINES

As a historical precursor to the abuse of *KEL* machines, we look back on the abuse of Internet to spread mass hysteria and violence that has strengthened wars and social and global unrest. In the current social setting, the ugly news catches more attention than beneficial news and it is to advantage of the media owner to feed the emotional explosives than to explain and solicit the virtues of restrained and orderly transition to a more advanced society. In a sense the beneficial use of *kel* machines need as much precaution as the use of Intelligent Internet network services. The greater complexity (thus the cost) of these machines is likely to curtail the abuse by hate-mongers, mafia, thugs, drug dealers, sex predators, etc.

CONCLUSIONS

A new methodology for processing knowledge is presented in this presented whereby any functionality in the knowledge domain is broken down into one or more (verb) functions by one or more (noun) objects in a predefined and stylized (convolution) fashion. The methodology is the same as in any conventional machine wherein the laws of arithmetic and logic are broken down into finer and finer processes that are executable in the hardware environment. The fundamental concepts for the organization, hardware, the software, and the firmware of the new *kel* machines are developed and presented here. The *kel* (knowledge element) machine needs specific architecture, memory organizations, bus structure, and switches to perform the interwoven and elaborate task to handle small and large *kels*.

The chip design and the time sequence flow of processes need greater consideration than those in typical computers. The recursion of verb-function on multiplicity of noun-object is akin the multiply and add functions in array processors and in the graphical processors. The design of *kel* processors can become (almost) as complex as the design of various new generations of processors combined into one processor or to design the *kel* processor as a plug-in unit for a new breed of social computers.

REFERENCES

[1] Maslow A. Farther reaches of human nature. New York: Viking Press; 1971. Also see, Maslow AH. A theory of human motivation. Psychol. Rev. 1943;50:370–396. Also see, Maslow AH. Motivation and personality. 3rd ed. New York: Harper & Row; 1970.
[2] Ahamed SV. Next generation knowledge machines. Elsevier Insights; 2014.
[3] Bass L, Clements P. Software architecture in practice. SUI Series in Software Design. Addison Wesley.
[4] Giloi WK, editor. Firmware Engineering: Seminar veranstaltet von der gemeinsamen Fachgrupe Mikroprogrammierung des GI Fachausschusses 3/4 und des NTG-Fachausschusses. (German and English Edition.). Springer; 1980.
[5] Ahamed SV. Intelligent Internet knowledge networks. Processing of concepts and wisdom. John Wiley & Sons; 2006.
[6] Ahamed SV. Social impact of intelligent telecommunication networks. In: Proc. of Pacific Telecommunications Conference. Honolulu, January 18–22, 1987, pp. 407–414.

ELEMENTS OF KNOWLEDGE IN SOCIETIES

CHAPTER SUMMARY

This chapter deals with the constant underlying movement of the elements of knowledge. Finely fragmented cogent, coherent, and connected particles of knowledge derived from larger bodies of knowledge traverse the mental spaces as atoms negotiate the chemical space. Both elements form bondages with other elements of compatible kind and form larger molecules, strings, and complex structures. Some of these larger, longer strings are more robust and stable than others and become elementary particles of even larger and even longer strings. The dictum of chemical elements is governed by the numbers and properties published in the Periodic Table. The syntactic and semantic rules for knowledge elements are flexible, adaptive, and dynamic, but coherent and cogent to make the mental space orderly, constructive, and creative. The routine textbook rules of chemistry become programs for knowledge machines to generate significant larger and longer strings of knowledge. Such machines emulate the behavior of finely fragments elements of knowledge, and their logical bondages with each other create and invent new, diversified and beneficial knowledge. These strings of knowledge form cohesive bonds between minds, thus establishing a continuity of rhythm of thought and compassion across cultures and societies.

Elements of knowledge thus become the numbers, alphabets, words, and symbols for a new generation of knowledge machines. Such elements can be stored, processed, arithmetically and logically enhanced, modified, and altered in the memory units, caches, processors, and switches of knowledge and network machines. This chapter explores these concepts from philosophic and ethical perspectives, and uses the discipline of knowledge at the frail boundary between "good" and "bad."

24.1 INTRODUCTION

Elements of knowledge (shortened as *kels* to represent knowledge elements) exhibit laws of chemistry as the chemical elements' bond with other elements and generate new compounds and molecules. In the domain of knowledge, the laws of convolution with other *kels* are flexible and adaptive, but maintain rationality for the mind to perceive knowledge in its microscopic or macroscopic formats in the real world and the mental space. Both the real world and mental space spans nations, cultures, and societies.

Knowledge in human activity blends like chemistry within species in nature. In most instances, larger bodies of knowledge are composed, enhanced, used, and utilized to benefit the existence of society. The fundamental precept behind all the widespread generalities is that lives of all species is based on dynamic actions of objects that make life feasible by prolonged strings of actions continually in the time dimension. Objects and actions trigger the mind into a

Evolution of Knowledge Science. DOI: http://dx.doi.org/10.1016/B978-0-12-805478-9.00024-8

life-form based on the answers to seven basic questions: why, who, what, how, when, how long, and where. The mental coordinates are established. Information is processed and knowledge is acquired. The long cycle from prior knowledge to the derived new knowledge continues ad infinitum.

The strife between good and evil is the theme of vicissitudes in lives. The inner self that refuses to accept anything but the best leads to the search for the best for each one (i.e., each noun-object(s), *no* or *no's*) with honor, justice and dignity accomplishing the each one of the deeds (i.e., each verb-function(s), *vf* or *vf's*) in a tactical and socially acceptable way (*). In a nutshell, the theme of activity becomes *(no →* → vf) or (no(s) →*s → vf(s))* in a time sequence that a machine can execute with probabilistic result(s). The central processor unit (CPU) of such a machine follows a series of executable statements that can be written down as $\{\sum ((no\rightarrow * \rightarrow vf))$ from *"t"* to *"t + Δt"* in real time. The motivation (why) for the *no* (who), the (what) actions (*vf's*) in real-time duration, *"t"* to *"t + Δt"* (when and how long) and a probable outcome after an interval are established.

The parameters listed above are entirely programmable as operators, operands, and operational codes in machines. The machine emulates the actions, behavior, and modality. The most probable outcome is stacked away to be combined with other executable statements. The series of actions can thus optimized for the most desirable (expected) result from any social, corporate, national, or any strategic result.

24.2 INCORPORATION OF HUMAN FACTORS

The expenditure of any of the numerous forms (physiological, mental, emotional, etc.) of human energy to function causes its depletion and reduces the tendency to remain active indefinitely. A sense of balance between the extra expenditure of resources and the expected gain in the marginal utility that is thus derived curtails excessive effort in any given direction. The balance becomes global and a sense of fairness and justice prompts most humans to be generous and positive based on gratification and peace. The Second Law of Microeconomics becomes the basis for human race to progress in a positive direction.

In the other direction, when resources are limited the conflict between self-interest and fairness starts to surface. The fears of the future sometimes dominate to obliterate the glory of being righteous in the past. Greed and negativity sets in. The first and second need levels from the Maslow's Need Pyramid [1] projected into the future cast an grim shadow over the fourth and fifth levels of need-gratifications from the past. Fear of fear makes the insecure drown in greed, hate, and violence. There is a scientific basis for the negative spiral of decay in ethics and morality. When greed receives its negative energy from a blend of hate and violence, greed catalyzes the two later traits, which in turn accelerate the former trait. The angular acceleration of the spiral even more thus causes a collapse of ethics and morality commonly seen in the societies.[1]

---

[1]It is almost feasible for the social scientists to write a set of equations for torque, angular momentum, angular acceleration, social resistance, the net resulting difference between positive and negative moments (product of tangential and axial force times the radial distance from the social axis of a culture or a nation). Unfortunately, these entities are dynamic, but the modern computing systems are well programmed to analyze the trends, causes, and their countermeasures of the finite incremental changes in the society over a period of time.

24.3 **ADAPTATION BY THE MACHINE**

The knowledge machine is more than a communications tool. It has all the potential of being an intelligent partner to interact and act as a highly logical human or a highly emotional companion. During training the machine, the machine acquires the personality of the "other" interactive human. The machine personality is augmented by internet knowledge bases that provide validity and verification to provide answers for the saint (with positive priming of the machine functions (vf(s)) and connectivity to intellectual and verified *KBs*).

Conversely, a negatively primed machine can also provide for the mafia and thugs by connectivity to mafia and their associated knowledge bases. In addition, the machine also acquires the most desirable interface for the interacting human based on the "mood" of the user, just as a therapist would adjust the sessions based on the attitude of a patient. Human temperament though highly variable is accommodated by appropriate macro commands at the interface.

The rest of the chapter is divided in two major sections. Section 24.4 presents the emulation of the elite processes for the social betterment by the practice of truthful, virtuous, and beautiful deeds in the society. Section 24.5 deals with the emulation of the deceitful, arrogant, aggressive, and hate-ridden actions of the perverse groups of the population, for social erosion of established ethics and morals. Appropriately, designed machines can address both sides of the human nature.

24.4 **THE POSITIVE AND BENEVOLENT SIDE OF HUMAN ACTIVITY**

Like fire that can provide warmth and comfort, it can also be used to burn and destroy. In most instances, the knowledge machine is used to process *kels* for social and human betterment. By altering the software, firmware, macros, and executable routines, the same hardware can serve as tools of mafia, thugs, and robbers for espionage and social unrest.

In pursuing the role of a knowledge machine in positive directions, we present the role of a doctor (a benevolent noun object) from the role of truthful one in Quadrant I of Figure 24.1. The concepts behind the actions allow wide latitude to make the objects (doctor in the case), their functions (seeking to invent), in a positive way (to benefit the society). Such objects and actions may occur in any nation, any culture, and any society. In this vein, the teachings of Aristotle and Plato (in the Knowledge domain, see the Loop T, Quadrant I, in Fig. 24.1) are bonded to Beauty and Healing (in the *kel* domain; see Loop B, Quadrant II, in Fig. 24.1), and so on in Quadrants III and IV, till the innovation of the Magnetic Resonance Imaging Systems. Historically, the bonding takes place in the minds of the innovators and inventors (such as, Edison, Bell, Shockley, Townsend, Bardeen, Ampere) and in the minds of contributors such as Gandhi, Carter, and Fleming who seek to benefit[2] of humanity.

In particular Figure 24.1 blends the concepts borrowed from the writings of Aristotle (as he documented them in 300 BC) [2] emphasizing the ideas of Truth, Virtue, and Beauty) that advance

---

[2]Numerous figures with the imagery of Figure 24.1 can be constructed for most situations in most cultures. The domain of knowledge is vast enough to cover the entirety of all Internet knowledge bases and more. This figure is illustrative for those who wish to invent based on a mathematical and scientific basis and contribute based on social and human betterment.

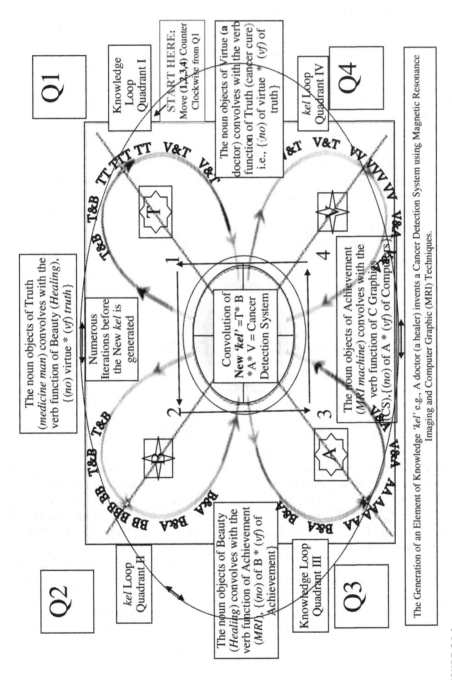

FIGURE 24.1

The Generation of an Element of Knowledge 'kel' e.g., A doctor (a healer) invents a Cancer Detection System using Magnetic Resonance Imaging and Computer Graphic (MRI) Techniques.

Example of the deployment the noun-objects (NO's) of one discipline with the verb-functions (VF's) of another discipline to generate, enhance, modify, invent new knowledge elements or kels in a similar or an entirely new discipline. Please see the text about the convolutions of T, B, V that result in the advancement of the society with the invention of the MRI systems [3].

human society, and thus ends up with Magnetic Resonance Imaging System (MRI) invented [3] in of the twentieth century to diagnose cancerous tissues in the human body. Please note the noun-objects (*no's*) and verb-functions (*vf's*) of and Achievement Beauty, Virtue, and Truth; i.e., (A, B, T, and V) can assume many forms. The imagination and creativity of the user is challenged in this figure. In order to trigger the movement, we tabulate some of the possible the *no's* of A, B, T, and V in Table 24.1 and some of the possible *vf's* in Table 24.1.

24.4.1 INCLUSIVENESS AND RICHNESS OF *KELS*

In scanning Table 24.1, many of the *no's*, *vf's* and (*s) are common because one no can have the attributes of others. For example, an intellectual may also be virtuous or benevolent can also be goal seeking and persistent. The attributes of the noun-objects form linkages and bondages with other noun-objects, or the deeds of the *vf's* can reinforce each other. Generally, most people have a single personality and do not sway between good and bad dramatically over short intervals. The story of Dr. Jekyll and Mr. Hyde is a classic case of imagination of Mr. R. L. Stevenson [4]. In reality, schizophrenics are generally hospitalized and the Table 24.1 attributes are not applicable to such extreme cases.

24.4.2 EXPULSION AND EXCLUSIVENESS OF *KELS*

However, opposite attributes of noun-objects and verb-function tend to become exclusive like cruelty and kindness or a saint and a thug. In the recent past there have been increasing cases where supposedly respectable humans have turned out to be thugs (and mafia types) and violated the public trust. The actions of few individuals in the recent history indicate the presence of negativity-ridden *KELs* in the society. For example, the Andersen [7], and Global Crossing executives [8], Nixon during Watergate years [9], Nixon and Johnson over the Vietnam war [10], Clinton and Monica Lewinsky [11] indicate that such *KELS* do not disappear by simply ignoring them. These *KELS* need to be included in the appropriate knowledge bases such that the knowledge machines are forewarned that such *KELS* can and may reappear in the future.

24.4.3 MOVEMENTS OF *KELS*

All knowledge elements or *kels* shift, move, and oscillate in the mental and social spaces. Tiny and microscopic or gross and cosmic suffer from intellectual and social forces. Natural and artificial forces govern their movements. Resident in nature and human minds, *kels* evolve, mature, and die unless they are preserved in some form or the other. The personality of objects is reflected by the knowledge within them. *Kels* can be natural, created, and altered by the forces in nature and/or artificial similarly created and altered by machine operating with AI-based rules and agents.

To some extent *kel* exhibit the propertied on physical objects that respond to mechanical forces. Direction of movement and acceleration of *kels* is derived from the resultant vector of force acting on them. Their mass and inertia can offer certain unique psychological and social properties especially when they are resident in the human mind. Even though the rules are not precise as the laws of physics, the concepts can be translated. In this vein, the universal factors (such as the human tendencies the lean toward good (seeking truth, virtue or beauty and order,

Table 24.1 Some of the suggested possible noun-objects (*no's*) and verb-functions (*vf's*) corresponding to Figure 24.1 and A, B, T, and V for a positive or "good" knowledge

		(Possible) Noun-Objects no(s)	(Possible) Verb-Function *vf*(s)	Laws of Convolution (*'s)
A	A C H I E V E M E N T	**Worldly** (humans and machines) Wealthy, affluent, prosperous, rich, financially secure, profiteers, self-interest groups **Scientific** Intellectuals, elite, researchers, dedicated, innovators, pioneers, etc.	**Worldly** (deeds and processes) Planning, organization, command, control, [5] deception, propaganda, thievery **Scientific** Research skills, contribute, persistence, goal seeking, etc.	**Worldly** (VARIATIONS) Corporate ethics, behavior, controlled aggression, greed, ruthlessness, self-interest, self-love **Scientific** Pursuit of science, laws of nature and mathematics, goal = {NO(s) (*s) VF (s)}
B	B E A U T Y	**Worldly** (humans) Celebrities, models, pageanists **Scientific** Scholars, famous, researchers, contributors, inventors, poets, painters, etc.	**Worldly** (actions and deeds) Acting, pageantry, modeling, personality enhancement, etc. **Scientific** Research skills, contribute, persistence, goal seeking, etc. Authentic, original innovations, etc.	**Worldly** (VARIATIONS) Show-personality behavior, appealing mannerisms **Scientific** Accuracy of statement, formulations, equations and time (li/less)ness of ideas, goal = {NO(s) (*s) VF(s)}
V	V I R T U E	**Worldly** (humans and machines) Social workers, charity leaders, etc. **Scientific** Philosophers, theologians, sufispreachers, reformers **Spiritual** Saint, clergy, priest, preacher, monks, rabbis, etc.	**Worldly** (deeds and processes) Benevolent, rewarding, love **Scientific** Truth in religions, beauty in deedCharitable deeds, selfless help **Spiritual** Divine deeds of monks, sufis, preachers, rabbis, imams, clergy, etc.	**Worldly** (VARIATIONS) Benevolence, selfless love **Scientific** Utilization of resources, honor, fairness, justice **Spiritual** Dedication, humility, forgiveness, acceptance goal = {NO(s) (*s) VF (s)}
T	T R U T H	**Worldly** (Humans and Machines) Sufis, religious, dedicated humans intelligent and social machines **Scientific** (humans and machines) Scholars, fame, intellectual, contributors, inventors, pioneers, intelligent knowledge systems **Spiritual** Spiritualist, universalists, inter-disciplinarians, etc.	**Worldly** (deeds and processes) Long-term deeds in education, charity, guidance, betterment **Scientific** Search for truth in sciences, fundamental equations, religions, beauty, charitable deeds, helping **Spiritual** Divine deeds of monks, sufis, preachers, rabbis, imams, monks, etc.	**Worldly** (VARIATIONS) Benevolence, untainted love for others **Scientific** Utilization of scientific resources, pursuit of honor, fairness and justice **Spiritual** Dedication, humility, forgiveness, acceptance goal = {NO(s) (*s) VF (s)}

Table Note: The table suggests positive traits for A, B, T, and V in the society. Positive noun-objects (no's), verb-functions (vf's), and their convolutions (*s) are tabulated. It is also possible to build similar table for other achievers, writers, sportsmen, teachers, etc. Noun-Objects (no's) are generally human beings, corporations, organizations, churches, mosques, synagogues, and/or charitable organization, etc. verb-functions (vf's) are generally negotiations, peaceful settlements, love, construction, reconstruction, etc. and their convolutions (*) are with sympathy, kindness, human and civil rights, understanding, and responsibility. When A, B, T, and V are present in the society and nations, everyone who can act will become a catalyst for the progress and invent new ways (convolutions) to honest, sincere, benevolent, and becomes an instrument in exponentially nurturing A, B, T, and V toward larger and more stable KELS of themselves.

Basic   NOUN OBJECTS   VERB FUNCTIONS   CONVOLUTIONS
Knowledge } $= \Sigma.\Sigma...\Sigma(no's(Who?) \rightarrow$ $vf's(What?) \rightarrow$ $*'s(How?))$
                                                                    Operations

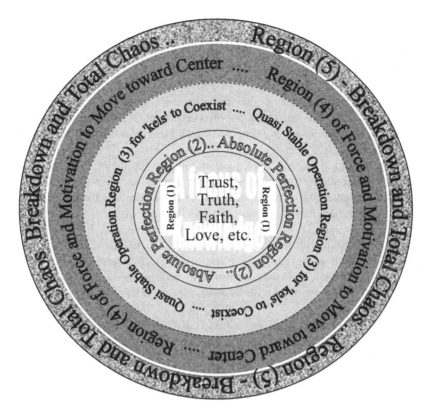

FIGURE 24.2

Depiction of the region of quasi-stability in the knowledge domain for knowledge elements "kels." Inner most circle portrays a focus (yellow print) around which kels gravitate. Typical such foci are trust, truth, love, and faith. Leaning toward the positive side such foci actions (VFs), for the betterment of society. Examples are Maxwell's or Schrödinger's equations, Ampere's or Faraday's laws, periodic tables. Typical negative foci are mistrust, falsehood, hate, and disbelief. Perfect knowledge to house any one or more of these foci is generally rarely achieved and a region of quasi stability of kels is reached in practice. For example, chemical reactions can be formulated in numerous ways (by atomic/molecular weights, valency, energy, bondage, etc.) and most ways are satisfactory; kels for both formulations can coexist. When the kels are pushed toward the outer circles, an extent of uncertainty, doubt, lack of confidence, and probability starts to creep in until total chaos is reached in the outer most annulus. At both extremes neither perfection is practical nor total chaos is tolerated and all knowledge and its kels lies where quasi-stability between knowledge(s) between numerous disciplines is reached. Different angles subtended by radial lines at the center of the focus of knowledge designate different disciplines.

justice and fairness) that influence human nature and social attitudes become applicable in the "*kel* space." After all, *kels* make up the integrated knowledge in objects that governs its constitution and behavior.

This concept is represented in Figure 24.2. The inner most core depicts the focus of knowledge. Five outer regions are indicated as: region (2) that holds the absolute perfection, region (3) that depicts an annular region for *kels* to coexist, region (4) that holds the natural and "good" nature of objects to be "perfect," and region (5) that breaks down every rule to be good and forces objects to become chaotic.

The ideal inner core of the good and socially beneficial knowledge leaning toward absolute trust, truth, faith, love, etc. is enclosed in a region of perfection. The region of *kels* to maintain a dynamic balance occurs in an annular region between the regions of absolute perfection and an inherent region of internal forces that seeks out the perfection. Reality lies near the circumference of a conceptual circle midway between the perfection and the inner motivation that seeks out perfection an very imperfect world of reality.

Kels simply float around in the region of quasi-stability where they can coexist with other *kels*. All the *kels* in this quasi-stable region constitute the impression (knowledge) of reality in the human mind. Like the impressions of reality that ebb and flow, the *kels* that form the knowledge in objects and govern their behavior, the *kels* also ebb and flow likewise.

Figure 24.3 depicts the progress of the society in the Internet age. In the top segment of the figure, the slow and systematic movement is depicted. Computers and networks facilitate the transition from one node to next in a scientific and logical progression. All the sciences and reasoning is used to make the enhancement from one node to the next with room for enhancement and modification. The movement ends in ethics (E) for the community and wisdom (W) for the general public.

When the progress in the knowledge domain is well ordered, the knowledge elements (*kels to BoKs*) also move in an orderly and methodical fashion to generate large bodies of well-founded knowledge culminating in the practice of Truth Virtue and Beauty represented as TVB in the lower section of Figure 24.3.

24.5 THE NEGATIVE AND DESTRUCTIVE SIDE OF HUMAN ACTIVITY

While the scientific progress has been impressive over the last century and contributed to the betterment of health and welfare of the society, the abuse of technologies has been destructive, devastating, and demeaning for the populous especially in the underdeveloped nations. The abuse of technology is funded by taxes in the developed nations and this technology exported to "friendly nations" at the drop of a hat who can abuse the destructive technology in an even more destructive fashion! This vicious cycle of abusive technology is not only cruel but propagates all the noun-objects and verb-function of deception (D), arrogance (and aggression, A), hate (H) [6], and shame (S).[3] In order to present the entire picture, we include this section in this paper that is antithetical to concepts in Section 24.2. The truth, beauty, virtue [2], and achievement of Section 24.2 are annihilated to make room for political and monetary gains of greedy individuals, states, and nations. We present facts without arousing emotions and should be considered as scientific part of events brought about by neglect of human rights, dignity, and honor.

---

[3]We present this section for the sake of completeness. Most authors abstain from presenting this side of human nature, hoping it will just go away. Historically, this bleak nature of behavior repeats in many forms and gets worse over the millennium. Evil does not die; it is reborn as a new species of deception, aggression, and hate bringing shame and dishonor to the society.

The Knowledge Node During the Progressive Phase in the Society

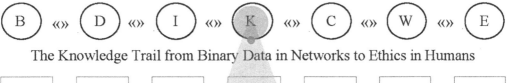

The Knowledge Trail from Binary Data in Networks to Ethics in Humans

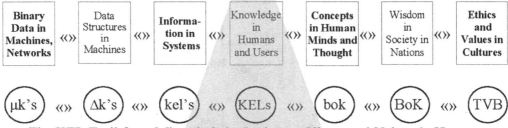

The KEL Trail from Micro-kels in Society to Virtue and Values in Humans

FIGURE 24.3

The forward movement of the society through the all-prevalent Internet and the high-speed networks that guide human activities toward an ethical society (top section of the figure) and the movement of knowledge elements (lower section of the figure) in the minds and society at large that enhance the values and virtues in nations and cultures.

In Figure 24.4, the noun-objects (*no's*) are generally individuals (war mongers, paranoids, robbers, murderers, mafia, cartels, etc.), the verb-functions (*vf's*) are generally spreading turmoil and unrest, burning and looting, rape and murder, etc., and their convolutions (*) are with ruthlessness, cruelty, hate, etc. The noun-objects (*no's*) (such as mafia, thugs, terrorists, terrorist nations, etc.), verb-functions (*vf's*) (such as ruthlessness, violence, terror, drone-bombers), and their convolutions (*'s*) (such as ways of racists, murderers, looters, killers) become dominant. When deception is tolerated in the society and nations, everyone who can act to become a catalyst to cheat, exploit, and hate thus becoming an instrument in exponentially enhancing D, A, S, and H toward larger but less stable and destructive *KELS* of themselves. Decay and negativity both are propagated and each human noun-object invents (and even machines can invent) new ways (convolutions) to deceive, cheat, and hide behind every "waterfall of lies."

Nuclear weapons, machine guns, laser guided missiles, drones, MIGs, mirage bombers, dynamite, satellite spy systems, etc. are computer-based machine counterparts of misguided human noun-objects. Computers become programmable tools of misery as technologies become abusive and destructive. In Table II portraying the negative image of Table I present the opposite extreme of the nature of human

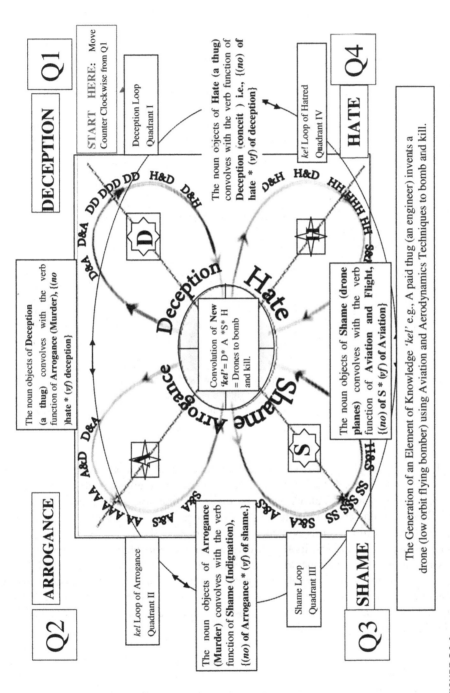

FIGURE 24.4

Example of the deployment the noun-objects (no's) of one discipline with the verb-functions (vf's) of another discipline to generate, new knowledge elements or kels in a similar or an entirely new discipline (drone Technology). Please see the text about the convolutions of D, A, H (Deception, Arrogance, Hate) that result in the Disgrace for the Society with the destructive Drone Systems.

beings. By comparing Tables I and II, it becomes clear that right can be depicted as wrong and vice versa; and evil can be portrayed as good, and vice versa. The human nature is flexible enough to adapt to the two extremes and vision can be fooled to "see" the white as black and vice versa. The sense of direction for the future can be easily reversed in the mind of young and restless. Age fortifies wisdom from past and from experience; youth offers strength and courage to dabble with the future. We propose a "wise" machine to channel the "courageous" toward a web-based knowledge positioning system that is firmly placed guidance for the mind to be efficient and optimal in the choice between "conversations" and "gossip;" "fact" and "fiction," "significant" and "trivia," "sense" and "nonsense," "reality and imagination," "truth and false," and "good and bad," etc.

24.6 INTERNET-BASED KNOWLEDGE POSITIONING SYSTEM (*KPS*)

As much as GPS can provide immediate access to physical coordinates, a knowledge positioning system provides knowledge coordinates and inform the users of where the knowledge is coming from and where it is leading based on the Internet knowledge bases (*IKBs*). The accuracy of any *kel* is based on the principle of triangulation from at least two well-founded knowledge bases. When activated, the *KPS* offers also the six mental coordinates (who, what, how, where, when, and how long) for any *kel*. Since all *kels* are dynamic, they can decay and deteriorate unless other *kels* interact to move toward a more desirable position. The *KPS* will prioritize *kels* from a utilitarian consideration unless the user may deliberately junk the *kel*. For example, gossip/junk knowledge can be allowed to be dumped/annihilated by the *KPS*. Spam *kels* are separated by filters barring junk noun objects, verb-functions, and the convolutions. For example, a spam email is a junk *kel* filtered by its own elements; its noun-object(s), its verb-functions, and its convolution(s). A deceptive claim, from a sales agency, asking to buy a particular item, can be discarded by 90% of the buyers who have bought a similar item in the last 60 days.

Useful knowledge is linked to other useful *kels* and junk *kels* may be cross linked to prior junk *kels* or allowed to die a natural decay in the mind by not remembering them. The *KPS* acts a mind cleanser by shelving the useful and/or positive *kels* and by junking the useless and/or negative *kels*. The human mind functions as a *kel* machine but the *KPS* provides some initial cleansing of *kels*.

Knowledge positioning systems (*KPS*) act as outposts between good and bad by analyzing the characteristic, of the *kels* that are in between by comparing the long, and short-term social rewards of each *kel* individually, and each cluster of *kels* dynamically. Every *no's*, *vf's*, and *'s* of every *kel* is examined individually and collectively. The expected marginal gain and loss (in this case the marginal reward and the expected risk) are evaluated by the *KAP* for every user. This deployment of the *KPS* is similar to the use of user-preference tables in an IPOD/Android device and becomes an extension of the mind set. Some of the proposed *no's*, *vf's*, and *'s* of the *kels* are presented in Tables 24.1 and 24.2. Such tables can be customized to most human activities that are essentially "good" and conversely "bad." In calibrating the *KPS*, the facts are based on history and the analysis is based on projection of the *kels*, their use or their abuse, their expected utility and their expected risk. The *KPS* functions thus, based on facts and their inference based on economic predictions of expected utility or risk to weigh and consider both. Maximizing the expected utility and/or minimizing the risk are both standard procedures in economics.

Table 24.2 *Some of the historic* noun-objects (*no's*) and verb-functions (*vf's*) corresponding to Figure 24.2 and *D, A, A, S* and *H* for a negative or "bad" knowledge

		(Possible) Noun-Objects *no(s)*	(Possible) Verb-Function *vf(s)*	Laws of Convolution (*'s)
D	D E C E P T I O N	**Worldly** (humans and machines) mercenaries, money launderers, agitators, paid killers; drones, MIGs, heat seeking missiles, machine guns, stealth bombers	**Worldly** (deeds and processes) Scientific but deceptive acts, spy activity, seek and kill, robbery, deception, false propaganda, thievery	**Worldly** (VARIATIONS) Aggression, greed, Self-love, ruthlessness, self-justification, righteousnessself-interest with aggression
		Scientific Unethical, opportunity seekers, false claimers to inventions, patents, originality and authorship,. etc,	**Scientific** Greed of wealth, power, political position, gain and self-illusion, etc.	**Scientific** Stealing and exploitation, abuse of power, position, money; personal gain = *{no(s) (*'s) vf(s)}*
A	A R R O G A N C E	**Worldly** (humans) Politicians, presidents, CFO's, and CEO's, who have brought shame to humanity by being aggressive,	Worldly (actions and deeds) Acting, pageantry, lying, dishonesty, self-justification	**Worldly** (VARIATIONS) Show-dual personality behavior, barbaric minds
		Scientific Self-proclaimed scholars, deceptive authors, stealers, false inventors, propagandists, etc.	**Scientific** False claims to inventions, patents, discoveries, drugs and prizes, etc.	**Scientific** false statements, dishonest formulations, exploitation, deceit, misrepresentations; personal gain = *{no(s) (*'s) vf(s)}*
A	S H A M E	**Worldly** (humans and machines) Hitler(s), Mao(s), War Lords, Mafia Heads, Genghis Khans, Nixon(s), slave traders, conquistadors, mirage bombers, machine guns, etc.	**Worldly** (deeds and processes) Ruthless inconsideration, dishonesty, self righteousness, indulgence and aggression. Dumb and inhuman machines.	**Worldly** (VARIATIONS) Destruction of life and habitat, senseless brutality
		Scientific Military industrial complex of 70's and 80's, war colleges, spy centers, etc.	**Scientific** Cruel exploitation of technology, authority, aimless murders and killings, state funded terrorism	**Scientific** Abuse of resources, power, public funds and elected positions
		Spiritual Mercenary bishops, clergy, monks, disoriented heads of state	**Spiritual** False trials, burning of Joan of Arc, Spanish Inquisition, false accusations and cruelty that followed, etc.	**Spiritual** No gain except the selfish short glory of the shameful; personal gain = *{no(s) (*'s) vf(s)}*
H	H A T E	**Worldly** (humans and machines) Racists, bigots, dogmatists, slave drivers and traders, war robots, satellite-based spy systems and bombers, etc.	**Worldly** (deeds and processes) Long-term deeds of cruelty, hate, murder, rape and killings	**Worldly** (VARIATIONS) War- like dictum, seek and destroy approach, infliction of injury, favor of damage
		Scientific (humans and machines) Hate machines that maximize injury and damage	**Scientific** Search for personal gain and opportunism, practice of greed, destruction of morality and ethics	**Scientific** utilization of science and weapons resources, pursuit of horror, and terrorism; personal gain = *{no(s) (*'s) vf(s)}*

24.7 INSTABILITY DURING DISORDER AND CHAOS

Human mind is sensitive to disarray and is influenced by disorder. Heightened by alarm, the mind jumps into frenzy only to cascade behavior into ruthlessness and conduct into cruelty. History has proven this shortcoming of human nature again and again. When the knowledge trail in Figure 24.3 starts to reverse, the trend can become rapid and deterioration can become exponential. Frenzy becomes fanatic and decency becomes degenerate. Decades of thoughtful achievements are blown to smithereens, and cultural reputations are "sold for a song." Eyes pop out for a loaf of bread, and modesty is molested for a drink.

In Figure 24.5, we portray the chaotic state of affairs where knowledge becomes willful arrogance and ignorance to drown ethics in a pail of water and torture Guantanamo prisoners (in the George W. Bush style of Presidency) for crimes they did not commit. Ethics can become "kill for fun" and "bomb for blast," at a very binary level depicted by the longest arrow (*a to b*) in the top part of Figure 24.5.

In the early phases of this ethical decay, the trend is slow but insidious and the reversal is gradual from node to node. During the middle stages, a sense of chaos starts to appear and the knowledge elements start to show greater disorder than behavior as portrayed in the lower part of Figure 24.5.

CONCLUSIONS

In this chapter, we have traced the role of knowledge in the conflict between "good" and "bad" in a mathematical and computational framework. The human judgment plays a decisive role in processing the knowledge gathered over the eons and guides the actions of the human being leaning in either direction but trying to navigate to a straight path between the two to avoid excessive dominance of either one. In the short term, fear ridden concepts derived from hastily acquired knowledge based on biased information has brought about the worst of human behavior and nations leaning toward aggression, selfishness and intolerance. Alternatively, concepts based on longer-term cyclic nature of forces in Nature have provided a basis for trust, understanding, and love. Myopic vision of the immediate present can become detrimental to the evolution of a better individual just as much fragmented perspective of current events can blind the longer term view. The good and the bad stand side by side for anyone to decide for one's own self.

The role of knowledge processing in unbiased machine systems forces the machines to derive their wisdom based on learning the past, interpreting the past, and reasoning toward the wise choice between good and bad. Knowledge elements gravitate based on the chronology of events leading toward perpetration and continued existence or toward transient gratification and self-consumption. Unfortunately, authenticated brand of unbiased machines can get tainted by humans in favor the short-term gratifications. A definitive code of ethics that favors the balanced role of humans becomes the most desirable outcome of any knowledge machine based on observation of the historical events. The history of humankind may repeat leading to a more evolved species of an entirely different kind or a more atrocious species of prehistoric beasts awaiting another meteor to strike!

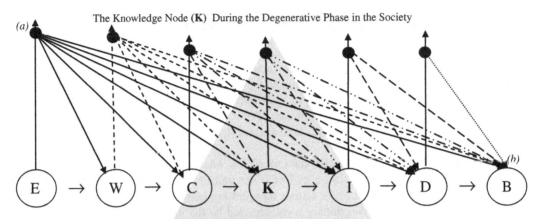

(a) Chaotic and Zig-zag shifts between the nodes of the Knowledge Trail, leading to the degeneration of Ethics (E), Wisdom (W), Concepts (C), Knowledge (K), Information (I) to garbage such as Spam and Gossip in Binary bits (B). Movement of knowledge elements or *kels* follow a chaotic movement during the breakdown of Ethics and Wisdom (such as during war, civil unrest, famine or during invasions) in society.

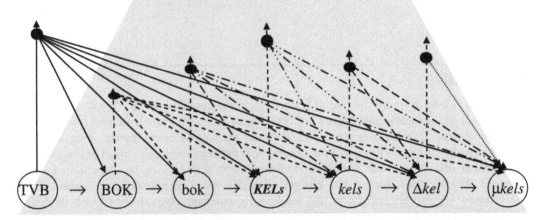

Enhanced Chaotic and added Zig-zag shifts between the nodes of the *KEL* Trail. Objects and human actions do no follow any orderly patterns causing severe social disorder (such as during WW I and II periods in US, or during the French Revolution, or the Spanish Inquisition)

FIGURE 24.5

Backward movement of the society through the Internet and the high-speed networks that accelerate the human activities toward a degenerative society (a) and the movement of knowledge elements (b) in the minds and society at large that further degrade the social and ethical values in nations and cultures.

REFERENCES

[1] Maslow AH. A theory of human motivation. Psychol. Rev 1943;50:370–96. Also see, Maslow AH. Motivation and personality. New York: Harper & Row; 1970 and Maslow A. Farther reaches of human nature. New York: Viking Press; 1971.

[2] Internet Encyclopedia of Philosophy, Aristotle (384–322 B.C.E.), <http://www.iep.utm.edu/aristotl/>, accessed March 1, 2015.

[3] Damadian RV. Apparatus and method for detecting cancer in tissue. US Patent February 5, 1974;3 (789):832 for the Invention of MRI. Also see Westbrook C. MRI in practice. 4th ed. Wiley-Blackwell; Hoboken, NJ, 2011.

[4] Stevenson RL. Dr Jekyll and Hyde Mr. Dover Thrift Editions; Dover Publications; Mineola, NY, 1991.

[5] Drucker PF. The practice of management. Harper Business; 2006.

[6] IEP, Internet Encyclopedia of Philosophy, <http://www.iep.utm.edu/aris-eth/>, accessed March 15, 2015.

[7] Ley Toffler B, Reingold J. Final accounting: ambition, greed and the fall of Arthur Andersen. New York: Crown Business; 2004.

[8] PBS.org, The Long Fall of Global Crossing, <http://www.pbs.org/newshour/bb/business-jan-june02-crossing_3-21/>; March 21, 2002. Also see, Callahan D. The cheating culture: why more Americans are doing wrong to get ahead. Mariner Books; 2004.

[9] Sussman B. The great coverup: Nixon and the scandal of Watergate. <www.watergate.info> 1995–2006. Also see Schmitz DF, Richard Nixon and the Vietnam War. Rowman & Littlefield; Washington, 2014.

[10] Taylor D. <http://www.bbc.com/news/magazine-21768668> Johnson and Vietnam war, The Lyndon Johnson tapes: Richard Nixon's "treason," accessed March 22, 2013. Also see, Berman L. No peace, no honor: Nixon, Kissinger, and the betrayal in Vietnam. Touchtone; New York, 2002.

[11] *Washington Post* and Starr K. The Starr evidence: the complete text of the grand jury testimony of President Clinton and Monica Lewinsky; Washington Post, Washington, 1998.

ROLE OF HUMAN DISCRETION IN SOCIETY AND ITS IMPACT ON ECOSYSTEMS

25

CHAPTER SUMMARY

In this chapter, we explore the local and global monitoring systems now in use, to monitor the cultural health and ethics of organizations, societies, and nations. Scanning, tracking, and extrapolating techniques are deployed to monitor the events influencing social movements in nations and organizational ethics in corporations. In conjunction with knowledge and wisdom machines, the Internet-based knowledge bases are queried to document the nature and number of incidences of cultural violations. Cultural violations in social settings (such as drug abuse, crimes, arrests, bribery, corruptions, murder, rape, nudity) that are routinely reported by news agencies and are an excellent barometer of the cultural snapshot of a nation, a community, or a society.

A statistical analysis of the incidents reveals the trend, geographical distributions and frequency of major and minor violations. Further the rate of change of such up or down trends of the violations are indicative of the cultural, cross-cultural, and counter-cultural forces in the environment. In this chapter, we further explore the type of positive forces that have given rise to great innovations (such as the backbone data networks, the Internet, wireless technologies, etc.) to benefit the society. We also report the methodology for awareness and accounting of negative force that result from cross/counter cultural forces (such as apathy, discontent, discord, denial of social rights, Presidential abuse of use, mass brutalities, illegal occupation of nations, obstruction of Justice). The use of networks combining the continuous scanning and analysis of the positive and negative events by social monitoring systems, the knowledge, and wisdom machines indicate the severity of impending changes in any culture. A fair and unbiased appraisal and the following action become crucial in mentoring the positive change and countering the negative forces. The need for National Cultural Accounting Agency (CAA) becomes as important as the need for the Central Intelligence Agency (CIA) especially in the Internet era. The system proposed is akin to the Tsunami warning systems to alert the public in the low-lying areas of any given region.

25.1 INTRODUCTION

Thoughtful deeds have shaped the global attire of civilizations. Beautiful faces emerge rarely but shine brightly for many centuries. These incidents result from the massive aggregation of positive efforts over sustained durations. Durations those have an aura of joy and happiness by being supportive of nature and society. Profound act of at most discretions sustain the profuse life on this planet are relatively few but cast an extended image of progress for many decades. In contrast,

Evolution of Knowledge Science. DOI: http://dx.doi.org/10.1016/B978-0-12-805478-9.00025-X

recklessness and indiscretion have shortened duration and reduced the chances of collective collaboration of human effort by weaving the threads of vice and greed in the attire of civilization around the world. Conflictive nature of humans with nature and society has impoverished everyone. Species are driven to extinction like lives are driven to death in a daze of confusion and horror. More civilizations have come and gone than those that have left a mark of progress and global harmony.

Like words on paper, thoughts are adrift in minds. Collectively, both have massive influence on the direction of the efforts of nations, societies, and organizations. Such efforts swing in both directions either to nurture nature to live and thrive or to drive it to agony and death. Humans against nature can slowly kill it. Like every human, nature follows her own cycles, though they are much longer and sometimes self-renewable. The evolution of the human species and the growth of western civilizations are but a tiniest fraction of most natural cycles.

The man-made cycles of the exploitation of nature are not exactly zero nor entirely negligible. The worldwide use of abusive technologies in bombs, missiles, nuclear weapons, depletion of the Ozone layer [6], etc. is now threatening the very long term of survival of the human race in some regions of the world. Nuclear armament of nations is not disarmed.[1] The profiteering from sale and profusion of offensive weapons is a way to wealth of the military-industrial complexes thriving in most "civilized nations."

In this chapter, we propose a decisive role that knowledge science and technology can play in restoring a balance between insatiable human greed and unforgiving backlash of nature. The integration of computer, information, and network technologies with the accumulated wisdom of the prior generations, now embedded in the Internet knowledge bases is perhaps the only hope of restoring a sane society from the greed for global dominance and power of the armed nations. The knowledge machines when they are not corrupted by political power or military money, moderate the course of wisdom-assisted actions for humans and nature to live a longer an7d healthier life around the globe.

25.2 **LONGEVITY OF ECOSYSTEMS**

Life is a complex mutually supportive web of relationships. The structure and constitution of these relationships have been explored by many philosophers from the ancient Greek civilizations to modern social historian and thinkers such as Gertrude Himmelfarb [1]. Economists such as Adam Smith [2] also preach about the polarity between the wealthy and the needy. The price of modern civilizations is based on the uneven distribution of wealth. Marx [3] loudly complains against the aggressive role of the wealthy in gathering more wealth for self-consumption in luxuries. Most self-consumers soon become greedy enough to impoverish the poor furthermore. Individuals, corporations, cultures, societies, and social groups become trapped in this web of wealth brightening one side of culture coin whilst the toilsome majority constitutes the dreary side of the same coin. Wealth is zero-sum entity whereas knowledge is not. Learning to live is to live to learn not to be trapped.

Most of the recent nations and organizations that rise to power have their objectives in the accumulation of massive wealth. Such acquisitions of wealth are rarely earned; they are grabbed, robbed, or nabbed by the barrage of words in the UN Security Council and weapons of war in

---

[1]United States and Russia are the worst offenders with about 7000+warheads each. United States is the only country to have used nuclear bombs in Japan and spends more money on its nuclear weapons than all countries combined!

battlefields. Such illegal grabbing, robbery, and nabbing are sometimes developed in a mad race for arms in Siberian camps, military bases, or well-funded war academies. These tactics form the bases of more illicit wealth and greater immorality in gathering such wealth. The egoistic nature of few aggressive politicians like Stalin, Mao Tse-tung, and Bush pushes nations like Russia, China, and the United States who exploit nature, sciences, and people to make gratify their shrunken egos. Yet the world respects such cruel "leaders" without regard to the rape against human rights and justice. Greatest of victories follow the noblest deeds of virtue for humankind. Filling their barren egos is like swallowing fire in their empty selves.

The renowned words of Lincoln "Government of the people, by the people, for the people" become verbal deceptions to power and "Wealth to me, by my military allies, for my greed!" The parallelism was proven by Cheney's Halliburton Corporation that amassed Billions of dollars[2] during the Iraq War under Bush! Destructive technologies for bombs and missiles [4] and nuclear weapons [5] are funded more than efforts for clean air for humankind and the further depletion of the Ozone layer [6]. These issues are posing real threats to the survival of the human race in some regions of the world.

At least two symbolic faces of the culture emerge in any nation, corporation, or society, including the church and religious organizations all seeking zero-sum entities such as wealth, power, and/or fame. The conflict is as clear as callous greed for money, power, authority, and control on one side. On the other more elegant side are the pursuit of social accord, selfless-love, concern, equality, and justice for the others. Though human nature fosters both sides, discretion, moderation, and balance perhaps constitute the three-dimensional fulcrum. This is the purpose of knowledge and wisdom machines still to arrive in a decade or two.

While the philosophers argue about the topics and society, we propose to build knowledge machines [7, 8] to be sensibly discreet, culturally moderate, and dynamically balanced based on computational algorithms and intelligent knowledge bases around the world. This computer-aided and knowledge-based social balance is never still or static but hovers around a multidimensional fulcrum without catastrophic jerks or massive swings that cause civilizations to become extinct.

Humans perhaps play the greatest and decisive role in altering the course of social and environmental events. Human discretion and conscious awareness influence their pivotal role. Information, education, and the derived knowledge form a basis for the human role to be cogent, coherent, complete, and cohesive in the ideal conditions and to conserve and manage the changes in local and global ecosystems. The nearest ecosystems are influenced first and the influence spreads into the wider arena. Families, corporations, societies, communities, and cultures are gradually manipulated by the wider participation in either (a) forward beneficial or (b) negative detrimental direction. When direction is established and movement have become epidemic, the blockage and reversal are never complete. Countercultures get as firmly ingrained as the originals. Even so, the composition of a culture has many flavors and the culture once lost will be lost forever. A new culture can be as different as a child being different from the parents. The genes of social organizations carry their distinctive code that influences every aspect of their existence. Similarities may exist but features can be noticeably different except in organizations that are fundamentally different, such as the Eskimo society and the Aztec tribes. In a social sense, human attitudes can be and are as different as apples and oranges from the same orchard. These attitudes are not genetic or inherited but acquired and cultivated. Deliberation and discretion thus play an active role in most social organizations and cultures to flex the attitude to be positive.

---

[2]Please see https://en.wikipedia.org/wiki/Halliburton and the web site https://www.quora.com/How-much-money-did-Dick-Cheney-mak....?

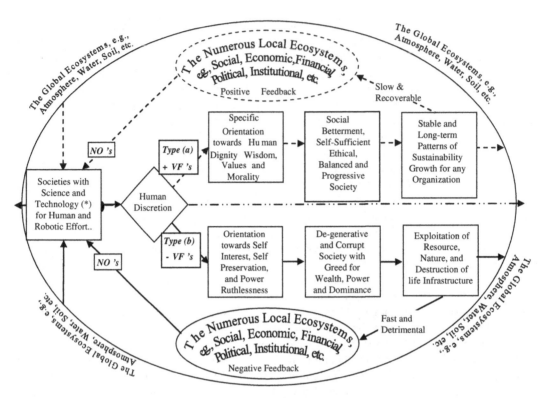

FIGURE 25.1

Key role of human discretion that swings the course of actions (+VF or −VF) for being wise and ethical or being shrewd and exploitive. The classic writings of early economists such as Adam Smith call for economy to move forward by preaching nations and industries to gather wealth and power but fail to point to the limitations of Nature and resources of global humankind (NO's) to be exploited (*'s). The foundation of global ecology is left in the swamps of ignorance, even though natural resources are a zero-sum entity. The concept of social justice is discarded causally by the distribution of paycheck to the toiling majority. The basis of capitalism is less blameworthy than the lack of discretion on the part of leaders responsible for change in nations and organizations.

In free spirited societies and organization, discretion plays a dominant trend-setter. When knowledge machines are programmed to emulate and possibly predict behavior of individuals, organizations, and societies, considerable uncertainty arises due to the differences in human nature. The behavior of sane and rational individuals and groups can only be estimated with good confidence based on the data, information, and knowledge gathered over a long periods. Based on this reasoning, we suggest two tendencies: (a) the compassionate and the benevolent and (b) the cruel and brutal. These are the two extremes human nature. The later tendencies of human entities and flimsy and are not irrefutable laws (like the laws of Maxwell or Schrödinger in Physics) but are noticeable in the disposi-tion of the attitude such as greed and self justification for global dominance, wealth, corporate policies, and their actions.

The actions (verb-functions or vfs and VFs) of these two groups affect the society differently and depicted in Figure 25.1. The dashed lines in the top of the Figure lead to social stability and perhaps more gradual changes in the social ecosystems that host the organizations and the solid lines in the lower half of this figure lead to rapid gain in wealth, power, authority, and control but deplete the infrastructure of natural and human resources: in fact they do not stop at robbing human dignity of others. Such opportunists are plentiful in society but are well camouflaged in their jobs and salesmanship.

25.3 THE SEVEN NODES TOWARD POSITIVE SOCIAL CHANGE

In the former case with Type (a) of predisposition (see Fig. 25.1), stability and recovery from the necessary changes are much more promising by an orderly scientific orientation and a set of well implemented transition procedures. Fortunately, the sign posts and anchor points are well established in both computer and network sciences. When mapped in a conformal basis, these target areas in social/behavioral and knowledge sciences start to become evident. In this era of computer and communication technologies, the binary bits (Node B) to encode data and its structure (Node D) and organized data structures as information (Node I) are firmly established. The seven stages of progress are highlighted as the B, D, I, K, C, W, and E nodes in the top half of Figure 25.2.

During this stage of infancy of knowledge science and social sciences, the targeted areas are identified in Figure 25.1 as concept (Node C), wisdom (W), moving ethics and values (E), all three firmly based in knowledge (Node K) bases around the world. The relentless human mind will never cease to derive fine steps between these nodes or to invent the hardware and algorithms to achieve them to build science-based concept bases (CBs), society-based wisdom bases (WBs), and cultural-based ethics/morality bases (EBs) to be posted on Internet-II and Internet-III. Such bases will become as common as electronic dictionaries and encyclopedias, now posted on the Internet. Personal discretion and creativity are not hampered by these new bases; instead, they are channeled into a positive frame.

25.4 SEVEN NODES TOWARD NEGATIVE SOCIAL CHANGE

In the latter case with Type (b) of predisposition (see Fig. 25.1), the downward slide of the counter-culture (of 1980s in the United States) is depicted. The born-free spirit of the baby-boom-era adults then (1980s) in the prime of their lives had successfully launched the challenge to an established framework of wisdom and ethics and replaced them with self-centered oracles and self-made ethics. This change of the "educated and elite" is depicted in the lower half of Figures 25.1 and 25.2. The aftermath is the litter in culture with nudity, prone TV shows, "Russian brides" for pastime, and sex-slaves for trade. The seven stages of negative social change are depicted as D/D, N/D, S/S, A/A, G/P, O/K, and B/C in the lower section of Figure 25.2.

Figure 25.2 depicts the details in the movements of the culture cross-culture and counterculture. In the top half, the established norms of the conservative culture are mapped. In the lower half, the forces of the counterculture are shown. Whereas the nodes in the establish culture are noun-objects, the nodes from the counterculture are verb-functions trying to dislodge the very foundation of concepts on which ethics are founded. Generally the tendencies toward counterculture emerge after the

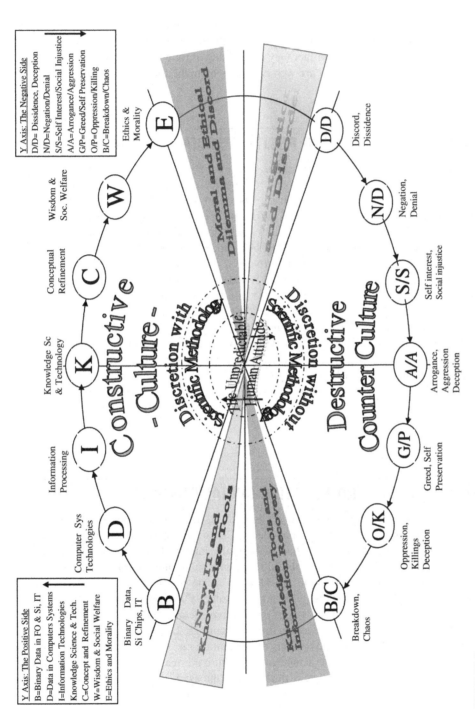

FIGURE 25.2

The role of computer systems and networks in quadrant I (i e., $+X$ and $+Y$) is projected into quadrant II (i e., $-X$ and $+Y$) to make machines more human in finding new knowledge from information, concepts from knowledge, wisdom from concepts and ethics from wisdom. Knowledge machines to help resolve additional human limitations in the lower two quadrants of the figure are proposed.

populous in a culture has acquired apathy and discontent. The seven nodes of counterculture are presented as follows.

25.4.1 **THE D/D NODE**

The first node is marked as D/D (for disillusion/discord, disarray/dissidence, disharmony, and disobedience). This state appears when the wisdom is discarded, and ethics are challenged. This stage follows a slow (or even a violent) collapse of the ethics and morality of the prior era. This tendency in society parallels the tendencies in free spirited humans who seek postmarital relations and in children who discard the parental guidance during childhood. Be it a search of new planets or be it a mere quest for a challenge, the spirit of adventure can prove to be necessary, or it can prove to be disastrous. Gradual and rational changes are goal of wise humans and wisdom machines. Transitions that are a part of nature, generally occur to favor growth and variety in life forms during evolutionary era of species.

25.4.2 **THE N/D NODE**

Order, structure, and social setting are the key constituents that give rise to discipline and culture. All three are evident in the foundation of sciences, development of technologies, and in migration from one node to the next in the top section of Figure 25.2. In a converse mode, negation of order and denial of logic (N/D) can become chaotic during the up rise of the counterculture. Such countercultures have become uncontrolled and unruly leading to short 2013 Tiananmen Square in China or as the prolonged resistance movement (1942—47) to force the British to quit India.

Countercultures need a well-defined course toward social betterment to become a positive culture but a well defined course to destroy ethic and values (see Node E in Fig. 25.2) can only be detrimental. Self-fulfilling goals charted against nature are even more devastating. Nature as global resource can be depleted by reckless spending or extreme greed.

25.4.3 **THE S/S NODE**

When order and structure are disrupted (see Node 2) in the society the self-interest of the mid-culture starts to become evident. Social injustices become prevalent and become justifiable. Left unabated, such exploitations and practices can last for many decades and even centuries such as those in the South Africa after the De Beers family took over the diamond mines in 1888. Other examples of British and Portuguese exploitation existed in India before 1947 amidst the chaos and bloodshed they have themselves created.

25.4.4 **THE A/A NODE**

During this phase, the arrogance and aggression by either culture are frequent. The French arrogance in the Polynesian regions and British reign of terror in South Africa speaks of the high handedness in occupied regions. Insolence of the immoral and aggression of the armed members in either culture sets the stage for public phobia of the future. History has repeated itself during the Marxist regimes and then again during the two Russian revolutions (February and Bolshevik,

1917). All counter cultural movements are not famous but their character lingers even in minor sociological events such as the city and county elections where the transition is legal and gradual. The arrogant and aggressive get gradually replaced. The basic nature of the population leans toward harmony rather than horror.

25.4.5 THE G/P NODE

Greed and self-preservation marked as (G/P) in Figure 25.2 are extreme recurrences of the earlier (S/S) node depicting self interest and social injustice. Dominant members of the two conflicting cultures resort to illegal and unacceptable practices and behavior to rescue their positions and status. Such extreme behavior is also common in business and in society when one administration is being taken over by the other. Ethics are trashed and self-preservation lasts over long periods.

25.4.6 THE O/K NODE

Brutality, oppression, and killing can coexist with the three prior needs to extend the chaos in a fallen culture. However, if the counterculture is for human betterment and is toward justice, these three nodes are quickly suppressed and the more stable ethical practices quickly take over.

In some instances, such as during Spanish Inquisition started in 1478 by the Catholic Monarch Ferdinand II of Aragon and Isabella I of Castile, provided the Catholic popes and clergy an excuse to seize the assets of lawful citizens, exile people, and commit murders. The duration was agonizing and painful.

Humans and machines learn from the past but machine retain historic wounds unleashed on civilizations indefinitely unless the subversive nature of a few humans is bent upon repeating such atrocities. It is our contention that unadulterated wisdom machines [8] will forewarn sensible human beings of disgrace of similar actions. Such machines can be programmed to block such highhanded humans who can bring shame to humanity by freezing their income and assets.

25.4.7 THE B/C NODE

Breakdown and chaos are the final and extreme truncation of the conflict of cultures. At this node the laws of jungle govern the savage society. Due to its extreme nature, chaos is short lived and normality returns by willful and deliberate actions of the ruling majority. The balanced outlook of few dictates the constitution for the future. The US Constitution (signed on September 17, 1787) was created to increase the federal authority and yet to protect the basic rights of citizens.

Conflicts are resolved by compromise and the expected rewards in the future overcome the greed for immediate resolution of needs. By and large, society finds a way out of the chaos even though the solution many not be optimal or least painful. The role of knowledge and wisdom machines is to support the human beings in a scientific and artificially intelligent fashion much like the modern computers that help the medical profession by Internet-based medical bases around the world. The bias and the self-interest of humans are practically eliminated. Stability of the solutions and fairness are achievable to needs of opposing societies and cultures, humans and nature, labor and management, etc.

CONCLUSIONS

The use of advanced computer and communication technologies that have made the Internet available in (almost) every household is proposed to monitor the slow and insidious social and cultural trends. Information processing by itself is inadequate to identify the drifting patterns in society. Artificial Intelligence (AI) tools and technologies embedded in knowledge and wisdom machines [7,8] become powerful enough to analyze and track social profiles of nations, communities, societies, and organizations. Together with content-based Internets (i.e., the Internet II and possibly the Internet III), these machines can scan the social horizons like planetary telescopic systems scan for movements in the cosmic horizons. The computer vision (CV) software and routines need to be tracked and registered with the ethical and cultural profiles of social and national organizations.

Being realistic about the potential of the future machine and being concerned with the downward trends in the society, it is challenge to the elite to consider the unthinkable: that unadulterated mind and wisdom machines (see Chapter 29) enforce ethical and moral standards upon the ruthless, the destructive and the greedy segment of populations that transgress human rights, social justice and who abuse their power and authority. After all, the Judiciary within every nation has such a task clearly delineated. The new breed of machines propels the notions of scholars and saints with the words of the Constitution and with the teachings in the Bill of Rights.

REFERENCES

[1] Himmelfarb G. One nation, two cultures: a searching examination of American society in the aftermath of our revolution. Vintage; 2001.
[2] Smith A. The wealth of nations. Buffalo, NY: Prometheus Books; 1991.
[3] Karl Marx. *"Das Kapital"*, Samual Moore (Translator), CreateSpace Independent Publishing Platform of Amazon.com; http://www.amazon.com, 2011.
[4] See Internet Websites, <https://en.wikipedia.org/wiki/Ballistic_missile>, <https://en.wikipedia.org/wiki/Intercontinental_ballistic_missile>.
[5] See <https://en.wikipedia.org/wiki/IAnti_ballistic_missile>, for missiles, ICBM's, and anti-ballistic missiles. Web pages accessed July 15, 2015. See the UN Webpage <http://www.un.org/disarmament/WMD/Nuclear/> accessed June 2015. Also see <http://www.icanw.org/the-facts/nuclear-arsenals/> Page accessed June 2015.
[6] See National Geographic Website, <http://environment.nationalgeographic.com/environment/globalwarming/ozone-depletion-overview/>, page accessed June 2015.
[7] Ahamed SV. Intelligent Internet knowledge networks. Hoboken, NJ: Wiley Interscience; 2007.
[8] Ahamed SV. Computational framework for knowledge. Hoboken: Wiley; 2009.

SECTION

PREFACE

III

PART II, SECTION III, SUMMARY

Section 03 with five chapters (26 to 30) deals with the migration of computer-based knowledge machines to socially oriented mind and medical machines. Though both sets of machines are hardware and computer oriented, the knowledge machines deal with rationality and programming to solve generic problems on a scientific and quantitative basis, whereas the socially oriented mind machines driven by individual needs of the human users, and as medical machines derived from the condition and status of physiological (or even emotional) health of any user. The former category of machines operates on universal noun-objects, verb-functions and their convolutions. The latter category of machines operates on the relation between the individual user in relation to the society and environments. Personal knowledge bases are coupled with Internet knowledge bases of healthy and well adjusted human beings. To some extent, the approach is modeled from the work of Maslow, who presented the statistical studies of healthy and well adjusted successful people in the society and constructed his pyramid of needs. In this part, we compare the medical evaluation of any users' status the mind (chapter 29) and body (chapter 30) to modify, enhance and surpass the "average" mind quotient and bodily health condition. Both machines offer users scientific-and knowledge- advantages over Internet users by incorporating built-in tools of creativity and mechanized selection and access to Internet Knowledge bases to supplement the resources of their uneven minds.

Human adaptability and creativity deserve the intellectual supremacy that processors and media cannot deliver. Programmed performance has its distinct limitations for the nature and depth of the solutions offered. The social pathways that accompany the neuron nets offer the beauty and variations that human beings flavor are relish. The variety of the human solutions is the expression of intelligence that people expect and deserve to circumvent the crevasses of boredom. In this arena of human agility, machine fall behind humans as humans have fallen behind in the areas of processing and communication.

Children, adults, fun seekers and game players are becoming more sophisticated. The expectations from devices, switches and the communication media are high. Though this trend is not evolutionary, it is very human to compete with gadgets and chip designers still have a challenge in offering the best solutions to the social situations that human being face in the daily life. Humanist machines that imitate behavioral tendencies are not social machines that construe the local and global nature of social problems of individuals and societies. Further, they intelligently construct a satisfactory solution, if not an optimal solution to such problem(s).

Being functionally akin to the global positioning systems (GPS) that offer roadways to specific destinations, the social machines offer numerous possible solutions to specific social problems or between two social situations between human beings or knowledge centric objects. The solutions are tailored to the traits of the users, their past preferences and social tendencies. The solutions form the starting basis for the user to fine tune and may not be optimal every time. The social machines adapt to current socioeconomic conditions, and the solution remains rational in a global fashion thus saving time and energy to resolve most social problems that abound.

SCIENTIFIC FOUNDATIONS OF KNOWLEDGE

26

CHAPTER SUMMARY

In this chapter, we propose that knowledge can be initially designed like any scientific object such a rudimentary automobile, airplane, or spacecraft. The premise is based on the theme that a specific body of knowledge rests on the embedded noun objects and the structural relation between these key-groups of knowledge centric objects (*KCOs*). The events, interactions, and forces in the society alter such *KCOs* and their structural relationships. The design of knowledge deploys a very pragmatic approach that knowledge based on these key objects, their interrelationships, and their interactions can be processed by knowledge machines. To this extent, we follow pragmatism (see Rows 5 and 6 in Table 12.1B) proposed by John Dewey and Nathan Crick (see Section 12.2.6), but we also propose that knowledge undergoes dynamic changes in the society, the minds of human beings, and the knowledge structures stored in the memories and knowledge banks of the machine and the Internet. Structures of knowledge can be altered in the knowledge processing units of knowledge machines much like data structures are altered in the central processor units of traditional computers.

In a covert fashion, the design of *any* object (any object at all) has some piece of information or knowledge that it communicates and thus, the science of knowledge is invariably linked with the science of *all* objects. The validity of this axiom lies its converse, i.e., objects that do not have *any* linkage to *any* knowledge are non-entities. The scientific foundation of knowledge is the science of all objects that encompasses physical sciences and metaphysical considerations.

26.1 INTRODUCTION

To a large extent, society processes knowledge in a clandestine and continual fashion. The social processes modify prior knowledge at numerous levels ranging from gossip to creative problem solving. These processes update the bodies of knowledge (*BoKs*). The mind stashes away these *BoKs* and updates the memory. At the lowest levels, gossip and rumors are plentiful and at the highest levels, profound scientific contributions heighten the pinnacles of wisdom. Human mind handles these accordingly. Knowledge machines simulate such knowledge dynamics in the society and follow certain intrinsic flow patterns to make the flow of knowledge organized, structured, scientific, useful, and possibly benevolent to the society. Left unattended and ignored, knowledge can assume hideous dimensions and confusing shapes that rattle human perceptions.

Human endeavor and knowledge are securely intertwined. Total independence of either is nearly impossible since both have a continuum of the neural paths in the mind and space, and the continuity of time in reality; both change accordingly. The rate of change of knowledge alters the mental

Evolution of Knowledge Science. DOI: http://dx.doi.org/10.1016/B978-0-12-805478-9.00026-1

state and the vice versa and to this extent change in one is driven by the energy in the other. The evolution of computer systems over the last few decades has altered this balance slightly. We have learned to alter the status of either one incrementally but for short durations. Computation without comprehension is as utterly useless as thought without confirmation.

Scientific representation, validation, attestation, and verification enhance the utility of any thought process. Amidst the latter processes, mathematics, computation, programming, and numerical corroboration with other observations start to gain foothold. The entire structure from human thought to derived social value becomes a discipline. Knowledge provides a background of continuum in the entire discipline and humans manipulate knowledge as much as comprehension manipulates human action. The long feedback can become frustrating to differentiate between cause and effect. In order to avoid dead ends in knowledge science, we suggest building bridges in the well-established islands of knowledge where sciences have made deep in roads and highways. For example, science and spirituality may not be directly connected, but the human mind-soul relation provides a link. Before Charles Darwin, evolution of species and forces of nature were not directly linked, but the logical basis of his reasoning provided the basis for accepting his flawless logic.

Where there has been no utility in mere thought process, humans have enjoyed tittle-tattle, chit-chat, hearsay, gossip, rumor, and even scandal at the lowest end of knowledge processing (*KP*). Conversely, when there is universal significance in thought processes of individuals, societies, nations, and human kind, the flavor of KP becomes significant enough to bring about breakthroughs (e.g., the steam engine, transistor, fiber optics) and revolutions (French, industrial, knowledge, network, etc.). All aspects of all sciences are invoked at the higher end of *KP*. The convergence of thought needs the concurrence of truth drawn from all disciplines. Human constructs are crossing barriers in knowledge thus altering the structure and bounds of knowledge to navigate the mind born free that knows no structure nor any bounds.

26.2 INFRASTRUCTURE OF SCIENCES

Knowledge is basis of science and science is organization of knowledge. Knowledge and science form a bonded pair to pursue progress. Embedded in this synergy is the underlying commitment that human values and ethics will be preserved and enhanced. In a sense, knowledge has evolved to serve humankind. More than ever before complete, precise, and incisive knowledge holds the key toward being successful, optimal, and efficient. Unsubstantiated knowledge can soon become embarrassing, misleading, dangerous, destructive, and devastating.

When knowledge is considered as a resource and as utilitarian, its accuracy and its preservation become essential. Left unattended and unprocessed, even basic scientific and benevolent knowledge can become gossip and rumor; conversely, the myths and legends may become laws and norms in the society. Such transpositions are abundant in history and numerous cults have left painful memories in the pages of Western society. In a more immediate sense and in the context of the Internet age, high speed networks add an additional element of complexity to the social transactions and transpositions and can become weapons of mass deception rather than backbones of constructive communication.

Physics leads into electricity and magnetism and then into electrical engineering. Being procedural, quantitative, and pragmatic, it becomes feasible to navigate directly into electrical

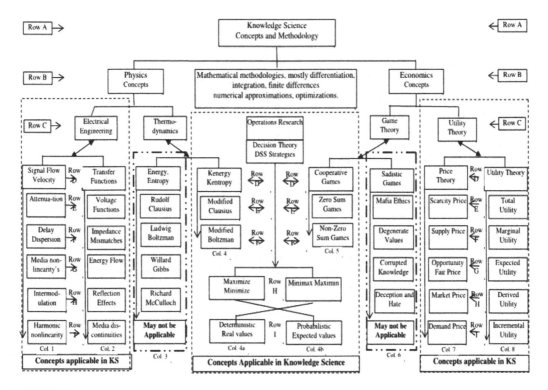

FIGURE 26.1

Conceptual-platform matrix for knowledge science (*KS*) derived from scientific perspective of physicists and electrical engineers (columns 1–4) as much as it is derived from behavioral perspective of economists and game theorists (columns 4–8). These intertwined concepts in the knowledge domain are discussed in Section 5.

engineering, signal transmission, and processing at the outset. Being human and behavior minded, it becomes feasible to navigate directly into Marshall's utility theory and then into von Neumann's game theory. At the broad intersection of the two major disciplines, the domain of knowledge sciences can be discovered with relative ease. The quantitative issues are addressed by (the laws) of physics and the behavioral issues are guided by (the laws) of economics. Figure 26.1 depicts the resources in different disciplines that form a broad overview of knowledge science.

26.3 PLATFORM OF PURE SCIENCES

26.3.1 ROLE OF PHYSICS

Physics provides deep insights of concepts and a rich methodology for quantitative verifications and leads into the technologies that have proved valuable to the society. In pursuing the role of physics to establish knowledge science, electrical engineering, and signal processing become prime contributors and depicted as columns 1 and 2 of Figure 26.1.

Most of these tools and techniques from pure science and applied sciences may not be directly compatible for the analysis and quantification of knowledge (*KCOs* and *BoKs*) nor the knowledge elements (*vfs'*, **'s*, and *ns'*). However, when appropriately transformed into knowledge domain from own domains, the noun objects (*KCOs*, *BoKs*, and *ns'*) start to exhibit similar relationships. For example, the change of structure from KCO_i to KCO_{i+1} would need energy. This energy would be appropriately measured as human (or machine) work at a given level of expertise for "*t*" seconds.

As an example if a *KCO* represented as ($F = m.a$) needed five years of Newton's time, then the energy of the *KCO* would be five (Newton-caliber)-years, etc. On the other hand, if a knowledge machine was used to derive this equation and it took one day of knowledge machine, then the energy of the *KCO* would be one modern-*KM* day.

As another example if it took 50 years for the naked human eye (KCO_i) to identify the rings of Saturn and it takes 10 minutes of the radio telescope (KCO_{i+1}) at Mauna Kea (Hawaii) to detect the rings, then the *kenergy* of Saturn rings is 50 (naked-eye-caliber-retina processor) years or 10 (Mauna kea-caliber image processor) minutes. Equating the two timings, the processor power of Mauna Kea radio telescope entity is 2.628 million ($= 50 \times 365 \times 24 \times 60/10$) times faster than the naked eye retina processor to be able to detect ring type configurations elsewhere, etc. Linearity is assumed in this case. When human ingenuity and intelligence are involved, the transformation of time scales becomes personality and creativity dependent.

On an incremental basis, if a student in a state i (i.e., a typical high school graduate or KCO_i) needs to be transformed to a state i+1 (i.e., a college graduate or KCO_{i+1}), the extra energy required would be 4 years (freshman to senior level) years at each of the four levels of learning. Stated alternatively, if the level of learning is averaged as the sophomore-junior caliber level, then it take 4 years of learning (=work done or power of the student at the middle level multiplied by 4 years of time) by the sophomore-junior caliber student.

26.3.2 ROLE OF ELECTRICAL ENGINEERING

Electrical engineering offers the extensive rigor of most well-known scientists who have contributed to the measurement of power and energy. The unit of power has been established since the days of James Watt (1736–1819). This unit of power range from lowest (femtowatt (10^{-15} of a watt)) to the highest (petawatt (10^{15} watts)). The range for energy is also very wide from femtowatt-secs to terawatt-hrs or even petawatt-centuries. All these derived units fall back on the unit of power of one watt or W, i.e., one Joule per second. It becomes advantageous to find if this chain of reasoning of the early scientists will lead to customized units of power and energy in the knowledge domain. The units for *kenergy* are derived from the writings of Clausius [1,2], Boltzman [3,4], Gibbs [5,6], and MaCulloch [2] in the field of thermodynamics (see boxes at rows C, D, E, F in column 3 of Figure 26.1).

Signal transmission and processing bears a good deal in common with knowledge flow and KP. Both signals and knowledge suffer degradations and distortions (attenuation and dispersion), both get contaminated and get cleansed, both get transmitted and get recovered, both suffer losses and leakages, and both need power and energy to propagate. Accordingly, there is sufficient overlap between the two realms of signal flow and knowledge flow. In pursuing the mechanisms behind the signal and knowledge flows, entities such as voltages (nominal, maximum, and effective values), currents (nominal, maximum, and effective values), impedances (Ohmic values), signal to noise ratios (*SNRs*), losses (resistive wattages), phase shifts, power and energy (transmit and received), reflections, and phase distortions bear notable anomalies in the knowledge and information domain. The methodologies of signal transmission in electrical circuits and media are used to derive the transformation matrix for the social media as information and knowledge traverse such social media. The nature of the matrix is presented in Ref. [7]. See boxes at rows C through I in columns 1 and 2 of Figure 26.1.

This signal flow in electrical engineering and knowledge flow in social media is explained when two objects *n1* and *n2* interact in a humanistic machine. If objects *n1* and *n2* have similar characteristics and work in a non-resistive mode, the information and knowledge content will flow from *n1* to *n2* and vice versa without distortions, reflections, attenuation, and dispersion. This is a direct corollary of the equations in data and signal flow through transmission lines, circuits, and electromagnetic fields.

Additionally, the magnitude and phase of reflected and transmitted signals bear established algebraic relations [8] to the differences in the media characteristics. An estimation of the refraction and reflection effects of any given *KCO* or *BoK*, at the boundary of two inhomogeneous social media (e.g., two different cultural environments), is feasible by a comparison of the transformation matrices for the media surrounding the boundary.

26.4 ROLE OF THERMODYNAMICS

This offshoot of physics becomes instrumental in accommodating the highly variable nature of human beings and social entities. Thermodynamics offers a framework to instill the initial knowledge level of *n1* and *n2* and the individual characteristics of both. Thermodynamics plays the desirable role in tailoring the programs for machines to individual human entities that deploy them. In an oblique framework, heat flow also imitates knowledge flow, but all the laws of thermodynamics (especially, the specifying the conservation of energy (and heat)) are not applicable in the knowledge domain.

However, it is possible to view the *kenergy* of *n1* in relation to the changes of *kentropy* in *n2* via a transfer-function. Such transfer-functions are generally used in signal flow analysis where active circuit component can and do amplify the signal levels. The admixture of concepts and (mathematical) methodologies from electrical engineering and thermodynamics will permit a knowledge scientist to follow the flow of *KCOs* and *BoKs* from different objects (*n1* and *n2*) and be precise about the changes in the *kenergies* and *kentropies*. The framework of thermodynamics offers an excellent platform to deal with (k)energy and (k)entropy. Even though the second laws of thermodynamics are not applicable in the knowledge domain, the concepts of energy and entropy find abundant commonality. When knowledge centric objects interact and find an operational stability, the energies of the driving entity play a significant part in altering the entropy of the reacting entity and vice versa. When the definition of Clausius [1,2] and the derivations of Boltzmann [4,6] are brought to bear in the way human and social entities should be treated as unique "objects," then the interaction between "who" (an unique *KCO*) deals with "whom" (another unique *KCO*) can be interjected as particular coefficients of "who" and "whom."

26.5 PLATFORM OF SOCIAL SCIENCE

26.5.1 ROLE OF ECONOMICS

The laws of economics find a quick entry in knowledge sciences. To a large extent, humans treat knowledge as an economic entity. In a pragmatic sense, knowledge has value, it has a price, and it yields utility. Aspects from numerous price theories in economics and the utility theory of Marshall's [9] and then the marginal utility theories [10] shed light upon the way humans deal, achieve, manage, and utilize all utilitarian objects including knowledge, See rows C through I of columns 7 and 8 of Figure 26.1. When humans control machines to explore the knowledge domain, the machines provide a mathematical framework wherein the expected utility of the effort is maximized in one or numerous dimensions.

Decision theory (from operations research or OR) lurks in the knowledge ware programs and their behavioral libraries. When the utility is not deterministic and can only be expected, the game theory brings in the individualistic character of a particular human or of a particular social entity. In a very pragmatic sense, knowledge needs management and utility of knowledge needs maximization according to Marshall. In a very humanistic sense, knowledge needs to benefit and satisfy the individual and social character of the entities that use the machines.

26.5.2 ROLE OF GAME THEORY

Morgenstern and von Neumann [11] have initially formulated game theory to shed some light upon the way humans deal, achieve, utilize, manage, and utilize knowledge. When humans control machines to explore the knowledge domain, the machines provide a mathematical framework wherein the expected utility of the effort is maximized in one or numerous dimensions.

The game theory concepts impact decision theory (from operations research or OR) in two areas; in the deterministic setting the most economic decisions become readily evident and in the nondeterministic setting, situational and estimation of gathered evidence also enter the decision-making process, but in a probabilistic sense. Such approaches are common in medical field when the doctors start to investigate other clues that either substantiate or refute the partial decisions about the prior conclusions.

Typically, knowledge-ware programs and their behavioral libraries would provide some direction to this type of decision-making based on past experience and "best" guess. The chances of making the correct decision can only be increased but not assured. In a very pragmatic sense, knowledge libraries need updating and management. This role of knowledge science becomes even more precarious when the *KCOs* play a (intelligent) conflictive games without any "rules of the game" except to be opportunistic and deceptive. This part of the knowledge science dealing with the negative side of humans and "negative" knowledge is depicted in column 6 of Figure 26.1. The laws of affirmative knowledge cannot be simply reversed to plough through this column and the negative creativity starts to fuel a very undesirable negative humanistic machine.

26.5.3 INTEGRATION OF TWO PLATFORMS

Integration of the pure sciences, physics in particular (Dewey Decimal System or DDS 530), and electrical engineering (DDS 620) with social sciences, economics in particular (DDS 330), is possible because of universal tools and techniques of mathematics, computer sciences, and knowledge sciences that run through all these disciplines. Social behavior (DDS 304) and social interactions (DDS 302) also play a role in knowledge sciences because humanistic objects (*KCOs*) treat knowledge as a utilitarian commodity. Behavioral patterns of social entities and objects become important in the emulation of such (*KCOs*). Unfortunately, the mathematical tools and procedures are not well documented in the DDS 302 and DDS 304, but some of the behavioral modes can be emulated as programmable computer processes [7].

26.5.4 ROLE OF MATHEMATICS

Calculus plays the most comprehensive role, even though operations research, game theory, probability and statistics (if they are considered as branches of mathematics) also influence the specialized techniques for the knowledge domain. Differentiation, integration, and partial differential equations have established inroads in econometrics, micro, and macroeconomics. Almost all topics in economics deploy differentiation, partial differentiation, and/or finite differentials of economic quantities. As it is knowledge sciences, economics deals with objects and entities that are dynamic and constantly changing making mathematics, its tools and techniques transparent between the disciplines. But more than that, the concepts and patterns behind behavior also experience commonality.

Integration leads to cumulative effects of and upon economic objects in economics and *KCOs* in knowledge science. The effect of time is handled by time series analysis and discreet algebraic methods in economics and analysis of observed data. Both these methods find applicability in knowledge science via the observation of social and individual knowledge centric objects. For example, if an active noun object *n1* initiates a verb function (v) or a convolution of verb functions (*v's*) directed toward a noun object *n2*, then a time series analysis of the behavior of *n2* will reflect the effectiveness of one strategy for implementing versus another, or the effects of one teaching methodology versus another, and so on.

Almost all aspects of the mathematics appear applicable in knowledge sciences. In most other discipline, the role of nonlinear effect may not be as predominant as those in knowledge sciences. Human and social *KCOs* display the most variable characteristic responses to verb function (*v's*) or a convolution of verb functions (**v's*). The incremental changes in *kenergy* and *kentropy* can also display large swings and nonlinear effects.

26.5.5 ROLE OF COMPUTER SCIENCE

During the seminal stages knowledge science, the methodologies for designing and constructing comprehensive software systems are readily applicable. The whole array of software associated the almost all branches of computer science (e.g., knowledge base system design, knowledge management, library systems, AI, and intelligent systems) will find way into knowledge science and its management. The use of existing computer sciences (S) and its deployment will become essential for knowledge sciences (*KS*). After all *KS* is a superstructure atop CS.

26.5.6 ROLE OF KNOWLEDGE-WARE

The tools for signal flow analysis are not established for the flow of knowledge in humanistic sciences. However, the exchanges of energies and entropies between interacting objects may be analyzed in reasonable detail and with fair accuracy by falling back to laws of thermodynamics. Great deal of caution is necessary because there is no law of knowledge that preserves *kenergy*. Knowledge (energy) that is shared is not depleted at the source. For this reason, the laws of thermodynamics cannot be indiscriminately pushed into knowledge science. To some extent knowledge science is unique even though there are threads of reasoning akin to those in physics (especially electrical engineering and thermodynamics), signal processing, transmission theory, and finally economics.

To the extent that there is considerable framework of electrical engineering that can lead to the core of knowledge science, we deploy the treatment of these parameters such as voltages, currents, power, energy, attenuation, dispersion. To the extent that there is some methodologies of thermodynamics that can lead to the computation of *kenergy* and *kentropy*, we deploy the treatment of the thermodynamic parameters such as energy and entropy. To the extent that there are concepts from signal processing and transmission engineering such as echo cancellation, equalization, feedback stabilization, and noise reduction, we deploy to the signal processing text in Ref. [8] and transmission engineering texts such as Ref. [12]. To the extent that *KCOs* and noun objects find their equilibrium with other *KCOs* and noun objects, based on the laws of marginal utility and utility theory, we refer to any elementary text [13] in economics.

26.6 FRAMEWORK OF KNOWLEDGE

In the information age, the frontiers of knowledge reach far and wide and across many disciplines and integrate their boundaries. Internet space has no geographical or subject precincts. The IP address permits global navigation. On the human side, knowledge being primordial encompasses the human mind completely. However, knowledge overloads can almost drown the senses. In a balanced proportion with human perception, knowledge nourishes the mind. When the overall human comprehension is intact, it is comprehension that encompasses knowledge. Knowledge and comprehension play out a beautiful embrace at each others' door steps. This symbiotic interdependence can last a life time, each stretching the bounds of the other.

Rather than be carried in a philosophic encounter, we propose a pragmatic and diagrammatic approach that establishes a reasonable pause in the deep embrace between knowledge and perception to explore the synergy between the two. Knowledge becomes the foundation of perception for an interval of time and then perception becomes the foundation of expansion of knowledge for the next interval which in turn calls for greater perception. Incremental gain in knowledge brings in new paradoxes for the mind to perceive. The cycle rotates in both directions for the individuals and civilizations to grow and expand. This dual cycle repeats till human being(s) refuses to learn and know anymore, and the cycle can become unidirectional till the accumulated knowledge from the past is depleted and society becomes stagnant and no new knowledge is generated. During the downfall of nations and cultures, the rise of cults and self-interest groups becomes evident. These destructive organizations become cancerous to the very society that once nurtured them.

History reminds us of many alarming regimes; Hitler's Germany (1933–1945) [14], Stalins' Russia (1922–1953) [15], Mao's China (1949–1959) [16], etc. Disintegration, dismay, decay, death, and devastation have followed. Given an opportunity, knowledge incubates and grows in creative minds in spite of harsh environments. Pharaoh's Egypt produced marvelous structures and Ottomans' Morocco produced many fine artistic forms. The cycle pauses for a short enough

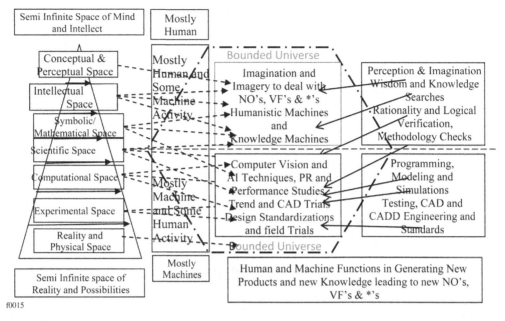

f0015

FIGURE 26.2

Diagram to illustrate the role of nouns, verbs, convolutions, knowledge centric objects, and bodies of knowledge
in the derivation of new knowledge from old knowledge and the reality. The human mind and then the
knowledge machines and humanistic machines play the pivotal role of the creation of new knowledge.

interval and produces masterpieces of many cultures or the ruins, death, and destruction of wars,
both evident in Europe.

In the knowledge domain, the role of computers and networks has become dominant through
late last century. More recently the impact of knowledge networks, Internet I and II has become
dominant. The ceaseless struggle between human minds and machines penetrates the perceptual,
mostly human space at the high end and the purely computational space at the low end. A snapshot
of this constant ebb and flow of knowledge between the humans and machines is depicted in
Figure 26.2.

Seven spaces are shown in the pyramid. The human mind may occupy any one space for a
lifetime or move freely to explore all the seven spaces. If the upward movement in this pyramid
constitutes on direction of the cycle, then the downward movement depicts the other. When
these movements are made harmonious and smooth, then the accumulated knowledge spills into the
reality for solving the problems that face an individual or a society. Conversely, when problems
are fed into the knowledge and conceptual spaces to gain global wisdom, they become an integral
part of human life to move forward.

Wars, social upheavals, and sheer indulgence on the part of individuals and nations disrupt the
ebb and flow of knowledge into an uneven and almost haphazard reality. Conversely, the ill-
conditioned knowledge bases during disruptions cause turmoil and a restless society. Willful
moderation for this delicate balance between the surplus of knowledge and the needs of self and

society can be sensed, moderated, and controlled by individuals for themselves and by knowledge machines for communities and nations.

A normal flow of information/knowledge from the numerous knowledge centers (e.g., universities, libraries, research centers) of a nation becomes indicative of "health of knowledge" of the nation. By the same token, the analysis of the flow of information/knowledge from mafia strongholds, porno institutions, nightclubs, casinos, bars, etc., becomes indicative of sickness in society. Such indicators are in use for fiscal policy settings. The economic indicators are constantly monitored and balanced to provide a healthy flow of monies within the nation. In the corporate environment, the balance sheets provide a strong clue about the health and stability of a corporation. In the same vein, an activity sheet of the major knowledge functions (e.g., inventions, innovations, novelty, and range of products) within a corporation provides a snap shot of creativity. If it deviates from a bench mark setting, a knowledge machine (*KM*) [7] will identify the opportunities for innovation and progress. More than that, the *KM* can formulate creative convolutions of the past verb function and current noun objects that show promise of desirable changes.

26.7 HIERARCHIES OF OBJECTS AND ACTIONS

Objects in knowledge space can become as numerous as symbols in computational space. Both need further characterization. Symbols in the computer space, have been classified as numbers (integers, floating point, double precision, etc.), dimensioned arrays, matrices, etc. In addition, these symbols are tailored to a problem at hand. In the knowledge space, objects may contain and encompass other objects, and subordinate objects may enclose leaf objects. To this extent, recursion of objects would be a desirable feature in the knowledge space as recursion of symbols in computational space of higher level scientific application programs.

In following the structure of graphs, if the node object is placed at the top of an object hierarchy and named as "knowledge centric object" or *KCO*, then the second-level objects can be called the "bodies of knowledge" or *BoKs*, and the third-level object can be called a "noun object," NO, or simply an object n. Thus, in a give knowledge space the *KCO*, *BoKs*, and *n's* constitute a simple graph that is indicative of the structure of knowledge in KOC. A possible depiction of the generalized object hierarchy is shown in Figure 26.3.

In following the classifications one step further in the organization of functions in the CPU of a computer [17], the traditional operation codes are also classified and encoded. Operation codes (OPCs) [18] exist for numerical operands, logical operands, matrices, I/O entities, etc. In the same vein, if actions in the knowledge space are classified, then the hierarchical order of actions can be written as convolution (*), action, interaction, and a verb function or verb (v). A possible depiction of the generalized action hierarchy (convolutions, actions, interactions, Verb functions, verbs, etc.) is shown in Figure 26.4.

26.8 KNOWLEDGE: A SCIENTIFIC ENTITY

The interpretation of any given *BoK* in the human mind can be highly variable. In the psychological interpretations of events, the mind sorts and relates the different events in a systematic fashion. It also disintegrates complex bodies of knowledge into their constituents to a predetermined

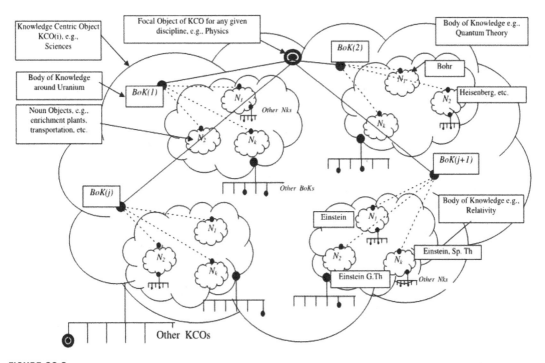

FIGURE 26.3

Depiction of any super object and the other constituting objects that contribute to the super object. The number of levels can vary significantly from one super object to another and is indicative of the depth of known objects in any discipline. Generally the routine problems in most disciplines can be investigated by three levels of representation of objects. (See Figure 26.5)

(depending on the knowledge quotient or *KQ*) levels up and down and relates the current event with the other objects existing in the knowledge bank(s). A trained human mind also deals with the *BoKs* in an efficient and orderly way order to relate and retrieve them. A photographic image of a complex *KCO* consisting of numerous constituting *KCOs* their relations, and their attributes and connectivity's can become as cumbersome as tracing the neural pathways in the brain.

In order to instill an external order, a conceptual graph may be constructed in the computational space of machines with the data structures in their memories representing these *KCOs*. In the development of other disciplines, symbols, and representations are used in the conceptual space of humans and the topological space of mathematics.

Knowledge manipulations may not approach the complete rigor of mathematical operations and transformations but may be traced and tracked like the tasks and transformations in managerial sciences and production engineering. For example, building an airplane is neither entirely mathematical nor wholly random actions. However, the intermediary space between the two extremes is occupied by the discipline of computer-aided design or CAD techniques in engineering.

In this vein, a complex knowledge object may be traced, tracked, modified, and built as a scientific entity that has order, structure, flow and methodology. In order to facilitate this methodology,

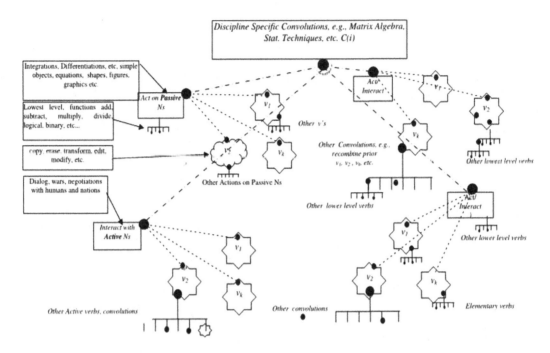

FIGURE 26.4

Depiction of a high level convolution (verb function) and the other supporting verbs such as acts, actions, verb functions, verbs that contribute to the high level convolution. The number of levels can vary significantly from one super convolution to another and is indicative of the depth of technology or processes in that discipline. Generally the routine processes in most disciplines can be investigated by three levels of processes.

we propose two sets of axioms. The first set deals with the structure of knowledge and the second set deals with the flow of knowledge. Both sets are derived from reality and based on laws of mathematics to construct low level *KCOs* (like optimized macros and library routines for computer systems), intermediate level *KCOs* (like I/O routine, mathematical functions and specialized processes for selected operations), higher-level *KCOs* (like elementary application programs, connectivity's and communications), and finally the complex *KCOs* that may represent new and innovative tasks. For example, building a spacecraft from the existing laws of aerodynamics in the atmosphere of earth, and then the basic laws of space flight, etc., would need a series of (v's, *s, and n's) specialized for the space craft as a complex *KCO*. Similar examples exist in social, managerial and political environments.

The implications of these two sets of axioms based on reality can be far reaching. They also carve out a methodology to administer changes in *KCOs* that humans or a society may impose. Thus, the axioms form a basis to evolve major modules of knowledge-ware (KW atop HW, SW, and FW) for a humanistic machine. At the outset, knowledge may appear as an abstract and virtual entity but being channeled into appropriate levels of the knowledge space as being composed of interrelated *KCOs*, major *BoKs*, these noun objects soon start to appear as plants and shrubs in a garden rather than trees in a forest.

26.9 STATE OF KNOWLEDGE

Knowledge like life spans microorganisms to macrocosms. From a single gene to a vast galaxy, the implicit knowledge is the basis for existence. The activities of organisms form the theme for their ongoing existence. In the humanistic domain, knowledge within the human mind is the microcosm with order and structure for gratifying the needs necessary to the survival of self, species, and society. These constitute the primary needs. Pursuit of gratifying higher level of needs (psychological, emotional, and spiritual) constitutes a secondary tier of activities. In a sense, knowledge gets clustered around objects (noun objects, n's) that play a role (verb functions, v's) in satisfying the primary needs and then the subordinate needs.

The procedure for the need satisfaction is an ordeal in its own right; subsequently, all aspects of knowledge to implement the mechanisms to satisfy such needs, except the most rudimentary needs, can become tedious and complex. In being thoughtful and algorithmic in implementation process, humans follow certain tracks and follow (verbs, v's), their most direct (convolutions,*'s) highways[1] and byways in the gratification process involving one or more objects (nouns, n's). In general, the satisfaction of any need demands an expenditure of energy and the process of iterative convergence of the final solution is depicted in Figure 26.5. The noun objects and the acceptable verb functions (associated with these groups of KCOs, BOKs, and Nos) are each examined, reexamined, and cross-examined until an adequate solution is found or a new noun object is invented on the right-hand side of Figure 26.5.

The state of knowledge in human mind is generally pragmatic and feasible, though less than perfect and optimal. Humans find a workable solution and then try to refine it. In a sense, humans learn (acquire knowledge) to live and live to learn.

26.9.1 HIGHWAYS AND BYWAYS

The binary encoding of information has altered our lives. Preservation of information and the derived knowledge both become feasible in any form of modern storage media inexpensively, efficiently, and error-free. Transportation becomes equally amenable to any signal carrying media cheaply, effectively, and free of errors. The highways and byways for information and knowledge are only a click away in a networked society as much as a thought process is a twinkle away in an open mind.

Science and society have made unprecedented progress in the last few decades. Together they bring the accuracy of mathematics and the power of the knowledge in thought that creates new knowledge. The gain of knowledge in the small world we live is thus a double exponential. The processing of this new knowledge to blend with the prior knowledge becomes as essential as the blending of reason with wisdom in order to preserve a sane society. Failures to develop deploy and universalize the structure and use of gainful wisdom from new knowledge are to open the doors to knowledge wars. It appears almost like stepping into the footsteps of Hitler [14], Stalin [15], and Mao [16] who stepped onto death sentences and military wars.

---

[1]In the words of an Indian poet who pleads: Know the passages within your heart, You may traverse many times to sort, The shadows of those who dart, In and out till it is time to part.

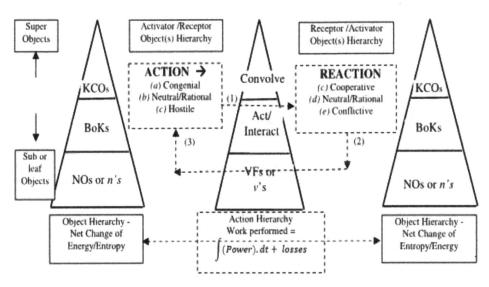

FIGURE 26.5

Representation of most active and passive actions, interactions, verb functions, verbs, and processes that are feasible between super objects, knowledge centric objects, bodies of knowledge, nouns, and noun objects. There are corresponding changes in energies and entropies of objects as a result of actions in the associated the numerous space shown in Figure 26.2.

Based on the immediate societies and adjoining communities, the highways and bye ways of communication provide enough means for a healthy competition. Spam and unwanted emails offer sufficiently low level annoyance. Universities compete for students; businesses compete for clients, etc.; wars rarely emerge. However, pushed into next two layers (nations and worlds) of organizational entities, the use of knowledge to fight unjust wars is eminently feasible.

26.9.2 NATIONS OF KNOWLEDGE

Nations at war are an ongoing scenario. Greed and malice are never too far from humans who deploy mathematics and science to suit. Special-interest groups (SIGs) and self-propagators who are close enough to both groups (the DAH group; deception, arrogance, and hate and the SET group; science, economics, and technology) will deploy SET into DAH, and vice versa. Nations of knowledge in conflict emerge and knowledge wars (based on nuclear, petroleum, refinery, techniques) develop. The wisdom component is missing in both groups. Unabated, history of intellectual slave-trade and religion-for-sale will become business enterprises assuming new names in the future knowledge society. The handwriting is already on the walls of corporate headquarters of many a mobster.

Global fiber-optic networks and transoceanic dense wave-length division multiplexed highway systems serve the intents of SIGs as well as needs of the societies. The access to power of deployment of these potent computer and communication technologies without the temper or discipline to evaluate the global impact is an open-door way to the death of a society. Only a few notables of the past (Lincoln, Kennedy, Carter, Einstein, Tesla, Marshall, and alike) have brought immense social rewards without personal gain, even without global information highways.

26.9.3 WORLD OF KNOWLEDGE

Astronomy and space exploration have shrunk our world and proven that science and knowledge are indeed universal. They bring the far reaches of the universe on to HDTV screens. The sensors to scan the universe and networks to communicate obey the laws of physics and mathematics embedded within a framework of knowledge with order and discipline. The expansion of information is phenomenal in comparison with our capacity to process the newly acquired information.

The need for processing knowledge is urgent while traditional computers are idling away tracking junk information and hype knowledge. The proof of this scenario is the lack of human-ware to reach over the under-deployed supercomputers in scientific laboratories and unlit fibers buried in the oceans. The world of knowledge surrounds us willing to be a subservient partner for the scientists and knowledge machinists who can deploy the hardware, software, firmware, knowledgeware, and finally the human ware that intellectually surrounds the unused silicon chips in the laboratories and optical fiber lying deep in the ocean beds.

26.9.4 UNIVERSE OF KNOWLEDGE

Knowledge is alive but not well everywhere. It almost has a life form adapting surviving everywhere. It can assume all the attributes ranging from being healthy to sick, half-dead to gloriously alive. The classification of the type of knowledge ailments, though feasible, is beyond the scope of this book. However, the dynamics of knowledge that deals with healthy changes in knowledge centric objects (*KCOs*) as they flow through the vines of society can be studied by scientific methodologies. During the ebb and flow, such as knowledge centric objects can get damaged, become distorted, and become disconnected with the neighboring objects, thus losing their identity, cohesion, and structure. This analogy with medical sciences starts to get too fuzzy too quickly.

However, the analogy can be meaningfully extended in physics and electrical engineering. Some of the major contribution in EE, signal processing, and basic physics start to shed light on the possible degradation and degeneration of knowledge as it flows through society. After all, wave shapes and electrical signals carry information. They do get distorted and lose their shape. They are restored and original information is reconstructed. In coding theory, electrical signal wave shapes and their relative positioning with respect to each other carry the original information. In a similar setting, when information and knowledge pass through society, the *KCOs*, their structure, and their interrelations start to get altered. Reconstruction and restoration of the signals for the ultimate recovery of data (and thus the embedded information) are a major discipline in and the design of communications systems and networks components.

When the concepts from transmission theory from electrical engineering (EE) are projected into the knowledge domain, the extent of degradation and distortion can be measured in terms of signal to noise ratio (SNR). It is indicative of the quality of received information as it passes through any transmission media. When *KCOs* flow through a social media (such as human groups, corporations, cultures), the extent of degradation of the *KCOs*, their interrelationships, and their attributes is indicative of the nature and character of that social media. Originally embedded knowledge at the source and its representation after much media distortion become indicative of the nature or bias in the media. Knowledge machines can perform such checks and reveal the SNRs in a free society, a biased society, or a subversive society. In reality, such incidents occur too frequently to be ignored. In the recent instances, during Mao's regime in China, dissemination of scriptures was banned; during the Watergate scandal of *Nixons'* era, White House tapes were conveniently destroyed; during the Iraq war of the Bush and Cheney Administration, the *KCOs* (names of torturers and the tortured) of the Guantanamo Bay prison were blocked from news media. History bears painful scars from the past when the flow of truth-bearing *KCOs* is deceptively distorted, blocked, and/or adulterated. Such distortions have occurred too frequently to be ignored.

The analogy cannot be taken too far because the classical laws of physics and EE can be too rigid and in addition well defined. On the other hand, the social laws and interpersonal interpretation are ill-defined and fuzzy. Fuzzy and unclear, such laws might be, they are not irrational, false, or significantly inaccurate. To this extent, we follow the concepts for the flow of signals in transmission media and derive the general framework but discard them when the rules become inapplicable to the flow of *KCOs*. Signal flow analysis in digital subscriber lines, fiber-optic, and satellite systems use the laws of physics and EE but combine the results from various groups of environments by the laws of statistics to interpret the system performance of a given environment. In essence, the scientific foundation is established firmly, and the applications are built atop the equations in physics and EE.

CONCLUSIONS

In this chapter, we present a framework of knowledge based on reality that noun objects drive verb functions. When verb-functions are convolved with noun objects, action, order, and life start to take shape. In humanistic systems, the energy to drive such verb function arises for the human needs and in machine/robotic systems, the energy is channeled by application programs and software from energy/monetary reserves available as resources. Complex verb-functions can be decomposed elementary human actions in the human environment and to operation code level in knowledge processors. Humans and machines can thus coexist in close proximity monitoring the local and global accuracy, computation and viability of solutions.

The flow of knowledge from humans and machines is tied to the awareness and use of knowledge centric objects (*KCOs*) between minds and as flow of data-structures between machines. Such *KCOs* initiate, enhance, modify, and terminate verb-functions to restore orderly transactions between human beings and machines. Such transactions exist everywhere from classrooms, hospitals, and banks.

Further in this chapter, we present a basis for customizing mathematical techniques and measures for gauging, extrapolating and exploiting past and current knowledge to meaningfully deploy it into the future. Physics and electrical engineering from the hard sciences are integrated with economics and operations research from social sciences and decision theory. The role of knowledge-oriented mathematics, computer sciences and knowledgeware atop of software, firmware, and human-ware are delineated to make knowledge machines regiment, compute, and evaluate and offer solutions to human and global problems.

REFERENCES

[1] Clausius R. On the motive power of heat, and on the laws which can be deduced from it for the theory of heat. Poggendorff's Annalen der Physick; 1850. LXXIX (Dover Reprint). ISBN 0-486-59065-8. See also Clausius R, Carnot S, Kelvin BWT. Thermodynamics: Memoirs by Carnot, Clausius, and Thomson. Nabu Press; April 20, 2010, and Rezakhanlou F, Villani C. Entropy methods for the Boltzmann equation. In: Golse F, Olla S, editors. Lectures from a special semester at the Centre Émile Borel. Paris: Institut H. Poincaré; 2001 (Lecture Notes in Mathematics).

[2] McCulloch RS. Treatise on the mechanical theory of heat and its applications to the steam-engine, etc. D. Van Nostrand; 1876. Also see Greven A, et al., editors, Entropy (Princeton studies in applied mathematics). Princeton University Press; 2003, and Swinburne J. Entropy: Thermodynamics from an engineer's standpoint, and the reversibility of thermodynamics [1904]. Cornell University Library; 2009.

[3] Vandome F, Mcbrewster A, Miller J. Boltzmann constant. Alphascript Publishing; 2010.

[4] Jaynes ET. The Gibbs paradox. In: Smith CR, Erickson GJ, Neudorfer PO, editors. Maximum entropy and Bayesian methods. Dordrecht: Kluwer Academic; 1992. p. 1–22.

[5] Ben-Naim A. On the so-called Gibbs paradox and on the real paradox. Entropy 2007;9:132–6, ISSN 1099-4300.

[6] Jaynes ET. Gibbs vs. Boltzmann entropies. American Journal of Physics 1965;33:391–8.

[7] Ahamed S. Computational framework of knowledge: intelligent behavior of machines. Hoboken (NJ): John Wiley and Sons.

[8] Bell Laboratories. Transmission systems for communications. Western Electric Co; 1982.

[9] Marshall A. Principles of economics. Nabu Press; 2010.

[10] Tamura H. Human psychology and economic fluctuations: a new basic theory of human economics. Palgrave Macmillan; 2006.

[11] Neumann J, von, Morgenstern O. Theory of games and economic behavior. Princeton Classic Editions; 2007.

[12] Ahamed S, Lawrence VB. Design and engineering of intelligent communication systems. Kluwer Academic Publishers; 1997.

[13] Parsons S. Money, time and rationality. In Weber M. editor. Austrian connections, Routledge studies in the history of economics; 2003.

[14] Veranov M. The third Reich at war – The rise and fall of Hilter's awesome military machine. Magpie Books; 2004.

[15] Radzinskii E. Stalin: The first in-depth biography based on explosive new documents from Russia's secret archives. Anchor Books; 1997.

[16] Ostermann C, editor. The Cold War international history project. Woodrow Wilson International Center For Scholars; February 2002, also see Changes in Zedong M. Attitude toward the Indochina War, 1949–1973, Working Paper No. 34, Translated by Qiang Zhai.

[17] Hayes JP. Computer architecture and organization. 2nd ed. New York: McGraw Hill; 1988, see also, Stone HS, et al., Introduction to computer architecture, computer science series, New York: Science Research Associates; 1980; Stallings W, Computer organization and architecture. New York: Macmillan; 1987.

[18] Rudd WG. Assembly level programming and the IBM 360 and 370 computers. Englewood Cliffs (NJ): Prentice Hall; 1976, See also, Detmer RC, Introduction to 80x86 assembly level language and computer architecture. Sudbury, MA: Jones and Bartlett Publishers; 2001.

REAL SPACE, KNOWLEDGE SPACE AND COMPUTATIONAL SPACE

27

CHAPTER SUMMARY

In this chapter, we propose that the intersection(s) of perceptual and computational spaces lies in the reality of the physical space. Reality is perceived by the senses and reinforced by rationality to instill order and predictability of effects that follow their causes, the ensuing actions, and their effects. Reality, understanding, actions, and their effects thus get chain linked in a circular mode. Knowledge space hosts the understanding and comprehension of the physical space and resides in neural space in the brain. Computational space is an imagery of the two prior spaces that resides temporarily in the magnetic, semiconductor locations during the emulation and execution phases of the problems encountered in dealing with real-space scenarios. This document elaborates on the connectivity of these three spaces by symbols and equations to manipulate and optimize the actions in the real space and to solve real-life problems.

Programming and software tools permit the problem-solvers to link any increment of knowledge, forward and backward in time, space, methodology, and mind. The logical ties to neighboring objects permit the computers to seek out the logic that has tied similar objects in the past from the Internet knowledge bases. In a similar vein, the machines seek out the actions that surround any particular object or similar objects and the scientific basis (such as gravitation, magnetism, chemical affinity, Maxwell's equations, polarity) by which they combine. In unison new elements of knowledge, however, large or small they may be, are created and stored away in the knowledge bases for future use in solving social and/or humanistic problems. This approach seeks venues and alternative those that are generally overlooked by purely human effort. The approach makes the machine processes (at CPU clock-rates) synergistic with the human thought processes (at mind-specific contemplative rates). These two processes are generally not in synchronism because of the computer clock ticks much faster than the triggering clock of neural cells. Thus a time warp between the computer and mind becomes necessary.

27.1 INTRODUCTION

Objects in nature are constantly arranged and rearranged as a result of internal or external forces and actions upon them and within them. Actions cause change in the status and entropy of all objects however, small or large the change maybe. Since there is no object that does not undergo change, there is some action or a set of actions inherently and inadvertently acting upon every object. An object without one or more verbs to act upon is a nonentity and a verb without one or more corresponding nouns to be acted upon is virtual. These truisms are as valid during the Big Bang as they will be during the collapse of the universe.

Evolution of Knowledge Science. DOI: http://dx.doi.org/10.1016/B978-0-12-805478-9.00027-3

431

Objects in nature and their inevitable changes are the basis of theory of knowledge. Changes occur over measurable and discernible parameters. It is the rate of change and innate forces in nature or the environment that brings about the change in the state of any object and science knowledge tracks such changes with reasonable accuracy. The validation of the normal usual equations relating the measurable parameters (such as mass and momentum, force and movement, torque and rotation, energy and inertia) becomes necessary. As the real objects fill the physical space; hypotheses, concepts, and notions fill the intellectual space; humans, their needs, and their innovations fill the social space. This chapter extends the domain of (statistical and probabilistic) computations coupled with the AI techniques to extend the frontiers of knowledge and to derive notions leading on to practical solutions of real-life problems in a satisfactory fashion, though not exactly. This is achieved by connecting the knowledge to solve with the best way to solve based on the syntactic and semantic issues of the situation and the origin of the problem.

27.2 ANATOMY OF SOCIAL INTERACTIONS

Social interactions are the basis of human relations. In order to be precise and computational, the interaction needs a framework and a blueprint even though the format may be violated on many occasions, there a basic theme that can be formally programmed for social machines. The computational space follows this pattern in time dimension thus following space-time coordinates in the memories, processors, and peripherals of the social machines. This space can be traversed, reversed, and optimized for efficient replicas of social interactions, even though social interactions in the real and neural spaces are irreversible in the time dimension.

In formalizing the steps of a typical dyadic social interaction, we present the following steps presented as a noun object *no1* initiates a verb function *vf* and the mode of interaction is establishes as *. This basic elementary process is represented as (*no1* * *vf*). Further, broken down this process is written down as:

$$(no1 * 12\ vf12\ no2);\ \text{or as}\ (no1\ vf12^* \rightarrow no2)\cdot$$

This element of any elementary transactional process can be written as:

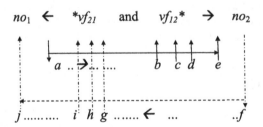

A forward process (full lines) with *a* through *e* steps is followed by a backward process (dashed lines) with *f* through *j* steps. This elemental transaction is repeated many times to depict an entire interaction between any two noun objects *no1* and *no2*.

A more detailed diagram of the interactive elemental process is depicted in Figure 27.1. The dyadic nature of the process is embedded in the symmetry of the diagram. The nature and the

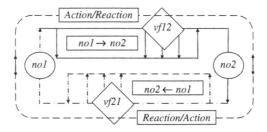

FIGURE 27.1

Representation of an element of an interactive process. The verb functions are drawn from *vf* knowledge bases appropriate to the nature of noun objects *no1* and *no 2*.

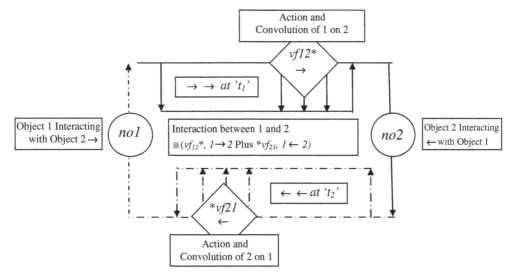

FIGURE 27.2

Detailed representations of interactive processes that constitute most mundane to the most scientific and sophisticated interactions. The timing of transactions and their durations may be unimportant in this representation in the computer space. However, the processing, inference, deductions, and implications are context driven. The supplementary information necessary for processing are derived from knowledge bases for the noun objects (*no's*), verb functions (*vf's*), and their convolutions (**'s*).

roles of noun object *no1* and *no2* are transposable and repeated numerous times to represent an entire dialog, debate, or any interactive process. The size of the transaction is inconsequential and the process can be repeated indefinitely on the Processor Units of computers.

A comprehensive and programmable model including the time and its effect is shown in Figure 27.2. The convolution (*) symbol depicts the nature of the verb function. The verb qualifier indicates the "tone" of the transaction. For example, a doctor t may diagnose an ailment or cure an treat the ailment, or a teacher may coach or educate a student, etc. The machine would then search the appropriate base(s) to proceed/compute the effect.

The time and duration of the transactions are incorporated by "*t*" dimension associated with the verb functions vf_{12} *and* vf_{21}. The necessity for time elements depends on the nature and context of the interactions involving verb functions in the real space (RS). For example, in forensics studies the nature of actions, the timing and the duration of the verb functions vf's can become crucial. These parameters are used in conjunction with other prior and later events to complete the transactions that make or break an entire case of social/corporate interactions.

27.3 SYMBOLIC REPRESENTATIONS OF INTERACTIONS

The human mind crosses numerous boundaries of real social and knowledge spaces during interactions. It traverses these spaces to make human discourse interesting, meaningful and to exchange knowledge in an efficient fashion. We propose that such interactions being complex, time and situation dependent be represented in a symbolic format such as *((n * v)* or *(n→*v))* for simple transactions and suitably modified for complex and compound transactions. Accordingly social processes are classified as follows.

27.3.1 SIMPLE SOCIAL PROCESSES

(n * v) A noun executes a verb; e.g., human strolls; human walks; human runs, human flees.

(n →*v) A noun with a modified verb; human runs fast; human slows down to standstill, etc., *(n* → v)*, e.g., human run and gets tired. The noun acts upon itself.

27.3.2 COMPLEX PROCESSES (DYADIC)

$(n1^* \rightarrow v\ n2)$ Teacher *(n1)* instructs *(*v)* student *(n2)*

$(n1^* \rightarrow v\ n2)$ Teacher severely reprimands *(* → v)* student *(n2)*

27.3.3 COMPOUND PROCESSES (TRIADIC)

$(n1 \rightarrow {}^*v \rightarrow {}^*v \rightarrow n2 => \rightarrow n3)$

Hydrogen explodes *(→*v)* during combination *(→*v)* with oxygen *(n2)* to form *(=> → n3)* water vapor; double modifier for *v*. Another example is

$((n1 \rightarrow {}^*v\ n2)(n1 \rightarrow {}^*v)^*n2 => v))$

Master *(n1)* whips *(→*v)* slave *(n2)* (and makes *(n1→*v)* her *(n2)* *cry* *(=>v)*. (Two simple sentences).

The same expression in the symbolic language

$((n1 \rightarrow {}^*v\ n2)(n1 \rightarrow {}^*v)^*n2 => v))$ can be used for

Master apologizes to slave and makes her feel good, etc. The nature of *v's* becomes different.

27.3.4 COMPLETE FORM FOR DYADIC INTERACTION(S)

In general, interactions between *no1* and *no2* can be written as

$$(no_1 \leftrightarrow {}^*_1 \leftrightarrow vf \leftrightarrow {}^*_2 \leftrightarrow no_2)$$

The knowledge machine compiles this symbolic expression as and assigns the direction of the vector-verb vf_{12} as vector 1 to 2 and vector-verb vf_{21} as vector 2 to 1.

27.4 THE ARROW SYMBOL AND ITS VARIATIONS

The simple interactive processes can be depicted by the single arrow convention for both forward and backward effects. For example, $\rightarrow$ represents a forward knowledge process, i.e., effect of the prior element on the following element, and $\leftarrow$ represents a backward knowledge process, i.e., effect of the following element on the prior element. However, social and machine generated objects can be classified into three major categories: (a) Passive, (b) Active/Reactive, and (c) Intelligent. Passive objects are generally inanimate and respond to the verb function according to laws of natural and material sciences and react in a preset fashion. For example, when water is heated, it vaporizes and forms steam, active and reactive noun objects act in a contextual fashion and become situation dependent. For example, when iron is heated with sulfur, it forms iron sulfide and when iron is heated with carbon it forms steel with altogether different properties from those of iron sulfide.

Finally, when an intelligent object such as a human being is stressed sufficiently, the reaction can be to radically change the nature of noun object itself, the convolution of forces that cause the stress and the other intelligent objects that are driving the forces to cause the stress and even to change the settings that give rise to the stress. This is generally the case when the two parties are in a severe conflict as in war, divorce, etc. situations. Accordingly, the arrow symbols are modified for these instances and depicted in Table 27.1.

In view of the many forms of responses from *no2* the symbolic representation of

$$(no1 \leftarrow {}^*1 \leftarrow vf_{21} \leftarrow {}^*2 \leftarrow no2)$$

shown in the lower part of Figure 27.3 should be rewritten as

$$(no_1 \quad \twoheadleftarrow {}^*_1 \quad \twoheadleftarrow vf_{21} \quad \twoheadleftarrow {}^*_2 \quad \twoheadleftarrow no_2)$$

processes "instructs" the knowledge machine to seek and search the local or Internet knowledge bases depending on the context of the interaction. For example, if Obama decides on an embargo ($\rightarrow$) of Russian beef in the Middle East, then Putin can decide to block US electronic chip-sets in Russia, as a resistive reaction with the symbol:

Further, Putin can deploy shooting down US planes in the Gulf regions with reactive behavior with a symbol: Irrational behavior of this nature endangering society ⬤⊣⊢ has been documented numerous times in history. For example, US decided to drop nuclear bombs on Japanese cities in response to the attack on Pearl Harbor; the early settlers in the North Western territories killed large tribes of Native American Indians in response to a few clashes with the new immigrants, etc.

Table 27.1 Variations of a Dyadic Interactive Processes when two Participants *no1* and *no2* Engage by Verb Functions *vf₁₂** & *vf₂₁** Respectively

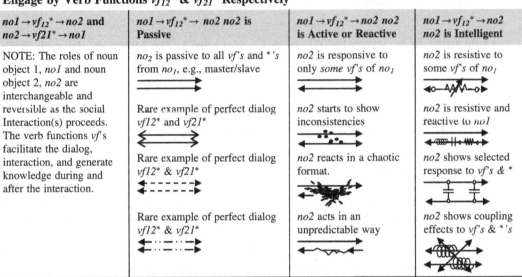

no1 → vf₁₂* → no2 and *no2 → vf21* → no1*	*no1 → vf₁₂* → no2 no2* is Passive	*no1 → vf₁₂* → no2 no2* is Active or Reactive	*no1 → vf₁₂* → no2 no2* is Intelligent
NOTE: The roles of noun object 1, *no1* and noun object 2, *no2* are interchangeable and reversible as the social Interaction(s) proceeds. The verb functions *vf*'s facilitate the dialog, interaction, and generate knowledge during and after the interaction.	*no₂* is passive to all *vf*'s and ***'s from *no₁*, e.g., master/slave	*no2* is responsive to only *some vf*'s of *no₁*	*no2* is resistive to some *vf*'s of *no₁*
	Rare example of perfect dialog *vf12** and *vf21**	*no2* starts to show inconsistencies	*no2* is resistive and reactive to *no1*
	Rare example of perfect dialog *vf12** & *vf21**	*no2* reacts in a chaotic format.	*no2* shows selected response to *vf*'s & ***
	Rare example of perfect dialog *vf12** & *vf21**	*no2* acts in an unpredictable way	*no2* shows coupling effects to *vf*'s & ***'s

Table Note: This table illustrates the types of dyadic interactive processes between two arbitrary noun objects no1 *and* no2. *However, the outcome is not always predictable. The responses of* no2 *and/or* no1 *are shown by the modification of the arrows. In a symbolic representation, the type of interaction can be encoded by the arrows used. Perfect interactions are shown in column 2 and the practical representations are shown in columns 3 and 4. Reactive behavior of the participants is common in practice. A knowledge machine attempts to reshape the dialog to a rational interaction as far as it is feasible by the AI algorithms that are programmed in the knowledge-ware of the machine.*

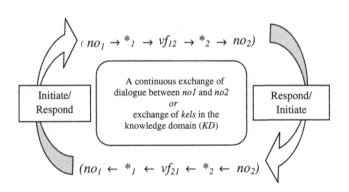

FIGURE 27.3

Representation of real time events to symbolic knowledge domain representation for the knowledge machine to analyze, modify, optimize based on prior experience(s) in Knowledge bases.

On the other hand, parallel o—WWW—o examples of cooperative behavior are also represented by intelligent behavior for the enhancement or peace rather than prolonging conflictive and irrational behavior presented in the numerous elements in columns 3 and 4 of Table 27.1. For example, Nikita Khrushchev pursued a policy of peaceful coexistence with the West despite the years of cold war and Kennedy's threats over the Cuban Missile Crisis; Gandhi offered a graceful exit from India for the British despite their massive detentions, public flogging, and brutal killing in Africa and in India, etc.

27.5 SEVEN CONCURRENT AND COEXISTING SPACES

Psychological spaces in mind are as essential as organs in the body. Each has one or more specific purpose, though sometimes overlapping. Partitioning mental space preserves order and classifying them instills conformity within each space. Seven such spaces (NS, MS, PsS, KS, SoS, CS, and finally PhS) are proposed in the chapter and depicted in Figure 27.4. The first five (NS, MS, SoS,

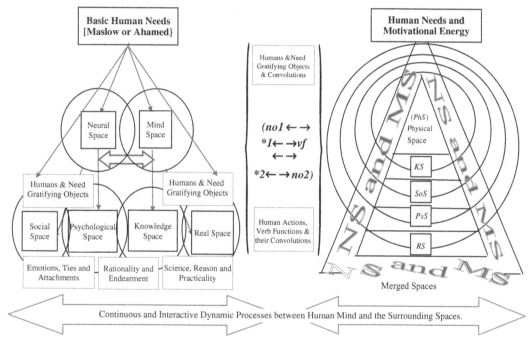

FIGURE 27.4

A depiction of seven (Neural (NS), Mental (MS), Social (SoS), Psychological PSS), Knowledge (KS), Computational (CS), and Physical or Real (RS)) spaces and their hierarchy. Being totally interconnected the human mind, these space navigate human activities in real space in an orderly and coherent fashion. Information and knowledge flow in and out of KS and is simulated in the computational environment. The computer space adds an additional dimension of rationality (and possibly wisdom) to the solution of deeply seated inherent problems in real space, such as conservation of resources, peaceful coexistence, preservation of environment, harmony with nature.

PsS, and *KS*) spaces depicted in the second and third tiers are completely interconnected as the neural nets in the human brain. Expertise to be optimal in the deployment of the rules governing these spaces is a lifelong learning and adjustment process. The derived knowledge offers the venues to learn from the past civilizations, to be cognizant of the present socioeconomic environment and to be cautious for the future for the frail nature we all share.

The four spaces (*MS*, *SoS*, *PsS*, and *KS*) lie in the perception of human minds. The seven spaces depicted in Figure 27.4 are necessary to emulate the mental functions in the mind and they are elaborated as follows:

27.6 THE HIERARCHY OF SPACES

The organization of the brain is not completely understood. To be practical in context to the discussion in this chapter, we present simplistic overview of the organization of the seven spaces as follows.

1. The Neural Space (*NS*): is embedded in the neural physiological structure of the brain. It is the basis of the human mind and most of the primary and secondary function spring from the organization and clustering of neurons in the configuration of neural nets in the brain and body.
2. The Mental Space (*MS*): is formed be the interconnected clusters of neurons that make up nodes of the mental images of objects in the physical space.
3. The Psychological Space (*PsS*): hosts the emotions of living creatures for the animate and inanimate objects. Being at the third intermediate level, this space is swayed in either direction turning bitterly savage or showing acts of great mercy. The space is intricately tied to the needs of the living organisms that range from the lower survival needs to the highest spiritual needs. At the lowest levels bitterness merged arrogance has brought the worst behavior of humans and nations. Examples occur during British role in world wars and during the period of French and Italian Inquisitions in Europe.
4. The Knowledge Space(s) (*KS*): merges long-term welfare of the society with proven rationality in the physical space (see *PhS*). This unique blend of sciences and disciplines offers tolerance and peace rather than rob and kill. The recent advances in computer and network technologies have propelled knowledge space into new horizons of cultural integration. Finally over the turn of the century, human thought has broken the barrier of selfishness and hate and gradually approached the frontiers of understanding by distinguishing between "good" and "evil," even though some humans and nations abuse the newer technologies by greedily pursuing private fortunes and self-acclaimed glory. The purpose of this chapter is to provide a machine-assisted quantified overview for human and national conduct rather than a hasty rush toward emotional behavior.
5. The Social Space(s) (*SoS*): accommodates the consideration and orientation of human self with respect to other human beings and establishes the social distances between human beings. The laws governing interactive forces between objects are evolved and modified in this space. As in physical space the location of objects can shift and can be adjusted, objects in social spaced can also be altered and adjusted. Unlike physical and astronomical objects that show a gravitational pull, social objects can be attracted or driven apart. Like objects generally attract each other like "birds of the same feather flock together" and conversely, "birds if different feather fight each other" (e.g., hawks and vultures), in a social context.

The forces and their nature exhibit peculiar characteristics in this social space. When social distances become too small, attraction can reverse its flavor as it is proverbially stated that "familiarity breeds contempt." Very short distance can reverse attraction to repulsion and love to hate, especially when the resources to share are restricted. Hence, the laws of social spaces need intricate and delicate programming instructions for the knowledge machine to arrange and rearrange objects in tight and congested social spaces

6. The Computational Space (*CS*): is allocated in computer systems to store "noun objects" and to store the operational codes associated with noun objects. Executable programs are usually held in active "core" locations of the machine during the execution phase with at least two segments in each instruction: (a) the address(es) where the objects are held in the memory and (b) the operation code specifying which preselected verb-function will be performed in the CPU(s) of the machine. Large varieties of devices and technologies exist for storing data, information, programs, their addresses, and addresses of nouns.

    When knowledge is fragmented sufficiently, its three main components (a) the noun object (s), (no or no's), (b) the associated verb function(s), (*vf* or *vf*'s), and (c) the convolution(s), (* or *'s) are also stored in the computer systems. Computational space thus assumes many forms and formats in computer systems. When the laws of handling computational space are exact and well defined, this space in computers is very precise, superfast, and extremely well managed in almost all computer systems and knowledge machines. This level of sophistication perhaps does not exist in any of the other six spaces presented in this section.

7. The Physical Space: is reality. Virtual space may exist in other spaces but reality dominates the senses. The x, y, z, and t (r, θ, φ, t, *etc.*) coordinates are connected via human senses and the perceptual reinforcement offers rationality to human thought. Since the evolution of life, real space has formed the platform of existence. On the microscopic scale, the accuracy of the coordinate systems is now supplemented by laser and nanotechnologies deployed in VLSI industry. On the macroscopic scale, light years provide an estimation of large cosmic distances. Both extremes of physical dimensions are programmable in the computer space and are processed with the central processor units of midsized computer facilities.

27.7 SWITCHED NETWORK CONNECTIVITY IN COMMUNICATIONS
27.7.1 OVERVIEW

Network switching systems in telecommunication systems are precise and dependable. Electronic switching systems (ESSs) execute the process commands from call-processing software system(s) in central office computers. The most attractive feature of the ESSs is that they are massively parallel processor oriented and each processor can handle any task within any one of the millions of call that the large ESSs can handle simultaneously. In fact, this feature is essential for their deployment in all the public domain communication networks! In the numerous spaces that the human find can function such massive parallel processing in not currently feasible, yet the subconscious handles some extent of parallel activities, such as reflex actions, hunger pangs, pattern recognition, and natural intelligence. The electronic nature of the ESS functions is entirely different from the neural electro-chemistry and neural network-pulses in the human body, even though similar pattern may (and do) exist. Connectivity's in the mind are also time and use dependent and the neural connections are invoked, assembled at the beginning of social events and intellectual activities and then disassemble and discharged at the end of the activity or activities. Spaces are dynamically connected in the perceptual spaces as switching systems are dynamically liked in the spaces of the mind. Pathways and by ways in perception are mapped into the channel routing maps that the tasks of the communication network operating system.

27.7.2 PROCESSES INVOKED AND THEIR EXECUTION

27.7.2.1 Switched network systems

In the simplest case of a call from one user to another, the call-er and the call-ed parties' identification (ID) are entered as inputs the call-processing software. Caller identification segment of the software scans for the call-er ID digits and the cal-led ID digits or addresses of the call-ed party. The communication connectivity segment of the software dispatched the call-ed address from the call-er central offices or switching center, the call-ed central office finds an available channel to the call-ed party and the "ring-signal" is sent for the part to receive the call. The call-er and the call-ed switching system both monitor the call during the connect time and at the end from either party, dispatch the command to disconnect the call circuit at both central offices or switching systems. The system returns to normal ready to receive other calls from callers. In other cases (such as VoIP, SONET, digital channels over ATM networks), the procedures are more complex and require numerous other segments of the "call processing software" that are tailored to the type of call, grade of service, media type (twisted wire pairs, fiber optic, cable, etc.).

Digital technology has dominated the switching systems since the inception of first ESS in 1965 [1]. Since the mid-1960s, innumerable American, European, and Japanese switch manufactures have made the switching of communication channels inexpensive and entirely programmable. The grand success of the switching technology results from these units being addressable from communication software and it executes the network commands as dependably as computers can execute numerical, logical, or database instructions.

The more effective ESS units in the United States have seven powerful features that permit its use in most of the networks for generic services and interconnectivity. These features include (a) each ESS unit is a single system that can serve all the applications: operator, local, toll, and international; (b) each ESS unit provides for digital switching between numerous subscriber loop carrier systems and interexchange carrier circuits (the T family or the E family), making the transition to ISDN easy and elegant. It also interfaces with the analog interexchange systems; (c) each ESS unit has a modular approach in the hardware and software design, which permits adding newer devices as technology evolves and which allows itself to interface with the older generation switching systems (e.g., the 4ESS switch or the older 5ESS systems); (d) each ESS unit's hardware modularity permits gradual growth as the network and service demands increase. This permits a cost-effective deployment of Central Office resources; (e) each ESS unit, being mostly digital in devices and its control, it has a reliability comparable to, if not better than, most computer systems. Extra error correction stages and parallel functionality of the CPUs permit quick and dependable retractability of any call processing step(s); (f) for each ESS unit, the computer orientation of the switch design permits local and centralized maintenance by running diagnostics in any module, combined modules, extended subsystems or global systems. The operations, engineering, and maintenance (OE&M) functions become much simpler; (g) The 5ESS operating system, being modular and encoded in a higher level language (the C language), permits Central Office capabilities to be added easily. The system is portable and modular to be customized to the particular Central Office need. New digital services (such as VoIP, secure data, and FTP transfers) and new intelligent network services within the SSPs can be accommodated by altering the flow control within the call-processing environment; such network services can include the detection of the trigger condition, data-base lookup in a network information data base (NID) or invoking an intelligent peripheral (IP), or exercising a service logic program (SLP). Numerous other digital switches also exist. In Europe, e.g., Siemens' EWSD® and Ericsson's AXE® systems perform comparable functions. Equivalent systems in Japan have also been built and function with similar precision and dependability.

Simple and elaborate versions of ESS are available in most national telecomm environment. These ESS units contend with both the all type of (cable, wireless, satellite, SONET, ATM, etc.) networks and their functionalities. In addition, this newer ESS platforms permit enhanced processing capabilities (such as caller-ID, call-waiting, grade of service), as they exist in the recent intelligent network environments, and servicing capabilities with operations, administration, maintenance and provisioning (OAM&P). Servicing capabilities include handling many millions of channels. Remote-switching modules with line capacities of 20,000 lines, wireless services, etc., are also programmable. The provisioning aspect is unique to most of the recently designed ESS platforms for the United States and Europe. The reliability of the 5ESS platform is better than that of most computer facilities and recorded to be at zero failure in the first seven months of its installation in eight countries.

Typical connectivity from any user to any other network user is shown in Figure 27.5. The communication is bidirectional (in both directions) and occurs as long as both users remain connected and the connection path gets dismantled by the program termination routines in the ESS of either party.

27.7.2.2 Perceptual spaces in the human mind

The connectivity and flexibility of addressing does not exist in addressing the five inter-related spaces (*NS*, *MS*, *PsS*, *KS*, and *SoS*) of human perception. Organization and programming to interconnect is an individual and learned trait in human being.

A definitive numbering system for the perceptual spaces in the mind, like the Dewey Decimal System (DSS), will resolve this problem. When computers are used to program robotic minds, the computer space (*CS*) will permit the programming methodology and tools from digital networks to be imported to bring the discipline to neural programming. This approach will also help the machines to model the human mind and learn from how a machine with an artificially intelligent (AI-based) mind will solve, resolve, and try again to handle problems in the five NS, *MS*, *PsS*, *KS*, and *SoS*) interrelated spaces as shown in Figure 27.6.

The accuracy and dependability of the modern networks is imported in the organization, order and structure of the human mind. The five perceptual spaces are also assigned memory locations in the computer and processes are programmed as CPU instructions. If perceptions are treated as organized spaces and their contents, the functions of the human mind alters these perceptions. The dynamic mapping of the mind is accurately represented as the content of the computer memory at the assigned locations. Since the memory contents can be optimized for optimum performance of functions, the computer can suggest the human mind to act according

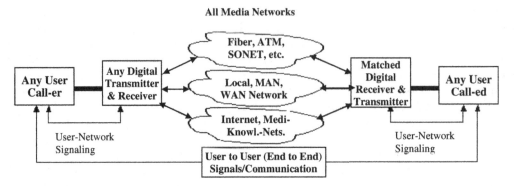

FIGURE 27.5

Built-in processes and functions in most communication environments currently in use. The details of Fiber, ATM, SONET, etc. networks are presented in Chapter 15 of Ref [1].

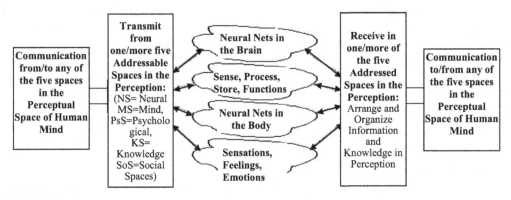

FIGURE 27.6

Suggested model for communication between the various spaces in mind based on the communication model for the digital data and networks. The protocol and procedural steps in the communication space are highly evolved and standardized. Such protocols and procedures in the "mind machine" will emulate the mind functions in the machines.

to the science of knowledge-based algorithms. The suggested model acts in unison with human thoughts that alters the perceptions but in a structured and optimal fashion and trains the mind to function optimally.

When the emerging knowledge-nets or medi-nets are integrated into individual personal spaces of the users and elite members of the Internet and knowledge society, the function of mind get, simplified to accomplish tasks germane to the needs to live. Creativity and innovation are very much in the human realm, while the machine works (at an almost human level) to perform the Operation, Administration and Maintenance or OA&M functions [2], and Operations, Engineering & Administration or OE&M functions [3] to gratify the lower four levels of Maslows' need pyramid [4]. Knowledge robots and medical robots will act as second level of human minds.

27.7.3 SWITCHING ASPECTS

27.7.3.1 Communication networks

In the optical networks, the switching is accomplished by digital cross-connect systems (DCS) and add drop multiplexors (ADM) shown in Figures 27.7 (a) and (b). These programmable units reside in SONET rings [5] and carry any type of data over short, long, and global distances with great

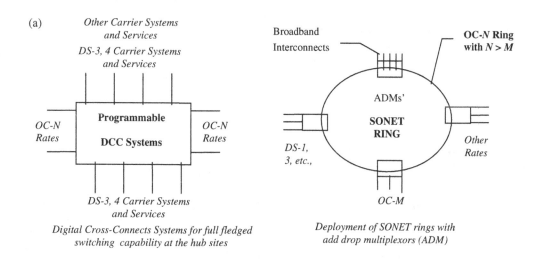

Digital Cross-Connects Systems for full fledged switching capability at the hub sites

Deployment of SONET rings with add drop multiplexors (ADM)

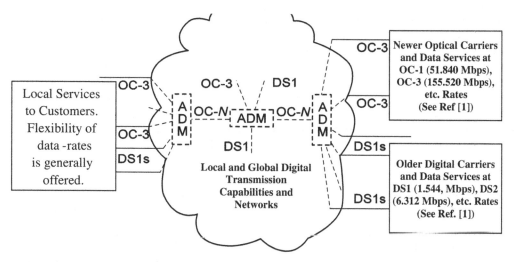

FIGURE 27.7

Cross-connects, add drop multiplexors (ADMs) and SONET digital rings for carrying data in communication networks.

accuracy and dependability. Data rates are generally much higher than the digitally encoded PCM [6] rates of 64 kbps or less.

27.7.3.2 Perceptual networks atop neural nets

Perceptual networks have not been identified nor labeled via the human nervous system, even though the senses are capable of performing intricate pattern recognition functions in speech, sight, touch, etc. Neural nets in the brain that actually process the sensory information still remain unexplored. The interconnectivity of the perceptual spaces in the mind and the functions of the neural nets in the brain is still a topic to be explored and understood. For this reason, we offer little to learn from communication networks to be transfused into the five (*NS, MS, PsS, KS, and SoS*) perceptual spaces in the mind.

CONCLUSIONS

The five (*NS, MS, SoS, PsS,* and *KS*) spaces depicted in the intermediate tiers of Figure 27.4 constitute completely connected neural nets in the human brain. Though not totally understood, they can be augmented by computer and network spaces, both represented as *CS*. Social space is one of the more complicated spaces to map into computer space and to organize it as systematically as the knowledge and science spaces. Since the social space forms the basis of gratifying the emotional, intellectual and psychological needs of most human beings, the application programs for dealing with this space have the most linkages into other spaces.

Individuals with the modern technology and connectivity to the Internets I, II, and III that have evolved for decades are thus drawn into the larger cultures of sciences and civilizations and become a recipient of laws of sciences that have evolved for centuries, values, and ethics that have matured for eons and pave the way for generations of societies still to come.

The sixth and seventh (*CS* and *RS*) spaces form the basis of reality we all live in and well imaged in the five mental spaces listed above. In this framework, reality is artificially mapped into the mind. The computational space permits the arrangement and order to prevail in a systematic and organized fashion. In a sense, the important and essential aspects of reality form the critical action-nodes in the mind and the main neural nodes in the brain. The organizational methodology of the computer sciences is thus extended into organization of the mind and over time and practice gets shifted into the organization of the neural nodes in the brain.

REFERENCES

[1] Ahamed SV, Lawrence VB. Design and engineering of intelligent communication systems. Boston: Kluwer Academic Publishers; 1998.
[2] Ahamed SV, Lawrence VB. Intelligent broadband multimedia networks. Boston: Kluwer Academic Publishers; 1997.

[3] Bell Telephone Laboratories. Engineering and operations in the Bell System. Indiana: Western Electric Co.; 1982.

[4] Maslow AH. A theory of human motivation. Psychol. Rev. 1943;50:370–6.

[5] Sandesara NB, Ritchie GR, Engel-Smith B. Plans and considerations for SONET deployment. IEEE Commun. Mag. 1990; Aug26–33. See also Bellcore, SONET Add-drop multiplex equipment (SONET ADM) Generic Criteria, TR-TSY-000496, Issue 2, 1989.

[6] Bell Telephone Laboratories. Transmission systems for communication. 5th ed. Murray Hill (NJ): Bell Telephone Laboratories; 1982.

APPENDIX 27A **SYMBOLS FOR KNOWLEDGE SPACE**
27A.1 ARROWS

→	Forward knowledge process, i.e., effect of the prior element on the following element.
←	Backward knowledge process, i.e., effect of the following element on the prior element.
→ =	Generates a result, or results. Can also modify the following verb v or a noun n in all spaces
= →	Or modifies the status in knowledge space but on the prior n or v, in knowledge spaces
← = →	Generates a result, or results in a verb v or a noun n, and in both directions

27A.2 NOUNS

n	A noun object or a simply a noun, no, NO, kco, or KCO, etc. and associated with both * and v. All nouns do not interact with all verbs and vice versa.
n'	The status of n after the process (n*v): n' = n, if the process does not affect n; e.g., nop in assembly level programs of plain old computer systems (*Italicization of n's and v's does not have any significance*).

27A.3 CONVOLUTIONS

*	A convolution process of interaction with n or v, usually occurs between n and v or v and n that can be unidirectional (i.e., * →, or ← *) or bidirectional (i.e., ← * →) in its general form. This function of this symbol is contextual, syntactic, and semantic; and it can depend on n and/or v. The time forwardness is depicted by the direction of the arrow for the effect of the convolution.
*'	The status of convolution * after the process (n*v): *' = *, if the process does not affect *

27A.4 VERBS

v	a verb function or simply a verb associated with n and *. All verbs do not interact with all nouns and vice versa. When attempted in illegal context the knowledge machine generates an error message.
v'	The status of the verb v after the process (n * v): v' = v, if the process does not affect v. (*Italicization of n's and v's does not have any significance*).

27A.5 KNOWLEDGE ELEMENTS

kel One or more elements of knowledge (in the knowledge space) associated

kels or with (n^*v), one or more *kels*, are generated during or after the process

KELs $= (n^*v)$. (*Italicization of n's and v's does not have any significance*).

27A.6 PROCESSES

$(n * v)$ A process in the real world that generates an effect in the real world and also generates a *kel* in the knowledge space. It has variations as $(n \leftarrow^* v)$, $(n *\rightarrow v)$, *or as* $(n\rightarrow^*\leftarrow v)$

27A.7 SPACES

RS Physical and Real space with $(x, y, z, t; r, \theta, \varphi, t; r, \theta, h, t;$ etc.) coordinates in which reality occurs

NS Neural space for thought and comprehension; it is real space in the physiological sense

SoS Social Space for humans and KCOs in dealing with social problems

SS Memory systems space in computer and network systems for computational tools, algorithms, etc.

MS Mental space derivative from NS

PS Psychological space with emotional ties to physical or mental objects, convolutions and verbs

KS Knowledge space(s): Subset(s) of mental space in the human mind, or superset/subset of the memory allocated for knowledge functions in knowledge machines. The main memory is thus tiered into three layers, operational or systems space, a knowledge space, and a real/simulation/application space for computing in the real physical/computational space (see Figure 27.1). Human beings routinely deploy different KSs to store knowledge accumulated in differ disciplines, or about totally unrelated noun objects. During solutions of knowledge-based problems, these spaces (RS and PS, RS and SS) get interdependent and work coherently to solve knowledge-based problems or create new knowledge which can be mapped into real world as inventions or modification of existing systems. Mapping back and forth from RS from and to KS are both feasible in knowledge machines as much as mapping to and back from SS to RS.

27A.8 INCREMENTAL CHANGES IN THE STATUS OF N, * AND V

φ An incremental change associated with the process $(n * v)$ in the real space RS ≢ 0, but finite however small or large it may be and equals $(n' \sim n; *' \sim *;$ or $v' \sim v)$; φ can be sub-microscopic or super-cosmic

ψ A corresponding change associated with the process $(n *v)$ in the knowledge space KS ≢ 0, but finite however small or large it may be and corresponds to real space change $(n' \sim n; *' \sim *;$ or $v' \sim v)$; ψ can be tiny and incomprehensible or engulf the entire neural space (NS).

27A.9 TIME

t Time in all spaces. Reversal of 't' is not possible in real space and MS but is feasible in KS, SS. Also used as a symbol in analog and continuous functions

δt or Δt Time to complete any process in the real and/or knowledge spaces.

T A span of time and $= \sum \delta t$ or Δt, Numerical operation is possible in all spaces.

27A.10 PROCESSES

27A.10.1 The convolution processes

Convolution processes in social and human environments are unique to the extent that they are syntactic, semantic, and individualistic. The parsing of the command embedded in the generic instruction (n * v) selects the nature of the convolution between n and v. For example, the nature of love between a mother and child is very different from that between a husband and wife, even though the noun object in mother's role is the same physical person (noun) in the wife's role. It is somewhat comparable to the convolution of two series expansion of functions f(x) and f'(x), where every element in the series expansion of f(x) interacts with each of the elements in the expansion of f'(x), and generated a specific element after the convolution. Even so, in social processes, the similarity is not valid because the nature of the elements in f(x) can influence the nature of elements in f'(x) thus giving a different result for different mother's love to the child or a different result for different wife's love to the husband or vice versa.

However, if a knowledge base is queried to get the expected attributes of a particular mother's affection to the child (with its own attributes), then a consistency of behavior can be expected with a certain degree of confidence. Thus, knowledge-bases play a significant role in most of the generic social process (n * v). In drawing a similarity between the mathematical processing and humanistic processing, convolution processes are significantly different. In the former case, there is a precise sequence of invariable steps that can be programmed as a series of numerical/logic operation codes (opcs) for the CPU of a machine, In the later case, the sequence of step are adaptive to the syntactic, semantics, and individualistic to the social process (n * v) conveyed to social processing unit (SPU) that rides atop of the knowledge operation code (kopc) to be executed in the knowledge processing unit or the KPU of a knowledge machine. Hence, the code (n * v) has three levels of decoding to generate (a) the social machine code, (b) the knowledge machine code, and (c) the numerical/logic code for the CPU. Knowledge-base lookup is an essential step in most social processing programs. Simple convolutions are common in scientific processing. Such convolutions used with Laplace Transform of the convolution of two functions and in the solution of differential equations (Duhamel's principle). Convolutions are also used in evaluating other transforms. The solutions of scientific problems have a clear and definitive methodology. Interactive solutions are also feasible but along particular tracts.

In a the social domain, considerable caution is necessary due to nonlinearities and emotional responses of the participants. These cannot be reduced to precise numerical responses, but estimated for particular social noun objects under particular contexts by looking up their behavioral responses from their individual knowledge bases. Such personal bases are generally stored in individual's hand held devices or their PCs. For example, individuals prefer certain foods, the company of selected individuals, and/or shopping habits and such preferences and their numerical values of the likes and dislikes can be used to evaluate the economic return for the value to their effort in getting a near optimal solution.

As another example consider a user command to the social machine, "Say the things you used to say and make the world go away." The social machine will respond by remembering and reciting the most effective statements it had conjured from its knowledge bases and made the user feel good. If such knowledge bases do not exist, it will search the Internet bases for users down in the blues and pick the context for the user and recite (via audiovisual signals) them to the user. Such responses can be as effective as the word of a psychologist who treats depressed patients to relieve anxiety or pangs of fear. Rationality replaces anxiety from the prior encounters with fear and emotions. This is possible use of a social knowledge-based machine.

Simple social processes

*(n * v)*   A noun executes a verb; e.g., human strolls; human walks; human runs, human flees, etc.
(n → v)*   A noun with a modified verb; human runs fast; human slows down to standstill, etc., *(n *→v)* e.g., human run and gets tired

Complex processes

*(n1 * v n2)*   Teacher (n1) instructs (*v) student
*(n2) (n1 *→v n2)*   Teacher severely reprimands (*→v) student

Compound processes

*(n1 →*v →* v → n2 = > →n3)*

Hydrogen explodes (→ *v) during combination (→ * v) with oxygen (n2) to form water vapor (=> → n3)

*((n1 →*v n2) (n1 →* v) *n2 = > v)*

Master (n1) whips (→*v) slave (n2) (and makes (n1 →* v) her (n2) cry (= > v).
(Two simple sentences)

The same expression in the symbolic language
*((n1 →*v n2) (n1 →* v) *n2= > v)* also can be used for Master apologizes to slave and makes her feel good, etc. The nature of v's becomes different.

Complete form for dyadic interaction(s) between *no1* and *no2*

$$(no1 \leftrightarrow *1 \leftrightarrow vf \leftrightarrow *2 \leftrightarrow no2)$$

The knowledge machine compiles the symbolic expression as and assigns the direction of the vector-verb *vf12* as vector 1 to 2 and vector-verb *vf21* as vector 2 to 1.

27A.11 THE ARROW SYMBOL AND ITS VARIATIONS

The simple interactive processes can be depicted by the single arrow convention for both forward and backward effects. For example, → represents a forward knowledge process, i.e., effect of the prior element on the following element, and ← represents a backward knowledge process, i.e., effect of the following element on the prior element. However, social and machine generated objects can be classified into three major categories: (a) Passive, (b) Active/Reactive, and (c) Intelligent. Passive objects are generally inanimate and respond to the verb function according to laws of natural and material sciences and react in a preset fashion. For example, when water is heated, it vaporizes and forms steam. Active and reactive noun objects act in a contextual fashion and become situation dependent. For example, when iron is heated with sulfur, it forms iron sulfide and when iron is heated with carbon it forms steel with altogether different properties from those of iron sulfide. Finally, when an intelligent object such as a human being is stressed sufficiently, the reaction can be to radically change the nature of stress (noun object), the convolution of forces that cause the stress and the (other intelligent objects) that are driving the forces to cause the stress and even to change the settings that give rise to the stress. Accordingly, the arrow symbols are modified for these instances and depicted in Table 27.1.

In social settings, the behavioral variations of participants *no1* and *no2* are shown when the participant act in perfect and imperfect relationships. The column 2 is the rarest case when the participants are in perfect harmony all the time. Columns 3 and 4 are more practical when the moods and external variable affect the behavior (e.g., relation between spouses). Column 3, rows 4 and 5 indicate disharmony and eventual conflict that can lead to termination (e.g., boss-employee, husband-wife) of relations. Column 4 indicates some predictability of the responses from the participants that can lead to a long term continued partnership with adjustments of Intelligent objects *no1* and *no2*, which is the case in almost all relationships. While filter theory in electrical engineering offers clues to smoothing the transient effects in circuits, a similar strategy in social interactions can lead to a less "stressful" tolerance of sharp corners in human behavior.

27A.12 HIGHER LEVEL KNOWLEDGE INSTRUCTIONS

At a very superficial level, the consummation of a male and female chromosomes that results in creation of a new genetic cell of the unborn infant is represented in symbolic language as (*no1* (male chromosome) * v (consummation with) → *no2* (female chromosome) = > *no3* (genetic cell of the infant)). At a detailed level, all the knowledge in reproductive biology is encompassed in this rudimentary representation; the symbols *no1*, *, v, *no2*, and *no3* need to allocated according to the level of detail. At a even more detailed level, the symbolic representation can become more elaborate but the encoding of the interactive processes is feasible. When programmed appropriately, knowledge machines can decode higher level knowledge statements and fill all the Internet-based knowledge levels and the symbols in great detail. This principle is used extensively in decoding high level scientific/business instruction(s) in plain old computer systems as the higher level command is fragmented into micro-coded subroutines.

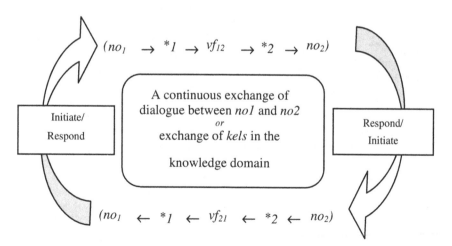

$$(no_1 \rightarrow {}^*1 \rightarrow vf_{12} \rightarrow {}^*2 \rightarrow no_2)$$

Initiate/
Respond

A continuous exchange of
dialogue between *no1* and *no2*
or
exchange of *kels* in the
knowledge domain

Respond/
Initiate

$$(no_1 \leftarrow {}^*1 \leftarrow vf_{21} \leftarrow {}^*2 \leftarrow no_2)$$

FIGURE 27A.1

Representation of real time events to symbolic knowledge domain representation for the knowledge machine to analyze, modify, optimize based on prior experience(s) in KB's.

CHAPTER 27 REAL SPACE, KNOWLEDGE SPACE

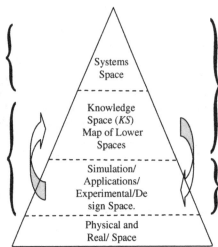

In human beings this Neural space is generally dedicated for body and physiological functions

Feedback from Ethics, Concept, and Wisdom Bases into KS: In human beings this space is for peripheral nervous, sensory system human memory, I/O and control to control actions, behavior and Design.

Reality of the physical Space

Systems Space

Knowledge Space (*KS*) Map of Lower Spaces

Simulation/ Applications/ Experimental/De sign Space.

Physical and Real/ Space

Network and Machine OS, Internets I, II and III Connectivity, and to Local KBs'; Local, Network and Operating System, Tools and Libraries

Local and Network Database Connectivity, CAD, AP, Tools and Resources

Robotic, Mechanical, Machine or Physical Space

FIGURE 27A.2

Organization of the computer space to track social interactions and their effects in the other perceptual spaces.

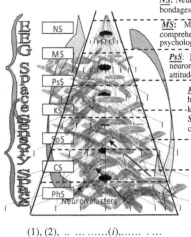

NS: Neural Space for biological neural nets, chemical and structural bondages of neurons, stem cells, and axons within body and brain.

MS: Mental Space derived from *NS* for thought and comprehension; it is real and reversible space in the physiological and psychological bondage. Laws of physiology and biochemistry

PsS: Psychological Space with emotional ties, connectivity of neuron clusters to physical and mental noun objects (*no's*); attitudes and temperament with convolutions (**'s*) and real or

KS: Knowledge Space(s): Subset(s) of Mental Space *MS* in the human mind, or superset/subset of the memory allocated for knowledge functions in *CS*. Laws for the manipulation of

SoS: Social Space for humans and large and small knowledge centric objects (*kco's*) in dealing with social and environmental

CS: Computer System Space in computers and networks operating systems. Laws and organizations of computer and network systems apply with computational tools,

PhS: Physical Space: Laws of mechanics, physics, engineering and sciences to deal with reality and abstraction. Irreversibility of the time dimension is a fundamental requirement in the physical space *PhS*

(1), (2), ...(*i*),...... ....
.......(*n*)
Noun objects in Physical Space and Corresponding Anchor Points in Mind

Connectivity and Overlap of Seven Spaces due to Social Interactions and the movement of Mental Anchors associated with Noun Objects. Sensory Space and Neural Space and their overlap is shown on the left side of the Figure.

Symbolic Representation of an Anchor in the Mind or a Neuron Cluster in the Brain

Representation of the Constant Shifts of Mental Anchors due to Social Interaction(s)

FIGURE 27A.3

Movement of noun objects by verb functions (black arrows) during social interactions.

GENERAL STRUCTURE OF KNOWLEDGE ($NO^* \rightarrow VF$ AND $VF^* \rightarrow NO$)

28

CHAPTER SUMMARY

In this chapter, we present a matrix approach to the uneven flow of knowledge in social and cultural settings. Based on the fact that knowledge is always in a state of transition and flows from one or more social or a natural source(s) to one or more receptors, the delay and dispersion of knowledge is related to the media characteristics represented as a matrix. The source and receptor characteristics also play a part in the communication of one element of knowledge (symbolized as a *kel*). These *kels* being of any size and nature can be integrated in a coherent and cogent fashion to make microscopic or macroscopic bodies of knowledge in organized, structured, and sensible knowledge in the human minds and in addressable segments of knowledge bases in networks and on the Internet. Small and large bodies of knowledge (symbolized as *boks*) can thus be organized, reorganized; processed and reprocessed; retrieved and stored; adjusted and organized; and optimized and enhanced to suit the reality of most social and scientific settings.

When perfect knowledge is being perceived, we present nine basic questions that are logical centered around the active verbs (symbolized as *vfs*), participating nouns (symbolized as *nos*), and their interrelations (symbolized as $*s$ or convolutions) that constitute the pursued knowledge. In answering these questions entirely, a framework of perfect knowledge will be gained, if the answers have a scientific basis or explanation. In real life situations, partial answers to a selected subset of these nine questions are generally sufficient to carry on a function or a dialog in a pragmatic sense. Answers to one or two of the nine questions do not present significant, useful, or pertinent knowledge and such answers generally degrade the quality of knowledge. The methodology and framework are presentment in detail to expand and to enhance the pursued knowledge to a targeted goal, even though it may not by an optimum or a perfect goal.

28.1 INTRODUCTION

Knowledge has been an integral part of all life forms since millennia. Modern machine offer new tools and technologies to use and reuse knowledge in ever expanding ways. Their positive deployment has helped human progress as much as its abuse has caused wars, destruction, and social stagnation. In hindsight, abuse has always retarded the flow towards the betterment of society. Numerous social scientists have highlighted the cause and effect relation of the social forces on the human inertia to the toil make building elegant knowledge and social environments.

Evolution of Knowledge Science. DOI: http://dx.doi.org/10.1016/B978-0-12-805478-9.00028-5

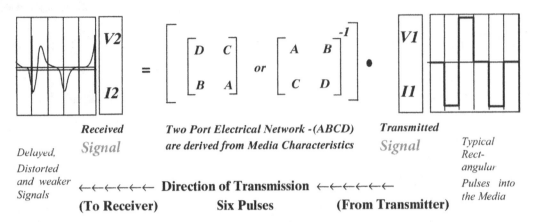

$$
\begin{bmatrix} V2 \\ I2 \end{bmatrix} = \left(\begin{bmatrix} D & C \\ B & A \end{bmatrix} \ or \ \begin{bmatrix} A & B \\ C & D \end{bmatrix}^{-1} \right) \bullet \begin{bmatrix} V1 \\ I1 \end{bmatrix}
$$

Received **Two Port Electrical Network -(ABCD)** *Transmitted* *Typical*
Signal *are derived from Media Characteristics* *Signal* *Rect-*

Delayed, *angular*
Distorted
and weaker ←←←←← **Direction of Transmission** ←←←←← *Pulses into*
Signals *the Media*
(To Receiver) **Six Pulses** **(From Transmitter)**

FIGURE 28.1

Transmission of signals through a electric medium that causes degradation. The elements of the ABCD matrix [2] can be accurately computed from the characteristic of the medium or combination of different media.

A universal platform for the integration of social science is desirable to make knowledge a science and then to use the computer, network, and Internet technologies to accelerate the positive social movement in spite of the social resistance by reason and methodology, rather than by force and violence. The positive use conserves human energy and offers lasting solutions.

In this vein, we suggest the use of machines that can serve as computer-aided knowledge systems that handle the rationale and logistics behind the deployment of constructive knowledge. A mathematical framework is also proposed that can formulate the basis of discovering knowledge behind the obvious information to make the proposed solutions enduring and sustainable. Longer-lasting stable solutions to most knowledge-based problems make the investment in knowledge science attractive.

28.2 METHODOLOGY BASED ON COMMUNICATION SCIENCE

28.2.1 ELECTRIC TRANSMISSION

In the modern digitized network environments, the information bearing binary signals over transmission media are transmitted and received to exchange knowledge. The typical representation of such binary signals (encoded in the AMI (alternate mark inversion) code) over twisted wire pairs in the subscriber environment of typical telephone networks, are shown in Figure 28.1. The encoded optical signals in the modern fiber optic networks have different shapes and are not presented here. In (almost) all communication networks, the information is encoded as waveforms and these waveforms suffer delay, distortion, and loss of energy as they traverse the media [1]. Such delays and distortions can be significant.

28.2.2 COMMUNICATION OF KNOWLEDGE

The equivalent configuration in the knowledge domain for the transmission and reception of *kels* over a social media can be written in Figure 28.2.

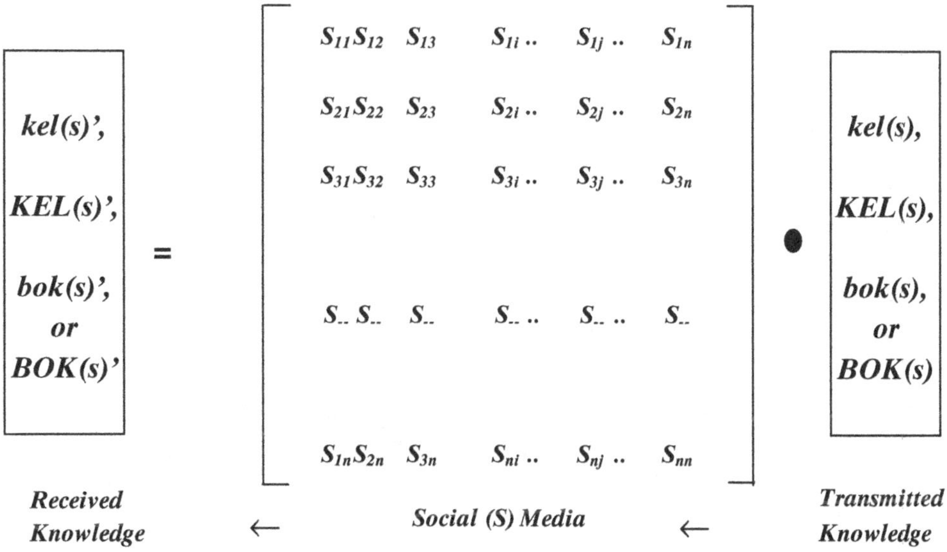

$$
\begin{bmatrix} kel(s)', \\ \\ KEL(s)', \\ \\ bok(s)', \\ or \\ BOK(s)' \end{bmatrix}
=
\begin{bmatrix}
S_{11}S_{12} & S_{13} & S_{1i} .. & S_{1j} .. & S_{1n} \\
S_{21}S_{22} & S_{23} & S_{2i} .. & S_{2j} .. & S_{2n} \\
S_{31}S_{32} & S_{33} & S_{3i} .. & S_{3j} .. & S_{3n} \\
\\
S_{..}S_{..} & S_{..} & S_{...} .. & S_{...} .. & S_{..} \\
\\
S_{1n}S_{2n} & S_{3n} & S_{ni} .. & S_{nj} .. & S_{nn}
\end{bmatrix}
\bullet
\begin{bmatrix} kel(s), \\ \\ KEL(s), \\ \\ bok(s), \\ or \\ BOK(s) \end{bmatrix}
$$

Received   *Social (S) Media*   *Transmitted*
Knowledge   ←   ←   *Knowledge*

FIGURE 28.2

Transmission of *kels* through a social medium that causes their degradation. The elements of the S matrix shown above do not have a formal representation and the knowledge recovery is less than perfect. However, the receiver can process the received *kels* and reconstruct the transmitted knowledge well enough to comprehend the content.

Correspondingly for the machine media, the matrix elements "S" in section 28.2.2 are placed as "M" elements and the equation for the reconstructed knowledge at the receiver end, is written in Figure 28.3.

The delay in the social media cannot be undone, and all communication systems suffer from the setback. Delay in social and human communications systems can be very long slowly depriving the utility of the original knowledge. In some cases when the original knowledge is based on extreme truisms, immortal beauty, and/or universal virtue, the knowledge itself assumes a flavor of immortality. For example, Boolean algebra, Tesla's conception of rotating electromagnetic fields in polyphase motors, Rumi's verses, Buddha's teachings carry their own validity, appeal, and integrity after many centuries. The converse statement is equally true; e.g., Bush's lies about the weapons of mass destruction (WMD) in Iraq followed by Tony Blair's acts of a war based on falsehood; Vietcong's brutalities and Ku Klux Klan's assertion of white supremacy have all brought unwarranted disarray into the world. The matrix of communication is frail, time dependent, and it can materially change the contents of any body of knowledge (BOK or bok). Knowledge machines deserve to be made secure against the abuse by manipulative folks!.

The emotional and value of knowledge content becomes dependent on the Social (S) Media matrix that can drastically alter received signals. Then this matrix is tuned with average transmitter (e.g., a newscaster), average unbiased media channel (e.g., a university broadcast system), and an average unbiased receptor (e.g., a typical college student), then the chances are that the received signal is a faithful replica of the transmitted signal. But this situation is hypothetical and in reality every received element of knowledge gets tainted to some extent other. However in vast majority of cases, the receivers generally get enough coherent knowledge to exchange ideas in human dialogs.

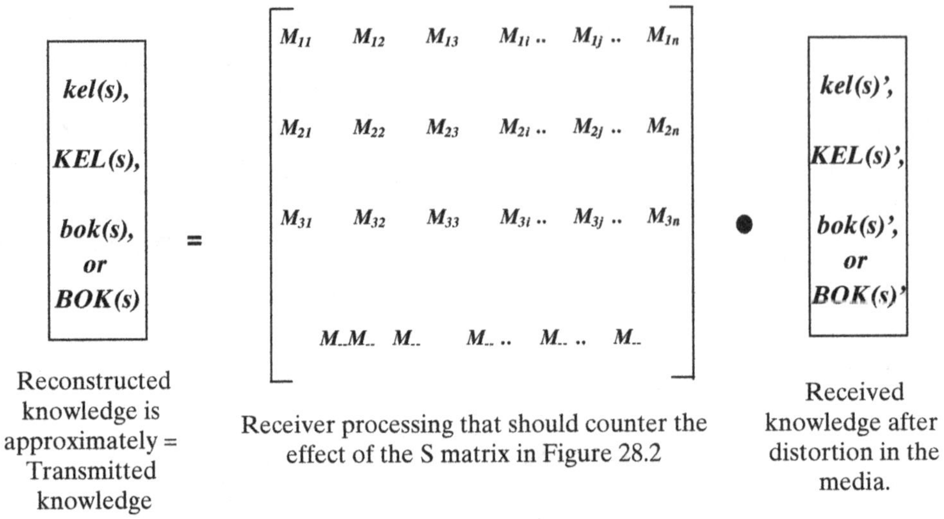

$$
\begin{bmatrix} kel(s), \\ \\ KEL(s), \\ \\ bok(s), \\ or \\ BOK(s) \end{bmatrix}
=
\begin{bmatrix}
M_{11} & M_{12} & M_{13} & M_{1i}\,.. & M_{1j}\,.. & M_{1n} \\
\\
M_{21} & M_{22} & M_{23} & M_{2i}\,.. & M_{2j}\,.. & M_{2n} \\
\\
M_{31} & M_{32} & M_{33} & M_{3i}\,.. & M_{3j}\,.. & M_{3n} \\
\\
& M..M..\; M.. & & M..\,.. & M..\,.. & M..
\end{bmatrix}
\bullet
\begin{bmatrix} kel(s)', \\ \\ KEL(s)', \\ \\ bok(s)', \\ or \\ BOK(s)' \end{bmatrix}
$$

Reconstructed knowledge is approximately = Transmitted knowledge

Receiver processing that should counter the effect of the S matrix in Figure 28.2

Received knowledge after distortion in the media.

FIGURE 28.3

Machine processing of the received knowledge that tends to undo the effect of distortion in the social media. Ideally the M matrix should be the inverse of the S matrix. Self-equalizing equalizers in receivers [3] machine can rarely (almost never) satisfy this stringent requirement, even though the human mind attempts to counter the media effects by being judicious.

28.3 SEVEN BASIC QUESTIONS TO COMPLETE KNOWLEDGE

Knowledge any stage is imperfect; imperfect and incomplete may be, it still conveys necessary information to abide by the laws to survive, live, and even progress by controlled measure(s) over finite durations of time. In a limited sense, order and organization appears to dominate what is known in answers to a set of logical questions about anything, any time anywhere and in any social and cultural context. The saving grace lies in refraining from asking question(s) that intellect cannot resolve and the mind cannot perceive. Human and mental resources are constrained, if resources are not the limit, life-span is.

In a very rational way one can seek the answers to Why? What? How? Who? Where? When? Duration (or how long?) for any element of knowledge, only to be frustrated that innate and unrestrained curiosity has no logical or totally rational end. Combination of these questions posed together will only cause more frustration for the mind and disarray in the thoughts. When appropriately constrained, the answers to these questions lead to well structured and duly ordered solutions of many scientific and social problems. Given any body of knowledge about anything, an intelligent human or machine can query in at least seven different ways (each by itself or in combination(s)) repeatedly to reach the frail edge of what is known.

In the knowledge domain, where every microscopic element of knowledge rests in a noun object, a verb function to and from other noun objects, in appropriate convolutions, has no immunity from these questions. However, this quest leads to a few guide posts. The answers to at least some of the questions form a stable neural net in the brain to encompass a noun-object, a verb-function, or a convolution in their own rights that can form linkage to such other cluster(s) and the neural net can grow larger and larger and become more and more stable. If the answers are derives based on science, truisms, social benefits, and economic principles, then the borders of rationality are pushed deeper and deeper in the neural nets in the brain; the personality becomes stable and larger tasks (verb-functions) can be accomplished more effectively and more efficiently with larger and larger noun-objects in a refined and orderly fashion.

In a gross and macroscopic form, the fundamental question (Why?) and its answer lead to life itself: since every living member of every species has to sustain its life form, all energies stem from this essential requirement. Physical, psychological, social, intellectual, etc., venues have been carved out for the orderly flow of these energies over the eons of existence. More recently, computers and networks have altered the flow and storage of knowledge that permits the channeling of these energies in optimal and efficient ways to achieve sets of goals and ambitions. The role of the new advances in technologies become crucial in finding innovations, sciences, and technologies to help mankind a more elated and more civil way to live and exist with nature without destroying it.

28.3.1 MACHINE AND NETWORK ENVIRONMENTS

In the most environments, searching for the answers to the seven basic question leads to objects and things; their actions and accomplishments; and the way in which these objects do what they have to do or what they have done. Knowledge starts here! Embedded in related objects, actions, and how they blend. Stated more precisely, every module or element of knowledge (*kel*) is founded in one or more noun-objects, one or more verb-functions, and their respective convolutions.

When knowledge elements are broken down into their own building blocks, machines become invaluable in reaching targeted goals of speed, efficiency, and accuracy. Computers, networks, and digital systems in the knowledge era have the innate ability to handle knowledge at its lowest to its highest levels in three distinctive ways as follows:

i.   Machines can and do grip and load the noun objects (*nos*) from their very rudimentary form as cellular and microscopic objects to large bodies of knowledge as (*BOKs* as books, knowledge bases (*KBs*), tables, series, texts, etc., as operands by bringing them (or their address(es)) to the Operand Registers (ORs).

ii. Machines have the innate ability to construct and construe verb functions (*vfs*) from nano-, micro-, midsized to macro, to cosmic processes, etc., as operation code by hardware, micro-programmable, or macroprogrammable codes by bringing them (or their address(es)) to the Instruction Registers (IRs).

iii. Machines have the innate ability to lookup a context-dependent table that selects the appropriate convolution (or a set of convolutions) to combine one or more elements of knowledge or *kel*(s) and assemble a series of context dependent micro instructions. Machines move the result or its (address(es)) to the output register(s) or (ORs).

All the software tools and methodologies currently used in computer engineering become applicable in the knowledge domain as knowledge-ware tools and methodologies in building and designing major knowledge-ware systems. We present the conceptual bridge between computer sciences and knowledge science in Table 28.1.

28.3.2 HUMAN AND SOCIAL ENVIRONMENTS

In the human environments, searching for the answers to the seven basic question leads to noun-objects, verb-functions, and their convolutions that have significance to the processes

Table 28.1 Seven Logical Questions and Their Implications in the Machine and Network Environments

Question/Partial Answers	Machine and Network Response	Objects (machines), Actions (execute), and Appropriate Convolutions (programs)
1. Why? Simply to continue life form	To Generate, Examine, Manipulate, etc.	Solutions and resolve (routine and special) problems; Information, logical, business, social, etc., issues
2. What? Computer Systems	Computers, Robots, Systems, Networks	Application and scientific programs; Procedures, OS SW, HW/SW/FW/structures
3. How? Procedures and Creativity	Computer and Machine Aided, Robotic Systems	Design and Derive general instructions for machines, their repetitive patterns, protocol, and OSI instructions, etc.
4. Who? HW, Know. Machines	Machine and Knowledge Systems	HW and machine, corporate, cultural configurations, etc.
5. Where? (x, y, z), (r, θ, φ), etc.	Controlled or Open space environments	Local machine, and (LANs, WANs, global, etc.) network and INTERNET
6. When? Past, present or future 't'	During execution or Realtime, extended time applns.	Execution-phase time Line, start to end, discrete, or continuous time setting
7. Duration? 'Δt'	Execution, loopback, Internet response time, etc.	Execution time for machines, network process time to execute Internet and machine instructions

and communications of knowledge elements. Typical answers of these questions in the human and social domain are presented in Table 28.2.

28.3.3 SUPERPOSITION OF MACHINE AND SOCIAL ENVIRONMENTS

An ideal machine-supported social setting is feasible if the machines will completely or partially execute the requirements of Table 28.2 by the programs and functions in Table 28.1. This ideal state of machine compliance is perhaps not likely to be realized quickly, but the machines can become more human rather than the humans become more robotic.

When Tables 28.1 and 28.2 are merged, from a conceptual and functional perspective, the blending is event by the devices and the device technology in rows 2 and 4 or both the tables. The prolonged investment to make the devices, computers, and networks faster and real-time oriented is evident by comparing Rows 6 and 7 of both tables.

28.3.4 EBB AND FLOW OF KNOWLEDGE

The velocity of flow of knowledge is as variable and dynamic as life itself. Static knowledge is no knowledge; instead it is indicative of a coma-static mind and body of any object or entity. More ever, the velocity is neither uniform in time or in space. Hence, the velocity of flow of objects, the rate of flow of activities, and the rate of change of their convolutions all play a role in the flow.

Objects and their activities are equally important in all aspects of social and machine tasks. The pattern of the ebb and flow of verb functions, noun objects, and their convolutions are depicted in Figure 28.4. There is a commonality in their flow and they are rarely synchronized.

Table 28.2 Seven Logical Questions and Their Implications in the Current Social and Human Environments

Question/Partial Answers	Human and Social Entities	Objects (entities), Actions (perform) and Appropriate, Orderly and Organized (functions)
1. Why? Support of Life Functions.	To support gratification of Needs to live and excel	Basic Needs: Freud (3-Layer), Maslow (5-Layer), Ahamed (7-Layer), (Carl Jung, Marx and Mead, Smith, Keynes)
2. What? All forms of Digital Systems	All communication and computing interfaces	Preloaded or Down Loaded Programs in Devices that follow scientific, social, search, and their algorithms.
3. How? Procedures Creativity.	Clicks and/or Operation of the devices and Gadgets	Learn and Use the preloaded programs in social and communication devices.
4. Who? Handheld Know. Systems	Generally Self or Partnering Individual or organization	Human(s) and organization(s) partnering with other social entities are involved
5. Where? (x, y, z) 't' (Spatial), etc.	The current location is generally implied	Distance is generally not an issue because of the network/Internet connectivity
6. When? Past, Present, or Future "t"	Present (Now) emphasized (Again and again)	This is situation and problem dependent parameter
7. Duration? 'Δt'	As Fast as Possible (Again and again)	Execution times for the devices and transit times in the network or Internet and to complete transactions.

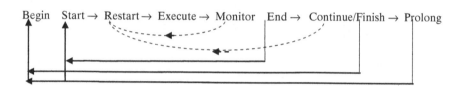

(a) What (vf) and What Action?

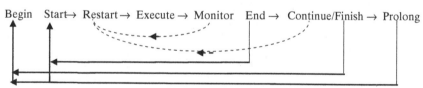

(b) Who (no) and Who is involved?

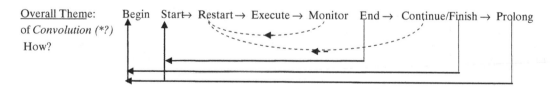

(c) How (*) and How are vf and no convolved?

FIGURE 28.4

Similarity of processes governing the ebb and flow of *vfs* (actions), *nos* (nouns), and **s*.

28.4 ZERO, PARTIAL, AND IMPERFECT KNOWLEDGE SYNDROME

The scenario for the state of knowledge at any instant of time can be represented effectively by a matrix. Isolated and inactive knowledge is similar to a buried treasure or inactive wealth in locked accounts. The circulation of knowledge is as vital to the society as the circulation of wealth is essential to the economy. Knowledge in circulation needs its transmission and its reception, and the transitional effects of the media and culture can be embedded in the matrix for its representation. This matrix can also be used for including the effects of the delay, distortion and cultural effect as knowledge is communicated. Knowledge without communion is lifeless and worthless. The velocity of flow of knowledge is embedded in the neural nets, communication nets, and the Internets that facilitate its flow.

In Figure 28.5 the status of three knowledge elements of knowledge,[1] Δk or *kel* is depicted. Three building blocks of any *kel* are (a) the noun objects, (b) the verb functions, and (c) their

Rece- Trans ptor mitter	What (*vf*)
What? (*vf*) (action)	A

(a) verb function *vf*, by itself has $\Delta k = 0$ or

kel =0; e.g., eats

Rece- Trans ptor mitter	What (*vf*)	Who (*no*)
What? (*vf*) (action)	A	C
Who? (*no*) (human; Corp.)	G	I

(b) a verb (*vf*) and a noun (*no*) combined Δk = incomplete. e.g., man eats.

Rece- Trans ptor mitter	What (*vf*)	How (***)	Who (*no*)
What? (*vf*) (action)	A	B	C
	Human Discretion		
How? (*) (legal, ethical, etc)	D	E	F
	Human Discretion		
Who? (*no*) (human; Corp.)	G	H	I
	Human Discretion		

(c) a verb (*vf*), its convolution (***), and a noun (*no*) combined makes $\Delta k = no*vf$ complete. e. g., "man quickly eats"; the placement of * is important to state Δk in a sensible way. For example, $\Delta k = vf*no$ would be interpreted as "eats quickly man" and makes no human sense. (See footnote 2). To this extent the accuracy of *kels* needs to be preserved.

<u>Note:</u> Media distortions can cause delay and dispersion effect of *vfs, *s* and *nos*.

Transmitter Δks

Δks Matrix

Receiver $\Delta k's$

A Two Port Network [4]. For imperfect media $\Delta ks \neq \Delta k's$

FIGURE 28.5

Knowledge is in a state of transition and flow from one state to the next. Accordingly, the *kels* have to traverse some definitive form of media; human to human, cell to cell, society to society, during the flow of *kels* undergoes some change. Any received *kel* need not be the same as the transmitted *kel* due to the media characteristics that can cause delay and dispersion in the properties of *vfs, nos,* and **s* that are uniquely blended to make the transmitted kel.

[1] *kels* can be of any size or form. In their pico-, nano-, or micro-format, they pertain to the microscopic universe of cells, biological organisms, and sub-microscopic entities, in their macro forms they pertain to earthly spaces, cosmic universe, in their humanistic formats, they pertain the humans, societies, cultures, and social entities. The combinatorial laws of *kels* can become radically different in different formats but retain an order and methodology in their own particular structure.

carefully placed convolutions. When intelligently chosen and appropriately placed, the resulting *kels* can combine, recombine, split, and regroup as elements in nature or human in society. These *kels* also carry quantifiable amount of knowledge in them. For example, the *kels* that make up a body of knowledge in the brain of an astronaut are of a different nature and far greater in number than the *kels* in the brain of an ant. Neuron cells in the brain bring order and organization to the knowledge in any body of knowledge that can be manipulated and restructured in the mind.

28.4.1 ZERO, INCOMPLETE, FINITE, AND PARTIAL KNOWLEDGE

In Figure 28.5, three variations of *kels* are shown. The zero knowledge entity shown in Figure 28.4 (a) has only one of the three building blocks, *vf*(s), *no*(s), or *(s), and does not carry any knowledge. These are alike the sounds of vowels or consonants that do not make spoken words. The incomplete *kels* depicted in Figure 28.4(b) can carry two of the three building blocks. The complete *kels* with at least three blocks make some sense,[2] though not entire sense. Perfect knowledge being impossible the limited knowledge starts to become partially useful.

When the matrix elements A; A and I; and A, E, I are unity with the other terms being zero in the matrices, (a), (b) and (c) in Figure 28.5, then *vf'*, *'*, and *no'* are equal to *vf*, *, and *no* respectively, and the media delay and distortions are each equal to zero. This is a rare instance in reality.

The transmitted knowledge element has the form *kel* and is represented as

$$kel = vf^*no.$$

The received knowledge element has the form and is represented as

$$kel' = vf'^{*'}no'.$$

The expanded form of the proposed representation will be as follows:

$$\mathbf{vf'} = \mathbf{A} .. \ vf + \mathbf{D}^* + \mathbf{G}.no; \quad {*'} = \mathbf{B} \cdot vf + \mathbf{E} \cdot {*} + \mathbf{H} \cdot no, \text{and } no' = \mathbf{C} .. \ vf + \mathbf{F}^* + \mathbf{I} \cdot no;$$

The received *kel* can thus be computed and reconstructed.

28.4.2 HUMAN DISCRETION AND UNCERTAINTIES

See Figures 28.6 and 28.7.

28.5 COMPLETE KNOWLEDGE AND KNOWLEDGE MATRIX (KMAT)

Perfection is abstract as much as truth is universal or as much as virtue is immortal. Even though human beings do not achieve perfection, universality, or immortality, yet most humans seek the perfection. In a sense, the imaginary becomes concrete enough to pursue in real life. Knowledge follows a similar trail in minds. Viewed from this perspective, knowledge is practical, effective, and essential even though the boundaries of knowledge are abstract, universal, and

---

[2]knowledge and sense are inherently coupled. Nonsense knowledge is doomed to quick and through extinction. The knowledge embedded in the neurons has to couple with similar other *kels* to form bigger and more stable *KELs*. Unlinked and unrelated *kels* are soon forgotten and their traces are removed from memory.

Role of Uncertainties in Knowledge flow due to Human Discretion		
What? (*vf*) (action)	Human Discretion		
	A	B	C
How? (*) (legal, ethical, etc)	Human Discretion		
	D	E	F
Who? (*no*) (human; Corp.)	Human Discretion		
	G	H	I

FIGURE 28.6

Human discretion has entered almost all social transactions because of the uncertainties about what action (vf) will take, how the action will be implemented (*), and who the human being is within the realm of human discretion and circumstances.

immortal yet driving perfection, completeness, and universality of knowledge inside the human realm. Here, granularity offers a quick path to quantization; and knowledge can leave a firm trail in sciences and in human minds as much as $0°$ A (or $-273°C$) offers a firm anchor in the mind temperature even though it has never been measured. Complete, perfect, and absolute knowledge about anything is out of the human or computational realms. In a sense, the capacity of the brain with approximately $10-12$ billion neurons is a limited resource as much as the number of seconds (or microseconds) is limited in an average lifetime. Fusing the two, to form a knowledge space is bigger abstraction for knowledge to being all-alive and live to being all-knowledgeable.

In order to be practical[3] and concrete, we suggest a limited structure in nine dimensions (or directions) for almost sensible and practical knowledge. Three main groups (fundamental, discretionary, and secondary) with three subcategories in each are depicted in Figures 28.7 and 28.8.

The role of human discretion is included in the 9×9 matrix elements H11 through H99. In this figure, two additional rows and columns (to validate the effects of Nature and Culture) are add at the outside of the 7×7 matrix that is generated by the seven basic questions pertaining to complete knowledge. These rows and columns facilitate the anchoring of knowledge in nature and in culture since both these influences are usually out of control. For example, in another cosmic world and in another culture, these 81 (9×9) parameters can have entirely different forms and formats.

In the limited excursions of routine human activities, the answers to questions in a sub-matrix (typically (3×3) like (Who? What? and When?) or ((What? How? and Who?), see the red sub-matrix in Fig. 28.6) and generally suffice. In context of this chapter, an element of knowledge *kel* is represented as (*kel = vf * no*), and in a generic format, the matrix can extend beyond the (H44, H45, H46; H54, H55, H56; H64, H65, H66) sub-matrix.

---

[3]We abandon the philosophic and mystic treatment of knowledge as being boundless and infinite, but relay on the art of classification or ontology to classify knowledge and further relay on the science of epistemology to relate and quantify the relationships. In the knowledge domain, extreme care is necessary to make the knowledge representation as accurate as possible.

kels, KELS boks,BoKs	Rows / Columns	Nat-ure	Cult-ural	Why	What	How	Who	Wh-ere	When	Dura-tion
FUNDA-METAL KELs	Nature & Environ (forces, energies,)	H11	H12	H13	H14	H15	H16	H17	H18	H19
	Cultural (social, custom, rule)	H21	H22	H23	H24	H25	H26	H27	H28	H29
	Why? (reason, cause, etc.)	H31	H32	H33	H34	H35	H36	H37	H38	H39
ESSEN-TIAL KELs	What? (action)	H41	H42	H43	H44 A	H45 B	H46 C	H47	H48	H49
	How? (legal, ethical, etc)	H51	H52	H53	H54 D	H55 E	H56 F	H57	H58	H59
	Who? (human; Corporate,etc.)	H61	H62	H63	H64 G	H65 H	H66 I	H67	H68	H69
SECOND-ARY KELs	Where? $(x,y,z);(r,\theta,\varphi)$	H71	H72	H73	H74	H75	H76	H77	H78	H79
	When? (t)	H81	H82	H83	H84	H85	H86	H87	H88	H89
	Duration? (Δt)	H91	H92	H93	H94	H95	H96	H97	H98	H99

Table III Generic Matrix for the Generation and Computation for the   Flow of Knowledge

FIGURE 28.7

Human discretion has entered almost all social transactions because of the uncertainties about what action (vf) will take, how the action will be implemented ($*$), and who the human being is. We include the effects of these uncertainties by replacing H_{44}, H_{45}, H_{46}; H_{54}, H_{55}, H_{56}; and H_{64}, H_{65}, H_{66}, by A through I, respectively. These parameters A through I are learned by deploying Artificial Intelligence programs and the flow of knowledge through the Internet. Internet II and III provide reasonable basis for estimating the parameters A through I. Probability and confidence levels thus enter in predicting the flow and processing of knowledge in social situations. Allocation of the matrix elements "H" for evaluating the flow of knowledge in different social and cultural settings and over periods of time by querying the context of the specified and machine generated knowledge elements. Humans and machines may not be accurately determined the 'H' values in reality but the undetermined "H'" indicate where the knowledge is incomplete.

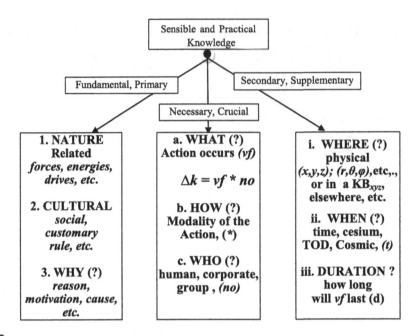

FIGURE 28.8

Routine activities of social entities for the rest of this chapter arbitrarily subdivide into three groups for classification. Other classifications are also distinctly feasible and can be made application and situation dependent. For example in the medical profession, the patient care can be partitioned as out-patient care, hospitalized-care and intensive-care, etc. The sub-headings will be logically replaced.

CONCLUSIONS

This chapter presents a semi-mathematical basis for evaluating the probabilistic flow of knowledge in cultures and social organizations and over time. A matrix representation for the media and time is proposed. The elements of the matrix determine the nature, the velocity, and the distortion in the tiny or large elements of knowledge. Distortions such as attenuation, dispersion, and delay can most likely be attempted by the accurate determination of the matrix elements. At this stage of the evolution of knowledge science, the exact computation of the (9×9) matrix (see Table III) is not definitive. But the proposed approach is applicable to a more precise and programmable framework of knowledge sciences. It is our contention that knowledge science can inherit the methodologies, approaches, and approximations that have made networks and the Internet as dependable. Though not infallible, communication and global networks function within the limits of accuracy and acceptability. The knowledge content of the information flow can also be monitored by knowledge machines at various space, time, and cultural nodes of this space-time-culture-flow-chart for knowledge. This offers a good chance that the (morally, ethically, and sexually) corrupted spam and marketing media deception can be removed from the Internet.

A national agency similar to the Federal agency that oversees the enforcement for blocking of annoying and marketing telephone calls is feasible when the content analysis of the most offensive spammers and websites are examined periodically. An ethical sense in the morality of a nation can indeed be brought back in corrupted cultures corporations, websites, and social entities by knowledge machines-programming tools and techniques.

REFERENCES

[1] Miller MJ, Ahamed SV. Digital transmission systems and networks. Applications, vol. II. Rockville, MD: Computer Science Press; 1988.

[2] Chapter 6 and 7 in Ahamed SV, Lawrence VB. Design and engineering of intelligent communication systems. Boston: Kluwer Academic Publishers; 1997.

[3] Chapter 7 in Ahamed SV, Lawrence VB. Design and engineering of intelligent communication systems. Boston: Kluwer Academic Publishers; 1997.

[4] Messerschmitt DG. A transmission line modeling program written in C. IEEE Journal on Selected Areas in Communications 1984;SAC-2(1) (January):148−53.

THE ARCHITECTURE OF A MIND-MACHINE

CHAPTER SUMMARY

In this chapter, we take bold step and propose the unthinkable: The genesis of a Customizable Mind-Machine. Thought that stems from the mind is deeply seated in a biological framework of neurons. The biological origin lies in the marvel of evolution over the eons and refined ever so fast, faster than in the prior centuries. Three (a, b, and c), triadic objects are ceaselessly at work. At a personal level (a) mind, knowledge, and machines have been intertwined like inspiration, words, and language since the dawn of the human evolution and more recently, (b) technology, manufacturing, and economics have formed a hub of progress, (c) wealth, global marketing, and insatiable needs of humans and civilization. These triadic cycles of nine essential objects of human existence are spinning quicker and quicker every year. The Internet offers the mind no choice but to leap and soar over history and over the globe. Alternatively, human mind can sink deeper and deeper into ignorance and oblivion. More recently, the Artificial Intelligence at work in the Internet had challenged the natural intelligence at the cognizance level in the mind to find its way to breakthroughs and innovations.

We integrate functions of the mind with the processing of knowledge in the hardware of machines by freely traversing the neural, mental, physical, psychological, social, knowledge, and computational spaces. The laws of neural biology and mind, laws of knowledge and social sciences, and finally the laws of physics and mechanics in each of the spaces are unique and executed by distinctive processors for each space. Much as mind rules over matter, the triad of mind, space, and time creates a human-space that rules over the Relativistic-space of matter, space, and time.

29.1 INTRODUCTION

The marvels of nature have challenged understanding since the inception of human mind. It remains a philosophic issue if we evolve to understand nature or nature that will shape our understanding. Be as it may, the modern age make scientific thinking and modern machines the prime movers toward progress. The inroads of scientific thinking can be pushed deeper into structure of nature to explore more of its hidden microstructure. Supplemented by the numerous inroads in biological neural sciences (biology), the functioning of mind (psychology), the organization of the society (sociology), knowledge science (knowledge machines) and physical/real spaces (physics and chemistry), and the principles in computer science offer the broad perspective of a much larger Super-space, of Mind, Matter, Space and Time.

In this chapter, we cross the borders of disciplines without violating them. The embedded and proven truth in each subject is reinforced, and notions are dispelled. The pursuit of perfect order is surrendered for

Evolution of Knowledge Science. DOI: http://dx.doi.org/10.1016/B978-0-12-805478-9.00029-7

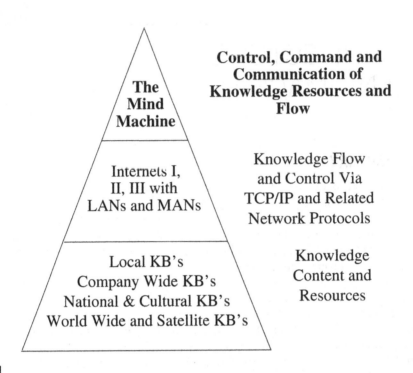

FIGURE 29.1

Hierarchy and Foundation of a Mind Machine. Control and Command for this machine is dispatched at the highest layer. The application programs and the lower two layers access the content and the methodology to solve the humanist problem based on AI and ES systems distributed in the local, corporate, and global networks. Communication is provided by the middle layer by deploying the protocol already established in Internet and backbone networks.

a more mundane quest of working knowledge to build enriched structures in this Super-space. After all the imperfect physics of Newton solved many a gravitational problem before Einstein modified it (ever so slightly). Ampere and Gauss had formulated their own rudimentary laws before Maxwell integrated them.

Internet society leaves no time for such prolonged developments and the evolving knowledge science plays out its own important role. Intelligent Internets constantly update knowledge and knowledge plays its fundamental role in the accurate functioning of the mind-machine. This interdependence is represented in Figure 29.1 and its three layer structure.

29.2 THE CONCEPTUAL FRAMEWORK

Human life deals with reality of making ends meet in biological, psychological, mental, and social domains. Need and gratification are operative for both objects and actions. The domain laws are variable in order to acquire objects to gratify and to perform the actions on objects that gratify. We apply this basic universalism in all disciplines to deal with reality. When the laws are firm and rigid, they are programmed as equations, when they are not totally rigid, firm, and mathematical, the methodology is programmed and when the laws are even more variable, the AI tools and techniques (CG, PR, CV, ES, and IA) from computer sciences are deployed to cross the interdisciplinary borders.

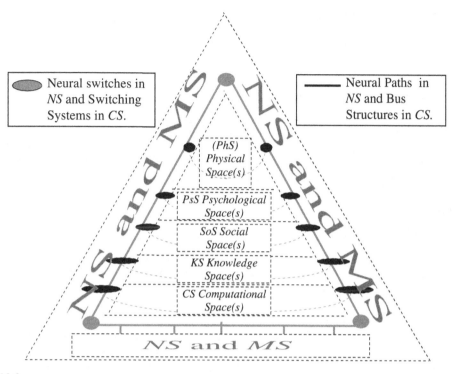

FIGURE 29.2

Organization of spaces in the mind-machine replicates the real and perceptual spaces as they develop in a human being. NS and MS represent Neural and Mental Spaces.

For example, to cross the boundary between mind and knowledge, the outer reaches of laws of perception of need gratifying objects (e.g., a home, a spouse, an institution) are supplemented by the knowledge about the laws for pattern recognition (PR) for objects that look like a structure (e.g., a hut, a house, a mansion, a castle for the home; a member of opposite sex, an eligible partner, a member of the household). As another example, to cross the boundary between social and psychological spaces (see Figure 29.2), the telephone numbers/SMS access for social contacts and the PDA/PC/wireless access procedures stored in the computer space are invoked. In addition, boundaries can be crossed by standard operating procedures stored in the mind space (see Figure 29.2).

29.3 SEVEN HIERARCHICAL SPACES

The function of the human brain is a marvel of evolutionary adaptation. Understanding all the complexities, all at once is self-defeatist. However, the piecewise and systematic integration is feasible. The complete integration needs multi-dimensional interwoven spaces not easily represented in the two dimensional of paper. Thus, to deal with the representation of such spaces in the two dimensions of the paper, we suggest a three-step solution: (a) a topographical identification of each of the spaces, (b) their hierarchy, and (c) their interconnectivities. These steps are implemented in following sections A, B, and C.

29.3.1 TOPOGRAPHICAL IDENTIFICATION OF SEVEN SPACES

Identification of mind-space(s) permits them to be mapped in the computer space(s). Among the many possible of perceptual spaces in the mind, at least seven spaces are identified in the following subsections.

1. **The Neural-Biological Space of the Brain**.
   Even though the electro chemical and ionic processes may not be precisely mapped, the effect is evident in behavior and action of human beings. This space is unique to the extent that almost all other functions are subservient the activity in the brain. The conscious, subconscious, mundane to the sophisticated are embedded and encoded in this space. Any machine to emulate the mind can lodge its central computational VLSI, their algorithms, and their microcode in this hyper-dimensional space of the neural biological space of the brain.

2. **Mind-Space(s)**.
   Human activity is a by-product of heredity and environmental influences such as training, education, personality traits. These functions are distinct from the biological and physiological functions even though definite linkages exist. The conscious mental processes that account for most willful and external behavior and actions can be encoded and accommodated in this mind-space. Such controlled behavior is amenable to computer SW, utilities, macros, and microcode.

3. **Physical Space(s)**.
   Physical reality anchors the mind. Real spaces provide room for existence of the physiological body. Two branches exist: (3a) Personal Physiological Body Space and (3b) Shared Physical Real Space.
   (3a) Laws of physics are not directly applicable to the human objects and physiological bodies. However, the principles have been embedded and engendered in physiology, dealing with heart, skeletal, muscular, circulatory, and muscle-tendon systems of each human. The somewhat complex procedures in orthopedics, kinematics, and physical balance also are housed in this space.
   (3b) Laws of particle and rigid dynamics, movement, rotation, floatation, etc., in mechanics and physics are precise and mathematical. These laws are applicable while working with physical noun objects in real space, provide validity to verb functions such as move, shift, rotate, turn, etc. for physical objects. Interconnectivity and validity become apparent but invalid if a child attempts the climb mount Everest or a when a dead person attempts to swim the English Channel. Such laws and their practicality in real space are the most programmable in the sub-computer system that emulates the real shared physical spaces.

4. **Psychological and Emotional Space(s)**.
   Freud [1], Jung [2], Maslow [3], and others have provided a basis for the stability and dynamics within the confines of human psyche. Motivation and effort are elegantly coupled; the origin of verb function upon noun objects (including ones-own self) can be realistically traced to the psychological energies associated with the individual personality type. Machines that emulate processes in this space can only be semi-numerical and based on pattern recognition (PR) of behavioral tendencies of individuals and personality types.

5. **Social Space(s)**.
   These spaces are individual and culturally dependent. Family, friends, and people correlations (stored in the individual's private knowledge banks) are checked by the mind-machine to

permit/block, verify further to safeguard the security and knowledge operation[1] [4] such as (no*vf) or (vf*no) during the execution of knowledge programs in the machine.

6. **Knowledge Space(s).**

Knowledge space(s) is perhaps the most encompassing space(s), only next to the neural-biological and mental space(s) in the human brain. Knowledge-space/time reaches everywhere in the cosmic world and reaches forward and backward in the time domain and complimented by the Internet technologies and protocol. In predicting future events, an element of uncertainty needs to be estimated and incorporated. These two steps become essential. The programming of knowledge function is at least an order of magnitude more complex than the scientific and business programming and still in its infancy as scientific programming was during the 1950s.

7. **Computer/Computational Space(s).**

Computer-space holds the rationality in sciences as programs. Systemization of many disciplines can be programmed and stacked in the physical computer space. Computer space and its architectural arrangement permit the control of two subspaces: (a) the space for operating systems, background programs, utilities, etc. and (b) active core memory for the currently executing programs. Both the active core and disk systems participate in the programs to be executed in all the other spaces. Whereas the computer space refers to all storage space in the specific mind-machine, the computational space refers to memory coordinates (such as hi mem and lo mem) for the currently executing program. This separation of memory/disk space prevents accidental contamination of programs by other unauthorized programs. However, the mind-machine may reference and scan related spaces with appropriate and authorized linkages presented in subsection C.

29.3.2 HIERARCHY OF PERCEPTUAL SPACES

The hierarchy of the seven spaces and the subspaces becomes complex and interwoven. It becomes an architectural diagram rather than the typical pyramids that Freud [1] and Maslow [3] use. Spaces are by nature more far reaching than concepts and notions that Freud and Maslow depict in their pyramids, but their concepts and notions are housed in these spaces.

In Figure 29.2, a conceptual representation and a possible hierarchy of these seven spaces (from neural, mental, physical, psychological, social, knowledge, and computational spaces) is presented. The hyper-dimensional, the neural-biological space, (NS) and mind space (MS) enclose the other five spaces. Being essential for existence, the physical space (PhS) is closely interdependent on NS and MS. The notion of reality is firmly seated in this triad of spaces as infants start to grab things (and even as adults grab wealth).

The psychological space (PsS) and social space (SoS) form the linkages and associations in the prior spatial triad through the inner self and through the external world. Reinforced by human senses, the two inner perception of reality and physical presence of objects and other need gratifying objects form the foundation of rationality in children during infancy. Passions and a higher

---

[1]Knowledge processing is based on the truism that an increment of knowledge ($\pm\Delta k$) is generated every-time, every-place, every-circumstance that a verb function (vf) convolutes (*) with a noun object (no), i.e., $\{(vf^*no) \rightarrow \pm\Delta k\}$. Conversely, when any no convolutes (*) with a vf, i.e., $\{(no^*vf) \rightarrow \pm\Delta k\}$, it also generates an increment of knowledge (Δk). This incremental knowledge adds or subtracts from the original knowledge k.

sense of (positive/negative, good/evil, use/abuse, love/hate, etc.) ethics evolve in the prior five spaces (see Figure 29.1). These linkages and interrelations are shown as black ellipses in Figure 29.2. The Freudian and Maslowian human being is resident in these five spaces even though neither Freud nor Maslow dwell deep into neural-biological space(s).

Knowledge space (KS) and computational spaces (CS) are relatively new and the modern society cannot function well without the awareness and intense power and deployment of both. Von Neumann and the Internet technologies have changed the prior five spaces and the architectural relations that used to exists before these two shield for the knowledge worker. Life has turned faster and more precise without being too dependent on Freud or Maslow. Their seminal work is now embedded in the downloaded knowledge space (KS). The knowledge worker of the 21st century lives in these two lower most layers with the Internet-based knowledge bases as the shield to hide behind till any malfunction in the other five layers sends the superfast knowledge driven worker to the psychiatrist or/and the cardiologist.

29.3.3 INTERCONNECTIVITY OF THE SEVEN SPACES

Spatial interconnectivity in the brain is not comprehended at present. However, nature has endowed the ability to travel these spaces at will and in good precision. Functionally, the interconnectivity of the seven space and the clusters in the brain may represented diagrammatically in Figure 29.3.

The need for such a presentation (Figure 29.3) is to arrange the functional modules of the mind-machine with addressable active memories and disk storage sub-systems. The diagram associates the functions in the mind with the processes (and processing programs and their data) in the machine with the respective storage spaces allocated. Processes and programs are retrieved from these addressable spaces in the computer system(s) of the mind-machine. Results are also stored in the corresponding memory/disk locations.

The bondage between the spaces is tightly interwoven with the flow of neural currents stemming from mental activity. These currents are simulated as control signals stemming from the knowledge-based operation codes (*kopc's*) of knowledge programs on mind-machines. Within the mind, the inter-connectivity of the neural currents occurs at the velocity of thought. In the computational space, the linkages can only occur as the knowledge programs are executed in the machine. The real-time simulations in the mind-machine are severely limited by the speed of knowledge processor units (*KPU's*). From a design perspective, the neural speeds in the mind healthy individuals are lightning-speed faster than clock rates to trigger the VLSI chips.

The structure and methodology of knowledge programming is reflected by the order and sequencing of verb functions (*vf's*) that are executed by noun objects (*no's*) on other noun objects. The symbolic nodes represented by *vf's*, *no's*, and their logistically appropriate convolutions (**'s*) constitute the vital links between the mental space and the machine space. The mind operates on need gratifying objects in virtual space, whereas the mind-machine deals with the data structure of humans, their needs, and of the need gratifying objects in the control memory, main memory of the computers, and the disk spaces of the global Internet knowledge bases. The flow of knowledge is presented as the flow of knowledge elements or *kels* from the various space is depicted in Figure 29.3.

In the knowledge domain, the composition of elemental knowledge elements (or *kels* or Δk) is formulated as

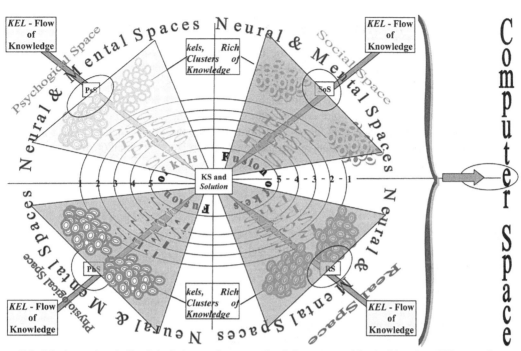

Kel is defined as an element of knowledge that occurs when a noun object (no) executes a verb function (vf) or when a VF is executed on a no. and represented as $\Delta k_{12} = (no_1 \rightarrow *_1 \rightarrow vf_{12} \rightarrow *_2 \rightarrow no_2)$ or as $\Delta k_{21} = (no_2 \rightarrow *_2 \rightarrow vf_2 \rightarrow *_1 \rightarrow no_1)$

FIGURE 29.3

Flow of Knowledge elements or kels during the solution of a problem into the Knowledge Space the inner most ellipse where the fusion of small and large kels (from the social, psychological, physiological, and real spaces) occurs to blend into the solution of the problem.

$$\Delta k_{12} = (no_1 \rightarrow *_1 \rightarrow vf_{12} \rightarrow *_2 \rightarrow no_2) \text{ or as } \Delta k_{21} = (no_2 \rightarrow *_2 \rightarrow vf_2 \rightarrow *_1 \rightarrow no_1)$$

and the lower four spaces (psychological, social, knowledge, and computational spaces) are interconnected via by *vfs* and *nos*, in the physical space (*PhS*) to the neural space (*NS*), and the mental (*MS*). The cycling and the recycling of the various spaces occurs in the mind via the physical, physiological, and/or real space. Elements of knowledge, objects, and actions play the most critical, decisive, and vital roles.

In the human environments, the solution to small and large problems consists of find the best solution to the immediate problems. Knowledge from all spaces and dimension flows to find the best solution. A typical flow of knowledge elements is depicted in Figure 29.3. Five ellipses are shown surrounding the knowledge space that hold the final and/or near-final solution and the *kels* flow through these ellipses from rich clusters of *kels* for the four (psychological, physical, real, and social) spaces and get filtered again and again to yields workable and feasible solution.

29.4 DETAILS OF KNOWLEDGE SPACE(S) IN THE MIND-MACHINE

Fortunately knowledge has been classified by the Dewey Decimal Classification (DDC) and by the Library of Congress (LoC) classification (see Figures 29.4–29.6). When the DDC classified knowledge segments in the world knowledge banks (KBs) are dynamically grouped and stored in mind-machine, then the six segments of the mind-machine (Figure 29.4) bear a direct correspondence with addresses of the KBs that hold corresponding data in the world knowledge banks; the Internets, LANS, and WANS serve as knowledge highways for the mind-machine. The real-space (i.e., the environmental) data is accessed by the personal/customized data bank(s) for the user, the corporation, the community, the nation, etc.

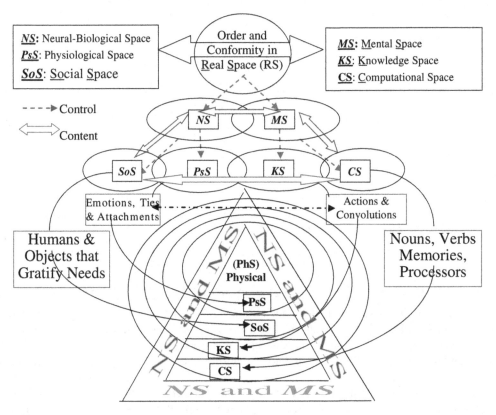

FIGURE 29.4

Depiction of the mental objects and the associated thought processes as they are occur to gratify human needs. Their connectivity to the mind-machine computational objects and their processes via the six perceived spaces in the brain, mind, physical, psyche, social, and knowledge spaces is also shown. The computational space(s) (i.e., CS) is the more malleable and controlled space(s) in the mind-machine.

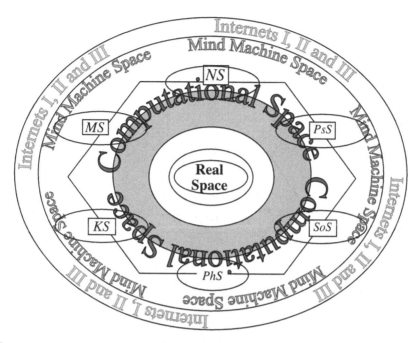

FIGURE 29.5

Mapping of the space(s) in mind and society with the addressable space(s) in the mind-machine.

The mind-machine is thus sufficiently interconnected to solve human, corporate, communal, national, etc., problems on a realistic basis (see *RS* and *CS* in Figures 29.5–29.7). The results become dynamic and change as the environment, the external, and internal conditions change. It is assumed that the machine processes data faster than the changes in the data. Many machines that deal with Stock Market also function on this assumption.

Machines become incapacitated when nature that controls the environment that moves faster than what the machines can predict even for a few seconds. Typically, Tsunami and hurricane warning systems, stock market analyzers, etc., all suffer from similar restrictions.

29.5 THE ARCHITECTURAL HARDWARE

The functions in each of the six spaces (*NS* through *PsS*) are confined to each of the 60° segments and the central ellipse RS holds the real space. Parameters and processes may communicate with each other via the computational space just as segments of human mind would communicate via the central and peripheral nervous system. The representation is complete with only one reality space (*RS*), but many perceptions of one reality (even though reality may be dynamic) can coexist in the *NS* and *MS*.

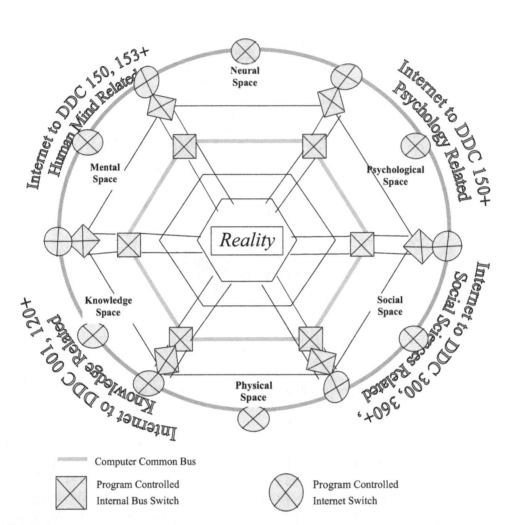

FIGURE 29.6

Correlation between knowledge classification and the storage spaces in the mind-machine. The architecture is generic enough to force a mind-machine as a social-machine, a community machine or a nation machine. The subject matters and local knowledge bases need to be primed with appropriate knowledge and data. Most general purpose computers can function as scientific computers, business machines, MIS machines, etc.

The concepts depicted in Figures 29.4 and 29.5 are integrated in the architecture shown in Figure 29.6. The real space(s) is replaced by the computational space(s) at the center of the figure. This space emulates the functions in the real space(s) based on the laws derived from the worldwide knowledge bases accessed via the Internets and Local Nets. The neural, mind, biological, psychological, physical, and the knowledge ($vf*no$) laws are implemented by the localized (or imported) programs, thus offering a scientific foundation for the results generated by the mind-machine.

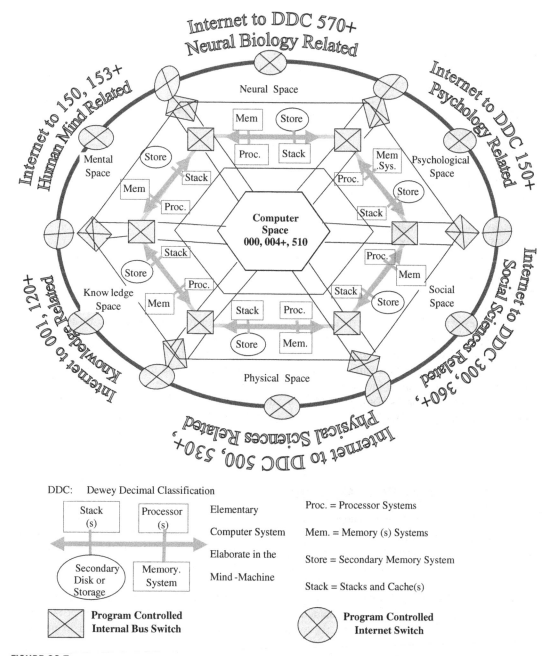

FIGURE 29.7

Realization of mind-machine with active command, control, and communication [5] (CCC) from a centralized machine in the computational space. A series of six subservient computers are suggested for this machine configuration, but the number, type, and nature of the slave machines can be tailored to suit the environment and the (humanistic) issues that the machine is attempting to resolve. The architecture and the CCC are essentially the same for most humanist machines, or management information systems [6].

29.6 THE INTERNET PARADIGM

The realization of this machine can be systematically achieved by a collection of independent computer systems, but working in unison under the command, control, and communication dictated by the Operating System of the highest level of the mind-machine (see Figure 29.7). Command and control are achieved at this OS layer. The communication is achieved by the program controlled local-bus and the Internet switches embedded in Figures 29.4 and 29.5, and shown in Figure 29.6.

Processing becomes context driven. Both the local laws and AI driven routines dictate the opcodes (*opc's*, *kopc's*, *oopc's*, etc.) and the operands (*opr's*, *kopr's*, *oopr's*, etc.) for the local and the central processors of the computational space(s).

It appears that the best machine may be realized by a master computer driving a series of very intelligent slave computers. The analogy is almost complete as a dictator CEO drives a series of highly skilled, naturally intelligent executives in a corporation or as Captain Kirk adaptively instructs a group of artificially intelligent non-robotic Spochs and a set of highly professional humanist doctors in a Star-Knowledge-Ship environment.

The evolution of the human mind is as mysterious as it is miraculous. The mind itself is as mystical as it is marvelous. Attempt to precisely simulate all the thought processes and native creativity can only be futile. In the absence of anything that approaches, these many beautiful aspect of human activity (thinking and creativity), we propose a feasible architectural arrangement of AI based machines with local and Internet addressing capability to force the machine to address the seven perceptual spaces (Section 29.3) of a knowledge worker in the Internet society. Future enhancements and modifications appear mandatory. In fact the multi-artificially-intelligent (MAI) processor capability for multiple environments (ME) or MAIME [4] and multiprocessing in subservient computer systems can be included by any skilled computer architect.

A proposal of this sort is somewhat like an attempt to trace planetary orbits in the times of Galileo without the tools of radio astronomy. Subsequent attempts have been more optimal and precise. The introduction of handheld mind-machines are as near as the 2020s or 2030s.

29.7 A DERIVED MEDICAL MACHINE

In Figure 29.8, we present an amended mind-machine to serve the as a medicine machine. In a medical machine, the six peripheral computers in Figure 29.7 are tailored to emulate the nervous (Nervous System), circulatory (Heart; Coronary and Anatomical), skeletal (Skelt.), muscular (Muscle and Tissue), blood (Blood), and digestive (Digestive.) systems, while the central computation system represents the neural-biological-space machine within the brain.

The human body and physiology are also highly evolved and developed. The six subservient elements of the anatomy are generally inadequate for any practical medicine machine. It becomes necessary to increase the number from six to the number of medical-courses[2] offered in medical

---

[2]Specialized courses, electives, and training taken by students make every professional unique. One standard medicine machine cannot serve all medical professionals just as one computer system cannot serve all research/business users. Even though computer systems can be architecturally alike, the software, utilities, and application programs make every machine unique in its own right. The underlying architectural framework of a medicine machine is introduced and proposed in this chapter.

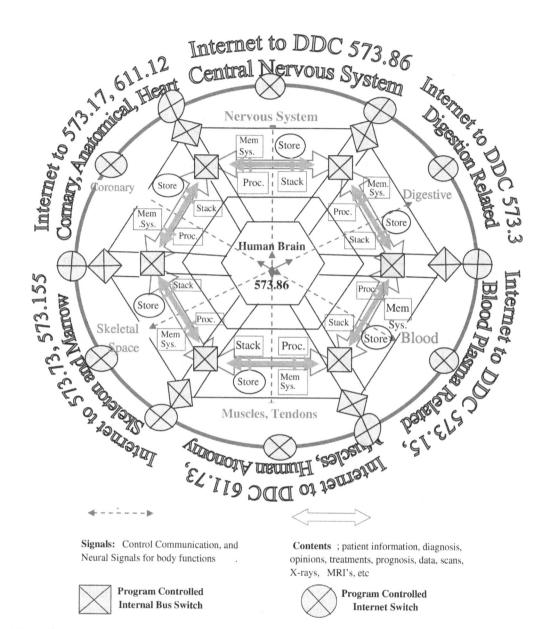

FIGURE 29.8

Configuration of medical machine based on the architectural features of a mind-machine. The Dewey Decimal Classification (DDC) numbers are modified accordingly.

colleges. Assuming that about thirty to forty such courses and course materials make a realistic collection of courses to graduate, we propose *at least* twenty subservient computer systems, thus making the diagram quite complex. However, a cluster of twenty (plus) computers is routinely handled in cluster computing. The system might be slow but the clock rates have increased by orders of magnitude over the last few decades.

It is interesting to note that the architectural arrangement is indeed generic. For example, a specialist can have the associated sub-specialties information and knowledge in each of the subsystems with one machine to serve as the patient specific machine. The individual history, preferences, and personal data are then retrieved and matched to the world-wide knowledge, treatments, care, and procedures. We foresee that wearable customized medical machines can be imprinted when the mind-machine contents are downloaded into generic VLSI chips. Such medical machines will scan the activity of organs and stimulate them as the mental functions become weak because of age or injury. This procedure is already practiced when the hearing-loss characteristics of an individual are used to build customized hearing aids. Most of the routine activities are made available by the medicine machine to the medical staff and the expertise (if needed) is then researched in unusual circumstances for further deliberation.

The layout, architecture, and the hardware of the medical machine have been retained from Figure 29.7, but modified to cope with medical imaging and diagnostic data needs, the rate of flow of objects, and enhanced interactivity between the medical community and the larger personal knowledge bases of the patients. The four essential elements of this computer (memory (Mem), storages (Sto), stacks and cache(s), and Processors (Pro)) also final readjustments are tailored to suit the specialized needs, the medical staff and administration preferences, hospital requirements, accounting and billing standards.

CONCLUSIONS

In this chapter, we have proposed and introduced a generic architecture of a mind-machine. It is based on the human physiology to the extent that the brain controls, commands, and communicates (borrowed from Peter Druckers' Concept of Management, see Chapters 2 and 14) with other subservient organs and their control mechanisms within the human body. The notion of numerous spaces is also introduced in this chapter. Actions and processes occur in these spaces on need-gratifying objects resident in their respective spaces to generate elements of knowledge or *kels*.

Such kels can be addressed, cascaded, and stacked (borrowed from von Neumanns' concept of the Princeton Institute of Advanced Study (IAS) computer) to generate major structure of significant knowledge. Although the spaces are interlaced, they have well-defined themes, functions, and stability criteria of their own, both individually and collectively. The number, types, and the architectures of the subservient machines are application dependent. For example, in a transmutation of the proposed mind-machine will suit corporation environments with subservient computers for finance, accounting, production, marketing, management information and Information Technology systems, human resources, etc. In fact, it would lead to fully fledged executive process control systems within the corporation. In fact, numerous executive information systems [7,8] try to emulate some of the functions of the mind-machine.

The proposed architecture is complete and intelligent since this computer-based system incorporates and tailors the function based on the individual history of the user(s) and the particular environment wherein it is deployed. It is dynamic and vigilant constantly checking for innovations and enhancements in the global knowledge bases. Every step in the solution is reinforced by scientific/mathematical principle(s), methodology, and/or documented procedure(s) in local and/or global knowledge bases.

REFERENCES

[1] Freud S, Strachey J, Gay P. The ego and the Id [The standard edition of the complete psychological works of Sigmund Freud]. Standard Edition W. W. Norton & Company; September 1990.
[2] Freud S. Carl gustav jung letters. Abr. edition Princeton: Princeton University Press; 1994.
[3] Maslow A. Toward a psychology of being. 2nd edition. New York: Van Nostrand Reinhold; May 1982.
[4] Ahamed S. Computational framework of knowledge: Intelligent behavior of machines. Hoboken, USA: John Wiley and Sons; 2009.
[5] Chapter 14, Section14.3.4.1, "From Drucker to Formm via von Neumann".
[6] Lucas Jr. H. Inside the future: Surviving the technology revolution. Santa Barbara, CA: Praeger Publisher; 2008.
[7] SAP solutions, and eLearning, Feltham, Middlesex, UK: SAP (UK) Limited; 2002.
[8] Gillespie R, Gillespie J. PeopleSoft developer's handbook. New York: McGraw Hill; 1999, also see Rowley, R. PeopleSoft v.8: A look under the hood of a major software upgrade, White Paper, PeopleSoft Knowledge Base, 2005.

THE ARCHITECTURE OF A MEDICAL MACHINE

30

CHAPTER SUMMARY

In the medical profession, absolute certainty is a folly, especially for treatment of patients. Any strategy for possible cure is built on steps upon step and stage upon stage. Computers and Internet access provide a good basis for improving the procedure(s) for treatment. Refuting the accuracy of the initial intuition of medical staff is well accomplished by definitive checks and counter-checks by the medical machines. A simple lookup in a symptoms-database is unacceptable in the modern era of artificial intelligence and global expertise. Medical machines deliver their finding based on the particular inputs and the results of global diagnostic procedures. When the machines have access to the patient history and the current symptoms, then the collective diagnostic-expertise of a large community of medical professionals is deployed to validate its findings. Connectivity to patient data and access to the diagnostic expertise is supplemented by analysis and interpretation of the ongoing treatments, and their results provides the medical team greater confidence in the effectiveness or treatment. Step by step estimation of the confidence in analysis and the probability of cure are also provided. Though there is not absolute certainty, the range of error is successively reduced to near zero level by effectively deploying the most recent tools and techniques in medicine for most of the ailments.

To some extent, the VLSI design teams have improved their confidence in the manufacture of silicon chips to almost 100% by enhanced analysis programs, modification of the chip designs, and then reanalysis of the VLSI design to reach an infallible (well almost infallible) chips with many millions of transistors. Response of humans and organs to drugs and procedures are less dependable, but it appears that there is room for improvement by falling back on the rigor and discipline of the systems designers and computer aided medical systems. During the late 20th century, corporations and auto manufactures experienced poor performance in meeting the realistic requirements for quality and delivery till the American and German manufacturers (Ford and Volkswagen) introduced the discipline of mass production. In the medical field, it appears the discipline of medical sciences, deployment of computer, network technologies, and the insights corporate visionaries need a coherent blending to hasten the innovations still to happen in the medical field. In perspective, physics, silicon, and wafer technologies, logic and mathematics have been successfully blended to offer the computer and network technologies that now a reality in the Internet age.

30.1 INTRODUCTION

Medical sciences have been well founded in most societies. Medical expertise has been diversified and widely spread through nations and the globe. The influence of computers and networks has

Evolution of Knowledge Science. DOI: http://dx.doi.org/10.1016/B978-0-12-805478-9.00030-3

been equally dominant. Accuracy and total recall coupled with speed and accessibility are the rewards of the Silicon industry and the Fiber Optic technology. In a sense, the synchrony of many disciplines that have influenced the society is impressive and most industries have greatly benefitted from digital technologies that arise from inexpensive Silicon chips and transoceanic fiber optic information highways [1].

Computer science and technology has shaped and accelerated every discipline. Art and music also have become the recipients of modern digital era; computer-generated sculptures look attractive and symphonies sound great. The VLSI and global network technologies have changed the lives of the commoners and elite alike. These products of artificial intelligence in machines are only logical strides for the cross section of population that can see through the science behind logic in electronic circuits and principles of total internal reflection in microscopic strands of fiber in global networks.

In the medical field, both semiconductor and fiber optic technologies hold a promise of extensive rewards over the next two or three decades. Fiber optic cable offer physicians to look into the organ of the body and surgeons perform micro-surgery. Guess work and intuition of most medical practitioner is supplemented by machine-derived logical inferences, based on conclusive derivations with highest accuracy. Three implications follow: (i) the results, even though they may be subjective, are more trustworthy, (ii) the medical teams treating the patients have the confidence based on the expertise of numerous authorities based on the Internet knowledge bases, and (iii) the evidence for medical opinions is firmly founded on documentable evidence. The machine unfailingly depends on the medical records of each particular patient, the medical history, and the treatment of patient symptoms and conditions by leading experts in the field. Local application programs based on their use can prolong the life span of not so terminally ill patients. Even such estimations will be based on the expert opinion of numerous authorities that these AI-based application programs can access. One such system was developed at the City University of New York and its potential was reported in 2006 [2].

Artificial intelligence, high-speed processors, and wide-band networks are all necessary to implement the system of (utmost) accuracy, (global) expertise, and (perhaps) devoid of all human errors. Human judgment still remains atop machine inferences and machine intelligence. The medical profession being the most ethical and dedicated removed from other professions and politics stands to benefit most.

30.2 EIGHT STAGES IN THE LIFE OF ANY KNOWLEDGE CYCLE

Knowledge has an active life span. Arising from its creation by intelligently combining the objects and their functions, new knowledge is generated in all shapes and forms. However, useful knowledge is dictated by its use that is outdated turns stale and gets discarded. One such depiction with eight stages is presented in Figure 30.1.

In the medical field, the commercial use of knowledge is highly valued by the patients and profiteering drug industry. Without any competition on the supply side, drugs can become prohibitive expensive like the diamond industry that limits its crown cuts of diamonds. The European liessez faire liessez passé economics [3] has only made the American drug industry very rich and prosperous.

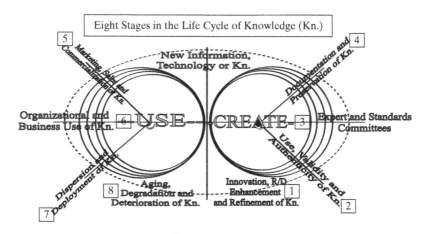

FIGURE 30.1

Beginning at Stage 1 (see 1 in square text-box), useful knowledge undergoes maturity at stages 5 and 6 and is eventually replaced by new knowledge that better serves the society. Innovation and standardization are shown on the right side and use and deployment are shown on the left side.

Medical staff and new drugs are generally in high demand throughout the world. Patented medicines generally bring in high returns and all the eight stages in the knowledge cycle (Figure 30.1) can be identified. In other less rewarding fields, some of the eight stages may be obscured.

30.3 MEDICAL MACHINES IN INTERNET SOCIETY

Medical services have long turned to the use of billing, information, and routine program-based diagnostic services. Computers for such routine functions are much like accounting and book-keeping machines in financial and banking services. Low level logic functions used in such programs have been the privy of electronic circuits since mid-1900s. The refinement and sophistication of Artificial Intelligence (such as pattern recognition, intelligent agents, robotics, content analysis, and intelligent switching) has yet to appear in the highly human-dominated environments. Isolated examples of the use of AI techniques (such as expert systems in Mycin and NeoMycin; and Cancer Detection in Magnetic Image Resonance) have made an impact since the days of Shortcliff [4] and [5].

Digital storage and network technology have provided the medical community with accurate and documented information. But these support services are user requested. The machine and networks are mere tools and mechanisms in a very dull and subservient way. The machines can indeed be intelligent medical assistants that are predictive and anticipative of the tools, techniques, and procedures of the doctors and staff without being either overbearing or intrusive.

The learning programs in the machines will offer the assistance only when and if needed as a trained medical assistant would provide. The role of the Internet will be to verify accuracy, authenticity, and degree of importance to the particular situation. New medical tools, procedures, and

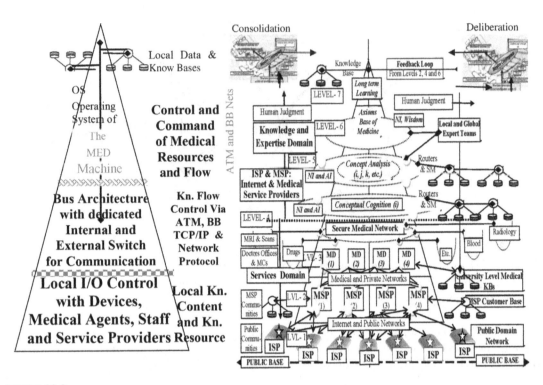

FIGURE 30.2

Overlay and connectivity of the medical machine (preferably one for every hospital) or medical center with access to global and national medical knowledge bases. See Figure 30.3 for details at the 7th Level.

drugs will catch the attention of the doctors or stored away for the doctors to retrieve if they wish. These new machines will act as very intelligent medical assistants with access to medical textbook, medical cook-book, and medical source-book knowledge. All aspects of the medical noun-objects (mnos), medical verb-functions (mvfs), and their (m*s) medicine-based convolutions will be generated and kept as background information should the staff wishes the examine it or improve any aspect of the practice.

In Figure 30.1, a hierarchy of the roles of the medical machine, communication networks, and the medical-ware is depicted on the left side as the expertise gets deployed from the top layer to bottom layer. The depiction is based on the accumulation of knowledge on the right side in Figures 30.1 and 30.2 in the professional setting to its dispersion in the commercial and business settings on the left side.

The role medical machine at level I is akin to the role of the Operating Systems in computers. The role of communication in the asynchronous telecommunication mode (ATM [6]), broadband (BB) networks, and the Internet at Level II becomes crucial in exploring and exploiting all the medical knowledge and information useful in any local hospital or medical center. Finally, at Level III, the devices that actually communicate with the medical agents complete flow of knowledge from experts to the eventual users.

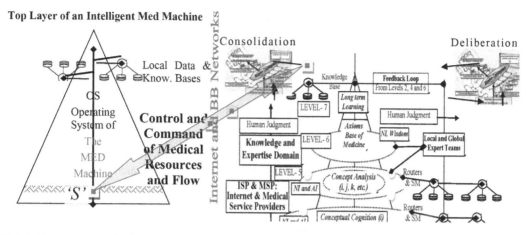

FIGURE 30.3

Embedded C^{3}I (Command, Control, Communication with Intelligence) in the Operating System of the Medical Machine with its own switch 'S' that connects to the evolved knowledge bases of the medical community in the hospital over a dedicated and secure LAN or over the broadband or Internet of the Global medical community. (See Figure 30.2 for the complete details.)

On the right side, the accumulation of expert knowledge, derived from the practice of medicine at the physicians at level 3, is shown. A valid profile of the entire expertise in the profession is built at level 7 after detailed analysis and inspection of the validity and use for the knowledge to be accumulated in the knowledge bases. This knowledge is then accessed by the doctors and staff for local problem solving or for treatment of patients.

30.4 EXISTING MEDICAL EXPERTISE AND ITS DEPLOYMENT

Medical history has a long time line, rich variety, and extreme diversity. Dating far back as 3300 years BC to stem cell biology, the practice of modern medicine spans mind, culture, and society as much as consciousness encompasses body, mind, and soul. Perhaps the human mind links the two universes as much as knowledge links objects and actions suitably coupled together. Only imagination can say, if it were to speak!

In the world of reality and in the dawn of digital age, systematic consolidation of new addition with the prior knowledge and then the deliberation of its possible deployment can add a step toward progress of the society. Depicted in the top right of Figure 30.3, the underlying accumulation of the knowledge base results from looking back and visualizing forward. In the medical field, there is no room for myopia in the hind sight and no reservation for imagination in the foresight.

The analysis and management of medical information is similar to the management information systems (MIS) in corporate environments but with much more sophistication and intelligence. Some of the intelligent MIS (IMIS) and data support systems (IDSS) that are taught in business-oriented schools and universities hold the principles that can be imported into the intelligent management of medical information systems or IMMIS.

Typically, the MIS environments are based on the executive command, managerial control, and artful communication for managing businesses and corporations. When the artificial intelligence (AI) principles are embedded the routine operations of managing the financial (such as payroll), operations (such as inventory control), production aspects (such as job-scheduling), and human resources (such as hiring, terminations of employees), the system acquires a flavor Intelligent MIS or IMIS.

In the design of IMMIS, all the security and privacy aspects of patient data and medical records gain prime importance. The automatic scanning for newer drugs, technologies, and procedures can be instituted in larger hospital and medical centers. To some extent, the library information services of a typical university will also become a part of the IMMIS for university and/or teaching hospitals.

30.5 MICRO-, MINI-, AND MAINFRAME MEDICAL MACHINES

The computing scenario has the experience of growing through minicomputers to personal computers and also growing through PCs to microcomputers and communication devices. Minicomputers attracted great disfavor from main frame computer manufactures just as the wireless communication devices (for voice communication) were frowned by AT&T during late 1950s. The resistance offered by both (then IBMs and AT&Ts) were mere setbacks for the modern handheld devices now used extensively for both computing and communication. Introduction of pattern recognition techniques, intelligent agents, and automatic regulation of the control mechanism need to be instilled to make the three format (micro, midi, and maxi) of the medical machines.

30.5.1 MICRO MEDICAL CHIPS

In perspective, the medical machine would do well to jump deep into the era of micro medical wearable devices. Such devices are already appearing to monitor the pulse, blood pressure, glucose level, anxiety level, etc., for individual patients. These devices are the dumb equivalents of the abacus or slide rules of the olden days. Devices for current era and through the next few decades should be able to up load the health status of all border line patients every day/week/month detailing the medical statistics and be able to down load the opinions and advice of online medical staff in any modern health service center. If the medical center has a maxi-medical machine, then the computerized transaction should yield the same benefits as a doctor's visit for the patient. The operating cost of the modern health service center will get shared by a large population of patients and the doctors' offices and visits will get slowly eliminated. It is our estimate that the medical machines will do as well as the doctors for the outpatient but at a small percentage of the cost.

The emergency room care and the need for doctors personal attention is not likely to be substituted by the medical machines, but the percentage of panic stricken patients is likely to be reduced since the medical machine can address the patient concern on a hourly/daily basis. As the instrumentation capacity of the wearable micro-medical chips goes up, the uploaded information is likely to be more accurate and revealing the patient condition to the medical machines than the verbal communication between the patients and the doctors. If the medical machine fails to get all the information from the implanted chip or if the chip needs to be reprogrammed for additional data collection, it can always schedule a doctors' visit or prescribe an alternate wearable chip. The current technology is capable of performing such instrumentation, uploading accumulated medical data from patients, and down loading expert diagnostic and remedial procedures and prescriptions from modern medical machines and networks.

To some extent, the automobile and aircraft maintenance crews have adopted such data gathering and transmission techniques to check the condition of the engines and safety of the vehicles by examining the data accumulated in the onboard-chips. Seismic-studies staff uses such procedures to monitor tremors and tidal waves. In a sense, the health industry can adopt the methodology for verifying the vital statistics (blood pressure, pulse, temperature, brain activity, EKGs, EEGs, etc.) and numerical test results (e.g., blood sugar reading, anxiety level, metabolism, etc.) generated by diagnostic laboratories. When the medical programmers develop enough skill that has evolved in the scientific communities to analyze VLSI designs, the Medical Industry Complex of medicine can be streamlined as the Semiconductor Industry Complex!

30.5.2 MIDI MEDICAL HOME DEVICES

Computer systems do not have firm rules for classification based on size. In this realm, integrating micros can lead to midis and reintegrating micros once more can lead to the computing power and capacity of main frames, even though it may not be the most economical alternative. In the medical realm, the standards and interfaces for the organ-chips and the cardiac-chips have not been established and it appears that the medical-industry complex of drug manufacturer, the drug retailers, the hospital communities, etc., seeking to maximize their profits[1] are unlikely to participate in such International standards' committees and to abide by them.

Elaborate devices and mini systems can be assembled from microchips. Integration of electronic chips to desktop configuration or to wearable wafer-scale integrated patches can also be designed to counter the nature of the disease, the complexity of ailment, or the patient condition. There is no way to guarantee that such midi-medical devices and systems will cure or totally check the onslaught of every disease or ailment for every patient just as nor team of physicians and medical expertise can avert the finality of every patient. However, such midi-medicaldevices can offer relief from pain and suffering to individual patients and to those who can afford such systems. The care of very sick or very ill patients can be somewhat automated by machine aided medical systems. Such effort may appear unattractive depending on the current state of technology, but becomes a viable proposition as VLSI technology starts to cut deep inroads into medical device technologies.

One possible advantage of the table-top system that operates on a wireless home network is that the individual medical chips can be assembled on a universal microcomputer CPU board. The medical chips will then have identified chip space for the cardio-muscular system, the circulatory system, the nervous system, etc. Such printed circuit boards will imitate the body functions in the flow of electric currents and signals throughout the PC board. When such patterns of current and signals are communicated to robots, the robots will function as low level human beings.

Nature has provided the bee-colony as a chemical equivalent of the proposed midi-medical system that heals itself, finds and invents new ways to migrate, live, and thrive in the most adverse circumstances. Other examples also exist where the species (such as the wolf packs in the Yellowstone National Park, or the dingo-dog packs in Australia, the elephant herds in Sri Lanka,

---

[1]The vintage AT&T steadfastly refused to join the ITU for many years to standardize protocols, signal levels, and interfaces for long time till the ITU was firmly established and the AT&T clout was ripped by the antitrust litigation in 1984.

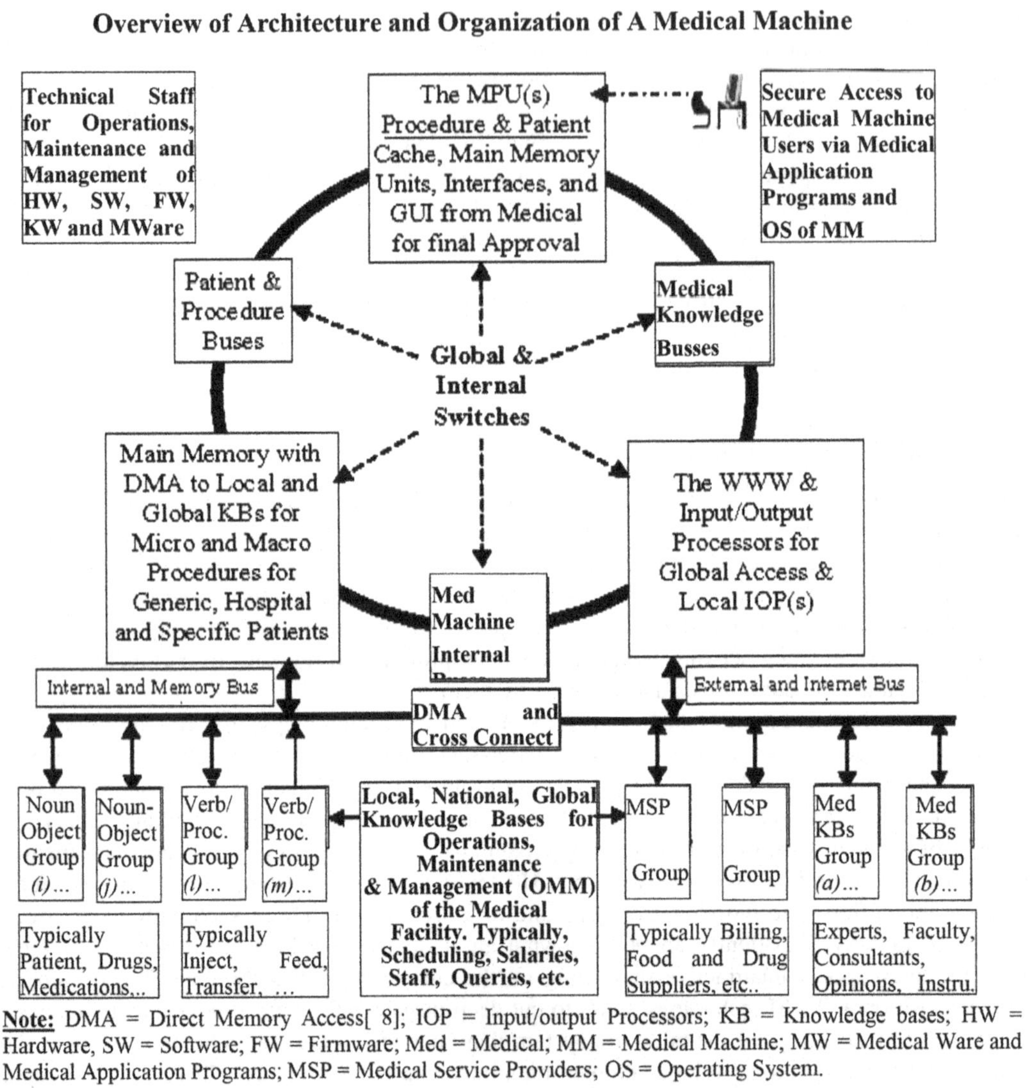
Overview of Architecture and Organization of A Medical Machine
Technical Staff for Operations, Maintenance and Management of HW, SW, FW, KW and MWare
The MPU(s) Procedure & Patient Cache, Main Memory Units, Interfaces, and GUI from Medical for final Approval
Secure Access to Medical Machine Users via Medical Application Programs and OS of MM
Patient & Procedure Buses
Medical Knowledge Busses
Global & Internal Switches
Main Memory with DMA to Local and Global KBs for Micro and Macro Procedures for Generic, Hospital and Specific Patients
The WWW & Input/Output Processors for Global Access & Local IOP(s)
Med Machine Internal
Internal and Memory Bus
DMA and Cross Connect
External and Internet Bus
Noun Object Group (i)...
Noun-Object Group (j)...
Verb/ Proc. Group (l)...
Verb/ Proc. Group (m)...
Local, National, Global Knowledge Bases for Operations, Maintenance & Management (OMM) of the Medical Facility. Typically, Scheduling, Salaries, Staff, Queries, etc.
MSP Group
MSP Group
Med KBs Group (a)...
Med KBs Group (b)...
Typically Patient, Drugs, Medications,..
Typically Inject, Feed, Transfer, ...
Typically Billing, Food and Drug Suppliers, etc..
Experts, Faculty, Consultants, Opinions, Instru.
Note: DMA = Direct Memory Access[8]; IOP = Input/output Processors; KB = Knowledge bases; HW = Hardware, SW = Software; FW = Firmware; Med = Medical; MM = Medical Machine; MW = Medical Ware and Medical Application Programs; MSP = Medical Service Providers; OS = Operating System.

FIGURE 30.4

Initial configuration of a Medical Machine from a Functional and Access consideration. Detailed explanations of the interconnectivity of the components are presented in Refs. [7,8].

etc.), learn to coordinate and control their efforts and learn to communicate the strategy for survival and a better life per se. The size of the cluster or group is not crucial and the group functions as one organism. In the digital era of the modern times, the mail delivery and their tracking systems provide immediate information on the status of noun-objects such as letters and packets and the verb-function(s) that is being performed at any instant of time.

FIGURE 30.5

Configuration of the OS, MW, Application Programs, SW, etc., for the maxi-medical machine.

It is our contention that the medical machines are able to provide intelligent and pertinent information about patients, their ailments, the status of every organ in the body (noun-objects), the medical-functions, the change of status, the effect of drugs, the test results, doctors' diagnosis, and all the pertinent information based on the AI algorithms to draw information, validate, and verify (the verb-functions) it, and further answer the questions that very intelligent human doctors ask while treating patients. A centralized main machine facility and many thousands of peripheral devices connected to intelligent Internets and broadband networks will perform accordingly. The medical-ware, the knowledge-ware, and the security coding are necessary to be positioned atop, software, firmware, hardware, and network. The operating system of the medical machine to command and control medical processes and the underlying net-ware to monitor the underlying communicate function appropriately to maintain synchronism and synergy in the many billions of processes necessary for every patient and for every doctor everyday. During this second decade of the 21st century, these requirements are quite realizable.

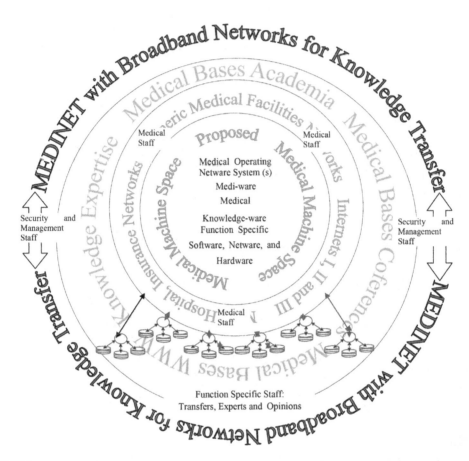

FIGURE 30.6

Configuration of the Medinet with the architecture of data and knowledge bases and their interconnectivities. Private addressing capabilities can be set up in the design of the Medical operating system.

30.5.3 MAXI MAINFRAME MEDICAL MACHINES

Mainframe computer were introduced during the 1950 s when the major corporations realized the potential rewards for industry and organizations. It was logical that these mainframes would yield substantial returns to the vendors and corporations alike. In the medical field, patients and doctors form as less organized community. Hospitals and medical centers being privately owned and well funded do not face as much competitive pressures. The goal of providing public services overshadows major innovations coming from hospitals. The free-enterprise-environment of prevalent for other services providers had been subdued, if not absent for the providers of medical services. Over the last few decades there is mounting pressure for the medical centers, hospitals, and doctors to provide excellent care and services, and as medical technology becomes less expensive, the lobbying for maintaining the status quo is likely to be broken down and the spirit of innovation will return to use new technologies and knowledge and make medical micro's, midi's, and even mainframe medical machines less expensive.

Like the telecommunications industry that faced major changes and reorganization during the last two decades of the 20th century subsequent to the Judge Green's rulings [6], the medical industry can benefit from Federal intervention and by importing combinations of decisive technologies from computer and communication sciences. Both these disciplines are vast and underutilized in the medical field.

System integration of medical information is routine as the integration of income and expenditure of individuals, corporations, communities, etc. Computer and medical science teams need to blend their expertise with the skills of AI and knowledge scientists to develop the medical application programs. Customization of the programs results in the individual needs of patients and doctors.

Maxi mainframes for medical services can accomplish numerous varieties of medical services from detailed organ health status to MRI-based CAT scans and dental X-rays for patients that are store in archives. All records are assembled as the tax or income records at one network based local/central facility and made available to authorized staff. Maxi systems are more economical and more efficient resulting in major saving for hospital, insurance companies, doctors, and patients. Chances of medical fraud and abuse are virtually eliminated. Medical statistics and trends are analyzed as the financial and economical statistics of communities, local areas, and nations.

30.6 FRAMEWORK OF NETWORK-BASED MEDICAL ENVIRONMENT (NBME)

NBME is based on a proposed backbone *medical network* (MEDINET), similar to NSFNET started by the National Science Foundation to encourage and initiate privately owned networks. The foundation of the Internet was thus established even though Internet is not privately owned. The details of the layout, interconnectivities, distribution of staff, and responsibilities are shown in Figure 30.7. When the funding, design, and implementation of a nationwide Medinet is complete, the medical service providers, patients, and public will benefit by the dispersion of authorized medical information, procedures, and authorizations, as the researcher, students, and academia benefitted from the NSFNET during the early 1980s.

30.6.1 MEDINET AND NSFNET

The initially installed super computers in 1984, during the vintage NSFNET [9] era[2] could tackle the medical access, problems and prescription of the current century. Diagnostic procedures and their access will be handled by the Medical Open System Interconnect (M-OSI) that functionally

---

[2]The startup of the NSF effort was modest and low-keyed in 1986. Both *CSNET* and NSF expanded the role of *NSFNET* and its access capabilities to all academic users. The government-owned wide-area networks became available to the public and academicians. The use of the was overwhelming and that commercial interest was made an integral part of the effort to enhance, modify, and evolve the multiple-networks interfaced (from the academic institutions and commercial enterprises) could benefit from the deployment of the communication networks. The extended use would "cost down for everybody." NSF had hoped for this was the ultimate goal. In 1988, the backbone-network was active with 170 campus networks. The T1 lines at 1.544 Mb/s to interconnect the centers were to be replaced by T3 lines at 44.736 Mb/s.

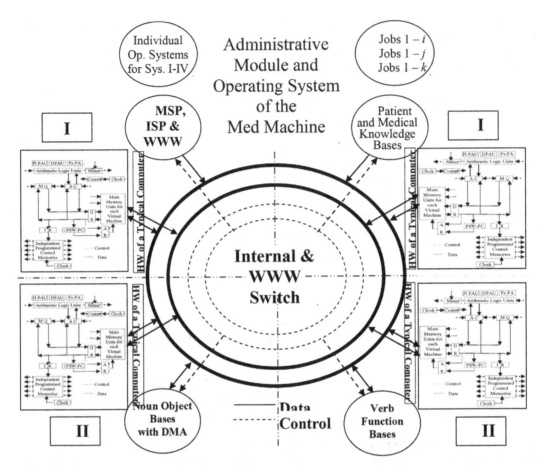

FIGURE 30.7

Multi-machine configuration to implement a midsized hospital-based medical system. An Architectural layout of a cluster of four computers (I-IV) based on conventional technology. Machines of this nature have been in existence for since mid-1980s. Such architectures can be tailored to specific applications such as weather tracking, deep space, and genome pattern explorations. The job queues refer to computational jobs waiting to be executed by the machine cluster. Jobs specific to any particular computer (I-IV) are assigned by the main operating System of the Cluster computer and the machine tasks specific to the each of the four machines are governed by their individual operating systems. The cluster data exchange takes place via the dual bus (concentric dark circles) and the control information flows via the dual bus arrangement (concentric dashed circles). DMA = direct memory access, ISP = Internet service provider(s), WWW = world wide web or the Internet, AC = accumulator, MQ = multiply/quotient register, AR = address register, DR = data reg, IR = instruction register, PSW = program status word used for multitasking, PC = program counter, FPAU = floating point arithmetic unit, DPAU = decimal point arithmetic unit, and Fx.PU = fixed point arithmetic unit.

resides over the traditional-communication Open System Interconnect (OSI [10]). The role of the National Science Foundation needs to be transfused in the National Health Foundation with financial leverage over the projected winners and losers over the next few decades. The rate of growth experienced by NSFNET during the 1980s is very unlikely for MEDINET because of the financial leverage held by the losers that will be emerge due to the proposed network. The medical community and the institutions would probably wish for no status quo because of the dominance that was held by the American Medical Association during the turn of the century.

30.6.2 WINNERS AND LOSERS

In a sense, the winners will be the public and society with enhanced authentic medical information, expert medical consultation, access to service provisioning, and the lowered medical costs as it is available in other countries. The medical profession would stand to gain since much of the intellectual talent will be diverted for solving serious issues (like cancer cure, the embryonic life, infantile deaths, etc.) to enhance medical sciences. Such beneficial effects were realized in the past when the attorney general launched antitrust litigation against the American Telephone and Telegraph Company [11] during 1980 s. The public use of networks and microwave communication has experienced a substantial growth since. The losers in the communication arena after the divestiture of AT&T seem to the top echelon of the management who occupied power and grandeur because of the monopoly of the corporation.

The losers in the provisioning of a *Centralized* MEDINET will be the medical insurance companies, the overpriced medical professionals, and the drug industries. Such consortiums with self-interest groups to manage the organizations will invariably resist a move toward Federal efforts toward supercomputer and network-based medical-environment (NBME). The financial implications will be enormous that can be funded only "by the people and for the people." Comparable investments of this nature and magnitude have been incurred in establishing the transportation, railroad, and shipping facilities around the nation and globe. The effort to build a *C*-MEDNET is long-term commitment for any Federal agency but sustained effort from the agencies, and the elite social group is likely to bear the reward in the future.

30.6.3 ARCHITECTURE AND ORGANIZATION (MULTI-MACHINE MODE)

A typical configuration of multiple-computer medical machine is shown in Figure 30.7. Multiple machines can be organized as a single medical machine especially if the patient demands and application programs start to increase rapidly. Multi-tasking can reduce the response time provided that most of the tasks will not require the services of any particular device or hardware attached to any one machine. The design methodology for multitasking is standardized in computer science and the design philosophy is applicable for multitasked, multiple-machine, medical machine. Specially trained computer personnel may become necessary to maintain and operate such complex machines. The functional organization and the human resource utilization in a typical local area network medical machine are shown in Figure 30.8.

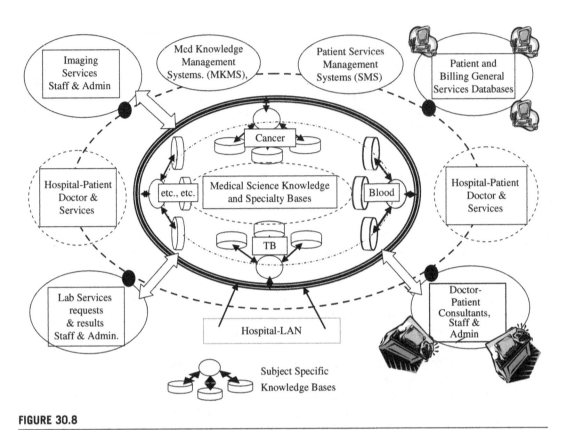

FIGURE 30.8

A local area network (LAN) implementation of the core hospital-based medical network for doctors, administrators and medical staff. MKMS = knowledge (medical) management systems. SMS = service/billing/admin management services.

30.7 GENERIC MEDICAL SYSTEMS AND THEIR NETWORKS

Medical networks can assume various formats. In a microscopic version, the network of medical records kept in doctors' offices and accessed by a group of local users qualifies as a miniature medical network. In more extended versions, hospital and insurance companies keep the records of their patients and clients.

Global medical databases are organized and strictly monitored for accuracy and completeness. The size of databases and the ability to access them for use access and its eventual use become serious concerns. An all-encompassing global medical database would be unfeasible and ineffective. However, a network of medical knowledge bases for a community, nation, or the globe holds scientific and social potential. In this section, the architectural configurations of hospital-based medical networks are presented along with the possibility of expansion to community, regional, or nation-based networks.

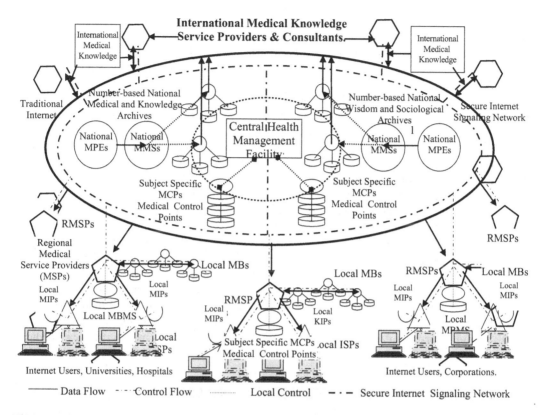

FIGURE 30.9

Framework of an intelligent Internet-based on IN concepts with traditional IN components. ISP = internet services providers; MIP = knowledge intelligent peripheral attached to ISP local network; RMSP = regional knowledge services providers; MB = knowledge base(s); MBMS = MB management systems; MCP = knowledge control point; MTP = knowledge transfer point; MMS = knowledge management system; MPE = knowledge provisioning environment; DDS = Dewey decimal system/Library of Congress system bases.

30.8 MED-BOTS FLOWCHARTS: PROCEDURES AND SUB-PROCEDURES

Medical robots have still to be incubated. In a dormant state, they exist in the minds of system integrators who can superpose robotics, all aspects of artificial intelligence, systems programming, and discrete medical procedural steps. In a sense, if the many steps medical practitioners take around the world can be conceptualized and summarized, we will have a programmable flowchart that a robot can use.

The undeniable truth is that every patient, doctor, and the treatment is unique at the final level of implementation. Conceptualizing permits system programmers to withdraw from the detail and capture the essential and critical steps which can perhaps be programmed even though there is no assurance it can be done with total accuracy and success. Human intelligence and judgment cannot be entirely duplicated, but the mundane tasks can be handed down to intelligent (robotic) medical aids and judgment can be based on the collected wisdom (stored in the knowledge banks) of world-wide-web of experts. A conceptual representation of fifteen such critical steps is presented in Figure 30.9 that superposes local and native intelligence with global and expert wisdom.

The medical processor performs the transactions, logical, and the contextual functions that are local in nature, and the knowledge-based, expert system-based, and generic functions are performed by the medical data banks. It is contemplated that the medical data banks perform their functions in conjunction with the search-engines associated with the medical data banks. The most logical place for these search-engines and other such hardware would be in the knowledge map (equivalent of the KCPs in Figure 30.9) of the knowledge bases in Figures 30.9 and 30.10.

Every sub-procedure is thus executed and the net result of the procedure is conveyed to the user (or the user program). The output is generated from sub-procedures, procedures, runs, and usage of the integrated medical system in an orderly and systematic fashion. Debugging of the integrated medical system functions becomes as easy as reading the registers and core dump of the medical processor unit or the registers and the core dump of the local processing units of the medical data banks.

The logical diagram for handling new or unexpected medical conditions is shown in Figure 30.10. This diagram is an appendage to the Figure 30.9. Invoked by local medical experts, additional analysis is tasked out to the medical operating system for scheduling and gathering the results for treatment or patient care. The programming steps necessary to incorporate new medical situations are represented in Figure 30.11.

30.8.1 INTELLIGENT NETWORK EMBODIMENT OF M6 EDINET

Medical processors necessary to implement the algorithmic flow-charts of Figures 30.9 and 30.10 include a memory and an administrative module, a knowledge module, a communication module, and switching modules necessary as shown in Figures 30.6, 30.7, 30.9, and 30.12. The knowledge modules execute a plurality of sub-processes. The communication module has software to further control communication between the subareas of the medical data banks and the knowledge module. It controls the sub-processes as they pertain to the inputted medical problem and organizes inputs and outputs of the sub-processes to execute the medical instruction. The processor also generates a medical diagnosis as the solution for a possible input of new medical problems. Medical machines and networks thus become inherently more complex than typical electronic switching systems (ESS's) and communication networks.

Several functions of the administrative module include keeping track of (1) which patient needs to be charged what fees and for which services; (2) which clinical lab needs to be paid, how much, for what services, and for which patient; and (3) accounts receivable and accounts payable for the hospital or medical center. The administrative module also allocates all resources to the appropriate needs within the hospital and performs the functions akin to the functions of an operating system in a computer environment. The hardware and executable software of the administrative module are the mechanism for the enforcement of overall optimality and a higher level of performance for the system. It also generates reports for hospital management to verify the accountability of every unit of the hospital or medical facility.

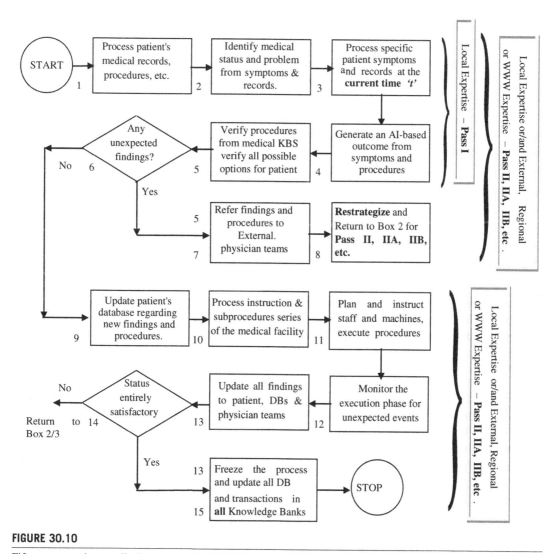

FIGURE 30.10

Fifteen-step patient medical process cycle (PMPC) for any patient at any medical facility.

The knowledge modules store up-to-date information from textbooks, academic information, and information-based on experience, and the distilled wisdom of medical profession: in short, all of the information that the medical teams can learn in universities, look up in medical journals, research in medical libraries, discover in medical conferences, and so on.

The communication module switches the appropriate query to the right knowledge base. This is done in accordance with preprogrammed instructions, such that the total network access time is minimized. The switching modules provide the pathways via the communication medium (i.e., electrical, microwave, fiber, satellite) on which the hospital-based system is built.

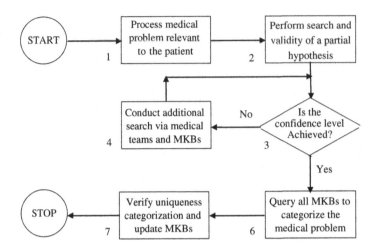

FIGURE 30.11

Steps in handling new medical situations in the medical facility.

The knowledge-based functions listed above are tailored to the specific patient information that is retrievable from general patient database and procedure/lab information from procedure/result analysis. Output reports from the integrated medical facility may be generated on-demand. Such essential functions are performed by component-configuration shown in Figure 30.6. In addition to the knowledge bus, there is one or more patient bus(s) connected to general patient database, and one or more procedure/lab bus(s) connected to a procedure/result centers. The output bus is connected to service facilities, which may include tissue work, therapy, blood work, and imaging, such as radiation and biopsy. The medical processor is connected to numerous patient access point units (Figure 30.2) that may be located at and operated from a remote location from the processor. These units include individual patient medical bases and input to the medical processor as well as output from the processor. These units monitor a patient's condition, input data, provide instructions to the patient, and alert the hospital staff and/or physician about changes in patient's condition.

In its proposed embodiments, the medical processor is connected to a number of authorized physician access point units. Through these units, physicians can access services facilities, procedure/result analysis, any or all medical data banks, the general patient database, and patient access point units. Physicians can also access these components through the medical processor as a direct user, or indirectly by query to the medical processor, whereby the medical processor utilizes whatever modules, memory, programs, subprograms, buses, and connected units and facilities as may be necessary or appropriate to respond to particular queries posed by the physician user. Authorized student access and use of integrated medical facility are thus feasible with appropriate security measure. In addition, the physician-based, remotely located physician access point units are connected to the medical processor for operating the processor from remote sources using the processor hardware modules connected to the processor.

30.8.2 HOSPITAL-BASED MEDICAL NETWORKS

A hospital-based integrated medical computer system for processing medical and patient information and for evolving medical knowledge, diagnoses, and prognoses is depicted in Figure 30.12.

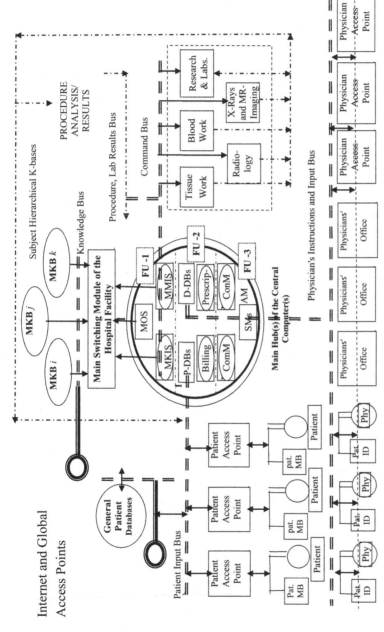

FIGURE 30.12

Depiction of the HW and functional blocks in a knowledge based Hospital or Medical Center computer and communications facility. Routine patient services are incorporated with the administration and management functions. The central information hub maybe a single super computer or a series of interconnected computers.

Acronyms: MOS = Medical Operating System, FU=Functional Unit; 1 for Knowledge-based functions of the machine: 2 for Routine Hospital functions: 3 for Communications in and out of the hospital facilities. P, and pat. = Patient related databases and DBs; D and Phy. = Doctor related activities and Databases, ComM = Communications module ConM=Connectivity and address search module, SM= Switching module(s), MKB = Local Medical Knowledge Bases, MKIS = Medical knowledge information system, MMIS= Hospital related management information system such as human resources, financial, academia/teaching, etc. DBMSs.

The system consists of a medical processor, including a memory, and a plurality of medical data banks to which it is connected. The medical processor and the medical data banks are designed to work in tandem for executing a plurality of instructions and/or obtaining information. Numerous processor hardware modules are connected to the medical processor.

The central hub of the hospital or medical center has three functional units: FU1, FU2, and FU3. There are three modules MOS function interdependently with the medical operating system, MKIS for global and Internet connectivity, and MMIS for the local hospital medical information systems, in FU1. The top Functional Unit, FU1, makes the system knowledge-based with the Medical Knowledge Information System (MKIS) that permits analysis, content based Internet search based on the local hospital functions and processes. MKIS also connects the machine with the Internet and Global access points.

Medical Operating Systems can be derived from typical multi machine and network operating systems, but with a special emphasis and priority for the medical functions, patient care, and physician control of specific medical tasks. Medical operation codes, macros and routines also need special consideration. A set of individual machines can be dynamically linked to perform a cluster medical machine or a single hub machine can be time-shared. This latter arrangement is not suitable for larger establishments and the response time can be long.

Medical Knowledge Bases and their subject specific bases hold an accurate record of the worldwide medical information, procedures and medications, etc. This expert-based AI system is used to update and verify doctors practices for the treatment of patients. This facility is comparable to the knowledge and information bases that hold the standard operating procedures (SOPs) in major corporations. Any variations are scrutinized and verified by the medical staff and/or experts. Patient and physician databases can be independent or interleaved with the medical functions specific to the medical functions.

The software in the Functional Unit FU3 includes a communication module (ComM), a switching module (SM), an administrative module (AM that resides within the Medical Operating System (MOS) in the hub of the central computer system(s), A knowledge module (KM) that resides in the Medical Knowledge Information System and shown as MKIS at the top section of the computer hub of Figure 30.12. This configuration is suitable for handling the traffic of a large community of hospitals or a local medical center. The capacity of the centralized Main Hub of the Hospital (See Figure 30.12) is made consistent with the expected service from the AM, KM, and SM. For small local clinics providing routine medical services, a standard server environment will suffice.

There are three hardware, firmware, and software modules in the processor. These modules function as a communication module—to control data communication between the other modules, the memory, and the medical processor. The effective communication from module to module is thus established. The hardware for the switching module(s) selects and switches between the various medical data banks for solving a particular problem. It also facilitates the administrative module to perform housekeeping functions, including multitasking control with resource allocation, real-time multitasking, and scheduling of tasks. Within a knowledge module (KM), the hardware performs knowledge processing functions and stores pertinent information in the medical data banks.

General patient databases, physician access point units, patient access point units, and service facilities are connected to the medical data banks and medical processor via several buses. In an alternative integrated medical computer system, numerous processors are included with their own memories and modules and are linked together to establish a processor net unit. This system can be used in a campus environment, where several buildings comprise the hospital or where several hospitals are interlinked over local area networks. One such configuration is shown in Figure 30.2. The nature of components and their capacities are matched to the variety of services provided, and sizes of the links and routers are matched to the expected client base that is served by the medical facilities.

CONCLUSIONS

In this chapter, we take the bold step of proposing the architecture(s) of a Network-Based Medical-Environment (NBME) to operate in a synchronous mode with a high-speed medical network (MEDINET). Founded on the design concepts of the National Science Foundation Network (NSFNET), the proposed backbone medical network spans nation-wide medical professionals, service-providers, medical experts and staff, and facilities. Complex series of patient care procedures, authorizations, strategies, and their accuracies are handled by AI based programs under the supervision of human control. The amount of detailed human processing and the associated costs are reduced considerably to make medical care affordable and Universal. Series of hardware architectures and details of critical software modules are presented to substantiate the validity of the concepts presented in this chapter.

The current state of computer and network technologies coupled with science of medicine and the state-of-art-derived AI tools to process knowledge in unison and synchronism is capable of providing very specific information and the knowledge derived from them, for the status of every patient and for every authorized doctor over secure networks. Very specific questions such as those addressed by very intelligent human doctors ask while treating patients will be answered very systematically and sensibly by centralized medical machines and their intelligent peripherals. Information and accurate inference gathering, validation, and verification will be transferred to the AI routines tailored and embedded in the medical-ware of such machines. It is our contention that the medical machines will follow the same evolutionary path toward personal medical machines (PMCs) and then onto wearable micro patch computers (PMWCs) as the main frame computers followed to desktop PCs and on to handheld devices for computing, communication and Internet. We also contend that the technology toward this migration is available awaiting a bold new enterprise to start the next major wave in computer aided personal medical technology.

The medical operation system supported by intelligent medical management-information-system will function and provides local and global knowledge about patient care and treatment. The proposed intelligent medical management information system, IMMIS will function as a sophisticated MIS that handles and services corporation needs and provides decision support for MEDINET corporation executives. Mainframe size medical machines may become necessary for service large hospitals and dedicated metropolitan area networks may become necessary for large campus-based hospital spread over urban area and a layer of Maxiframe size medical machines to address the national medical needs of large countries. The layered structure of the switching systems that handle the overall communication needs of the United States will serve as an excellent architectural framework for the MEDINET.

REFERENCES

[1] Ahamed SV. Chapter 2. The network perspective. Intelligent internet knowledge networks. Hoboken (NJ): John Wiley and Sons; 2006.

[2] Waraporn N, Ahamed SV. Intelligent medical search engine by knowledge machine. Proc. 3rd, Int. Conf. on Inf. Tech.: New Generations, IEEE Computer Society, Los Alamitos, CA. 2006. See also Waraporon N. Intelligent Medical Databases for Global Access, Ph.D. Dissertation at the Graduate Center of the City University of New York; 2006.

[3] An economic theory or plan in which a government does not have many laws or rules to control the buying and selling of goods and services. Available from: <http://dictionary.cambridge.org/us/dictionary/english/laissez-faire> [accessed April 2016].

[4] Shortcliffe E. MYCIN: Computer-based medical consultations. New York: American Elsevier; 1976. See also, Buchanan BG, Shortcliffe EH. Rule-based expert system: the Mycin experiment at Stanford heuristic programming project. Boston: Addison Wesley; 1984.

[5] Kintsch W, et al. About NeoMycin, Methods and tactics in cognitive science. Mahwah (NJ): Lawrence Erlbaum; 1984. See also, Buchanan BG, Shortcliffe EH. Rule-based expert system: the Mycin experiment at Stanford Heuristic programming project. Boston: Addison Wesley; 1984.

[6] Kearney JD. From the fall of the Bell System to the Telecommunications Act: Regulation of Telecommunications under Judge Greene, Judge Greene Ruling on Divestiture of AT&T, Marquette University Law School.

[7] Ahamed SV. Design and engineering of intelligent communication systems. Kluwer Academic Publishers; 1997.

[8] Hayes JP. Computer architecture and organization. 2nd ed. New York: McGraw Hill; 1988. See also, Stone HS et al., Introduction to computer architecture. Computer Science Series. New York: Science Research Associates; 1980. Stallings W. Computer organization and architecture. New York: Macmillan; 1987.

[9] The Internet – The Launch of NSFNET, www.nsf.gov/about/history/.../launch.htm, National Science Foundation.

[10] Ahamed SV. Design and engineering of intelligent communication systems. Kluwer Academic Publishers; 1997, see Chapter 15.

[11] Pinheiro J. AT&T divestiture & the telecommunications market. Berkeley Technol. Law J 1987;2(2) Fall September.

Acronyms for Knowledge Science

ACRONYMS
ARROWS

→ Forward knowledge process, i.e., effect of the prior element on the following element.

← Backward knowledge process, i.e., effect of the following element on the prior element.

= → Generates a result, or results. Can also modify the following verb v or a noun n in all spaces.

← = Or modifies the status in knowledge space but on the prior n or v, in knowledge spaces.

← = → Generates a result, or results, in a verb v or a noun n, and in both directions.

⊛ Convolution marker

* A convolution process of interaction with n or v, usually occurs between n and v or v and n that can be unidirectional (i.e., $*\rightarrow$, or $\leftarrow *$) or bidirectional (i.e., $\leftarrow * \rightarrow$) in its general form.

*' The status of convolution * after the process $(n * v)$: *' = *, if the process does not affect *

φ An incremental change associated with the process $(n * v)$ *in the real space RS* ≠ 0, but finite however small or large it may be and equals $(n' \sim n;$ *'$ \sim$ *; or $v' \sim v)$; φ can be submicroscopic or super-cosmic.

ψ A corresponding change associated with the process $(n * v)$ in the *knowledge space KS* ≠ 0, but finite however small or large it may be and corresponds to real space change $(n' \sim n;$ *'$ \sim$*; or $v' \sim v)$; ψ can be tiny and incomprehensible or engulf the entire neural space (NS).

μD Micro decode function

μmp Micro medical process instruction for the medical machine

1

1A Processor special communication processor for call-processing applications in electronic switching systems

2

2B + D ISDN Basic Rate

2B1Q Code two binary

2-D Trellis coding, two-dimensional $(x + i\,y)$ code algorithm for data communication

2 G and 2 G + Coding standards by ITU cordless telephone (CT) usage

3

3 G Third-generation wireless technologies for CT applications

3GPP Third-Generation Partnership Project

4

48 Octets playload in the ATM cell

4 A (ETS) Electronic Translator System

4 A Crossbar Toll System
4ESS AT&T Electronic Switching Systems of 1976. 5ESS Electronic Switching Systems 5 of 1982.
  5ESS-2000 A very compact Electronic Switching Systems for handling up to 2000 lines

5

5 octets ATM header block
  51.840 Mb/s. SONET-1 Rate 53 octets ATM cell size
5ESS A generic electronic switch for handling a wide variety of telephone switching services

8

800, 900, 700 Numbers reserved for special services
802.x, ITU Standards for packet switched networks
899 or 898 Numbers and numbers for specialized services to the customers

9

900 Services reversed charges special services network services
911 (Public emergency) service
9-row/13-row SONET frame configuration debates and deliberations

A

ABCD Transmission coefficients in electrical systems
ABC Transmission coefficients in Knowledge
-DEF Systems (A through I) operate on
-GHI *nos, *s,* and *vfs* embedded in *kels* (This matrix is A-I Matrix for human
  and humanistic noun objects)
AAL ATM Adaptation Layer
ABS Alternate billing service
ACS Administrative Communications and Switching modules in an ESS facility
ADCCP Advanced Data Communications Control Procedure
ADM Adaptive delta modulation
ADMs Add-Drop Multiplexers for the new and older generation networks
ADPCM Adaptive delta pulse code modulation
ADSL Asymmetric digital subscriber line
ADSL/HDSL Asymmetric digital subscriber line/highspeed digital subscriber line
ADSL + Specialized version of ADSL
AI Artificial intelligence
AIKN Advanced intelligent knowledge network
AIN Advanced Intelligent Network
AKS Adjunct knowledge processor
AKSP Adjunct knowledge processor for knowledge functions in knowledge environment

ALI Automatic location identification
ALKP Application Level (Knowledge) Programs
ALU ALU in the CPU and KPU environments
ALUs Arithmetic logic units in the CPU environment of a computer
AM Administrative module
AM Amplitude modulation
AM, CM, and SM Administrative, Communications, and Switching
AMPS Advanced mobile phone service
AND, OR, EXOR Logical functions
ANI Automatic number identification
ANS American National Standards Institute
AP Adjunct processor
APC Adaptive predictive code
APs Applications programs
AS Access stratum (RRC and UP)
ASN Adjunct service node
ASP Adjunct service processor
ASP Adjunct service point or adjunct service processor
AT&T American Telephone and Telegraph Company, (Vintage) no longer in existence
Atlantic Cables for data/voice services
Atlantis-2 One of the many Atlantic crossings for voice and data communication
ATM Asynchronous transfer mode for cell relay systems
Attr. Attribute or attributes of NOs
AuC Center for Authentication
AUs Arithmetic units embedded in the ALU and CPU environments.
AV Authentication vector
AW Artificial Wisdom
A-WAB Wisdom axiom base for the type A human being (philosopher)
AWC Area wide centrex

B

B Bearer channel of the ISDN
BAL Basic assembly language
BALK Basic assembly language knowledge instructions
BALM Basic assembly-level medical-instructions
BB Broadband
BC Bearer control
BCC Bell client companies
BCPN Business customer premises network
BCR Bell Communication Research
BISDN Broadband ISDN
BRCS Business/residence custom services
BRISDN Basic rate integrated services digital network (ISDN)
BS Base station
BX. 25 Special inter-office
BX. 25 Version of X. 25 protocol/network developed by Bell system

C

CACC Customer access and call control
CAD Computer-aided design
CAMA Centralized message accounting CANTAT-3, one of the numerous Trans
CANTAT-3 One of the numerous Trans-Atlantic Cables for data/voice services
CAT CAT scans
CATV Cable television
CCF INCM component
CCIS 6 or 7 Common Channel Interoffice Signaling 6 or 7
CCISS Common Channel Interoffice Signaling System
CCITT Consultative committee of the ITT CCS
CCS Common Channel Signaling
CCS7 Common Channel Signaling #7
CCSN Common Channel Signaling Network
CDMA Code division multiple access
CEPT Central European post and telegraph
CLASS Special group of IN/2 services provided by second generation INs
CM Communication module in intelligent networks (context dependent)
CM Control memory in CPUs (context dependent)
CMAC Customer mobile access control
CN Campus networks
CO Central offices
COMNET An event-based computer simulation program to evaluate network performance connection oriented transport protocol of the Internet architecture; reliable byte stream delivery service

Convolutions within kels, KELs

CPDFM Continuous phase discrete frequency modulation
CPM Critical path method
CPU Central Processor Unit
CSA Carrier serving area
CSPDN Circuit switched public data network
CT2 Cordless telephone second-generation telephone services
CT2 Cordless telephone second-generation
CT3 Enhanced CT2 telephone services toward the third generation

D

D Channel banks CO equipment for multiplexing and demultiplexing the DS0 and DS1 signals through the circuit switched networks
DACS Digital access cross connect systems
DB Database
dB deciBell
DBAS Database administration system
DBM Database management
DBMS Database management system
DCPN Domestic customer premises network
DCS Digital cross connect systems in the SONET environment

DDS Dewey decimal system
DDS Digital data services (in context to digital transmission systems)
DDSN Digital derived services network
DECT Digital European cordless telecommunication digital network (ISDN)
DMA Direct memory access
DMS Nippon's telephone and telegraph
DNS Domain name system
DPSK Differential PSK
DPU Display processor
DPUs/GPUs Display/graphics processor units
DS D-system digital hierarchy in Americas
DS0 Digital signal 0 is 64 kb/s channel at the lowest level of digital hierarchy
DS1 Digital signal 1 is 1.544 Mb/s signal with 24 DS0 channels + signaling bits, also known as T1 signal
DS1, DS1C, DS2, DS3 American digital hierarchy
DS1C Digital signal 1 C is at 3.152 Mb/s
DS2 Digital signal 2 is at 6.312 Mb/s also known as T2 signal
DS3 Digital signal 3 is at 44.736 Mb/s
DSD Direct services dialing
DSDC Direct services dialing capabilities
DSL Digital subscriber line
DSS Decision support system
DWDM Dense WDM

E

E1CEPT Digital hierarchy signals at 2.048 Mb/s
E2, E3 CEPT Digital hierarchy signals
EC Echo cancellation
EIR Equipment identity register
EO End office
EPC Evolved packet core
E System European digital hierarchy for data transmission
ePDG Evolved Packet Data Gateway
ERMES European radio messaging
ERS Emergency response service
ES Expert Systems
ESS Electronic switching systems
ETSI European Telecommunications
E-UTRAN Evolved UTRAN
EWSD A series of ESS facilities built by Siemens

F

FC Functional components
FCC Federal Communications Commission
FCs Functional components of the intelligent network conceptual model
FDE Fetch, decode, execute cycle of any

FDM Frequency division multiplex
FEPs Front-end processors of the SCP
FH-DPSK Frequency hopped differential phase shift keying modulation
FLAG One of the numerous transoceanic fiber-optic networks
FM Frequency modulation
FM Functional modules
FO Fiber optic
FORTRAN One of scientific programming languages
FPLMTS Future public land mobile telecommunications
FRS Federal Reserve System
FSK Coherent frequency shift keying
FTTC Fiber to the curb distribution data/voice/video

G

Gb/s Gigabits per second optical rates in FO networks
GERAN GSM EDGE Radio Access Network
GMSK Gaussian Minimum Shift Keying
GNS Green Number Services
GPGPU General purpose GPU
GPRS Global packet radio services
GPU Graphical processor unit
GSM Global system for mobile communication
GTFM Gaussian timed frequency modulation
GUI Graphical user interface
GUMTS Generic Universal Mobile Telephone Systems

H

HD Hamming distance
HDLC High-level data link control
HDSL High-speed digital subscriber line
HDTV High-definition TV
HLL Higher level language
HLR Home Location Register
HSS Home Subs. Subsystem

I

IAS Institute of Advanced Study known for von Neumann's SPC machine
IC Integrated circuits (context dependent)
ICC Interexchange carriers in network environments
IETS Interim European technical standard
IKN Intelligent knowledge network
IKPS, I-KPS Intelligent, Internet-based, or IN-based knowledge processing system
IKW Intelligent-knowledge-ware
IM Inter-modulation

IMF International Monetary Fund
IMN Intelligent medical network
IMS IP Multimedia Subsystem
IMS Intelligent medical systems
IMTS Improved mobile telephone service
IN Intelligent Networks
IN/1 First-generation intelligent network
IN/1 + enhanced version of the IN/1 IN/2, second-generation IN
IN/1 + Enhanced version of the IN/1
IN/2 Second-generation IN
INCM Intelligent network conceptual model
INOs Intelligent Noun Objects
INTERN An AI program for medical diagnostics Internet-based, or IN-based knowledge processing system
INWATS Inward wide area telecommunication services
IOPs Input/output Processors
IP Intelligent Peripheral of Intelligent Networks IN/2
IP Internet protocol that provides a connectionless best effort delivery service across the Internet
IP Intelligent Peripheral of Internet Protocol
IPTV Internet protocol TV
ISDN Integrated services digital network
ISI Inter-symbol interference
ISN Information storage node
ISO International standards organization
ISP Internet service provider
IT Information Technology
ITU International Telecommunications Union

J

JCL Job control language
JDC Japanese digital cellular

K

Knowledge elements

kel One or more elements of knowledge (in the knowledge space) associated
kels or with *(n * v)* One or more *kels* are generated during or after the process
KELs *(n * v)*
KAP Knowledge-action-process
kb/s Kilobits per second
KBMS Knowledge base management system
KBs Knowledge bases
KCO Knowledge Centric Objects
KCP Knowledge control point
KCPU A hardware unit to accomplish knowledge functions and CPU functions
KD Knowledge domain

KF Knowledge functions in knowledge environment
KIP Knowledge intelligent peripheral
KIR Knowledge instruction register
KLP Knowledge logic programs
KM Knowledge machine
KMM Knowledge management module
KMs and WMs Knowledge machines and Wisdom Machines
KMS Knowledge management systems
KN Knowledge network
Kompilation Compilation of knowledge programs
kopc Knowledge operation code
kopcode Operation code within BAL knowledge instructions
KP Knowledge processing
KPE Knowledge processing environment
KPS Knowledge processing systems
KPU Knowledge processing unit
KSCP Knowledge services control point
KSS Knowledge management systems
KTP Knowledge transfer point

L

LA Lexical analysis
LAN Local area network
LATA Local Access and Transport Area
LECs Local Exchange Carriers
LED Light emitting diode
LoC Library of Congress
LPC Linear predictive coding
LT Line termination
LTE Long-Term Evolution for NGMN

M

MAC Medium Access Control
MAN Metropolitan area network
MAP Medical Application Programs
MAS Memory administration system
Mb/s Megabits per second
MCN Mobile control node
MCOs Medical-centric objects
MCPN Mobile customer premises network
MDB Medical database
ME Mobile Equipment and hand phones
MFs Micro procedures (*vf*) on micro medical (*mno*) or knowledge objects (*no*)
MIMD Multiple instruction multiple data CPU architecture
MIMO Multiple instruction multiple object

MIN Medical intelligent network

MIS/DSS Management Information/decision Support Systems

MISD Multiple instruction single data CPU architecture

MISO Multiple instruction single object KPU architecture

MJ Early wireless system introduced by AT&T in the 450 MHz band, circa 1970 s

MK Early wireless system introduced by AT&T in the 150 MHz band, circa 1970 s

MKCO Medical knowledge-centric object

MKCP Medical knowledge control point

MKI-MO Multiple knowledge instruction Multiple Object

MKI-SO Multiple knowledge instruction Single Object

MKNs Medical Knowledge Networks

MKPU Multiple object KPU architecture

MKTP Medical knowledge transfer point

MLAP Medical Language Assembly Program

MME Mobility Management Entity

MMOS Operating systems for medical and object functions

MNMS Medical network management systems

mno Medical noun-object

MNO' Newly synthesized medical noun object

mno_k Medical noun object k

mopc Medical operation code with *moprs* medical operands

mopc Medical operation code

moprs Medical operands

MP Medical Processors

MPC Medical program code

MPF(s) Major medical program functions

$MPF \circledast MNO$ Major medical function convolved on a major medical noun-object

$mpf_i \circledast_j mno_k$ Minor medical function convolved on a minor medical noun object

MPU Medical processor unit

MRI Magnetic resonance imaging

MSI Medium scale integration

MSMS Medical services management system

MSPs Medical Service Providers

MTP Message Transfer Part

MTS Mobile telephone service

MTSO Mobile telephone switching office

MUA Mobile user agent

MVFs Major medical verb functions

MW Medical ware

MYCIN An artificially intelligent SW system for medical diagnostics

N

Nouns

n A noun object or a simply a noun, *no, NO, kco, or KCO, etc.* and associated with both * and *v*. All nouns do not interact with all verbs *and vice versa*

n' The status of *n* after the process *(n * v): n' = n*, if the process does not affect *n*; e.g., *nop* in assembly level programs of plain old computer systems

n* * *v A process in the real world that generates an effect in the real world and also generates a kel in the knowledge space. It has variations as ($n \leftarrow^* v$), ($n *\rightarrow v$), or as ($n \leftarrow^* \rightarrow v$)

n* ✕ *m $m \times n$ matrix operations or convolutions

NA Node administration

NADC North American Digital Cellular

NAS Non-Access Stratum

NCOM Network communication unit

NCP Network Control Point

NGMN Next-Generation Mobile Network

NIDB Network information database

NIH National Institute of Health

NKSP Network knowledge service providers

NNI Network-to-network interface

NO Noun-object

NOs and VFs Noun-Objects and Verb-Functions

NPU A numerical processor unit working with imprecise rule for manipulating the attributes of objects in KPU

NRM Network resource manager

NT-1 and NT-2 Network terminations 1 and 2 for ISDN services

O

OA&M Operations, administration, and maintenance

OAM&P Operations, administration, maintenance and provisioning

OC Optical carrier designation

OC-12, OC-48, OC-192 Optical carrier data rates

OC-*n* Optical carrier systems in the SONET environment

OMAP Operations and maintenance applications part

ONN Off-network node

OOL Object-oriented languages

OOP Object-oriented programs

OOP Object oriented programs

OPP Object processors

opc Operation code

OPNET A discrete event networks simulation package

opr Operand

OPU Object processor unit

OR OR logical function

OR Operations research

OSI Open Systems Interconnect

OSS Operation Support System

P

PBXs Private branch exchanges

PC Paging control

PCM Pulse code modulation

PCP Processor control point

PCRF Policy and Charging Rules Function
PCS Personal communication services
PCU Program control unit
PDCP Packet Data Control Protocol
PDN Packet Data network
PDNGW or PGW Packet Data Network Gateway
PE Paging entity
PIN Personal Identification Number (in computer and network service environments)
PIN Personal intelligent network (in intelligent network environments)
PLCP Physical layer convergence protocol
PLMN Public Land-Mobile Network
PMPC Patient medical process cycle
PMR Private mobile radio in UK
PON Passive optical network
POTS Plain old telephone service
PPNs and EPNs Processor port network and expansion port network
PPV Pay per view
PR Pattern recognition
PROCEDURER An HW unit that executes micro procedures (*vf*) on micro medical (*mno*) or knowledge objects (*no*)
PS Packet-switch
PSK Phase-shift keying
PSPDN Packet switched public data network
PSTN Public switched telephone network
PUCI Protection against Unsolicited Communication in IMS
PVN Private virtual network

Q

QAM Quadrature amplitude modulation
QoK Quality of knowledge
QoS Quality of service
QPSK Quadrature phase-shift keying
QPSK Band-limited quadrature phase-shift keying
QPSKM Quadrature phase-shift keying modulation
QPSK Quadrature phase-shift keying

R

RACE Research and development for Advanced Communication in Europe
RAN Radio Access Network
RAT Radio Access Tandem
RBOC Regional Bell Operating Company
RDTs Remote data terminals
RF Radio frequency
RLC Radio Link Control
RLC Radio Link Control
ROM Read only memory
RRC Radio Resource Control

S

S, T, U, and V ISDN standardized interfaces
SAE System Architecture Evolution
SAFE Spanning the globe, a global network
SAN Storage area networks
SAP One of a series of intelligent MIS and EIS programming systems
SAT-3/WASC One of the newer fiber-optic transoceanic network
SAT-3/WASC/SAFE One of the newer fiber-optic transoceanic network
SCCP Signaling connection control point
SCE Service creation environment
SCP Service Control Point
SDLC Synchronous Data Link Control
SDN Software defined network
SDSL Symmetric DSL
SDTV Standard TV
SEA-ME-WE 2 Segments of the fiber-optic transoceanic network
SEA-ME-WE 3 Spanning the globe fiber-optic transoceanic network
SEAS Signaling, engineering, and administration system
SGSN Serving Gateway Support Node Serving
SGW Serving Gateway
SIMD Single instruction single data CPU architecture
SIMO Single object KPU architecture
SIP Service intelligent peripheral
SLCS Subscriber-loop carrier systems
SLI Service logic interpreter
SLP Service logic programs
SM Switching Module
SM 'S' Interface for the Mobile Roamer
SMDS Switched multi-megabit digital service
SMS Service management system (in conventional INs)
SMSI Simplified message service interface
SNI Service network interface
SNMP Simple network management protocol
SNR Signal-to-noise ratio
SONET Synchronous optical network SONET/SDH

SOCIAL PROCESSES SIMPLE SOCIAL PROCESSES

(n * v) A noun executes a verb; e.g., human strolls, human walks, human runs, human flees
(n →* v) A noun with a modified verb, human runs fast, human slows down to or standstill, etc. *(n *→v)*, e.g., human run and gets tired

COMPLEX SOCIAL PROCESSES

(n1 * v n2) Teacher *(n1)* instructs *(*v)* student *(n2)*
(n1 *→v n2) Teacher severely reprimands *(*→v)* student

COMPOUND SOCIAL PROCESSES

$(n1 \to {}^*v \to {}^* v \to n2 \; = > \; \to n3)$ Hydrogen explodes $(\to {}^*v)$ during combination $(\to^* v)$ with oxygen *(n2)* to form water vapor $(= > \to n3)$

$((n1 \to {}^*v \; n2) \; (n1 \to^* v) \; {}^*n2 \; = > \; v)$ Master *(n1)* whips $(\to {}^*v)$ slave *(n2)* (and makes $(n1 \to {}^* v)$ her *(n2)* cry $(= > v)$. (Two simple sentences)

SOCIAL PROCESS SYMBOLIC LANGUAGE

$((n1 \to {}^*v \; n2) \; (n1 \to^* v) \; {}^*n2 \; = > \; v)$ also can be used for master apologizes to slave and makes her feel good, etc. The nature of *v's* becomes different

SPACES

RS Physical and real space with $(x, y, z, t; r, \theta, \varphi, t; r, \theta, h, t;$ etc.) coordinates in which reality occurs

NS Neural space for thought and comprehension; it is real space in the physiological sense

SoS Social space for humans and KCOs in dealing with social problems

SS Memory systems space in computer and network systems for computational tools, algorithms, etc.

MS Mental space derivative from NS

PS Psychological space with emotional ties to physical or mental objects, convolutions and verbs

KS Knowledge space(s): subset(s) of mental space in the human mind, or superset/subset of the memory allocated for knowledge functions in knowledge machines

SPC Service control point (in conventional INs)

SPSO Single process single object KPU architecture

SS Switching system

SS7 Signaling System 7

SSB Single side band

SSB-F/A Single sideband frequency/amplitude

SSI Small-scale integration

SSKO Single Simple Knowledge Object

SSLI Special services logical interface

SSP Service Switching Point

SST Spread spectrum transmission

STM-*i* STM-*i* designation, with $i \; (= n/3)$ for the STS-*n* designation

STP Service Transfer Point

STPs Signal transfer points (in conventional INs)

STS Synchronous Transport Signal

STS-*n* Synchronous transport signal at level *n*

SW Switch for the mobile telephone/wireless environment

T

T1 Signal at DS1 rate of 1.544 Mb/s

TAT-8, TAT-9 Global Optical Networks

TCP/IP Transmission control protocol, connection-oriented transport protocol of the Internet architecture; reliable byte stream delivery service. IP Internet protocol that provides a connectionless best effort delivery service across the Internet

TCPAP Transactions capabilities applications part
TDMA Time division multiple access
TE Terminal equipment
TEm Terminal equipment − microwave

TIME

t Time in all spaces. Reversal of 't' is not possible in real space and MS but is feasible in KS, SS. Also used as a symbol in analog and continuous functions
δt **or** Δt Time to complete any process in the real and/or knowledge spaces
T A span of time and $= \sum \delta t$ or Δt, Numerical time dependent operations are possible in all spaces
TINA TMN + IN Telecommunication management network + intelligent network
TMM Transaction management machine
TPC-5 Trans Pacific cables toward the third generation

U

U, T, and S Interfaces for ISDN
UCI Universal customer interface
UE User Equipment
UIS Universal Information Services
UISN Universal Information Services Network
UMTS Universal Mobile Telecommunication System
UNIX A powerful operating systems developed by Bell System to operate ESS type of telecommunication nodes and network functions. It is generic enough to operate most computing environments
UNMA Universal network management architecture
UOS Universal operating system
UP User Plane
UPT Universal personal telecommunication
USIM Universal Subscriber ID Module
USIN Universal services intelligent network proposed by AT&T during late 1980 s, but never finally implemented.
USN Universal Services Nodes
UTRAN Terrestrial Radio Access Network

V

Verbs

v A verb function or simply a verb associated with n and *. All verbs do not interact with all nouns *and vice versa*. When attempted in illegal context the knowledge machine generates an error message
v' The status of the verb v after the process $(n * v)$: $v' = v$, if the process does not affect v
VCs Virtual circuits through the network environments
VDSL Variable rate DSL, one of the numerous versions of the digital subscriber lines
VF Generic verb function
VFN Vendor feature node
VHDSL Very high-speed DSL

VLSI Very large-scale integration for IC chips
VoIP Voice over Internet deploying established IPs
VSAT Very small aperture terminals
VSELP Vector sum excited linear prediction
VT Virtual terminal

W

WAN Wide area network
WARC World Administrative Radio Conference
WC Wire center of a typical switching node where the subscriber line terminate at the central office
WDM Wavelength division multiplex for FO transmission
WWW World Wide Web

X

X. 21 One of the earlier packet data protocols
X.25 ITU Recommendation that specifies the interface between users data equipment (DTE) and the packet-switching data circuit terminating equipment

Z

Z_0 Characteristic impedance of transmission media

Epilogue: Transitional Knowledge Field Theory (KFT)

EPILOGUE SUMMARY

This epilogue presents a platform for a more precise Science of Knowledge in the real space, even though it appears well founded in the knowledge space. Extrapolations deep into knowledge space (*KS*) and knowledge domains (*KD*) are presented. The mathematical tools and methodology are borrowed from other disciplines thus providing an initial entry into knowledge field theory. With careful deliberations and willful insight, some of the concepts from vector algebra and vector operators such as *del, grad, div, curl, curl-of-curl* are interpreted in *KD*, though not as precisely as their representations in traditional field theory or in Physics. In many instances, even though these operators carry a sense of interpretation, they reach mental dead ends. However, these mathematical operators only provide a foothold into treating knowledge on a scientific basis, assigning a degree of numerical measures and imposing a degree of mathematical formalism.

The *Laplace, Poisson, Quasi-Poissonian Equations, Divergence Theorem and Gauss's Law, and Stokes Theorem* are transfused into *KD* and knowledge space. These incursions shed new light in the formalism, as they are applicable in the knowledge domain. These transfused concepts revive the basic awareness that knowledge fields exist in knowledge space like fields in electromagnetism (*EM*) and in other thermal or fluid mechanics problems in real space. Long before civilizations, the *EM* fields have existed and only recently discovered in the cosmic world. Knowledge fields penetrate and travel through minds as *EM* waves penetrate objects and traverse through space. Total reception and partial and total shielding are as feasible for movement of knowledge in minds as they are feasible for *EM* fields in circuits and antenna spaces.

In this epilogue, we explore the shadows of strict formalism of Physics and vector algebra in the deep trenches of knowledge spaces and its science. The extent of transfusion between the two disciplines is restricted to the pragmatism of interpreted concepts and the equations. Though incomplete, the unison of the two disciplines offers pathways in the uncharted knowledge space, and conversely it offers the universality of knowledge into the realm of vector fields in physics.

E.1 INTRODUCTION

The activities of all biological life forms revolve around their needs [1], need structures [2], and pyramids [3]. An *N*-group(s) of "objects" coupled with appropriate *V*-group(s) of "actions" or verbs gratifies the needs of all organisms. Knowledge about such objects and verbs and life are as tightly

519

intertwined to make it a continuous process. All forms of life thus learn to live and to keep living. The struggle for knowledge is innate in all organisms. When groups of nouns and verbs are treated as vector entities or tensors, they are orthogonal in nature in most cases. The knowledge space soon becomes hyper-dimensional due to the complexities of needs, the "noun-groups," and their associated "verb-groups." Though complex and hyper-dimensional, needs, objects, and verbs are tractable and linkable in the computer spaces of modern machines.

Correlation between physics and knowledge appears evident since physics is passed on as knowledge about "things" and "actions" around the things. Noun-things are as essential to all life forms as the associated verb-actions in, out, and around these noun-things. Total absence of either one (noun-things or verb-actions) is lifelessness and lack of consciousness. Further, as much as the E and M fields are orthogonal in the electromagnetic field space, the N-group(s) of objects is orthogonal to the V-group(s) of functions, thus generating a velocity component to knowledge flows in the knowledge domain.

To accommodate this truism, we restate that all life activities are motivated by some open or underlying need of the organism. Such motivations trigger the biological energy manifest as the physical, mental, emotional, and/or spiritual need. Realistic perspectives by Freud [4], Maslow [5], and Ahamed [6] have been presented, stating that the need structures for all organisms ranging from animals to philosophers do exist. All approaches emphasize that (biological) *"objects"* always have to *"do"* something or the other sooner or later, even if it is "no action" for a little while. Thus, the science of no action by a object is worthless physics and becomes dead as null-knowledge science.

E.2 MARSHAL AND NEWTON INTO KNOWLEDGE SPACE

Change is perpetual in all environments. Every minutia of change needs energy derived from the difference between the force to exist as-is and the force to change. If a perceptual distance is placed between the status of any object at "t" and its status at "$t + \Delta t$," then the basis of energy is derived as the product of the resultant force causing the change of status ($=$"Δs") times the distance. On the one hand, there is the vector force ($F1$) to preserve the status of any object in its current form and on the other is a vector sum ($F2$) of the forces to change the status of the object. The interaction yields a resultant force ($F1 \sim F2$) that brings about the change. The two forces $F1$ and $F2$ counter, alter, adjust, and shape each other almost giving the object a sensation of life. These vector forces are never perfectly equal nor perfectly opposite for prolonged durations.

If the utility of the object at its status $S1$ at "t" is $U1$ and the utility at status $S2$ at "$t + \Delta t$," is $U2$, then (according to Marshall's utility theory) the price in the change of utility ($U1 \sim U2$) is the cost of energy incurred in the change is ($F1 \sim F2$) times Δs.[1] This generalization of the Newtonian concept that energy is force times distance into the social and knowledge domains is feasible. It is presumed that nature, human beings, circumstances, and machines, originate and supply the energy for change. In the older cultures, human spirit and glow have served to implant the primal "concepts" for the energy for change. The path from concept to its implementation human effort is embedded in discipline and endurance.

However, through the 1970s to the current era, machines have assisted human effort and creativity enormously. Computer graphic and computer vision both facilitate the upsurge of knowledge and hence the creativity that follows. The environmental-input process is faster, more efficient, and more detailed by providing neural inputs directly into the optic nerve that is 10 times larger than the auditory nerve. The more recent advances in the binocular vision, 3-D graphics, and gaming devices can only sharpen the human response. The truisms that living organisms (noun-objects) have needs that such need gratification(s) do exist and support life by actions and interactions (verb-functions) on and by the surrounding objects run through this book and in this epilogue.

E.3 NOUN-OBJECT AND VERB-FUNCTION FIELD GROUPS

Two key constituting vectors in the knowledge domain are (a) the "noun-field-group(s)" of noun-objects (or simply *Ns*) that humans *have to have* in order to gratify their needs and (b) the "verb-field-group(s)" of verb-functions (or simply *Vs*) that humans *have to do* with the *Ns* to quench their needs. These two groups, the *Ns* and the *Vs*, provide for the "knowledge-energy" transfers or knowledge flow in society that can be picked up by the reception (antenna) characteristics of the recipients (such as humans, animals, live-stock, and all life forms).

Knowledge potential is a dominant parameter in the knowledge domain. Much as electric and magnetic potentials (E and M potentials) introduced during the inception of electromagnetic field theory, we propose knowledge potential (*KnP*) to introduce the Field Theory of Knowledge. This knowledge potential *K* (shortened as *KnP*) is indicative of the knowledge potentials of knowledge-centric objects, or *KCOs*, in its own particular direction.[2] It is derived from the "work-done" or "energy-spent" in acquiring that potential in the educational/learning/training sequence(s) of a *KCO* learning the particular discipline, trait, trade, specialization, profession, expertise, etc. In essence, this *K* is similar to the energy spent or acquired by electrically or magnetically[3] "charged bodies." This parameter is also indicative of the "capacity" of any *KCO* to do the "work" in the direction of the expertise and/or training. *KCOs* can be quite generic ranging from an animal, an individual, a corporation, a society, a culture, a nation, etc.; the mere existence of a *KCO* is indicative of some work having been done to create it. It implies that any *KCO* has some *K* associated with it. For example, each of the tiniest objects such as a cell, a microbe, a viruse, a bacteria, each has its own genetic imprint and an effort to take it to its current state. The particular *K* is thus associated with each of the objects. In addition, an atom has a nuclear structure and order; it has a distinct *K* signature associated with it.

In assigning the *educational* knowledge potential (*KnP*) of a human being, it was suggested [7] that *KnP* of a high school graduate be assigned a 0 degrees K such that college and higher education/training can have reasonable positive measures of *KnP*. However, the dimensionality of a human can be in numerous directions such as art, musical talent, dance, and theatrics. These are indeed typical dimensions of *K* for humans in the Dewey Decimal Classification (*DDC*) [8] or the

Library of Congress (LoC) [9] classification. These many scalars present the vector of K. The numerical values of these scalars are indicative of the expertise in those directions. For example, a nuclear scientist may have a typical *KnP* value of 500 degrees K (see Ref. [10]) with a PhD in the direction of nuclear sciences but have a *KnP* of typical value of 120 degrees K (as much as a typical college graduate in all sciences) in the direction of biological sciences. The directionality of knowledge thus starts to play its own specific role in enforcing a vectorial direction to knowledge.

In comparison with a 3D, rectangular physical object may measure (*x*, *y*, and *z*) inches in the X, Y, and Z dimensions of *x.y.z* cubic inches of physical volume. In the knowledge domain, a new PhD graduate may have achieved *KnP* of 500 degrees K (*KnP*) in the direction of the specific direction of specialization (such as *EM* Field Theory with a DDS identifier of QC661.K648 (1990), see Ref. [11]), with five years (Y) of training with Doctoral Faculty and achieved 5 patentable claims of creativity (C). The cubic educational volume of this particular PhD thus becomes 12,500 *KYC* [10].

E.4 CONTOUR OF UNIVERSAL BUT ILLUSIVE KNOWLEDGE

Impression of perfect knowledge is a fleeting imagination. The fragment of conceived knowledge is as fragmented as the weight of a biological body in the entire weight of the universe. However, this fragment of knowledge being a part of the universal knowledge carries its *genetic imprint* of the parent "perfect knowledge." Thus, the knowledge "K" multiplied by a unit vector along the direction (i.e., a universal DDS classification of "K") indicates an endpoint. When such endpoints located in a hyper-dimensional space(s) of all knowledge(s) of all species, at all times are collected and connected at any one instant of time (which is outright impossible), then the contour of the illusive knowledge(s) can be (only) imagined as the extrapolation of the *genetic imprint*. Extrapolations are pushed to outer limits of infinite space(s) to reach the contour(s) of many knowledge(s). Such processes are no longer mathematical but existent even in the neural nets within the brain. If such hyper-dimensional contours exist, then the surface integral over the entire contour *may be* zero[4] or are they?

We revert to the scientific realm of dealing with fragmented and conceivable knowledge in sciences and physics where reality of the physical space dominates reason, judgment, and mathematics. In this confined space the localized algebra of the four-dimensional world where the operators *del, grad, div, curl, Laplacian*, etc. have their severe limitations but together yield a deeper perspective of knowledge that lies ahead is to be explored. In the Knowledge domain, these operators have much deeper implications.

E.5 OVERLAP BETWEEN PHYSICS AND KNOWLEDGE SCIENCE

Physical spaces and knowledge space do not completely overlap. Totally conformal transformations are not feasible even though the thread of rationality runs through both spaces. Knowledge space being far more encompassing than physical space molds the personalities of different *KCOs*, species, and humans in the real space.

Fields of many natures exist in nature. Electric fields (as in cloud formations), thermal fields with heat-flow-temperature gradients (as in volcanic flows), fluid mechanics fields with pressure-velocity gradients (as in oceanic waves), electromagnetic fields (as in the cosmic objects), MRI fields with various penetration rates in healthy and cancerous tissues, etc., are known to exist. Some of these fields have been harnessed for human betterment and benefit. In the same vein, knowledge fields that exist around and about highly knowledge-centric objects (*KCOs*, such as scientists, scholars, saints, gurus, corporations, cultures and even knowledge banks) can be indicative of the knowledge flow to and from various large *KCOs* to and from tiniest knowledge-centric objects (*kcos*). As in the case of flow of electrical energy, a difference of electric potential (or voltage) is necessary; a certain difference between the knowledge potentials (*KnPs*) is necessary along the direction of knowledge flow. The flow of knowledge is sometimes haphazard compared the quantized flow of current perpendicular to the equipotential lines. The laws of precise and formal mathematics start to fall apart if they are pushed too far in the knowledge domain. To an extent, the flow of current between two electrical objects can get randomly excited and influenced by local conditions (as in lightning discharges from the clouds) by the directions of energy; the current flow can also become haphazard.

Knowledge flow also exhibits such variations when two or more *KCOs* are brought in close (enough) proximity. Edison and Bell are known to have fierce exchanges; Tesla and Westinghouse have quarreled about poly-phase rotating magnetic fields, etc. To a lesser extent, when any number of *KCOs* cross paths, trails of knowledge are blazed but soon forgotten.

E5.1 IDEALIZED ETHER SPACE AND PRISTINE KNOWLEDGE SPACE

Knowledge fields (in particular, the *N* fields) surround *KCOs* and *kcos*, noun-things, noun-objects, and their groups. Knowledge fields (in particular, the *V* fields) surround *VFs* and *vfs*, verb-functions, verb-actions, and their groups. Together, in an appropriate syntactical and semantic context, they foster the flow of *intelligent* knowledge. They exist like electromagnetic fields (i.e., the E and M fields) that surround all active electric and magnetically charged bodies or the thermal field around hot bodies. Such knowledge fields travel through the minds as *EM* waves traverse through objects and space as short and long strings[5] [11] pass through objects.

Two key constituting vectors in the knowledge domain are the "noun-field-group(s)" of noun-objects (or simply *Ns* that humans need to gratify their needs) and the "verb-field-group(s)" of Verb-Functions (or simply *Vs* that humans do with the *Ns* to quench their needs). As much as the E and M fields are orthogonal in physics, the *N*-group(s) of "noun things" is orthogonal to the *V*-group(s) of "verb actions." This orthogonal pair generates a velocity component for the knowledge vector *K* in the knowledge space providing for the "knowledge-energy" transfer or flow in society.

The energy can be picked up by the "tuned" antenna characteristics of the recipients (such as humans, animals, live-stock, and all life forms). This mode of communication in the *EM* field theory by the propagation of the Poynting vector (P = E × H) [12] becomes applicable in the knowledge domain as the knowledge vector ($K = N \times V$). The knowledge domain being decisively more complex than free space for *EM* waves, the group velocities of the *N* and *V* vectors need to be addressed. The permeability and permitivity (i.e., μ_0 and e_0) coefficients for ideal free space translate as μ_{k0} and ε_{k0} flavor in an *uncorrupted* knowledge space. The velocity of knowledge propagation depends on the knowledge media characteristics. It can range from being (almost) infinite[6] between two perfect minds (in total synchrony) to become zero in the corrupted knowledge spaces such as news media and spam-full the Internet. Corrupt knowledge media can offer very high N and V "resistivities" (the dissipative components that accompany μ_{k0} and ε_{k0}) for noun-object groups and verb-function groups, respectively.

E5.2 SOCIAL PERMEABILITY OF N'S AND PERMITIVITY OF V'S

The velocity of the knowledge vector K in knowledge space becomes feasible as the velocity of the (Poynting) vector in the Ether space. The vectors that become dominant in the ether space are E and M; the vectors that are decisive in knowledge space are N and V. The velocity of light determined as $[1.0/(\text{Sq.root}(\mu_0 \cdot \varepsilon_0)]$ has an analogous basis as $[1.0/(\text{Sq.root}(\mu_{k0} \cdot \varepsilon_{k0}))]$ for the velocity of knowledge or v_k. But, the gurus and saints of the spiritual world have not determined the μ_{k0} and ε_{k0} thus stalling the precision of the numbers into knowledge science. By as it may, one can pragmatically circumvent this knowledge block by assuming it as *indeterminate* for the time being. If the knowledge is encoded as encoded data riding over the *EM* fields (as it is practiced now), then the vector velocity of knowledge becomes the vector velocity of light in free space in the Poynting vector direction.

Social media characteristics are generally biased and content driven. In the pristine knowledge space that does not distort knowledge willingly and wantonly, v_k can be very *indeterminately* high[7] and offers no attenuation nor distortion to the N and V vectors and to knowledge flow. Conversely, v_k can degenerate to zero in some social settings where delay, distortion, and attenuation are infinitely high.

Typically, the commercial and biased social media offers the higher "resistivities" to the flow of true and pristine knowledge, but simultaneously amplify, exaggerate, and publicize spam, deception, and fraud. This social tendency when reflected in the domain of physics leads to a medium for light that makes the velocity of light depend on its wavelength, or (λ). It is observed in fiber optics and known as dispersion (i.e., different velocities for different colors) leading to the widening of the transmitted pulses of laser optical sources of light. Dispersion is also dominant in copper and cable media offering different delays for different frequencies present in signal carrying voltage pluses [13].

In the social domain, dispersion of Ns and Vs is highly dramatic and can ever reverse from positive to negative values depending upon the content of knowledge. These types of media characteristics are unknown in traditional physics of fiber optics and pulse transmission in metallic media even though they may occur in galactic regions. The Ns and Vs vectors that are essential to carry the knowledge vector K suffer dramatically in corrupted social settings. Very much as truth and authenticity are unique in the knowledge domain, there are infinite variations of delays, deceptions, corruptions, and spam.

E.6 ROLE OF *GRAD, DIV, CURL, CURL-OF-CURL* IN THE KNOWLEDGE DOMAIN

The vector operators' *grad, div, curl, curl-of-curl*, etc. have a conceptual basis and elegantly tie the findings of many scientists like Ampere, Gauss, Gilbert, Galvani, etc. Electromagnetic fields being four (x, y, z, and t) dimensions are relatively simpler to formulate. The dimensionalities of knowledge (*DDC* and *LoC* classification) offer innumerable dimensions, even though there is considerable overlap. Further the knowledge is quantized and offers statistical properties that call for its treatment based on *kuantum* (see Chapter 17) theory of knowledge. The use of vector operations in the knowledge domain for precision of results is not to be expected as much as the transfusion of concepts from mathematics to knowledge. Appendix A details some of the implication of Gradient (grad) of the K, the divergence (*div*) of vectors N and V, and velocity of the vector K. The implications of *Curl* and *Curl-of-Curl* are no immediately evident. It is possible that the partial differential (*Laplace, Quasi-Laplace, Poisson,* and *Quasi-Poisson*) equations *will* shed some deeper understanding of the multidimensional vector knowledge potentials (*KnPs*) of complex knowledge centric objects *KCOs* and *kcos*.

E.6.1 IDEALIZED KNOWLEDGE FIELDS AND FLOW

Under ideal conditions, the knowledge fields in knowledge space start to exhibit the characteristics of electric fields in real space as shown in Figure E.1. When a positively charged *KCO* ($K+$) starts a dialogue with an ideal receptor of similar character, then the field distribution for knowledge flow can be akin to the field and flux distribution in an ideal capacitor. In reality, the distribution is far from this ideal. Media, culture, social, national, regional, and human characteristics enter the knowledge flow distribution. For example, if the four quadrants I, II, III and IV in Figure E.2 have different resistive, and dielectric properties, the field pattern gets effected accordingly. In the knowledge space, the surrounding media properties influence the flow of knowledge energy or the kenergy flow is curtailed or accentuated accordingly. The flow can also be enhanced if the media amplifies the N, the *V*, and/or * vectors.

The flow of knowledge in knowledge space can become even more elaborate when the knowledge fields are to be traced in the real space. In the four quadrants of Figure E.3, further influences

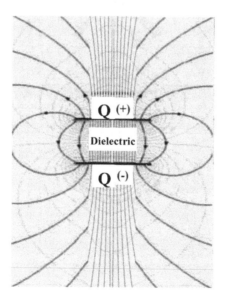

FIGURE E.1

Knowledge field closely approximated by an electrostatic field pattern. The electric properties are assumed to be uniform in the region.

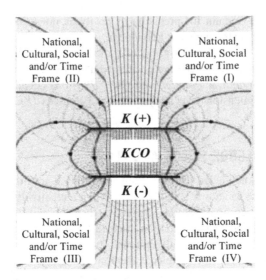

FIGURE E.2

Knowledge flow in real world where it experiences effects of national, cultural, social, and time variations. Kenergy and knowledge power can both change dramatically.

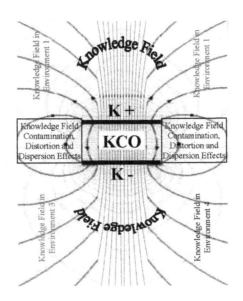

FIGURE E.3

Knowledge fields in regions with widely varying characteristics in and out of the KCO that exhibits +K KnP and −K KnP. The distortion and dispersion effect change the character of Knowledge from time to time and from culture to culture.

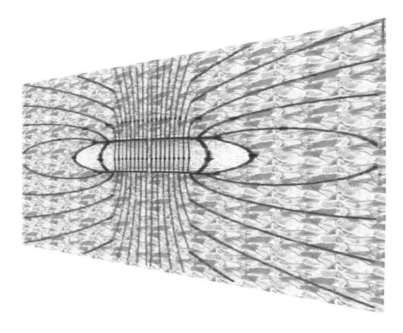

FIGURE E.4

Knowledge flow within small regions (designated by the different contours and colors in the figure). The isolated regions can show different properties of knowledge like the species show different adaptations in geographic regions of the world.

by the distortion and dispersion effects of the media are depicted. The knowledge flow and fields are severely affected. The individual *KCO* that holds the plus *K* and the minus *K* knowledge potentials with retention and bias characteristics will also distort the knowledge fields.

In Figure E.4 the passages of time and expansion of the three vectors (*N*, *, and *V*) are shown from left to right. The colors indicate the influence of the different, national, cultural, and social influences. The effects can be oscillatory in the time domain or in the cultures. The net effect is that the old knowledge can assume a new contour again, and the new knowledge can become old stuff in a different culture, etc.

Knowledge flows within small regions are designated by the different contours and colors in Figure E.4. The isolated regions can show different properties of knowledge like the species show different adaptations in geographic regions around the world. This figure depicts the true character of knowledge as it varies over different time spans and in different regions around the world and universe.

E.7 LAPLACE AND POISSON EQUATIONS IN KNOWLEDGE SPACES

Simpler versions of these two equations are too simplistic for the *KD*. Linear magneto-static and electrostatic fields are well represented by these equations. Since knowledge potential is introduced as *KnP*, the vector of multidimensional vector *K* has to be conceived as the vector potential A for magnetic flux (in Webers/sq meter). Such a vector remains unconceivable in the *KD*. However, some analogies prevail and explored further in Appendix EB.

Length of Lines indicates Physical Distance

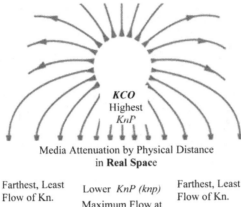

Media Attenuation by Physical Distance
in **Real Space**

Farthest, Least
Flow of Kn.

A

Lower *KnP (knp)*

Maximum Flow at

Center i. e., Least

Physical Separation

Farthest, Least
Flow of Kn.

B

FIGURE E.5

Knowledge flow curves from *KCO* to audience physically separated from *KCO*. The media resistance is high at the edges A and B, thus attenuating the knowledge flow.

Some of the simpler distributions of *KnP* are presented in Figures E.5, E.6, and E.7. Consider a teacher, a professor, a preacher, etc. (a given *KCO* with a high *KnP*) presents the subject matter in any given *DDS* classification (a given direction) to a class, students, parish (a group with an average *KnP* lower than that of the *KCO*). The flow of knowledge and the corresponding equipotential *KnP* contours are depicted in Figure E.5 and E.6.

Media resistance and human resistance both affect the flow of knowledge in different ways, and the flow of knowledge can be altered considerably by both types of resistances. In the real world both resistances are present, and the knowledge flow gets unevenly distributed with places (*x, y,* and *z* coordinates) and time ("*t*") coordinate.

In Figure E.7, the uneven flow of knowledge from a highly *KnP* charged *KCO* to a group of lesser charge *kcos*. Both the knowledge flow and equi-knowledge-potential lines in knowledge space are portrayed from a real-life situation where exchange of knowledge occurs. In such cases, the knowledge-flow gets irregular but not haphazard. Participants have unequal knowledge potentials in any discipline, and each member receives unequal knowledge over a finite duration. This situation depicts any generic real-world situation where the information received is a function of time and or the physical space that the member occupies with respect to the *KCO*. The media characteristics (such as room acoustics, background noise, passer-by distractions) also influence the total *kenergy* in the knowledge that is communicated or exchanged.

In this figure, irregular mesh of knowledge flow (red lines) and *equi-knowledge* potential (black and red lines) are shown, rather imprecisely. These two sets of lines are not orthogonal but intersect at irregular and oblique angles because of the more complex nature of knowledge flow that assumes the flavor of compressible fluid flow at instant "*t*" but can change its favor to

Length of Lines indicates Resistance to Knowledge

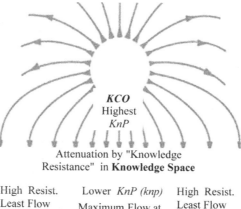

KCO
Highest
KnP

Attenuation by "Knowledge
Resistance" in **Knowledge Space**

High Resist.   Lower *KnP (knp)*   High Resist.
Least Flow   Maximum Flow at   Least Flow

                    Center,i. e., Least
C   Kn. Resistances   D

FIGURE E.6

Knowledge flow curves from *KCO* to audience psychologically separated from *KCO*. The human resistance is high at the edges C and D, thus attenuating the knowledge flow.

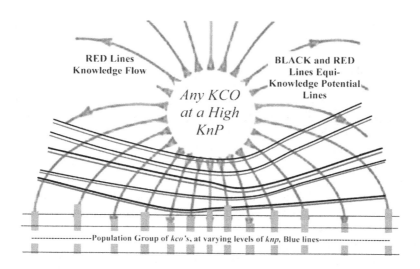

RED Lines
Knowledge Flow

BLACK and RED
Lines Equi-
Knowledge Potential
Lines

*Any KCO
at a High
KnP*

--------------------Population Group of *kco's*, at varying levels of *knp*, Blue lines--------------------

FIGURE E.7

Knowledge flow and equi-knowledge-potential lines in knowledge space are portrayed from a real-life class room situation or a conference room situation. The audience (i.e., *kcos*) has unequal knowledge potentials and each member receives unequal knowledge over a period of time. This situation is the most generic real-world situation where the information received is a function of time and or the physical space that the member occupies with respect to the *KCO*. The knowledge flow gets irregular but not haphazard.

noncompressible or even expansionary fluids in very short duration "Δt." Being dynamic in nature, it becomes almost questionable if the traditional field theory from Physics and EM fields can be forcefully applied in the knowledge domain. From an analytical perspective, the formulation appears dreadfully complex, but from a computation perspective, the super-fast processors of the twenty-first century can track the fast movements of knowledge in the knowledge space and depict them the graphical space controlled by the high-speed graphical processor units of the modern computers.

CONCLUSIONS

The basis of this epilog is the fact that all human activities (actions and verbs or Vs) are based on their deficit needs. Stated alternatively, deficit needs provide the motivation for human activities. Elements of knowledge that are derived from the convolution of noun-objects (Ns) with verb-functions are essential for *all* insidious activities of *all* life forms. Actions are initiated and executed by all biological organisms (Ns) and are directed toward objects and actions. In this chapter, we have introduced the concept of group velocities of Ns or "noun-things" and of Vs or "verb-actions." In an appropriate context, and together, Ns and Vs form convolutions that materially affect the knowledge content being generated and/or modified. These vectors, N and V, face a range of "transmission characteristics" in the social media for the flow of knowledge. The knowledge vector K becomes orthogonal to the N and V vectors as accounts for transfer of knowledge energy as much as the Poynting vector carries the energy in EM fields. The formalism of electric and EM fields cannot be brute forced through the knowledge space, even though the methodology is applicable. The vector K can suffer highly variable delays, distortions, and dispersion effects for knowledge as it flows through classrooms, gatherings, societies, and cultures.

This epilog should be conceived as conceptual and seminal rather than conclusive and final in the science of knowledge. Knowledge about knowledge becomes twice as illusive. Hence this segment of the book provides a grip on treating knowledge as the "work-done" or "energy expended" in achieving that potential of knowledge or knowledge potential KnP. Emotional, psychological, physical, and mental energies are all integrated in the estimation of the "work-done." The extent of achievement of KnP thus becomes a personal endeavor of the individual. In an education setting, where education is essentially streamlined from high school level to doctoral level, the work done depends on the student caliber (i.e., the GPA), the number of semester-months and type of faculty—student interactions. Any particular student can thus have different ranges for the KnP at the bachelor, masters, and doctoral levels. The direction of this KnP is classified by the subject and/or area of specialization. The KnP energy can now be expended (without loss or depleting it) in other problem-solving environments.

Human neurobiological framework does not offer permanent retention of KnP achieved once; instead, it is continuously fluctuating in any given direction and gets drained over longer periods. It is modified by events and interaction, by Internet surfing and by IPOD browsing. The KnP is comparable to any other quantitative measure (such as temperature, blood pressure, pulse-rate) of human health. Only certain ranges have been standardized. Being energy oriented KnP can be generated, acquired, and transformed, even though the laws of conservation of energy (from traditional physics) are not entirely applicable. Muck like human health, KnP can degenerate and can be even destroyed by abuse, neglect, and drugs.

CONCLUDING REMARKS

It is doubtful if knowledge field theory yields immediate results in the real and physical space and in an entirely pragmatic world. However, in the knowledge space, such knowledge-fields and the knowledge-based operators (*grad, curl, div, curl grad*, etc.) govern the flow of knowledge in a direction of flow from + ve charged *KCOs* to less charged ± *kcos* in any given direction of knowledge (defined by the *DDS* or *LoC* classification). Such transfers of knowledge occur in classrooms, shrines, churches, and synagogues. The least resistance to the flow is facilitated by the neurons ready to receive the "discharge of knowledge." Such paths channel human thoughts in a context of symbolic operators and operations on knowledge vectors, nouns, verbs, and their convolutions.

It appears illogical to dismiss the knowledge flow theory as nonexistent or irrelevant in the deep knowledge spaces of the mind, as it is impossible to write-off electromagnetic field theory in deep cosmic spaces. The knowledge fields around many eminent scholars and scientists are known to exist and are evident in scientific dialogs. In most cases, the knowledge space surrounding humans and life-forms carries the concepts in the knowledge, that are more permanent than the words that carry the message. We submit to the readers to weigh and consider the concepts presented in this epilogue, in light of their own experience that are indeed "bodies of personal knowledge" that can come back at different times, in different places and, in different shapes and sizes. The strings ("Strings" as in String Theory) of continuity are entrenched in the concepts and wisdom that knowledge machines can isolate, process and enhance.

NOTES

1. This truism is based in the Newton's Law that "work done" equals force times displacement. In this case the force is the difference between the force to retain the status quo of any noun-thing and force to change the status of the noun-thing, and the displacement is the change of status.
2. Since there are numerous directions of knowledge, any particular *KCO* may have numerous scalar potential of Ks each for the particular direction chosen, such as social skill, educational achievement, job skill, and training.
3. All the accepted notions and equations from *EM* field theory are neither (entirely) feasible nor (entirely) applicable in knowledge field theory (*KFT*) in the knowledge space. However, the concepts can be transmuted and commuted. To some extent these concepts are also transferable. For example, the *EM* equation (Div B = 0, or ∇ dot B or ∇. B = 0) becomes irrational in KFT, even though the notions of (H = Grad M or H = ∇M and the Divergence Theorem) may be applicable. They provide a basis for the many direction(s) of expertise in the many directions and dimensions of knowledge. An entirely new set of mathematical rules evolves just for the KFT.
4. Perhaps only the gurus and monks may decipher the genesis of this illusive knowledge.
5. String Theory is a recent branch of physics detailed to some extent in the Website http://www.nuclecu. unam.mx/ ~ alberto/physics/string.html.
6. Velocity exceeding the velocity of light are conceivable when an ideally perfect tuned super-recipient gets the knowledge accurately before the sender has even transmitted a given "body of knowledge" or *BoK*. Perhaps, telepathy and inspirations travel at extreme speeds faster than the *EM* waves that carry encoded information and knowledge.
7. In the absence of any scientific knowledge as to how "noun-groups" and "verb-actions" are communicated, this indeterminacy is postponed until a breakthrough in telepathy; inspirations or revelations are conceived, transmitted, and documented in literature.
8. Rationalized MKS system is generally used for the quantification of this equation in electrical systems.
9. The symbols in these two equations are explained fully in Ref. [14, 15].

REFERENCES

[1] Coate RA, Rosati JA. The power of human needs in world society. Boulder: Lynne Rienner Publishers; 1988. Also see, Maslow AH. A theory of human motivation. Psychol. Rev. 1943;50:370–396.

[2] Maslow AH. Toward a psychology of being. 2nd ed. Van Nostrand Reinhold; 1982.

[3] Ahamed SV. Need pyramid of the information age human being. International Society of Political Psychology (ISSP) Scientific Meeting, Toronto, Canada, July 3–6, 2005. Also see, Need structure of organizations and corporations.

[4] Freud Sigmund. Carl Gustav Jung Letters. Abr. ed. Princeton University Press; 1994.

[5] Maslow AH. A theory of human motivation. Psychol. Rev. 1943;50:370–96. Also see, Maslow A. Farther reaches of human nature. New York: Viking Press; 1971.

[6] Ahamed SV. An enhanced need pyramid for the information age human being. In: Proc. of the Fifth Hawaii International Conference, Fifth International Conference on Business, Hawaii, May 26–29, 2005.

[7] Ahamed SV. Next generation knowledge machines. Waltham, MA: Elsevier Insights Book; 2014. Chapter 11.

[8] OCLC, Dewey decimal classification and relative index. 22nd ed. Dublin, OH: OCLC; 2003. See also, Comaroni JP. Dewey decimal classification. 18th ed. Albany, NY: Forest Press; 1976.

[9] United States Government, Library of Congress Classification. <http://catalog.loc.gov>, accessed June 2013.

[10] Ahamed SV. Computational framework for knowledge. Hoboken, NJ: John Wiley and Sons, Inc; 2009.

[11] Kong JA. Theory of electromagnetic waves. New York: Wiley; 1975. https://searchworks.stanford.edu/view/577625

[12] Kraus JD, Carver KR. Electromagnetics. McGraw-Hill; 1973.

[13] Ahamed SV, Lawrence VB. Design and engineering of intelligent communication systems. Boston: Kluwer Academic Publishers; 1997.

[14] Ahamed SV. Accelerated convergence of numerical solution of linear and non-linear field problems. Comp. J. 1965;8:73–6.

[15] Ahamed SV. Application of the acceleration of convergence technique to numerical solution of linear and nonlinear vector field problems with numerous sources. Int. J. Eng. Sci. 1970;8(5):403–13.

[16] Botis M. MATLAB program for the numerical solution of Duhamel convolution integral. Bulletin of the Transylvania University of Brasov 2012;5(54).

APPENDIX EA VECTOR OPERATORS IN KNOWLEDGE DOMAIN

Vector operators combine measurement with directionality. Formalism and formalization are both concisely embedded in the representation and equations. It appears that knowledge domain cannot entirely accommodate the rigor of mathematics, but to the extent that it is possible, new interpretations cast new concepts.

The operator *del* offers a magnitude and direction of the steepest gradient for the knowledge potential. Any knowledge-centric object (*KCO*) does indeed have such gradients, especially because the directions of knowledge are formalized in the *DDC* [8] and *LoC* [9] classifications. During the interaction of two *KCOs* the bidirectional flow of knowledge can be mutually rewarding provided the directions are slightly different, thus generating new knowledge in-between the two directions. Totally opposing directions can lead to conflicts and dialectics. In reality, the precise measure is not feasible and direct conflicts are generally skirted to provide for meaningful interactions in social situations.

The operator *div* (and the surface integral) offers insight into the fluctuation of the knowledge and of the "noun-thing" and "verb-function" groups. To the extent that these two vectors fluctuate, there is some social agent or social agitation to cause the change. In an enclosed social sphere or setting (such as culture, society), the extents of fluctuation of N or V groups are related to the "divergence" of the influence of social agents responsible for the change inside the sphere or setting. The delay, dispersion, and the attenuation are influence by this "measure" of divergence. The velocity of flow of knowledge is also influenced by the presence/divergence of the social agents.

The operator *curl* (or contour integral) may offer insight into the "work done" in acquiring the *KnP* of any particular *KCO*. Further, *curl* in a two-dimensional space, becomes too restrictive for even the smallest knowledge-centric object (*kco*). However, in the super-space of knowledge, the integral form of *curl* (after Stoke's theorem) becomes a valuable tool.

For example, the knowledge crossing the surface contour around any (*KCO* or *kco*) is influenced by other *kco's* within the surface, to the extent that they influence the *Ns* vector and the *Vs* vector that convey the knowledge across the surface. In particular, the quasi-Poissonian equation for knowledge flow or distribution also indicates the "flux of knowledge" through and around heterogeneous knowledge media.

In other cases, the contours for integration can be vast and diversified, and the duration of integration may be the college years for students or a lifetime for the gurus and monks. The units and measure of the work-done depend on "force of acquisition" (or nature of training) and along the "pathways of struggle" (or experience during acquisition). Both the two measurements can be highly variable, controversial, and debatable.

APPENDIX EB LAPLACE AND POISSON EQUATIONS IN KNOWLEDGE DOMAIN

These two operations have direct influence on the flow velocity and direction of knowledge since the coefficients μ_{k0} and ε_{k0} for the group velocities of *Ns* and *Vs*. The two socially variable coefficients can alter delays, distortions, and attenuations to *Ns*, *Vs*, and/or both. Unlike the coefficient (μ_0 and ε_0 for free space) in physics, these two parameters can reverse and fluctuate violently in different cultures and societies causing social storms. Magnetic and electric storms have been observed in distant worlds throughout the universe. Such dramatic variations of (μ_0 and ε_0) may exist in other worlds.

EB.1 GENERIC FORM OF POISSON EQUATIONS

In the general format Poisson equation has the form:

$$\nabla^2 \varphi = f.$$

And in three-dimensional coordinates, Poisson equation has the form:

$$\left(\frac{\partial^2}{\partial x^2} + \frac{\partial^2}{\partial y^2} + \frac{\partial^2}{\partial z^2} \right) \varphi(x, y, z) = f(x, y, z).$$

Laplace equation is simply a special case of Poisson's equation when $f = 0$. The gravitational field can be represented by this equation as:

$$\nabla^2 \phi = 4\pi \, G\rho.$$

In the absence of the electromagnetic fields, the equation for electrostatic assumes the form:

$$\nabla^2 \varphi = -\frac{\rho_f}{\varepsilon}.$$

where ρ_f is the charge density and ε is the permittivity of the free space and equal to

$$\frac{10^{-9}}{36\pi} C^2 N^{-1} m^{-2} \approx 8.854\ 187\ 817 \times 10^{-12} C^2 N^{-1} m^{-2}.$$

Such equations can be solved analytically (for simple geometric configurations) and by iterative methods for fields in complex geometries and when the media properties are not uniform and/or nonlinear.

For the (non-time varying) *electrostatic* fields with nonlinear distribution of the permittivity, the quasi-Poisson equation for two dimensions has the form.

$$\frac{\partial}{\partial x}\left\{\varepsilon \cdot \frac{\partial \varphi_z}{\partial x}\right\} + \frac{\partial}{\partial y}\left\{\varepsilon \cdot \frac{\partial \varphi_z}{\partial y}\right\} = -\rho_z$$

For the (non-time varying) *electro-magneto-static* fields with nonlinear distribution of the permeability, the quasi-Poisson equation in two dimensions has the form

$$\frac{\partial}{\partial x}\left\{\frac{1}{\mu} \cdot \frac{\partial A_z}{\partial x}\right\} + \frac{\partial}{\partial y}\left\{\frac{1}{\mu} \cdot \frac{\partial A_z}{\partial y}\right\} = -J_z$$

EB.2 VECTOR OPERATORS IN THE KNOWLEDGE DOMAIN

For the sake of managing the Poisson problem in the knowledge space, let us assume that noun, convolution, and verb vectors from Section E.3 are orthogonal as the x, y, and z axes in Cartesian coordinate system with unit vectors i, j, and k in the three composite vectors N, *, and V. This is an initial approximation and should be treated as such. It becomes necessary to introduce a new vector parameters K (for Knowledge) and force the operators grad, div, and curl upon K.

The operator *grad* operating on K thus becomes:

$$i\frac{\partial K}{\partial N} + j\frac{\partial K}{\partial *} + k\frac{\partial K}{\partial V}.$$

The operator *div grad* operating on K thus becomes:

$$\frac{\partial^2 K}{\partial N^2} + \frac{\partial^2 K}{\partial *^2} + \frac{\partial^2 K}{\partial V^2}.$$

and the Laplace's operator *div grad* becomes:

$$\frac{\partial^2 K}{\partial N^2} + \frac{\partial^2 K}{\partial *^2} + \frac{\partial^2 K}{\partial V^2} = \nabla^2 K$$

The operator *curl curl* ($\nabla \times \nabla K$) tentatively becomes:

$$\begin{vmatrix} i & j & k \\ \dfrac{\partial}{\partial N} & \dfrac{\partial}{\partial *} & \dfrac{\partial}{\partial V} \\ K_n & K_* & K_v \end{vmatrix}$$

The operator ∇^2 with vector operand $K = K_n i + K_* j + K_v k$ becomes

$$\nabla^2 K_n i + \nabla^2 K_* j + \nabla^2 K_v k.$$

Other operators such as *grad div, div curl, curl* of *curl* may be similarly derived for the vector K. It is not evident how these operators can be used for knowledge fields in the knowledge space but not in the real space. Parallelisms between the two spaces exist, but the precision is lost.

The simplest formulations in "static knowledge field" (comparable to static magnetic and static electric fields) are presented here, even though there are many complex versions of the two operations in the real domain of knowledge. Linear superposition theorems, uniform conductance and susceptance, uniform characteristics-impedances, and their independence are not applicable here.

In particular, we present quasi-Poisson equation based on simple three-dimensional (x, y, z) magneto-static field[8] problems [13] and transfuse it to the equivalent quasi-Poissonian equation for "noun-things" in the knowledge domain (*KD*). The correspondence to M field equation is indicated first and field equation for "noun-things" is presented next.

$$\frac{\partial}{\partial x}\left\{ \frac{1}{\mu} \cdot \frac{\partial A_z}{\partial x} \right\} + \frac{\partial}{\partial y}\left\{ \frac{1}{\mu} \cdot \frac{\partial A_z}{\partial y} \right\} = -J_Z$$

This equation is converted to it integral format by using Stokes theorem and written as

$$\int^{contour} H \cdot dl = \iint^{surface} J \cdot ds \quad \text{or} \quad \int^{countour} H \cdot dl = \int^{surface} J \cdot ds$$

In the differential equation, the vector A_z is enclosed magnetic flux perpendicular to the (x, y) plane and J_z is the magnetizing current density in the z direction. In the integral equation, dl is the length of an increment of the contour ($x + iy$) and ds is an element of the surface[9] and J is the current density in the enclosed surface.

EB.3 KNOWLEDGE ENERGY BALANCE EQUATIONS

Volume integral if any *KCO* or NO can be written as the surface integral of the knowledge escaping or decaving from that object:

$$\iiint_v K_v \cdot dv = \iint_s K_s \cdot ds$$

where K_v is the knowledge density per unit volume, and K_s is the surface density of knowledge crossing the surface enclosing that volume or the *KCO* or NO. An equivalent equation for "verb-actions" is feasible. If the two vectors are indeed orthogonal as the E and the M vectors in the *EM* fields, then they (i.e., Ns and Vs) in combination produce a "Knowledge Vector (or *KV*)" and offer its velocity. In the *KD*, the orthogonality is not guaranteed. However, for very short durations orthogonality may assumed, and the velocity for that duration remains constant. By adapting Duhamel's integral [16], the velocity of KV through a heterogeneous social medium can be computed. These seminal concepts need further investigation and more rigorous mathematical proofs.

For example, if an organism "needs" nutrition, then there are groups of numerous nourishments (noun-things) that are dynamic in the environment. Similarly, there are sets of dynamic verb-actions. These verb-actions are also dynamic in the environment. When coupled by appropriate convolutions (*'s), the Ns and Vs generate two basic results: (a) to gratify the need and (b) generate new knowledge vector KV as a cubic volume generated by the three arrays of Ns, *s, and Vs. Further, the velocity of gratification and the velocity of the knowledge flow become available.

Index

Note: Page numbers followed by "*f*" and "*t*" refer to figures and tables, respectively.

Rudimentary knowledge, 67–68

S

SAP. *See* Systems, Applications, and Products (SAP)
Satellite controlled systems, 70
Satellite networks, 34
Science, economics, and technology (SET), 293
Science of knowledge. *See* Knowledge science (KS)
Science-based CBs. *See* Science-based concept bases (Science-based CBs)
Science-based concept bases (Science-based CBs), 389
Scientific foundations of knowledge. *See also* Knowledge (K)
    entity, 404–406
    framework of knowledge, 402–404, 403*f*
    hierarchies of objects and actions, 404, 405*f*
    infrastructure of sciences, 396–397
    platform
        of pure sciences, 397–399
        of social science, 400–402
    state of knowledge, 407–410
        highways and byways, 408
        nations of knowledge, 408
        universe of knowledge, 409–410
        world of knowledge, 409
    thermodynamics, 399
Scientific/business applications, instruction formats for, 173
SCP. *See* Service switching point (SCP)
SDH. *See* Synchronous digital hierarchies (SDH)
Secondary memories (SMs), 34
Security measurement, 83
Self Interest/Social Injustice node (S/S node), 391*f*, 392–393
Self-interest groups (SIGs), 58, 292
Self–regeneration of knowledge, 359
Semantic rules, 311
Semiconductor technologies, 464
Seminal energy for change in knowledge domain, 85–86
Service logic program (SLP), 421–422
Service switching point (SCP), 26
Services management systems (SMS), 26
SET. *See* Science, economics, and technology (SET)
Short messaging system (SMS), 152–153
Shunt elements for signal flow, 285, 287*f*
SI. *See* Staffing and implementation (SI)
Signal flow, 398–399
    analysis, 287
    in conventional circuits, 283–284
    inductive and capacitive elements, 284–285, 284*f*, 285*f*
    series elements, 284, 287*f*
    shunt elements, 285
    theory, 119
Signal to noise ratios (SNRs), 398–399, 409–410
Signal transmission, 398–399

SIGs. *See* Self-interest groups (SIGs); Special-interest groups (SIGs)
Silicon atom, 353
Simple social processes, 415, 429
Single instruction single data (SISD), 367
Single process, single object processor (SPSO), 183–184, 184*f*, 185*f*
    processors and machines, 184–187
Single VF Multiple NOs (SVMN), 172
Single VF Single NO (SVSN), 172
Single-process, multiple-objects (SPMO), 183–185
SISD. *See* Single instruction single data (SISD)
SLP. *See* Service logic program (SLP)
SMs. *See* Secondary memories (SMs)
SMS. *See* Services management systems (SMS); Short messaging system (SMS)
SMs. *See* Switching modules (SMs)
SNRs. *See* Signal to noise ratios (SNRs)
Social awareness, 4
Social decay of nations and cultures, 50–51
Social interaction
    foundations, 208, 209*f*
    social interaction-based processing, 314
Social lais sez-faire, 61
Social machine(s), 9–11, 56, 207, 242, 312–314, 313*f*
    mediation by, 255
Social media, 286
    and human interactions, 224–229, 225*f*
        from block diagrams to devices, 225–226
        separation of reason and emotion, 226–229, 227*f*, 228*f*
    knowledge flow and distortions, 289–291
Social norms
    change
        in social status of organism, 62*f*
        in spaces, 59
        in status in society, 63*f*
    grouping of machine and human functions, 64*f*
    noise in social setting, 59–60
    oscillation of, 57–65
        social lais sez-faire, 61
        social supervision, 61–65
    social energy and ensuing shifts, 57–58
Social processor unit (SPU), 193, 280, 312, 366, 428
    features, 195–197
Social progress (SP), 41, 179–182, 181*f*, 183*f*, 208
Social psychology, 96
Social realities
    beneficial and constructive role, 56
    detrimental and exploitive role, 56–57
Social science(s), 207
    computer science, 401
    economics, 400
    game theory, 400

Printed in the United States
By Bookmasters